POWER AND SOCIETY

Greater New York
at the
Turn of the Century

Columbia History of Urban Life
Kenneth T. Jackson, General Editor

POWER AND SOCIETY

Greater New York at the Turn of the Century

WITHDRAWN

DAVID C. HAMMACK

New York   Columbia University Press

Columbia University Press Morningside Edition 1987
Columbia University Press
New York   Guildford, Surrey

Library of Congress Cataloging-in-Publication Data

Hammack, David C.
  Power and society.

  (Columbia history of urban life)
  Reprint. Originally published: New York : Russell
Sage Foundation, 1982.
  Bibliography: p.
  Includes index.
  1. New York (N.Y.)—Politics and government—To 1898.
  2. New York (N.Y.)—Politics and government—1898–1951.
  3. New York (N.Y.)—Economic conditions.   4. New York
(N.Y.)—Social conditions.   I. Title.
  [F128.47.H2   1987]   974.7'1041   87-13222
  ISBN 0-231-06641-4 (pbk.)

This book has been published by arrangement with Basic Books, Inc.
All rights reserved.

For LSH

CONTENTS

PART I

On the Historical Study of Power

PART II

Greater New York, 1880–1910

PART III
Mayoral Politics

PART IV
Major Policy Decisions

Contents

PART V

The Distribution of Power in Greater New York

LIST OF TABLES

LIST OF MAPS

LIST OF ILLUSTRATIONS

PREFACE

BETWEEN 1880 and 1910 Greater New York became the first American metropolis to assume a modern character. Nineteenth-century New York had been a great mercantile center; by 1895 corporate managers were displacing merchants and the city's economy was demanding more specialists, more white-collar workers, more semiskilled laborers. New York had always been remarkable for its social heterogeneity; by the 1890s its Anglo-Protestant social elite was both internally divided and challenged by competing German Christian and German Jewish social elites. Like all great ports New York had long contained small colonies of people from many nations; massive migrations after 1880 turned several of these colonies into vast communities that were larger than most cities in Ireland, Germany, Italy, Austria-Hungary, or Russia. Increasingly segregated by income and ethnicity, New Yorkers lived in a city whose central business district was expanding rapidly into skyscraper office buildings, whose extensive tenement-house areas were growing more crowded, and whose suburbs were spreading rapidly outward along proliferating rail and rapid transit lines. Seeking to adapt to—and to control—these changes, the region's public and private institutions grew larger, more numerous, more specialized, more bureaucratic, more reliant on expertise.

Several of these distinct changes have attracted their historians; this book offers a comprehensive account of New York's transformation in an effort to understand the relation between that transformation and the distribution of power. Drawing on the "new social history" and on economic history, it describes the ways in which the identities of the region's major interest groups—and the wealth, the organizations, and the cultural resources they controlled—changed during these years. Drawing on social science as well as on history, it assesses the effectiveness of these interest groups in their efforts to shape events and trends in the metropolis.

A single narrative could never capture the kaleidoscopic change that characterized New York in this period. Instead, this book is organized into topical chapters grouped in five parts. Power was as controversial at the turn of the century as it is today: hence Part I explores the views of late nineteenth-century New Yorkers and explains the approach adopted here. The emergence of the modern metropolitan region is a notable story in its own right, so the separate chapters of Part II tell that story and consider the impact of economic and of social change on the region's population and interest groups. Because the mayor and other elected and party officials played important roles in the making of policy, the three chapters of Part III offer a new interpretation of the tangled and long neglected period of mayoral politics between the downfall of the Tweed Ring in 1871 and the re-emergence of Tammany Hall in 1903. To determine how the broad economic, social, and political changes identified in Parts II and III affected the distribution of power, the chapters of Part IV describe the making of three of the most important of the policy decisions that helped create the metropolitan region: the consolidation of the five boroughs into Greater New York, the planning and financing of the first subway, and the centralization of Manhattan's public school system. Part V, in conclusion, draws all these distinct stories together into a comprehensive account of the distribution of power in the first modern American metropolis.

ACKNOWLEDGMENTS

AN EXTRAORDINARY TEACHER, C. Wayne Altree, launched me on the journey that led to this book when he suggested that an eleventh grade student in Portland, Oregon, read *The Autobiography of Lincoln Steffens*, a work that describes another westerner's encounters with New York. I have accumulated many other debts along the way. At Harvard, Samuel Beer and Frederick Jaher suggested, in the general education course Social Sciences 2, that it might be possible to pursue both history and theory. At Reed College, David B. Tyack demonstrated what might be done with the history of education, Dorothy Johansen encouraged my interest in urban history, and John Tomsich insisted on the significance of culture. And at Columbia University, Sigmund Diamond, Stuart Bruchey, Walter P. Metzger, and David J. Rothman exemplified several approaches that a historian might adopt in approaching the social sciences, and Wallace S. Sayre offered advice on my proposed research design.

For financial support that gave me the opportunity to develop my own approach, I am indebted to Columbia University, to a New York State Herbert H. Lehman graduate fellowship, and to the Russell Sage Foundation. I am especially indebted to the Foundation for assistance that permitted me to secure a reduced teaching load and then a few weeks of absolutely uninterrupted time necessary for the completion of this book. At a critical juncture the generous hospitality of the Ossabaw Island Project in Georgia provided ideal working conditions in which to recast four chapters. The Department of History and the Committee on Research on the Humanities and the Social Sciences of Princeton University and the Russell Sage Foundation helped defray travel, research, and typing expenses.

My family has also provided stimulation and support of many kinds; this book would have been very different without the help and influence of my parents, Charles W. and Dorothy Morgan Hammack, of Floyd Morgan Hammack, and of Maurice, Cylia, and Jonathan Shils. If it were not for the delightful distractions of Peter and Elizabeth, it might have appeared earlier. If it had not been for Lory's efforts, it might not have appeared at all.

New York City's fine research libraries and librarians made it possible for me to pursue almost every line that seemed likely to prove fruitful. I am especially indebted to Kenneth A. Lohf of Columbia University's Rare Book and Manuscript Library, and to the Butler, Columbiana, Law School, and Teachers' College Libraries at Columbia; to the helpful librarians and the rich manuscript, pamphlet, newspaper, and book collections of the New York Public Library, Astor, Lenox, and Tilden Foundations, and to Thomas A. Dunnings and the New-York Historical Society. In the years before the fiscal crisis of the 1970s almost closed his agency, James Katsaros and his assistants located many useful items in the Municipal Archives and Records Center of the City of New York. Elsewhere in the city, librarians at the Long Island Historical Society, the Museum of the City of New York, the Dun and Bradstreet Business Library, the Chamber of Commerce of the State of New York, and the Union League Club gave access to relevant materials. Upstate, the libraries of the State of New York at Albany, Cornell University, and the George Arents Research Library at Syracuse University all provided valuable sources; Sister Marguerita Smith, Associate Archivist of the Archives of the Archdiocese of New York at St. Joseph's Seminary in Dunwoodie, New York, courteously answered my queries. I am also indebted to the librarians and collections at Princeton and Yale Universities, the Princeton Theological Seminary, Williams College, the Library of Congress, the State Historical Society of Wisconsin, and the Bodleian Library at Oxford University. Mr. Thomas D. Green and Mrs. Edward M. Pulling kindly permitted me to examine papers they have since placed in established manuscript collections. David Goldsweig helped me secure important information about the history of several New York City law firms.

Chapter One makes use, in revised form, of some of the material that I published in two articles: "Problems in the Historical Study of Power in the Cities and Towns of the United States, 1800–1960," *American Historical Review* 83 (1978), and "Elite Perceptions of Power in the Cities of the United States, 1880–1900: The Evidence of James Bryce, Moisei Ostrogorski, and their American Informants," *Journal of Urban History* 4 (1978). I wish to thank the editors of those journals for permission to use that earlier work.

At Lehman College of the City University of New York and at Princeton, a succession of bright and challenging students provided welcome criticism and stimulation. Several Princetonians—graduate students Dina Copelman and Leonard Rosenband and undergraduates Patricia Braverman, Julia

Cloud, Joshua Greene, Michael Schill, and Elaine Soffer—also served as able research assistants, helping me to identify and locate useful sources and information. Isobel Abelson helped in research, typed much of one draft, and gave valued encouragement.

Many scholars have generously taken time to read and comment on part or all of this book. Sustaining a venerable Columbia tradition, a number of my fellow graduate students at Columbia—Paula Fass, John Harper, Aaron Halberstam, Wilber R. Miller, and Harold Wechsler—gave several chapters their earliest and most rigorous reading. At Princeton, Arthur S. Link, Alan Anderson, James M. Banner, Jr., Linda Lewin, Carl E. Schorske, Nancy J. Weiss, and R. Sean Wilentz offered some incisive observations, and Jameson W. Doig and James M. Polachek each made especially helpful comments on two chapters. Carl V. Harris provided an incisive critique of the entire manuscript; W. Elliot Brownlee, Clyde Griffen, Samuel Haber, Richard L. McCormick, Samuel McSeveney, Harold Perkin, and David B. Tyack all made valuable suggestions about parts of it. At the Russell Sage Foundation, Bernard R. Gifford early saw merit in this project; Herbert Morton and Byron E. Shafer showed me how to clarify several tables and more than one section of the text; and Priscilla Lewis expedited the production process. For their grasp of essentials and meticulous attention to detail I am greatly indebted to Richard A. Boscarino, who made the maps, and to Shirley Diamond, who compiled the index.

Three historians have given exceptional assistance, reading and commenting on the book at several stages. Kenneth T. Jackson shared his wide-ranging knowledge of urban history and suggested that I increase my references to other American cities and sharpen my own arguments. Stuart Bruchey introduced me to economic history, scrutinized two versions of the manuscript, and provided a challenging example through the comprehensiveness and clarity of his own work. Above all, I wish to thank Sigmund Diamond. His seminar provided the ideal setting in which to define my initial approach to this book. His advice in the early stages was both incisive and restrained. And his energy, learning, and commitment to the search for knowledge set an exacting standard.

It is a great pleasure to acknowledge that all this assistance is responsible for much of the merit of this book. Candor and pride of authorship compel me to add that I did not accept all the advice that was offered and that I alone am responsible for the evidence and argument presented in the pages that follow.

PART I

On the Historical Study of Power

CHAPTER 1

CONTEMPORARY PERCEPTIONS,

HISTORICAL PROBLEMS

FROM the Declaration of Independence and the *Federalist Papers* through the Voting Rights Acts of 1965 and 1970, the distribution of power has been a dominant theme in American history. Equality of power, universal participation in public affairs, a government responsive to all citizens—these are fundamental American ideals. In the nineteenth century, Europeans saw political equality as more characteristic of the United States than equality of opportunity, status, or wealth. In the years since Emancipation, political equality, at least in the minimal sense of "one man one vote," has often been seen as an essential first step in any campaign for racial equality, economic justice, or the fair treatment of women. Americans have generally accepted the distinctions, most fully developed by Max Weber, among power, wealth, and status. But in their awareness of the close connection between power and the most stubborn social problems in the United States, Americans have never been so ready as some European observers to conclude that the distribution of power matched the national ideal; objections to the excessive power of the rich, the well born, or the politically favored few have formed a continuing thread in public debate on the character of American life.

This debate has focused especially sharply on American cities. Contemporary observers from the 1870s through the First World War and again from the 1950s on, as well as political scientists and sociologists from the 1950s to the present, have argued vigorously about the distribution of power in the cities. Historians, with some notable recent exceptions, have held aloof from this debate, choosing until recently to approach the matter incidentally in the course of broader investigations; as a result

they have treated power indirectly, implicitly, and incompletely. Much
of the best recent work on nineteenth-century communities has neglected
power to emphasize other dimensions of social life and has sought to
shift attention from the elite to the "inarticulate."

The historical neglect of power has been unfortunate. Power is as important to community life as wealth and status; many of the central issues
in the history of any community concern the relationship of wealth and
status to power. The powerless may face difficulties fully as unpleasant
as those of the poor or the outcast. Yet as many recent works have insisted,
the three conditions need not always afflict the same people: Unskilled
workers, agricultural laborers, new immigrants, and even slaves, it is said,
have exerted sufficient power to shape the worlds they inhabited and
to justify a sense of collective pride. For the most part, they exerted
power in their local communities.[1]

When historians of American communities have touched on the question of power, they have usually adopted one of several competing interpretations of the history of power distribution since the eighteenth century. One group of interpretations stresses the continuing domination
of elites; these interpretations differ in their accounts of the nature and
unity of the elites in various kinds of communities at different times.
The other interpretations all argue that power has been widely if not
equally distributed, differing as they find the concentration of power in
American communities unchanging, increasing, or decreasing over time.

Stated in their full detail, these interpretations are quite complex and
involve, for many writers, fundamental political beliefs and commitments.
It is difficult even to frame generally acceptable definitions for such terms
as "power" and "community," or to devise generally acceptable methods
for their study. Steven Lukes, the English student of society and politics,
has insisted that power is "an essentially contested concept" for which
any definition, and any research strategy, is "inextricably tied to a given
set of (probably unacknowledged) value-assumptions."[2] Lukes puts the
point very strongly, but there is no doubt that it is difficult to study
power or that there is no unambiguous and generally accepted way to
produce a series of coefficients for the distribution of power similar to
those economists have produced for the distribution of wealth.

These difficulties should not discourage the historical study of community power; power is a difficult and controversial subject because it is
important. Because it is controversial, however, and because we will need
a number of studies in different places at different times before we can
hope to construct a general history of community power in the United
States or to test generalizations about the determinants of different distri-

butions of power, we must be explicit about definitions, assumptions, and methods. Since the political and social scientists have already contributed valuable studies of power in particular communities from the 1920s on, it is appropriate to make use of the social science literature in devising a historical approach to the subject. Fortunately a few historians—most notably Estelle Feinstein, Carl V. Harris, and J. Rogers Hollingsworth and Ellen Jane Hollingsworth—have already begun this task.[3]

With few exceptions, empirically oriented social scientists have accepted one or another variant of Max Weber's definition of power as "the chance of a man or of a number of men to realize their own will in a communal action even against the resistance of others who are participating in the action."[4] Under this definition, power is a relative term, and one person may be said to exert more power than another when he or she attains his or her objective, whether opposition develops or not, whether the result is achieved publicly or behind the scenes, and whether or not others regard the result as legitimate. Power may be exercised by individuals or collectivities, from families to voluntary associations to social classes.[5] The competing individuals and collectivities define their own preferences. They may compete in any institutional arena: the family, the business firm, the church, the city, the state, or the nation. Finally, power is to be distinguished from potential power. A patrician class which withdraws from civic life may possess wealth, ability, and high social standing, but it cannot be said to be powerful unless it successfully employs its resources in an effort to secure the policies or nominations it prefers. Because it clarifies issues of these kinds, Weber's definition is the most satisfactory one for empirical historical research.

This book examines the distribution of power in one community, the portion of the New York metropolitan region that lay within the State of New York during the last twenty years of the nineteenth century. Historical reality precludes the assignment of absolutely precise geographical, institutional, or temporal boundaries. The New York metropolitan region certainly extended into New Jersey, and for many purposes into Connecticut as well; its New York State portion extended well beyond the boundaries of New York City, Brooklyn, and Long Island City before 1898 and included substantial territory omitted from Greater New York after 1898. Decisions affecting the people of the New York metropolitan region were made by the Federal government in Washington, D. C., by foreign governments, by a wide variety of local governments, and by business firms located in and out of Greater New York—and abroad. In general, this study examines decisions taken by the governments and political

organizations of New York City and New York State between 1886 and
1903. Because decisions made during the 1890s often had their origins
in the 1880s and frequently had their greatest impact after 1900, this
study places them in the context of the city's economic, social, and political history between 1880 and 1910. And it examines city and state governmental policies that were of deep concern to—and attracted the vigorous
participation of—the region's business firms, churches, and charitable
organizations as well as its voters in general.

New York is not America; it would make little sense to seek to generalize
from New York to all American communities. But as the largest and
economically most central urban community in the United States, Greater
New York provides an essential locale for evaluating the conflicting interpretations of power. Although those interpretations diverge at many
points, they all agree that an important turning point or crisis in the
distribution of power occurred at the end of the nineteenth century,
and that both the size and the degree of economic development in a
community had important effects on the distribution of power within
it. Since Greater New York provides the extreme case of rapid and large-
scale urbanization, evidence about the distribution of power within it
is essential if we are to determine the impact of urbanization on power.

Greater New York's sheer size also argues for its inclusion in any comprehensive assessment of the history of community power. During the
critical period between 1890 and 1910 New York City contained one of
every nine persons who lived in a place of more than 2,500 people
in the entire United States; the area within forty miles of New York's
City Hall contained more than one of every six. Chicago, whose rapid
growth in these years is legendary, was only half as large as New York in
1910.

New York's central role in American life during these years provides
a further argument for the importance of knowledge about the distribution
of power within it. Its conspicuous role as the largest city in the most
important swing state in every presidential election between 1876 and
1900 focused local attention on politics and power in the metropolis,
placing even its local affairs in the center of the national stage. New
York dominated the nation's system of cities, serving as the center of
national and international networks in communication, finance, trade,
business management, and the professions. As a result its distribution
of power, like its other social conditions, ideas, and practices, attracted
national attention and exerted the influence of warning, precept, and
example over the residents of urban communities in all parts of the
country.

Genteel Decline, Patrician Elitism, Economic Elitism, Government by Syndicate, and Other Perceptions

The distribution of power was a matter of absorbing, even passionate, concern to New Yorkers as to other Americans during the last third of the nineteenth century. The city of the Tweed Ring and of Tammany Hall, increasingly dominant in investment banking, publishing, and law, New York was inevitably at the center of the national debate on municipal government. Opinion leaders in these fields repeatedly turned to municipal government as the one great unsettled—and unsettling—national question. Nor was the debate confined to the economic elite. Henry George was attracted to New York as the place where he could most effectively publicize his ideas about the urban problem. And it was from a base in New York City that Samuel Gompers finally gained control of the American Federation of Labor in 1896 and that Morris Hillquit and others sought to launch an American socialist party.

Contemporary New Yorkers held a wide variety of opinions about the distribution of power in the metropolis. We cannot conduct a retrospective opinion survey to determine exactly how the various views were distributed among the city's economic and social groups, but our best evidence suggests that opinion varied, then as now, largely along economic lines. Few late nineteenth-century New Yorkers doubted that their city's numerous wealthy individuals and increasingly numerous wealthy corporations were powerful. But many among the wealthy complained that universal manhood suffrage imposed real limits on the power of the economic elite. Political leaders indirectly agreed, arguing that they did their best to respond to all constituents. Most of those who were both wealthy and well educated, however, attributed at least potentially dominant power to a diverse aggregation of the rich, the well born, the best educated, and the most able, and asserted that such "best men" limited their own power by failing to exert themselves. Less concerned about the abstract virtue of local government, business leaders were increasingly willing to leave political offices to professional politicians and to seek their own ends through lobbying. The distribution of power perceived by various New Yorkers may well have reflected expectations and conventional wisdom more than it reflected reality. But to the very considerable extent that beliefs affect actions, perceptions did shape the real distribution of power.

Some prominent members of New York's economic elites disliked the limits which they believed poor voters imposed on their power. By the

1860s wealthy merchants no longer dominated the city council.[6] At first, the professional politicians who replaced them attracted widespread criticism. George Templeton Strong, the famous diarist, protested as early as 1868 that "the New Yorker belongs to a community worse governed by lower and baser blackguard scum than any city in Western Christendom, or in the world."[7] Three years later Strong intemperately denounced the city's "blackguard Celtic tyrants" as members of a "race not remarkable for its love of other people's liberties."[8] Charles Loring Brace insisted that life and property, not mere liberty, were under threat. In *The Dangerous Classes of New York*, he asserted in 1872 that "the 'roughs' who sustain the ward politicians, and frighten honest voters [were] ready for any offense or crime, however degraded or bloody."[9] Invoking the still fresh image of the Paris Commune, Brace wrote ominously

> All these great masses of destitute, miserable and criminal persons believe that for ages the rich have had all the good things of life, while to them have been left the evil things. Capital to them is the tyrant.
> Let but Law lift its hand from them for a season, or let the civilizing influences of American life fail to reach them, and, if the opportunity offered, we should see an explosion from this class which might leave this city in ashes and blood.[10]

During the great depression of the nineties still another alarmist quoted housing reformer Jacob Riis to the grim effect that New York City's tenements "hold within their clutch the wealth and business of New York, hold them at their mercy in the day of mob-rule and wrath."[11]

A large portion of the wealthy New Yorkers active in municipal affairs from the 1870s through the 1890s objected to universal manhood suffrage not because it fostered a dangerous democracy, but because, in their view, it permitted unsavory bosses, often in league with upstart plutocrats, to push aside gentlemen of the old school and take control of the city's public offices. As E. L. Godkin, the most widely read exponent of this theory of Genteel Decline, put it during the reform campaign of 1894, New York City was "governed today by three or four men of foreign birth, who are very illiterate, are sprung from the dregs of foreign population, have never pursued any regular calling . . . and who now set the criticism of the intelligent and educated classes at defiance."[12] One of Godkin's subthemes, announced in 1890 and employed more and more widely in reform campaigns over the next twenty years, was the charge that the city's politicians, especially those in Tammany Hall, prospered through a corrupt alliance with the most immoral of criminals: receivers of stolen goods, illicit sellers of liquor and narcotics, pimps and prostitutes, professional gamblers.[13]

Godkin would also have agreed with Elihu Root, who asserted in 1915 that during the last two decades of the nineteenth century the Republican boss, "Mr. Platt [,] ruled the state. . . . It was not the governor; it was not the legislature; it was not any elected officers; it was Mr. Platt."[14] Critics increasingly accused Platt of corrupt dealings with great railroad, insurance, and other corporations.[15] As active participants in the political rough-and-tumble themselves, both Godkin and Root understood that successful politicians were by no means always of impoverished immigrant stock. Thomas C. Platt, though of modest family background, was a native-born, Yale-educated Protestant. But Platt was also a consummate machine politician.[16]

In fact, Godkin's version of the theory of Genteel Decline was largely a pessimistic elaboration of a view widely expounded by American lawyers in the 1870s and 1880s. Simon Sterne, a remarkable New York City attorney, developed the most vigorous statement of this view in response to the Tweed Ring scandal. Insisting that "a city is at one and the same time a decentralized portion of the general government of the state and a cooperative organization of property owners for the administration of private property," Sterne argued in a widely cited article that the American failure to recognize this distinction lay at the basis of the municipal problem. Although the citizens at large did have a legitimate interest in the police and the public health, as he put it, they had no such interest in the management of public works. "In applying the doctrine of universal suffrage indiscriminately to the management of mere property interests as well as to governmental functions," he concluded, "a state of affairs has been created in American cities by which the great mass of nontaxpayers and unthrifty inhabitants obtain the control of all these expenditures relating to property, in which they have, it is true, a remote interest, but no direct pecuniary interest, and which puts the taxpayers at the mercy of the tax eaters."[17]

Hermann E. von Holst, the distinguished German writer on American law and government, made the same point in 1887 when he wrote that as municipal officers came to be "elected directly by the people, the vote of the lowest scamp counted just as much as that of the greatest merchant prince."[18] The result, as Sterne observed, was to give "the handlings of vast sums of money (in the city of New York upwards of $30,000,000 a year) to the political organizations. . . ."[19] Sterne, like his fellow members of the influential 1876 Tilden Commission on municipal government in New York, urged that the best solution was to give taxpayers an effective veto over municipal expenditures. In the absence of a taxpayer veto, the courts, influenced by legal commentators who

shared Sterne's outlook, themselves frequently imposed limits on municipal activities and expenditures, not only in New York but in other states
as well during the thirty or forty years after 1870.[20]

The view that venal bosses controlled urban politics was not limited
to those who identified with a declining elite of gentlemen or with property owners who felt especially hard-pressed. Henry George, the popular
advocate of radical tax reform, said much the same thing in his classic,
Progress and Poverty. As he quoted himself during his 1886 campaign
for the New York mayoralty:

> In all the great American cities there is to-day as clearly defined a ruling class
> as in the most aristocratic countries of the world . . . Who are these men?
> The wise, the good, the learned—men who have earned the confidence of
> their fellow-citizens by the purity of their lives, the splendor of their talents,
> their probity in public trusts, their deep study of the problems of government?
> No; they are gamblers, saloon-keepers, pugilists, or worse, who have made a
> trade of controlling votes, and of buying and selling offices and official acts.
> . . . It is through these men that rich corporations and powerful pecuniary
> interests can pack the Senate and the Bench with their creatures.[21]

Others deprecated the power of the bosses even further, asserting that
rich individuals or rich corporations—increasingly toward the end of the
century—ruled the city and ruled it quite directly. Conrad Carl, a New
York City tailor, informed a committee of the United States Senate in
1883 that "the millionaire corrupts the courts and legislation. . . . The
dangerous classes are not to be found in tenement houses . . . but in
mansions and villas."[22] Henry George, whose 1886 Labor party campaign
attracted by far the largest vote of any mayoral campaign organized from
the left in those years, declared that his was a movement of "the masses
against the classes." To judge from contemporary interviews with his
followers and accounts of his campaign, his views on the distribution
of power were widely shared by his supporters.[23] He certainly aroused
the enthusiasm of a notable coalition whose leaders included advocates
of his single tax idea, of the Irish Land League, of socialism, and of "pure
and simple" trade unionism. George himself asserted that American workers were rapidly giving up their traditional belief that republican political
institutions gave them sufficient power to protect their interests. By 1879,
he insisted, workers had come to understand that the unequal distribution
of private property in land produced "all the injustices which distort
and endanger modern development . . . , rear the tenement house with
the palace . . . and compel us to build prisons as we open new schools."[24]

During the late 1870s and well into the 1880s labor leader Samuel Gompers largely shared George's views. In later years Gompers usually refrained from sweeping generalizations about power and society because he preferred to deal with one concrete issue at a time. But in his autobiography he recalled that he had helped draft an 1875 statement attributing "the greater part of the intellectual, moral, and economic degradation that afflicts society" to "the present degraded dependence of the working man upon the capitalist for the means of livelihood. . . ." Gompers supported George's 1886 Labor party campaign out of outrage at political and judicial support for capital, and devoted his entire career to the creation of an effective economic and political bargaining unit for workers.[25] It seems likely that in late nineteenth-century New York, just as in the midwestern towns recently studied by sociologists William H. Form and Joan Rytina, the workingmen who had the fewest years of formal education and received the lowest wages were the most likely to believe that "big businessmen really run the government in this country."[26] Yet then as now, this view was by no means confined to the poor. Three years after his defeat in the 1886 mayoral election, Theodore Roosevelt—at the time out of elective office—wrote to his close friend Henry Cabot Lodge that he "would like above all else to go into politics . . . , but that seems impossible, especially with such a number of very wealthy competitors."[27]

The belief of both rich and poor that the political machines had illegitimately usurped power over the city or had sold the city out to the highest bidder, derived to a large extent from the antiparty sentiment that had been widely held in the United States since the eighteenth century. According to this view, organized, permanently established political parties served not to represent legitimate interests and to develop responsible leaders and candidates for office, but to introduce faction and discord where there should be unity and harmony. The antiparty view continued to shape perceptions of local politics through the nineteenth century.[28] Strikingly, most well-to-do and well-educated New Yorkers, so far as we can tell, not only accepted this view as an ideal, but also believed that it provided an adequate account of reality. Despite the alarm of George Templeton Strong and Charles Loring Brace, the well-turned arguments of E. L. Godkin and Henry George, and the reasoned concern for the rights of property offered by Simon Sterne and H. E. von Holst, most New Yorkers who paid close attention to public affairs in the last twenty years of the century believed that a small, wealthy, patrician elite dominated their city, or could dominate if it chose.[29] This view found its fullest and most influential statement in James Bryce's classic *The Ameri-*

can Commonwealth, first published in 1888. Bryce interpreted modern conditions in terms far more favorable to the rights of property than did von Holst. In Bryce's view, the experience of Western Europe since the Roman Republic had shown that

> when in a large country . . . the sphere of government widens, when adminis-
> tration is more complex and more closely interlaced with the interests of the
> community at large . . . [then] the business of a nation falls into the hands
> of men eminent by rank, wealth, and ability, who form a sort of governing
> class, largely hereditary.[30]

Although he quickly learned that the "best men," as he called the members of the "governing class," usually did not hold office in American cities, Bryce found a way to reconcile American facts with his European expectations. Following the views of leading lawyers, university administrators, journalists, and wealthy reformers in New York and a dozen other cities, Bryce developed a Patrician Elitist account of power that can be summarized in five points:

1. American cities of the late nineteenth century contained two powerful elites: the new capitalists, and the established social, economic, and educated elite Bryce called the "best men."
2. These elites were the true rulers; political party leaders and officeholders were subordinate to them.
3. Both the capitalists and the best men exerted influence on every issue they deemed important; the capitalists, however, were concerned only with a narrow range of issues that directly affected their own economic interests, while the best men often opted out of political life because they understood neither their duty nor their highest self interest.
4. The capitalists sought to rule in their own economic interest, but the best men pursued the general interest of the community as a whole.
5. Serious conflict occurred between the best men and the capitalists; the bosses had no independent base of power; the poor, the immigrants and the blacks were ciphers. If the best men would only exert themselves, they would gain the support of "well-conducted men of small means" and of the politically active poor, and would take power in America's cities.[31]

Bryce's account was not merely his own invention. He conducted an astonishingly voluminous and comprehensive correspondence with well-educated and well-informed professional men in New York (as well as other cities) during the 1880s and 1890s, and his description of power largely reflected their views. With the single exception of Godkin and one or two of his older associates on *The Nation*, Bryce's New York informants agreed that the "best men" could gain and hold power if they would do the necessary work. Even Godkin was cautiously optimistic on this point during the 1880s; despite his worries about the mob, Charles Loring Brace agreed.[32] And George William Curtis and Richard Watson Gilder, two of the most influential of the genteel editors, remained cheerfully confident into the 1890s.[33]

Most of Bryce's best informants, especially the younger ones, were, moreover, even more secure than he himself in the belief that the "best men" could rule New York. Theodore Roosevelt was pleased that Bryce had rejected "the 'tyranny of the majority' theory," but disappointed that *The American Commonwealth* did not go further. "You do not show," he wrote Bryce in 1888, "that in good city districts the 'machine' is also generally good. Thus in our three N.Y. districts, the 'brownstone front' ones, we have good machines . . . the assemblymen and aldermen are all gentlemen—club men, of 'Knickerbocker' ancestry, including a Hamilton, a Van Rensselaer, etc., etc. In none of these districts is there the least difficulty, now, in a decent man's getting into the machine. . . ."[34] A few years later Frank J. Goodnow, already a prominent political scientist, concluded "that even in New York the community has a moral sense which is capable of being outraged and which when outraged is strong enough to drive our corrupt politicians out of office."[35] By 1897 Albert Shaw, the brilliant young editor of the widely read *American Review of Reviews*, could claim that "we are governed in this city today, and governed splendidly, by the New York Chamber of Commerce."[36] Edward P. Clark, one of Godkin's assistants at *The Nation*, had added, in 1896, that "our 'intelligent classes' have been saddling on the 'ignorant foreign vote' a responsibility for our ills that did not properly belong to it."[37] Even after his defeat in the 1897 mayoral election, Columbia University President Seth Low retained what Bryce had called an "inspiring faith in political progress." Describing his strong showing as an independent, Low wrote, "We have awakened an amount of civic spirit and civic pride in the people of this metropolis which exceeds anything that has been known here. If 10 righteous men could save Sodom, it is not too much to hope that 150,000 men who were ready to turn aside the strong appeal of party for the city's sake will yet bring about good government in the City of New York."[38] Four years later, Low's election as mayor of New York seemed to vindicate his optimism.

The Patrician Elitist account of power was accepted more widely than any other among well-educated and well-to-do men in New York affairs at the end of the century, but it did not go unchallenged. The Patrician Elitists shared with those who accepted the inevitability of Genteel Decline the notion that New York, like other American cities, possessed established elites whose virtue was as unquestioned as their "wealth, rank, and ability." But not everyone was willing to accept such a notion. Moisei Ostrogorski, who visited New York City when Bryce's *American Commonwealth* was at the height of its fame, devoted much of his shrewd study, *Democracy and the Organization of Political Parties,* to an implicit critique of Patrician Elitist theory and the pretensions of the "best men." On the basis of conversations with a number of leading men as well as wide reading and direct observation, Ostrogorski adopted the skeptical view that American politics, city politics above all, was simply "a business in the ordinary sense of the word," and that it was difficult if not impossible to identify a general interest.[39]

Ostrogorski did agree that the "best men" should govern, but he asserted that such men were rare in the United States. "The eminently materialistic spirit that animates the prosperous and wealthy classes," he wrote, disqualified lawyers, newspaper editors, and other professional men from conducting themselves as disinterested patricians concerned for the welfare of their city as a whole.[40] In his view, municipal reform candidates "were not successful in bridging the gulf between the people and the rich." Indeed, "reform clubs were only 'bourgeois associations'" that often "aimed deliberately" to exclude the poor from membership. The reformers "tried to bind together the 'classes,' not exactly against the 'masses' as such, but against the masses who, [by supporting] plundering politicians-. . . allowed serious injury to be inflicted on the propertied classes."[41]

Though Ostrogorski criticized Patrician Elitism, he did not object to its elitist elements. He assumed that the propertied, especially the very wealthy, held power, but he did not deny a place to those who possessed "rank and ability" in addition to wealth. What he did deny was the claim that the wealthy could be divided into the "best men" and the "capitalists," and the further claim that since such "best men" would govern in the common interest, they would win the support of the poor in a fair election. Whereas Bryce insisted on the independent power conferred by social standing, virtue, and ability, Ostrogorski asserted that in the United States power was exclusively a function of wealth. His own account, which was almost a pure statement of Economic Elitism, can be stated in four points:

1. A capitalist elite ruled America's cities at the end of the nineteenth century. The established social and professional elite was employed by, allied with, led by, and effectively part of the capitalist elite.
2. Political party leaders and officeholders were subordinate to this elite but could not easily be displaced.
3. The capitalist elite exerted influence on every issue important to its economic interest, which did not often reflect the public interest.

4. The bosses mediated between the capitalists and the masses of voters; the voters were not ignorant of their own self interest. Potential conflict was between the propertied classes and the propertyless. When bosses failed to prevent this conflict from breaking out or allied themselves with the propertyless, the propertied classes successfully rallied to protect their economic interests.[42]

Bryce and his New York correspondents objected that Ostrogorski's account of American parties was too grim and one-sided. But they admitted that "he combines a profound knowledge of political philosophy with a personal knowledge of living politicians." According to *The Nation*, Ostrogorski knew "the Platt machine" as thoroughly as he knew Plato's *Republic*.[43] *Democracy and the Organization of Political Parties* offered a disturbing challenge to the comfortable Patrician Elitism of *The American Commonwealth.*

We know much less about Ostrogorski's informants than we do about Bryce's. Since his papers have been lost, we must rely on his footnotes, which contain the usual references to *The Nation* and comparable journals of elite political and professional opinion, and on scattered bits of evidence indicating that he spoke directly with many well-informed Americans, including several whom Bryce did not meet.[44] Ostrogorski's clear-eyed approach to politics provoked a cool response from his genteel American reviewers, but by the 1890s his leading ideas had already been widely anticipated by hardheaded business leaders and lawyers in New York.

These men saw the emergence of the political machine and the tendency of professional politicians to take over public offices previously held by wealthy merchants as aspects of the increasingly fine division of labor that was coming to characterize American society as a whole. Those who wished to be effective, they argued, must accept and adapt to the new order in which some men specialized in politics just as others specialized in business management or the professions.

In an extraordinarily sophisticated 1893 defense of Tammany Hall, for example, Daniel Greenleaf Thompson, a successful lawyer and a leading American exponent of Herbert Spencer's social Darwinism, argued that the Democratic machine provided New York City with the "government by syndicate" that it needed. "The syndicate," he pointed out, "is a business combination for business ends," and as such was responsive both to the voters who demanded respect and representation and to the businessmen who sought "commercial prosperity."[45] Ambitious for wealth and social advancement themselves, Tammany leaders were well aware, Thompson concluded, that "any movement materially disturbing the so-

cial order would result in the disintegration of the organization itself:
Any serious attempt to disturb the existing status by revolutionary methods would be thwarted at once."[46] Though an Amherst graduate and a
respectable member of literary and legal society in New York, Thompson
left no room in his scheme for the "best men" or for a belief that American
politics might realize an elevated notion of the general interest, and his
work was received by the genteel press with a stony silence.[47]

But Thompson was by no means an isolated eccentric.[48] Ignored by
the political and religious weeklies, his Government by Syndicate ideas
were quickly picked up by the city's business and trade papers. In 1894
the *Real Estate Record and Builder's Guide* insisted that only a tough,
possibly even high-handed oligarchy or "directorate," similar to the one
that ran the Pennsylvania Railroad, could effectively manage New York
City.[49] Two years later the New York-based *Banker's Magazine* suggested
that "even the system of bosses in politics . . . has its usefulness and
reason for being." Mercenary though they were, bosses simply responded
to the needs of the propertyless citizens for employment and a friend
in court, and to the need of "financial corporations" for the protection
of "a Rob Roy who could control the legislative marauders."[50] Thompson
had argued that in large cities, "there is more governing to be done,
and it pays better," and "with a heterogeneous population and with everybody busy with his own affairs, there is greater apparent need of someone
who will make a specialty of administration of public affairs."[51] Citing
the special personal qualities necessary for public leadership, the *Banker's
Magazine* agreed. Neither businessmen, professional men, nor college professors, it argued, possessed the personal qualities of a successful politician.
Success in politics required that one apply his forces "cunningly, quietly,
in a manner to give least offense," that he seek to lead men by "appeals
to their self-interest or by protracted argument," and that he "must always
seem to follow rather than to lead."[52]

The professional politicians themselves, though they did occasionally
admit to "working for my pocket all the time" or to taking advantage
of "opportunities," also insisted on this interpretation of their role. Tammany district leader George Washington Plunkitt made the point with
cynical indirection when he asserted that if a leader wished to hold his
district, he had simply to "study human nature and act accordin'."[53]
Paul Leicester Ford, the best-selling contemporary novelist, gave a very
different emphasis to the point in his widely read novel *The Honorable
Peter Stirling*, when he asserted that a successful politician had only to
be a good Christian: "Christ enumerated the great truth of democratic
government when he said, 'He that would be the greatest among you,

shall be the servant of all.' "[54] Thomas Gilroy, a key Tammany organization man and one-term mayor of New York, is said to have exclaimed
of the political parts in *Peter Stirling*, "Isn't it all damn so!"[55] Writing
of New York City in particular, journalist Henry Jones Ford put this
standard defense of the party system most directly: "So far as the appearance of representative character in party organization is concerned, it is
generally greatest when its subjection to professional management is
greatest."[56]

Accepting the fact "that in our great cities, with their unorganized
masses of voters, a political oligarchy has grown up," and that "government is at least as complicated as a business, and requires at least as
much attention as the making of hats or of shoes," two of New York
City's most prominent legal publicists had anticipated Thompson's Government by Syndicate views as early as the 1880s.[57] In 1884 J. Bleeker
Miller devoted a long and learned treatise to the proposition that the
city's labor, property owners', "trade, business, and professional organizations need, and before long will surely have representation in our city,
state, and national legislatures," as well as guild-like "self-government
and control over their own members." To judge from their current efforts
to lobby the state legislature, he added, such organizations had "been
every year taking a more direct interest in legislation."[58] Simon Sterne,
who often served as a lobbyist for such leading business organizations
as the Chamber of Commerce of the State of New York and the New
York Board of Trade and Transportation, pushed Miller's proposal a step
further in an 1885 address before the Constitution Club. The medieval
guilds, he argued, had provided "a sort of Chamber of Commerce government." New York City might "get back to something of that kind" if
its citizens would "stop organizing on the basis of arbitrary population
and organize on the basis of interests, and let the elected few or the
chosen few, who are at the top of those interests, *ipso facto*, go into
government."[59]

Sterne was not happy about the fact that "the division of labor has
created a politician class," and he believed that the politicians were generally men who had been unsuccessful in business and who had unjustifiably
displaced successful businessmen in public office. Like J. Bleeker Miller
he also believed that prosperous business and professional men were able
to achieve their objectives by other means. The Government by Syndicate
theory led Thompson, Sterne, and Miller to views very much like those
of Ostrogorski. Certainly their lack of concern for the morality of municipal policy, their view that the professional politician was merely a broker,
and their confidence that the wealthy could indeed gain their ends without

holding office themselves all resembled Ostrogorski's views more than Bryce's. Perhaps because Thompson, Sterne, and Miller were so closely involved with New York's local affairs, they differed from Ostrogorski only in their insistence on the view that the city's wealthy men were deeply divided by conflicting economic interests.

The study of attitudes cannot tell us all we want to know about the actual distribution of power. Attitudes, after all, are only indirect evidence, often supplied by those who may be relying on hearsay or conjecture or who may be repeating statements they know to be false. The opinions quoted in the previous pages were all written for particular purposes, under particular circumstances. Differing assessments of the distribution of power may in fact have reflected the observers' unstated definitions of power; yet we cannot now be certain how any of the observers actually defined power.[60]

Despite these difficulties, both the views of contemporaries and the theories elaborated by Godkin, George, Bryce, Ostrogorski, and Thompson raise some important questions about the distribution of power in late nineteenth-century New York. Very few contemporaries doubted that the city's wealthy men could dominate local affairs when they cared to do so. Yet much of the evidence seems to indicate that effective power was widely distributed. The poor apparently tended to believe that the rich had their own way, but the rich—or at least the relatively well-off—seem to have disagreed widely among themselves. Many of them, especially in the 1870s and early 1880s, found in their experience some reason to fear the power of the mob, the labor unions, and the politicians. In their public statements, at least, many politicians and journalists agreed that officeholders and party leaders did play important roles, that they took into account the interests of the poor as well as the rich, and that they did not neglect their own interests. Union organizers were similarly confident of their potential ability to exercise power. Yet to the considerable extent that they shared Bryce's Patrician Elitism, men of inherited wealth, culture, and professional attainments insisted that family, education, and ability—as well as money—served as sources of power. Other members of the city's economic elites endorsed Ostrogorski's baldfaced Economic Elitism. Conceivably all these observations reflected real experiences. The poor, although less powerful than the rich, did have the vote; the rich had diverse interests and several distinct bases of power.[61]

Accurate or not, these beliefs had consequences. Sterne, von Holst, and other lawyers, law writers, and jurists successfully sought to enhance the power of property owners by insisting that property owners had in fact lost power to "tax eating" politicians and their irresponsible, impoverished constituents.[62] Henry George used his claim that power had passed into the hands of the grasping few as part of a remarkably successful rallying cry to mobilize voters for his mayoral and reform crusades. Gompers effectively used his beliefs about power to forge an influential interest group of skilled workers. Businessmen who accepted Thompson's analysis remained content with a division of labor that left politics to the professionals. But the men of wealth and education who shared the Patrician Elitist account of power also possessed a valuable intellectual resource. Confident in their fundamental power as well as in their righteousness, they were encouraged to seek power more frequently and with a more confident enthusiasm than they would otherwise have done.[63] Acting as if they were powerful, they sometimes shaped events simply by stepping forward when no one else took the initiative. The confidence of the wealthy may also have discouraged potential opponents; when opponents believed that wealth conferred power, that belief itself must have discouraged them from acting. It was only prudent for those who believed that they lacked power to avoid conflict; they thus avoided giving offense, escaped clear-cut defeat, and left the degree of their weakness untested.

In an age that witnessed both Henry George's formidable challenge and successful Tammany campaigns based on the slogan "To Hell With Reform," many voters and politicians clearly disregarded the patricians' claims to social and cultural superiority. Nevertheless, many acknowledged the Patricians' continuing power. The evidence of opinion is not the last word about the distribution of power in Greater New York: It is incomplete, somewhat inconsistent, and of uncertain import. But it does raise interesting questions. The wealthy and well-informed usually assumed that wealth and status conferred power. But their persistent concern about the power of the electorate, the roles of the political parties, the attitudes of the immigrants, and the virtue of the various economic elites all suggest, at the least, that the wealthy could not simply dominate without exerting themselves.

Power and the Historians

Historians of New York and other cities in the late nineteenth century have generally adopted one or another of the contemporary interpretations of power. The first generation of urban historians—including Arthur M. Schlesinger, Allan Nevins, and many of their students—mostly followed

James Bryce and his American friends in adopting the Patrician Elitist view.[64] Richard Hofstadter, Frederic C. Jaher, Stow Persons, and others who have relied heavily on the evidence of intellectual history have been more impressed by Godkin's perception of an ineluctable Genteel Decline.[65] Gabriel Almond, Gabriel Kolko, and James Weinstein have adopted various versions of Ostrogorski's Economic Elitism.[66] All of these interpretations stress the effect of social and economic change on the power of the rich and well-born. They differ from one another largely on one question: Did economic change reinforce the power of established groups, or did it generate distinctive new elites to challenge those who inherited their wealth and position?

Other historians, often on the basis of cities smaller than New York, have argued by contrast that great wealth and high social standing were not the only sources of power, and that small businessmen, middle-class home buyers, immigrants, skilled workers, and adherents of certain religious persuasions exercised significant power on issues of great importance to themselves. Business historians from Robert K. Lamb to Charles Glaab and Julius Rubin have been at pains to show that entrepreneurial elites were limited by other business and community interest groups.[67] Oscar Handlin, Herbert Gutman, and others who stress the solidarity of immigrant or laboring communities have often found such groups capable of exercising considerable power.[68] Most students of local politics have assumed that power over local nominations and policies was quite widely dispersed. Some have further agreed with Robert K. Merton (and Daniel Greenleaf Thompson, Henry Jones Ford, and Lincoln Steffens) that the political machine served important functions for the poor and the immigrants as well as for businessmen and the consumers of vice. Others have followed Richard C. Wade's hypothesis that the machine was the product of class conflict between poor urban centers and their wealthy peripheries.[69] And recent interpretations of the "ethno-religious" basis of nineteenth-century voting patterns have suggested that Lutherans, Catholics, and evangelical Protestants all successfully insisted that local political organizations listen to their demands.[70]

Most of those who detect some diversity among the holders of power in late nineteenth-century cities do not speculate as to the impact of increasing urbanization and economic development on the distribution of power. One of the few who has written on this problem is Samuel P. Hays. According to Hays, the last half of the nineteenth century saw "the decentralization of urban life into an ever-increasing number of sub-units, each with relatively autonomous institutions and each with a separate political voice in urban government."[71] The result was a continuous increase in the diversity of power wielders in most cities. But in his view the "vertical integration" of American society since about 1890 together with the "reform movements of the twentieth century" which have been dominated by economic and professional elites, have increasingly centralized power in the upper third of the "social and political order."[72]

Many other historians still believe that the municipal reforms of the Progressive Era, like many aspects of the New Deal and even the Great Society, have had the effect of distributing power more widely in the urban communities as well as at other levels of American society. In this view, industrialization, rural-urban migration, immigration, and the increasing scale of organization in American life, together with a series of reforms in the political process, left ordinary people not only with grievances but also with opportunities to organize and gain an increased share of power.[73] Similarly a number of political and social scientists, notably Terry N. Clark, John Walton, and Michael Aiken, have suggested that the social transformations associated with urbanization and economic development in the twentieth century have encouraged a more "pluralistic" distribution of power in which, as Nelson Polsby and Wallace Sayre put it,

> participation in decision-making is limited to a relatively few members of the community, but only within the constraints of a bargaining process among competing elites and of an underlying consensus supplied by a much larger percentage of the local population, whose approval may be difficult to secure.[74]

According to these writers, in the years since World War II such a pluralistic distribution of power most frequently has been found in cities characterized by large size, greater social heterogeneity, more economic diversity, absentee ownership of local economic enterprises, a larger number of voluntary associations, and a higher level of citizen participation in local politics, as well as by nonreformed local political institutions.[75]

The Analysis of Major Decisions

The several interpretations of power in New York and other late nineteenth-century American cities conflict at many points: Which of them best fits the facts? If we define power in Max Weber's terms as "the chance of a man or of a number of men to realize their own will in a communal action even against the resistance of others who are participating in the action," the best approach is that suggested by political scientist Robert Dahl: the "careful examination of a series of concrete decisions."[76] The study of decision making requires the direct observation of the exercise of power; other methods measure power more indirectly. By comparing several decisions, we can determine whether the persons or groups that dominate one decision have any power over others, and we can draw conclusions about the "scope" of their power. The fact that a decision is made assures that alternatives, some possibly preferred by members of the community, were rejected. Analysis of decisions thus permits conclusions about the relative ability of participants to overcome opposition— conclusions about the "strength" and "extent" of their power.[77] Finally, the analysis-of-decisions approach makes few assumptions about the central problem of community power research, namely the relationships between power and such resources as wealth, occupation, status, or knowledge.

Since no historian can study all decisions taken in a large community during even a limited period of time, it is necessary to be selective.[78] The most efficient approach requires the choice of major decisions. While there will always be room for discussion as to which decisions are "major," several criteria seem appropriate. A major decision affects a relatively and absolutely large number of people, either by affecting the distribution of a large quantity of valued resources, by changing the way policies are established and administered, or by affecting the values, beliefs, and information that constitute the climate of opinion within which proposals are considered. A major decision is one viewed as unusually important by contemporary and later experts, by reputedly powerful groups in the community, or by large segments of the community's population. A major decision takes several years to resolve.[79] It is not necessarily resolvable within the community's local government or even within the community itself.[80] The most important decisions may be "non-decisions" which keep significant ideas off the public agenda.[81]

Analysis of decisions of this sort, from three or four distinct areas of community life (for example, decisions that are primarily political, economic, and cultural), permits conclusions to be drawn as to the existence or absence of a single, unified, dominant power elite. No power elite could ignore or permit itself to be excluded from such important decisions. At the same time, because major decisions evoke the widest participation and produce the fullest historical sources, they provide the best opportunity to evaluate the power of rising elites and non-elite groups. Since this approach makes no assumptions about the powers of officials or the significance of government forms and boundaries, a series of studies carried out on these lines would permit comparisons over time and space, between communities with differing local institutions.

Recently some contrasting methods for the study of power have gained widespread support. Several writers, including Peter Bachrach, Morton Baratz, Matthew Crenson, and Steven Lukes, have argued that to focus sharply on the decision-making process may be to ignore important aspects of the distribution of power.[82] They insist that we must consider how, through institutions and values, "some issues are organized into politics while others are organized out," and how some actors use behind-the-scenes techniques to manipulate the underlying consensus and "define the situation" so as to suppress proposals inimical to their own interests and even persuade people to act against their own self-interest.[83] Carl Harris has recently observed that inherited historical circumstances often give some political actors special advantages.[84] Similarly, as Carl J. Friedrich insisted, even well-established elites may themselves respond to a barely visible form of power when they shape their behavior in accordance with the anticipated reactions of their constituents, publics, or subjects.[85] These aspects of power must certainly be taken into account; studies that ignore them are incomplete and likely to be naïve. But the "hidden faces" of power constitute in effect a set of resources that may or may not prove useful in particular circumstances. Evidence of their importance can best be sought through the analysis of decisions.

Other social scientists have urged that attention be shifted from the decision-making process to its results, for example, in levels of taxation and expenditure. Fiscal data are available for long periods of time for New York and other nineteenth-century communities; as J. Rogers Hollingsworth and Ellen Jane Hollingsworth have shown, it can be quantified and put on a comparative basis.[86] But, to paraphrase Robert Burns, men's best-laid plans often go awry. Since a decision may fail to accomplish its author's intent, to shift attention from the decision-making process to outcomes is to abandon the study of power. Like King Lear, a powerful man may act so as to harm himself and those he seeks to assist; the complexity of social relations makes it difficult indeed to know who will benefit from a particular decision. Even those who clearly do benefit from historic or institutionalized circumstances may be more fortunate than powerful. Indeed, they may even be unfortunate, like those who inherit conspicuous privilege on the eve of a revolution.

In another approach, several historians and social scientists have sought to use the holding of public or voluntary association office as an indicator of power.[87] But while it is true that an office may be a valuable resource to one who seeks to exert power, much of the controversy over late nineteenth-century municipal affairs had to do with the difference between official appearance and reality. The possessor of a resource may lack the ability or the will to use it effectively; not every president has made good use of his "bully pulpit." People in nineteenth-century American cities often asked whether the mayor did not owe his position, and his allegiance, to a boss, a kingmaker, or a "Warwick." Was he controlled by a power behind the throne, a gray eminence, a caucus, a kitchen cabinet? Was he a mere *locum tenens*, a placeholder acting for an unseen principal, a "flugelman" playing someone else's tune, a "yellow dog" who was merely standing in for an acknowledged boss, or a "cat's paw" whose role was to draw politicians' chestnuts out of the fire?[88] Were the capitalists, too shrewd to waste time with the front man, making their deals with the ring behind the scenes? No study of power can ignore those who held public or voluntary association office, but their power must be defined and demonstrated.

An influential group of historians has insisted in recent years on the distinction between the history of "events" and the history of "structures."[89] This distinction has served a most valuable purpose, directing attention away from what had long been an excessive historical preoccupation with discrete events and great men. Calling attention to the interconnectedness of history and the significance of social life, this approach has encouraged a spate of remarkable studies of the history of economic development, of society, the family, the stages of life, culture, and slowly changing mentalities.[90] For the study of power, however, an excessively sharp distinction between superficial event and underlying structure can be misleading. The best way to uncover the underlying structures of power is through the analysis of events—of the great decisions that most clearly reveal how power is distributed among the members of a society.

Greater New York as a Decision-Making Arena

New York City's population at the end of the nineteenth century, compared with that of other cities, was unusually large, diverse, and changing. The metropolis contained more than its share of the very wealthy, of the bankers, lawyers, and others who provided professional services to business, and of small businesses. Its wealthiest residents belonged to an unusually complex set of exclusive social clubs; its social life and pattern of social prestige were unusually complicated by the presence of many large ethnic groups.

Taken together with the various contemporary and historical views described above, these facts suggest a series of questions about the distribution of power in the metropolitan region. Was there a single economic elite, able to work out a common program and put it into effect? Or were there several competing elites in constant conflict with one another? Did one of these elites consist of "best men," or the "cultivated classes?" Was there a clear distinction between the *nouveau riche* and the established rich? If the economic elites were divided along lines of economic interest or cultural allegiance, how was power distributed among them? What role did experts play in the city's affairs? Did experts enjoy any independent power, or were they clearly subordinate to the economic elites? Did less wealthy businessmen, those concerned with strictly local markets, have an independent share of power? To what extent did the mayor and other officeholders dominate? How much power did party leaders enjoy, and whose interests did they serve? How was power distributed among such other groups as homeowners, middle-class neighborhood associations, organized labor, municipal employees, unorganized labor, the poor? How did ethnic and religious affiliation affect the distribution of power in the middle and lower economic ranks?

This book approaches these questions by examining the behavior of participants and non-participants in four sets of major decisions. Using census data and a variety of other statistical and literary information, chapters two and three identify and assess the resources of the metropolitan region's increasingly diverse economic and social groups. Emphasizing the relatively well-documented distribution of economic resources in Greater New York's population, these chapters also consider the distribution of cultural, organizational, and political resources. Subsequent chapters then consider whether these economic and social groups sought to exert power in local affairs and assess their relative success in realizing their preferences in major political, economic, and cultural decisions.

Between 1886 and 1903 the irregular, interrupted, yet extremely large increases in the New York metropolitan region's population and prosperity produced deeply felt doubts and severe conflicts. In response, several of the region's elites sought to persuade local and state agencies to adopt a series of new policies and governmental arrangements designed to bolster New York's economic position and to moderate hostility between classes and cultural groups. Economic elites in particular sought to use government agencies to improve the city's facilities for trade and transportation;

to bring order to the metropolitan markets for mortgages, municipal bonds, and real estate; to improve the living conditions and the training of workers; to discourage tendencies toward socialism, tax reform, and cultural diversity; and to increase the efficiency and effectiveness of local government for dealing with major social and economic problems. Some economic and political elites were concerned above all with the course of national policy on matters such as the tariff, the gold standard, and international expansion, and sought to use New York State's large share in the Electoral College to influence presidential elections. Other economic and political elites objected to each of the policies proposed. And political, religious, ethnic, small business, civil service, and labor leaders responded to the economic and social elites' initiatives with efforts to protect themselves and their constituents, and even to turn the elites' initiatives to their own advantage. In the resulting controversies, New York City assumed the physical dimensions and much of the institutional shape it has retained to the present.

Three of the most important controversies began in the late 1880s and led to sets of major decisions between 1894 and 1900. These decisions included the creation of Greater New York, the planning and financing of the first rapid transit subway line, and the centralization of the public school system in Manhattan and the Bronx. Economic elites (including groups of wealthy individuals, corporation owners and officers, leaders of business and professional associations, and the philanthropists behind organized charity), assisted in each case by experts, worked out the proposals that led to these decisions. But local and state government actions were also required in each case. The city's mayors were rarely innovators or leaders in the formulation of policy, but they did play important political and administrative roles. The nomination of candidates for the eight mayoral elections between 1886 and 1903 thus constitutes a fourth set of major decisions during these years.

Together, these decisions significantly affected the distribution of economic, political, and cultural resources, and rearranged the institutions through which future decisions would be made. Each decision took about ten years to complete, received a great deal of publicity, and became an issue in electoral politics. To develop the evidence needed for conclusions about the distribution of power, each chapter dealing with these decisions presents a narrative that establishes the decision's impact on the city's various economic and social groups, the preferences developed by each group at each stage in the decision-making process, the economic, social, and cultural resources each group brought to bear, and the chronological sequence of events. The narratives demonstrate that a few individuals played leading roles in the making of each decision. But biographical sketches also demonstrate that each of these individuals gained his or her decision-making role through membership in one or more of the competing economic, social, or political groups. Because of the complexity of local political developments during these years and the fact that no satisfactory history of them has yet laid a ground-work, three chapters of the book are devoted to mayoral nominations.

The evidence suggests that in the late nineteenth century the metropolitan region's power was strongly concentrated in the hands of a number of competing economic and social elites. These elites are distinguishable, although their membership fluctuated and sometimes overlapped. The economic elites were so numerous, and so frequently in conflict with one another, that other groups, less wealthy but well organized, were also able to exert significant influence on their own behalf. The political party organizations were the most notable of these less wealthy groups, but on occasion others—including neighborhood economic associations, the Catholic Church, organized Jews and Protestants, and even organized labor and school teachers—were able to gain their own ends or at least to defend their own interests.

We have no comparable study of New York in the 1830s, 1850s, or 1870s, but our best evidence suggests that power was still more strongly concentrated in the hands of the very wealthy during the antebellum years. Wallace Sayre and Herbert Kaufman's study of decision making in New York during the 1950s argues that by then power was much more widely dispersed. Competition among the very wealthy at the end of the nineteenth century may very well have opened the way to a wider distribution of power among well organized though individually less wealthy pressure groups in the twentieth century.

PART II

Greater New York, 1880-1910

CHAPTER 2

ECONOMIC CHANGE

AND CONTINUITY

NEW YORK harbor provided the symbolic image of the metropolis and its economy until some years after the turn of the century. Approaching Manhattan on steamships from Europe or on ferries from the great railroad terminals in Jersey City and Hoboken, visitors in the 1880s and 1890s were impressed by the harbor's great sheets of protected water, crowded with the traffic of tramp steamers, sailing vessels, ferries, barges, and lighters bearing railroad cars and goods in transit. The harbor was fringed with ramshackle docks that stretched for miles in the deep water around the lower third of Manhattan and were scattered along the shallow Jersey, Staten Island, and Long Island shores, reaching from Gowanus Bay to Greenpoint in Brooklyn, on around Long Island City to College Point in Queens County, and up the Harlem River toward Westchester. Behind the docks loomed acres of warehouses and grain elevators, coal dumps, stoneyards and petroleum storage tanks, gashouses and abbatoirs, vast sugar mills and breweries, and a few great factories producing complex mechanical contrivances. Apart from several massive, squat, outdated fortresses, only the Brooklyn Bridge and the Statue of Liberty, completed within three years of each other in the mid-eighties, dominated the natural features and shipping of the harbor.[1] Increasing numbers of tall steel-frame office buildings were erected in Manhattan after 1888, but the skyline did not replace the harbor as New York's symbol until after 1910 or 1915.[2] Until then, ocean-borne commerce still appeared to dominate finance and corporate headquarters in the metropolitan economy.

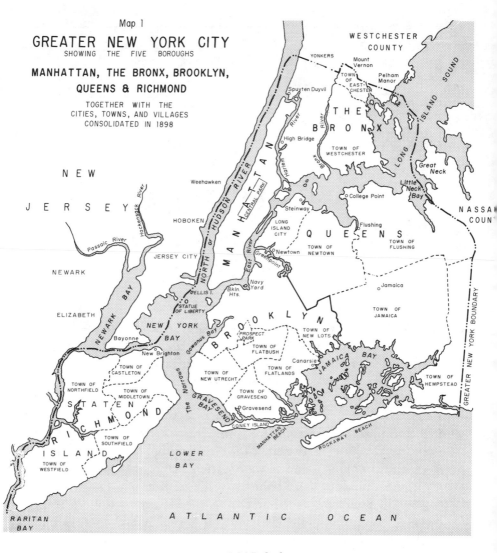

Map 1

GREATER NEW YORK CITY
SHOWING THE FIVE BOROUGHS

MANHATTAN, THE BRONX, BROOKLYN,
QUEENS & RICHMOND

TOGETHER WITH THE
CITIES, TOWNS, AND VILLAGES
CONSOLIDATED IN 1898

MAP 2-1

The Greater New York Region, 1898

But behind the façade of continuity, the metropolitan region was going through an economic transformation so complex, so fundamental, and so pervasive that it permanently altered the basis of politics and decision making. One of the most astonishing products of the nineteenth century, New York was at the center of the profound economic changes that were sweeping the western world. In 1880 Greater New York was still a mercantile city, with a largely German-, Irish-, and American-born population of two million engaged in the financial, commercial, and manufacturing activities appropriate to the *entrepôt* that handled the lion's share of America's trade with the Atlantic world. By 1910 the metropolis was more extensively involved in the management of American industry than in the Atlantic trade, and while its own manufacturing sector remained healthy, it produced a considerably narrower range of goods. The five million people engaged in these activities of 1910 were Russian-Jewish, Italian, and Austro-Hungarian as well as German, Irish, and American-born.

These changes kept Greater New York in its dominant position as the largest urban region and the most important central business district in the nation's system of cities. Despite its emergence as the great center for corporate headquarters in these years, manufacturing in the city itself remained in the hands of small firms, many of which did not incorporate. Yet its specialization in several fields enabled New York to remain by far the most important and diverse manufacturing center in the nation, even as its relative dominance in manufacturing, like its relative dominance in trade and finance, began to decline. Employment in business management and in legal and other professional services, and in services and trade for the nation's largest and wealthiest urban market made up for these relative declines. In 1910 as in 1880 Greater New York contained about one out of every eight city- and town-dwellers in the United States.[3]

The key to Greater New York's continuing national dominance in these years lay in its long-established advantages as the center of communication, trade, and finance both within the United States and between the United States and Europe. In the eighteenth and early nineteenth centuries these advantages had chiefly been supplied by nature and by the economic demography of colonial America; New York's unsurpassed harbor lay between the intensively developed and heavily populated New England and Chesapeake regions. Through the nineteenth century New York's central position brought added advantages: scheduled shipping service to Europe (from 1807) and the Atlantic coast, the Erie Canal (1825), and then railroad lines to the interior; superior market-making facilities;

New York City from the Battery to Fulton Street, in snapshots taken from the same location on the Brooklyn waterfront in 1881, 1893, and 1906. These views sum up the city's economic transformation. *From top to bottom:* The Trinity Church steeple rises above four-story mercantile buildings and sailing ships in 1881. The massive Produce Exchange tower joins the church steeple in 1893, but both are challenged by several tall structures already under construction. In 1906 an entirely new skyline composed of corporate and financial office buildings blocks the view of both the church and the merchants' Produce Exchange. The sailing ships of 1881 have largely given way to railroad barges and a ship with sails set has become a rare sight, not to be missed by the amateur photographer. (Collection of Mrs. A. C. Johnson, Courtesy of the Museum of the City of New York)

and finally the largest American collection of specialized experts capable of providing financial, legal, professional, and technical services. These commercial advantages simultaneously brought to New York the greatest concentration of wealth in the United States. By the middle of the century the metropolis was drawing to itself the largest share of those who sought capital, whether or not they also wanted advice. The enormous capital demands of the railroads after 1850, of the mining and petroleum industries after 1870, and of manufacturing corporations after 1895 attracted them all to New York.

This economic history provides the essential background for a study of power in the late nineteenth-century metropolis because it determined who, with what economic resources and what motives, was present to seek power. Greater New York's economic history produced not one but several economic elites. In the mercantile city of 1880 these elites still consisted of merchants, commercial and investment bankers, railroad entrepreneurs, great urban landowners, and lawyers. Of these, the merchants and the lawyers were the most prominent and the most active in public affairs, although individually such extraordinarily wealthy railroad men as Cornelius Vanderbilt and Jay Gould could exert great political influence. By 1910 the economic elites included investment bankers, insurance executives, and industrialists, as well as commercial bankers, railroad and utility entrepreneurs, lawyers and other professional and technical experts, great landowners, retail as well as wholesale merchants—and "capitalists" who were investing mercantile or railroad fortunes in a variety of new industries. Wholesale merchants and commercial bankers provided some direction to local affairs right to the end of the nineteenth century, but the merchants faded from the scene after 1900. No single group replaced them.

As New York intensified its role as the central control point for American business, its economic elites became increasingly diverse and were more and more inclined to look outward rather than at the metropolis itself. Nationally, investment bankers and manufacturers replaced merchants as the leading economic elites. But although manufacturing continued to be a leading component of the city's economy, it produced only a few great fortunes; after 1880 the New York pattern of large numbers of small producers grew stronger than ever. As a result, the headquarters city for American manufacturing did not produce a manufacturing elite of its own. Instead, it became ever more complex and internally divided. Its increasingly large and diverse economic elites found it impossible to develop and support a single economic program.

Merchants, Bankers, and Manufacturers: The Impact
of the Corporation

As the historical geographer Allan R. Pred has shown, New York had
become the central place in the circulation of commercial and political
information in the United States as early as the 1780s.[4] Taking advantage
of their access to fresher and fuller information, their more regular communication with European and southern ports, and their central location
in the rapidly developing region between Boston and Baltimore, New
York's merchants made their city the leading port in the nation before
1800. The development of the Hudson Valley of upstate New York and
then of the Great Lakes region, all tapped by the Erie Canal, strengthened
the city's position.[5] By 1830 New York Port was handling 37 percent
by value of the nation's foreign trade, and the proportion continued to
increase until 1870, when it reached 57 percent. But with the shift of
population to the west and with the emergence of Chicago, St. Louis,
San Francisco, and other interior commercial cities, a long, slow decline
set in. Shortly after 1890 the port's share fell below 50 percent, and by
1900 it was about 47 percent, though in absolute value it had continued
to climb. New York's share of foreign trade tonnage had never been as
high as its share of the value, because other ports, notably Philadelphia
and Norfolk, handled much more ore, crude petroleum, and coal. On
the other hand New York's trade in processed and manufactured goods
requiring careful handling was disproportionately large, and its share of
imports remained above half the national total until after 1910.[6] (See
tables 2–1 and 2–2.)

        Contemporary merchants were distressed at the port's relative decline,
as the share of Chicago and other regional distribution centers rose after
1870. The merchants often placed the blame for their decline on the
railroads, which they accused of pricing policies that discriminated against
New York.[7] Through government regulation the merchants could hope
to do something about the railroads. But their relative decline was fundamentally part of an inexorable erosion in the merchant's position in the
American economy during the fifty years following the Civil War. Before
the war, merchants had financed and coordinated the activities of manufacturers, most of whom operated on a small and precarious scale. But
war profits and new facilities for raising capital enabled the most successful
manufacturers to dispense with the merchant's financial services. For a
while merchants made up some of the lost ground by increasing their

TABLE 2-1
Imports and Exports through the Port of New York, 1790–1910

Year	Total Value	Percentage of U.S. Trade
1790	$ 2,505,465	5.7
1800	14,045,079	8.6
1810	17,242,330	11.3
1820	13,163,244	9.1
1830	55,322,053	36.8
1840	94,704,830	39.5
1850	163,836,064	71.2
1860	311,358,064	45.3
1870	477,663,559	57.6
1880	852,497,243	56.6
1890	865,478,484	52.7
1900	1,056,071,753	47.0
1910	1,624,493,354	47.4

SOURCES: Eaward E. Pratt, *Industrial Causes of Congestion in New York City* (New York: Columbia University Press, 1911), p. 37; Benjamin Chinitz, *Freight and the Metropolis* (Cambridge: Harvard University Press, 1960), p. 19; *Annual Reports* of the Chamber of Commerce of the State of New York; *The Manual of Statistics* (New York, 1910), p. 1015.

TABLE 2-2
Imports and Exports through the Port of New York, 1880–1900

Year	Percentage of Total U.S. Imports, by Value	Percentage of Total U.S. Exports, by Value
1880	68	46
1890	68	40.5
1900	62	36

SOURCES: See table 2–1.

specialization in marketing. But during the last two decades of the century the increasing technological sophistication of many industries and the rise of large manufacturers serving increasingly concentrated urban markets made the traditional wholesale merchant obsolete.[8] In the early nineties a leading guidebook noted that New York's old-fashioned merchant, whose counting-house and sales-room were attached to his warehouse, confronted a "prodigious growth of brokers," as commodities "formerly sold by actual inspection" came to be sold "on faith or by sample" at one of the new commodity exchanges.[9] By the early twentieth century many independent wholesalers had been forced out of business entirely, their places taken by brokers, by the sales offices of vertically integrated manufacturing firms, and by the purchasing agents of the great department stores. While the great merchants retained their prominence in New York affairs through the 1890s, by 1910 they had fallen far behind.

Greater New York's own manufacturing enterprises, closely tied to the port, also began to fall off in national importance during these years. According to one estimate, the region's share of all production workers in the United States hovered around 16 percent during the 1880s, but fell to about 14 percent after 1900 as it entered a long, slow decline.[10] Some large manufacturers, particularly those engaged in processing bulky imported raw materials such as copper ore and molasses and in preparing paint, chemicals, petroleum, rubber goods, leather belting, soap, and distilled and brewed liquors for distribution and export, retained large plants in the metropolis, though high rents and crowded streets were driving them out of Manhattan. Other large factories producing printing presses, pumps, clocks, pianos, and other mechanical contrivances remained in Manhattan and Brooklyn, near their markets and their workers. By 1910 most large manufacturers were seeking to move to the region's outskirts, if not out of the region altogether.[11]

Thus the national trend toward the concentration of industries in a limited number of locations where producers could turn out large quantities at prices low enough both to permit regional and even national distribution and to encourage the takeover of markets previously held by smaller local firms generally worked to the disadvantage of New York's manufacturers.[12] But in three great groups of industries—clothing, printing and publishing, and specialty and luxury goods—entrepreneurs found that the metropolitan region gave them significant competitive advantages. As one leading manufacturer explained to a Columbia University investigator in about 1910, "those industries which produce products of a standard pattern can locate anywhere . . . but industries whose products differ with each particular order must be located in or very near their market, in order to be under the constant supervision of their customers."[13]

The industries that thrived in the New York region were also able to benefit from the intensely urban qualities of the metropolis—the rich variety and freshness of information about fashions and market conditions in Europe and throughout the United States, the incredibly varied and apparently limitless supply of labor, the presence of bankers, brokers, jobbers, wholesalers, and other business services in endless variety, and the availability of imported raw and semifinished materials. The total number of industrial wage earners employed in Greater New York grew from 275,000 to over 554,000 between 1880 and 1910; clothing, printing and publishing, and the specialty and luxury industries accounted for more than 70 percent of this increase, as they raised their share of the manufacturing labor force from 41 percent to well over 55 percent (see table 2–3).[14]

But the expansion of these industries was not accompanied by the emergence of a new group of industrial giants determined to shape the affairs of the metropolis. In Cleveland, Pittsburgh, Chicago, Philadelphia, Birmingham, and Milwaukee, the era of large-scale production was also the era of giant factories managed by national corporations in iron and

TABLE 2–3

Industrial Wage Earners in Greater New York, 1880 and 1910, by Industry

Industry	1880		1910		Number of Jobs Added, 1880–1910	Percentage of Jobs Added, 1880–1910
	Number	percent	Number	percent		
Clothing and Related Products	81,291	30	217,894	39	136,603	49
Printing and Publishing	17,680	6	50,841	9	33,161	12
Specialty and Luxury Items	14,352	5	37,598	7	23,246	8
Metal Working	29,272	11	62,598	11	33,326	12
Food Processing	10,099	4	31,722	6	21,620	8
Other Expanding Industries	3,656	1	30,722	6	27,066	10
Subtotal	156,805	57	431,372	78	275,022	99
Other Industries	118,134	43	122,630	22	4,496	1
All Industries	274,939	100	554,002	100	279,518	100

SOURCE: United States Census of Manufactures, 1880 and 1910.

steel, textiles and knit goods, and meat packing.[15] New York City attracted corporate headquarters, but it did not attract large factories. Instead, the number of firms producing clothing and related products increased even more rapidly than the number of production workers, so that in 1910 the average clothing manufacturer in greater New York employed about a third fewer workers than had his predecessor thirty years earlier. In printing and publishing and in the specialty and luxury industries the ratio of firms to workers remained constant. Again, the intensely urban character of New York's industries—the elaborate division of labor throughout the metropolis, the availability of services and supplies in any quantity needed, and the concentration of many firms in a small space—encouraged the proliferation of small, interdependent producers, each specializing in a particular process or product. This gave New York a relatively large number of entrepreneurs in its leading industries, increasing the likelihood that at least some would be making the styles preferred by buyers from every section of the nation, and so adding to its competitive advantage in its own fields (see table 2–4). But the division of Greater New York's expanding industries into a multitude of small firms also meant that they produced few dominant figures with the resources to take a leading part in local affairs.

If the metropolitan region's economic elites included declining proportions of merchants and smaller proportions of wealthy manufacturers than total manufacturing output might have suggested, they also contained far more than their share of those who provided financial, professional, and technical services to business. Initially located in New York as an adjunct to commerce, these activities had taken on a life of their own by the middle of the nineteenth century. Their concentration in one city proved to be self-enhancing, as the superiority of the metropolis as a place to raise capital, gather investment information, and obtain supporting services continued undisputed.[16] By the 1890s if not before, the varied forms of expertise available in Greater New York were at least as important as the facilities of the port itself in attracting new business.

From the final demise of the Second Bank of the United States in 1836 banking, many forms of insurance, and other financial services to foreign and domestic trade increasingly concentrated in New York. By the 1850s, 600 of the nation's 700 commercial banks sought to expedite both domestic and foreign commercial transactions by keeping permanent balances in New York.[17] During the same decade the New York Stock Exchange emerged as the national marketplace for railroad stocks and bonds.[18] Mining and petroleum securities found their central mart in New York by the 1880s. Investment banking in other fields was still

TABLE 2-4

Leading Manufacturing Industries in Greater New York, 1909, by Number of Employees and Size of Firm in New York State

Industry	Employees in Greater New York		Distribution of Employees among Smallest and Largest Firms in New York State		Percentage of Employees In New York State Working in Greater New York
	Number	Percentage of All Employees	Percentage in Firms with 51 or Fewer Employees	Percentage in Firms with 250 or More Employees	
Women's Clothing	110,567	16	49	9	96
Men's Clothing	77,553	11.8	44	24	74
Printing & Publishing	74,118	11	37	33	78
Foundries & Machine Shops	29,200	4	26	38	39
Tobacco	26,664	4	31	45	74
Millinery	24,712	4	55	3	97
Bread & Bakery Products	20,041	3	69	15	69
Copper, Tin, & Sheet Iron	11,399	2	32	40	66
Fur Goods	10,719	2	79	0	95
Artificial Feathers & Flowers	9,759	2	52	4	52

SOURCE: U.S. Census of Manufactures, 1909, pp. 858–71, 886–91.

somewhat dispersed; Jay Cooke managed his enormous and innovative sale of Civil War era U.S. government bonds to a mass public from his Philadelphia headquarters, and as late as the mid-nineties Boston provided the best market for industrial securities.[19] But manufacturing companies were much smaller and more closely held than railroads until the great merger movement of the early twentieth century, and then the New York Stock Exchange eagerly absorbed the industrials.[20]

New York's investment bankers themselves were few in number, but by the 1890s their wealth and their impact on the national economy were already legendary. The greatest of these firms was of course Drexel, Morgan & Co., later J. P. Morgan & Co., which had its origins in the commerce of Philadelphia, Baltimore, and especially Boston. Others, like Morton, Bliss & Co., had roots in New England commerce. Two or three, including Winslow, Lanier & Co., Vermilye & Co., and Spencer Trask & Co., had old banking connections in New York. An increasingly important third group, including Seligman Brothers, Kuhn, Loeb & Co., and Lehman Brothers, stemmed from the successful mercantile activities of German-Jewish immigrants of the 1840s.[21] Boston firms, notably Lee, Higginson & Co., and Kidder, Peabody & Co., also operated in New York as did investment bankers based in Scotland (John S. Kennedy & Co., later J. Kennedy Tod & Co.), London (Baring Brothers, which worked through a Boston or New York representative), and the continent (notably the Rothschilds, through their New York affiliate August Belmont & Co., and Speyer & Co.).[22] By the 1880s these firms were no longer simply selling stocks and bonds on commission. They were also advising railroads and, within a few years, industrial corporations as to the terms for selling their stocks and bonds. By the mid-nineties the investment bankers were doing more still, as they reshaped the physical and organizational structure as well as the finances of the American railroad network in the wake of depression-induced bankruptcies. After 1895 they performed similar services for the great industrial corporations.[23]

A few of New York's great commercial banks, notably the National City Bank, joined in the activities of investment banking. But commercial banking as a whole in New York was itself not immune to the changes sweeping the American economy at the end of the nineteenth century. By the early 1880s Chicago had outgrown its dependence on New York and had begun to lend directly to borrowers in the metropolis. The National Bank Act of 1863 had assigned to New York alone the status of a central reserve city; in 1887 Chicago bankers persuaded Congress to raise their city and St. Louis to that level. New York's share of the national volume of bank clearings had been 63.3 percent in 1875; by 1900 it

was only 46.8 percent, while Chicago's share doubled from 5 percent to
10.8 percent. As Michael P. Conzen has demonstrated, "the dominant
trend [in commercial banking] between 1881 and 1910 was a progressive
multiplication of correspondent linkages within the urban system in addition to [or instead of] obligatory links with New York." In earlier years
most banks had direct links with New York, but now many, especially
in New England, the Midwest, and the Far West, tied themselves to Chicago or other regional centers, with the result that "important financial
business was no longer automatically routed through New York." In 1876,
Conzen found, 96.0 percent of all banks in the nation's twenty-four largest
cities kept correspondent accounts in New York; the proportion had
dropped to 91.6 percent by 1881 and to 83.4 percent in 1910. By 1910
Boston, Philadelphia, St. Louis and San Francisco also enjoyed strong
banking linkages with other large cities.[24]

New York remained by far the most important banking center, with
pervasive ties to other banks throughout the United States, but after
1880 it had to make room for a rapidly maturing network of intermediate
financial centers. As a contributor to the *Journal of Political Economy*
(edited at the University of Chicago) put it in 1913, there was "ample
evidence" that in banking New York's growth was "less rapid than that
of other sections of the country, and that other cities are now relatively
of more importance than in the past."[25] In 1890 the census reported
that 22 percent of all bankers in the United States lived in Greater New
York; by 1910 the proportion had dropped to 10 percent.[26]

Nonfinancial business services followed the merchants and bankers,
becoming so well established that they continued to expand even after
commerce and banking ceased to increase their share of the nation's business. The city's lawyers had helped create interstate railroad systems from
the 1840s; they gradually specialized their practices and expanded their
firms until, in the 1890s, the very large Wall Street law firm had become
a national institution, and New York lawyers were ready to help New
York bankers reorganize railroads and create national corporations in the
wake of the 1893–1897 depression.[27] New York had also become the
chief center for the offices of architects, consulting engineers, industrial
designers, and other experts. By 1890 New York's leading position in
these fields was strong enough to show clearly in the published statistics
of the U.S. Census (see table 2–5). Not only did the metropolis contain
the largest concentrations of persons engaged in professional and financial
services, but even in relation to its size New York had more technical
and professional experts than any other large city in the United States.

As the national corporations took shape after 1880, many of them also

TABLE 2–5

Percentage of All U.S. Workers in Selected Professional and Managerial Occupations in the Five Largest Cities, 1890 and 1910

Occupation	Year	Greater New York	Chicago	Philadelphia	Boston	St. Louis
All Occupations	1890	4.42	2.02	2.05	.90	.82
	1910	5.64	2.61	1.86	.83	.84
Architects:	1890	n.a.				
	1910	13.60	4.74	2.64	1.85	1.87
Designers	1890	n.a.				
	1910	15.40	6.56	5.60	1.86	1.42
Engineers	1890	8.60	3.25	3.70	2.07	1.49
	1910	7.17	2.66	1.69	.95	.92
Authors,	(1880)	10.10	2.70	2.94	1.93	1.87
Editors,	1910	12.60	4.52	2.25	1.77	1.19
Reporters						
Lawyers	1890	5.71	2.39	1.93	.85	.73
	1910	9.29	3.40	1.61	1.19	.99
Insurance	(1880)	12.00	2.85	3.24	2.30	1.72
	1910	8.35	. 3.65	3.30	1.00	1.49
Bankers &	1890	22.40	7.35	5.76	3.01	2.48
Brokers	1910	10.24	4.12	2.07	1.07	1.05
Manufacturers	1890	12.00	5.69	6.36	1.99	2.33
	1910	14.30	4.47	4.16	1.13	1.26

n.a. = not available

SOURCES: Department of the Interior, Census Office, *Statistics of the Population of the United States at the Tenth Census* (June 1, 1880), Washington, D.C., 1883, Tables XXXII and XXXVI; same author, *Report on Population of the United States at the Eleventh Census* (1890), Part II, Tables 84 and 118; Department of Commerce, Bureau of the Census, Thirteenth Census of the United States (1910) Volume IV, *Population: Occupation Statistics*, Tables I and III. I am indebted to Professor Margo Conk for the conversation that led to the construction of this table. Figures are not strictly comparable between different census years because of changes in census definitions, classifications, and procedures. The figure for engineers includes "civil, mechanical, electrical and mining" engineers and surveyors in 1890, "civil and mining engineers and surveyors" in 1910. No figure for "authors, editors, and reporters" was published in 1890, but the 1880 census gave a figure for "journalists" which is used here. The 1880 category "in insurance," also omitted in 1890, probably included some clerical and secretarial occupations; the 1910 figures are for "insurance agents and officials." No explicit change in the definition of the category seems to account for the precipitate decline in New York's share of bankers and brokers; perhaps this represents a real expansion of banking facilities outside New York City. The 1890 figure for "manufacturers, publishers, etc.," is paired in this table with the 1910 figure for "manufacturers and officials." Because it is derived from the census of population, not a census of employing firms, the data in this table refers to the location of residence, not the location of work, reported by workers in these professional and managerial occupations.

located in New York, so that as New York's dominance in wholesaling, foreign trade, and banking receded, it became the headquarters for American industry. By 1895 corporate offices were as disproportionately concentrated in the metropolitan region as were the bankers and professionals: In that year Greater New York contained fully 298 mercantile and manufacturing firms worth more than one million dollars; Chicago, with a

population about half as large, had only 82, Philadelphia had 69, and
Boston 64.[28] The bankers and lawyers who had initially congregated in
New York to serve commerce could also serve—as well as create—corporations. Corporate leaders in large numbers found that New York offered
by far the best combination of marketing facilities, commercial information, and financial, professional, and technical services. Experts in any
of these fields could be hired in the New York labor market, and if a
corporation did not wish to employ a highly specialized patent attorney,
accountant, or mining engineer, the metropolis provided an incomparable
concentration of professional and consulting firms, all available for face-
to-face discussions and ready to provide services as needed "under the
constant supervision of their customers."

Wealthy individuals, many of them engaged in managing their own
investments, also gravitated to New York to take advantage of its business
facilities as well as its social life. Sometimes their move was part of the
shift toward the creation of the great national manufacturing corporations.
The pattern was already well established by the early eighties; it was to
the Windsor Hotel in New York, not to a steel factory in Pittsburgh,
that Andrew Carnegie called Henry Clay Frick when he was ready to
take Frick and Connellsville Coke into the Carnegie Steel Company in
1881.[29] Carnegie had come to New York because his best customers, the
railroads, were there already. Railroad magnates seeking to direct freight
away from the metropolis often hammered out their agreements in its
hotels. By 1883 John D. Rockefeller and Colis P. Huntington had followed
Carnegie, as had Montana mining millionaire William A. Clark and many
others.[30] According to a careful New York *Tribune* survey of 1892, designed not to parade New York's wealth but to prove that most American
fortunes were obtained without the aid of the protective tariff, Greater
New York contained 1,265 millionaires, 30 percent of all millionaires
in the United States. Another 12 percent lived in the nearby New York
State portion of the metropolitan region, and still more lived in southern
Connecticut and northern New Jersey.[31] These figures suggest that the
concentration of American wealth in New York rivaled the contemporary
concentration of British wealth in London.[32]

Some of these shifting relationships among Greater New York's economic elites can be described in quantitative terms. So much wealth in
so many different forms was concentrated in Greater New York that it
is almost impossible to inventory it all. But the effects on local elites of
the relative decline of New York's national position in shipping, finance,
and manufacturing, and of the city's rapid emergence as the headquarters

TABLE 2–6

Assets of Firms in Major Industries in
Greater New York, 1880, 1895, and 1910

Industry	Assets of Median Firm (in thousands)			Number of Firms With $1,000,000 or More in Assets		
	1880	*1895*	*1910*	*1880*	*1895*	*1910*
Railroads	27,000	40,000	400,000	8	9	6
Life Insurance	5,816	14,200	43,302	10	11	10
Utilities	n.a.	13,250	31,844	n.a.	8	24
Trust Companies	8,860	8,460	18,645	10	25	44
National Banks	6,674	7,824	11,820	52	53	43
Savings Banks	4,210	6,833	8,300	25	30	47
State Banks	4,210	1,520	5,146	25	44	45
Fire, Marine, and Title Insurance	439	506	1,125	12	16	21
Private Bankers & Brokers	75	75	1,000	27	67	102
Shipping and Foreign Trade	35	35	35	20	45	60
Wholesaling	35	35	200	36	32	75
Manufacturing:						
National Firm:	5	35	200	11	32	330
New York Firm:	5	5	5	32	70	198
Garments	1	1	5	0	0	0
Retailers	1	1	1	0	11	27
Construction	1	1	1	0	0	0
Other	—	—	—	4	7	9

n.a. = not available
SOURCES: *Annual Reports* of the Superintendent of the Bank Department, State of New York; *Annual Reports* of the Superintendent of the Insurance Department, State of New York; *Annual Reports* of the United States Controller of the Currency; *The Manual of Statistics* (New York: 1883, 1895, 1910); R. G. Dun & Company, *Reference Book (and Key) Containing Ratings of Merchants, Manufacturers, and Traders Generally, Throughout the United States & Canada* (New York: 1880, 1895, 1910). Median ratings for private bankers and brokers and all subsequent entries are based on an 0.8 percent sample of all firms rated for New York City and Brooklyn in the *Reference Books* for January 1880 and 1895, and for Greater New York in 1910. Numbers of firms rated at $1,000,000 or more in 1880 and 1895 are by actual count; for 1910 the numbers are the result of a 33 percent sample of such firms.

for national corporations, were clearly evident in R. G. Dun & Company's widely used credit ratings for firms of "merchants, manufacturers, and traders generally" and in related directories of bankers, insurance companies, and railroads (see table 2–6).[33] In 1880 wholesale merchants, importers and exporters, and firms of national and private bankers and brokers constituted fully 60 percent of the 196 firms with headquarters in Greater

New York rated at a "pecuniary strength" or capitalized at more than one million dollars. Merchants and bankers still supplied 50 percent of the 410 million-dollar firms in 1895, while the proportion of manufacturers had grown slightly, and the great department stores had broken into the group.

Much more dramatic changes had come about by 1910, when those engaged in foreign and domestic trade and banking had fallen to just over a quarter of the 971 million-dollar firms while the proportion in manufacturing mushroomed to 54 percent. More than half of these manufacturing firms, moreover, were in fact the New York offices, often the headquarters, of corporations whose actual production facilities were located elsewhere. In 1880 only 11 percent of the million-dollar manufacturing, wholesaling, and banking firms located in New York had branches or were themselves branches of firms located in other U.S. cities; the proportion nearly doubled to 21 percent by 1895, and then almost tripled to 58 percent by 1910. Railroad companies already had many offices in New York in 1880, but they followed a similar pattern over the ensuing thirty years. As late as 1895 many of the railroads retained only a stock and bond transfer office, usually provided by a bank, in New York. But by 1910 many railroads had their own offices, performing a wider variety of functions, in the metropolis.[34] As Greater New York came increasingly to serve as the center for American business, the significance to the city of foreign trade declined. In 1880, 7 percent—one in fourteen—of the city's million-dollar firms had a foreign branch; by 1910 the proportion had declined to ½ of 1 percent.

New York's economic elites can be ranked somewhat more precisely in terms of their capital (see tables 2–6 and 2–7). The railroads—above all the New York Central and the Erie, but also the several profitable lines tying New York with Pennsylvania coal fields—controlled by far the greatest investments; the New York Central claimed to be paying interest and dividends on $140,000,000 in 1883 and on almost $500,-000,000 in 1910. Municipal utilities, including streetcar and elevated railroad lines as well as the gas companies and the rapidly expanding Edison Electric Company, claimed to represent investments ranging from $7,000,000 to $65,000,000 in 1895. Some of the very largest manufacturers, bankers, insurers, and holders of real estate managed equally large amounts of capital. Firms in each of these groups increased their capital rapidly enough over the thirty years to retain their relative places, as did many of the largest savings banks, trust companies, and commercial banks.[35]

Private bankers and brokers and national manufacturers represented

TABLE 2–7

Percentages of Large and Small Firms in Selected Economic Sectors in Greater New York, 1880, 1895, and 1910

Economic Sector	1880 Assets $10,000 or less	1880 Assets $125,000 or more	1895 Assets $10,000 or less	1895 Assets $125,000 or more	1910 Assets $10,000 or less	1910 Assets $125,000 or more
Banking and Whole-saling	55	14	50	25	41	18
General Manufacturing	63	4	65	7	64	7
Garment Manufacturing	74	0	80	0	55	8
Construction	74	0	100	0	93	0
Retailing	86	2	91	3	96	1
Entire Sample	70	3	71	8	71	8

SOURCE: R. G. Dun & Company, *Reference Book (And Key) Containing Ratings of Merchants, Manufacturers and Traders Generally, throughout the United States & Canada,* (New York: 1880, 1895, 1910). These figures are based on an 0.8 percent sample of all firms listed for New York City and Brooklyn in the January, 1880 and 1895 volumes, and for Greater New York in the January, 1910, volume. Since the numbers of firms in some categories, such as construction, are very small, these percentages should be taken as suggestive rather than definitive.

much smaller capital investments through 1895, but both vaulted up to a very high level by 1910, when R. G. Dun and Company assessed the median firm of private bankers and brokers at more than $1 million, and the median national manufacturer at $200,000. Many commercial banks and insurance companies did not increase in size, however, though they continued to represent eight or ten times as much capital as did most firms engaged in foreign and domestic trade. Greater New York's shippers and wholesalers were slow to incorporate and managed relatively small amounts of capital. Yet the median wholesaler's "pecuniary strength" remained seven times that of the median New York City manufacturer.

These shifts reflected vigorous conflict and competition among the metropolitan region's economic elites, but they did not reflect clear and persistent class distinctions. Following some contemporary critics of the "soulless corporation," sociologist Daniel Bell has described the economic transformations of this era as the grand "breakup of family capitalism" through the aggressive tactics of the investment bankers. "By their intervention," Bell asserted, "the investment bankers, in effect, tore up the social roots of the capitalist order. By installing professional managers— with no proprietary stakes themselves in the enterprise, unable therefore to pass along their power automatically to their sons, and accountable to outside controllers—the bankers effected a radical separation of prop-

TABLE 2–8
Sources of Million-Dollar Fortunes in Greater New York,
1892 and 1902

Economic Activity	1892 (percent)	1902 (percent)
Banking, Brokerage	13.7	21.7
Railroads	3.4	7.0
Oil, Mining	1.7	3.3
Wholesaling, Importing	26.5	25.0
Shipping	6.8	3.7
Ship Building	1.7	0.2
Processing (brewing, sugar refining, metal refining, tanning)	7.7	3.1
Manufacturing	13.7	9.8
Publishing	5.9	0.6
Real Estate	12.0	11.4
Retail Trade, Hotels, Storage	2.6	1.8
Street Railroads, Contracting Utilities	0.9	0.6
Law	1.8	6.8
Commercial Services	0.9	0.4

SOURCES: *The Tribune Monthly*, vol. 4, 1892, and *The New York World Almanac and Encyclopedia*, 1902, pp. 141–43, both reprinted in Ratner, *New Light on the History of Great American Fortunes*. The 1892 figures are based on a sample including the first name for New York City and Brooklyn and every tenth living and economically active individual thereafter; the 1902 figures are based on the 522 individuals for whom an economic characterization was supplied, with the 183 "capitalists," "corporate directors," and "financiers" redistributed in accordance with the distribution of the 78.6 percent of them who were listed in the *Tribune*'s 1892 list. Columns do not add to 100 percent due to rounding.

erty and family."[36] Although he pointed out a real change, Bell exaggerated the element of class conflict.

An examination of New York City's largest fortunes demonstrates the point. In 1892, according to the New York *Tribune*, about 43 percent of the millionaires living in New York City and Brooklyn had accumulated their wealth primarily in the port's traditional shipping, processing, and wholesaling activities; ten years later, to judge from a less complete list published by the New York *World*, these traditional activities were producing at most only 32 percent of the city's fortunes (see table 2–8). Under the economic conditions of the 1890s, banking, railroads, mining, and law had all become more effective ways to wealth. Recognizing that fact, the possessors of at least a third of the commercial fortunes of 1892 were seeking, ten years later, to shift their money into new fields. By 1902 the *World* was describing 37 percent of the city's millionaires not in the unambiguous language ("banker," "commission merchant," "dry-goods importer," "railroad investor," "real estate investor") employed by the *Tribune,* but in the vague terms "capitalist," "corporate director," and "financier." A comparison of the two lists reveals that about half of those described as capitalists and corporate directors in 1902 owed their wealth to commercial activities carried on before 1892, and that another fifth derived their fortunes from railroad investments.

What was happening in New York City, then, was not an investment banker assault on an established mercantile class, but a decisive transformation of a mercantile economy into a modern industrial economy. In the mercantile economy, most large fortunes were held by the leading merchants, bankers, manufacturers and processors, or their heirs, often in the form of real estate. In the modern economy, ownership is increasingly separated from management, and the wealthiest men and women seek to diversify their investments. In New York, this transformation was accomplished with a remarkable continuity of personnel. The data on the city's millionaires demonstrate a central but often neglected point made by the classic studies of William Miller, Frances W. Gregory and Irene D. Neu, and Mabel Newcomer. The investment bankers, law firms, railroads, and national manufacturing corporations that increasingly crowded New York's merchants to one side recruited about 60 percent of their own leaders from those merchants' sons and from the sons of the merchants, bankers, and lawyers who had dominated eastern cities and towns, including New York, during the middle third of the century.[37] Most of the investment banking firms themselves had started out as mercantile enterprises.[38] Over the course of the 1890s they functioned in large part to help men and women who had built up or inherited large fortunes to take profits out of family businesses and to diversify their investments. Far from promoting conflict among various economic elites, the investment bankers reduced conflict and increased the city's economic complexity by encouraging many wealthy people to invest in railroads *and* in mining *and* in a variety of industrial corporations.[39]

In seeking high returns, New York bankers and investors often joined in new if not speculative ventures. The city's wealthiest financiers, for example, were heavily involved from the very beginning in the electrical manufacturing industry, as they had been in railroads and the telegraph.[40] The men who owned Greater New York's banks, real estate fortunes, leading mercantile houses, and law firms, and who managed the great national corporations were interrelated and associated with one another in a variety of complex ways. These interrelationships tended to blur and diffuse the equally important conflicts that grew out of their particular economic interests.

Business and Professional Services: The Proliferation
of Expertise

In addition to their wealth, economic elites may possess many other sorts of resources. Greater New York's economic elites enjoyed extraordinarily good access to expertise and information, and they were often able to exert a good deal of control over the distribution of those resources. But as the city became more and more heterogeneous, many of them lost their ability to appeal to the local public as the spokesmen for widely shared cultural or religious values, as opposed to narrow economic interests. Their skill as business organizers constituted an important resource. But their diverse economic interests led them to create a fragmented set of business and professional organizations. By the 1890s they no longer shared a set of common notions about the proper role of government in the economy. Diversity of interests, fragmented organizations, and competing notions of political economy all worked to diffuse their formidable economic resources.

The diverging, often conflicting lines of economic interest in Greater New York were reflected in its business organizations. The most important of these, and through the 1890s the most important organization in the Greater city, was the Chamber of Commerce of the State of New York, a body which aspired, in the words of the *Sun,* to serve as "the parliament" of the region's business interests.[41] Composed of just one thousand men "well established by success and wealth," the Chamber was most often in the public eye on the occasions when it offered the city's respects to distinguished foreigners, in conscious counterpart to the way the Lord Mayor and the London Corporation received notables in the Guildhall. The wealth of its members, the prestige of its ancient charter, the strength of its record of support for aggressive measures to advance New York's commercial interests, and the fact that several of its leaders were elected to New York's mayoralty in the thirty years following the ouster of the Tweed Ring in 1872, all combined to secure for the Chamber an acknowledged leadership among business organizations.[42] But even at the height of its career during the 1880s and 1890s, the Chamber of Commerce was not without rivals.

Among merchants, the most important rival through the 1890s was the New-York Board of Trade and Transportation, organized in 1873, as the New-York Cheap Transportation Association. Largely composed of importers and wholesalers, the Board of Trade, in contrast to the Chamber of Commerce, was neither so diverse and internally divided by the inclusion of many exporters and bankers, nor so constrained by the membership of the owners of the New York Central and other railroads. The Board of Trade and Transportation played an important part in bringing about the famous Hepburn Committee investigation of railroad pricing policies alleged to be working against New York City, and then in creating the Interstate Commerce Commission.[43] It continued to provide a forum for the discussion of transportation, tariff, and related matters through the 1890s, though its members divided sharply over a number of local issues.

Many members of the Board of Trade also belonged to the Chamber of Commerce and to another of the city's numerous exchanges as well. The most prominent was the New York Produce Exchange, whose elaborate Italian Renaissance building was one of the most striking landmarks in downtown New York.[44] Besides providing facilities for trading in grain, the Produce Exchange—like the cotton and coffee exchanges—took positions from time to time on matters affecting transportation, taxation, and the cost and quality of local government.[45] The Reform Club, which produced a notable series of pamphlets proclaiming the virtues of free trade and the gold standard in the early nineties, was another rival to the Chamber of Commerce and the Board of Trade. The Merchants Association, initially set up by wholesalers to attract and assist dry goods buyers, became a more successful rival for influence over local government after 1900.[46] The New York Stock Exchange and comparable organizations of brokers, bankers, and insurance men took public positions much less frequently;[47] individuals in these fields preferred to speak out through the Chamber of Commerce or through single-purpose movements, or to avoid public statements altogether. In addition to numerous neighborhood bodies, New York's real estate operators also supported two competing city-wide organizations during the 1890s; the Real Estate Exchange, the oldest and best-established of these, was itself bitterly divided over both business and municipal policy.[48] Despite their overlapping interests, the various business organizations could not agree to pursue a common policy even on so fundamental and general a matter as transportation.[49]

Lawyers were often called in to formulate public statements for these commercial bodies, although lawyers as such were barred from membership in the Chamber of Commerce.[50] Lawyers prospered more than any other group of professional or technical experts in late nineteenth-century New York, yet they spoke with an increasingly divided voice and shared the stage with an increasingly large number of competing experts as the century drew to a close. As late as the 1870s, New York City's lawyers, nearly all of whom still carried on comprehensive practices out of two- or three-man firms, retained a near monopoly on the expertise necessary to formulate municipal policy.[51] Under those circumstances the profession's elite enjoyed general support when it set up the Association of the Bar of the City of New York "for the purpose of maintaining the honor and dignity of the bar," in the wake of judicial scandals revealed during the Tweed Ring exposure.[52] Through its efforts to review all judicial nominations and much of the legislation affecting New York City, the association played a very visible public role throughout the period. But by the end of the century the large new Wall Street firms that specialized in corporate matters had come to dominate the association to the exclusion of trial lawyers and others, especially those of a non-Anglo-Saxon background, who had already begun to move toward the creation of the rival New York County Bar Association.[53] In the tradition of *pro bono publico* work, many lawyers contributed to the resolution of public problems, but by the 1890s the prosperous corporate firms could dominate in this field; some firms would even assign a young partner almost full time to devising and monitoring legislation in such fields as civil service or voting reform, municipal administration, or public education.[54] Yet even the elite lawyers did not speak with a single voice, and they often found themselves in conflict with their less prominent colleagues.

Even more significantly, by the 1890s New York City's lawyers as a group were losing the near-monopoly over municipal expertise they had so long enjoyed. In technical matters, of course, they had always deferred to doctors and to the architects and engineers who followed the lawyers in setting up large consulting firms in the city during the 1880s and 1890s.[55] In questions requiring specialized knowledge of politics or administration, lawyers had always contended with journalists, whose literary skills, knowledge of the city, and editorial duties enabled them to develop public policy proposals of their own, as well as to determine which other ideas would be reported, and in what ways. In the last decade of the century, lawyers were further crowded aside by graduates of the new university programs in public law and administration, economics, social welfare, and education who were taking positions in the city's universities, welfare agencies, and editorial boards and developing their own policy ideas there.[56]

Altogether, in the provision of professional and technical services as in the organization of business, New York underwent a fundamental transformation during the 1890s. By the end of the decade, professional and technical experts were more specialized and more highly trained. They worked out of more fully developed institutions that reflected a greater division of labor and often a greater separation between the expert and the client who paid for his expertise. Lawyers, doctors, and engineers had never been merely spokesmen for the interests and perceptions of the city's elites. By 1900 several factors—their greater number and diversity, increasingly specialized training, stronger sense of belonging to national professions, and increasingly diverse work settings—encouraged experts to develop independent policy preferences that did not necessarily coincide with those held by New York's other economic elites.

Municipal *Laissez-faire vs.* Municipal Mercantilism

Despite the rapid growth of the region as a whole, several of Greater New York's economic elites faced serious challenges in the eighties and nineties. The great merchants, the local commercial and savings bankers, and the owners of New York real estate all felt they had reason to fear that the region was not growing fast enough. Drawing on the strong local tradition of municipal mercantilism, spokesmen for some of these elites sought to devise a strategy to protect their advantages. But they could not persuade all of the economic elites to help them put their strategy into practice.

As New York's commercial and manufacturing dominance began to recede, as merchants lost their exalted economic role, and as the nation's population moved westward, the advantages arising from the location of the metropolis began to seem fragile and intangible. The city's strengths in market making, information, commercial services, and professional expertise all reinforced its claim to be the nation's central business district. But these activities, like the city's made-to-order manufacturing enterprises, were highly mobile; they required relatively small investments in fixed capital; and they were affected less by transportation costs than by the economies of concentration and access to buyers. Both nationwide economic activities of coordination and control and New York's garment, printing, and luxury manufacturing industries were constrained to locate in the nation's leading business center, wherever it might be found. It was widely and not unreasonably believed that if Chicago, for example, were to become the most populous city in the United States, it would attract the American branches of European banking and export firms and gradually replace New York as the nation's chief commercial, financial, and communications center. Much of New York's corporate headquarters and manufacturing activity would follow, it was thought, with disastrous consequences for property values and for established professional firms.[57]

To counteract these dangers many merchants and landowners were increasingly eager to invoke the spirit of Alexander Hamilton and DeWitt Clinton on behalf of municipal enterprise. This tradition was so strong that the Reform Club—which served as the most vigorous local advocate of free trade and was heavily supported by W. R. Grace and the other great merchants—encouraged a prolonged and serious discussion of municipal socialism in the pages of its quarterly, *Municipal Affairs*, between 1896 and 1902.[58] The Hamiltonian program of the eighties and nineties provided a strong stimulus to some of the proposals that led to the major decisions considered in this book—the creation of Greater New York as an omnicompetent agency for the development of the region and its port, the rapid transit subway as a means of opening new areas to settlement and reducing both travel and transport costs in the metropolis, and the centralization of the public school system as essential to the production of a disciplined, literate labor force. Related proposals were intended to upgrade the labor force through better standards of health and housing, to increase the efficiency of municipal government, and to expand the region's cultural institutions.

New York's venerable tradition of municipal mercantilism retained and even increased its vigor between the 1880s and the First World War, as it merged with the new corporate liberalism and with the public health and social welfare professionalism characteristic of the twentieth century.[59] But many corporate and professional leaders ignored or opposed the Hamiltonian proposals of the nineties as irrelevant or inimical to their interests. Not one of the proposals received unified support from the region's economic elites. Unlike the merchants, the managers of far-flung national railroad and manufacturing corporations had no particular interest in the continued commercial viability of Greater New York. Some of the landowners believed that the region's economic advantages were solid enough; the Astors and many others who had inherited large blocks of Manhattan property saw no reason to pay higher taxes or to submit to inconvenience for the sake of improvements that might benefit them only indirectly. They preferred to sit tight and profit from the general rise in values.[60] Many merchants, despite their increasing difficulties, were so deeply committed to an orthodox *laissez-faire* that they objected in principle to any government intervention in the economy.[61]

Still other members of Greater New York's economic elites did not press for governmental intervention in the economy, because their cultural or religious commitments led them to conclude that the great causes for concern were social, moral, or political. These wealthy men and women variously saw the region's overriding problem as its increasing ethnic and religious heterogeneity, the decline of religion and the rise of immorality, the demise of deference, or the rise of socialism or anarchism. Increasing numbers of wealthy people were ready to invoke the notions of *noblesse oblige,* Christian Duty, or potential class conflict as arguments for government intervention into social, cultural, and moral affairs. The result was a great expansion of the range of human activity brought under public discussion and made subject to public policy. But the city did not have a single, unified economic elite capable of bringing forward a comprehensive, unified program. Instead, its distinct elites offered a host of competing and mutually antagonistic economic, political, charitable, and cultural initiatives. Moreover, the same economic forces that had produced such diversity and complexity in New York's economic elites had also attracted an increasingly diverse, complex, and non-Anglo-Saxon labor force to the city. And in New York, the workers were also voters who could directly or indirectly affect the fate of the elites' proposals.

The New York *Sun* asserted enthusiastically in 1892 that "the best, the brightest, the strongest minds of the country are drawn to New York, [producing] a stimulus which leads to greater organization of efforts than are planned in other cities."[62] Populists and others at the time made much the same point in their bitter attacks on New York, protesting that the metropolis dominated the nation's economy as "the money kings of Wall Street," aided by the city's lawyers and accountants, exploited honest producers from Maine to Georgia, and from Kansas to California.[63] Such protests accurately though imprecisely reflected Greater New York's central economic position. They also emphasized the fact that Greater New York contained significantly more wealthy men, even in proportion to its population, than any other urban region in America. Yet these men did not constitute a unified economic elite. Divided along lines of diverse and sometimes conflicting economic interest, their very numbers and diversity encouraged them to divide again and again along cross-cutting lines of social style and cultural allegiance. The result was to fragment their formidable resources. And the economic forces that brought men of wealth to Greater New York simultaneously brought unusually large numbers of white-collar and prosperous manual workers. Though these people were themselves divided and re-divided along economic, social, and cultural lines, many of them believed their interests differed from those of the economic elites, and made remarkable "organization of efforts" to secure their own ends. Through their political, commercial, occupational, ethnic, and religious organizations they frequently exerted significant influence on events.

CHAPTER 3

SOCIAL TRANSFORMATIONS

THE ECONOMIC CHANGES that simultaneously brought an extraordinary concentration of wealth to late nineteenth-century New York and
divided its owners into distinct elites were closely associated with social
and cultural changes that divided the very rich still further. Those same
economic and social changes also attracted a rapidly growing and increasingly heterogeneous middle- and lower-income population to the metropolis. The ethnic and religious diversity of this population exacerbated the
cultural divisions among the wealthy, further reducing the value of cultural resources the wealthy had long enjoyed. Gradually but unmistakably
the region's economic, social, cultural, and political resources were becoming more widely dispersed among its population as a whole.

Economic centrality attracted to the metropolis far more than its share
of wealthy men: so many, possessing such varied interests and outlooks,
that they separated into several disparate and sometimes competing economic elites. Their sheer numbers, together with their increasingly diverse
regional and ethnic origins, similarly made it impossible for them to coalesce into a single social elite or hierarchy of elites: The half-dozen leading
social elites that emerged by the mid-nineties jostled one another in a
vain and uneasy quest for precedence. And as the region's population
became more and more diverse, each social elite found that it could look
for deference only from a more and more restricted portion of the whole.
Economic and social distinctions cut across one another at different angles,
producing an increasingly complex and fragmented congeries of elite and
nonelite economic and social groups.

The several economic and social elites controlled a very large proportion
of Greater New York's wealth, prestige, cultural symbols, information,
and other resources, but others in the metropolis possessed increasingly
significant material, social, and cultural resources of their own. In New
York, as in London, the emphasis of the metropolitan economy on service
activities and specialized manufactures assured the region of an unusually

large middle-income population. New York's less wealthy professional
men, small manufacturers, petty entrepreneurs, and myriad officials, semi-
professionals, and technicians comprised an increasing proportion of its
population. Collectively if not individually they controlled an increasing
share of its wealth as well as a great many organizations. Increasingly
they also shared ethnic and religious identity with the skilled, semiskilled,
and unskilled manual workers who constituted just over two-thirds of
Greater New York's population in 1880 and just over three-fifths in 1910.
The middle-income groups, like the wealthy, were subdivided into many
neighborhood, ethnic, and religious subgroups. But more frequently than
the rich in these years, the city's middle-income residents were learning
to work together across communal lines. In an increasingly divided city,
their cosmopolitanism became a valuable resource, enabling some of them,
particularly those of Irish and German stock, to exert a significant impact
on local policy.

The region's large population of manual workers also produced its own
elites, including several competing groups of labor union officials. Many
skilled workers in particular earned good incomes, belonged to vigorous
trade unions, and sought with increasing success to take part in local
politics. Large numbers of semiskilled garment workers succeeded in organizing during the decade after 1900, and they too played an increasingly
effective part in politics. Even the unskilled possessed the ability to vote,
to strike, to plead for relief, to threaten, or simply to move away. As
the sources of immigration shifted and the workers became more and
more diverse, their ability to employ each of these tactics, like their respon-
siveness to appeals from one social or religious elite, changed.

Greater New York thus presented an increasingly difficult challenge
to any group that sought to shape its affairs. Businessmen, machine politicians, patrician reformers, religious zealots, trade union organizers, and
radical socialists all found it impossible to operate in the same way from
decade to decade, let alone create lasting coalitions capable of shaping
the region's affairs.

Light, Shadow, and Moving Up: Contemporary Perceptions of New York Society

Contemporaries sought to make sense of late nineteenth-century New
York's social structure by stressing its extremes, its concentration of oppo-
sites, its paradoxical contrasts. As early as 1872 one popular account of

the "Lights and Shadows of New York" asserted that "there are but two classes in the city—the poor and the rich. The middle class, which is so numerous in other cities, hardly exists at all here. . . ."[1] In 1893 the first edition of Baedeker's guide to the United States admitted that New York was "the wealthiest city of the New World, and inferior in commercial and financial importance to London alone among the cities of the globe." But Baedeker also singled out the city's high proportion of immigrants and its (comparatively not especially high) death rate as two of its most significant social statistics.[2] Theodore Dreiser stated the contemporary perception with his characteristic emphasis on the struggle for survival: The city displayed a "sharp, and at the same time immense, contrast between the dull and the shrewd, the strong and the weak, the rich and the poor, the wise and the ignorant." The strong, Dreiser thought, "were so very strong, and the weak so very, very weak—and so very, very many."[3]

The compelling images of Fifth Avenue and the tenement house reinforced the contemporary perception, and have combined with the striking language of contemporary journalists and reformers to make the New York of this period one of the most widely known, if not one of the most accurately understood, of America's historic cities. Fifth Avenue reached its height as the street of fashion in the nineties, when for more than three miles above Washington Square it was lined with costly houses, hotels, shops, clubs, and richly furnished places of worship. Following a mile and a half of respectable brownstones, a marble mansion at 34th Street, which dry-goods millionaire A. T. Stewart had not lived loi g enough to occupy, served wealthy Democrats as the Manhattan Club and announced the beginning of the plutocratic regions. Rich Republicans gathered in the "magnificent specimen of Queen Anne architecture" that housed the Union League Club at 39th Street, and a white marble and brick Italian Renaissance palazzo announced the presence of the Metropolitan or "millionaires" Club at 60th.[4] Above 51st Street the half-dozen Vanderbilt residences and the gleaming French Renaissance palaces of Col. John Jacob Astor, H. O. Havemeyer, and Elbridge T. Gerry, each of which occupied at least half a block, set a national standard for ostentatious domestic architecture.[5] At 55th Street stood "Dr. Hall's" Presbyterian Church, singled out as a leading sight not for its architecture but because its eloquent pastor was "said to preach to £50,000,000 every Sunday."[6]

Jacob Riis provided the classic image of the tenements and their immigrant inhabitants. "When last arraigned before the bar of public justice" as Riis put it in 1890, the tenement was technically defined as a building, generally one of a long row, built of brick, twenty-five feet wide, sixty feet deep, and four to six stories high, containing a saloon or shop at street level and four families on each floor occupying "one or two dark closets, used as bedrooms, with a living room twelve feet by ten." The staircase was "too often a dark well in the center of the house and no direct through ventilation is possible. . . ." Dark, foul, and unhealthy, tenement house districts had "crept up from the Fourth Ward slums and the Five Points the whole length of the island, and have polluted the Annexed District [later the South Bronx] to the Westchester Line." Crowding out all other housing in the lower wards, tenements lay "along both rivers, like a ball and chain tied to the foot of each street." As early as 1890 the tenements were already "filling up Harlem with their restless, pent-up multitudes"—multitudes that were still almost entirely white. Altogether, Riis asserted, "the tenements to-day are New York, harboring three-fourths of its population."[7]

The power and persistence of these images of the late nineteenth-century metropolis as a community of bright lights and dark shadows have made us too receptive to the contemporary emphasis on extremes and paradoxical contrasts. This emphasis distorts through omission. New York's size and its role as a great Atlantic port brought it more than its share of millionaires and exotic immigrants, and these of course impressed both visitors and writers looking for what Dreiser called "the color of a great city." Contemporary writers consciously stressed the city's chiaroscuro; speaking of New York's literary possibilities, Basil March, editor-protagonist of William Dean Howells's 1890 *A Hazard of New Fortunes* observed that "those phases of low life are immensely picturesque. Of course we must try to get the contrasts of luxury for the sake of the full effect."[8] The large numbers of rich and poor in close proximity, moreover, provided an irresistible text for moralists and reformers. But the separation of rich and poor into distinct neighborhoods also underlined for contemporaries the general process by which people in late nineteenth-century American cities were segregating themselves into homogeneous residential neighborhoods finely calibrated according to income. Like nineteenth-century London, nineteenth-century New York City contained a disproportionate share of the nation's middle as well as its upper classes.[9] New York's extremes were particularly striking, but the foreignness of its population and the dazzling display of wealth on Fifth Avenue should not obscure the presence of many apartments and neighborhoods for the middle and the better-paid working classes.

On his visit to America in 1904–1905 after years of travel throughout Europe, Henry James was struck in Central Park more than anywhere else with the brilliant "air of hard prosperity, the ruthlessly pushed-up and promoted look worn by men, women, and children alike." All, he added, were enjoying "their rise in the social scale, with that absence of acknowledging flutter, that serenity of assurance, which marks [those] accustomed, and who always quite expect, to 'move up.' "[10] The knowledgeable and worldly New York *Sun* observed in 1892 that as the immigrants became "prosperous in any degree" they moved uptown, creating "foreign quarters . . . where the people are thoroughly prosperous and comfortable."[11] Since these quarters contained a largely foreign-stock population, living as Europeans did in apartments—often defined technically as tenement houses but in fact far more comfortable then the tenements of classic image—rather than American style in single-family houses, they were often confused with tenement districts. Riis was aware of the significant social and economic distinctions among the city's residential areas, but he obscured them in his desire to emphasize the need to do something for the "other half," and especially for the "submerged tenth."[12]

About half the city's population did live in tenement houses, and many of these were every bit as bad as Riis described them. As late as 1902 in Manhattan 6,763 houses, containing perhaps 300,000 people or more than 10 percent of the city's population, were still without inside toilets; many of their primitive "school sinks," or privies, were flushed in such a way as to contaminate the water supplied to the single tap on each floor.[13] At least another 10 percent lived in conditions only marginally better. Yet at the same time 30 percent of Manhattan's 38,732 tenements rented for an average of $4 or more per room monthly, well above the basic rent of $10 for three rooms or $12 for four which prevailed in the least expensive and most discussed 20 percent of the tenements.[14] Neither tenements nor brownstones were well-lit in Manhattan, but the more expensive tenement buildings, many of which were put up on the Jewish Lower East Side after the mid-80s, were new, clean, and fitted with reasonably adequate plumbing, heating, ventilating, and fire-protection devices.[15] On his 1905 visit to New York Henry James found, to his surprise, that a lower east side tenement could provide "conditions so little sordid, so highly 'evolved' [as a] fire-proof staircase, a thing of scientific surfaces, impenetrable to the microbe, and above all plated . . . with white marble of a goodly grain."[16] Those who lived for a time in the worst tenements did on occasion move to better quarters. Thomas Kessner has recently argued that their chance of doing so was greater in New York than in most other cities of the period.[17] Even Dreiser observed, at the end of his harrowing account of "the toilers of the tenements," that "Broadway from Thirty-fourth Street south, to say nothing of many other streets, is lined with the signs of those who have overcome the money difficulty of lives begun under these conditions."[18]

In the nineties, the presence of fairly well-off German, British, native-born, and even Irish skilled workers, clerks, and tradesmen in New York was symbolized not by the confusing image of their living quarters, but by pictures of their playgrounds—Broadway, Madison Square Garden, the race tracks. Richard Harding Davis, the contemporary best-selling novelist, once described how a disgraced police commissioner, exiled to Tangiers, yearned to return to the neighborhood of Tammany Hall on Fourteenth Street, on a June evening,

> when the boys are sitting out on the steps in front of the Hall, and just take a drink at Ed Lally's, just for luck. . . . I don't know nothing better than Fourteenth Street of a summer evening, with all the people crowding into Pastor's on one side of the Hall and the Third Avenue L cars running by on the other. That's a gay sight, ain't it now? With all the girls coming in and out of Thiess's, and the sidewalks crowded. One of them warm nights when you have to have the windows open, and you can hear the music in at Pastor's, and the audience clapping their hands. That's great, isn't it?[19]

Dreiser himself described a related scene at Manhattan Beach, a summer resort near Coney Island. Less constrained by limited space and the cost of permanent construction, New York's summer resorts reflected the city's middle-level distinctions more obviously than did its residential neighborhoods. Manhattan Beach was neither Newport nor Coney Island, but "served a world which was plainly between the two," a world somewhat more prosperous than that which frequented Tony Pastor's Music Hall. "The clerk and his prettiest girl, the actress and her admirer, the actor and his playmate, brokers, small and exclusive tradesmen, men of obvious political or commercial position, their wives, daughters, relatives, and friends, [all frequented] this much above average resort." New to the metropolis at the time, Dreiser found the scene astonishing. "I never saw so many prosperous-looking people in one place," he wrote later, "more with better and smarter clothes, even though they were a little showy. The straw hat with its blue or striped ribbon, the flannel suit, with its accompanying white shoes, light cane, the pearl-gray derby, the check suit, the diamond and pearly pin in necktie, the silk shirt. . . ." Thomas C. Platt, "easy boss" of the state Republican Party, summered at the Oriental Hotel in Manhattan Beach, and was to be seen, together with "almost the entire company of New York and Brooklyn bosses, basking in the shade and enjoying the beautiful view and the breezes." Leading businessmen and entertainers joined the politicians, and "lolled and greeted and chatted," until by "dusk it seemed as though nearly all had nodded or spoken to each other," and could take time to listen to the music of "Seidl's great symphony orchestra and Sousa's band," to enjoy the fireworks that shot out over the ocean every evening, and to take in "the beauty of it all, the wonder, the airy, insubstantial, almost transparent quality of it all!"[20]

Five Social Elites

The popular contemporary image reduced New York's social structure to a single, stable pyramid, with two competing groups, the old established families and the *nouveau riche*, struggling for control of its pinnacle. Yet socially as well as economically New York was a city in the process of fragmentation. Powerful economic forces disrupted the New York merchant's world, attracted men of wealth from all over the world, threw up the great national corporations, and drew in hundreds of thousands of immigrants. These same economic sources produced an increasingly disparate and disrupted social reality.

Economic interests divided the rich in one set of ways; social and religious distinctions and prejudices increasingly divided them in another. A virulent wave of anti-Semitism produced the most profound social distinction, as Jews were increasingly separated from gentiles during these years. But only a few of the very wealthiest German-Americans gained membership in the higher of the social circles dominated by British-American Protestants; this was the great period of an independent and almost self-sufficient German world within New York. Protestants of British background were themselves increasingly divided into at least three distinct, if overlapping, social elites, in which prestige was based, respectively, on wealth, ancestry, and cultural achievement. The British-American Protestants as a whole excluded the Jews and most of the Germans from their most elite organizations; they themselves were not so clearly excluded from organizations they wished to join.

But in the heterogeneous and rapidly growing metropolis, wealth, philanthropy, and even cultural achievement were more honored than ancestry, and in these respects Jews and Germans could certainly hold their own. By the mid-nineties, Greater New York had five distinct social elites of comparable wealth and prestige: three consisted of British-American Protestants—those who most valued wealth, ancestry, or cultivation—others consisted of German Christians and German Jews. As the numbers of very wealthy men increased, their social cohesion declined, and they were unable to augment their economic resources with the cultural and organizational resources that might have been generated by a single hierarchy of social prestige and organizations.

The proliferating religious and ethnic distinctions of late nineteenth-century New York show up dramatically both in the gross census figures on the national background of men in the top occupations, and in the finer detail revealed through scrutiny of the names associated with the most heavily capitalized firms. In 1900, when fewer than 25 percent of the city's employed male residents had been born in the United States of American, Canadian, or British-born parents, over 55 percent of its bankers, wholesalers, and professional men were the sons of parents born in those English-speaking nations. Germans contributed the next largest group to the economic elite; in 1900, when 25 percent of all males who gave an occupation were of German parentage, 19 percent of those in the highest status occupations had German-born parents. An important section of the German group was Jewish; others were both Protestant and Catholic, though it is difficult to determine in what proportions. First- and second-generation Irishmen constituted 21 percent of all occupied males but only 10 percent of those in banking, wholesaling, and the professions, while the newly arrived, mostly Jewish Russians, Poles, and Austro-Hungarians comprised 13 percent of the male labor force and already over 6 percent of those in elite occupations (see table 3–1). The predominance of men with British backgrounds among the economic elite was even more evident at the top of occupational groups, as is clear when we consider the national origins indicated by the names of the most prosperous firms (see table 3–2). It is appropriate to speak of the ethnicity of particular firms, for few Germans and no Jews were to be found in the largest law firms, banks, and corporations headed by those of British origin. Instead, most Germans and nearly all Jews formed their own firms, which in turn usually included no outsiders.[21]

Jews were increasingly excluded from the social life of New York's wealthiest Protestants. German Jews had organized separate clubs, including the *Harmonie* (1852), the Progress (1864), and the Fidelio (1870), almost from the date of their first arrival in large numbers, but Jews had joined with Germans in the *Liederkranz* singing society, organized in 1847, and had been among those who founded the Union League Club to support the northern cause during the Civil War. Yet as early as 1854 the Arion Society had split off from the *Liederkranz,* and in 1892 the trend toward increasing segregation of Jews culminated in the

Social Transformations 67

TABLE 3–1
Ethnic Backgrounds of Males in High White-Collar Occupations
in Greater New York, 1890 and 1900

	1890		1900	
Ethnic Group	Number	Percent	Number	Percent
Native White, Native Parents	11,370	53.4	17,020	45.1
Native White, Foreign Parents	5,052	23.7	n.a.	n.a.
Great Britain and Canada	1,339	6.3	3,644	9.7
Germany	1,576	7.4	7,075	18.8
Ireland	912	4.3	3,892	10.3
Sweden, Norway, Denmark	162	0.8	417	1.1
Russia and Poland	n.a.		1,369	3.6
Austria-Hungary	n.a.		1,015	2.7
Italy	n.a.		442	1.1
Black	n.a.		194	0.5
Totals	21,311	95.9	37,728	92.5

n.a. = not available
SOURCES: Department of the Interior, Census Office, *Report on the Population of the United States at the 11th Census*, (Washington, D.C., 1897), Part II, pp. 640–41, 704–05; and Department of Commerce and Labor, Bureau of the Census, *Special Reports: Occupations at the Twelfth Census*, (Washington, D.C.; 1904), pp. 634–41. High white-collar occupations included here are engineers, lawyers, doctors, and "bankers, brokers, and officials of banks, etc." in 1890; and architects, clergymen, dentists, engineers, lawyers, doctors, bankers and brokers, and merchants and dealers (wholesale) in 1900. Data are not strictly comparable because the "native white, foreign parents" category of 1890 was omitted in 1900 and the "born in Great Britain," "born in Germany," and similar categories of 1890 were replaced by "born to mothers born in Great Britain," "born to mothers born in Germany," and similar categories in 1900. Percentage columns do not add to 100 because the census did not provide data on every ethnic group, and because some very small groups have been omitted from this table.

blackballing of Theodore Seligman from the Union League Club and in the consequent decision of his father and the remaining Jewish members to resign *en bloc*.[22] None of the Jewish clubs was even mentioned in most contemporary lists of the city's social clubs; their members were excluded from both the *Social Register* and the rival *Society-List and Club Register*. No Jews were among the "400" invited to Mrs. Astor's famous 1892 ball.[23] The increasing social segregation of Jews in these years is further suggested by the fact that when Edwin Einstein ran for Congress on the Republican ticket in 1878, he was described as a German; in 1892, when he ran for Mayor on the same party line, he was identified as a Jew.[24]

The increasingly isolated social situation of the Jews stands out, but religious and ethnic ancestry played an increasingly important role in all aspects of New York's social life. German gentiles had possessed their own organizations from the founding of the small and exclusive *Deutscher*

TABLE 3–2

Ethnicity of Greater New York's Mercantile, Manufacturing, and Private
Banking Firms, 1880, 1895, and 1910

	1880		1895		1910	
	All Firms (%)	AA-rated Firms (%)	All Firms (%)	AA-rated Firms (%)	All Firms (%)	AA-rated Firms (%)
British	52	78	36	63	32	65
German	32	17	50	25	50	27
Irish	9	0	8	2	4	1
Eastern European Jewish	0	0	2	0	4	0
Italian	0	0	1	0	3	0
Other	6	5	4	10	7	7
Totals	99	100	101	100	100	100
	Sample Size	Total of AA-Firms	Sample Size	Total of AA-Firms	Sample Size	Sample Size
Firms with Patronyms	233	126	325	233	420	179
Firms with no Patronym	6	12	20	65	45	88
Grand Total	239	138	345	298	465	267

SOURCE: R. G. Dun & Company, *Reference Book (And Key) Containing Ratings of Merchants, Manufacturers and Traders Generally Throughout the United States and Canada* (New York, January 1880, 1895, and 1910). These figures are based on a 0.8 percent sample of all firms in New York City and Brooklyn in 1880 and 1895, and of all firms in Greater New York in 1910; as well as a complete count of AA-rated firms in 1880 and 1895 and a 33 percent sample of such firms in 1910. An AA rating, indicating a "pecuniary strength" of more than $1,000,000, was the top rating. Ethnicity of names is the author's best guess in each case. The increasing number of corporations, and of firms not named after their proprietors, diminishes the usefulness of the figures over time. Columns may not add to 100 percent due to rounding.

Verein in 1842 and the *Liederkranz* in 1847; although the *Deutscher Verein* and forty of its members were listed in the 1896 *Social Register*, only sixteen of those members, several of whom had only indirect connections with the German community, belonged to other exclusive social clubs.[25] The *Social Register* listed neither the *Liederkranz* nor the Arion Society among the seventy-one clubs it deemed distinguished in 1896. These organizations, together with a host of German musical, gymnastic, and shooting societies, flourished throughout the period. The Arion Society, as the largest and most inclusive of all, stood in these years as "the leading German social organization of the United States," or at least of Greater New York.[26] Few of the Irish could join in social competition at the top levels of wealth, although the Catholic Club (organized in 1871 and listed in the *Social Register*) and the Xavier Club served Catholics of all national backgrounds, and the less pretentious St. Patrick's Club and the Gaelic Society advanced social ambitions as well as the causes of Irish culture and benevolence.[27]

Social and cultural distinctions were also drawn among Protestants of Dutch and British origin in late nineteenth-century New York, though with less rigor than the distinctions that separated them from the Germans, or Jews from gentiles. Retrospective commentators have often sought to identify the single "social ladder" that described the distribution of prestige in the metropolis.[28] But the most perceptive contemporary observers understood that no single ladder could be found. In *The Age of Innocence*, set in the 1890s, Edith Wharton asserted that "New York, as far back as the mind of man could travel, had been divided into the two great fundamental groups of the Mingotts and Mansons and all their class, who cared about eating and clothes and money, and the Archer-Newland-van-der-Luyden tribe, who were devoted to travel, horticulture, and the best fiction."[29] She made one of her characters add that "when I was a girl, we knew everybody between the Battery and Canal Street; and only the people one knew had carriages. It was perfectly easy to place anyone then; now one can't tell, and I prefer not to try."[30]

Wharton's fictional character had reached a great age by the 1890s; the journalist Junius Henry Browne had anticipated her view as early as 1869, when the effects of New York's great scale, enormous wealth, and rapid growth on the distribution of prestige were already apparent. "No society in the world," Browne insisted, "has more divisions and subdivisions than ours—more ramifications and inter-ramifications—more circles within circles—more segments and parts of segments."[31] Protestants with social pretensions in New York were divided into at least five distinct sets, as Browne perceptively suggested: the "old Knickerbockers," the

Oswald Ottendorfer, publisher of the *New Yorker Staats Zeitung,* from a 1905 painting by A. Muller-Ury. This is one of the most striking of the many similar portraits made for the Chamber of Commerce of the State of New York (now the New York Chamber of Commerce and Industry) between 1880 and 1910. A leading German-American Democrat and philanthropist, Ottendorfer was listed in the *Social Register* as a member of the Century Association and of the (Democratic) Manhattan, the (low-tariff) Reform, and the (good government) City Clubs—but not as a member of the *Deutscher Verein*, the Union, or the Metropolitan. (Courtesy of Pach Brothers; original painting in the collection of the Chamber of Commerce and Industry)

"livers upon others' means" whose inherited wealth was sometimes three or four generations old, the "cultivatedly comfortable," the "new rich," and the "mere adventurers."[32] In a social geography that might have been invented by Lewis Carroll each of the first four of these sets confidently looked down upon the others.

Nor was it easy to determine who belonged to each set. Like all Americans, New Yorkers lacked the clarity and publicity of titles and an Honors List. As a result, as Frederic C. Jaher has noted, American social elites and their historians must rely on such "intangible" symbols of social prestige as "the multiplication of family ties, of inheritances, of memberships in patrician organizations," and the like.[33] Intangibles resist measurement; Jaher finds it "impossible to determine exactly when families became Knickerbockers or Brahmin."[34] Jaher concludes that Boston and Philadelphia developed collections of families "that possessed intergenerational continuity and group solidarity and dominated the business, social, and cultural activities of their cities until the end of the nineteenth century."[35] But the leading families of New York's colonial and federal periods lacked "the institutional and kinship protection of patriciates in the other two cities" and had to cope with much larger numbers of *arrivistes* when their city grew far more rapidly than its competitors. As a result, "New York's upper classes in general possessed neither solidarity nor continuity."[36] In 1892, according to Jaher's estimates, fully one third of Boston's millionaires were Brahmins: but only 18 percent of New York's millionaires were Knickerbockers.[37]

A common contemporary view had it that "culture will admit to the charmed circle in Boston," and "in Philadelphia the door is closed to all pretensions except those of family, [but] money buys a ready social recognition in New York."[38] Mrs. Burton Harrison, herself a migrant to the metropolis, observed in her 1896 edition of Martha Lamb's classic *History of the City of New York* that nearly everyone with social pretensions engaged in "our struggle for great wealth" and knew all about "the dropping out of public consideration of those who do not maintain it."[39] In fact New York's social institutions did not on the whole draw a strict line against wealthy newcomers. Henry James, an exquisitely precise witness on such a point, found New York's clubs notable for their hospitality and openness, in contrast to the closed, "consecrated egoism" of clubs in London.[40] Great hostesses like Mrs. Astor made it one of their chief objectives, at least after the 1870s, to bring the right sort of newly rich families into contact with the more favored of the old.[41]

But money alone did not confer undisputed social prestige. New York was so large and so central to the nation as a whole that it was influenced by the social fashions of every section. By the mid-nineties New York had developed three distinguishable though overlapping Protestant social elites, each characterized by one of the three most celebrated social traits: "family," wealth, and culture. Perhaps a thousand or more families sought to be numbered among the "400" defined by social arbiter Ward McAllister as the city's leading elite in the 1890s.[42] These families showed up again and again on the guest lists for the fancy dinners and balls that made up the New York season. As Gabriel Almond once pointed out, these affairs were devoted exclusively to social display; even in the depression winter of 1893–94 they continued with undiminished flamboyance, rarely pretending to serve a charitable or cultural purpose.[43] McAllister's standards were wealth and family, and the fact that his services were much in demand is itself evidence of the newness and uncertainty of one sector of New York society. But McAllister's standards were not universally accepted. As *The Nation* sarcastically observed in 1892, McAllister "occasionally [alluded to] 'manners,' as things which will do an Exclusive no harm, but makes in none of his works any mention of education. This, and the correct use of the local language, are, no doubt, required in most countries as a qualification for a life among 'the brightest and best,' and they perhaps ought to be required here."[44]

Characteristically, *The Nation* overstated its case. Wealth was no doubt the most publicized criterion for social standing in New York, but ancestry and culture had their own devotees. The three principles of discrimination emerge clearly in an analysis of club memberships. Since (as E. Digby Baltzell has observed) clubs chose their members through an elaborate process of sponsorship and election, club membership served as a better index of social standing than presence on a single hostess's guest list. The leading clubs were for men only, but this simply reflected the fact that family prestige was almost entirely determined through the male line.[45] Lacking other indicators of status, New York's men joined social clubs not simply out of habit or because they wished to use their facilities, but "by way of reference or passport to high social circles."[46] To be sure of their social credentials, wealthy New Yorkers often joined three, four, or as many as fifteen clubs. The leading clubs of the 1890s can be divided into five groups, according to their emphasis on wealth, ancestry, culture, politics, or sport. Membership in the top clubs of the first three groups no doubt carried more social prestige than membership even in the New York or the Sewanhanka Corinthian yacht clubs, but clubs in the first three groups cannot be placed on a single hierarchy of prestige.

The Union Club, established in 1836, was the oldest of the exclusive social clubs still flourishing in the 1890s. Composed both of men from established families and of successful newcomers during its first thirty-five years, it had become too broadly inclusive to suit one group of its members, who split off to form the Knickerbocker Club in 1871. This, like the St. Nicholas Club and the less prestigious Holland Society (1885) insisted quite rigidly on descent from a colonial ancestor as a qualification for membership. Meanwhile the Union Club continued to thrive as an institution devoted to the circulation of elites, or as *Harper's Weekly* put it in 1890, to serving both "the shipping merchant, the dealer in his own wares, and the banker, who put their money into substantial brick and stone houses," and the newer "commission merchant and the broker, who invest their profits in railroad and telegraph securities."[47] The Metropolitan, which under the presidency of J. P. Morgan was by far the most successful of the new clubs organized by well-known million-aires during the eighties and nineties, paid still less attention to family background and, like the equally wealthy and older though socially less notable New York Club, had "no public functions whatever."[48]

The Century Association (founded in 1847) headed the third group of exclusive clubs, those serving the "cultivated." Others of this type included the University, Aldine, Lotos, the short-lived Fellowcraft, and the Nineteenth Century. All of these provided appropriate settings for meetings among men of letters, lawyers and other professional men, publishers, editors, and cultivated business men, and university administrators and professors. The Century was "formal," serious, and most exclusive; the Lotos was "sprightly" and sometimes frivolous, the Fellowcraft excessively snobbish, and the Nineteenth Century, which met in members' homes, at Sherry's restaurant, or in the Metropolitan Museum of Art, had women among its officers.[49] Brooklyn had its own clubs, which varied along similar lines.

Membership patterns confirm the point that New York's clubs cannot be fitted onto a single social hierarchy. It is true that those who belonged to several leading clubs were most likely by far to indicate that they received mail at the Union Club, if they belonged to it (see table 3–3).[50] Yet of a random sample of 129 drawn from the 1896 *Social Register*, 70 percent of those who belonged to the Union or the Metropolitan— the most prestigious of the clubs devoted to wealth—did not belong to the Century or the University, the two leading clubs devoted to culture; and 66 percent did not belong to the two leading clubs devoted to ancestor-worship, the Knickerbocker and the St. Nicholas (see table 3–4). Similarly 72 percent of those who belonged to the cultural clubs did not belong to the great clubs devoted to wealth, and 89 percent did not belong to the ancestry clubs. Three-quarters of those who belonged to the Knicker-

TABLE 3-3

Club Membership Patterns among Seven Greater New York Social and Economic Elites, 1892–96 (in percentages)

Club Type and Name	Social Register 1896 (n=129)		Officers and Directors of AA Firms 1895 (n=577)		World Millionaires 1894 (n=769)		Chamber of Commerce 1896 (n=101)		Patriarchs (1896) and 1892 Astor Guests (n=100)		Charity Officers and Directors 1896 (n=79)		Deutscher Verein 1896 (n=40)	
	Belonging	Members Listing First	Belonging	Members Listing First	Belonging	Members Listing First	Belonging	Members Listing First	Belonging	Members Listing First	Belonging	Members Listing First	Belonging	Members Listing First
In Social Register	100		37		60		55		74		56		100	
Wealth:														
Union	17	82	8	80	17	79	17	82	55	84	11	100	12	80
Metropolitan	11	15	9	30	21	16	20	30	57	9	26	24	12	20
Calumet	5	86	1	33	1	33	2	50	6	50	0	—	2	100
New York	2	3	2	31	4	16	1	0	3	0	0	—	20	38
Ancestry:														
Knickerbocker	5	71	3	15	8	35	4	0	37	41	5	50	0	—
St. Nicholas	5	14	1	10	5	0	7	28	20	0	3	0	0	—
Culture:														
University	17	65	5	33	6	21	8	25	24	8	31	48	2	0
Century	10	77	6	28	11	23	6	0	27	26	43	53	7	33
Politics:														
Union League	13	50	10	68	16	49	27	44	27	26	15	42	7	0
Manhattan	9	75	5	34	7	29	10	50	1	10	8	14	12	60
City	6	11	5	3	8	1	9	0	20	0	30	4	5	0
Reform	6	25	4	8	3	3	11	0	5	0	15	8	25	10

SOURCES: Persons included in the Social Register indicated the club at which they received mail by listing that club first. The 1896 Social Register New York sample includes the first name listed on the first and every third page. That volume also lists the "patriarchs" of the Assembly Balls" on page 444 (the 1896 Social Register was compiled in November, 1895). The New York Times listed many of the guests at Mrs. Astor's famous ball and published Ward McAllister's longer list (of 273 individuals) on February 16, 1892. The New York World published its list of 769 reputed millionaires on October 7, 1894. (The World characteristically used a social prestige criterion in selecting names for its list; 60 percent of those on the Tribune Monthly's longer June, 1892 list, were listed the Social Register. But the club membership patterns of the two lists were very similar.) R. G. Dun & Co.'s Reference Book identified the firms with a "pecuniary strength" of more than $1,000,000, the Directory of Directors and Trow's Business Directory identified their partners, chairmen, and presidents. The 1896 Chamber of Commerce sample includes the first and every tenth name from the list of members published in the Chamber's 1895–96 Annual Report, pp. 113–35. The charity officers and directors are those of the Charity Organization Society, the Society for Improving the Condition of the Poor, and the New York Mission ...

TABLE 3-4

Patterns of Membership in Clubs Emphasizing Wealth, Ancestry, and Culture, among Six Greater New York Social and Economic Elites, 1892–1896

(in percentages)

Membership Pattern	Social Register 1896	Officers and Directors of AA Firms 1895	World Million- aires 1895	Chamber of Commerce 1896	Patriarchs (1896) and 1892 Astor Guests	Charity Officers & Directors 1896
Members of Clubs Emphasizing Wealth	(n = 30)	(n = 143)	(n = 278)	(n = 37)	(n = 74)	(n = 25)
but not Culture	70	71	62	78	61	8
but not Ancestry	66	50	54	73	42	76
but neither Culture nor Ancestry	43		36	57	30	8
Members of Clubs Emphasizing Ancestry	(n = 12)	(n = 90)	(n = 190)	(n = 21)	(n = 51)	(n = 7)
but not Wealth	25	54	32	57	16	29
but not Culture	66	73	65	86	51	14
but neither Wealth nor Culture	25		26	57	6	14
Members of Clubs Emphasizing Culture	(n = 36)	(n = 65)	(n = 130)	(n = 12)	(n = 40)	(n = 43)
but not Wealth	72	38	23	58	15	44
but not Ancestry	89	65	52	83	38	84
but neither Wealth nor Ancestry	69		17	33	8	42

SOURCES: See table 3–3. For this table, only two clubs of each type have been considered: the Union, Metropolitan, Knickerbocker, St. Nicholas, Century, and University.

bocker or the St. Nicholas did belong to the Union or the Metropolitan, but two-thirds did *not* belong to the Century or the University. As table 3–4 shows, these patterns characterized economic as well as social elites. In short, the clubs devoted to wealth and to culture incorporated quite distinct, though overlapping, sets of members. The strictly old-family clubs (which were of much more recent vintage than the Union or the Century) had fewer members and were more closely allied to the wealthy than to the cultural clubs.

In short, the city's various economic and social elites followed diverse patterns of club membership. Although the very wealthy played leading roles in commercial affairs, in high society, and in the city's charities, the same wealthy people were not active in all three areas. Perhaps half of the city's millionaires belonged to none of the leading clubs. Reputed millionaires who did join a club were two or three times more likely to belong to a club emphasizing wealth than to one emphasizing culture. Those who were especially active in mercantile affairs as members of the Chamber of Commerce were just a little more likely than other wealthy men to join a club that emphasized wealth and just a little less likely to join a club emphasizing culture. The social leaders who served as patriarchs for the city's Assembly Balls and who were included among the "400" publicly invited to Mrs. Astor's 1892 party belonged to the largest numbers of both the wealth-celebrating and the ancestor-worshiping clubs. The officers and directors of the city's leading Protestant charities, by contrast, were six times more likely to belong to a cultural than to an ancestor-worshiping club, and were no more likely to belong to a millionaire's club than was an ordinary millionaire.

By the 1890s, continuing social fragmentation had created a situation in which Greater New York's exclusive social clubs served more to divide than to unify wealthy Protestants in the metropolis. The simple presence of such large and increasing numbers of clubs reduced the likelihood of casual meetings among men of divergent tastes; in smaller, less fragmented cities, a single leading club could serve as a convenient place for unplanned encounters and informal discussions and negotiations. A single leading club or set of clubs might have encouraged the development of a single notion of upper-class behavior and social responsibility.

One notion of this sort found expression on the occasion of the death of Charles Howland Russell, a prominent member of the city's Protestant cultural elite. The descendent of a 1640 founder of Woburn, Massachusetts (and the son of a director of several railroads), Russell attended private school, Harvard, and Columbia Law School; began work with the leading Wall Street firm of Evarts, Southmayd, and Choate; married the

daughter of Episcopal Bishop Henry Codman Potter; and went on to practice law with Grover Cleveland and John W. Davis and to become president of the Society of Mayflower Descendents. When he died, a friend
wrote of him "he belonged emphatically to his own class and he gave
the world what his class in its best sense can give, and that freely and
generously: courage, courtesy, justice, serious thought, culture, ripe wisdom, loyalty to people as to ideals, never a commercial judgment, never
a selfish or mean action."[51] But instead of encouraging this or any other
single notion of upper-class behavior, New York's clubs fostered divergent
norms: One set nourished a reclusive clannishness; another provided the
setting for conspicuous consumption of a public-be-damned variety; a
third supported what a visiting English Liberal approvingly called "the
very earnest, philanthropic, public-spirited class."[52]

So far as public policy was concerned, the most important social distinction lay between the first two of these groups and the third. Greater
New York's charities and philanthropies provided the most important
social—and public—activities for the "earnest, public-spirited class." Poor
relief, legal and medical services for the poor, libraries, and museums
were all provided through private voluntary associations; as an astute
contemporary observer insisted, these associations were "a part of the
de facto government" of Greater New York.[53]

The Charity Organization Society, set up by Mrs. Josephine Shaw Lowell
in 1882, played the most innovative role among New York's charitable
associations during the 1880s and 1890s, seeking to bring a degree of
order to the chaotically fragmented charitable enterprises of the metropolis. Right from the beginning Mrs. Lowell found it difficult to secure
the support she wanted. "What we need," she lamented in an early letter,
"are more men with the tradition of public service like so many of the
'nobility and gentry' of England."[54] Yet, although her insistence that much
traditional charity was "wasteful" and did "harm by encouraging pauperism and imposture, and that "so important a business as the administration
of charity has become in New York City requires to be carried on on
business principles," appealed to some potential donors, it offended others.
She failed to gain the support of many men and women of established
wealth who remained loyal to their fathers' approaches to charity—or
who adopted the truly Darwinian view that all charity is pernicious.
Among the forty-three male officers and directors of the C.O.S. in 1895,
only one had been invited to Mrs. Astor's 1892 ball for the "400," and
only one was among the "patriarchs" of New York society. The men
who supported Protestant voluntary organizations had already become a

distinct minority of the city's wealthy by the mid-1880s, when by one count fewer than 20 percent of the professionals and corporate managers listed in local Blue Books were active in such bodies.[55]

Religious and ethnic distinctions also divided those who played leading roles in Greater New York's charities. Through an "absolutely non-sectarian, non-political, and cosmopolitan" approach, the C.O.S. did bring "more than 500 churches and societies and upwards of 1000 private families into its fold," persuading many charitable organizations to move into the United Charities Building after 1893.[56] But although one or two Catholics, Jews, and Germans sat among its directors, C.O.S. "non-sectarianism" was limited, as is suggested by the organization's close relationship to the emphatically Protestant Mission and Tract and Children's Aid societies. In fact, C.O.S. cosmopolitans and Mission and Tract Society enthusiasts cooperated effectively because they shared an optimistic belief in their duty to approximate the Kingdom of God on earth through converting the ungodly, suppressing the vicious, and relieving the miserable.

Catholic charities did cooperate with the C.O.S., but they were coordinated by the Society of St. Vincent de Paul, so far as its funds permitted, and Catholics remained skeptical when many Protestants sought, in the late 1890s, to divide the entire island of Manhattan into "parishes," each served by a single Protestant church. German Jews also had their own central organization, the United Hebrew Charities, as well as many independent organizations. From the 1880s on, east European Jews set up their own independent charities as quickly as they could.[57] Legal aid and many other charitable services were provided by separate German-American organizations.[58]

These distinctions reflected conflict as well as a division of labor within and between New York City's major religious and cultural groups. Many of the charitable organizations, particularly those that cared for orphans, received substantial support from New York State and its municipalities under arrangements that were written into fundamental law after heated debate at the 1894 state constitutional convention.[59] The privately managed museums, libraries, botanical gardens, and zoos of New York and Brooklyn also received municipal land and financial support in these years.[60] Such arrangements placed the charitable and cultural organizations in competition with one another for allocations of public money. They also encouraged the private institutions of the city's "*de facto government*" to seek official government support for a great variety of divergent and conflicting policies, ranging from strategies to cope with the "tramp problem" to a proposal to open museums on Sundays. Protestants found themselves on both sides of many of these disputes.[61] So did Catholics and Jews, who also disagreed among themselves as to the wisdom of setting up their own systems of elementary and secondary schools, and as to the proper qualifications for paid positions in their charitable organizations.[62]

The proliferation and the formal development of these organizations further increased the diversity of participants in New York's public policy debates. As charitable, educational, and cultural agencies of all kinds created more and more paid positions, they hired more and more experts to fill them. The experts, often university-trained, brought their own policy preferences with them. And the charitable and religious organizations provided wealthy women with the one field in which they could actively and directly participate in forming public policy.

Economic and social change brought so many wealthy people, of such diverse economic interests, cultural affiliations, and social persuasions to late nineteenth-century New York that they fit on no single social pyramid. There were Jewish and German social elites, and at least three distinct social elites among Protestants of British ancestry. While some of these elites differed only superficially from one another, there were deep cultural and religious divisions among the very wealthy, and these divisions had striking consequences. Most fundamentally, they made it impossible for Greater New York's economic elites to coalesce into a unified, self-conscious, social group that could settle on a single set of cultural, social, religious, and economic policies. By exemplifying and supporting widely shared values and by rendering conspicuous service to the poor and to the community at large, such a group might have won a settled and generally acknowledged standing as the leading social class, deserving of respect and deference. It would then have been able to add formidable social and cultural resources to its already extraordinary wealth and would have been an irresistible force in local affairs. Instead, social and cultural division and conflict among the wealthy limited the ability of individuals, of particular economic elites, and of the group as a whole to define objectives and to make the most effective use of its enormous resources in local affairs.

White-Collar Workers and Entrepreneurs

To the extent that Greater New York's economic and social elites sought to influence the decisions of local, state, or national officials in an era of universal manhood suffrage and nearly universal voter turnout, they had to contend for power not only with one another, but with less affluent groups as well. Drawing on the growing numbers of prosperous white-collar and skilled workers, middle-class organizations mustered increasingly substantial economic, social, cultural, and political resources. As the Germans and the Irish moved up the occupational scale they produced their own, largely middle-income leaders. East European Jews also found their own leaders, first among German Jews but quite rapidly among the more successful of their own group. Ethnic self-consciousness, together with the increasing prosperity of some members in each ethnic group, led larger and larger proportions of the city's residents to look away from the British Protestant social elites for leaders. Ethnic and religious divisions fragmented the poorer as well as the richer sections of the city's social order. But even a loose sense of belonging to an ethnic group in America often permitted organization on a scale broader than that encouraged by village parochialism, and by the 1890s some of the city's middle-class Irish and German political leaders had developed a remarkably cosmopolitan culture that enabled them to mobilize large numbers of voters—and organizations—behind their demands for influence over municipal policy.

In an urban community like Greater New York at the end of the nineteenth century, most people did not own their own homes, and knowledge and skill determined a large portion of the reward to labor. Thus occupation is a better clue to the general distribution of material resources than other available indicators.[63] By this criterion, it appears that on the whole the accumulated wealth, skill, and incomes enjoyed by the mass of the region's population improved significantly between 1880 and 1910. Unfortunately the constantly changing census categories and the incompleteness of the published census returns make it impossible to be precise about the degree of improvement. It is also clear that during that period, nearly half of the region's people lived poorly and that the most wretched suffered a grievously high rate of disease and death.

The contemporary notion that New York City had no middle class was never consistent with the more accurate belief that the city was the capital of American business. The contemporary observers assumed that the city's middle class had fled to the suburbs—in 1892 some estimated that half of those who worked in Manhattan lived elsewhere. But in fact a large and increasing proportion of the labor force in Manhattan as well as other parts of Greater New York engaged in nonmanual occupations between 1880 and 1910. According to the quite complete and detailed figures of the 1910 U.S. Census, just short of 37 percent of all males who gave an occupation followed professional, managerial, clerical,

TABLE 3–5

White-Collar Workers as a Percentage of Male Residents in Greater New York and in Manhattan and the Bronx, 1890 and 1900

	1890		1900	
Skill Level	*Greater New York*	*Manhattan and the Bronx*	*Greater New York*	*Manhattan and the Bronx*
High White Collar	2.8	2.8	3.4	3.6
Middle and Low White Collar	28.1	27.8	29.5	28.3

SOURCES: U.S. Department of the Interior, Census Office, *Report on the Population of the United States at the Eleventh Census*, Part II (Washington, D.C., 1897), Part II, pp. 640–41, 704–5; U.S. Department of Commerce and Labor, Bureau of the Census, Special Reports, *Occupations at the Twelfth Census* (Washington, D.C., 1904), pp. 634–60.

or entrepreneurial pursuits. The less complete figures for "selected occupations" published in earlier years suggest that less than 31 percent in 1890 and about 32 percent in 1900 fit into similar nonmanual classifications (see table 3–5).

While Manhattan clearly had many more office jobs than the outer parts of the region, and many of its workers commuted to work from homes in Brooklyn and New Jersey, the proportion of Manhattan's residents who told census enumerators that they followed nonmanual callings was consistently as high as the proportion in other boroughs of Greater New York. As the population of Brooklyn and other outer areas grew between 1890 and 1910, Manhattan's share of white-collar workers (like its proportion of all workers living in the metropolitan region) dropped from two-thirds to one-half, but the total number of its white-collar workers rose from 153,000 to 292,000. Even allowing for the probably significant undercounting of the poor, particularly in the much-criticized 1890 census of New York City, both Manhattan and Greater New York as a whole had a middle class of substantial proportions.

As the proportion of men in nonmanual occupations rose, the proportion in manual occupations fell. Within the manual group, however, not all trends were toward higher skills, higher incomes, greater safety, and steadier employment. The most highly skilled workers were also the best organized, the best paid, and among the most steadily employed. But (as table 3–6 shows) the proportion of Greater New York's resident males who were classified in skilled occupations did not increase between 1890

125th Street, looking east from the el at 8th Avenue, 1893. The main business street of one of Greater New York's several middle-income residential neighborhoods, this stretch of 125th Street was home to *Dickson's Uptown Weekly* and the Hamilton Bank, two of the organizations that opposed school centralization and the creation of Greater New York as contrary to Harlem's interests. (Courtesy of the Museum of the City of New York)

and 1900. Those left to the residual category, "laborers not otherwise specified," declined slightly between 1880 and 1900, but the category was abandoned in a great expansion of the occupational classification in 1910, when as many as 13 percent of those whose occupations were enumerated were described as "laborers" of one sort or another. As the occupational titles listed in the published census became more finely detailed, as the proportions working as servants and apprentices declined, and as the garment industry expanded, the numbers in semiskilled occupations grew until in 1910 about a third of Greater New York's male workers were described as cigar makers, draymen, tailors, and the like.

Distinctions based on national origin cut an increasingly erratic pattern across the occupational groups in Greater New York between 1880 and 1910 (see table 3–6). The 1880 pattern—with American- and British-born Protestants predominant at the top yet still scattered up and down the occupational scale, with a largely German middle class, with German

TABLE 3-6

Skill Levels of Men of Specified National Backgrounds in Greater New York, 1890–1900
(in percentages)

Skill Level	Year	All Occupied Males	Native White, Native Parents	Great Britain and English Canada	Germany	Ireland	Sweden, Norway, Denmark	Russia and Poland	Austria and Hungary	Italy
High White Collar	1890	2.8	8.6	3.2	1.1	0.9	1.3	n.a.	n.a.	n.a.
	1900	3.4	8.7	5.1	2.3	1.7	1.8	1.5	1.9	0.6
Middle and Low White Collar	1890	28.1	41.5	25.9	26.4	17.5	14.4	n.a.	n.a.	n.a.
	1900	29.5	42.8	36.8	31.4	21.3	13.4	29.9	25.6	16.6
Skilled	1890	21.2	21.7	39.2	26.6	22.1	31.4	n.a.	n.a.	n.a.
	1900	20.8	18.5	28.8	25.0	22.0	39.0	12.6	14.8	11.9
Semiskilled	1890	26.7	16.3	16.4	32.6	23.9	30.9	n.a.	n.a.	n.a.
	1900	28.4	18.3	16.6	26.8	27.8	27.0	44.2	44.5	30.4
Laborer	1890	9.8	2.9	5.8	5.2	29.2	10.9	n.a.	n.a.	n.a.
	1900	9.4	3.2	3.8	5.3	17.7	8.5	5.7	4.4	30.3

n.a. = not available

SOURCES: See table 3–5. Most figures are not strictly comparable between years, both because the category "native born, foreign parent" was eliminated by the use of the criterion "birthplace of mother" instead of "place of birth" for assigning people to ethnic groups in 1900, and because the census employed somewhat different occupational titles in the two years. Every effort has been made to assign the same occupations to the same skill levels in each year. Where possible, the 1910 census description of occupations as skilled, semiskilled, or unskilled has been followed in assigning occupations to skill levels. Columns do not add to 100 percent because the table uses the census figures for the total number of men in each national group and for the number of men in each group who were reported as following selected occupations; the census did not publish data on the national origins of men in every occupation. The reported occupations engaged about 90 percent of the men in each national group; the range was from 88.9 percent from Sweden, Norway, and Denmark in 1890, to 93.9 percent from Russia and Poland in 1900. The consistency of the procedures used in compiling the groups and for both censuses, and the consistency of the difference between census totals for adult males and for reported occupations in all groups, suggest th̲.... all provide meaningful information.

and Irish skilled workers, and with Irish and Scandinavian laborers and dockworkers—vanished in the next fifteen years. As the Protestant social elite separated into distinct sets and was forced to make room for rival Jewish and German social elites, the ethnic origins of those on the lower levels of the occupational scale became more and more diverse, with cultural divisions setting in along both horizontal and vertical dimensions. After 1880 the British and the Germans moved steadily into the higher white-collar and skilled trades. The Irish, by contrast, achieved a foothold as entrepreneurs by 1890 but lost some of it thereafter and improved their representation in white-collar ranks by greatly adding to their numbers in lower-level managerial and clerical occupations. As a group, the Irish moved very slowly out of unskilled and semiskilled occupations. The Scandinavians remained under-represented in white-collar callings, but more concentrated in skilled and semiskilled trades than any other group.

While the ethnic groups already established in New York made only gradual changes in their occupational position, newcomers rearranged the entire pattern (see table 3–7). By 1900 the region's bankers, wholesalers, and professional men were still predominantly of native American and British background, with a large minority of German origin. But those who followed semiprofessional, managerial, and clerical pursuits were as likely to be German as native American, and a large minority was Irish. On the other hand, among entrepreneurs (including manufacturers, shopkeepers, peddlers, restaurant and bar-keepers, and livery stable proprietors), almost a third was of German background, over 20 percent was eastern European, 15 percent native American, and 12 percent Irish in parentage. Workers in skilled and most semiskilled trades were still predominantly German and Irish, with a large representation of the native-American and British groups and small proportions from Italy and eastern Europe. The largely semiskilled garment workers of 1900 were by contrast overwhelmingly eastern European and German in origin; and laborers were Irish, Italian, and German in proportions of 39 percent, 22 percent, and 14 percent. In sum, the native Americans and British were heavily overrepresented at the top; Germans were solidly ensconced in the middle; Irish were well represented in the clerical, skilled, and semiskilled ranks and had almost double their share of laborers; eastern Europeans were over-represented in the entrepreneurial ranks and dominated the garment trades; and Italians were well represented only among petty entrepreneurs and garment workers and had three times their share of laborers.

Of the newer immigrants, both the Russians and Poles and the Austro-Hungarians entered Greater New York with larger proportions in the

TABLE 3–7
National Backgrounds of Men at Specified Skill Levels in Greater New York, 1900
(in percentages)

	All Occupied Males	High White Collar	Semi-professional and Managerial	Clerical	Entrepreneurial	Skilled	Semi-skilled	Garment	Laborers
Native White, Native Parents	17.7	45.1	30.2	32.9	14.8	15.7	13.9	1.4	6.8
Great Britain and English Canada	6.5	9.7	9.2	9.2	6.1	9.1	4.5	1.0	2.6
Germany	24.9	18.8	25.3	23.4	31.3	29.9	25.4	16.1	13.9
Ireland	21.1	10.3	14.6	20.6	11.7	23.0	25.4	2.3	39.3
Sweden, Norway, Denmark	2.1	1.1	0.9	1.1	0.9	3.9	2.1	1.5	1.9
Russia and Poland	8.1	3.6	6.4	3.4	14.1	4.9	4.1	44.5	4.9
Austria and Hungary	4.9	2.7	3.8	2.1	6.7	3.5	4.1	21.5	2.3
Italy	6.7	1.1	1.8	0.9	8.1	3.8	7.0	7.7	21.6
Other	8.0	7.6	7.8	6.4	6.3	6.2	13.5	4.0	6.7

SOURCE: See table 3–6.

white-collar ranks than the Irish or the Scandinavians, but with much smaller proportions in the skilled trades. The Italians, of whom over 60 percent were in unskilled or semiskilled occupations in 1900, entered at the bottom. Contrary to most impressionistic accounts, the eastern Europeans, most of whom were newly arrived Jews who had fled pogroms and persecution, already claimed 94 percent of their share of white-collar occupations. While this figure includes large numbers of peddlers, small shopkeepers, and marginal garment contractors, it would be 81 percent if the peddlers were excluded, and the comparable figures for other national groups also include many saloon and livery stable keepers, barbers, and petty tradesmen who were no more prosperous.[64] This background helps explain and confirm Thomas Kessner's recent conclusion that New York's Jewish immigrants enjoyed remarkable upward occupational mobility during these years.[65] In other communities the arrival of new immigrant groups often pushed older groups up the occupational ladder, but in Greater New York the new immigrants themselves supplied foremen and petty proprietors as well as factory hands for a new industry, the manufacture of ready-to-wear clothing, which indirectly drove many German tailors and Irish dressmakers out of work.[66]

Entrepreneurs constituted a separate group, distinct from others in white-collar categories. Although entrepreneurs varied greatly, most peddlers, shopkeepers, and small manufacturers worked with their own hands in small establishments. As late as 1910 R. G. Dun & Company rated 96 percent of the retailers and 64 percent of the manufacturers, as opposed to only 41 percent of the wholesalers and bankers, at a pecuniary strength of less than $10,000 (see table 2–6). A 10 percent return (which would have been very high in an era of 5 percent bonds) on a $10,000 investment would have produced just under $20 per week, hardly a handsome income. Moreover, the Dun ratings did not even record the existence of the thousands of peddlers and hundreds of garment contractors included by the census among the city's 107,000 "retail dealers" and 34,000 manufacturers.[67] Slender resources and an extremely competitive business environment made these firms vulnerable to failure, forcing them to be concerned above all with keeping costs down and discouraging their owners and managers from taking any large view of the problems facing their industries, let alone those facing the region as a whole.

The economic resources of middle-income New Yorkers varied widely, but even the most prosperous had to organize to participate effectively in local affairs. Ethnic background clearly exerted a strong influence on the distribution of occupations in the city, yet in many cases both employ-

ers and employees organized along lines of economic interest, not national
origins. In this as in other respects the public life of middle-income New
York was remarkably cosmopolitan. Building contractors, brewers, bankers, jewelers, and the larger printers and publishers—all of whom had
to deal with effective craft unions—had their own organizations, which
functioned throughout the period on a city- or region-wide basis and
without overt reference to national distinctions.[68]

In other fields—particularly clothing, specialty, and luxury goods,
where trade unions were weak—manufacturers seem to have had no established representative or coordinating organizations until after 1900 or
later.[69] In practice, many of the small manufacturers in these fields were
only quasiindependent, depending in a very traditional way upon great
merchants for orders and credit just as many contractors depended upon
public officials for construction work.[70] The business relationships between manufacturers and merchants were of course based largely on competition in terms of prices, quality, and reliability, and competition frequently involved cutthroat tactics. But price differences must often have
been slight, permitting established contacts or personal ties to play an
important role in many deals, as Abraham Cahan emphasized in *The
Rise of David Levinsky*, his classic novel about the garment industry.[71]
The dependence of many small manufacturers upon the patronage of
commercial magnates probably intensified in the years after 1880, as the
average size of the firms in the rapidly expanding garment industries
failed to increase.[72]

In these industries, the numerous small manufacturers found their leaders among those substantial merchants who had a considerable interest
in the prosperity of the region's garment and specialty industries and
who sought to defend and assist those industries in the public arena.
But this arrangement did not always work to the interest of the small
entrepreneur. In a series of disputes in the garment industry after 1909,
for example, leading mercantile and financial figures intervened on behalf
of garment workers who were seeking better wages, better working conditions, and unionization. Apparently the magnates believed that the long-
run interests of both the industry and the metropolitan region as a whole
would be served best by stable labor relations and somewhat improved
incomes and health for the garment workers. Since many of the small
manufacturers could expect their "long run" to last only a few years,
they could not take so broad a view of their labor problems. Yet when
they wished to influence those who often spoke most effectively for their
industry, the eastern European Jews who were rapidly moving into the

clothing business had to make their cases to American-born Protestants of British background and to German Protestants as well as to German Jews.[73]

Most of Greater New York's retail merchants had even fewer capital resources than the small manufacturers. This economic weakness was reflected in the paucity of retailers' organizations and even in the name of the Retail Dealers Protective Association, one of the few retailers' groups listed in the very thorough *Eagle Almanac* directory for 1899.[74] Nevertheless some of the larger retailers, together with builders and real estate dealers, organized effective local chambers of commerce in several sections of the greater city. Such organizations were particularly strong on the West Side of Manhattan, in Harlem, on the North Side (later the Bronx), and in Brooklyn and some of its outlying business districts. Rapidly built up during the 1890s, these areas competed directly with one another. Their promoters and retailers, many with close ties to the political parties, sought to persuade municipal officials to provide the improved transportation facilities, school buildings, and police and sanitation services necessary to attract new residents.[75] The businessmen and the residents of these middle-income residential areas were quite mixed in terms of national origin; in 1899, central Harlem alone boasted twenty-five Protestant churches (five of them Lutheran), eight Catholic churches, and five synagogues.[76] Greater New York's white-collar workers also organized themselves into occupational associations, and these too cut across ethnic lines. Public school teachers and administrators, for example, had several distinct and well-established associations that divided along the lines of gender and bureaucratic rank, not ethnicity or religion.[77]

Middle-income New Yorkers also created a host of charitable, mutual protection, and self-help organizations, and these often followed national-origin lines. The innumerable German organizations constituted a world unto themselves, as did the east European Jewish organizations described so well by Moses Rischin in *The Promised City*.[78] Mutual benefit, insurance, and labor organizations exerted such a strong attraction on American Catholics, in New York as elsewhere, that Church leaders successfully pressed for a relaxation of the Vatican ban on membership in secret societies; but Catholic authorities encouraged membership in the Knights of Columbus and continued to discourage Catholics from joining non-Catholic organizations that bore the slightest resemblance to the Masonic Order.[79] Reflecting the slight and precarious prosperity of their members, most of these organizations emphasized sociability and basic insurance. But some of them, particularly those most closely affiliated with religious groups and those prosperous enough to engage in charitable activity, sought to influence local and state policies in such fields as education and social welfare.[80]

These ethnic and religious associations did not always agree with one another, of course; some of the state's most severe political conflicts in the 1880s and 1890s brought Protestants and Catholics into conflict. On some occasions Catholics, Protestants, and Jews quarreled among themselves. Yet identification with an ethnic group often raised an immigrant's sights from the parochial concerns of his *landsmanschaft,* as Arthur Goren has demonstrated in his study of the *Kehilla,* the umbrella organization created by New York's Jews as a means of coping with anti-Semitism. However, although many mutual-benefit associations were ethnically based, the most successful were nonsectarian and broadly inclusive in philosophy, even when their local branches took on an ethnic cast. In 1901 the four largest mutual benefit associations, all of them nonsectarian, claimed over 134,000 members in Greater New York.[81]

By then, the memory of the violent Protestant-Catholic confrontations of the 1850s, '60s, and '70s was fading as German and Irish Catholics and Protestants found ways to work together. By then, too, middle-income Germans and Irishmen were abandoning crowded, one-nationality immigrant districts to live together in "surburban" uptown neighborhoods. Tammany Hall had begun to produce ethnically balanced tickets in the 1880s, and by 1904 George Washington Plunkitt and others had perfected the techniques of inclusive politics.[82] By the 1890s many of Greater New York's most effective neighborhood and political leaders had achieved prominence not as the champions of one group against the others, but as mediators able, as one of them put it during the school centralization controversy of the nineties, to "harmonize" religious and ethnic group conflicts.[83] Working through Tammany, through mutual-benefit and charitable organizations, neighborhood improvement associations, churches, and labor unions, uptown Irishmen and Germans and downtown Jews forged a new set of local elites in these years.[84] Alternately calling on a common background and on a cosmopolitan appeal, these elites posed a serious threat to the cultural as well as the political leadership of the very wealthy.

Manual Workers

If the economic resources of Greater New York's entrepreneurs and white-collar workers were often limited, those of its manual workers were frequently meager indeed. Yet the standard of living varied widely among the region's manual workers. Skilled workers—especially those engaged in operating stationary or locomotive engines and in the printing, building, and stone-, metal-, and woodworking industries—possessed scarce and valuable skills and well-established unions that assured them of relatively steady work, short hours, and high wages.[85] Most unions lost members during hard times, but in 1900, just three years after the Great Depression of the mid-nineties, about 60 percent of the region's skilled workers be- ✓ longed to a union. Despite the depression, men in New York City's organized building, stoneworking, and woodworking trades all secured the eight-hour day during the nineties, while the printers and many metal workers also succeeded in reducing the length of their work day.[86]

Taking account of layoffs, workers in all these trades were earning on the average between $13 and $16 weekly in the prosperous years at the end of the century; engineers and firemen, shipbuilders, and printers, most of whom worked longer days, earned more.[87] In Greater New York such a wage enabled a man to provide good food and decent clothing for his family, to pay union dues and purchase a little insurance, and to rent three or four rooms in a relatively new, clean, and comfortable tenement building or Brooklyn row house away from the unhealthy gashouse and slaughterhouse districts along the Hudson and East rivers.[88] By 1910 two-thirds of the manual workers who worked below Fourteenth Street and earned more than $14 a week lived away from the ancient slums near their workplaces, as did over half of those who earned less than $10.[89] (See map 3–1 for population densities and map 3–2 for health data on districts in Manhattan.) Many of the better-paid workers who lived below Fourteenth Street lived in the comparatively good housing available in the German district between Broadway and the Bowery above Houston Street in the 1890s and in the central parts of the Jewish Lower East Side after 1900.[90] (See map 3–3 for the ethnic make-up of Manhattan districts.)

Semiskilled workers rarely earned more than $10 a week, and until 1909, when the International Ladies Garment Workers Union and others, in a "spectacular conquest," brought more than 250,000 clothing workers into union ranks, they were rarely organized.[91] Ill-paid, unorganized, lacking job security, semiskilled and unskilled workers together made up New York's other half. In the best of health and the best of times, a semiskilled worker could hardly feed and clothe his family and pay the rent. Almost always compelled to work ten or eleven, even twelve hours a day, six days a week, the semiskilled worker was forced to live near his work; in Manhattan that often meant paying a rent that reflected the high price of land near an overcrowded industrial district.[92] Unskilled laborers and widows were still worse off. In 1894 one investigator encountered the following families living in two-room apartments on Essex Street on the lower east side:[93]

A Polish Jew, his "wife and four children; occupation, baster; wages received, $12 per week for seven months of the year; rent, $8 per month; clothing $75 per year, savings, nothing."
A Polish Jew, his "wife and six children; occupation, expressman; wages received, about $8 per week; rent, $9 per month; clothing $100 per year; savings, nothing."
A Russian Jew, his "wife and two children; occupation, laborer; wages received, $1 per day; time lost for want of employment, two days per week; rent, $7 per month; savings, nothing."

Another investigator found that an even still harsher pattern prevailed among Italians living on Mott and Spring streets:[94]

Tenement of 3 rooms, rent $12 per month, husband, wife, 4 daughters (eldest 18), two sons, and 8 male lodgers. Total, 16.
Tenement of 2 rooms, $8 per month, widow, son and 9 male lodgers.
Tenement of 3 rooms, rent $9 per month, husband, wife, 1 daughter (age 18), 2 sons, married lodger, wife, 3 daughters (14 and 16), son and 4 young men lodgers. Total, 15 persons.

Still another investigator wrote of the Bohemian cigar makers who lived in the vicinity of 72nd Street and First Avenue, "I cannot describe the condition of the people making the cigars in the same room in which they live, cook and eat their meals and sleep. Yet they have to pay for three small dirty rooms $11 or $12 monthly. I found several cases, where the heads of the families and other adult members were unemployed, others again, who earn' from $3 to $5 a week, and I found only a very few, who said they have enough work and earn enough."[95]

These accounts of rents and household patterns are representative, as tables 3–8 and 3–9 make clear. While these miserable conditions prevailed at the depths of a great depression and eased somewhat after 1897, only the garment workers among the semiskilled were able to establish effective unions before the 1930s. Strenuous efforts to organize teamsters, transit workers, and hotel and restaurant employees between 1910 and 1916 all failed.[96]

To some extent Greater New York's manual workers were able to supplement their economic resources with cultural, ideological, and organizational resources, and with their votes. Michael Gordon has shown, for example, how the Irish made use of their traditional practice of boycotting,

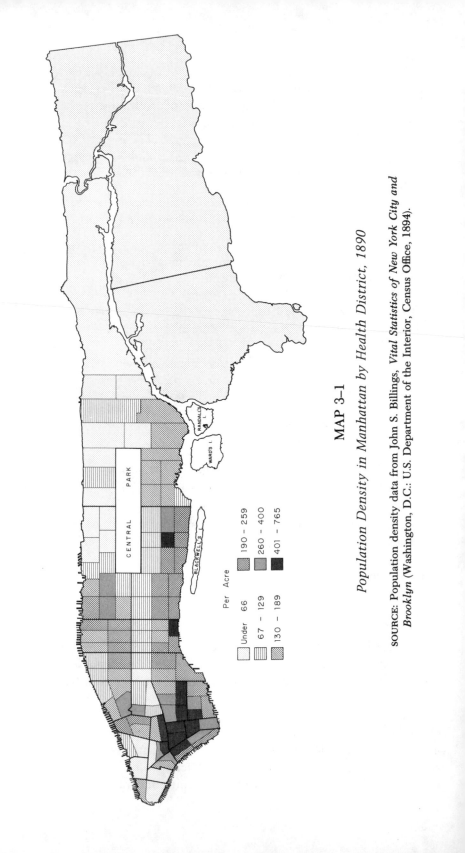

MAP 3–1

Population Density in Manhattan by Health District, 1890

SOURCE: Population density data from John S. Billings, *Vital Statistics of New York City and Brooklyn* (Washington, D.C.: U.S. Department of the Interior, Census Office, 1894).

Per Acre

Under 66

67 – 129

130 – 189

190 – 259

260 – 400

401 – 765

CENTRAL PARK

BLACKWELL'S I.

WARD'S I.

RANDALL'S I.

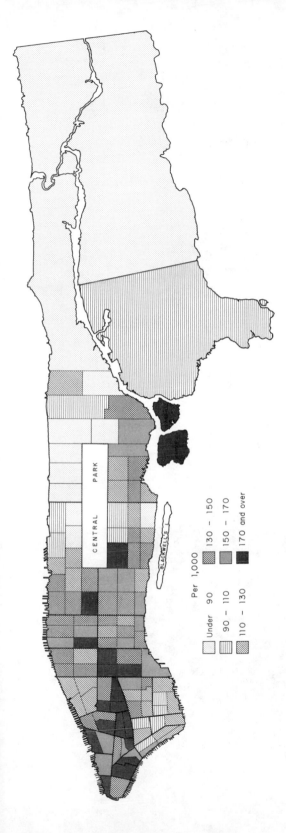

MAP 3-2

Death Rates of Children under Five Years of Age in Manhattan, by
Health District, 1885–1890

Data on the death rates of children provide the best indirect measure of the relative poverty or prosperity of each district, in part because it controls for the varying age distributions in different districts. Considered together with map 3-1, this map indicates that the highest early childhood death rates did not occur in the city's most crowded areas.

SOURCE: See map 3-1.

CENTRAL PARK

BLACKWELL'S I.

Per 1,000

Under 90
90 – 110
110 – 130
130 – 150
150 – 170
170 and over

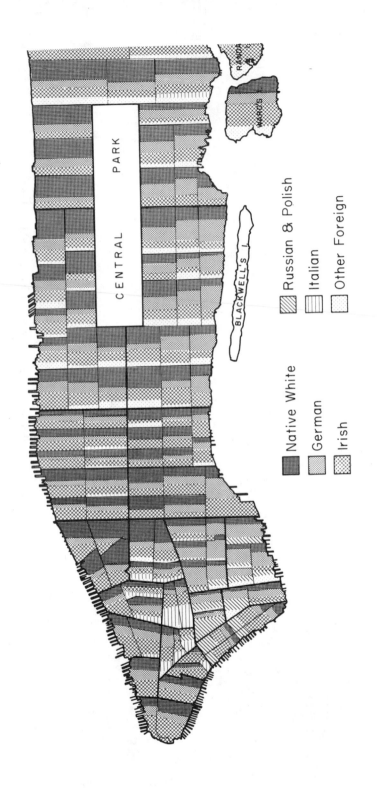

CENTRAL PARK

BLACKWELL'S I.

RANDALLS I.

WARD'S I.

Native White

German

Irish

Russian & Polish

Italian

Other Foreign

MAP 3–3

Principal Ethnic Groups in Manhattan by Health District, 1890

This map is in effect a composite of more than 100 bar graphs. Each health district in Manhattan below 180th Street is shaded in bars of varying darkness to show the proportion of its residents belonging to one of six ethnic and nationality groups. Within each district, the bars are layered from light (other foreign) to dark (native white), without regard for actual residential locations. Thus the map shows a concentration of Germans in the districts between Grand and 14th Streets east of the Bowery, but does not show where members of that group lived within each district. Membership in each group was derived from a census question as to place of birth; hence "native whites" include the U.S.-born children of white immigrants. A group was not indicated if it failed to constitute at least 10% of the population in a district. Note that native whites and German and Irish immigrants lived in almost every district, including most of the heavily Italian and Eastern European districts below 14th Street.

SOURCE: See map 3-1.

Hester Street at Norfolk Street, 1898. New brick buildings (including the new Public School 42 in the background on the right with a prominent cornice) and intense market activity, involving the buying and selling of dressmakers' supplies as well as food and clothing, reflect the economic vitality of the lower east side. (Courtesy of the New-York Historical Society, New York City)

the ostracizing of those who collaborated with British landlords, to punish strikebreakers. When this tactic drew vehement denunciation as un-American and proved less effective in a great city than in small towns and villages, the Irish and other workers adapted it to the "do not buy" approach still employed by labor unions against the products of offending manufacturers.[97] As Gordon's example suggests, such cultural resources often became more valuable after workers had been in the United States long enough to adapt them to American conditions. Jewish workers could sometimes draw on a different cultural trait, the sense of communal responsibility in a hostile world. As Moses Rischin has observed, during a bakers' strike the *Jewish Daily Forward* urged that all participants consider the community's reputation in the city as a whole:[98]

TABLE 3–8

Tenement Houses by Average Monthly Rent Paid per Apartment,
Manhattan Wards 1–22 and Brooklyn, 1902

Manhattan Ward	Percentage of Population in Tenement houses (%)	Under $3 (%)	$3–$3.50 (%)	$3.50–$4 (%)	$4–$5 (%)	$5 or more (%)
1	48.3	n.a.	n.a.	n.a.	n.a.	n.a.
2	21.3	n.a.	n.a.	n.a.	n.a.	n.a.
3	46.9	n.a.	n.a.	n.a.	n.a.	n.a.
4	65.8	26	28	28	14	4
5	68.9	12	31	28	23	6
6	79.8	11	15	31	35	8
7	91.0	13	21	28	26	12
8	76.3	12	20	30	27	11
9	70.6	11	19	24	31	15
10	85.7	7	20	36	32	5
11	93.8	24	31	29	14	3
12	78.3	30	24	19	18	9
13	93.2	14	29	31	22	4
14	81.0	7	17	37	36	3
15	54.5	8	15	24	29	24
16	62.3	13	17	21	30	19
17	83.7	9	23	32	26	10
18	66.8	27	29	22	12	10
19	75.5	34	28	16	13	9
20	73.9	30	24	19	17	10
21	64.1	26	23	23	16	12
22	71.6	24	22	16	18	20
All Manhattan	77.5	23	24	22	20	11
Brooklyn	n.a.	81	10	5	3	1

n.a. = not available

SOURCE: First *Report* of the Tenement House Department of the City of New York, 1902.

It is wholly a domestic matter with us. The workmen are ours and the bosses are ours, and we alone are the customers. . . . Let us show the world that when a struggle like this occurs in our midst, we settle the question in a feeling of justice and human sympathy—that we settle the issue in favor of the workmen and their just demands.

The networks for the exchange of information regarding employment opportunities, wages, and the like that flourished in every trade provided another cultural resource. A 1910 survey elicited protests from more than one manufacturer against the ease with which his employees used such information to play employers off against their competitors.[99]

The shifting fortunes of New York's labor organizations provide our

TABLE 3–9

*Number of Rooms and Average Monthly Rent Paid for Tenement Apartments
in Three Lower East Side Districts, 1894*

Number of Rooms	"German Quarter"		"Jewish Quarter"		"Italian Quarter"	
	Families Occupying[a]	Average Rent Paid	Families Occupying[a]	Average Rent Paid	Families Occupying[a]	Average Rent Paid
1	1%	$ 5.43	2%	$ 4.51	2.5%	$ 5.19
2	24	9.62	35	7.98	42	7.93
3	36	13.61	39	11.92	37	10.98
4	26	18.19	18	15.96	13	16.20
5	7	26.17	3	18.65	3	22.58
6 or more	8	46.42	3	37.97	3	36.19
Ratio of Children to Families	1.72		2.25		2.68	
Ratio of Lodgers to Families	0.42		0.36		1.48	

[a] Columns may not add to 100 percent because of rounding.
SOURCE: Robert Graham, *Social Statistics of a City Parish* (New York: Church Temperance Society, 1894). Of the many surveys of tenement house conditions made during the 1890s this is the only one that gives figures for the average rent paid for apartments of a specified size, or that provides detailed comparisons between districts. These districts were part of St. Augustine's Cure, Trinity Parish. The "German Quarter" (in which 40 percent of the population had been born in Germany and which was 31 percent Catholic, 33 percent Lutheran, and 10 percent Jewish) was bounded by the Bowery, East 5th Street, Avenue A, and East Houston Street. The "Jewish Quarter" (in which 43 percent of the population consisted of "Russian, Polish, and German Jews" by birth and 10 percent was German, and which was 70 percent Jewish, 10 percent Catholic and 10 percent Lutheran) was bounded by the Bowery, East Houston Street, Essex Street, and Hester Street. The "Italian Quarter" (in which 58 percent of the population had been born in Italy and 94 percent was Catholic) was bounded by the Bowery, East Houston Street, Broadway, and Canal Street.

best evidence of the relative strength of the ideological perspectives that competed for working-class followers. Although workers became more and more diverse in their ethnic origins between 1880 and 1910, the ideological and organizational pattern became somewhat simpler as larger and larger portions of the city's workers adopted one or another of the two most successful views: "pure and simple" American Federation of Labor unionism and the social democratic tradition.

As unions revived after 1882, New York's workers joined a wide array of groups that formed and fell out of alliances with bewildering frequency. By far the largest of the early groups was District Assembly 49 of the Knights of Labor, a body that was itself made up of disparate subgroups, including idealistic cooperationists, believers in the transcendent unity of head- and hand-workers alike, socialists, and craft unionists. District

TABLE 3–10

Wage Earners' Support for Labor Unions, Lodges, and Religious
Organizations, New York City, 1907

				Percentage Contributing Regularly to			
Nationality	Number of Families	Median Income	Average Contribution	Labor Union	Lodge, etc.	Church or Synagogue	None of These
Austrian	32	$850	$15.55	22	63	56	6
Russian	57	750	15.30	37	54	63	7
Bohemian	14	750	26.45	36	86	71	7
Irish	24	850	14.93	29	13	88	8
German	39	950	15.41	21	39	62	15
United States (White)	67	850	11.51	25	30	61	22
United States (Black)	28	750	6.89	18	36	39	25
Italian	57	750	8.64	23	26	25	44
All Nationalities	318		13.58	26	40	55	20

SOURCE: Robert Coit Chapin, *The Standard of Living Among Workingmen's Families in New York City* (New York: The Russell Sage Foundation, 1909), pp. 45 and 208. These figures were produced by a casual but not statistically random survey, conducted by trained interviewers armed with a very detailed schedule of questions; they are valuable but certainly not definitive. The purpose of the study was to determine what comfortable workingmen's families in general—not the average family or the family in particular occupations, or of particular national backgrounds—spent for specified objects.

Assembly 49 supplied half the 120,000 members of the Central Labor Union in 1885; independent craft unions and German socialist unions provided the rest.[100] Politically divided among competing German and English socialist, eastern, and southern European syndicalist and anarchist, Irish land reform, and American single tax, low tariff, and protectionist persuasions, the workers' movements reached a peak of confusion, fragmentation, and conflict during the depression of the mid-nineties. But the separation of union organizing from party politics, the success of Gompers's pure and simple unionism—emphasizing higher wages and better working conditions—in the skilled trades, and the decline of ethnic divisions within the labor movement introduced some clarity by 1900.[101]

By the mid-nineties, as Moses Rischin has pointed out, "German and English-speaking unionists were coming together despite jurisdictional conflicts," and labor organizations were reflecting the ethnic heterogeneity of most city neighborhoods (see map 3–3). In 1900 "the German Central Labor Federation and the Irish Central Labor Union merged to form the Central Federated Union. . . ."[102] Pure and simple unionism formed the basis for these mergers, as Gompers and the craft unions turned away from socialism to the independent political tactic of rewarding friends and punishing enemies.[103]

On a per capita basis the material resources of Greater New York's manual workers probably improved somewhat between 1880 and 1910, despite the fact that a smaller proportion remained in the skilled trades and a larger proportion had become semiskilled by the latter year. But there is no question that trade unions—making use of the workers' diverse cultural resources, decreasing parochialism, and widespread adoption of the tactics if not the ideology of pure and simple unionism—had become much more effective. (For one indication of the support unions had secured by 1907, see table 3–10.) Labor economists have cast doubt on the proposition that unions raise wages, but they surely do provide workers with spokesmen. Between 1880 and 1910 the workers' spokesmen in the metropolis gained a stronger base and a clearer, if less comprehensively radical voice.[104]

Artisan-Republican Rhetoric, the Sporting Style, the Kingdom of God, and Other Political Strategies

When those who belonged to Greater New York's economic elites wished to influence state or municipal officials, they had to take account of the influence their poorer fellow citizens exerted at the polls. Poor and middle-income New Yorkers apparently believed that the vote was one of their most valuable resources, and they used it assiduously. In 1888, when the national presidential election turnout was 62 percent in the south and 73 percent in the nonsouthern states, the New York City turnout was 86 percent of the eligible native-born and naturalized male population over 21 years of age. In 1890 a ballot reform law intended to reduce voting among illiterates was passed in New York State, but in 1892 New York City again produced an 86 percent turnout, while nationally the proportions declined to 58 percent in the south and 70 percent elsewhere. In 1901 about 74 percent of Greater New York's eligible voters participated even in an off-year mayoral election; comparable figures in the 1900 presidential election were only 29 percent in the south, where the movement to disenfranchise blacks and poor whites had been very effective, and 65 percent in nonsouthern states.[105]

Since the wealthiest men in Greater New York were predominantly of native-born stock, they were at a cultural disadvantage at the polls. In 1890 only 21 percent of those eligible to vote in New York City were the American-born sons of American-born mothers; the comparable figure in Brooklyn was just 29 percent.[106] For Greater New York as a whole in 1900, the figure was less than 23 percent.[107] The native-born of native parents were largely Protestant; but the region as a whole was heavily Catholic and increasingly Jewish. Cultural differences made it difficult to translate a clear predominance of material resources into political influence.

Some of the very wealthy did seek a basis for cross-cultural and cross-class coalitions. In 1886 iron manufacturer and merchant Abram S. Hewitt successfully rode into the mayor's office on the old-fashioned argument that in a republic artisans and manufacturers are fellow producers.[108] During the 1880s and 1890s and after, William C. Whitney, Thomas Fortune Ryan, August Belmont, and other utilities millionaires employed a sporting style—entertaining on a large scale, providing racetracks and thoroughbreds, offering "drinks all around," contributing to Tammany Hall relief committees, and in other ways underwriting popular customs and exemplifying widely shared values—with such success that Greater New York's politics often resembled those of London in the same period.[109] But Hewitt's artisan-republican rhetoric rapidly lost currency after 1886, and the sporting style required a cosmopolitan outlook and a sure touch as well as the willingness to spend a great deal of money. And it often proved self-limiting. Wealthy men who appealed to Irish and German workers on the basis of a shared love of horse racing, gambling, and whiskey, could not hope to be equally successful among eastern European Jews and Italians, who preferred other forms of entertainment. And when German-Jewish magnates began to play similarly conspicuous roles among their poorer co-religionists in the nineties, they found themselves pushed and pulled away from their economic peers among gentiles of German and British background.

The sporting style also clashed with the earnestly public-spirited, ostensibly rational, often deeply religious approach to local affairs that came easily to well-educated Protestant bankers, merchants, corporate leaders, and professional men—and their wives and sisters. Such people disliked the easy camaraderie of the race track and Fourteenth Street: Their dislike made a Tammany Hall plan to build a trotting-horse raceway in Central Park one of the great "scandals" of the early 1890s. A millennial desire to establish the Kingdom of God on Earth often animated the earnestly public-spirited approach, making it incompatible with the objectives of wealthy as well as impoverished devotees of the sporting style or with those of many Catholics and Jews. Morris K. Jesup, a merchant whose wealth and standing were recognized in his election to a vice presidency of the Chamber of Commerce, was one of the most notable of those who discovered that enthusiasm for extreme Protestant measures often provoked a divided reaction from prosperous businessmen. Jesup found that many members of the Chamber were willing to join in his financial support for the New York Mission and Tract Society and for Anthony Comstock's intrusive Society for the Suppression of Vice. But others opposed those organizations' aggressive efforts to convert the Jews and regulate behavior. Jesup's experience persuaded him to invoke commercial arguments, not religious or moral ones, when he sought to persuade the Chamber to demand a more rigorous enforcement of the blue laws. "If life and property are not safe in this city," he insisted, "if people cannot come here from afar and feel that their lives are cared for, that the great temptations and evils we all know about in New York are not proscribed, if New York once gets the name and the fame of having no justice in it, then I would like to know what business the Chamber of Commerce could expect to do in the future."[110] Many merchants rejected his view.

A Kingdom of God Protestantism also influenced many of those who created the settlement houses of the nineties, encouraging the optimism and the ambitions that led the leaders of at least one Episcopalian settlement to assert that their neighborhood was really quite godly, that most if its inhabitants were "people associated in some way with a church."[111] But many settlement house workers were engaged in a systematic effort to comprehend and relieve social ills as well as to promote their religion, and they found it easy to work with more secular men and women who were seeking to advance the causes of efficiency, expertise, and a predictable bureaucracy in municipal affairs.[112]

The earnestly public-spirited approach probably seemed familiar and persuasive to the increasingly numerous native-American, German-American, and even Irish-American white-collar employees of the region's banks, insurance companies, and national corporations. But the rise of white-collar employment in New York had less influence on the voters than it might seem, because as the number of bookkeeping and clerical jobs increased, more and more of them, particularly in the rapidly expanding new corporations, were taken by women.[113] The corporations, with their comparatively long-term perspective and rational, bureaucratic style, consequently exerted the influence of an employer over a smaller portion of Greater New York's male electorate than the amount of their capital and the total number of their employees might suggest. Yet the presence of relatively large proportions of German-Americans and eastern European immigrants in nonmanual occupations provided potential allies to those who sought improved public schools or more even-handed administration of the laws—as long as the Protestant impulse toward proselytizing and the rigid enforcement of blue laws could be kept in check.

The sporting style and the earnestly public-spirited approach gave some of Greater New York's wealthiest men the basis for appeals to their poorer fellow citizens, but neither religion nor national culture provided the region's wealthy Protestants with a set of symbols or institutions through which they could easily appeal to the group pride, the material needs, or the deference of their community's German and Irish, Lutheran and Catholic, white-collar and skilled workers. On the contrary, Irish hatred of the British made "Anglomaniac!" an effective slur in New York politics. Only the Germans were well represented up and down the occupational ladder, but when the German economic elite sought to appeal to German white-collar and manual workers, it had to contend with the fact that German Protestants, Catholics, and Jews were present in different proportions at each occupational level.

Greater New York's extraordinary social and ethnic diversity both divided the rich from one another and made it difficult for them to appeal for the votes or the deference of their poorer fellow citizens. But these factors created difficulties for all New Yorkers. Differences in religious, ethnic, and even home-town background divided people at all occupational levels. Manual workers were perhaps more widely divided over economic strategy during the eighties and nineties than at any time in American history, and their disagreements reached an unusual intensity in New York. And many nonmanual workers, especially the small entrepreneurs in the region's largest industries, found themselves continually off balance as they were caught up in rapid, unpredictable, increasingly competitive change. Only in the cases of the American and British Protestants at the top, the eastern European Jews in the garment trades, and smaller groups of German and Irish skilled workers did significant numbers of people share both economic position and cultural background, so that they could employ a shared culture for purposes of political or economic organization. In general, appeals for concerted economic action had to be made across cultural lines, just as appeals for cultural or religious action had to be made across economic lines. Since the ethnic mix varied from one occupational level to another, moreover, a rhetorical style or organizational strategy that worked at one level was often ineffective at another.

No single group held sufficient economic, organizational, and cultural resources to dominate Greater New York at the end of the nineteenth century. The region's size and its position at the top of the national system of cities brought to it a disproportionately large number of wealthy people. But the economic interests of the city's wealthiest people had rapidly proliferated: whereas in 1880 most fortunes stemmed from mercantile and banking activities, by 1910 wealth was more likely to be derived from railroads, mining, national manufacturing corporations, investment banking, and law. As economic activities became more and more various, the region attracted an unusually large and increasingly diverse concentration of professional and technical experts. The factors that drew both the wealthy and the experts to Greater New York encouraged them to divide themselves into a number of distinct though overlapping economic elites. As the rich and the expert grew richer and more numerous, social and cultural differences encouraged them to divide yet again into quite separate social elites. These internal divisions made it impossible for the city's wealthiest people to form a single dominant elite, capable of working out a unified economic, cultural, and political agenda for the metropolis.

Instead, wealthy and well-educated men and women produced a variety of economic, cultural, and political initiatives. But the increasing size and diversity of Greater New York's middle- and lower-income population made it still more difficult for the rich to appeal for social deference or political support. The region's middle-income population was also unusually large, and by the nineties was producing a vigorous and remarkably cosmopolitan generation of German- and Irish-stock leaders in Tammany Hall, the Catholic Church, the labor movement, the lodges, neighborhood chambers of commerce, and other self-help organizations. Yet these middle-income leaders, like the rich and the expert, had to deal both with a demanding and increasingly well-organized lower-income German, Irish, and Scandinavian population and with large and rapidly growing new groups of Italians and Jews.

E. L. Godkin's notion that the rich, the well born, and the cultivated were in eclipse seems implausible. Men of this sort possessed extraordinary resources and dominated the boards of the charitable agencies that constituted an important part of the region's "*de facto* government." Moisei Ostrogorski's argument that the cultivated and the merely rich could not be distinguished from one another was a clever taunt that failed to take account of real differences in values and patterns of association. But James Bryce's competing view that the rich could be divided neatly into "best men" and "capitalists" and that the former could gain power simply by stepping forward to accept the support of a deferential citizenry, failed to reflect a much more complex reality. The social basis for deference had largely disappeared and effective resources were more widely distributed than Bryce understood. Yet any of the contemporary theories about power—Godkin's Genteel Decline, Bryce's Patrician Elitism, Ostro-gorski's Economic Elitism, Daniel Greenleaf Thompson's Government by Syndicate—may have been correct. Resources were not distributed as God-kin, Bryce, or Ostrogorski assumed. But the distribution of resources is not necessarily the same as the distribution of power over the making of decisions.

PART III

Mayoral Politics

CHAPTER 4

TRADITION AND REALITY

IF POWER is the ability to influence the outcomes of decisions, the possessors of high political office are no more certain of power than are the possessors of great fortunes. The office holder, like the rich person, enjoys only a resource that may help to gain desired ends. But although an examination of electoral politics cannot by itself yield sufficient evidence to permit conclusions about the distribution of power in a community, no study of the distribution of power in an American city can ignore mayoral politics. The roles of American mayors have varied from time to time and from place to place, but the mayor has almost always played an important part in his city's affairs. Whatever the mayor's influence on decisions, mayoral politics defines much of the context in which decisions are made.

In the last third of the nineteenth century the mayoralty of New York was the city's most important elective office, even though it had not yet become the "great prize" that Wallace Sayre and Herbert Kaufman found it to be when they published their classic *Governing New York City* in 1960.[1] In the wake of the Tweed Ring and of a series of aldermanic scandals in the early 1880s, the theory that controlled the design of the city's government centralized a great deal of power in the mayor's hands, but limited his ability to use that power to give positive and continuous direction to municipal affairs. A short, two-year term of office made the mayor responsible to the electorate, but it also made him responsible to those who controlled nominations. The mayor played a leading role in the preparation of the municipal budget, but he shared this responsibility with the elected comptroller and the other members of the Board of Estimate. He had to approve most actions of the City Council, but nearly all important changes in policy for the city—and for the region as a whole—were made by the state legislature in Albany.

Yet the mayor did gain increased powers over state legislation and over city commissioners in the mid-nineties and again after 1900. Further, as the symbolic head of the city he was indisputably the region's most visible public official. He enjoyed numerous opportunities—election campaigns, annual messages, making appointments, ceremonial or crisis occasions— to define issues and to shape the region's agenda. Through his powers of appointment he strongly affected the quality of the city's services, the careers of its officials, and the fate of its political organizations. As a result, the office of mayor served as the focal point of the city's politics; one of the chief tests of any political organization's strength was its ability to influence a nomination for mayor.[2]

The years 1886–1903 form a coherent transitional period in New York City's political history, but they should be understood in the context of social and political changes that date back to the overthrow of the Tweed Ring in the early 1870s. Adopting the perceptions and social biases of contemporary partisans, historians and political scientists have almost universally retained the traditional view that mayoral politics in late nineteenth-century New York was an essentially static conflict between "bosses" and "reformers." This view greatly oversimplifies and misinterprets the character of the city's political actors and organizations. A more realistic understanding of mayoral politics is essential to an accurate understanding of the distribution of power.

In reality, the city's politics reflected the increasing complexity of its economic and social life, with the years between 1886 and 1903 serving as a Transition Period between the merchant-dominated polity of an earlier era and the Tammany-managed city of the first third of the twentieth century. In the earlier years, merchants dominated municipal politics just as they dominated the municipal economy, and after the 1870 ouster of the Tweed Ring they dominated quite openly. During what can be called the Era of the Swallowtails, 1872–1886, every man elected Mayor of New York City was a prominent merchant who owed his nomination to the most important politically active group of Democrats among the merchants, bankers, and lawyers who directed the city's economy. During the Transition Period, local politics became much more complicated and uncertain, as a newly effective and broadly based Tammany Hall nominated the winners in four of six mayoral elections, and a changing coalition of disparate economic, political, charitable, and labor elites mounted two successful and three effective but unsuccessful campaigns. Tammany did much better during this period than it had done in the past, but it did not firmly establish its dominance until 1903, when it launched its one great age, an age that lasted until 1933.

The wealth they had gained through nonpolitical careers (and inheritances) made the Swallowtails (so-called after their penchant for frock coats) independent of party discipline and enabled them to purchase the assiduous assistance of others. But they were also serious, dedicated, and effective politicians. As the city's economy became more complex, attracting larger and larger numbers of wealthy owners and managers of national railroad, mining, and manufacturing corporations, the wealthy Swallowtail Democrats fell into increasingly severe internal disagreements, abandoned their alliances with professional politicians in the assembly districts, and found themselves confronted by stronger and stronger groups of wealthy Republicans and municipal nonpartisans. From the late 1880s into the early 1900s, deeply held religious and cultural commitments further divided the politically active among the wealthy, as tolerant *laissez-faire* liberals and exponents of the sporting style argued and competed with increasing numbers of aggressive Protestant blue stockings and with progressive social Christians over the election strategy most appropriate to the city. And all of these groups of wealthy men (and a few wealthy women) had to deal not only with increasingly well-organized and self-sufficient Tammany Hall and Republican party organizations, but also with a thriving and politically active labor movement. The great theme of the period was not the static battle between bosses and reformers, but the increasing diversity of the political organizations that could influence mayoral nominations.

Four Campaign Scenes

Theodore Roosevelt contributed one of the best-known statements of the traditional view. "Almost immediately after leaving Harvard in 1880," he wrote in his brilliantly persuasive *Autobiography*, "I began to take an interest in politics. . . . The men I knew best were the men in the clubs of social pretension and the men of cultivated taste and easy life. Although the Twenty-first [Assembly District] was known as one of the silk-stocking districts of town, when I began to make inquiries as to the whereabouts of the local Republican organization and the means of joining it, my friends laughed at me and told me that politics were 'low'; that I would find them run by saloon-keepers, horse-car conductors, and the like." In a story designed to exaggerate the significance of his career, Roosevelt asserts that he replied, "If this were true it merely meant that the people I knew did not belong to the governing class, and that the other people did—and that I intended to be one of the governing class."[3] Tammany district leader George Washington Plunkitt indirectly supported Roosevelt's contention that wealthy and well-educated men were rarely to be found in the city's political circles: Most reformers were "mornin' glories—looked lovely in the mornin' and withered up in a short time, while the regular machines went on flourishin' forever. . . . The fact is," Plunkitt concluded, "that a reformer can't last in politics."[4] Yet in 1889 Roosevelt complained, in a private letter to his close friend Henry Cabot Lodge, that although he "would like above all things to go into politics . . . in this part of the State that seems impossible, especially with such a number of very wealthy competitors."[5] And Plunkitt, who wished to emphasize his own (considerable) achievements and to discourage troublesome reformers, also observed that "bluff counts a lot in politics."

Four scenes—two from the mayoral campaign of 1886, two from the campaign of 1897—convey a more accurate impression of the changing character of metropolitan politics in these years.

The most extraordinary mayoral campaign of the late nineteenth century was waged by organized labor on behalf of Henry George in 1886, and the most striking event of the George campaign was a great parade, held on Saturday, October 30.[6] As though to deny suggestions that George's supporters were irrational anarchists and to affirm that organized labor was ready to play a mature and serious part in local politics, the editors of George's campaign newspaper emphasized the paraders' large numbers and sober earnestness:

> Between six and eight o'clock in the evening, trade unions, Henry George clubs, and district associations were marching from all parts of the city to rendezvous in the streets running out from the Bowery; and sharp at eight the Printers' Legion led the line toward Union Square. Before the march began a mist commenced to fall, and in half an hour a heavy rain-storm set in which continued till midnight. Nevertheless, though the men were drenched, the procession moved on between deep double lines of sympathetic and enthusiastic spectators. . . .
>
> In front of the cottage at Union Square the procession passed rapidly in an almost solid mass. It was estimated that ten thousand people stood upon the street here to observe the review. Henry George, surrounded by a crowd of his supporters, reviewed the procession as it rushed by. Each body of men in passing cheered the candidate, and as the parade lasted two hours, one continuous shout from eight till ten o'clock greeted the ears of Mr. George.
>
> Most political processions are equipped by the candidates. Thousands of dollars are spent for uniforms, torches, and transparencies [illuminated signs].

But upon this procession no money was expended except what each man spent for himself. There were no gayly decked wagons, no uniforms, and but few torches, and the transparencies were made by the men who carried them. Trades organizations carried union banners, and fantastic emblems were here and there displayed. Some of the bodies marched in darkness, without torches, music, transparencies, emblems, or banners. No one could watch the parade and not feel its significance. . . . There was an earnestness about it all, which renewed the courage of those who participated, and their friends who looked on, and admonished the politicians that a new era in politics had indeed begun.[7]

The more colorful account on the front page of the next day's New York *World* noted that Patrick Ford, editor of the *Irish World and American Industrial Liberator;* German-American leader Theodore Von Bremsen; and several minor Democratic politicians had joined George on the platform at Union Square, where "calcium lights and colored fires" lit the scene. According to the *World,* delegations from at least fifty unions of skilled and semiskilled workers joined George's political supporters in the ranks behind the printers. Especially notable were the large bodies of tailors, plumbers, Progressive Painters (led by a "knight in armor"), brass workers, framers (carrying a large red flag), street railway workers, tobacco workers (carrying torches and Roman candles), Cuban cigar makers, Italian fruit handlers, and Bohemian single taxers. German coopers, carrying a huge broom (with which to sweep the election) brought up the rear.

Many of the marchers, including forty plumbers and a large number of Samuel Gompers's tobacco workers, carried slogans and symbols on illuminated transparencies. To judge from the *World*'s account, the slogans made three points. First, many supported traditional artisan virtues: "No Charity: We Want Fair and Square Justice;" "We Are Striving to Elevate Our Craft." Second, others insisted that workers simply sought long-established republican rights: "The Spirit of '76 Still Lives!" "The Workers of The City Are Not Anarchists!" Third, and most significantly for the future, the largest number of signs militantly insisted on labor's new political goals: "Boycott the Enemies of Labor!" "No More White Terror! Down With Bribable Judges, Corrupt Legislators, and Vile Police Despotism!" "Reorganization of Society Independent of Boss, Priest, or Loafer!" and Henry George's own appeal for "Honest Labor Against Thieving Landlords and Politicians—The Land Belongs to the people!"[8]

The Tammany Hall meeting held four days earlier to rally support for Abram S. Hewitt, George's Democratic opponent, provided a scene that was almost equally astonishing to contemporaries. During the fifteen

years since the 1871 ouster of the Tweed Ring, Tammany had been forced
into a secondary role, for most New York Democratic affairs were managed
by the wealthy merchants and lawyers who constituted the Swallowtail
Democrats. Hewitt was that group's most astute and energetic leader.
As the *World* observed, the notable point about Hewitt's rally was simply
the fact that "men were present who had never been inside of Tammany
Hall before, and there were others there who had been strangers to it
for years." In addition to the current Swallowtail and Tammany leaders,
Hewitt was supported on the platform by Swallowtail ex-mayors Edward
Cooper and Franklin Edson, and by dedicated anti-Tammany publishers
Joseph Pulitzer of the *World* and Oswald Ottendorfer of the *New Yorker
Staats-Zeitung.* Two millionaires who had sought the Tammany nomination served as vice presidents for the meeting, as did Tammany Swallow-
tails August Belmont, the banker; Roswell P. Flower, the broker and railroad investor; and Jacob Ruppert, the brewer. Two other Tammany
swallowtails, Joseph J. O'Donahue, a tea and coffee importer, and Eugene
Kelly, a drygoods merchant-turned-banker, opened the meeting.

But although Swallowtail Democrats were much in evidence, this was
by no means entirely a rich man's meeting. As if to emphasize that Tammany district leaders were now in charge, the organization's meticulous
secretary, Thomas F. Gilroy (whose impoverished mother had brought
him from Ireland to New York at the age of five), read the list of vice
presidents. Altogether, the appearance of these men at a Tammany meeting was a spectacle capable of attracting a crowd that overflowed from
the Hall's 5,000 seats down the stairways and out into Fourteenth Street
below. The crowd was a cross-section of New York; almost half of it,
according to Pulitzer's pro-Hewitt *World*, consisted of "working men."[9]

Hewitt had been nominated because he, better than anyone else, possessed the intelligence, the speaking ability, the ideological vision, and
the public standing necessary to give a compelling argument against
George. Most of those in the hall had come to hear his carefully constructed speech, and they gave it their rapt attention. Hewitt began with
a series of significant asides—acknowledging the many years that had
passed since he had been inside "this familiar hall," referring obliquely
to the "dynamite" exployed by the "anarchists" at Haymarket Square,
nodding to a Tammany committee that had "done so much for the rights
of Ireland," and lightly dismissing George's assertion that he was serving
as the politicians' "tool." But in an effort to meet many George voters
on their own ground, Hewitt devoted the bulk of his address to a celebration of the liberty and opportunity that permitted American workingmen
and manufacturers alike to create and accumulate wealth.

"All over the world," Hewitt insisted, "men are looking to this land as the great example of what may be done for the elevation of the masses." America's success, he suggested, derived from two sources: "free government" and the efforts of "the honest working people who have brought up their families in the fear of God, have accumulated money to buy a house and have laid together some provision for their old age." He added, "Among these is a certain number and class of men who, by their exertions, have achieved an honest competence. . . . Now these are the people who have a hard battle to fight in this country, and for whom I have fought."

George, he insisted, would restrict the freedom of Americans by introducing the labor-discipline technique of shunning into politics as well as labor relations: "Do you understand what that means? Do you understand that the horrors of the prison-house, the odium of the stripes and bars is preferable to the condition of that man who is turned out like Ishmael from the society of his fellow workmen?" And George's "single tax" policy would exempt the buildings which constituted the "accumulated capital" of millionaires and raise the rents paid by honest workingmen and small manufacturers. As a life-long opponent of tariffs and other taxes on consumer goods and income, as a beneficiary of and life-long spokesman for free public education and for scholarships to private schools like his own family's Cooper Union, and as a persuasive advocate of responsible charity, Hewitt concluded, he himself was best able to promote "individual liberty" and "the best possible equality, which is that a large portion of the community are in comfortable circumstances, honest in character and charitable in action."[10]

Once Hewitt had spoken, Tammany's own W. Bourke Cochran, a young Irish-American already well known as an orator, made his way to the rostrum amid "cheers and a Tammany tiger" to endorse and echo Hewitt's refrain: In America, above all in a New York City illuminated by the Statue of Liberty, "labor will find an easy market, and it will be housed and fed in comfort." Moreover, "there are no classes where all are equal at the ballot box." A vote for Hewitt was a vote for "Liberty, prosperity, and order."[11]

By the mid-nineties the most important group of wealthy men in New York City's politics consisted not of Democratic merchants and bankers, but of a diverse assortment of bankers, investors, merchants, lawyers and other professionals, and Protestant church and charity leaders. In 1897, following protracted, painful and only partly successful negotiations among themselves and with various established organizations, a substantial group set up the Citizens' Union, a third party intended to be active only in municipal affairs, and settled on Columbia University President Seth Low (heir to a Brooklyn mercantile fortune and one-time Republican mayor of Brooklyn) to head their ticket. The rally they held in Cooper Union's Great Hall on October 6, 1897, to kick off Low's mayoral campaign, revealed more than they intended about their movement.

Treating the occasion as a solemn civic ceremony, a well-dressed, "intelligent-looking" crowd of about 4,000 men and 500 women filled the hall to overflowing. Citizens' Union leaders and their wives crowded the stage, and the entire assemblage assumed a "thoughtful, considerate" air as it awaited Low's arrival. When the candidate, accompanied by his wife and escorted by Bar Association President Joseph Larocque, finally appeared, the crowd leapt to its feet, men cheering, women waving their handkerchiefs. But after acknowledging the cheers Low fell into his accustomed college-president demeanor: Remaining in full view of the audience throughout the preliminary speeches, he sat in a chair near the center of the stage, arms folded, frock coat buttoned, eyes on the orator of the moment—or gazing at the ceiling. His wife sat next to him, and next to her sat Mrs. William J. Schieffelin and other leaders of the Citizens' Union auxiliary. Among the many others on the stage were Chamber of Commerce president and Citizens' Union leader Charles Stewart Smith (a merchant-turned-banker, a Republican, and an earnest Presbyterian), Charity Organization Society leader Charles S. Fairchild (a banker and former Democratic Secretary of the Treasury), Wall Street lawyers Stephen H. Olin (an active school reformer) and Arthur Von Briesen (founder of the Legal Aid Society and German-American leader), and several minor Republican party leaders. This was a gathering of the wealthy—or at least the well-to-do—but in behavior, in tone, and in the prominent presence of so many women it resembled the annual meeting of the Mission and Tract Society far more than it resembled a meeting of the Union Club, let alone an ordinary political rally.

The wealthy and well-educated women who were now taking a public part in metropolitan reform politics contributed notable portions of enthusiasm, intelligence, and labor to Low's campaign, even though they could not vote and even though their very presence offended many, especially among the Germans, who retained traditional notions about woman's proper place. But they could not make up for the failure to secure Democratic, Republican, German, and labor support, or for the failure to reach out to the new eastern European Jewish and Italian communities. Fearful of offending Protestant leaders, businessmen, and editorial writers, Low and his associates delivered short, vacuous speeches that avoided the burning contemporary issues—liquor, labor recognition, ethnic-group recognition, municipal ownership, public services—leaving the impression that he was a narrow, humorless man and giving the missing groups no incentive, save fear of Tammany or Republican bossism, to vote for him.[12]

The Tammany ratification meeting held one week later presented a stark contrast to the Citizens' Union rally and the Tammany rally of 1886 but it was no more inclusive of outsiders. Tammany's financial backers, given prominent (if remote) places for themselves and their wives in "gaily decorated boxes" at the organization's 1886 nominating convention, now had no public role to play at all. Marshalled by their district leaders and attracted by bands and fireworks, "a tremendous crowd of men" filled the hall and surged around the three supplementary platforms set up on Fourteenth Street and Third Avenue. Inside, Hugh J. Grant, the lawyer and uptown real estate investor who had defeated Abram S. Hewitt in 1888 to become New York City's first Irish-American mayor, and who had lost to Strong in 1894, and John C. Sheehan, the contractor who was Tammany's nominal leader, led the procession to the platform. In the line behind them came street railroad promoter Lawson N. Fuller; Irish leader O'Donovan Rossa; Tammany congressmen Amos J. Cummings, George B. McClellan, Jr., and William Sulzer; Tammany district leaders "Barney" Martin, "Big Tom" Brennan, and Tom Grady; State Senator Jacob A. Cantor; Judge John Henry McCarthy; several leaders of Brooklyn's Willoughby Street counterpart to Tammany Hall; and Col. Asa Bird Gardiner, the Tammany candidate for district attorney.

These men included Protestants and Jews, native-born and German-Americans, as well as Irish Catholics; they retained ties to various parts of the Greater City; and they followed a variety of occupations. But each of them was admittedly, even proudly, a professional politician and a loyal Tammany organization man. Each one received hearty cheers as he reached the stage, but Sheehan, as leader of the organization, Grant, as its most reliable warhorse, and Gardiner, as a blueblood who had shouted "To Hell With Reform!" during a speech at the Wahatchie Club (an obscure Harlem branch of Tammany) received the most enthusiastic welcome.

The most remarkable absentees from Tammany's meeting were not its financial backers, but its real leader, Richard Croker, and his candidate for mayor, the obscure judge Robert A. Van Wyck. Croker avoided the meeting because he had not yet officially stepped back into the place he had relinquished to Sheehan following Grant's defeat three years earlier. Van Wyck did not appear because, according to Tammany, he had not had time to compose a letter of acceptance. According to Tammany's opponents, he failed to appear because, as Croker's "yellow dog," he had nothing to say. Former Mayor Thomas F. Gilroy, former Congressman Bourke Cochran, and former New York City Postmaster Charles W. Dayton, once the leading Democrat in Harlem, did not appear because they had fallen out with Croker and his current associates.

Appearances counted, because this meeting was more a spectacle than an oratorical occasion. Yet the oratory did reflect both the organization's determination to appeal to a variety of low- and middle-income pressure groups and to avenge recent insults. Tammany Secretary McGoldrick read the resolutions endorsing the (anti–blue law) "home rule" and "personal liberty planks;" the (pro-labor) anti-monopoly, cheap gas, municipal ownership–municipal control, and pro-public works planks; as well as the traditional low-tax and anti-nativism planks of the party's platform. Elmira's former assemblyman, John Stanchfield, withstood an intrepid cheer for Henry George and a passing band's rendition of "There'll Be a Hot Time in the Old Town To-Night" before he was able to get off his eulogy of Van Wyck. Congressman Cummings delivered a startling and inappropriate defense of Richard Croker, whose return from a horse-racing retirement in England had provoked a hail of newspaper abuse. And at last Thomas F. Grady, who had replaced Cochran as Tammany's favorite orator and who had been denied the district attorney nomination at the last minute, received "the only real Tammany yell of the night," dismissed Seth Low as an aristocrat, and brought down the house by concluding, with reference to the successful moralistic anti-Tammany campaign of 1894, "We want revenge. We want a terrible revenge. Such as will satisfy the indignation that we feel over the abuse that was levelled at honest men in official positions, and for the wrong that was done us. We want revenge for the lies they told, for the passions they excited. And it looks now as if we will get it!"[13]

The contrasts among these four election scenes reflect three fundamental long-term developments: increasing numbers, diversity, and conflict among the wealthy men active in local politics; increasing self-sufficiency within the Tammany and Republican machines; and increasing numbers of effective pressure groups representing the city's low- and middle-income population. In 1886 Swallowtail Democrats had played a dominant role in the making of the Tammany nomination; their counterparts had played the same role in the Republican party; and both regular parties had nominated wealthy men. Swallowtails continued to play important roles in both party organizations in 1897, but the Democrats among them had become few in number and the Citizens' Union was a fragile coalition supported by a much larger and more diverse collection of rich and well-off men and women. The professional politicians of Tammany Hall, like their Republican counterparts, had heartily acknowledged the Swallowtail role in 1886; but in 1897 they jealously excluded men of wealth from their public proceedings, insisting in every way possible on the competence and self-sufficiency of an organization that produced its own leaders from within. In 1886 the city's diverse labor organizations had put aside their considerable differences to mount an impressive campaign for Henry George and against established parties that appeared to serve only their enemies; in 1897 labor split five ways, as Tammany, the Republicans, and the Citizens' Union all sought and received more labor votes than either Henry George, Jr.'s Labor party or Daniel DeLeon's recently reorganized Socialist Labor party. Both Tammany and the Independent Labor party had appealed for the Irish vote in 1886; eleven years later all three of the city's comprehensive political organizations sought to deal with the insistent and irreconcilable demands of numerous German, eastern European, and evangelical Protestant organizations as well as with the Irish. Each of these long-term developments—the political fragmentation of the very wealthy, the increasing maturity of the political machines, and the proliferation of politically effective pressure groups among the rich, the middle-income, and the poor alike—requires exploration in some detail.

Factions and Rules

In the traditional view, mayoral elections in late nineteenth-century New York City were a series of contests between "professional politicians" and "reformers." This view assumes that Tammany Hall usually won elections and insists that fusion was always the key question: Would the reformers rouse themselves, unite with one another, and form an alliance with the Republicans? Many of the chief facts of the elections between 1886 and 1903, and indeed of elections all the way back to 1870, the last year of the Tweed Era, can be arranged to fit this view. Table 4–1 indicates that a "Tammany," a "reform," and a "Republican" candidate can be identified in almost every election, and that candidates in each column received significant shares of the vote.

But the information in table 4–1 also suggests some of the inadequacies of the traditional perspective. Between 1870 and 1886, for example, "re-

TABLE 4–1

Mayoral Elections in New York City, 1870–1903: The Traditional View

	Tammany Hall		Reform		Republican	
Year	Candidate	Percentage of Vote	Candidate	Percentage of Vote	Candidate	Percentage of Vote
1870	HALL	61	Ledwith	39	Ledwith	*
1872†	Lawrence	35	HAVEMEYER	39	HAVEMEYER	*
1874	WICKHAM	53	Ottendorfer	18	Wales	28
1876	ELY	66	ELY	*	Dix	34
1878	Schell	42	COOPER	56	COOPER	*
1880	GRACE	*	GRACE	50	Dowd	49
1882	EDSON	*	EDSON	55	Campbell	43
1884	Grant	38	GRACE	42	Gibbs	20
1886†	HEWITT	*	HEWITT	41	Roosevelt	27
1888	GRANT	42	Hewitt	26	Erhardt	27
1890	GRANT	53	Scott	43	Scott	*
1892	GILROY	61			Einstein	34
1894	Grant	40	STRONG	56	STRONG	*
1897	VAN WYCK	44	Low	29	Tracy	19
1901	Shepard	42	LOW	51	LOW	*
1903	McCLELLAN	52	Low	*	Low	42

CAPS indicate victorious candidates.

* Indicates endorsement of candidate nominated by another political force.

† In these years nominees who are not included on this chart received large numbers of votes.

SOURCES: Official election statistics published in the New York *City Record*, 1874–1903; the New York *Times*; the New York *Tribune Almanac*, 1874–1904. Elections for 1897, 1901, and 1903 were for mayor of the enlarged city of Greater New York.

formers" were more likely to fuse with Tammany than with the Republicans; and when Tammany did not join in a fusion campaign during those years, its candidate was usually defeated. Between 1870 and 1886 "reformers" won seven of the nine elections, and they won nine of the sixteen held over the thirty-three-year period as a whole. Even when Tammany candidates did begin to win with some regularity after 1886, they generally attracted less than 45 percent of the vote. The fact that it is possible to identify a "reform" candidate in every year save 1892, moreover, suggests that the reform movement was neither sporadic nor amateurish.

In fact, the traditional view both underestimates the success and the persistence of "reform" movements in late nineteenth-century New York and obscures the considerable variety of those movements. As table 4–2 shows, the "reform" nominations were produced not by a single continuous movement, but by distinct organizations that belonged to three separate political traditions. Tammany Hall and the New York County Re-

TABLE 4–2

Nominations for Mayor of New York City by Major Political Organizations, 1870–1903

Year	Tammany Hall		Apollo or Irving Hall Democrats		Gold Democrats		Citizens' Organizations		Republican Party Organization	
1870	HALL	61	Ledwith	39			Ledwith		Ledwith	
1872	Lawrence	35	O'Brien	27			HAVEMEYER	39	HAVEMEYER	
1874	WICKHAM	53			Ottendorfer	18			Wales	28
1876	ELY	66	ELY						Dix	34
1878	Schell	42	COOPER	56					COOPER	
1880	GRACE		GRACE	50					Dowd	49
1882	EDSON		EDSON		EDSON	55	Campbell	43	Campbell	
1884	Grant	38	GRACE		GRACE		GRACE	42	Gibbs	20
1886	HEWITT		George		HEWITT	41			Roosevelt	27
1888	GRANT	42			Hewitt	26	Hewitt		Erhardt	27
1890	GRANT	53			Scott	43	Scott		Scott	
1892	GILROY	61							Einstein	34
1894	Grant	40			STRONG		STRONG	56	STRONG	
1897	VAN WYCK	44			Low		Low	29	Tracy	19
1901	Shepard	42			LOW		LOW	51	LOW	
1903	McCLELLAN	52					Low		Low	42

CAPS indicate victorious candidates; numbers indicate each candidate's percentage of the total vote, listed in the column indicating his chief factional loyalty in the year of the election. Nominations in column 2 are for Apollo Hall in 1870 and 1872, for Irving Hall thereafter. Nominations in column 3 are for the Liberal Democracy in 1874; for the New York County Democracy in 1882, 1884, 1886, 1888, and 1890; and for the New York State Democracy in 1894, 1897, and 1901. The Citizens' nominations of 1870, 1872, and 1888 were *ad hoc*, one-campaign efforts; those of 1882 and 1884 reflected the independent organization of Democrat William R. Grace; that of 1890 was made by the People's Municipal League, of 1894 by the Committee of Seventy, and of 1897, 1901, and 1903 by the Citizens' Union.

SOURCES: See table 4–1.

publican organization were the most continuously active political organizations in the city, nominating or endorsing candidates in every election and maintaining both leadership cadres and effective networks of assembly district organizations. But non-Tammany Democrats, working now through the Apollo or Irving Hall organizations that sought to rival Tammany, now through the Gold Democrats' County and New York State Democracies, were almost equally persistent and well organized; between 1870 and 1886 they clearly dominated Tammany's mayoral selection process. The various "citizens' " movements were much more discontinuous in the earlier years, but with the successive and closely related campaigns of the People's Municipal League (1890), the Committee of Seventy (1894), and the Citizens' Union (1897, 1901, 1903), they competed with Tammany on nearly equal terms between 1894 and 1903. A still finer analysis of mayoral nominations would reveal that non-Tammany Democrats, nonorganization Republicans, and an increasing variety of labor and ethnic pressure groups played significant roles in elections throughout the period.

Three long-term social and economic trends clearly shaped this welter of shifting local factions. Wealthy swallowtail candidates, Republicans as well as Democrats, continued to appear throughout the entire period. As table 4–3 shows, rich men did not abandon politics: In 1897 two wealthy Republicans ran against a Tammany Democrat who sported a high-sounding Dutch name; in 1901 a future president of the Chamber of Commerce defeated a Wall Street lawyer whose partner was the president of the Association of the Bar; in 1903 a modestly wealthy Princeton graduate was the Tammany organization candidate. But rich men did become somewhat less dominant: Between 1870 and 1890 swallowtails received sixteen of the twenty-six major nominations for mayor: Between 1892 and 1903 they received five of eleven. Increasingly, the swallowtails were displaced by professional politicians who had worked their way up through their organizations' ranks. From 1884 on, Tammany turned to a swallowtail only under extreme duress, and the Republican organization pressed—with less success—for the same autonomy. As the swallowtails became somewhat less numerous (and more deeply divided among themselves), and as men who had devoted their entire career to politics moved more frequently to the head of the ticket, labor and ethnic group leaders were also able to increase their impact on mayoral nominations.

As table 4–4 shows, labor and socialist nominees had played almost no part at all in mayoral elections before the Henry George campaign of 1886. But although George's strong showing was clearly exceptional, it served to encourage independent Social Democratic and Socialist Labor campaigns that drew small but not insignificant votes in the succeeding years. The ethnically balanced ticket had not yet become a New York tradition, but ethnic as well as labor leaders did exert increasing influence over the selection of candidates.

The highly factionalized character local politics in New York City was encouraged by the laws that regulated nominations and elections. Throughout the period, state law stipulated that nominations to public office in New York City were to be made by party convention, not by direct primary. Accordingly, those who wished to influence nominations had to enroll as active members of a party, or set up a party of their own. Party creation was made easier by the fact that the law did not permit any organization to establish a legal claim to be "the" Democratic or "the" Republican Party: At one point three distinct city-wide organiza-

TABLE 4-3

Mayoral Nominees in New York City, 1870–1903: Socio-Political Types

Year	Tammany Hall	Apollo or Irving Hall Democrats	Gold Democrats	Citizens' Organizations	Republican Party Organization
1870	TAMMANY DEMOCRAT	Organization Democrat		Organization Democrat	Organization Democrat
1872	Swallowtail Democrat	Organization Democrat		SWALLOWTAIL DEMOCRAT	SWALLOWTAIL DEMOCRAT
1874	SWALLOWTAIL DEMOCRAT		Swallowtail Democrat		Swallowtail Republican
1876	SWALLOWTAIL DEMOCRAT	SWALLOWTAIL DEMOCRAT			Swallowtail Republican
1878	Swallowtail Democrat	SWALLOWTAIL DEMOCRAT			SWALLOWTAIL DEMOCRAT
1880	SWALLOWTAIL DEMOCRAT	SWALLOWTAIL DEMOCRAT			Swallowtail Republican
1882	SWALLOWTAIL DEMOCRAT	SWALLOWTAIL DEMOCRAT	SWALLOWTAIL DEMOCRAT	Swallowtail Democrat	Swallowtail Republican
1884	Tammany Democrat	SWALLOWTAIL DEMOCRAT	SWALLOWTAIL DEMOCRAT	SWALLOWTAIL DEMOCRAT	Organization Republican
1886	SWALLOWTAIL DEMOCRAT	Labor	SWALLOWTAIL DEMOCRAT		Swallowtail Republican
1888	TAMMANY DEMOCRAT		Swallowtail Democrat	Swallowtail Democrat	Organization Republican
1890	TAMMANY DEMOCRAT		Swallowtail Democrat	Swallowtail Democrat	Swallowtail Democrat
1892	TAMMANY DEMOCRAT				Organization Republican
1894	Tammany Democrat		SWALLOWTAIL REPUBLICAN	SWALLOWTAIL REPUBLICAN	SWALLOWTAIL REPUBLICAN
1897	TAMMANY DEMOCRAT		Swallowtail Republican	Swallowtail Republican	Organization Republican
1901	Swallowtail Democrat		SWALLOWTAIL REPUBLICAN	SWALLOWTAIL REPUBLICAN	SWALLOWTAIL REPUBLICAN
1903	TAMMANY DEMOCRAT			Swallowtail Republican	Swallowtail Republican

Tammany Democrat = Democrat who made his political career within Tammany Hall, Organization Democrat = Democrat who made his career within another assembly district–based Democratic organization, Swallowtail Democrat = Democrat who entered politics after a successful business or professional career, or with the sponsorship of wealthy business and professional men in politics, Organization Republican = Republican who made his career within the New York County Republican organization, Swallowtail Republican = Republican who entered politics after a successful business or professional career, or with the sponsorship of wealthy business and professional men. CAPS indicate successful candidate.

SOURCES: Candidate and faction sources indicated in table 4–1; biographical information derived from a wide variety of sources.

TABLE 4–4

Labor and Socialist Nominees for Mayor of
New York City, 1870–1903

Year	Greenback, United Labor, Social Demo-cratic Party		Socialist, Socialist Labor	
1870				
1872				
1874	Swinton	0.07		
1876				
1878	Headley	0.5	Jonas	1
1880				
1882	Franklin	1		
1884				
1886	George	31	George	
1888	Coogan	4	Jonas	1
1890	*		Delabar	2
1892			Jonas	2
1894	*		Sanial	3
1897	*George	4	Sanial	3
1901	*Hanford	2	Keinard	1
1903	Furman	3	Hunter	1

*Former leaders of the Henry George United Labor campaign of 1886 played an important role in organizing the People's Municipal League campaign of 1890, and less important but still significant roles in the Committee of Seventy and Citizens' Union campaigns of 1894, 1897, and 1901.

Numbers indicate each candidate's percentage of the total vote, listed in the column indicating his chief factional loyalty in the year of the election.

SOURCES: See table 4–1.

tions—Tammany Hall, Irving Hall, and the County Democracy—all claimed to be the dominant and legitimate representatives of the city's Democrats. Theoretically all members of a party were eligible to vote in its conventions. But in practice few voted, and each party organization was controlled by a small group of leaders. Municipal election authorities kept lists of the registered voters, but the parties themselves determined who was eligible to vote in their conventions. State law required that the party advertise the time and place of each convention well in advance; but the parties decided whether their basic unit was to be the tiny election district (precinct) or the assembly district, whether separate conventions should be held for each office, whether there should be two, three, or more tiers of conventions to select the delegates who would finally select

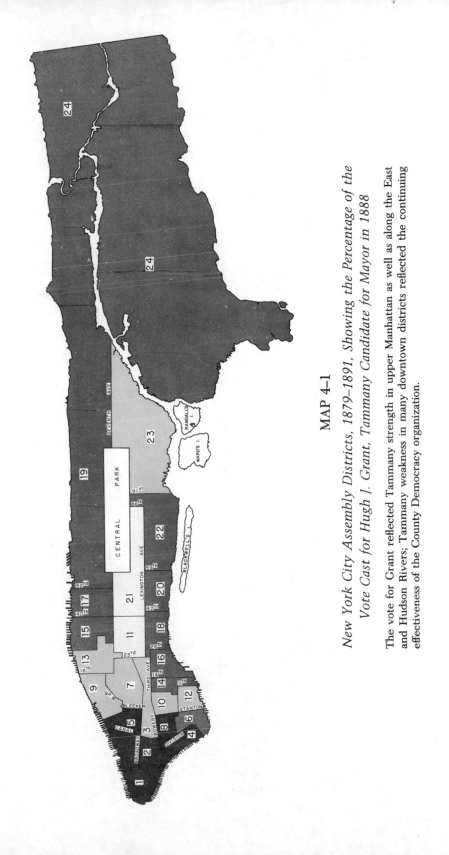

MAP 4-1

New York City Assembly Districts, 1879–1891, Showing the Percentage of the Vote Cast for Hugh J. Grant, Tammany Candidate for Mayor in 1888

The vote for Grant reflected Tammany strength in upper Manhattan as well as along the East and Hudson Rivers; Tammany weakness in many downtown districts reflected the continuing effectiveness of the County Democracy organization.

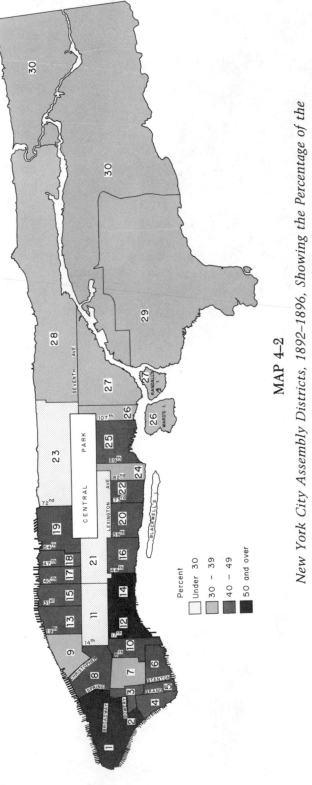

MAP 4-2

New York City Assembly Districts, 1892–1896, Showing the Percentage of the Vote Cast for Hugh J. Grant, Tammany Candidate for Mayor in 1894

Percent

Under 30

30 – 39

40 – 49

50 and over

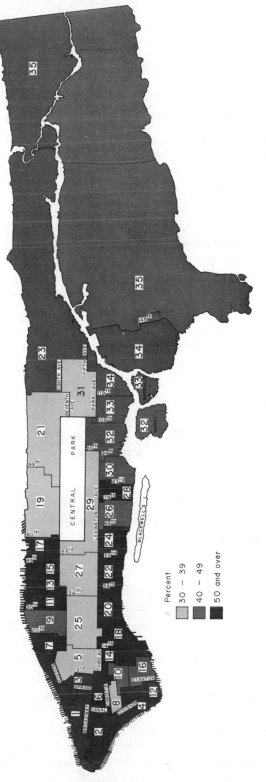

MAP 4-3

New York City Assembly Districts, 1897–1903, Showing the Percentage of the Vote Cast for Robert A. Van Wyck, Tammany Candidate for Mayor in 1897

The vote for Van Wyck reflected the consolidation of Tammany strength in the downtown and riverside districts, and the decline of Tammany's appeal on the upper west side.

candidates for city-wide office. Also, party officials supplied and counted the convention ballots.[14]

These provisions, together with increasingly vigorous central control over the district leaders, placed effective power over nominations in the hands of a few central officials within each party. On the other hand the central officials were elected by, and remained more than nominally responsible to, their assembly district leaders, who could and often did form factions to resist central direction, or shift allegiance from one city-wide party organization to another. Until 1890 district leaders also distributed the general-election ballots (which were printed at party expense), so they had opportunity to engage in their own brand of fusion politics and change or omit the names of candidates endorsed by their party as a whole. Central party officials could, and in extreme cases did, intervene to replace ineffective or uncooperative district leaders, but ultimately each district leader, whether imposed from above or not, had to win local election to retain his post. No party secured a consistent majority in local elections through this period, so no party could win a city-wide election without the fullest possible support of its district leaders and the endorsement of outside political, ethnic, or labor organizations.

During the 1890s political and economic interest groups in other states manipulated election rules to limit the participation of black, poor white, and immigrant voters.[15] The diversity of the city's interest groups and the unintended consequences of some of the new rules limited the effectiveness of similar efforts in New York. A vigorous campaign by Republicans and wealthy Democrats did produce an 1890 state law transferring the responsibility for printing and distributing general-election ballots to public authorities. This measure relieved the party organizations of one expense and to that extent made them less important. But the publicly printed ballot also strengthened the central authorities in each party because it reduced the ability of district leaders to strike the names of party-approved candidates from the ballots they distributed. The 1895 elimination of the "paster," a paper listing one or more names which a voter might attach to an official ballot, further reduced the district leaders' independence.

These party-strengthening consequences of the changes in New York's voting laws were unanticipated. But the printed ballot in New York further strengthened the parties by intent, because the Democrats successfully insisted that it list candidates by party line under symbols intelligible to illiterate voters. Given the diversity of the groups that engaged in New York elections, it is not surprising that the state did not adopt the antifusion laws that crippled third party efforts in many southern and midwestern states; and the adoption of such innovations as bipartisan election boards, mandatory registration, and a ninety-day waiting period for newly naturalized voters had little effect. Even after the 1898 introduction of state-managed primaries, the parties remained central to the nomination process and bore a good deal of its expense. Party leaders had to consider the effect of their nominations on party income as well as on district-leader and voter loyalty.[16]

These regulations and practices conferred an advantage on those who could employ large sums of money or highly disciplined organizations in the contest to control nominations. To a certain extent, each of these resources could be substituted for the other: Money could hire organizers, but an effective organization could reduce the need for money—and might successfully request or extort funds from those subject to its control. Votes had a much more indirect impact on nominations. A successful candidate for mayor usually had to be an effective vote-getter, and once elected he gained control of patronage resources that could be used to strengthen the party that had nominated him. Parties were thus encouraged to consider the voters' preferences. But the voters could only choose among the candidates offered by the political parties, which in turn were constrained to consider first the preferences of their constituent Assembly District organizations, of their financial backers, and of the economic, social, religious, and ethnic pressure groups that might aid or oppose their campaigns. Despite (and to some extent as an unintended consequence of) the ballot reform efforts of wealthy Democrats and Republicans, New York's voting rules reduced the importance of wealthy backers and increased the power of party leaders during the 1890s.

These patterns of participation and constraint dominated the entire period from 1870 to 1903 and were little affected by the annexation of parts of the Bronx to New York City in 1877 and 1895, or even by the consolidation of New York City with Brooklyn and the surrounding territory to form Greater New York in 1898. The highly factionalized pattern of New York City politics predated 1870, but it came to something of a conclusion in 1903. In that year a newly disciplined Tammany Hall, under the shrewd leadership of Charles Murphy, demonstrated its willingness to accommodate some of the mayoral preferences of swallowtails and labor leaders, took advantage of the city's voter shift toward the Democratic Party, exploited the party-strengthening aspects of the new voting laws, and established itself as the key broker in local politics.

CHAPTER 5

ECONOMIC ELITES AND

MAYORAL POLITICS

IN MOST American cities, members of the local economic elites held nearly all municipal offices until the 1840s, and although professional politicians began to move into the lower offices of the larger cities after that date, the office of mayor continued to be reserved for wealthy men until the end of the century. As the largest and most complex of all American cities, New York confirmed this pattern by following it at an accelerated pace. By one mode of reckoning, New York City's first professional-politician mayor was Fernando Wood, who took office in 1857.[1] But in this as in other respects New York is the exception that proves the rule. In response to Wood's election, a coalition of wealthy New York City Democrats and Republicans joined the upstate Republicans in the state legislature to deprive the city's mayor and council of control over most municipal functions, including most police, fire, health, and public works activities, between 1857 and 1870. Boss Tweed's nominee, the "elegant" A. Oakey Hall, became mayor in 1870, but the Tweed Ring scandals of that year made his term a brief and unhappy one, and permitted wealthy merchants to return to office.[2]

In the aftermath of the Tweed Ring scandals, a substantial group of the city's wealthiest men decided to become, in effect, professional politicians in their own right. Playing a continuously active part in local party affairs, a single economic and political elite—the Swallowtail Democrats—exerted substantial control over mayoral nominations between 1872 and 1886. These men, who included wealthy import-export and wholesale merchants, processors and manufacturers who relied on imported raw materials, bankers, railroad investors, and their lawyers, sought a coherent set of local, state, and national policies. Using New York City as their political base, they were remarkably successful in local politics through the 1880s and in national affairs through the 1890s. But as Greater New York's wealthy men increased in numbers and diversity, the Swallowtail Democrats found themselves challenged by competing economic elites and by conflicts over economic and cultural policy that they could not resolve. By the mid-1890s, New York City's economic elites were producing not one but several competing forces in local politics.

The Era of the Swallowtail Democrats

New York City's Swallowtail Democrats entered politics largely to secure lower tariffs, hard money, and federal assistance to commerce in the form of improved harbors, harbor defences, coastal surveys, and foreign consulates. In order to gain these objectives, they sought above all to influence Democratic presidential nominations. Several characteristics of New York State encouraged them to work through local politics. As the most populous state and the one whose voters were most evenly split between the two national parties, New York played a key role in presidential elections. Any man who had proven that he could run well in New York brought a considerable advantage to his party in a presidential campaign: Hence control over the Democratic Party in New York City, which provided the bulk of Democratic votes in the state, was exceptionally valuable to those who wished to influence national policy.[3]

With the presidential candidacies of Horatio Seymour in 1868, Charles O'Connor in 1872, and especially Samuel J. Tilden in 1876 and Grover Cleveland in 1884, 1888, and 1892—and with their support of William McKinley in 1896—the Swallowtails enjoyed remarkable success. Because they used New York City largely as a political base, Theodore Roosevelt was not far off the mark when, during his 1886 campaign for mayor, he insisted in his partisan way that "our City Government has been made a tender to National and State Party Government. . . . We are practically blackmailed to the extent of millions of dollars annually by a host of sinecurists whose return is rendered not in service to us but in protection and support to certain political leaders, candidates, and factions."[4] But the Swallowtail Democrats were also concerned with the city as taxpayers and as business or professional men, and their participation in its affairs was motivated by their desire for low taxes, efficient municipal administration, and municipal improvements to harbor, dock, street, and other commercial facilities.

The revolt against the Tweed Ring gave the Swallowtails their chance to take over. Led by attorneys Tilden, Seymour, and O'Connor, iron and steel merchants and manufacturers Edward Cooper and Abram S. Hewitt, and bankers August Belmont and Augustus Schell, a central group of Swallowtails sought to gain control over the city's Democratic Party by supporting "Honest John" Kelly in his effort to renovate Tammany Hall once Tweed had left it.[5] They controlled critically important resources: money (Swallowtail mayoral candidates personally contributed $20,000 or more to each campaign); social and business prestige (needed to reassure the city's creditors, taxpayers and voters); newspapers (notably the New York *Times*, the *Evening Post*, and the *New Yorker Staats Zeitung*); patronage (jobs and opportunities to make money in their own enterprises as well as in the federal, state, and city governments); and considerable political expertise. For many years they articulated a widely popular ideology that simultaneously embraced federal, state, and municipal aid to commerce and local development, low taxes, economic opportunity in a free labor market, government nonintervention in religious and cultural affairs, and the belief that they had a duty voluntarily to devote much of their wealth to the public good.[6]

Making effective use of these resources, the Swallowtail Democrats controlled mayoral politics between 1872 and 1886 through a calculated policy of alliance and conflict with New York City's political organizations. Swallowtails frequently disagreed among themselves, and they worked through a kaleidoscopically changing set of political factions. But their dominance can be discerned through the detail.

In 1872 the year immediately following the ouster of the Tweed Ring, Swallowtail Democrats divided among themselves but still managed to control each of the three nominations for mayor. Tammany, under the newly dominant Swallowtail-Kelly regime, put up attorney Abraham R. Lawrence. Another group of Swallowtails, which had been seeking to replace Tammany with the rival Apollo Hall organization, ran Apollo's leader, former Tammany sheriff James O'Brien. A third set of Swallowtails, believing that all Democratic organizations would and should be beaten in 1872, set up a "Citizens'" movement, joined the Republicans, and ran retired sugar merchant and banker William F. Havemeyer, a former Democratic mayor. Havemeyer won the election, but nearly all the Democratic Swallowtails then parted company with the Republican Party, and Tammany successfully regrouped. The organization secured election for two successive Swallowtail mayoral candidates, diamond merchant William H. Wickham and leather merchant Smith Ely, and for a time the alliance seemed firm. When some Swallowtails refused to return to the fold and in 1874 joined the independent campaign of Oswald Otten-dorfer, publisher of the distinguished *New Yorker Staats Zeitung,* Hewitt retorted that Wickham was good enough, adding that the party "comprises a great many elements, and if we limit ourselves in selecting candidates to first class bankers, and men of high social standing, such men will soon be left standing alone, and there will be no party left to put in the votes."[7]

The Swallowtail-Tammany alliance failed to survive Tilden's defeat in the 1876 presidential election. Unable to settle nomination and patron-age disputes with Kelly and wary of the increasing control he had gained, with their assistance, over Tammany district leaders, the central group of Swallowtails abandoned Tammany in 1878. At first they took over the Irving Hall organization which, under the leadership of the dashing John Morrissey, had replaced Apollo Hall as the city's second-ranking Democratic organization.[8] Despite Morrissey's unexpected death on the first of June 1878, the Irving Hall Swallowtails scored an immediate suc-cess, electing Edward Cooper to the mayoralty with a 20,000-vote plurality over Swallowtail Augustus Schell, who had remained in Tammany Hall. But Kelly made the defectors pay for their victory by refusing to renomi-nate Hewitt to his seat in Congress in 1878 and by splitting the party in order to deny election to the Swallowtails' candidate for governor in 1879.[9] Without a governor and with Tilden aging and in doubtful health, the Swallowtails failed to promote a viable candidate for the Democratic presidential nomination in 1880.[10] Constrained to cooperate in a presiden-tial year, most of the Irving Hall group followed the Tammany lead in nominating William R. Grace, a merchant and shipowner identified with no faction, for mayor. Wealthy and ambitious, Grace quickly became a political force in his own right. But he was attacked as a Catholic and friend of Cardinal McCloskey who might divert tax money to the parochial schools, and as a secret ally of Tammany Hall. With part of Irving Hall working for his opponent, Republican banker William R. Dowd, Grace won by only 3,045 votes. Hewitt, also backed by both Tammany and Irving Hall, returned to Congress.[11]

Continuing conflict with Kelly and dissatisfaction with Irving Hall fi-nally persuaded the central group of Swallowtails, led by Hewitt, Cooper, and lawyers William C. Whitney and E. Ellery Anderson, to set up a new political organization of their own, the New York County Democracy. They gave the County Democracy a remarkably intricate set of convention delegate-selection regulations, designed to increase the voters' control over nominations and to limit the professional district leaders. But Hewitt and his associates also understood that a full-scale political organization required a cadre of professionals, and they included a number of them in their organizing committee. In practice the County Democracy operated very much along the lines of Apollo, Irving, and Tammany halls.[12]

The County Democracy got off to a promising start in 1881, electing as many assemblymen as all of the city's other political organizations combined and returning Hewitt to Congress.[13] But internal frictions and external challenges then began to take their toll. In 1882 Tilden prevented Hewitt (who had managed Tilden's 1876 presidential campaign) from running for governor, and Tammany denied the nomination to the County Democracy's second choice, Allan Campbell, throwing its support to Grover Cleveland, whose origin in Buffalo had left him happily uninvolved in quarrels of the metropolis.[14] Determined to play a role in the election of a governor who would be a likely presidential candidate in 1884, the Swallowtails decided to support Cleveland after all, and united with Tammany to support the mayoral candidacy of their own Franklin Edson, president of the Produce Exchange. Campbell, who had expected to receive the County Democrats' mayoral nomination, insisted on running anyway as the candidate of an ad hoc "Citizens'" movement put together by Grace, dissident County Democrats, Chamber of Commerce attorney Simon Sterne, and several Republican Swallowtails. With the victories of Cleveland and Edson, both of whom favored the County Democrats in their appointments, the Democratic Swallowtails appeared to be well established.[15]

Tammany quickly grew dissatisfied with Cleveland's performance as governor, and it demanded a high price—support for the mayoral candidacy of Irish-American Hugh J. Grant, a Kelly protegé and professional Tammany man—in return for its wholehearted cooperation in Cleveland's 1884 presidential campaign. Refusing these terms, the Swallowtails patched up an alliance with Grace and the tattered remnants of Irving Hall. Grace attracted uptown and lower east side Tammany dissidents, as well as Republicans (including Theodore Roosevelt) who were unhappy with their own party's candidate, and won the three-way contest.[16] Cleveland also won and promptly selected veteran Swallowtail William C. Whitney, who had played a leading role in financing Cleveland's campaign, to be his Secretary of the Navy. Control of this post, with its great significance both to merchants in foreign trade and to those seeking patronage appointments at the Brooklyn Navy Yard, further strengthened the County Democracy.[17]

But internal difficulties continued to plague the Swallowtails, and these, together with the Henry George challenge of 1886, finally forced them to abandon their attempt to replace Tammany Hall with an organization that would remain firmly under their own control. Grace used his second term as mayor to build up his own organization and to undermine Hewitt-Cooper influence within the County Democracy, and that organization was further damaged when several of its district leaders were implicated in a major contracting scandal.[18] With Tammany in transition during John Kelly's long terminal illness, Whitney was careful to recognize its patronage claims as well as those of the County Democracy. But Tammany was also vulnerable: Kelly died in the summer of 1886 and his successor, Richard Croker, was rough and untried.[19] All Democrats agreed that only a united mayoral campaign could defeat George.

Tammany refused to consider either Grace (who wanted the nomination) or Cooper, because both men had done the organization a good deal of harm.[20] The County Democrats similarly rejected Tammany insiders like Grant, P. Henry Dugro, and Joseph J. O'Donohue.[21] Some Tammany leaders were tempted to take up the "independent" candidacies of O. B. Potter, a sewing machine manufacturer turned downtown real estate investor, or J. E. Simmons, a merchant turned banker and former president of the New York Stock Exchange, two Swallowtails who had not turned against the Hall. But the County Democracy responded coolly to their "booms," and Joseph Pulitzer's *World*, whose increasing circulation below 14th Street made its support critical in 1886, observed that neither a stock exchange president nor a landlord could oppose George effectively.[22] With Cleveland and Whitney pressing for union and the *World* suggesting that Hewitt might be "the best possible candidate," protracted discussions between Croker and his associates and Hewitt, Cooper, and their associates, finally produced a united nomination for Hewitt.[23] Protesting that they had been "euchered," the County Democracy's district leaders, only partly consoled by a share of the subordinate nominations, went along.[24] The Republicans saw Hewitt as simply another Democrat, refused to join him, and nominated Theodore Roosevelt.[25]

Hewitt made an excellent and successful candidate, but as mayor he proved to be a disaster for the County Democracy and a harbinger of Swallowtail decline. Despite his close association with Tilden, a calculating railroad lawyer whose friends had called him "Old Usufruct," Hewitt made an effective appeal to labor. His own father had been an artisan; he himself had become, through partnership with his brother-in-law Edward Cooper, a paternalistic ironmaster whose success enabled him to keep his mills open and his employment books full during recessions. He had responded to the strikes of 1877 by holding congressional hearings instead of denouncing labor out of hand, and he had even supported—

Abram S. Hewitt, about 1890. Hewitt's high standing is reflected in the fact that he is portrayed in at least two painted portraits, in a full-length sculpture (in the Chamber of Commerce collection), and on a gold medal. The expression in Hewitt's eyes in this photograph captures something of the intensity with which he engaged in public affairs. (Courtesy of the New-York Historical Society, New York City)

cautiously—labor's right to organize.[26] He managed the Cooper Union, a free technical institute and adult education center founded by Peter Cooper and supported almost entirely by the family. In language very like that of Henry George he criticized the Astor family for failing to devote to worthwhile public purposes the "unearned increment" in the value of its vast real estate holdings.[27] During the campaign Hewitt at least nodded in the direction of Irish rights and opposed George's Single Tax plan by suggesting that the city tax the mansions of its "rich people

. . . in order that the working-classes of the city may have a purer water, and a better supply of it, more recreation . . . more breathing places . . . better streets, better pavements," and better sanitation.[28]

Henry George did very well in the election, drawing over 68,000 votes and running especially well among second-generation Irish, Germans, and Jews. But Hewitt won with 90,552 votes, just over 41 percent of the total. Despite Tammany support Hewitt did very poorly among the second-generation Irish and even less well among Germans and Jews who lived in relatively prosperous districts. Political scientist Martin Shefter has shown that his strongest support came from Irish immigrants who in 1884 had given much of their vote to Grace on the County Democracy ballot, from Italians, and from Jews in the poor districts, who had gone heavily for Tammany.[29] Hewitt won pluralities in the County Democracy strongholds near the Battery; in the Tammany gashouse districts along the East River; and in the new middle-income districts uptown; and he also ran well in the silk stocking districts.[30] County Democracy and Tammany leaders in the Battery, Bowery, and gashouse districts were not reluctant to stuff ballot boxes and may well have helped Hewitt in that way.[31] But poor Catholics may also have been impressed by their Church's last-minute denunciation of George as a man whose ideas "would prove the ruin of the working men he professes to befriend,"[32] and by Hewitt's promises of conservative but visible improvements in living conditions in the tenement house regions.

Hewitt began his term in office by exchanging cordial messages with Archbishop Corrigan, by appointing Tammany Irishmen Croker, Morgan J. O'Brien, and H. P. Mulvaney to significant offices, and by pushing his schemes for sanitary reform and small parks in the slums as well as for a comprehensive scheme of harbor, street, and rapid transit improvements that would simultaneously aid commerce and provide large numbers of public works jobs.[33]

But the new mayor then fell apart under an irresistible combination of psychological and cultural pressures, and as he fell he took all the Swallowtail Democrats with him. Personally Hewitt was increasingly embittered by his failure to gain high national office despite abilities and a reputation that led Henry Adams to call him "the most useful public man in Washington." His long record of party leadership had failed to secure him his party's gubernatorial nomination in 1882 and again in 1885. His notable contributions to Cleveland's presidential campaign had not won him a cabinet post, and had not even produced what he considered to be routine patronage. At age sixty-four he could not expect to displace the younger president in the national elections of 1888 or 1892.[34] These personal pressures fell uniquely on Hewitt and may well help account for his growing tendency to indulge in impolitic, even vituperative outbursts. But like many of the Protestant, British-stock Swallowtails, he was also deeply affected by the religious revival that made it impossible to sustain an easy tolerance for cultural and religious differences.

Under these various personal and cultural pressures, Hewitt's behavior in office took a bizarre turn. After his initial recognition of Tammany claims he gave the Hall only one other significant appointment, and men with Irish names only two. Failing to overcome lengthy delays on his slum-improvement projects, he devoted his energies instead to efforts to clear the streets of peddlers and cartmen (in the interest of speeding the flow of heavy commercial traffic) and to close small saloons on Sundays.[35] These moves pleased the Chamber of Commerce and the evangelical Protestants, but they annoyed low-income drinkers and aspiring small businessmen, clerks, and laborers, as well as Tammany Hall.

Hewitt then indulged in an extraordinary series of gestures that hopelessly stamped the Swallowtails as bigoted, anti-labor, anti-immigrant, and elitist. He came out against the (already largely established) Saturday half-holiday for labor and denounced the Knights of Labor as a "secret conclave" whose leaders' support of the right to strike made them "worse than highwaymen." He dismissed the Grand Army of the Republic as no more than a lot of office seekers. And he publicly disposed of Cleveland, on the occasion of his renomination in 1888, as a man he did "not believe in."[36]

Still more dramatically, Hewitt curtly refused the request of two hundred Irish-American societies that he follow a twenty-seven-year-old tradition and review the St. Patrick's Day Parade in 1888.[37] In denying a subsequent city council proposal to fly the Irish flag from City Hall on March 17, the mayor observed that "the Irish furnish more than double the number of inmates" in the city's jails and alms houses than "would naturally belong to their proportion of the population." Turning an Irish argument against its authors, he argued "if it be right that Ireland should be governed by Irishmen, as France is governed by Frenchmen and Germany by Germans, then it is equally true that America should be governed by Americans, and that so far as the flag is the symbol of home rule, it, and it alone, should float from the seat of sovereignty."[38] One of the Irish leaders who invited Hewitt to review the St. Patrick's Day Parade had observed that "the majority of Irishmen vote the Democratic ticket, and your vote came largely from Irishmen, a considerable portion of whom belong to the societies who will parade on St. Patrick's Day." Profoundly offended at the suggestion that Irish-American organizations should expect to play a regular part in the city's politics, Hewitt thundered in return that "the danger line has been reached, when it must be decided whether American or foreign ideas are to rule in this city." Determined to secure a victory of "American ideas," he then devoted much of his term to advocating a literacy test for immigrants and a twenty-one year waiting period for naturalization.[39]

The County Democracy could not survive Hewitt's outbursts, and it rapidly disintegrated after 1888. But the Swallowtail Democrats did not immediately leave the scene. Although they had lost many of their most effective district leaders and alienated their wealthy Catholic, Jewish, German, and Irish colleagues, the Hewitt-Cooper group managed to run Hewitt for reelection in 1888, and to secure a remarkably large 26 percent of the vote for him.[40] In 1890 a group of Swallowtails played a prominent role in the effort to put together a new anti-Tammany movement, the People's Municipal League, and they played important though subordinate parts in anti-Tammany mayoral campaigns throughout the decade. But they never regained the position they had held in the seventies and eighties.

Although neither unchallenged nor undivided, the Democratic Swallowtails dominated mayoral politics in New York City during the 1880s. As Allan Nevins, long the most influential historian of this era, once observed, it required "John Kelly and the pugilist John Morrissey" to make the Swallowtails "acceptable to Irish voters."[41] But even under Kelly's most vigorous leadership Tammany was able to do little more than veto the nomination of men like Allan Campbell and Edward Cooper, to whom it was unalterably opposed, or to encourage the nomination of a Catholic such as William R. Grace; so long as the Swallowtails devoted themselves wholeheartedly to mayoral politics, Tammany was unable to elect anyone they opposed. Relying on their money, their social and business prestige, their credit with (and control over) the press, and their considerable political skill, they worked with equal effectiveness through Tammany, the opposing Apollo and Irving halls, and their own County Democracy to select (and supply) nearly every significant candidate for mayor between 1872 and 1888. Their influence began to wane, as Hewitt bitterly recognized, in part because Tammany developed independent sources of support and because labor and ethnic groups organized more effectively. But Swallowtail influence also declined because Hewitt and others succumbed to the cultural pressures of nativism and Evangelical millennialism, fragmenting and limiting the appeal of the Swallowtail movement itself.

Fragmentation

The Swallowtail Democrats dominated New York's local politics not only because they controlled essential political resources, but also because the city's other wealthy men acquiesced in their leadership. After 1886 the challenges of Republican competition—and of the political reform, moral reform, and social reform movements—deprived them of the general support they had enjoyed from the wealthy; the new competitors brought their own formidable resources into the political arena. Each of the new contenders for power over mayoral nominations requires a brief introduction.

Republican Swallowtails like Joseph Choate and Elihu Root had long played important parts in local affairs: Choate had launched Theodore Roosevelt's career back in 1880.[42] But in the mid-eighties the professional district leaders, under the leadership of state Republican boss Thomas C. Platt, moved to free themselves of Swallowtail control and to increase their ability to appeal to German and Jewish voters who were often alienated by Swallowtail attitudes. Wealthy Republican businessmen, Union League Club members, and Grand Army of the Republic veterans all responded by increasing their own political activity and by organizing anti-Platt assembly district organizations of their own. They became significant factors in local politics through their wealth, their organizations, the federal patronage they received from Harrison, McKinley, and Roosevelt (and state patronage from Governors Levi P. Morton, Frank S. Black, Roosevelt, and Benjamin B. Odell), their credit with the New York *Tribune,* the *Herald,* the *Times,* and other newspapers, their ability to cooperate with the Platt forces, and the increasing numbers of votes they could attract.[43]

By the early 1890s some wealthy and well-to-do Republicans, Democrats, and independents had resolved to pursue several political reform goals through nonpartisan, essentially pressure-group methods. The earliest and best-known of their goals was civil service reform, which had produced adequately financed and effective state and national organizations by the late 1880s. New York's City Reform Club, which sought to extend the civil service reform principle by evaluating the performance of the city's local and state legislators, persisted from 1886 into the mid-nineties. At that point its members and its activities were absorbed in the new City Club, which, together with affiliated Good Government Clubs in nearly every assembly district, sought to evaluate—and if necessary to replace—not only the city's legislators, but also its elected and appointed administrators. By 1895 the City Club and the Good Govern-ment Clubs together had on the order of a thousand active members.[44] In addition, the city's German-Americans had organized parallel organiza-tions to seek civil service reform, efficient and inexpensive government, and recognition of their own ability to fill important offices. In the 1880s German Democrats had separated from German Republicans to form the German-American Cleveland Union, but in the 1890s they came together into the German American Reform Union. By 1894 the GARU boasted suborganizations in twenty assembly districts, a presence in German and eastern European Jewish as well as German gentile areas, and over 25,000 enrolled members.[45] Altogether, the wealth, enthusiasm, numerical and organizational strength, and credibility of these professedly "nonpartisan" political pressure groups gave them considerable ability to influence mayo-ral nominations in the 1890s.

The Republican and Civil Service Reform–Good Government Club con-tributions to New York City politics are well known. But we have usually overlooked the still more significant contributions of the city's diverse moral and social reform movements, Protestant churches, Protestant and Jewish charities, and universities. Yet these movements and organizations explain a great deal about the mayoral politics of the decade. As New York became more and more heterogeneous in its ethnic and religious composition—with Catholics becoming more numerous, more prosperous, and better organized, and with eastern European Jews arriving in large numbers—the sixty-year-old struggle to establish the dominance of Protes-tant culture in the city came to seem almost hopelessly difficult. James Bryce reflected the view of many of his New York acquaintances when he responded to Richard Watson Gilder's 1894 Tenement House Report, "I wish it were possible to stop all Italian and Jewish immigration into the U.S. for the next ten years, if that could be done without hardship to the poor people. For your country is not getting a fair chance."[46]

At the same time, and only partly in response to the problems posed by immigration, both evangelical and social reform-minded Protestants in New York (as well as throughout the United States) were increasingly coming to believe that it was possible—indeed their absolute duty—to establish the Kingdom of God on earth, to create a thoroughly (Protestant) Christian state and social order.[47] These religious and cultural imperatives bore more heavily on some of the city's wealthy Protestants—including Abram S. Hewitt—than on others, and they bore only indirectly on Catho-lics and Jews. But they provoked a remarkable proliferation of moral and social reform activity and an extraordinary commitment of resources, ma-terial and organizational as well as cultural and symbolic.

The religious and charitable movements and organizations were most directly influential, of course, among the upper- and middle-income Protestants whose communities produced them, and among the Jews and Catholics who were most closely associated with Protestants. The churches and charities possessed eloquent spokesmen as well as wealthy backers who commanded attention and respect and who were able to influence many voters. Like the political reform organizations, the churches and charities also enjoyed good relationships with the press, especially the swallowtail-controlled New York *Times*, Godkin's *Evening Post*, Oswald Ottendorfer's *New Yorker Staats Zeitung*, and Pulitzer's *World*, as well as the widely read Protestant religious weeklies and the genteel weekly and monthly magazines. This easy access to publicity was exceedingly valuable in itself, not only for advocating principles and candidates, but also for keeping allies in line and tearing down the opposition: The moral reformers did not hesitate to denounce—from the pulpit, in the weeklies, and on the editorial pages—any Catholic, Jew, or Protestant who seemed to require attack.

Protestant moral reformers often found a less than ready audience among the poor, but Protestant and Jewish charitable, social reform, and educational organizations were able to reach many lower-income voters, not least through the distribution of material assistance. Increasing numbers of wealthy New Yorkers were contributing money for moral reform, education, or charity, and this money could be used to accomplish multiple objectives. Following the example of the ordinary political machines, the Charity Organization Society provided Thanksgiving dinners to striking garment workers during the cold November of 1895, and then allocated a share of its job tickets through the United Garment Workers Union.[48] As historian Clyde Griffen has pointed out, the (Episcopalian) Church Association for the Advancement of the Interests of Labor (CAIL) and the settlement houses (all of which were set up in the years immediately following the Henry George campaign of 1886) took a different approach, making serious efforts to meet, to learn from, and to assist workingmen and immigrants.[49] The Charity Organization Society and the settlement houses carried out a series of important tenement house investigations in the nineties, provoking some reform measures but also (quite intentionally) gathering favorable publicity for themselves.[50] It was through the CAIL that Seth Low joined Samuel Gompers in the New York Board of Mediation and Conciliation and earned a politically valuable reputation as a fair mediator of labor disputes.[51] The moral reformers also found that many poor immigrants were concerned about moral issues as well, especially judicial favoritism and prostitution.

The charitable societies, settlement houses, and universities also employed increasing numbers of highly trained men—and women—who were seeking public applications for their newly won expertise and who were ready to devote a great deal of effort to local politics. As Head Worker of the University Settlement Society, for example, James B. Reynolds made such assiduous political use of opportunities for dispensing patronage, lobbying, and electioneering that an annoyed Theodore Roosevelt could describe him, not unfairly, as "an ordinary election district captain."[52] Women did not have the vote, and their names were carefully kept off the published lists of political organizers so as not to provoke opponents of woman suffrage. But the charitable and religious societies, and associated pressure groups like the Ladies' Sanitary Reform Association, provided women with acceptable vehicles for activity in the public sphere. Significant numbers of women took advantage of the opportunity, and through these organizations they were able to play a significant part in local politics. Mrs. Josephine Shaw Lowell, who had led in the creation of the Charity Organization Society, also became one of the Citizens' Union's chief political managers.[53] Such women constituted a notable untapped political resource, but only political movements that allied themselves with the charities and the churches could make use of their intelligence, training, and energy.

Greater New York's proliferating upper- and middle-income political, charitable, moral reform, and religious movements made a variety of effective appeals to low- and middle-income voters. But unlike the Swallowtail Democrats, they could not offer a single, coherent, widely acceptable ideology. Instead, for the purpose of their independent mayoral campaigns they sought to paper over their differences with a formula that they repeated in one local election after another between 1888 and 1902. The formula began by asserting (over some Republican and Democratic objections) that municipal government was "the administration of a great business," not a "political" affair. Ideally, municipal elections should be separated from state and national elections, which did deal with properly partisan issues. "Municipal officers . . . should be independent of political parties, halls, bosses, and factions"; they "should be chosen solely for their business ability and personal integrity." Because it avoided specific programmatic commitments, this part of the program enjoyed the broadest support. Historian Melvin Holli has described it as the arid "structural" approach which in his view characterized municipal reform in New York City.[54]

But the independent formula always went on to say that as soon as the city had the right sort of officers, it should implement a series of "positive programs." Several of these were intended to serve local economic interests, but many of them were of the sort that Holli describes as "social" reform. In 1890, for example, the People's Municipal League platform called for better men not only for "the care of city property, the management of city franchises, [and] the collection and expenditure of city revenues," but also for "the development of systems of rapid transit, and the impartial and vigorous enforcement of labor legislation and of measures for the improvement of the homes of the industrial classes."[55]

Yet there was always a religious side to the "positive programs" as well. Settlement house leader James B. Reynolds put it moderately in 1897, asserting that while "nothing so much retards and cripples the work of religious, philanthropic, and educational institutions as the influence of corrupt politics and selfish politicians . . . no coadjutator to such movements is of equal value with . . . an intelligent and righteous administration."[56] But the Reverend Charles H. Parkhurst of the Madison Square Presbyterian Church and the Society for the Prevention of Crime used equally characteristic language when he denounced Tammany officials for their failure to cooperate in his anti-vice crusade: "There is not a form under which the devil disguises himself that so perplexes us in our efforts, or so bewilders us in the devising of our schemes as the polluted harpies that, under the pretense of governing this city, are feeding day and night on its quivering vitals. They are a lying, perjured, rum-soaked, and libidinous lot. . . . Every effort to make men respectable, honest, temperate, and sexually clean is a direct blow between the eyes of the Mayor and his whole gang of drunken and lecherous subordinates."[57]

Outbursts of this kind reflected sincere and deeply felt religious commitment. But they engendered a principled anti-Catholicism and an unyielding demand for blue-law policies that made coalition building difficult and that dismayed the Germans in particular. Frederick W. Holls, a prominent German-American Republican who worked closely both with Joseph Choate and Elihu Root and with the Charity Organization Society, wrote a Lutheran pastor and friend in 1897 that he had "hoped . . . for a. normal and orderly development of good city government . . . for better streets and docks, schools, parks, and municipal enterprises for the general good" from the Republican-Fusion reform administration of Mayor William L. Strong. But the Sunday closing issue had "upset the kettle of fish." "When I observe the antics of some clergymen," he concluded, "it is hard to be patient and to believe that, on the whole, the influence of the Church is not evil."[58] The difficulty lay in the religious origins of much of the demand for social reform. If God's will was to be done on earth, then it was necessary to feed the starving, clothe the naked, succor the sick, and cherish the children. But it was also necessary to smite the sinners with a wrathful hand. The same impulse that led many wealthy Protestants to seek an alliance with non-Protestant immigrants also made it impossible for them to sustain that alliance.

The Fusion Era

The Swallowtail Democrats and the other politically active wealthy men in New York had sought to influence mayoral nominations in one of two ways: through the control of a Democratic or Republican party organization complete with professional-politician district leaders, or through an ad hoc "Citizens' " movement put together to advocate a single candidacy. After 1886 many wealthy men continued to play important roles in the regular Republican and Democratic organizations. But others, caught up in the Protestant revival, sought to create a permanent citizens' movement that would seek to realize their conception of the City of God. Through diligent and hard-headed political work, they put together a succession of self-styled independent political organizations—the People's Municipal League, the Committee of Seventy, and the Citizens' Union. But the militant Protestants could never entirely ignore other political formations, which had their own economic, organizational, and electoral bases of support. The independent political organizations always contained discordant elements, and once these had sorted themselves out they still found it necessary to seek alliance with the regular Republican organization as well. For about ten years the independents were, as a whole, remarkably effective in winning votes. The result was a series of vigorous fusion campaigns in 1890, 1894, 1901, and 1903; an impressive independent campaign in 1897; and resounding fusion victories in 1894 and 1901. But the changing political loyalties and religious commitments of the voters, and the volatile nature of the political issues, prevented any faction from establishing a clear dominance within the fusion movement. By 1903 the Protestant revival had spent much of its political force, and most of the city's wealthy men were ready to return to the regular parties or to seek their goals through special-purpose pressure groups.

Abram S. Hewitt's 1888 campaign had combined the older forms. He retained the support of the considerable portions of the County Democracy that he and William R. Grace continued to influence, but he also had the backing of a citizens' committee consisting of Republicans, wealthy merchants who were beginning to finance Protestant moral reform crusades, and several leading real estate developers.[59] In view of his extraordinarily impolitic outbursts he ran surprisingly well, and he might have run even better if he could have secured greater support from the Swallowtail Democrats and their newspapers; the pro-Cleveland Germans; and such Republican Swallowtails as Elihu Root and Theodore Roosevelt.[60] In 1890 a group of Swallowtail Democrats sought to bring such a coalition together in the People's Municipal League (PML). The PML leadership included Swallowtails Wheeler H. Peckham, Charles S. Fairchild, and William B. Hornblower, German-American Democrat Gustav H. Schwab, civil service reformers A. C. Bernheim, Horace E. Deming, and Carl Schurz, social-reform-minded Protestant ministers R. Heber Newton, Howard Crosby, and D. Henry Van Dyck, and Independent Labor Party leaders James P. Archibald and Louis F. Post. The PML represented the last major nineteenth-century effort to bring about a *rapprochement* between wealthy Democrats, social reformers, and labor.[61]

The PML had no intention of working with Tammany Hall and no hope of appealing successfully to Irish Catholics. Archbishop Corrigan, who had given Hewitt important assistance in his 1886 campaign against Henry George, refused even to meet with PML representatives in 1890.[62] It was clear that the PML could win the mayoral election only if it brought the remaining County Democrats and the Republicans into a vigorous fusion campaign; its leaders, including Archibald and the Reverend Mr. Newton as well as Peckham and Schwab, accordingly entered into a long and difficult series of negotiations with those two organizations. As the skeptical *Herald* put it, the nominee "must be a Democrat to head the ticket, and according to the PML he must be an angel as well. The Republican members, unused to such tactics [and annoyed by the PML's 'spirit of gush'] soon grew weary and told the County Democrats, as it was their funeral, to go it alone."[63] Amid rumors that William R. Grace was somehow controlling the entire proceeding from behind the scenes, the negotiators finally agreed to nominate Francis M. Scott, a young Grace associate who had made a respectable if neither distinguished nor prominent record as an attorney and as one of two reform aqueduct commissioners appointed by Hewitt.[64] Most of the other top places also went to County Democrats.[65]

The Republicans, dissatisfied with the distribution of places, refused to work hard for this ticket, and the County Democrats failed even more than in 1888 to deliver the vote of the newest and poorest Irish immigrants.[66] Scott held the vote in the wealthy silk stocking districts, did quite well in some though not all of the lower east side districts with large Jewish populations, and with Archibald was pleased to see that the labor vote did not swing over to the Socialists. But most of the Irish vote went to Tammany; many Republicans and workers abstained; and Scott drew 61,443 fewer votes than had Hewitt, the Republican Erhardt, and labor's Coogan combined. Tammany, by contrast, polled slightly more votes than it had in 1888.[67] Future fusion campaigns would have to stimulate heartier Republican cooperation and take account of County Democracy weakness.

Although Schwab and other PML leaders and the County Democrats all hoped to mount another mayoral campaign in 1892, considerations of presidential politics prevented them from doing so. Fairchild, Grace, and other Swallowtail Democrats briefly used the remnants of the County Democracy organization in their successful effort to secure a third nomination for Cleveland, but they realistically discarded it in return for Tammany support for their presidential candidate at the general election.[68] Wealthy Republicans likewise supported a mayoral nominee selected by their party's regular local organization.[69]

But 1892 did see the launching of the Reverend Mr. Parkhurst's extraordinary anti-vice, anti-Tammany crusade. Armed with the results of a City Reform Club investigation into vice and police corruption as well as evidence gathered in his own guided tours of dives and brothels, Parkhurst and the *Times* urged the Republican-controlled state legislature to undertake a formal investigation.[70] Financed by the Chamber of Commerce of the State of New York (after Governor Roswell P. Flower, a Wall Street banker who had stayed with Tammany, vetoed an appropriation for the purpose), chaired by Republican State Senator Clarence Lexow of Nyack, and directed by County Democrat John W. Goff, the resulting investigation produced four thick volumes of testimony.[71] This testimony did not implicate top police or Tammany officials, and it included plenty of evidence that abuses long predated Tammany's current success. It revealed that police officers and some lower east side politicians (County Democrats as well as Tammany men) had imposed a complicated protection racket on gamblers and prostitutes. It established that Tammany officials sought to control the police department in their organization's own narrowly conceived interest. And Goff persuaded one Irish Catholic police captain to testify that he had been forced to pay $15,000 (to a County Democrat) for the promotion he had earned through examination.[72]

The Parkhurst crusade and the Lexow investigation set the stage for the second great fusion campaign, the Committee of Seventy movement of 1894. Reflecting the forces that had come to dominate among the independents, the Committee of Seventy was put together by leaders of the Chamber of Commerce of the State of New York and included the financial backers (though not the religious leaders) of the Protestant moral reform movements; Protestant and Jewish charity trustees (but not the social workers they employed); civil service reform and Good Government Club leaders; and the wealthy patrons of Republican, German-American reform, and to a lesser extent of Democratic political organizations.[73] In contrast to the mixed character of the People's Municipal League, the Committee of Seventy was an omnibus gathering of Swallowtails, led by the Chamber of Commerce, the Protestant moral reformers, and the anti-Platt Republicans.

The usual view follows Plunkitt of Tammany Hall in dismissing the independents of the 1890s as idealistic amateurs. But Committee of Seventy leaders were no more amateurish than the Cooper-Hewitt County Democrats of the seventies and early eighties had been. Before naming its ticket, the committee met in succession with all possible elements of a fusion campaign: the Republicans, the (city-wide) O'Brien and the (largely lower east side) Steckler factions that had broken with Tammany, the Grace-Fairchild "New York State Democracy" (which included a number of old County Democrats as well as single taxer Louis F. Post and labor leader James P. Archibald), and the expanded German-American Reform Union.[74] In evaluating mayoral candidates, the committee took careful account of each faction's preferences and political strength. The Democrats eliminated Parkhurst-backer and former Chamber president Charles Stewart Smith as too aggressively Protestant; the O'Brienites, the Stecklerites, and the Republicans eliminated State Democrat John W. Goff as belonging to the wrong faction; and the Committee of Seventy itself eliminated Republican politicians Horace Porter and Lemuel E. Quigg as insufficiently rich and righteous. Theodore Roosevelt had taken himself out of consideration because he "simply had not the funds to run"; Seth Low was reluctant to leave his post as president of Columbia University.[75] At last the committee proposed a ticket headed by William L. Strong, a millionaire dry goods merchant turned banker and former president of the Business Men's Republican Club. Strong could afford to contribute to his own campaign, had the backing of the effective anti-Platt Republican organizer, William Brookfield, and, following a conference about patronage, secured the grudging support of Platt himself.[76]

Committee of Seventy managers then made their nomination stick through an impressive exhibition of political sophistication and toughness. Swallowtail Democrats (in the GARU as well as in the State Democracy) and their organ, the New York *Times*, objected violently to the nomination of a partisan Republican and threatened to bolt the coalition if Tammany could be induced to nominate an acceptable candidate.[77] Tammany did offer the nomination to Cleveland Democrat Nathan Straus, the millionaire Macy's department store partner and Jewish philanthropist who was serving as parks commissioner under the Tammany administration.[78] But the Committee of Seventy countered by offering all subordinate places on its ticket to representatives of the various Democratic factions, stating that a defection by Swallowtail Democrats would force it to strike all their names, and threatening to join forces with the Republicans or if necessary to run its own Charles Stewart Smith as a spoiler.[79] Strong declared that he would not run without Democratic support, insisted that he had no intention of serving as the Republican organization's tool, assured the GARU that he would not countenance a "narrow minded construction of the excise and Sunday laws," and apparently made specific pledges of patronage to the Democrats.[80] According to GARU leaders Gustav H. Schwab and Theodore Sutro, and to Parkhurst, Swallowtails Grace and Fairchild then persuaded the State Democracy district leaders and the GARU to remain within the fold.[81] Under a discipline imposed by Republican Swallowtails like George Bliss and William Brookfield and endorsed by Platt, Republican district leaders also accepted the entire Committee of Seventy slate despite their great dissatisfaction with the allocation of its subordinate places.[82]

Nathan Straus's Tammany candidacy remained as the only obstacle to a clear run for fusion, so the Committee of Seventy quickly launched a ruthless campaign to drive him from the field. A long list of prominent merchants, bankers, and lawyers had praised Straus as a possible candidate before his nomination. But once the anti-Tammany Democratic factions had agreed upon Strong, an equally long list—including *Freundschaft* Club President Julius J. Frank, Swallowtail Democrat and Committee of Seventy member Simon Sterne, and other well-known Jews—deplored his candidacy as a "grave mistake" which implied that a morally corrupt Tammany might hope to receive the "Hebrew vote."[83] As if to emphasize

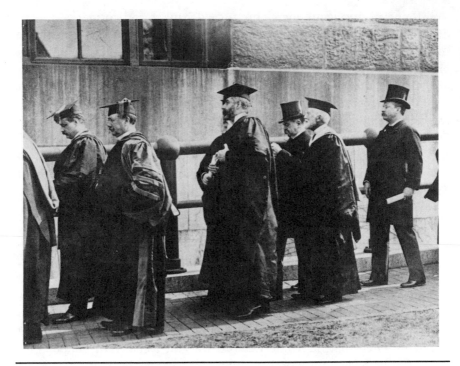

Left to right: Nicholas Murray Butler, Mayor Seth Low, Citizens' Union Chairman R. Fulton Cutting, J. H. Van Amringe *(behind Cutting)*, William C. Schermerhorn, German Ambassador Theodor von Holleben, and President Theodore Roosevelt, in procession at Butler's installation as president of Columbia University, April 19, 1902. Butler, Low, Cutting, Van Amringe, and Roosevelt simultaneously managed the University, Citizens' Union-Republican politics, and a section of organized charity. (Columbiana Collection, Courtesy of Columbia University)

the position in which Straus's candidacy would place Jewish honor, Parkhurst himself made a widely publicized appearance before Good Government Club X on the lower east side, taking advantage of the occasion to remind his audience that Jews had given valuable evidence to the Lexow Committee, to observe that they suffered more than their share of "the oppression, the cudgeling, and the thievery of the police department," and to urge them to support Strong.[84] The Committee of Seventy had successfully prevented the Democrats from putting together a unified slate and threatened to destroy Straus's reputation; three days later he and his disappointed Tammany sponsors found a face-saving way for him to withdraw.[85]

The Committee of Seventy changed the standard independent platform only by insisting that Tammany "corruption, inefficiency, and extrava-gance" threatened the "health and morality," the very "life and liberty" of rich and poor alike.[86] These claims, buttressed by Lexow revelations, depression distress, and the unified support of all factions combined to secure a solid victory for Strong. He received nearly 47,000 more votes than had the Republican candidate, Edwin Einstein, two years before, while Tammany's vote fell by nearly 65,000. The result reflected anti-Tammany sentiment in the midtown silk stocking districts and in the middle-income German and Jewish districts on the upper west side, in Harlem and Yorkville, and on the lower east side.[87] Despite the great show made by anti-Tammany Democrats, the pattern of Irish loyalty to Tammany Hall remained intact.[88]

Tough and sophisticated though it was, the Committee of Seventy had put together a coalition that was as fragile as it was diverse. Unlike his contemporaries Josiah Quincy in Boston and Hazen S. Pingree in Detroit, Strong was unable to reconcile the demands of his city's conflicting eco-nomic and cultural groups—for both economy and increased expenditure on education, welfare, and economic development; for both accommodat-ing the Germans and enforcing the Sunday closing laws; and for the distribution of the limited available patronage to representatives of all factions. By 1896 the coalition was coming apart at the seams.[89]

At this point the leaders of organized charity, who had played significant but subordinate roles in the People's Municipal League and the Committee of Seventy, stepped forward to take the lead in the creation of a third independent organization, the Citizens' Union. Guided by Charity Organi-zation Society President R. Fulton Cutting, the CU drew the core of its support from British and German Protestant and German Jewish charity trustees, and from the wealthy backers of the political and the Protestant moral reform movements.[90] Its leaders ignored suggestions that they seek organizational strength by incorporating the Union League Club–Brook-field anti-Platt Republicans or the Grace-Fairchild National (anti–Bryan Gold) Democracy and the similar Shepard Democracy in Brooklyn, and they were reluctant to work very closely with labor organizations.[91] In-stead, they named University Settlement Society Head Worker James B. Reynolds their executive director and made a determined effort to build an independent party on the narrowest base of any of the independent efforts—their own charitable, religious, moral and political reform movements.[92]

This relatively narrow and coherent base enabled the CU to persist through three mayoral campaigns, but it also limited its ability to forge winning coalitions. Cutting had declared that the "religion of the twenti-

eth century is destined to employ Government as one of its principal
instruments for the solution of social issues."[93] R. Heber Newton, rector
of All Souls' Episcopal Church and a veteran of the Henry George campaign, added, in a warm letter of encouragement, that he saw "no way
of permanently uplifting the condition of the masses of our people by
our private charity or helpfulness that does not lead on to the organization
of improved conditions under the direction of the municipality."[94] But
the CU also remained in close touch with Parkhurst, whose implacable
demand for Sunday closings alienated most German voters.[95] Although
Reynolds carefully cultivated Jewish voters on the lower east side, the
Jewish philanthropist Jacob A. Schiff had to explain to him, as late as
1896, that he had made a serious error in judgment when he permitted
Christians who were seeking to convert Jews to work out of the University
Settlement.[96]

Reynolds and his University Settlement associates had also cultivated
good relations with labor leaders in the garment and other trades, but
when he sought to bring them into the CU coalition, the *Times* (which
spoke for Democratic Swallowtails whose support was critical) protested
against discussions "where the hope is expressed that [the CU] will give
New York a candidate for mayor like PINGREE of Detroit, and where
the referendum, municipal operation of gas works, electric light plants,
railroads and telephones, and other fads that the halfbaked have picked
up from Prof. ELY and other Socialistic writers are expounded."[97] Ultimately most labor leaders followed Daniel Harris, president of the New
York State Branch of the American Federation of Labor, who withdrew
from the CU because he had "more regard for my standing in the estima-
tion of the working classes than whether Dick Croker or Tom Platt is
in control of the City Government."[98]

The Citizens' Union's narrow approach also alienated the Republicans.
Seth Low had been the CU's preferred candidate from the beginning,
and through the summer of 1897 it seemed that he might secure Republican support as well. It was true that Low had joined the mugwump revolt
in voting for Cleveland and against his own party's Blaine in 1884; but
that record might attract needed Swallowtail Democrats. He was president
of Columbia University, chairman of the Board of Trustees of the University Settlement Society, and a sponsor of the Church Association for
the Advancement of the Interests of Labor; thus he was clearly acceptable
to the philanthropists, charity workers, and religious reformers. He had
won a reputation for sympathy with organized labor; thus he might attract
its support. As a two-term Republican mayor of Brooklyn he had introduced notable civil service reform measures; thus he should be acceptable

to Brooklyn voters (who were now to vote for the mayor of part of Greater New York) and to the political reformers. And he was more closely allied with the Choate-Root-Theodore Roosevelt Swallowtails than with the Strong-Brookfield-Union League anti-Platt Republican organizers; so he might prove acceptable to Platt himself.[99]

So the Citizens' Union's leaders reasoned. But they refused to negotiate directly with any of the groups or factions whose support they sought.[100] Without a formal conference at the least, Platt and the regular Republicans, like most of organized labor, refused to join the Citizens' Union behind Low's candidacy.[101] Instead the regular Republican organization, supported by several of its wealthy backers and ultimately by President McKinley's Secretary of the Interior, Cornelius N. Bliss—and encouraged by the expectation of support from the many Republicans in the Brooklyn, Queens County, and Staten Island areas who would now vote for the mayor of newly formed Greater New York—ran Benjamin F. Tracy, a former Secretary of the Navy, Brooklyn man (and law partner of Platt's son) for mayor.[102] The pro-Bryan Democrats, single taxers, and many labor leaders, joining together in the "Jeffersonian Democracy," ran Henry George, thereby drawing off still another portion of the potential CU vote.[103] The Democratic Swallowtails, left with no place else to go, fell unhappily in line behind Low.[104]

For the Citizens' Union, the disappointing result reflected defections on all sides and a polarization of the vote along income lines. By comparison with the 1894 vote for Strong, the combined vote for Low and Tracy fell least in the relatively wealthy silk stocking districts in the center of Manhattan, on the upper east side and west side, in central Harlem, and in what was probably the most prosperous Jewish assembly district on the lower east side. Strong had not run well in the largely Irish districts along the Hudson River and in the mid–east side gashouse districts. Low suffered only an average loss there. But he did very badly indeed in the poorer areas of the lower east side and in every district that had a substantial German population.[105] Shefter's statistical analysis of election district returns confirms these observations: In comparison with 1894, the Germans (in the wealthier as well as the poorer election districts) and the poor of all ethnic backgrounds shifted most strongly to Tammany.[106] Low outpolled Tracy in every borough except Staten Island, where Tracy received a one vote plurality—demonstrating that the Citizens' Union could easily deny election to a Republican; but despite the great outpouring of CU literature and speakers, the support of several newspapers, and his long and well-respected career in the public eye, Low drew only 25 percent of the vote in Manhattan and less than 29 percent in the Greater

City (which included all of the present five boroughs) as a whole. Platt had also made his point that the CU could not win on its own. But the CU had established its right to name the fusion candidate: Tracy received only 18 percent of the Manhattan vote, and only 19 percent overall.

Three developments enabled the Citizens' Union to reassemble enough of the independent forces to win the mayoral election in 1901. The Tammany leaders who controlled the city after Van Wyck's victory in 1894 threw aside all restraint and cynically set out to make their fortunes, leaving themselves open to renewed attack for corruption, favoritism, and vice-mongering. Under the leadership of Episcopal Bishop Henry Codman Potter, the Protestant moral crusaders shifted their emphasis from Sunday sales of liquor to the much more widely effective issue of prostitution in the tenement house districts. And with Theodore Roosevelt's election—as governor, then vice president and then president—the independents gained an ally in a position to insist that the Republican organization work with them.

The Republican-controlled state legislature launched the campaign in 1899 with the only moderately successful Mazet Committee investigation into Tammany corruption and arrogance.[107] Bishop Potter then seized the initiative, passionately calling on Mayor Van Wyck "to save these people who are in a very real way committed to your charge from a living hell, defiling, deadly, damning, to which the criminal supineness of the constituted authorities, set up for the defence of decency and good order, threaten to doom us."[108] Repeating the tactics of 1894, Potter and other Protestant and Jewish religious, charity, and Chamber of Commerce leaders set up a Committee of Fifteen to expose and denounce Tammany complicity in police corruption.[109]

These tactics and resources again gave the religious and charity leaders within the independent movement the upper hand in the mayoral negotiations. With the support of Roosevelt and the Brooklyn Republicans, they turned aside the GARU-sponsored candidacy of Charles A. Schieren, a Republican who had served as fusion mayor of Brooklyn in 1894 and 1895, and nominated Low once again.[110] Low refused to run without united Republican support, and Platt, pressed by Roosevelt, finally agreed that it would be better to support Low than to build up a Democrat.[111] Many Democrats objected to the CU's increasingly Republican complexion, but ultimately several Swallowtails, the remnants of the National Democracy, the Jeffersonian Democracy, and several disaffected Tammany district leaders all joined the Republicans in a fusion campaign behind

Low.[112] Cutting insisted that the district attorney nomination go to William Travers Jerome, a freelance Democrat who had played the most active part in Bishop Potter's anti-prostitution crusade, but the CU recognized the other factions and cultural groups in its coalition by giving the remaining nominations to a French-German Catholic and National Democrat; to a Brooklyn Protestant Swallowtail Democrat; and to Tammany district leader Jacob A. Cantor, a Jew who had long worked closely with the city's leading merchants.[113] But not all Democrats were satisfied, and after extensive discussions, the Tammany nomination also went to a Swallowtail, Edward M. Shepard of Brooklyn.[114]

Conceding the Irish and the German Catholic vote to Tammany even in advance of the nominations, the Citizens' Union continued to stress the moral reform issues and shifted its platform just slightly to the left in an effort to appeal simultaneously to the middle- and upper-middle-income silk stocking districts, to Protestant Germans, and to the eastern European Jews on the lower east side. As former congressman and Grace associate John DeWitt Warner observed after the election, "the vital question in reform politics was as to how the 'East Side' vote can be won." Since much of the east side's population had come to New York "from European cities that are as progressive as we are backward" in providing adequate municipal services, Warner asserted, "the wage-earning masses, largely of foreign birth," were remarkably "enlightened and progressive in spirit." By contrast, "ignorance and narrowness" regarding municipal government prevailed among the city's "cultured and well-to-do classes."[115]

R. Fulton Cutting insisted that the CU won in 1901 because it earned the wage earners' confidence.[116] Yet it moved very cautiously to do so. It now called for municipal ownership of the city's water and some of its gas and electric utilities. But so did many Chamber of Commerce leaders who, like Low, saw improved service and municipal revenue possibilities—not lower prices for small consumers—in these ideas.[117] The CU added building code reform to its earlier demand for public health measures, but a Charity Organization Society Committee had already formulated this proposal in part as an explicit bid for lower east side votes.[118] And despite continued admonitions from the *Times*, the CU strengthened its committment to implement model labor relations practices for city employees.[119] But Warner was wrong to suggest that the CU ran a collectivist campaign directed to the lower east side in the *City Vigilant* and a traditional low-tax, antivice campaign "in the body of the reform press."[120] Under Parkhurst's continued control, the *City Vigilant* paid far more attention to moral reform than to municipal socialism. And while William

Travers Jerome, the CU's star campaigner on the lower east side, did not ignore such issues as cheap fares, tenement house reform, and school accommodations, he stressed the anti-prostitution theme. "I do not believe you can stop prostitution," he declared to a lower east side audience. "If there is one ounce of manhood in you, however, you will stop the police growing rich off the shame of fallen women. Is the honor of Jewish women sold for brass checks nothing to you?"[121]

In 1901 the CU-led fusion coalition used these issues to eke out a narrow victory. Running 14,000 votes behind Jerome, Low received a bare 50 percent of the total; in Manhattan and the Bronx he received only 48.7 percent and ran ahead of Shepard by fewer than 6,000 out of 333,093 votes cast. By comparison with the totals he and Tracy had run up together in 1897, Low made his greatest gains in the two Manhattan areas where the CU had pushed its 1901 campaign most energetically: the silk stocking districts and the Jewish lower east side. He also did better in German districts along the East River. But in Brooklyn his fusion candidacy attracted no more voters than had the separate CU and Republican candidacies in 1897: 54.5 percent for Low as against 34 percent for Low and 20 percent for Tracy in 1897.[122]

Seth Low's administration brought the transition era to an end. Like William L. Strong, he failed to recognize the patronage claims of all the factions that had supported him, and he chose to enforce the Sunday closing laws even though that action was bound to alienate the city's Germans.[123] Before he had been in office for a year, Low had abandoned his nonpartisan stance to campaign for the re-election of Republican Governor Benjamin B. Odell and to speak openly of his desire to help Roosevelt win the presidential election in 1904.[124] Through his patronage and political decisions, Low was in effect giving up the effort to sustain an independent municipal party in order to strengthen the Roosevelt-led Republicans. When the Democrats in his administration found him deaf to their objections, they left office and returned to their own party. As the incumbent mayor and as the president's choice, Low had the 1903 Citizens' Union nomination for the asking. But it had become merely the Republican nomination, and Low was soundly defeated.[125]

It was not mere partisanship that ended the political effectiveness of the Citizens' Union. That movement had always been made up of diverse and discordant elements. Its wealthy leaders and backers had sought mutually incompatible ends: low taxes *and* expanded municipal services, civil service reform *and* political recognition, *laissez-faire and* social reform, top priorities for expenditures on schools *and* on transportation, opposition to social welfare fads *and* the labor vote, the dry Sunday *and* the

German vote, a Protestant revival *and* the Jewish vote. After ten years and two mayoral administrations the advocates of these discordant objectives recognized that they could not be amalgamated into a single movement. Just at this time, national and local developments encouraged the city's wealthy men to return to the regular Democratic and Republican organizations. Locally, both regular party organizations had successfully avoided the tendency toward cultural exclusiveness that Protestant zeal and Anglo-American ethnocentrism had so often brought to the independent movement. By 1903 both of the regular parties could appeal for immigrant votes more effectively than could the Citizens' Union. Locally too, both the Democrats and the Republicans had new leaders who were willing to accommodate many of the wealthy men who had created the fusion coalitions.

After 1903, wealthy New Yorkers who had strong partisan commitments or who entertained an ambition to hold higher office returned to one of the two national parties.[126] Wealthy men who were deeply committed to particular moral reform, social reform, or economic goals henceforth abandoned the effort to create a permanent municipal party. But they did not abandon municipal politics. They had already created effective single-purpose pressure groups, and, as historian Richard S. Skolnik has observed, after 1903 they sought to use these groups, rather than an independent municipal party, to influence municipal affairs.[127] Yet there can be no doubt that their influence over mayoral nominations declined. In the 1880s the city's Swallowtail merchants and bankers had dominated mayoral politics, determining both the Democratic and the Republican nominations, supplying the candidates, limiting the issues to the *laissez-faire*, equal opportunity, commercial development objectives they favored. In the 1890s the city's wealthiest men had become more numerous and more diverse, and they sought much more, in cultural as well as economic terms, from the city government. They got much of what they wanted. But the logic of the city's economic and social development threw the rich into conflict with one another and created effective competing interests in the political parties and in the lower- and middle-income pressure groups. By the beginning of the twentieth century the city's wealthy men controlled the best-endowed pressure groups, but they could no longer hope to dominate mayoral politics.

CHAPTER 6

NON-ECONOMIC ELITES

AND MAYORAL POLITICS

BY the last decade of the nineteenth century the ability of Greater New York's economic elites to control mayoral nominations was severely limited by deep divisions among them. It was also limited by the increasing power of political, labor, and ethnic group leaders who could draw on significant resources of their own: rising prosperity for many of their constituents, effective organizations, and a developing core of values shared quite widely among the city's immigrant and second-generation residents. During the 1890s the most important of these leaders—who belonged to what might be called, serviceably if not elegantly, the city's non-economic elites—were found at the head of Tammany Hall and organized labor. This chapter examines their considerable impact on the mayoral nominations of the period.

Although they do not receive separate attention here, other non-economic elites also gained influence during these years. Professional Republican politicians in the city as well as in the state organization sought, with less success than Tammany leaders but by no means in vain, to gain autonomy from their wealthy backers through the use of tactics very much like those of their Democratic counterparts. They employed many of the techniques that appealed to Tammany—notably centralization of patronage and leadership and accommodation to a wide variety of pressure groups. Labor organizations constituted the most important of the non-economic elite pressure groups in this period, but religious and ethnic organizations produced by the city's middle- and lower-income population used similar techniques to veto proposed nominations and to shape the platforms on which the nominees stood. The rise and maturation of Tammany Hall and the development of labor organizations into effective pressure groups paralleled the experience of most non-economic elite groups in this period.

Tammany Hall: The Rise of the Professional Politician

The Swallowtail Democrats who moved into Tammany Hall following their 1871 ouster of Tweed found the organization difficult to control, and by 1878 most of them had moved out again, leaving Tammany to its own devices. The Swallowtails continued to rely on professional district leaders, but because they supplied the money, the public standing, the press coverage, the patronage, and much of the political expertise, they made the major decisions for Irving Hall, the County Democracy, and the State Democracy. A number of the Swallowtails were self-made men, but they had established themselves in commerce or law before turning to politics. Within Tammany after 1878, by contrast, men who made their mark first in politics controlled the organization, choosing their own city-wide leaders and developing their own candidates.

Technically, the Tammany Society was a private patriotic and benevolent association; Tammany Hall merely provided the chief meeting place for the New York County Democratic Committee. But Tammany was neither simple nor unchanging. In the 1870s Tammany was a congeries of independent, irresponsible assembly district organizations, each on the lookout for its own interests, ready to work for the individual or group that offered the highest price. As the city grew more complex, as its economic elites grew in size and diversity, as its ethnic mix grew richer, and as its white-collar and skilled workers produced more vigorous economic and social organizations, Tammany was transformed. By 1903 it had taken on the character of a modern political party. It had become quite autonomous, able to support itself without recourse to a few wealthy men, capable of producing effective leaders from its own ranks, reasonably coherent, increasingly disciplined, and successful not so much as the advocate of a particular stance toward public policy, but as a broker organization that specialized in the arts of policy compromise, ethnic conciliation, and political management. The increase in internal discipline played a key role in this transformation. But the styles of particular leaders, their growing control of significant resources, the changing ethnic origins of the voters, and the shifting activities and purposes of Swallowtail Democrats and Republicans all had their own impact on the pace, timing, and character of Tammany's development. The net effect was to shift the

Tammany Hall decorated for the gubernatorial election of 1891. The banners refer to the issues of rapid transit and Greater New York. The question, "Has the Seat of the Empire Gone to the West?," defiantly responds to the claim that Chicago would soon surpass New York City in population; a large New York City vote "on the 3rd of November" will put Chicago in its place. Tony Pastor's café is in the Tammany Hall basement, the Academy of Music is next door to the left. (Courtesy of the New-York Historical Society, New York City)

power to make mayoral nominations from the Swallowtails to the professional politicians in Tammany Hall and more broadly to increase the political impact of the city's middle- and lower-income voters, especially those represented by effective organizations.

"Honest John" Kelly, Tammany's first post-Tweed leader, dominated the first phase of the organization's transformation. Aided and abetted by the Swallowtails, he introduced a whole series of disciplines that Tweed had never even tried to employ. As political scientist Martin Shefter has recently shown, Kelly expelled unwanted men from assembly district committees, rejected district nominations, imposed nominations he preferred, allocated patronage strictly through the district leaders he had recognized, and withheld support from excessively independent elected officials.[1] A deeply impressed contemporary exclaimed that Kelly found Tammany "a horde. He left it a political army."[2]

Yet Kelly never controlled sufficient resources to shake off the influence of the Swallowtails. He owed his own elevation to the Tammany leadership to their influence, and it was Tilden and his associates who had first encouraged him to centralize control as a means of countering those who remained too closely associated with the Tweed Ring. When he turned those same techniques against the Swallowtails in the interest of Tammany autonomy, they drew back in alarm.[3] But even then Kelly knew that his organization could not supply creditable candidates from its own ranks. His first three mayoral nominees after the Swallowtail split in 1878 were themselves Swallowtail Democrats: banker Augustus Schell, who remained within Tammany; merchant William R. Grace, who had previously remained aloof from local politics; and Produce Exchange President Franklin Edson, who had played a minor part in the Irving Hall–County Democracy movement.[4]

And so long as the Swallowtails supported a well-organized, well-financed, city-wide body of Democrats that could serve as an alternative to Tammany Hall in local, state, and national elections, they were able to undermine Kelly's efforts to dominate. Expulsion and the withholding of patronage are effective weapons only to the extent that the organization employing them monopolizes political resources. By creating rival Democratic organizations, winning local elections, and securing critical appointments in the national government under Grover Cleveland, the Swallowtails denied Kelly the resources to carry out his centralizing intentions.[5]

Kelly's Tammany did manage to hold on to some of the county and judicial offices it had taken over during the Tweed era; Tammany men served as fire commissioners through most of the eighties, and Kelly himself served for several years as the city's comptroller. These resources did not permit Tammany to dominate. William M. Ivins, who served as city chamberlain under both Grace and Hewitt and wrote from long experience, observed in 1887 that "a single department" was "of itself enough to furnish the foundations of a Machine," provided that it supplied "a score of fair places for the superior politicians, and a laborers' pay-roll for the rank and file."[6] Through the eighties Irving Hall and County Democracy men retained control of the considerable construction and employment patronage of several departments, including parks, public works, water supply, and police, as well as the legal and clerical patronage of the corporation counsel's office.[7] Using this patronage, they sustained effective assembly district organizations throughout the city and mounted effective campaigns in the downtown and waterfront areas inhabited by the most recent Irish and German immigrants.[8] The existence of a rival Democratic organization had a destabilizing effect, encouraging opportunistic district leaders to continue their traditional tactic of playing competing organizations off against one another. In the face of increasing centralization within Tammany Hall, district leaders like Michael C. Murphy at the Battery, Timothy D. Sullivan and Timothy J. Campbell between the Bowery and South Street, Charles Steckler and John Reilly on the lower east side, George Washington Plunkitt and Henry Murray in Hell's Kitchen, Andrew J. White in Harlem, and Henry D. Purroy in the Annexed District (later the Bronx) were able, with Swallowtail support, to enjoy a good deal of independence.[9]

The Swallowtails deplored the independence and the rough tactics employed by these district leaders, but they did not scruple to make use of their services. With the aid of Murphy, Sullivan, Murray, White, and Purroy, for example, Grace did better among Irish immigrants in 1884 than did Hugh J. Grant, Kelly's first non-Swallowtail Irish Catholic candidate for mayor. According to Shefter, the vote for Grant actually *declined* by as much as 3.5 percent for every 10 percent increase in the proportion of Irish immigrants in an election district's population.[10] Because they provided a viable alternative, the Swallowtail Democrats were able to find allies among the district leaders, undermine Tammany efforts to establish effective discipline, and dominate mayoral politics.

Kelly never controlled sufficient resources to make his new discipline techniques effective, but the decision of Abram S. Hewitt and other Swallowtails to abandon local Democratic politics in order to pursue a Protestant millennium permitted his successors to complete the task he had begun. Kelly died in 1886; by 1889 Richard Croker, James J. Martin,

Mayor Hugh J. Grant—an exemplar of the sporting style—driving a trotting horse, 1891. Professional politicians who rose to the mayor's office were rarely portrayed in paint. In this case, Grant sought immortality at the hands of a none-too-expert painter of sporting scenes, rather than at those of one of the highly skilled European-trained artists who painted the members of the Chamber of Commerce. (Courtesy of the Museum of the City of New York)

Hugh J. Grant, and Thomas F. Gilroy—the "Big Four"—were widely hailed as the effective creators of a "New Tammany."

All of these men were professional politicians. Croker, who had been born in Ireland and received his education in the Fourth Avenue Tunnel Gang and the school of hard knocks, had used a volunteer firefighting company as the springboard for his political career. He succeeded through a combination of shrewdness, tenacity, loyalty, and a certain ability to cultivate the favor of such useful men as Hewitt and Kelly. By 1883 he had outlived the (almost certainly false) charge that he had murdered a political opponent during an 1874 campaign for Hewitt and other Tammany nominees; mayors Edson and Hewitt then appointed him to successive terms as fire commissioner.[11] Closer than any other Tammany man to Kelly in his last years, Croker simply stepped into the leadership in 1886. Martin, leader of the silk stocking 21st Assembly District in central Manhattan, had been a horsecar conductor, a clerk and *confidant* to Kelly in the comptroller's office, and Tammany's chief Albany lobbyist. He worked closely with Croker in managing the downtown district leaders.[12]

The other two members of the Big Four represented the somewhat more prosperous uptown crowd of Tammany district leaders who had made considerable investments in upper Manhattan real estate and street railroads. Hugh J. Grant was typical of those who had derived some of their wealth from nonpolitical activities. His father came to New York from Ireland, built up a string of successful saloons, and left his son a tidy inheritance. Grant graduated from St. Francis Xavier College and Columbia University Law School, traveled in Europe, and prepared for the bar under a well-connected Tammany lawyer. Devoting himself more to the management of his west side real estate holdings than to the practice of law, he began to win elections at an early age, became the leader of an upper west side assembly district, and developed close relations with Croker as well as with the uptown crowd. Thomas F. Gilroy, on the other hand, apparently started out with few advantages. His mother had brought him to New York from Ireland at the age of five or six, sent him to the city's common schools, and arranged a brief printer's apprenticeship. Gilroy then rose from the promising but humble position of Tweed's messenger boy through a series of county and court clerkships. By 1880 he owned—or occupied—at least two pieces of property. By 1886 he was under sheriff of New York County, leader of an upper east side assembly district, and chairman of the critically important Tammany Committee on Organization.[13]

Between roughly 1884 and 1894 the uptown group, working closely with Croker and Martin, dominated Tammany Hall. They were determined to avoid another round of effective intervention by the city's wealthiest men, to establish their own reputations for prudence and good business management, and to serve their own real estate, career, and patronage interests. To gain those objectives, they saw to it that Tammany's mayoral platforms stressed just two issues during these years: commitment to "firm, efficient, and honest government"—and low taxes—and opposition to "know-nothing" bigotry and xenophobia.[14] With the mayoral candidacies of Grant in 1884, 1888, 1890, and 1894, and Gilroy in 1892, and especially with their victories in 1888, 1890, and 1892, they were able to go a long way toward imposing those policies on Tammany as well as on the city.[15]

These policies, the increasing discipline within Tammany, and Swallowtail failures enabled the Big Four to win a series of elections and thereby to gain the resources they needed to impose central control over Tammany at last. For several years their victories only increased the power of the uptown group within the Big Four. When Grant won election in 1888, he gained control over the management and the patronage of more city departments than Kelly had dreamed of. These resources enabled his organization to shake off the Swallowtails for good.

In 1884, it was later charged, Croker had been willing to spend $180,000 to bribe the city's aldermen into supporting Grant, rather than the County Democrat favored by Mayor Edson, for commissioner of public works; but the deal had not come off.[16] In 1889 Mayor Grant could simply appoint Gilroy to that office. At the same time he could make James J. Martin one of the four police commissioners, name Croker himself to the post of city chamberlain, William Dalton (leader of the 15th A.D.) commissioner of street cleaning, and Edward J. Fitzpatrick (4th A.D.) excise commissioner. These men in turn could make Martin's brother Barney (7th A.D.) deputy commissioner of public works, and Edward Hagen (16th A.D.), deputy commissioner of street cleaning.[17]

With the return of Fire Commissioner Henry D. Purroy (24th A.D.) to Tammany, the organization enjoyed almost unlimited opportunities to send construction and carting work in the direction of contractors and livery stable owners John Reilly (14th A.D.), John McQuade (22nd A.D.), and Charles Welde (23rd A.D.), and to offer jobs to the unskilled and semiskilled workers who frequented the saloons of downtown district leaders Paddy Divver, Peter Mitchell, John Scannell, Daniel Hanley, and James Barker (A.D.s 2, 5, 11, 12, and 13) as well as those of Fitzpatrick, "Barney" Martin, John Reilly, and Dalton.[18] Men who sought skilled, clerical, or professional jobs were now well advised to join Charles F. Murphy's ancient Anawanda Club in the 16th district, Hugh Grant's long-established Narragansett Club in the 19th, or one of the many similar social-political clubs with Indian names that Tammany district leaders were setting up from one end of town to the other.[19]

These resources, together with the demise of the County Democracy, enabled Tammany's new leaders to employ Kelly's techniques with real effectiveness. In the absence of a rival Democratic organization, their control over patronage, nominations, and social facilities permitted them to impose a definitive discipline over their subordinates. No longer was it necessary for a Tammany leader to bribe a Democratic alderman. With central control assured, the leaders could confidently insist that officeholders contribute to the expenses of the organization. They could bargain directly with corporations or pressure groups that sought specific policies, then insist that subordinates accept the resulting agreement. And they could insist that subordinate officeholders refrain from making their own demands—or striking their own bargains—with those who needed protection or sought favors.[20] Altogether, central control made it possible for the Big Four to take the stage as statesmen, capable of building the city up honestly, efficiently, and with due regard to the interests of its varied ethnic and religious groups, and hence able to garner the prestige as well as the material resources that the Swallowtails had previously monopolized.

At least the Grant-Gilroy uptown group so hoped. In fact they were unable to rule with quite so firm a hand. Several of Tammany's long-established downtown district leaders cared far more for their personal incomes than for their reputations or for the stability of the organizations. And when the Big Four replaced some of them with former County Democrats, several of those also proved to be more rapacious than upright. Their continuing corruption left Tammany's newfound respectability vulnerable. In 1890 the Republican legislature's Fassett Committee investigation forced Grant to admit that on his election as sheriff in 1885, he had given Croker's two-year-old daughter at least $10,000 in cash; but he was able to brazen his way past this incident (little Flossie was his only goddaughter, Grant had inherited wealth but had no family of his own, and Croker was a "poor man") and win re-election.[21] But although both Grant and Gilroy had insisted that Tammany should impose a stricter discipline than Croker approved on the most corrupt and criminal of its downtown district leaders, neither of them was able to withstand the Lexow Committee's 1894 investigation into police corruption.[22] Together, the Lexow Committee and Parkhurst's indiscriminate attacks on Tammany morality were bound to damage the uptown leaders' standing in the business world and to embarrass them in their effort to make Tammany both a symbol of achievement and an aid to the aspirations of the city's Irish and German, Catholic, and Jewish communities. As the incumbent mayor in 1894, Gilroy clearly had to step down; when Grant lost the election that year, the uptown group (which had been losing strength in any case as more uptown voters turned to the Republican party) lost its ability to dominate the organization.[23] (For the declining Tammany vote in uptown districts, see maps 4–1, 4–2, and 4–3, pp. 125–127.)

The discrediting of the uptown group, together with the strong reaction against William L. Strong's mayoral administration, made possible the brief third stage in the maturation of Tammany Hall. Recognizing that he could dispense with other interests, Richard Croker delivered the organization into the hands of William C. Whitney and other street railroad promoters and contractors and of a set of unscrupulous downtown district leaders.[24] Hugh Grant was still willing to manage the 1897 mayoral campaign, Thomas F. Gilroy was still available to lend a hand, other uptown

Tammany leader Richard Croker (in bowler hat) with a group of unidentified associates, 1899. Intent on establishing an image of the evil boss, contemporary photographers usually portrayed Croker in a less flattering light than Byron has on this occasion. (Byron Collection, Courtesy of the Museum of the City of New York)

leaders stood in the wings, and many of the Grace-Fairchild Swallowtails were eager to reconstitute the Democratic Party on a more comprehensive and durable basis.[25] But once it became clear that the Republicans and the Citizens' Union would nominate competing candidates, everyone understood that Croker and his associates would select a puppet who would be responsive to them alone.[26] Quickly passing over Grant, Charles H. Truax, and P. Henry Dugro, each of whom possessed a great deal of experience and an independent base of support within Tammany, Croker arranged for the nomination to go to the pliable Robert A. Van Wyck, a little-known chief judge of the city court who possessed an aristocratic-sounding name but who enjoyed neither wealth nor significant district leader support. Van Wyck was certain to be Croker's creature.[27]

In the long run, Tammany's 1897 campaign was most noteworthy for the breadth of its appeal. Tammany speakers did not drop their traditional insistence on economic and social *laissez-faire:* Gilroy criticized the substantial increase in the city's budget and tax rate that had taken place under Mayor Strong, and district attorney candidate Asa Bird Gardner was by no means the only Tammany candidate who shouted "To Hell With Reform!"[28] But with this campaign Tammany began to present itself as a general advocate for organized low- and middle-income groups. Some of its spokesmen stressed its long-standing commitments to provide fair treatment for municipal employees, opportunities for local boys who were willing to work their way up through the ranks (not university-trained experts), an end to religious prejudice in the schools and in municipal government generally, and a reasonable approach to the Sunday drinking question. Others added new promises: to promote unionization, to seek lower gas rates, and to increase taxes on corporations.[29] Consciously countering the Citizens' Union's "best men" rhetoric, Tammany insisted that it—not the Chamber of Commerce or the Charity Organization Society— could supply the men best able to consider the interests of the city's varied population. With this new breadth of concern, Tammany tied its 1897 campaign themes together with very much the same rhetoric that political scientist Steven Kelman found in his content analysis of its 1903 campaign: "Common people don't need the 'better element' to run the city for them; Republicans insult the people by calling all Democrats thieves and gamblers; anti-elitism."[30]

The election results demonstrated the effectiveness of these arguments. Tammany won not only because the Citizens' Union and the Republicans split the vote, but also because it attracted a larger share of the poor voters regardless of their ethnic backgrounds. Van Wyck did least well in the relatively wealthy silk stocking districts in the center of Manhattan, on the upper east and upper west sides, in central Harlem, and in what was probably the most prosperous assembly district on the Jewish lower east side. He failed to gain a larger share of the Irish immigrant, Jewish, and other foreign-stock voters who lived in relatively prosperous districts. But he held the already very large vote in the largely Irish districts along the Hudson River and in the mid–east side's gashouse section and drew a substantially increased vote in the poorer areas of the lower east side and in every district that had a substantial German population.[31] Martin Shefter's detailed analysis of election district voting patterns confirms these observations.[32] Under Croker's leadership, and in the face of the fusion shift toward militant Protestantism, Tammany had successfully presented itself as the legitimate representative of, and broker among, the city's increasingly diverse lower- and middle-income ethnic groups.

This shift in Tammany's ideological and social stance was to become permanent, but Croker's leadership style dominated only for a brief period in the organization's history. Croker, not Van Wyck, became the effective manager of the city government in 1898. Operating without the restraint formerly imposed by Grant, Gilroy, and others in the uptown crowd who sought social and business recognition and had learned discipline in the lean years of the 1870s and 1880s, and taking advantage of the possibilities presented by the amalgamation of the local governments of Brooklyn, Queens, and Staten Island into Greater New York, the Boss and the district leaders he placed in every available office cheerfully set out to make their fortunes. Through sinecures, rigged contracts, kick-backs from favored bonding companies, legal, banking, sheriff's auction patronage, and "retainers" from business firms seeking favors or freedom from interference, most of them did very well indeed. And they were proud of themselves. Challenged by Parkhurst's associate, Frank Moss, during the Republican legislature's Mazet Committee hearings in 1899, Croker declared: "to the party belongs the spoils"; "we win and we expect everyone to stand by"; "we want the whole business if we can get it"; and "I am working for my pocket all the time, same as you!"[33]

Yet Tammany firms did do much of the work they were paid for, and, by contrast to the Tweed Ring's depredations, little of this graft affected the city's taxpayers, merchants, or large employers. For the most part Croker and his associates resisted the temptation to steal directly from the city. They continued to proclaim their devotion to low taxes and to a high rating for the city's bonds.[34] But their alliance with Whitney and other utilities magnates and their continuing commitment to *laissez-faire* prevented them from seeing that the economic interests represented in the Chamber of Commerce now sought a municipal government that would actively pursue the city's interests in such matters as transportation, the water supply, and public health. And Croker signally failed to keep the police out of trouble. These failures of management and policy brought his regime to an abrupt close.[35]

So long as Van Wyck remained in office Croker retained control within Tammany Hall, and in an effort to retrieve the situation he offered the 1901 mayoral nomination to Edward M. Shepard, a distinguished Swallow-tail Democrat from Brooklyn.[36] Shepard would not have been Croker's free choice. By choosing him, Croker was, in effect, acknowledging the limits of his own power, admitting that Tammany could dominate mayoral politics only if its leaders paid closer attention to the policy preferences of the city's economic elites and imposed a stricter discipline on their subordinates. Shepard stood for both actions, and his political skills, experience, and strong bases of support made it clear that if elected he would carry them out. The former ward of Abram S. Hewitt, he had become a successful Wall Street lawyer whose articulate advocacy of civil service reform, the gold standard, and honest elections, together with his effective county-wide political organization, had made him the most prominent independent Democrat in Brooklyn and one of the three or four most prominent in Greater New York. He had played a prominent role in the Cleveland and Gold Democratic movements and had opposed the Willoughby Street machine, Brooklyn's equivalent of Tammany Hall, by supporting the successful 1893 mayoral candidacy of Republican Charles A. Schieren and then by running for the office himself in 1895. In 1897 he had worked to bring the Henry George movement into Seth Low's campaign.

But Shepard opposed many Republican policies, identified himself thoroughly with the Democratic party, and had taken care not to offend the Irish or those who preferred the wet Sunday. Like Theodore Roosevelt, he was ambitious for higher office. A convinced and active anti-imperialist, he had joined with the regular Democratic organizations to support Bryan's presidential campaign in 1900.[37] As Croker must have understood perfectly well, Shepard would not have accepted the nomination unless he and his closest associates had believed that he could use the mayor's office to reform Tammany as well as to move into a prominent place within the Democratic mainstream. Shepard proved to be an effective candidate: Despite the incubus of the Van Wyck/Croker record, he retained almost as large a share of the vote as Van Wyck had drawn and lost to Low in Manhattan by only 6,000 votes. But he failed to prevent a further shift of votes in the silk stocking, German, and Jewish districts away from Tammany, or to increase the Democratic vote in Brooklyn.[38]

Shepard's nomination was the last, desperate stroke in Croker's career; his defeat forced Croker to retire from the scene. With his successor, the taciturn Charles F. Murphy, Tammany moved into its maturity. The son of poor immigrants who had made his way as a saloonkeeper and petty contractor and had worked his way up through the Tammany ranks, Murphy, like Croker before him, made his mark strictly as a professional politician. But he also learned from Croker's mistakes. A realist, Murphy used Tammany's resources and its now well-established disciplinary techniques to impose new principles that enabled his organization to dominate the city's mayoral politics for the next thirty years. He did not put an end to all corruption, but he did insist that Tammany officials avoid the gross and flagrant disregard for honesty and morality that characterized the behavior of many during Van Wyck's administration. He had no desire to abolish patronage appointments, but he accepted the need for expertise in such fields as public health and education as well as in finance. Recognizing that Tammany would be more stable if it served a wide range of constituencies, he sought to accommodate the policy preferences of diverse groups of businessmen, social reformers, and organized workers. And he was aware that it was in Tammany's own interest to select mayoral candidates who, like Shepard, enjoyed considerable personal stature and would satisfy non-Tammany groups that might otherwise seek to influence local politics more directly.[39]

Murphy's first mayoral nominee, Congressman George B. McClellan, Jr., reflected these principles. Bearer of the name of his father, the most famous Democratic general in the Union Army and the Democratic candidate for president in 1864, McClellan had begun life with considerable standing in New York City politics. He had also inherited a comfortable fortune. After graduating from Princeton and traveling for two years in Europe, he entered politics in New York, made his way among Tammany leaders with considerable shrewdness, and quickly became one of Croker's protégés. By 1903 he had served five terms in the United States Congress, where he established an impressive record for intelligence and independence.[40] These credentials made McClellan a widely acceptable mayoral candidate in 1903. Taking advantage of Low's mistakes, he won easily with 52 percent of the vote (Shepard had secured only 42 percent).[41]

Murphy had nominated McClellan because he satisfied a variety of constituencies and because he appeared to possess the stature to be his own man in office. To Murphy's chagrin, McClellan lived up to appearances. He pleased taxpayers by keeping waste and corruption to a minimum. He impressed the Chamber of Commerce by placing experts in charge of water supply, public health, and traffic matters and by resisting the demands of traction magnates. His management of the police department satisfied the Reverend Mr. Parkhurst without alienating the Germans. And he saw to it that the tenement house laws were strictly enforced. When Murphy objected that he was going too far in his effort to satisfy these diverse interests, McClellan dismissed appointees whose first loyalty was to Tammany and replaced them with men loyal to himself. In the end, Murphy was able to deny McClellan a nomination for a third term and to bring his political career to an early close.[42]

But although Tammany nominated McClellan's successor, William J. Gaynor, it chose him for the same reasons it had chosen McClellan, and he proved to be equally independent. The leaders of a mature Tammany were able to nominate New York City's mayors for so many years only after they had learned that they must consider other interests besides their own. Wallace Sayre and Herbert Kaufman observed that "the widespread and persistent myth that the New York mayoralty belongs most of the time to Tammany does not stand up . . . the mayoralty [may] much more accurately [be] described as Tammany's achilles' heel."[43] Between 1872 and 1903 this was true because the city's wealthiest men could always threaten to defeat a Tammany mayoral candidate with one of their own. After 1903 it was true because Tammany's own leaders had mastered the art—and recognized the necessity—of balancing the demands of the full range of the city's interest groups.

Organized Labor

The transformation of mayoral politics and the increasingly broad distribution of power over the nomination of mayors in late nineteenth-century New York City was the consequence not only of the fragmentation of the economic elites and the maturation of Tammany Hall, but also of the emergence of pressure groups representing the city's middle- and even low-income residents. In the 1870s such organizations had played a negligible part in local politics, but in the prosperous years after 1877 they rapidly increased in numbers and membership. The labor-sponsored Henry George campaign of 1886 marked a decisive turning point. As both of George's opponents, Abram Hewitt and Theodore Roosevelt, recognized, organized labor would henceforth be a force to reckon with in New York politics. By the mid-nineties labor and ethnic organizations were able to shape the platforms, influence the selection of candidates, and ultimately say a good deal about the chances for survival of the Democratic, the Republican, and the Citizens' Union parties themselves. The rise of organized labor is especially dramatic and well documented, but it was not essentially different from the emergence of lower- and middle-income ethnic, religious, and neighborhood commercial pressure groups of all kinds. All of these groups contributed to the transformation of the city, but all of them were themselves profoundly influenced by the city's character.

Neither organized labor nor other low- or middle-income interest groups played a significant part in mayoral politics during the 1870s. Greenback and Socialist parties did nominate mayoral candidates from time to time, yet none of them drew more than 1 percent of the vote and labor received scant attention from the Democratic and Republican managers. The city's skilled workers, like its Tammany Hall politicians, were just beginning to build a new set of vigorous grass-roots organizations. These organizations differed widely in the crafts they represented, in their ethnic composition, and in their views of the relative merits of the cooperationism espoused by the Knights of Labor, of several competing versions of socialism, and of "pure and simple" unionism as defined by Samuel Gompers and his American Federation of Labor associates. Despite their differences they enrolled more and more workers, and they coalesced into city-wide bodies that were increasingly effective as the nineteenth century drew to a close.

One of these city-wide bodies, the Central Labor Union (CLU), sponsored a labor candidate for mayor as early as 1882, barely a year after it was organized. But it failed to mount an effective campaign and drew only the usual 1 percent of the vote. Yet by this time labor organizations were expanding rapidly. In 1884 the CLU consisted of just 36 affiliated member organizations; in 1886 the number fluctuated between 120 and 207, and the total number of individuals connected with the CLU reached fifty or sixty thousand.[44] In September 1886, the *Sun,* by no means sympathetic to the movement, estimated that as many as forty thousand of these were registered voters. The Knights of Labor, with 415 local assemblies and almost sixty-eight thousand members in Greater New York's District Council 49, also grew rapidly during the mid-eighties, as did the socialists, whose numbers are very difficult to estimate.[45] Perhaps as many as half the unions that belonged to the Central Labor Union also belonged to the Knights of Labor; all together, the two bodies represented, in the autumn of 1886, about eighty thousand men.[46]

Whatever their disagreements with one another, all labor organizations agreed on the necessity for workers to organize and to develop the means to advance their interests. Neither employers nor municipal authorities had been willing to concede these points in the 1870s, and the result was increasing conflict, in New York City as everywhere throughout the industrial northeast and midwest. By the mid-eighties New York's unions were employing a wide variety of new tactics, including the demand for the closed shop, the consumer boycott, and the "Irish" boycott (the practice of shunning or "sending to Coventry" working men who refused union discipline).[47] Employers responded with lockouts, police harassment of pickets and union meetings, and vigorous use of courts that were willing to declare unions to be illegal conspiracies in restraint of trade. Recalling the campaign against strikers and boycotters forty years later, Samuel Gompers wrote that "in the spring of 1886 police brutality against New York workers became so flagrant that labor's patience reached the breaking point."[48]

The prosecution of the "Thiess boycotters" brought matters to a head. In the wake of an unsuccessful strike, the Carl Sahm Club of musicians, which was affiliated with District Council 49 of the Knights of Labor, had declared a boycott against George Thiess's music hall and beer garden on 14th Street, across from Tammany Hall. Waiters' and bartenders' unions affiliated with the Central Labor Union joined in the protest. Alarmed by their effective picketing, George Ehret, whose brewery supplied Thiess's, brought the parties together. As part of the resulting settlement, Thiess agreed to contribute $1,000 toward the expenses of the striking unions. But when he paid, the over-zealous Grand Jury intervened, declaring that the money had, in effect, been extorted. With the enthusiastic urging of Judge George C. Barrett, who owed his position to a joint Apollo Hall–Tammany Hall nomination, the five union leaders who had accepted Ehret's invitation to negotiate with Thiess were tried, convicted, and sentenced to terms ranging from eighteen to forty-four months.[49]

Organized labor responded with the Henry George campaign, the single most effective political initiative it has ever mounted in New York. At the initiative of the Central Labor Union, which had been pushing the use of the boycott, a wide variety of labor, radical, and reform organizations, including the Knights of Labor, several AFL affiliates, and the socialists, agreed to lay aside their considerable differences and create an Independent Labor party (ILP) as the instrument for mounting a protest against the use of courts and police to harass union organizers and boycotters. With little debate the ILP resolved to run a full slate of candidates in the forthcoming municipal elections.[50] Some of those who were moving toward "pure and simple" unionism, remembering the CLU's poor showing in the 1882 elections, supported the plan only reluctantly. But most union leaders, encouraged by John Swinton and other labor journalists and by the socialists, and convinced that an independent campaign was necessary "as a demonstration of protest," gave their wholehearted support.[51]

Henry George made an especially effective labor candidate in 1886 precisely because he could appeal—for the purpose of his first mayoral campaign—to the widest possible range of organizations and views. His emphasis on the centrality of land and the reform of property ownership—as well as the fact that the British had arrested him during a speaking tour of Ireland—attracted the Irish Land League. His proposal for a "single," heavy tax on land appealed to socialists as a first step toward the social control of property. At the same time, his proposal to do away with the tax on buildings and other improvements to land appealed to those, like George himself (and like most Democrats), who thought of themselves as individualists and who saw most taxes, like the tariff, as burdens on productive enterprise.[52] The peculiarly indeterminate character of George's views permitted the widest range of labor organizations to unite behind him, using his candidacy to make a point of their own: that public authorities and political parties must accept workingmen and their representatives as full participants in local affairs. Once Central Labor Union leader James P. Archibald proposed his name, the ILP gave no other candidate serious consideration.[53]

George proved to be as effective as he was acceptable. Enjoying the united and well-coordinated support of all those who had nominated him, he spoke before labor unions, Irish nationalists, Catholic parish fairs, middle-income social reformers, and single-tax clubs as well as at mass rallies from one end of the city to the other.[54] George's speeches applied his single-tax idea to the city's problems: New York City's workers lived in miserable, overcrowded, overpriced tenements because speculators held land off the market. A heavy tax on land would force them to release sufficient space to accommodate the city's people in decent single-family bungalows, and would yield sufficient revenue to permit the city to take over the elevated railroads and run them at no charge to their passengers and to greatly expand educational and recreational facilities.[55] George also publicized labor's demand for the right to conduct strikes and boycotts without police or legal interference.[56] And in response to Hewitt's jibe that his campaign encouraged class conflict, George retorted that "corrupt government is and always must be government of the men who have the money."[57] If his movement was a class movement, he insisted, it was a movement of the sort that the English Liberal, Herbert Gladstone, had called "a movement of the masses against robbery by the classes."[58] George was not fomenting class conflict, but he *was* insisting that workingmen be included in the body politic. The ILP saw to it that his views were widely distributed, both through a speakers' bureau organized by Samuel Gompers and through newspapers and broadsides edited by Louis F. Post and Fred C. Leubuscher, who later published an official history of the campaign.[59]

On the eve of the election Hewitt predicted that George would receive 70,000 or 80,000 votes; his information proved to be remarkably accurate, as George's official total was 68,110, about 31 percent of all votes cast.[60] As Martin Shefter has shown, George ran especially well among the second-generation Irish, the Germans, and the Jews.[61] He attracted more voters than Hewitt in five assembly districts—including the unpredictable

8th and 10th on the lower east side and the 15th and 17th in the west side's largely Irish Hell's Kitchen—that supported entrenched Tammany organizations.[62] George and his supporters argued that the Democrats had counted him out; one Democrat had reputedly asked, "How can George win? He has no inspectors of election!"[63] Yet George did best in the Tammany strongholds along the east and west sides. From one point of view, he lost because he carried too few of the votes among the newest Irish immigrants, a majority of whom followed the lead of County Democracy district leaders and the official position of the Catholic Church and voted for Hewitt.[64]

Despite his defeat, George jubilantly concluded that his campaign had made labor a distinct and effective force in the metropolis. "Never again," he declared, would "the politicians look upon the labor movement with contempt."[65] E. L. Godkin's *Nation* acknowledged, with characteristically exaggerated alarm, that "people now know that what with the boycotting Socialistic and Anarchist vote, and the 'crank' vote, there is in our city affairs a danger which it will not do to joke about. . . ."[66] But despite the *Nation's* fear and George's optimism, the unions, the Irish nationalist groups, the socialists, and the middle-class reform groups that had made up the Independent Labor Party were individually more important than the ILP itself. As a hostile but cool Theodore Roosevelt shrewdly observed after the election, the large vote for George did "not mean a new party, but, unfortunately, a new element to be bid for by the old parties."[67]

As Roosevelt foresaw, ILP unity had a short life. Under the pressure of New York City's cross-cutting ideological, ethnic, and religious pressures, the labor movement disintegrated into its constituent parts within just two years. In 1887 the single-taxers expelled the socialists and many of the German-speaking district organizations from what now became the United Labor Party, and the socialists, encouraged by Frederick Engels and by the British socialist M. H. Hyndman and supported by most of the Labor Party's German members, resumed the practice of nominating their own candidates.[68] Retaining much of its Irish support, though losing that of Patrick Ford, who now took his celebrated *Irish World* back into the Church, the United Labor Party ran George for a state office in 1887. He drew a respectable 72,000 votes but was disappointed when his New York City vote fell to just half its 1886 level.[69] Discouraged by his low vote, by his failure to reach the Germans, and by the increasingly harsh measures of opposition employed by Catholic Archbishop Michael A.

Corrigan, George decided in late 1887 that he could most effectively work for his ideals by dropping the single tax and taking up the issue of free trade.[70] His new purpose was to push the Democratic Party toward a more uncompromisingly low tariff policy. Led by the extraordinary Father Edward McGlynn, whose radical views on Ireland and labor had repeatedly provoked his Catholic superiors, the single-taxers in the Labor Party denounced George's plan to work with "the rotten Tammany Hall interwoven with the Catholic ecclesiastical machine" and expelled their most effective candidate.[71] In 1888 George stumped for Cleveland and free trade.[72] McGlynn's United Labor Party gave its mayoral nomination to J. J. Coogan, a furniture dealer who had offered futile competition to George in 1886 and who could afford to help finance his own campaign.[73] The Socialist Labor Party nominated Alexander Jonas, one of its best-known leaders. The Central Labor Union, which in 1887 had split almost evenly between the single-taxers, the socialists, and those who believed that the CLU should take no position at all, did not figure in the local campaign.[74]

Forty years later Samuel Gompers asserted that he had always doubted the wisdom of taking labor organizations into elective politics, and that after 1886 he "did not let the A.F. of L. become entangled in any partisan activity" in New York.[75] Yet in fact Gompers continued to play an active role in the United Labor Party through 1887, retaining close ties with George and seeking to turn the movement toward "tangible results."[76] It may very well have been his 1887 experience in labor-radical politics— together with simultaneous conflicts between his cigarmakers' union and the Knights of Labor and the Central Labor Union—that persuaded him to keep unions out of politics.[77] In New York City, at least, anyone who sought to put an effective labor party together had to contend with the fact that German workers who might support such a movement were likely to be caught up in German debates over the merits of Lasallean socialism; that Irish workers would disagree among themselves about such questions as Home Rule, the single tax, and the Clan-na-Gael as remedies for the problems of their homeland; that eastern European Jewish workers arrived in New York discussing the merits of syndicalism and anarchism; and that workers from other national backgrounds would similarly come to the local labor movement with views derived in substantial part from the radical movements specific to their homelands. Under these circumstances it was necessary but often vain to assert that socialism was an *international* movement. In the midst of New York's heady but endlessly contentious mixture of disparate national backgrounds and conflicting ideologies, it was not surprising that those who sought tangible results came to view direct involvement in electoral politics as inevitably divisive and futile.

Although it proved impossible to put together an effective, broadly-based labor party in New York, labor did not lose the recognition it had achieved in 1886. For about ten years after the debacle of 1888, several union leaders sought to advance labor's interests through an alliance with the social reformers who played a significant role in the People's Municipal League, the Committee of Seventy, and the Citizens' Union. Central Labor Union leader James P. Archibald and publicist Louis F. Post were among the initial organizers of the PML, and they played important roles throughout the PML's history. Archibald sat on the committee that refused the mayoral nomination to Edward Cooper (Cooper, Hewitt & Co. was in the midst of a strike) and conferred that nomination on Francis M. Scott.[78] According to the newspapers, it was at Archibald's request that the PML nominated John W. Goff as its candidate for district attorney.[79] Labor influence also shaped the platform planks that committed the PML to the proper "care of city property, the management of city franchises, the collection and expenditure of city revenues, the development of systems of rapid transit, and the impartial and vigorous enforcement of labor legislation and of measures for the improvement of the homes of the industrial classes."[80]

Although Archibald was listed as one of the members of the Committee of Seventy and although Goff had played a prominent role as the Lexow Committee's chief investigator and courtroom performer, labor played a much less prominent role in 1894. Archibald and Louis F. Post joined the State Democracy and no doubt gained some influence over the appointments Mayor Strong made from that organization.[81] But on the whole Strong's administration did not please labor, and the Citizens' Union had to make a special effort to retain labor support in 1897.[82] Out of deference to labor it agreed not to consider Sanitation Commissioner George E. Waring as a mayoral candidate, and it considered labor's views on the platform despite the continuing hostility of the New York *Times*, the *Evening Post*, and the Swallowtail Democrats. Seth Low's strengths included his support for unions,[83] his record as a labor mediator, and his work for effective and inexpensive rapid transit. Some unions, especially the largely Jewish garment workers' unions that Theodore Roosevelt, the Citizens' Union, and the Charity Organization Society had cultivated, went along with his nomination.[84] But all unions had grown stronger even as they had grown more diverse in the decade since 1886, and many

Father McGlynn speaking at the funeral of Henry George, as pictured in the New York *World,* November 1, 1897. A bust of George is placed on the platform next to the rostrum; Mayor William L. Strong and Citizens' Union mayoral candidate Seth Low are identified among the other dignitaries on the platform. Through its coverage of George's funeral, the *World* sought to persuade those who had been inclined to vote for George to switch to its favorite, Low. This may explain why the *World* chose not to identify the others on the platform. (Courtesy of the New-York Historical Society, New York City)

of their leaders took the opportunity of the 1897 Citizens' Union/Republican split to demand still more recognition. When they failed to get it, they mounted a second independent campaign, again behind the candidacy of Henry George.

It was generally understood that this second Henry George campaign was simply a protest; one Gold Democrat dismissed it not unfairly as "an indiscriminate jumble" of social reformers, single-taxers, union leaders, Bryan Democrats, and disappointed erstwhile Tammany men.[85] George died two days before the election, and although his son and namesake stood in for him, drawing 4 percent of the vote, we cannot know how many votes George himself might have received. The *World* described the massive crowds at his funeral and burial procession as comparable only to those for Lincoln.[86]

But in many ways the pro-labor planks of Tammany's 1897 mayoral platform were Henry George's most impressive memorial.[87] Concerned to demonstrate its devotion to economy, low taxes, and free enterprise, and perceiving labor organizations as a threat to its base among the second-generation Irish, Tammany had taken few steps toward a *rapprochement* with organized labor between 1886 and 1896. Instead, it presented itself as the workingman's friend and employed an increasingly strident rhetoric of opposition to the city's British-American Protestant upper class.[88] By 1897 labor pressure had become irresistible, and Tammany shifted its strategy, making a direct appeal for union support by explicitly endorsing several union demands.[89]

By 1900 the city's chief political organizations—the Republicans and the Citizens' Union as well as Tammany Hall—were all recognizing union demands in their platforms as well as in their criteria for determining the "availability" of potential mayoral candidates. Labor organizations characteristically responded in diverse ways. Both the Social Democrats, who retained a considerable German following and who supported George in 1897, and the Socialist Workers' Party, which under Daniel De Leon's leadership attracted significant eastern European Jewish support, continued to offer mayoral candidates after 1897.[90] But by the beginning of the twentieth century most union leaders, like the leaders of most other organized interest groups and most businessmen, kept aloof from direct participation in mayoral politics. Henceforth they would seek to advance their purposes, as Gompers put it, by "rewarding friends and punishing enemies" rather than by taking direct part in mayoral politics.[91]

The Transformation of Mayoral Politics, 1870–1903

Between 1880 and 1910 national and international economic and social forces transformed Greater New York from a British-American-, German-, and Irish-stock mercantile and financial center to a British-American-, German-, Irish-, eastern European Jewish-, and Italian-stock corporate, financial, mercantile, and manufacturing metropolis. These economic and social changes were directly reflected in the character of the groups and individuals who selected mayoral nominees. Above all, these changes hastened a shift from a politics based on the direct participation of particular economic and social elites, to a politics of competing elite and non-elite economic, social, and cultural interest groups mediated and managed by specialized professional politicians. This shift reflected increased diversity and conflict among the elite groups and the new determination of many wealthy people to seek to create an evangelical Protestant Kingdom of God on earth. It reflected the accumulation of increased economic, organizational, social, and cultural resources by the city's non-elite groups. And it reflected the impact of elective politics in an increasingly heterogeneous city: By the early twentieth century, neither the city's capitalists nor its Protestant charity leaders nor its labor leaders were acceptable to a large enough portion of the electorate to stand as serious candidates for mayor.

There can be no doubt that these changes in New York City's mayoral politics forced the city's economic and social elites to relinquish the direct control over local affairs that their predecessors had retained into the 1880s, and that by 1900 the city's low- and middle-income pressure groups were exerting increased influence over the selection of mayoral candidates and over the content of the platforms on which they ran. This dispersion of power was not the result of a general defeat or withdrawal of the economic and social elites. Rather, it was in large part the result of greatly increased diversity and fragmentation within those elites. Disagreeing with one another, the various economic and social elites limited one another's ability to control mayoral nominations and thereby created opportunities for the increasingly well-organized political parties and non-elite economic, social, and cultural interest groups. Yet even after 1900 the economic and social elites continued to exert an indirect influence over the Tammany and Republican mayoral nominations. And although mayoral elections attracted a very large share of the city's attention, the mayor was only one of the officials who determined municipal policy. Only an analysis of a series of major policy decisions can indicate the real significance of the position.

PART IV

Major Policy Decisions

CHAPTER 7

URBANIZATION POLICY:

THE CREATION OF

GREATER NEW YORK

ON JANUARY 1, 1898, state law consolidated old New York City, which had consisted only of Manhattan and what is now the south Bronx, with Brooklyn, Staten Island, and what then became the modern boroughs of the Bronx and Queens to form Greater New York. By any criterion this was one of the most important decisions ever taken in the metropolitan region. Touching at once on economic, political, social, and cultural life, consolidation established enduring new boundaries and institutions for the region and affected the relative value of the resources possessed by most of its residents. Consolidation was not a typical decision. But its singular importance provoked a very large proportion of the region's elites into action, leaving an unusually rich deposit of information about the ability of each to, in Max Weber's words, "realize its own will even against the resistance of others."

The region's long-established mercantile elite and its allies first advanced the Greater New York plan as part of a vision that would meet their most pressing economic needs. Many of the city's merchants and bankers believed that if a single municipal government could gain control over New York harbor and all the surrounding territory, it could promote the unified, comprehensive development of shipping, railroads, and related facilities in such a way as to aid both merchants and property owners. Suburban districts and the large city of Brooklyn would give up their autonomy, losing control over local taxes and expenditures, over their physical development, and over their social composition. But in return

they would be able to draw on the very considerable revenue and borrowing powers that old New York City derived from the presence of the
central business district and from its unusually expansive colonial charter.
According to the mercantile vision, consolidation would knit the region's
diverse municipalities into a coherent transportation system and a single,
uniformly well-serviced real estate market.

The mercantile elite possessed the economic and political resources
necessary to launch this plan and to control its discussion for many years.
But several groups of landowners and developers did not like the terms
of the proposed bargain. And the militantly Protestant portion of Brooklyn's social elite had its own vision, one that stressed the preservation
of Brooklyn as a "City of Churches" and a home of virtuous, hard-working,
church-going families.

The conflict of visions threw the Greater New York plan squarely into
the political arena, where its considerable political implications and the
necessity of state legislation would have brought it in any case. Deeply
experienced in political infighting, the original advocates of Greater New
York sought to minimize its political implications. But they could not
deny that consolidation would abolish the corporate identity of every
constituent municipality and create a new electorate, twice as large, even
more diverse, and much more evenly balanced between the two major
political parties than in any of the original communities. When pressed,
they offered a vague hope that consolidation would permit the construction of a reformed framework for municipal government. But this answer
hardly satisfied the Republican Party leaders who had to consider the
plan as it moved through the legislature. When it finally emerged, Greater
New York was as much the creation of the political leaders as it was of
the mercantile elite. The exact form of the new city's government satisfied
no one, but its boundaries, its division into boroughs, its uniform rate
of taxes and assessments, its unification of control over services, and its
potential—however rarely realized—for comprehensive planning on a regional scale, have all endured.

It is easy to see that consolidation affected the resources—economic,
political, and even social—of nearly every resident of the greater city,
but it is very difficult to measure with any precision just how far the
distribution of resources was altered. New York and Brooklyn were already
large and rapidly growing political units; voters in each city already realized that their individual votes counted for little. Political organizations
were more immediately affected by the need to operate in a larger unit.
But they found it possible to work out new alliances, and they were
buffeted more strongly by the shifting voting patterns of the mid-nineties

than by the change of boundaries. Consolidation may have hastened the
decline in the social prestige enjoyed by Brooklyn Heights, but Brooklyn
had always been a middle- and lower-income dormitory for New York.
Its social elite was already less wealthy and less fashionable, if not less
proud, than New York's. Even in the 1880s Brooklyn's New England
settlers were not numerous enough to impose the dry Sunday upon their
German and Irish fellow-citizens.

Consolidation did shift some of the cost of public works—bridges, highways, neighborhood schools, and fire stations—from real estate in the
outer boroughs to real estate in Manhattan. But the resulting benefits
are difficult to apportion. Landowners in the outer boroughs benefited,
and in many cases, so did their customers and tenants, who might well
have moved out from Manhattan. Manhattan capitalists also benefited;
for much of the money for development in the boroughs was provided
by Manhattan banks and insurance companies. Landowners, employers,
and retail merchants in Manhattan surely benefited from the general
growth of the metropolis and from the increasing numbers of potential
employees and customers who were able to live within a convenient
distance.

These considerations suggest that the enormous number of microeco-
nomic calculations needed to assign precise values to consolidation's economic impact would make a very doubtful contribution to knowledge.
Nevertheless it is clear that the decision was of the highest importance,
as contemporaries almost universally agreed. The New York *Times*, the
New York *Tribune*, and the Brooklyn *Eagle* made "Greater New York"
a major heading in their indices between 1893 and 1896; the *Evening
Post* devoted all space allotted to New York City in its rudimentary 1896
manuscript index to that issue alone.[1] In the course of these extensive
discussions, the region's economic elites produced an extraordinarily articulate statement of their competing visions of the metropolis and its future.

Placing Consolidation on the Agenda

No decision can be made until the idea behind it gains acceptance as a
possible course of action in the minds of those who have the power to
act. The idea that the region surrounding New York harbor ought to
have a single municipal government had a long history before 1898. Historian Sidney J. Pomerantz traced the notion back to the eighteenth century,
and others have found it implicit in the expansive powers which the

colonial Dongan Charter assigned to New York City.[2] In 1827, according
to one account, Brooklyn real estate promoters sought consolidation as
a means of tapping Manhattan for revenues to pay for Brooklyn improvements; in 1833 the New York City delegation in the state legislature
stopped a movement to assign a city charter to Brooklyn on the ground
that New York had an implicit right to expand to the east in its own
good time. Developers of what is now the Bronx sought to speed that
expansion in their direction during the 1870s, as did their counterparts
in Brooklyn during the 1880s, and in Brooklyn, Staten Island, Long Island
City, and the eastern Bronx in the 1890s.[3]

Political motives produced the most effective set of initiatives toward
consolidation before the 1890s. In 1857 the New York State legislature,
controlled by Republicans and anti-Tammany Democrats, sought to deprive Tammany Mayor Fernando Wood of patronage and to assure property
owners of more economical and more responsive service by creating a
Metropolitan Police Commission to take over the police departments of
New York, Kings, Richmond, and Westchester counties.[4] At the same
time the legislature set up the Central Park Commission to design and
construct the great park.[5] The state added a Metropolitan Fire Commission
in 1865 and Excise and Health commissions in 1866, all of them coextensive with the Police Commission.[6] In 1865 and 1866 the state also expanded the powers of the Central Park Commission, giving it control
over the street plan and most public works from 59th Street to the northern border of Westchester County. The state commissions were in large
part designed to take New York City's government away from its inhabitants; when the "Tweed Charter" of 1870 abolished the commissions,
they did not leave behind a favorable image of metropolitan government.[7]
In the early 1870s some of Tweed's opponents proposed the creation of
a metropolitan government for the region as a means of promoting its
growth and preventing the return of Tammany Hall. The only result
during that decade was the annexation of the south Bronx to the city
of New York.[8]

The effective movement for consolidation was not launched until 1888,
when it was proposed by the Chamber of Commerce of the State of New
York and elaborated by Andrew H. Green as part of his vision for promoting the planned, controlled, orderly, sustained growth of the metropolitan
region. Under a single, central municipal government, Green argued, new
construction and related municipal policies could be made to conform
to a rational, comprehensive plan that would protect and promote all
interests, especially those of the great landed estates and of the merchants
of the metropolis. Green and those who joined in advocating this idea

Tammany— anti consol

did not control its disposition by the legislature. Yet simply by initiating discussion with a carefully considered proposal, they shaped the public agenda, defining alternatives in such a way as to direct action in the direction they preferred.

Andrew H. Green played an extraordinary series of public roles in nineteenth-century New York. Since his private papers have been lost, a review of his career provides the context essential for understanding his role in the creation of Greater New York. Born into an atmosphere of middle-class respectability, learning, and Protestant piety in Worcester, Massachusetts, Green was sent to New York in 1835, at the age of fiteen, to receive a "thorough commercial training." Then, in his early twenties he changed his politics from Whig to soft-shell Democratic and his profession from commerce to law. In 1844 he began a lifelong association with Samuel J. Tilden, a great early "master-mind in consolidating independent [rail]roads and other business concerns on a profitable basis." Beginning as Tilden's student, Green became his assistant and then his partner and friend. In Tilden's office Green learned the craft of the corporate lawyer, the skill of an investment advisor, and the strategy of the manager of great estates.[9]

From the first, Andrew Green was also Tilden's political protégé and ally. In 1845, Green helped prevent Tammany Hall from striking Tilden's name from the assembly ticket; in 1848, probably with Tilden's aid, he was appointed ward school commissioner, and from 1855 through 1860 he served on the city's Board of Education. Quickly becoming known "for his punctilious regard for economy in the expenditures of the Board," in 1857 he won election to the first of two successive terms as the Board's president.[10] By this time he had become a vigorous spokesman for the interests of the city's property owners. In his major address to the Board of Education in 1857, he pointed out that New York City taxpayers contributed far more to the state's school fund than the city received from it and complained that "the valuations placed upon property throughout the State, are unequal and so palpably unjust, as to demand the immediate application of the simple remedy that would be furnished by . . . a Board of State Assessors, whose duty it would be to equalize the county valuations." His goals as president of the Board of Education, he added, were to "insure order, and economy."[11] These goals, together with a commitment to administrative efficiency and fairness as the means for carrying out large projects, characterized his entire career.

As his career evolved, Green became, in effect, the semiofficial and quite effective comprehensive planner for major public works in the metropolitan region. He held this position for the extraordinarily long period from his first major public appointments in 1857 to his death in 1903. In the former year Green became, presumably through Tilden's influence, a member of the Central Park Commission. As treasurer and then comptroller of Central Park he directed the Commission's activities for thirteen years, becoming its most important official.[12] Comparing him to the other commissioners, Frederick Law Olmsted, who could not abide Green's cautious, methodical, parsimonious, and politically astute ways, wrote that he did "a hundred times more work than all the rest put together."[13] It was Green's administrative and political skills, and his diplomatic approach to large property owners, as much as Olmsted's brilliant design talents, that led those who owned much of the real estate of upper Manhattan and lower Westchester County to ask the state legislature to give the Central Park Commission "absolute control" of public works planning for the area. The result, Olmsted later claimed, was "generally satisfactory, and . . . caused an enormous advance of the property of all those interested."[14]

Boss Tweed's "home rule" charter abolished the Central Park Commission, and Green briefly found himself an isolated member of New York City's Park Commission. But he quickly reappeared as a leader of the 1871 campaign against the Tweed Ring. After the city's chief creditors refused to purchase additional bonds and the Chamber of Commerce of the State of New York announced that Tweed and his associates were hopelessly corrupt, Green was the man chosen by anti-Tammany Democrats Tilden and William F. Havemeyer to replace Tweed's comptroller, "Slippery Dick" Connolly. During the next six years Green provided city records for Tilden's investigation and prosecution of the ring, sorted out the city's tangled finances, and sought to deny fraudulent claims for wages and other payments issued by the ring. Financiers who had refused the city's bonds agreed to take them, on condition that Green personally sign the notes.[15] Green's tenacious defense of the city's interests, as defined by those he called "the substantial people," made him so many enemies that in 1876 he refused to be considered as a candidate for mayor out of fear that those who disliked him would vote against Tilden, who headed the Democratic ticket as the candidate for president.[16]

Following his resignation as comptroller of New York City in 1876, Green remained active in Swallowtail Democratic politics. His lack of great wealth, his sometimes abrasive manner, or perhaps his close association with Tilden kept him out of the very top rank.[17] But his years of experience and his famous integrity, together with what Olmsted once called his "politico-commercial alliances," made him one of Greater New

York's leading advisors to landed estates, cultural institutions, and charities. He had a hand in nearly all the decisions regarding the location of
major public works, from bridges over the Harlem and Hudson rivers,
the Bronx Zoo, the American Museum of Natural History, and the New
York Public Library, to the private *Isabella Heimath* for respectable German widows, the new Tombs prison, and City Hall itself.[18] Considering
these duties together with his public works plans for the Central Park
Commission (1857–1870), the Greater New York Commission (1890–
1896), and the New York Commerce Commission (1898–1900), it is clear
that Green's role was much like that more recently filled by Robert Moses.

Opponents of Greater New York sometimes dismissed consolidation
as "Green's Hobby" and derided him as a monomaniac obsessed with a
crackpot nostrum.[19] But although he did develop a reputation for a crotch-
ety, difficult disposition, he never acted alone. Throughout his career
he took the city's property owners, taxpayers, and great merchants for
his clients, and sought to define policies that would work to their best
long-run interests. He did not simply act in a crude sense as the mere
agent of these clients; he often urged measures that they did not understand and even disliked. But he carefully took their interests into account,
and made his plans to suit their purposes. During a public career of nearly
fifty years he never lost their confidence.

Green first proposed the elements of his vision for Greater New York
in an 1868 *Communication* to the Central Park Commission. Two years
earlier he had urged the Commission to adopt a comprehensive plan for
the physical development of upper Manhattan. Green acknowledged that
such a plan would impose a network of streets and tramways, of water,
sewer, and gas lines, and of parks, and so would not permit individual
owners to develop their land as they saw fit. But he believed he could
persuade landowners that advance planning would serve both their individual interests and the common good. The authoritarian methods employed by Baron Haussmann in Paris were not appropriate in a free republic, but Haussmann's aesthetic and practical goals appealed to Green. In
the United States, he optimistically asserted, "a common interest of landed
ownership and a common perception of the most profitable use of the
land will generally assure symmetry in the plan of the city."[20] In 1868
Green sought to encourage a "common perception" of the most profitable
development of Greater New York as a whole. A general plan for the
region, he asserted, would reduce both present and future costs, help
owners develop their land, protect investors and taxpayers, and accommodate downtown real estate and mercantile interests as well. "It is not

too early," he concluded, "to endeavor to guide . . . the progress of improvements in Westchester in conjunction with those of this city, for
the ultimate best interests of both." For the future, New York should
look to union with Kings "and a part of Queens and Richmond" counties
"under one common municipal government."[21]

Green returned to this theme more cautiously in 1874, then dropped
it for a period of fifteen years.[22] The excesses of the Tweed Ring, quickly
followed by the panic of 1873 and the ensuing depression, soured investors
on municipal bonds and discouraged the large-scale planning of public
works. Then the long postwar deflation raised the real cost of borrowing,
making municipalities reluctant to reenter the capital markets. Instead
of taking on large-scale projects in new areas, New York, like other municipalities, sought to close gaps in existing water, sewer, and road systems,
and to pay the cost out of assessments and current tax income.[23] As a
manager of a large portion of "all the real estate of any value over which
New York must march in its necessary growth," as park commissioner,
Brooklyn Bridge trustee, and advocate of the Harlem Ship Canal, among
many other duties, Green remained the most important public works
coordinator in Greater New York.[24] But he was not a persistent advocate
of consolidation.

Instead, it was the Chamber of Commerce of the State of New York
that succeeded in placing the Greater New York idea on the public agenda
after 1887. In the autumn of that year a delegation from the Chamber
met with Mayor Abram S. Hewitt (who was himself one of the Chamber's
leading members) to point out that the crowded, filthy, pot-holed condition of the city's streets interfered with the movement of goods and the
keeping of appointments, adding to the expense of commerce in New
York and reducing the city's competitive advantage against other ports.[25]
Hewitt responded in his annual message of January 1888, by outlining
a vast, coordinated program of public improvements for the city's harbor,
docks, streets, street railway, and rapid transit facilities. To speed the
dispersion of the overcrowded slums and perhaps also to commend his
program to poorer voters and local contractors, Hewitt urged that these
improvements, especially rapid transit, be extended to Harlem and the
annexed portions of the Bronx. He concluded with a peroration on the
future of New York City that was to be echoed in proconsolidation appeals
over the next ten years:

> With its noble harbor protected from injury, and the channels of its approach
> straightened and deepened; with its wharves and docks made adequate for
> the easy transfer of the vast commerce of the country; with its streets properly

paved and cleaned, and protected from destructive upheavals, with cheap and
rapid transit throughout its length and breadth; with salubrious and attractive
parks in the centers of dense population; with a system of taxation so modified
that the capital of the world may be as free to come and go as the air of
heaven; the imagination can place no bounds to the future growth of this
city in business, wealth, and the blessings of civilization. Its imperial destiny
as the greatest city in the world is assured by natural causes, which cannot
be thwarted except by the folly and neglect of its inhabitants.[26]

Four months later the Chamber of Commerce devoted its *Annual Report*
to the future of New York City. Hewitt's public improvement program
should be welcomed, the Chamber said, because it served the needs of
the region's bankers as well as its merchants. Noting that the retirement
of the national debt had created a "large amount of floating capital,"
and that "the large sum held in New York [savings banks] is confined
. . . by our State Legislature to investment at home," the Chamber observed that insurance companies, savings banks, and trustees of estates
preferred to invest in "real estate and its improvement." Hewitt's public
works program would provide the public support essential for the prosperity of those investments. Noting that real estate development in the metropolitan region did not respect existing municipal lines, and picking up
Hewitt's imperial vision, the Chamber insisted that "nothing yet reached
in municipal grandeur is beyond the aspiration of New York" and concluded by asking rhetorically "if it be not the true policy to unite New-
York and all its environs under one general scheme of municipal rule."[27]
Leading publications quickly followed the Chamber's initiative. The
respected *Real Estate Record and Builder's Guide* praised Hewitt's "brilliant and remarkable message on public improvements" and came out
at once in support of the Chamber's proposal for municipal consolidation.
A comprehensive public works program was necessary, the *Record and
Guide* argued, if decent homes were to be provided for the metropolitan
region's rapidly growing population.[28] Commenting on the Chamber's pro-
posal, the New York *Times* implied that Hewitt himself had favored it.
Consolidation, said the *Times*, is "a question which often arises in the
minds of citizens of New York who have faith in its future growth and
in what Mayor Hewitt has called its 'imperial destiny.' "[29]
As though in response to a request from the Chamber of Commerce,
Andrew Green now reentered the consolidation discussion, appearing in
Albany in March 1889 to propose that the state legislature create a Greater
New York Commission to consider the question.[30] Although Green had
the added support of the *Sun*, his proposal ran into stiff resistance from
uptown New York real estate interests, who feared that consolidation

would divert resources away from their area and into Brooklyn. These interests had an effective spokesman in Hugh J. Grant, the uptown developer and Tammany politician who had just defeated Hewitt in the mayoral election of 1888.[31] They also comprised an important constituency for the *Record and Guide*, perhaps as a result, that paper tended to neglect consolidation after 1889. With most Brooklyn senators joining those sent by Tammany Hall, Green's consolidation commission bill was defeated in the senate.[32]

Armed with the renewed support of the Chamber of Commerce and with a new set of arguments, Green returned to Albany in 1890 and secured his point. His new appeal, received and printed as an official document by the assembly, repeated his earlier case for comprehensive planning. He added that the growth of rival centers had given a new urgency to his proposal. "London, Paris, Brooklyn, and Chicago," he wrote, had all "become great and prosperous, not alone by accumulation of number, within their first restricted bounds, but by expansion, annexation, and consolidation."[33] New York was in competition with these great centers of commerce, Green argued; consolidation would give it the means of holding its own.

Emphasizing problems that were of particular concern to the merchants in the Chamber of Commerce, Green argued that a unified city could do far more for the port than could the disparate efforts of New York City, Brooklyn, and the petty municipalities of Queens and Staten Island acting independently. A greater city embracing the entire New York State portion of the harbor could act without waiting for the state or national governments. It could maintain the channels of navigation, improve the docks and warehouses, and prevent garbage barges and mud scows from polluting the waters. And it could control all owners of waterfront property, including those "who by encroachment, appropriation, and misuse, deplete the general system [through] niggard scheme[s] of individual profit." A greater city could introduce a sort of zoning, setting aside specific areas in Staten Island, Brooklyn, Queens, and lower Westchester as well as Manhattan for "factories, docks, bridges, terminals and markets [so as to] economize space, promote convenience, and ensure dispatch." A greater city might even be able to help New York's merchants in their struggle with the railroads, preventing the railroads from engrossing vast stretches of waterfront and holding them off the market, encouraging new lines to serve the port, and even constructing a railroad bridge across the Hudson to reduce the cost of shipping imported and manufactured goods to the south and west. Employing the extraordinary proto-populist language that New York's merchants had used against the railroads since the mid-seventies, Green concluded that only a unified metropolitan government would enable "our unselfish, thoughtless peoples, and their fatuous municipalities" to carry on more than "desultory and futile war against the organized forces of relentless and absentee capitalism, resident in Boston, San Francisco, New Orleans, London, Paris or Frankfurt. . . ."[34]

Republican Assemblyman Frederick S. Gibbs, a small-time New York City manufacturer who had been his party's unsuccessful candidate for mayor in 1884, reintroduced Green's Greater New York Commission bill in 1890. This bill quickly passed in the assembly. Taking note of Green's new arguments, the Senate, controlled like the lower house by the Republicans, sent the bill to its Committee on Commerce and Navigation as well as to its Committee on Cities. Some Brooklyn senators still objected, but Green sent a determined lobbyist to Albany and secured the support of the *World* and the *Tribune* as well as the *Times*, the *Sun*, and even the *Record and Guide*. The bill passed in the form Green had proposed, except that it omitted the names of the commissioners. But after Democratic Governor David B. Hill had signed the bill into law he named five of Green's six nominees to the commission.[35] With the establishment of the Greater New York Commission, the Chamber of Commerce, Andrew H. Green, and their allies had succeeded in placing their plan on the public agenda in such a way that they would be able to shape the next stage of debate.

The Pro-consolidation Coalition

From its formation in 1890 through the autumn of 1894 Green's Greater New York Commission continued to hold center stage as the leading advocate and arbiter of plans for consolidation. The commission did not spend much time dealing with the merits of the idea; it was already favored by all of Governor Hill's appointees and most of those appointed by the mayors of New York and Brooklyn and by the boards of supervisors of Westchester, Queens, Kings, and Richmond counties. At their first official meeting the commissioners, already primed, elected Green their president; at their second meeting they declared themselves unanimously in favor of a union of all municipalities in the area he had proposed.[36]

By this very early act the Greater New York Commission established a key point: Greater New York would embrace all the New York State territory bordering on New York harbor, including the southern portion of Westchester, the western portion of Queens (after 1898 the eastern portion of that county became Nassau County), Staten Island, as well as all of New York and Kings counties. The decision to include so much of Queens County that both Little Neck Bay and Jamaica Bay were in the greater city, along with all of Staten Island, reflected the influence of the Chamber of Commerce and its desire for the control and development of the harbor. The counties of Kings and what became the Bronx had space enough for several decades of housing construction; New York and Brooklyn contained most of the population and would have constituted a city safely larger than Chicago. As Green insisted, only the harbor and its problems united all five counties.[37]

After their second meeting, however, the Greater New York Commissioners found themselves unable to agree on a course of action. Green would have preferred to move directly for consolidation under a strongly centralized government. But Kings County representatives were reluctant to move so quickly, and after Green briefly found one meeting "so unsatisfactory . . . that he told the members in plain terms that he would no longer undertake to provide a place of meeting for them," he dropped the effort to design a form of government.[38] Green also discovered that the decision to include all the territory bordering on New York harbor provoked some very stubborn opposition, especially from upper Manhattan, Bronx, and Brooklyn real estate interests who feared that so large a greater city would slight their particular sections, from party politicians who were reluctant to face the factional and voting bloc hazards of so large a jurisdiction, and from upstate politicians who had begun to fear the power of a monster metropolis.[39] Under these circumstances Green put aside any effort to secure a specific form of government and led the commission into a three-year campaign for public support. His aim was to produce an overwhelming referendum for consolidation, forcing the politicians and local real estate interests to go along.

Green concentrated most of his efforts during this campaign on Brooklyn, where he quickly found effective allies among merchants, bankers, and real estate developers. Providing the platform from which Edward C. Graves, a Brooklyn attorney, delivered an 1891 address, "How Taxes in Brooklyn Can Be Reduced One-Half by the Consolidation of the Cities of New York and Brooklyn," to set the theme, Green and his commission issued a call for concerted action.[40] Graves repeated and extended his argument in mid-January 1892. Four days later, the Brooklyn Real Estate Exchange endorsed consolidation.[41] And when Brooklyn representatives cast key votes against the commission's request for a consolidation referendum in the 1892 legislature, a prominent group of Brooklyn businessmen met to organize the Brooklyn Consolidation League as a home-grown advocate of the idea.

The thirty-nine men most prominently identified with the Consolidation League controlled substantial economic resources. At least ten of them were reputed millionaires. Eight belonged to the Chamber of Commerce of the State of New York; one of these, grain exporter Alexander E. Orr, was elected president of that body in 1895. Another, exporter Darwin R. James, was also president of the New York Board of Trade and Transportation; a third, Marshall S. Driggs, was chairman of the executive committee of the New York Board of Fire Underwriters. At least fourteen served as officers, directors, or partners in Manhattan banks, title or fire insurance companies, or law firms, or held similar positions with Brooklyn firms. Five were real estate dealers, nine were known locally as major real estate owners, three were presidents of streetcar lines, and four, including Abraham Abraham of Abraham and Straus, were large-scale retailers. Simply stated, the thirty-nine were prominent among the mercantile, financial, and real estate elites not simply of Brooklyn but of the metropolitan region as a whole.[42]

The Consolidation League's leaders possessed considerable political as well as economic resources. Most of them, led by A. E. Orr, were active Swallowtail Democrats, supporters of Grover Cleveland, and opponents of local Willoughby Street boss Hugh McLaughlin. By 1893 Brooklyn's Swallowtail Democrats had built vigorous political organizations of their own, with experienced cadres down to the precinct level in many wards, a number of patronage positions in the Brooklyn Navy Yard, the Post Office, and other local agencies controlled by President Cleveland, good relations with such papers as the Brooklyn *Eagle* and the New York *Times, World, Staats Zeitung,* and *Evening Post,* and a stable of effective stump speakers. One of their best speakers was William J. Gaynor. A future mayor of Greater New York, Gaynor was then a protegé of Coney Island and South Brooklyn developer William Ziegler.[43] In 1893 he brought his carefully cultivated reputation as a fighter for honest, economical government and his effective platform style to the Consolidation League's service. According to one contemporary account, Gaynor's speeches "gave impetus" to the consolidation movement "which it had not had before."[44] Happy to follow the activities of anti-McLaughlin Democrats even when they doubted the wisdom of consolidation, the *Eagle,* the *Times,* and other newspapers covered proconsolidation speeches by Gaynor and others in great detail. But the league did not rely solely on the press; it also printed and distributed its own literature. According to a contemporary celebration of the consolidation movement, "in all, over 2,000,000 pieces of literature were distributed in Brooklyn alone." League agents presented a copy of Edward Graves' pamphlet, "How Taxes in Brooklyn Can Be Reduced One-Half. . . ," to every person who emerged from the Brooklyn Bureau of Taxes and Assessments in 1893.[45]

Brooklyn's consolidationists employed their resources to gain several objectives. They sought reduced taxes for Brooklyn and a comprehensive approach to public works planning for the port and its region. But they also wanted some specific public works projects. One of these was a new bridge over the East River. Although Brooklyn Bridge had opened as recently as 1883, its walkways and tramcars already carried as many commuters as they could handle. Yet plans for a new bridge were stalled, in part because the developers of real estate in upper Manhattan opposed any move that would bring competing land onto the market and insisted that New York invest in their territory instead. Similar problems could be anticipated when Brooklyn, which was running short of water, sought access to New York City's plentiful Croton water supply. By making Brooklyn part of New York City's political system, consolidation would reduce, if not eliminate, jurisdictional squabbles over the control of water and the location of bridges and enable Brooklyn interests to demand their fair share of the greater city's resources.[46]

Brooklyn could not build a bridge to Manhattan on its own; indeed by 1892 it could do very little more than sustain routine services. During the early 1890s Ziegler, Gaynor, and other reformers protested against the size of Brooklyn's debt, charging that incompetent and corrupt officials left the city little to show for its expenditures.[47] According to Brooklyn reformers these charges applied even more fully to Gravesend and other county towns, and in 1894 they brought about the creation of a Greater Brooklyn, coextensive with Kings County, in the hope that its officials, elected in a glare of publicity on city-wide slates, would prove more worthy.[48]

But Kings County had already encountered resistance to its bonds in 1892, before the Panic of 1893 put a damper on all bond sales. The county towns had indeed issued bonds to a fare-thee-well, and after it absorbed their debts Greater Brooklyn found itself in debt up to the limit set by the state consititution.[49] Since the debt limit was simply a percentage of a municipality's assessed valuation, the only way to increase Brooklyn's borrowing capacity would have been to raise the assessments. But this would, in turn, have increased Brooklyn's share of the state tax, and property owners already objected that Brooklyn assessed them at rates substantially higher than those applied by New York.

Though it is difficult to compare parcels of property in two different cities and in widely separated sections of a metropolitan area, Brooklyn's residential property probably did pay taxes at a higher rate than Manhattan's, because Manhattan contained the central business district for the entire region and enjoyed special fiscal advantages. Altogether, the consolidationists probably did not exaggerate when they insisted that Brooklyn's property owners paid higher taxes and received less adequate services than their counterparts across the East River.[50]

Brooklyn consolidationists argued that the plan would bring about good government for the entire region as well as specific benefits for Brooklyn. By abolishing several local governments it would reduce the total number of public officials; by centralizing responsibility it would promote efficiency and accountability; by adding Brooklyn's virtuous population to the whole it would bring one million people who stood "steadfast for good government" into the greater city. Audaciously reversing the point, Gaynor insisted that consolidation would bring to Brooklyn what he was pleased to call New York City's more virtuous electorate. Brooklyn, he said, had "a lower sentiment concerning local government than any other city in this country or civilized Europe," because "the best part of our people in enterprise, brains, and skill go to New York every day." In New York, by contrast, the best people lived where they worked. "I am not sure," Gaynor concluded, "that public sentiment is not more powerful in New York City than in any city in the world."[51]

Gaynor no doubt had his tongue in his cheek when he made these pronouncements. But the notion that consolidation would advance the cause of good government had been part of the movement from the beginning and played an important role in its success.

Listening carefully to the Brooklyn Consolidation League's arguments, many New Yorkers asked why *they* should pay for the development of Brooklyn.[52] A group of distinguished advocates of municipal efficiency— Albert Shaw, Simon Sterne, and Dorman B. Eaton—provided the answer: Consolidation could provide the occasion to increase the participation of the "best men" in local affairs. As advisors to the financial institutions, law firms, business organizations, civic groups, and newspapers that supported "reform" and sought to define respectable policy in New York City, these men exerted considerable influence. Had they not seen potential advantages in consolidation they would have opposed it as a proposal for an unwieldy, expensive, Tammany-controlled monstrosity. Instead, they worked for consolidation behind the scenes, becoming so committed to the plan that they were unable at the end to establish an independent position in the public mind. Although they disliked the Greater New

York plan that was finally passed by the state legislature, they had lost their chance to oppose it effectively.

Albert Shaw was by far the most active advocate of consolidation among these men. Holder of one of the first Ph.D.'s granted by Johns Hopkins University, where he had studied with Woodrow Wilson and James Bryce, Shaw had been a newspaper editor and secretary to the Twin Cities Commerical Club in Minneapolis and had come to New York City in 1891 to edit the *American Review of Reviews.* His books, *Municipal Government in Great Britain* and *Municipal Government in Continental Europe,* established his reputation as an expert on municipal reform.[53]

Shaw believed that the best city government could be provided by the sort of men he believed dominated the councils of British cities "representatives of the best elements of business life . . . men of intelligence and character, and of practical conversance with affairs."[54] In the nineties, he saw in the new London County Council a model for Greater New York. The members of the first LCC, he wrote, "possessed as high an average of ability and distinction as the House of Commons. . . . It may interest New York, Boston, and Chicago readers," he added, "to be assured that there were no saloon keepers or ward bosses in this London council, over which Lord Rosebery presided as chairman, while the scientist-statesman Sir John Lubbock served as vice-chairman, and the distinguished London reformer, the late Mr. Firth, as deputy chairman."[55]

Shaw proposed that the government of Greater New York be designed along the lines of the LCC. Echoing the oligarchic assumptions of his mentor, James Bryce, Shaw wrote that "logically, the mayor must eventually swallow the council or the council must swallow the mayor, if political forces are to be accorded some degree of natural play."[56] In Shaw's view, the council should be made to prevail. A strong mayor, like the receiver of an ailing business corporation, could prevent wrongdoing and extravagance, but could not introduce "creative policy." A strong council whose members were "the fully empowered trustees through whom all the affairs of the municipal corporation are managed" would attract the city's "best men."[57] Such men could be elected even in New York, provided they could run at large, not from small, single-member districts, and provided the elections were conducted according to a system of proportional representation. Shaw was not simply a conservative structural reformer. He sought substantive social reforms as well and worked throughout the 1890s to persuade the city to undertake a variety of new programs, from municipal ownership of public utilities to the provision of better health and welfare services for the poor.[58] He did not trust Tammany to conduct these programs. But, committed to the patrician elitist perspective, he believed that if men like the leaders of the Chamber of Commerce could be elected to a powerful city council they would support progressive programs out of enlightened self-interest and Christian compassion, and would persuade other taxpayers and bondholders to go along.[59]

Shaw pushed his LCC idea vigorously between 1893 and 1896, arranging for the publication of articles about it in his own and other journals, advocating it in public testimony and addresses, and urging it on other reformers in private. Many of his listeners responded; he did not exaggerate when he later asserted that "the example of the London County Council, with its splendid array of men of distinction, ability, and zeal . . . unquestionably made a great impression upon the minds of many leading citizens of New York."[60]

No doubt some of Shaw's success was due to the compatibility of his approach with a strain of thought that dated back to the Tilden Commission of 1877. Rejecting the strong-mayor system and other proposals, that commission had boldly asserted that "the choice of the local guardians and trustees of the financial concerns of cities should be lodged with the taxpayers."[61] This proposal to limit the vote remained a tantalizing though unrealizable goal for New York's taxpayers. In 1885 Simon Sterne, the distinguished lawyer and widely respected writer on public affairs who had served on the Tilden Commission, suggested that a system of proportional representation might achieve the desired result. Sterne hoped to secure "a sort of Chamber of Commerce government" like that provided through the guilds of medieval cities. "We must," he urged, "stop organizing on the basis of arbitrary population and organize on the basis of interests, and let the elected few or the chosen few, who are at the top of these interests ipso facto go into government. Minority representation," he thought, "would accomplish this end," if it could be applied to the election of members for New York's City Council.[62]

To many advocates of economy and efficiency, Shaw's arguments about the virtues of the LCC seemed a useful and logical extension of the long-standing, frustrating effort to ensure that the best men controlled New York City's government. One of those who was most impressed was Dorman B. Eaton, who had been one of the architects of the metropolitan commissions that had governed Greater New York between 1857 and 1870. Acknowledging Shaw's contribution, Eaton urged that pride of place in the consolidated city's government be assigned to a single-chambered council of between forty-eight and sixty members, elected to staggered six-year terms, by a system of proportional representation from large districts, with "a majority—if a large majority all the better—of the members elected from the city at large—which would give superior men."[63] Andrew

H. Green himself wrote in 1896 of the relevance of the LCC, stating that for Greater New York "my own idea is that we should have a legislative body, constituted in such a way as to give it weight and influence, that will provide for local legislation here after consolidation has taken place, and that each locality . . . shall have its say in that legislative body."[64]

Despite his considerable success, however, Shaw found that "most American municipal reformers think that for the purpose of this country it is better that there should be a mayor elected directly by the people, charged with the appointing power, and given a larger discretion in his executive work." Faced with such resistance, he gave up his agitation for an LCC-style government for Greater New York. "So long as nineteen-twentieths of our most active reformers favor the plan of a strong mayor," he wrote in 1896, "I am not going to be an obstructionist for the sake of a theory."[65] Yet Shaw and the others who thought consolidation might permit sweeping charter revisions designed to increase the influence of the "best men" played an indirect, unintended, but significant role in Green's effort to generate public support. Green enjoyed great respect as a man of probity, but he was also known as the manager and agent of great estates and other interests; and the organizers of Brooklyn's Consolidation League were well-known as promoters of public works projects and were quite explicitly working for their own interests. Since Shaw, Eaton, and those who adopted their line had established themselves as independent advocates of municipal economy and efficiency, they were in a much better position to reassure taxpayers that consolidation might work to their advantage. Without their assurances, many property owners, bankers, lawyers, and journalists might have grown skeptical of the consolidation movement and organized to resist it. Shaw and many of those who had listened to him disliked Greater New York in its ultimate form. But they had helped it along and become identified with it, and they found themselves in an awkward and ineffective position when they sought to oppose it in 1896 and 1897.

By early 1893 Green and his associates had developed effective support among the merchants and bankers of Greater New York, the property owners of Brooklyn, and the advocates of municipal efficiency in Manhattan. But although these elites commanded considerable economic and political resources, including the ability to present the proposal on their own terms, they could not supply enough votes out of their own ranks to secure overwhelming support for a referendum on the issue. They used a fourth set of arguments to appeal to the voters at large.

In essence, the consolidationists touted their idea as a solution to the
tenement house problem, as the "remedy" for "poverty, disease, crime,
and mortality."[66] Edward C. Graves asserted that the potential tax benefits
would accrue to the working man as well as to the landowner, so that
"Brooklyn rentpayers, mechanics, and working people should favor the
consolidation" just as much as their landlords.[67] A Brooklyn real estate
journalist offered this argument in its fullest form:

> within the accessible limits of the present metropolis there is no land available
> for independent homes for the industrial and middle classes. An eminently
> worthy and numerically considerable part of the day population of New York
> City is made up of this class—the clerks, bookkeepers, salesmen, mechanics
> and other operatives in its hives of industry—many of whom prefer a modest
> free-standing cottage to a flat. Brooklyn has such houses at $25 per month,
> and 2-family houses at $10 per month.[68]

Once Brooklyn was made more accessible, many more such houses could
be built, creating jobs as well as relieving crowding in the slums.

Consolidationists phrased their slum-dispersing arguments to appeal to
those who feared socialism as well as to the poor. According to the *Real
Estate Record and Builder's Guide,* improved access to inexpensive single-
family housing would "help to separate . . . the industrious and self-
respecting poor . . . from the less regenerate people by whom they are
surrounded," and so "prevent unfortunate people from becoming essentially depraved."[69] The sale of small homes to working people encouraged
"a spirit of saving and investment . . . and in this direction [would do]
more to counteract anarchistic tendencies and to stiffen the backbone
of the nation than could ever be done by military or legislative
influences."[70] With consolidation, "New York will be the gainer . . .
in having thus added to its electoral constituency a strong intellectual
and moral element that will work for better government and thus counteract the politics of the slums."[71] As Albert Henschel put it to the readers
of the *World* and the *Sun,* consolidation simply meant "proper dwellings
for the people."[72] Developed by Green and his associates, these arguments
won significant support from labor leaders and effectively appealed to
large numbers of voters, some of whom expected to benefit only indirectly.

Referendum

Confident that their carefully developed arguments would secure an overwhelmingly favorable vote for consolidation, Green and his commission
pressed the legislature to authorize a referendum. When the legislature

refused to do so in 1892 and again in 1893, the consolidationists took increasingly vigorous action.[73] They lobbied, testified, and presented petitions in Albany. They used the municipal reform and tenement-relief arguments to secure additional support from religious leaders, social reformers, and Swallowtail Democrats, including Episcopal Bishop Henry Codman Potter of New York, the Methodist Epworth Club, the Baptist Social Union, Columbia University President Seth Low, and former Mayor William R. Grace.[74] Then, taking advantage of the impression that Greater New York was a reform supported by "good citizens" and opposed by machine politicians and petty developers, Brooklyn's consolidationists made support for the plan an issue in the successful anti-McLaughlin campaign of 1893. Supported by reform Democrats as well as by his fellow Republicans, Charles A. Schieren defeated McLaughlin's candidate for mayor; several proconsolidation assemblymen and state senators simultaneously defeated incumbents who had resisted the measure.[75] In 1894 the legislature approved Green's referendum measure by votes of 106 to 7 in the assembly and 18 to 7 in the senate, and Democratic Governor Roswell P. Flower immediately signed it into law.[76]

Green and his associates mounted a strenuous effort to secure a "large and favorable vote." Working behind the scenes, Green had already done everything he could to make the proposal so vague that every possible constituency could find something in it. In deference to the Chamber of Commerce and to his own sense of priorities, he had secured agreement from the legislature and the commissioners that Greater New York would include all the territory bordering on New York harbor. But he saw to it that other key issues remained unresolved. The growing political influence of the Brooklyn Consolidation League had not been sufficient to persuade him to include an official equal-taxes–equal-assessments clause, although privately he seems to have agreed to that condition.[77] Despite the strong desire of many municipal reformers—and his own preference—the referendum did not deal with the greater city's form of government. On the eve of the election, Green issued a statement in the name of the commission that not only acknowledged but also stressed the vagueness of the referendum; it allowed, he said, for "nothing more than a simple expression of opinion." Even "if every ballot in the city or town were cast in favor of consolidation, there would be no finality about it."[78] As presented to the voters, the consolidation scheme was as ambiguous as one of the pictures in a Rorschach test, and like a Rorschach test invited each voter to see his own preferences in it.

The consolidationists pursued this strategy in their active campaign as well as in their literature. Sampling opinion to determine where and

how to pitch their message, they sent speakers armed with different arguments into every corner of the metropolis.[79] They enlisted the aid of
civic associations, including the City Club and the Good Government
clubs of Manhattan, as well as commercial associations in outlying areas,
and they spoke directly to the voters themselves.[80] To make sure that
nobody failed to hear their message, they distributed hundreds of thousands of leaflets.[81] And they arranged for extensive support from the
Manhattan press. Green persuaded the *World,* the *Herald,* the *Sun,* the *Tribune,* and the *Times* to publish the commission's press releases and
broadsides *verbatim.* The *World,* which had by far the largest and most
loyal following below 14th Street, printed a proconsolidation catechism
on its front page every day for two weeks before the election.[82] The Lexow
Committee's revelations about vice and corruption among New York City's
policemen provoked increasing revulsion in Brooklyn, but the Consolidation League there simply redoubled its efforts.

Opposition came from two sources: the Brooklyn *Eagle,* which dreaded
the end of an independent existence for Brooklyn and abhorred the prospect of Tammany influence in Brooklyn's affairs, and Tammany itself.[83]
Tammany leaders had called for a referendum and had voted for the
measure in the legislature. Early in the spring the Tammany *Irish-American* had praised consolidation as a splendid plan, approved by Mayor
Gilroy, to keep New York's population larger than Chicago's—even large
enough to challenge London's!—and as the best way to provide efficient
government for the suburbs as well as two million homes for the residents
of overcrowded New York.[84] But the Lexow Committee hearings and the
Constitutional Convention controlled by anti-Tammany elements intervened. On election eve Tammany's "Instructions to Voters" said: Vote
the straight Democratic ticket, vote against all constitutional amendments,
vote for municipal construction of a rapid transit road, and do not vote
at all on other issues.[85] Many Manhattan real estate men also opposed
consolidation, but others welcomed the idea. The real estate interests
as a whole did not have a general impact on the election.[86]

Despite Tammany's change of heart the consolidationists encountered
little organized opposition. Although the Brooklyn newspapers opposed
consolidation, only the *Eagle* made a feature of its views.[87] Tammany,
engaged in a desperate struggle to defeat hostile constitutional amendments and to hold on to a few offices in the face of the Lexow disclosures
and an unusually effective reform campaign, largely ignored the consolidation issue. The outcome proved Green's strategy to have been sound
but risky: Consolidation secured a large majority of all the ballots cast
in the referendum, and a majority of some sort in every political unit

TABLE 7-1

The Vote on the 1894 Consolidation Referendum

District	For	Against	Defective
New York County	96,938	59,959	9,608
Kings County	64,744	64,467	255
Queens County	7,712	4,741	*
Richmond County	5,531	1,505	5
Town of Westchester	374	206	*
Town of Eastchester	620	621	*
Town of Pelham	251	153	*
	176,170	131,706	9,868

* None reported.
SOURCE: John Foord, *The Life and Public Services of Andrew H. Green* (New York: Doubleday, Page, & Co., 1913), p. 191. The Town of Mount Vernon also voted, negatively, on consolidation in 1894, but it was included in the referendum at the request of its residents: Neither Green nor the Greater New York Commission sought to include it.

he had sought to include. But Brooklyn, the key to the entire plan, supported consolidation by only the narrowest of margins: less than 300 votes out of 129,000 (see table 7-1).[88]

It is difficult to interpret this vote because the issue was presented in vague terms and also because, as Tammany feared and as anticonsolidationists later charged, many voters may have confused a vote for consolidation with a vote for the revised constitution.[89] But it appears that Green and his associates pitched their appeal effectively. In Manhattan and Brooklyn consolidation won strongest support from wealthy and middle-income citizens, the native-born, the German-Americans, and the more assimilated and prosperous of the German and Irish immigrants, especially those who supported Republican and Cleveland-Democratic candidates.[90] (See maps 7-1 and 7-2.) In addition, the proconsolidation vote was high in those parts of Brooklyn that most needed public improvements, and low in parts of New York City where residents feared that aid to Brooklyn would delay improvements they sought for themselves.[91] Across the thirty New York City assembly districts the vote in favor of consolidation correlated 0.769 with that for successful Republican-Fusion mayoral candidate William L. Strong, and 0.901 with the vote for the basic revision of the state constitution. Across the twenty-eight Brooklyn wards that existed both in 1893 and in 1894, the vote for consolidation correlated 0.694 with the vote for Charles A. Schieren and 0.394 with the reform Democrats' candidate for city treasurer.[92] In both cities the lowest vote for consolidation came from the poorest districts, where Democratic opposition to the new constitution apparently led most voters to reject consolida-

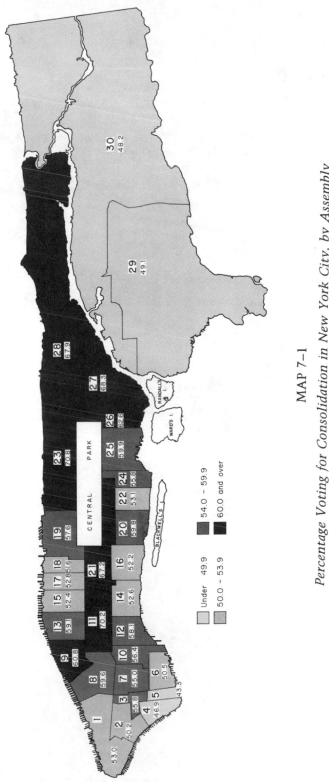

MAP 7–1

*Percentage Voting for Consolidation in New York City, by Assembly
District, 1894*

Under 49.9

50.0 – 53.9

54.0 – 59.9

60.0 and over

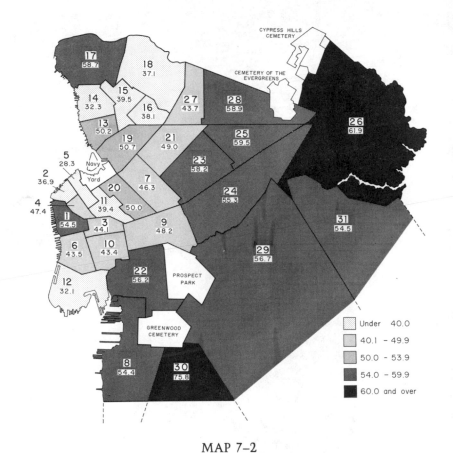

MAP 7-2

Percentage Voting for Consolidation in Brooklyn, by Ward, 1894

tion despite the promise that it would mean cheap houses for working people. The campaign to present consolidation as a step toward reformed government may very well have made a crucial contribution to the precariously slim majority in Brooklyn.

Brooklyn Opposition

Those who successfully brought consolidation through the 1894 referendum—hard-headed merchants, bankers, and real estate promoters, together with civic reformers of the "earnest, public-spirited class"—seemed on the verge of gaining most of their objectives when they encountered stern resistance from the defensive but effective Protestant social elite of Brooklyn. The *Record and Guide* had suggested that the political result of consolidation would be a quarrel "like two cats tied together by their tails and thrown over a clothesline." Fearing that result, many politicians also were eager to delay action until they had a clearer sense of political implications.[93] Brooklyn's defensive Protestants slowed down the drive for consolidation, dispelled the impression that the consolidationists represented *all* men of wealth and respectability, and gave the politicians the opening they sought.

Professing surprise at the proconsolidation majority in Brooklyn, some of that city's most prominent cultural and religious leaders organized a League of Loyal Citizens within a week of the election. A. A. Low, James O. Cleveland, and William C. Redfield played the most prominent parts in the league. They were closely supported by a group of Brooklyn Heights clergymen, including the Rev. Dr. Theodore L. Cuyler of the Lafayette Avenue Presbyterian Church, Richard S. Storrs of the Church of the Pilgrims, Lyman Abbott of Plymouth Church, Bishop A. N. Littlejohn of the Episcopal Diocese of Long Island, and Charles H. Hall, rector of Holy Trinity. Other leaders of the Loyal League included Robert D. Benedict, president of the New England Society in the City of Brooklyn; Truman J. Backus, head of the Packer Institute, a private finishing school for girls; William H. Maxwell, superintendent of the Brooklyn Public Schools; Alfred T. White, the reformer and philanthropist; and St. Clair McKelway, editor of the *Eagle*, whose conception of Brooklyn had made him a major Brooklyn institution in his own right.[94]

Like the consolidationists, leaders of the League of Loyal Citizens possessed considerable economic and political resources. At least five of them were reputed millionaires, eight were officers or directors of large New York City banks, thirteen held similar positions in Brooklyn banks, and ten were substantial mechants. Several held large investments in Brooklyn real estate and utilities; two of these, A. A. Low, and Henry E. Pierrepont, were among the wealthiest landowners in Brooklyn. Several of the anticonsolidationists were prominent anti-McLaughlin Democrats; others were prominent Republicans.[95]

What differentiated the Loyal Leaguers from the consolidationists was not their politics or their slightly larger number of inherited fortunes, but their vision of Brooklyn. All of them were deeply devoted to Brooklyn's Anglo-American Protestant institutions and to the way of life those institutions symbolized and encouraged. The Protestant institutions supplied eloquence, organizational ability, and other cultural resources to the Loyal League. But they also supplied a defensive motive that reduced the value of their resources; for all their eloquence, the league's spokesmen could only hope to win the Protestant half of Brooklyn's population to their standard. The consolidationists, by contrast, were much more diverse in ethnic origin; they included several politicians skilled in the art of cross-cultural politics; and they defined their cause in straightforward economic terms that had universal appeal.

William C. Redfield's pamphlet, *Taxes and Tenements*, summed up the Loyal League's objections to consolidation. Far from producing economical and efficient government, Redfield argued, consolidation would prove to be expensive. New York City did have a low tax rate, but that would not last for long. New York had already launched several costly projects, and consolidation would serve Brooklyn's purposes only if still more were added. But these projects would become hideously expensive because the monstrous size of the greater city would permit venal, slum-chosen public officials to operate hidden from the public eye.[96]

But like all Loyal League spokesmen, Redfield stressed the threat that an alien, impoverished tenement-house population posed to what he took to be the Brooklyn way of life. He urged each citizen of Brooklyn to "consider the character of the city and the citizens with whom he is asked to unite." That character was low. Redfield quoted Jacob Riis to make his point: " 'in the tenements all the influences make for evil;' " tenement districts were " 'the nurseries of pauperism and crime;' " they " 'touch[ed] family life with deadly moral contagion.' " A reliable authority—so Redfield asserted—estimated that Manhattan harbored as many as sixty thousand prostitutes. Riis had correctly observed that the tenement house districts were spreading and that they already " '[held] within their clutch the wealth and business of New York.' " Some consoli-

dationists had seen suburbanization as an antidote to the slums, but Redfield feared that the slums would overwhelm the suburbs. "There are,"
he noted, "more voters by far in the tenement houses of New York City
than in all of Brooklyn."[97]

The Rev. Dr. Storrs picked up the political point: "it is a question,"
he stated at one of the Loyal League's mass meetings, "whether good
government is possible in such an immense, shifting, heterogeneous population of three million . . . with a large proportion of recent immigrants,
and into which the political sewage of Europe is being dumped every
week (Applause)." Storrs, the "Chrysotom of Brooklyn," preferred to
rely on Brooklyn's "comparatively homogeneous population," two-thirds
of which had been "trained from childhood in American traditions, for
good local government."[98] Republican Mayor Frederick W. Wurster
bluntly raised the same issue in a private letter of 1896: "what will be
the chances for the maintenance of the public school system or the preservation of its integrity as . . . non-sectarian . . . if half the legislative
power of the state is put—as consolidation would put it—in the hands
of Tammany Hall?" Brooklyn, Wurster continued, "is largely a New England and American city. That element is large enough to assimilate any
foreign element in or coming to Brooklyn. Consequently, American customs and institutions—including the public schools—are maintained free
from evil influence . . . and the sentiment easily built up that makes
for good government."[99]

These quotations from Redfield, Storrs, and Wurster illustrate the Loyal
League's abhorrence of Manhattan. But, as their anti-Manhattan language
implied, the League also had a positive vision of Brooklyn as a city strong
in respectable Protestant values and institutions. The very titles of its
spokesmen made the point most eloquently. The Rev. Dr. Storrs argued
that Brooklyn had no need of bridges to improve its real estate:

> The only practicable way to make Brooklyn a fashionable place of residence,
> for people of the sort that we want, is to make it attractive because replete
> with fine institutions, with everything that intelligent men and women desire
> in the city of their homes: to make it attractive that it shall be fashionable
> for everyone to live in it except the billionaires: and, if the worst comes to
> the worst, we must try to get along without them. (Laughter)[100]

St. Clair McKelway's similar vision of Brooklyn as a bastion of prosperous, respectable Protestantism had made him much in demand as an after-
dinner speaker. To the Montauk Club in 1895, for example, he proclaimed:

> The identity of Brooklyn is indestructible. It always was a city of homes and
> churches. It is becoming a city of clubs as well. . . . The homes are the church

feeders. The churches are the home result. The clubs antagonize neither the churches nor the homes. Of the best Brooklyn clubs the reverend clergy are welcome members, and in the best of them space and provision are made for the special entertainment of the fairer and better sex.[101]

This passage is typical of McKelway's praise of Brooklyn for its homogeneous, hardworking, prosperous, "American" population, and for the churches, schools, institutes, clubs, and reform political movements this population supported. In another speech of 1893 he observed to a New York audience that "our Brooklyn is so domestic and lovely that Bishop Potter says New York wants it as a moral and spiritual infusion." He added, "we have no streets analogous to your Fifth Avenue, but neither have we any resembling those of your tenderloin district. With us are as yet no extremes of wealth or poverty; but the families of moderate means are becoming fewer with you."[102] Those views were so popular that he was called upon to give them at least six times every season from 1891 through 1896. In Brooklyn alone during these years he addressed the Twenty-third Regiment, the Vermont Society, the Montauk, Hamilton, and Union League clubs; the Long Island Business College, the YMCA, the Packer Institute, Miss Brown's Schools, and the Brooklyn Institute of Arts and Sciences; and dinners in honor of General Sherman, George William Curtis, Benjamin F. Tracy, General Grant, Hamilton, Lincoln, and Washington.[103]

Effective as it was, the Loyal League's vision of Brooklyn as a city of middle-class Protestant respectability ignored nearly half of the city's residents (see table 7–2). The vision was both partial and self-limiting. Compared to New York City, Brooklyn was slightly more native-born and Protestant, and it did have proportionately more residents whose mothers had been born in England, Wales, Scotland, Canada, and Scandinavia. New York had many more from eastern and southern Europe. But just about half the people in each city were children of Irish or German mothers. Presuming that the Roman Catholic population contained only those of Irish, French, Italian, and Bohemian origin, and half those of German origin, about 38 percent of Brooklyn's and 46 percent of New York's people followed that faith. Adding the Russians, Poles, and Hungarians, at least 52.7 percent of New York's but only about 40 percent of Brooklyn's population came from non-Protestant stock. Thus there were clear differences between the cities, but these were much less sharp than Loyal League spokesmen implied.

Making use of skills learned in business, politics, education, and religion, organizers of the League of Loyal Citizens employed a wide variety of techniques to mobilize resistance to consolidation. Among Brooklyn's

TABLE 7–2

Population of Brooklyn and of New York City, 1890: Birthplace and Parentage

	Brooklyn		New York City	
1. Birthplace of parents and color[1]	Number	Percentage	Number	Percentage
Total population 1890[2]	806,343	100.0	1,515,301	100.0
Native born White	534,672	66.2	852,641	56.3
2 Native parents	222,573	27.5	270,487	17.85
1 or 2 Foreign parents	312,099	38.8	582,154	38.5
Foreign born White	260,725	32.4	636,986	42
[Foreign born or Foreign born Parent]	572,824	71.2	1,219,140	80.3
"Colored"[3]	10,946	1.26	25,674	1.7

2. Birthplaces of mothers of whites	Brooklyn		New York City	
	Number	Percentage	Number	Percentage
Total	795,397	100.00	1,489,627	100.00
U.S.	268,097	33.7	334,727	22.4
Canada	7,200	0.9	9,647	0.64
England and Wales	50,379	6.3	55,572	3.72
Scotland	14,195	1.78	19,627	1.3
Ireland	196,372	24.7	399,348	26.8
Germany	195,663	24.6	403,784	27
Russia and Poland	7,581	0.95	80,235	5.4
Scandinavia	21,178	2.65	13,311	0.89
Italy	12,454	1.56	54,334	3.65
Other	24,275	3.4	105,916	7.18

[1] John S. Billings, *Vital Statistics of New York City and Brooklyn* (Washington, D.C.: U.S. Department of the Interior, Census Office, 1894), tables 5 and 80, pp. 6, 238–41.
[2] Total population includes Native Born White, Foreign Born White, and "Colored."
[3] In the "colored" category this study includes persons of oriental as well as black African descent.

Protestant majority they made the League itself a mass organization, claiming fifty thousand members by early February 1895. They published *Greater Brooklyn* periodically from April to November, as well as a steady stream of pamphlets, most of which reproduced the speeches delivered at anticonstitutional mass meetings.[104] They announced a prize of ten dollars for the best anticonsolidation essay by a child and gave a three-hundred-dollar prize for the best anticonsolidation song. And they launched a petition campaign that gathered over seventy-two thousand signatures, a good seven thousand more than the number of proconsolidation votes cast in Brooklyn in 1894.[105] Armed with this evidence of mass support, Loyal Leaguers attacked the legislature through testimony, letters, and direct lobbying.[106]

What the Loyal League sought was a new referendum or, as they put it, "resubmission," with the terms of consolidation spelled out in some detail.[107] Meanwhile, the reformers who had elected Mayor Schieren in Brooklyn and Mayor Strong in New York City found themselves engaged in difficult battles with their erstwhile allies among the Republican regulars who now controlled the state government. Shaw and the other municipal theorists found that they were not going to come to a consensus about the ideal frame of government for the greater city. And some of the Brooklyn consolidationists began to grow uneasy about the absence of a formal guarantee that consolidation would mean equal tax assessment rates throughout the greater city. From all of these sources there now came the demand for resubmission, or at least for an early disclosure of terms.

Boss Platt, Governor Morton, and the Legislature

In the six years from 1888 through 1894 the Chamber of Commerce, Andrew H. Green, the New York *Times*, and their associates in metropolitan New York's mercantile elite formulated the Greater New York idea, placed it on the region's public agenda, and brought it to the fore as a proposal that required definitive action. But they could control it no further. Green, like many of his merchant supporters, was a Democrat; in 1894 the Republican Party gained the upper hand in politics throughout the state. Effective though it was, Green's entirely commercial vision of civic greatness provoked continuing opposition from some New York real estate interests; more significantly, the referendum provoked the League of Loyal Citizens into a colorful demonstration of the fact that rival visions of the metropolis and its purposes commanded widespread middle-class support. Beset by these misfortunes and by illness, Green faded from the scene.

He was replaced by Thomas C. Platt, the acknowledged "easy boss" of the state's Republican Party. With the Republican victories of 1894 Platt reached, as he later observed, the strongest position he ever held in state politics—a position much like that achieved by Tammany leader Charles F. Murphy in 1903. After graduating from Yale, Platt had returned to his native town of Owego, in upstate Tioga County, to launch a political career. He rose rapidly, becoming a United States Senator in 1881 at the age of forty-seven. But then an embarrassingly unsuccessful political maneuver cost him his seat in the Senate, his political base,

Senator Thomas C. Platt at his U. S. Express Company offices, 1899. (Byron Collection, Courtesy of the Museum of the City of New York)

and part of his reputation. Platt set out to regain all three. Working with matchless patience and persistence he built up a network of loyal friends across upstate New York, cultivated machine Republicans in New York and Brooklyn, and found his way back to the role of acknowledged (though unofficial) leader of his party in the state. By the early nineties he had centralized control over the flow of both government and corporate patronage, and over the actions of subordinate party officials throughout the state. His permanent residence in Manhattan's fashionable Fifth Avenue Hotel had become the scene of weekly "Sunday school" meetings at which Platt gently but firmly led discussions of Republican policy. The legislature returned him to the U.S. Senate in 1893.[108]

An astute man of affairs, Platt made a good deal of money in the politically sensitive express and bonding businesses. But he was eager to regain social prestige as well as political power, and he shunned the vulgar forms of corruption. Instead, he sought recognition as a shrewd capitalist capable of energetic leadership on behalf of big business.[109] He had never been a puritanical man and by the 1890s he recognized, as a purely practical politician, that New York's Republicans could never win consistently if they insisted on closing German saloons on Sundays or embracing the nativist American Protective Association. But he also understood that they must retain the support of evangelical Protestants inclined to shift their allegiance from the Republicans to the Temperance party.[110]

Promoted by a mercantile elite and resisted by defensive evangelical Protestants, Greater New York raised just the sort of issues that Platt had to master if his party was to secure its new hold on the state and reelect him to the senate. Whatever the difficulties it posed, consolidation had become an "irrepressible movement;" Green and his associates had seen to that.[111] But Platt was blessed with the gifted politician's genius for finding opportunity where others see problems, and he found a way to make consolidation serve three of his purposes. First, he would make himself the "Father of Greater New York" and reap praise from the mercantile elite for promoting "the complete and rational development of the metropolis" so as to protect its "threatened . . . supremacy."[112] Second, he would use the reorganization required by consolidation to discipline troublesome independent Republicans in New York and if necessary in Brooklyn, making his control over the party still more secure. And third, he would gain for the Republican Party the prestige and the voter loyalty due a political organization capable of advancing the most fundamental economic interests of the metropolis. If everything fell into place, he might even be able to turn Greater New York into a solidly Republican municipality: Republican-fusion Mayor William L. Strong won 56.1 percent of the New York City vote in 1894, and Brooklyn gave Republican candidates 58 percent in 1893 and, even without fusion support, 54 percent in 1895.

Despite the increasing resistance, most informed observers believed that Greater New York would be set up in time for the 1900 census. Hoping to take advantage of the favorable referendum and to retain control of the movement, Green, supported by the New York *Times,* arrived in Albany on the first day of the 1895 legislature with a bill authorizing his commission, together with the mayors of Brooklyn and New York City, to devise a charter for the greater city. But the shift in state politics and the protests of the League of Loyal Citizens reduced Green's influence, and he found himself pushed somewhat to the side. Control of the issue now passed to the Republicans and in particular to Thomas C. Platt.

The Republicans were not yet ready to act. Unaccustomed to state-wide dominance and riven by conflicts between factions that had not yet determined their relative strength, Platt's party needed another year to decide what to do about consolidation. At the very beginning of the legislative session the newly elected Republican governor, Manhattan banker Levi P. Morton, countered Green's bill with one of his own, de-signed to empower him to replace Green's commission (which had, after all, been appointed by his Democratic predecessor) with a charter commis-sion of his own choosing. But the legislature ignored both Morton's bill and Green's. Within a few weeks conflict came to a head between New York City's new independent Republican mayor, William L. Strong, and the regular Republicans, led by Platt and New York County Republican Committee Chairman, Edward L. Lauterbach. Legislation directed at the police, the police courts, the schools, and the tenements of New York City was all, as the *Record and Guide* reported, " 'hung up,' pending the consummation by politicians of bargains."[113] In the midst of this battle Platt proposed, so the anti-Platt *Tribune* reported, to use the Greater New York plan as a pretext for reducing the mayors' powers, depriving them of patronage, or curtailing their terms of office.[114] Then toward the end of the session Platt's legislative managers, renouncing anti-inde-pendent intentions, stated that they would take up Morton's bill after all. As a pledge of their intent to raise consolidation above the level of petty factionalism, they amended Morton's bill to add Andrew H. Green's name as one of the commissioners.[115] But as Platt's aide, State Senator Clarence Lexow, recalled, the League of Loyal Citizens "held up . . . the ghost of Tammany domination . . . before the Republicans," and "cajoled" them "with promises and threatened with dire consequences to future party success, if the bill for consolidation was enacted into law."[116] At the last minute, a deal between Tammany senators and their Kings County colleagues, together with a Brooklyn Republican demand for resubmission, defeated the bill.[117]

By the end of 1895, Platt had decided to push consolidation through the next legislature regardless of opposition. He succeeded, but only after protracted negotiations and at the cost of important concessions to Gover-nor Morton and the expenditure of considerable political capital.

In mid-December Platt summoned Morton to a special Greater New York strategy session with Lauterbach, U.S. senator and Republican Party wheelhorse Frank Hiscock, and others at the home of Platt's close Brooklyn associate, former Secretary of the Navy Benjamin F. Tracy.[118] Within two weeks, Morton and Platt were in disagreement as to what had been decided; their letters reveal the ensuing bargaining process in vivid detail.

On December 31 Morton wrote Tracy that "some of our mutual friends" feared that the Republicans planned to use consolidation as a pretext for creating special temporary state commissions to take over a large portion of the patronage in New York and Brooklyn.[119] These friends had not confined themselves to private discussions; in December the *Record and Guide* and the *Times* reported that the Republican organization sought control of the police, fire, park, public works, and health departments because they provided many jobs and could be consolidated quickly, unlike those that could sue and be sued, like the school departments, and those that dealt with myriad details, like the offices for taxes and assessments.[120]

"This," Morton wrote Tracy, "was not my understanding of the proposition as presented at your house." Morton had been nominated governor as a compromise candidate, capable of working with Platt and his group, with militant upstate Protestants, and with the Protestant and business-Republican independents in New York City and Brooklyn. It was becoming clear, he observed, that Republicans in Brooklyn and in upstate New York would resist the creation of a monster city. Would it not be wise, he asked, to accede to the growing Brooklyn and New York City demand for resubmission?[121]

Tracy passed Morton's letter along to Platt, who responded angrily:

> When we sought and had the conference with you at General Tracy's house on this question, it was for the purpose of having definitely settled what your position would be on this great question. There could have been no misunderstanding on your part as to what was our intention, and purpose in the interview with you, because our entire program was definitely stated and thoroughly explained, and we went away from that conference understanding that you were in full accord and would stand by us to the end. Now, at the very opening of the legislature, as I have expressed it to you before, you "take to the woods" and are leaving us in the lurch.[122]

Platt was not impressed with the League of Loyal Citizens and the others who were calling for resubmission:

> Evidently the raid on you by Mr. Low and Company had its effect. You understood at the interview above referred to that this was likely to happen; that the enemies of the measure would do everything in their power to prevent the passage of this bill and would resort to just the arguments that they are using; and would do everything in their power to intimidate you. This was our reason for calling upon you, so that we might know that you would stand firmly by the programme. These men who have been visiting you from Brooklyn are, as you well know, the men who are the champions of the opposition. The great mass of the people, both in New York City and Brooklyn, who

favor consolidation, have not such a personal interest in the matter that they take the trouble to visit you and express their views. If it is necessary to deluge you with letters from good men in Brooklyn, in order to stiffen you up, it is a very easy matter to do it, and we can have large committees appointed to wait upon you with reference to that question.[123]

For all his bluster, Platt avoided the special metropolitan commission issue that had provoked Morton's letter in the first place. Morton noted this point in his response:

I like your entire frankness. . . . I consider myself wholly committed to the resolution for the adoption of the name of New York for the cities of New York and Brooklyn and for their ultimate consolidation, but I did not understand—as I said in my letter—that there was any intention or expectation of legislating out of office the present officials of the two cities until Jan. 1, 1898, when the full scheme should go into effect. I do not hesitate to say that I believe any attempt to cut short the tenure of office of existing officeholders would be to hazard and imperil the success of the whole movement.[124]

Platt had persuaded Morton to support Greater New York despite the opposition of Manhattan independents and militant Brooklyn Protestants. But Morton in turn had made it clear that he would use all the powers of his office to prevent the appointment of special commissioners. Platt was not yet willing to concede the point. During the following three months, New York City and Brooklyn newspapers frequently reported that Lauterbach and Platt planned to introduce "supplemental bills" to create the special state commissions. On February 4, for example, the *Eagle* quoted Lauterbach as

telling the Republicans in the Twenty-ninth district over the river last night that "the greater New York bills are sure to become laws, and that under them the men who had failed to recognize the existence of the majority of the county organization [that is, of Lauterbach's anti-Strong group], during the past year, will wonder if they exist when it comes to recognition in appointments for office . . ." Lauterbach did not attempt . . . to outline the laws to be made but he did say they will provide for the appointment by the governor of bi-partisan commissioners to govern the greater city to be created.[125]

In mid-March, Lauterbach attempted to persuade the governor to accept his commission plan in the form, as Morton described it, of supplemental measures "to legislate out of office present incumbents of some of the commissions or departmental offices in New York or Brooklyn, after and assuming the approval of the Greater New York resolution in its present form." Morton reminded Lauterbach that "it was the general impression and understanding" that the Greater New York bill, as amended by the senate, "covered all the legislation that it was intended to attempt upon that subject this year."[126] Undaunted, Lauterbach replied,

> the problem of a Greater New York can only be properly solved by the appointment of adinterim Commissioners who shall properly organize the great Departments Police, Fire, Health, and Public Works in the new territory, so that the incumbents of those places who shall be designated by the first Mayor elect of the Greater City shall enter upon their duties under favorable circumstances, [not in] chaos and confusion.[127]

Morton was unmoved. As he had observed, the "adinterim commissioner" idea provoked increased opposition in Brooklyn and New York, particularly among Republicans and independents allied with the mayoral regimes of Frederick W. Wurster and William L. Strong. Seeking to take advantage of the new resistance to consolidation, real estate interests in Manhattan and in the newly annexed district above the Harlem River redoubled their efforts. *Dickson's Uptown Weekly* protested, "if consolidation is effected, the money that should rightfully be expended on the North Side will be wasted on such unknown places as Flatlands, Fresh Pond, Canarsie, and the like."[128] Speaking more generally for Manhattan taxpayers, the *Real Estate Record and Builder's Guide* objected to the planning implications that Andrew Green had made basic to his proposal. In its 1896 form, at least, consolidation would throw an excessive burden of taxation on the older city. The plan violated the basic rules for successful annexations. The new territory did not already possess a population density and a degree of physical development comparable to that of the annexing city, and was not required to pay all the costs of its own paving, drainage, lighting, and poor relief. Properly, the *Record and Guide* insisted, the "united body" should undertake "only the great works which clearly benefit the city as a whole," including the major highways and bridges, trunk sewers, parks, and fire and police protection.[129] The *Record and Guide* favored the public control and planning of utilities and great public works, but it rejected comprehensive advance planning of suburbs as too expensive for the central city.

Consolidation's opponents thus gained strength. But they labored under severe handicaps. The League of Loyal Citizens "tackled every known consolidationist of prominence" in Brooklyn and claimed that its survey of legislative candidates in the November 1895 elections revealed "a very large majority" in favor of resubmission. Yet all three candidates for mayor of Brooklyn in that year, reflecting the views of the regular Democratic, reform-Democratic, and Republican organizations that had nominated them, favored consolidation if the terms could be made right for their city.[130]

In New York City, many of those who now spoke out against consolidation on the basis of adinterim commissioners had supported the movement in the past and could be dismissed as indecisive men who were now influenced by the positions they and their friends held under Mayor Strong. The Union League Club, which in 1896 decided to join the opposition for the first time,[131] continued to serve as a meeting place for Republican politicians and their financial backers, but its apparent anti-Semitism and its involvement in the anti-Platt Brookfield Republican movement had reduced its political importance. As leader of the regular Republican organization, Platt could also dismiss the opposition of Whitelaw Reid's independent Republican *Tribune,* of the Rev. Dr. Parkhurst's City Vigilance League, of the nonpartisan City Club, of Grace Democrat Francis M. Scott, and of the heavily Democratic German American Reform Union. And to new Chamber of Commerce objections he could respond that the Chamber had long supported the idea and opposed it only because it now seemed to threaten the Chamber's pet mayor.

While opposition continued to grow, moreover, the advocates of Greater New York largely held ranks. The Consolidation League, rallying new support from merchants, manufacturers, bankers, architects, builders, realtors, and street railway owners, easily matched the League of Loyal Citizens' two or three hundred pages of testimony before a legislative committee.[132] Green's Greater New York Commission continued its Albany lobby and retained the support of the *Times,* the *World,* and the *Sun.*[133] Prominent real estate men countered the arguments of *Dickson's Uptown Weekly* and the *Record and Guide.*[134] And Tammany Democrats, watching Republican maneuvers from the sidelines, waited for an opportunity to gain something with their votes.

Platt assessed the risks and decided to go ahead. He had arranged for his close associate, State Senator Clarence Lexow, to manage the Greater New York bill, and in March Lexow brought the bill to a vote. The measure was essentially the one offered by Governor Morton in 1895. It declared that all the territory included in Andrew H. Green's plan would be consolidated into a single municipality known as the City of New York on January 1, 1898; it empowered Governor Morton to appoint nine members to a new commission to draft a charter for the greater city; and it specified that the mayors of New York, Brooklyn, and Long Island City, the state engineer and the state attorney general, and Andrew H. Green were also to serve on the commission.[135] Lexow brushed aside an effort to remove the Queens County towns of Flushing, Jamaica, and Hempstead from the greater city.[136] He and Platt had no doubt hoped that Lexow's hearings into Tammany police corruption had won him such a firm reputation as a reformer that his name alone would quiet fears that this consolidation scheme would be used as cover for a patronage raid, but at the last minute he accepted two small amendments offered by Tammany Senator Jacob A. Cantor, who often cooperated with the Chamber of Commerce, designed to reduce the chance that adinterim commissioners would be made part of the scheme.[137] With Tammany support the amended bill easily passed in both houses of the legislature.[138]

But the mayors of New York and Brooklyn, exercising powers that Manhattan reformers had placed in the new state constitution, reviewed the bill, drafted formal messages of disapproval, and returned it to the legislature for repassage or burial. It went through the senate with ease, but then it nearly stuck in the assembly. Mustering all their political resources for the crucial vote, the League of Loyal Citizens and the Manhattan independents persuaded a large bloc of Brooklyn Republicans and several upstaters to vote no.[139] Seeing an opportunity to put Platt into a corner, about twenty Tammany Democrats who had voted yea in the first instance reversed themselves.[140] Twisting arms and making free use of political threats and promises, Platt forced the measure through. In addition to a few votes from upper Manhattan Democrats allied with Andrew H. Green and from three Brooklyn Republicans, Platt secured the almost unanimous support of the upstate Republican groups that formed the basis of his control over the party. As Lexow later declared, "it required all Senator Platt's energy, and the full weight of his influence throughout the state, to secure a constitutional majority." And it cost him part of his reputation as the easy boss who led by consensus.[141]

The opponents of the measure now concentrated their fire on the governor, urging him to veto the bill. Morton allowed them to rehearse their arguments once again, but his important discussions were held with Platt.[142] Platt had never renounced the "adinterim commission" idea, and some observers believed that he intended to have the legislature set up a special committee under Lexow to investigate and perhaps to take over several city departments in the summer of 1896. Morton apparently persuaded Platt to drop any such notion as part of the price for his signature.

The bill passed on April 22. On April 23 Platt wrote Morton, urging him to sign it "at as early a date as possible."[143] Then five days later Platt wrote the governor again, using a petulant tone and implying that Morton had denied him something:

I have learned a lesson, and that is never again to attempt to manage the affairs of another man's canvass, no matter how good a friend he may be. I shall go on and do my utmost to advance your interests in the present canvass for the Presidency, but I shall take special pains to give no assurances and make no promises for the future: then there will be no danger of accusations such as have come to my ears from men close to you, that I am "putting the Governor in a hole."[144]

Morton did not hesitate to keep up his end in this extraordinarily frank and articulate exchange. "Many letters are coming to me from Brooklyn and from old personal friends in New York, of the highest character and standing," he replied. "One of the most frequent and serious criticisms and objections urged against the bill is as to the methods that were used to force it through the assembly."[145] Persuaded that he could prevent the use of special commissions and select his own men for the commission, Morton drafted a message approving the legislation and sent it to Tracy for review.[146] On May 11, 1896, he signed the bill into law.[147]

A Temporary Resolution: The Greater New York Charter of 1898

With the preparation and passage of a charter for Greater New York, the mercantile and political forces that had controlled the consolidation movement struck a temporary resolution. Platt protected his own interests and those of the Republican Party; the charter made important concessions to Brooklyn and advanced no dangerously remarkable schemes of munici-pal reform. On the other hand Morton saw to it that nothing was done to disturb the independent administration of Mayor Strong in New York. And the charter provided for the inclusion of all the territory that Andrew H. Green had specified, for uniform rates of taxes and assessments, and for a strong central government with new if not striking powers to promote "the complete and rational development of the metropolis."

Under the new law, Governor Morton was to name nine men to the Charter Commission. On the day following the April meeting at which Morton made it clear for the last time that he would tolerate no "supple-mental legislation," Platt wrote sourly, "I shall not obtrude my advice or suggestions upon you any further unless they are sought"; and yet, "I think I am entitled to be considered in the selection of the Commission-ers under the Greater New York law by reason of the fact that I have

been instrumental more than any other man in securing its passage."
Morton responded that he would of course "be pleased to receive your
suggestions regarding the composition of the commission freely and
fully."[148] Morton also consulted others, including Benjamin F. Tracy,
Seth Low, and St. Clair McKelway.[149]

Platt insisted that McKelway not be named, and in fact the entire commission proved satisfactory to him.[150] Tracy, Brooklynites Stewart L.
Woodford and Silas B. Dutcher, and Queens County man Garret J. Garretson were all sensible Platt Republicans, as were the state engineer and
the state attorney general, who held their places *ex officio*; Brooklyn
Mayor Frederick W. Wurster could be brought into line.[151] Tammany
ex-Mayor Thomas F. Gilroy and Willoughby Street Democrat William
C. DeWitt were the sort of regular Democratic politicians whom Platt
found easy to work with; save for his unrealistically exalted ambitions,
Long Island City's Democratic mayor, Patrick J. Gleason, was much the
same.[152] Morton named two Manhattan attorneys, George M. Pinney and
the much-respected conservative expert on municipal law, John F. Dillon,
who were independent of Platt but were identified neither with the anti-
Platt factions nor with advanced notions of municipal reform.[153] Mayor
Strong, a member *ex officio*, had hoped that Morton would select Joseph
H. Choate, Elihu Root, or James C. Carter; instead, Morton named Seth
Low, president of Columbia University and former mayor of Brooklyn,
to serve as Strong's single reform-minded colleague.[154] Andrew Green,
by now both ill and out of touch with Swallowtail Democrats, was the
only representative of that group.[155] Woodford, conveniently enough, had
been president of the New England Society of Brooklyn and could be
described as a spokesman for the Brooklyn interests that had created the
League of Loyal Citizens. Labor organizations, which had played almost
no part in the movement, had no representative on the commission. As
Platt viewed it, the Charter Commission was entirely "safe," both as to
politics and as to policy.

Tracy, as Platt's closest associate and the leading Republican, was selected chairman of the Charter Commission at its first meeting.[156] Eager
to placate as many of the Brooklyn Republicans as possible, Morton, presumably at Platt's request, had given that city more than its share of
commissioners; they quickly moved to protect Brooklyn's interests by
approving provisions for equal taxes and assessments and by arranging
for the charter to go into effect in such a way that Brooklyn landowners
avoided taxes for the first six months. Brooklyn's desire for a continued
independence helped persuade the commission to adopt a borough form
of local government, with elected borough presidents in each of the five

major parts of the city; an alternative proposal for smaller, more coherent local units was rejected as inconsistent with the Brooklyn preference. And in response to one of the chief fears of the Brooklyn League of Loyal Citizens, as well as of Republican politicians like Mayor Wurster, each borough's schools were treated as a largely independent system.[157]

These measures were designed in part to restore the Republican Party's reputation in Brooklyn; the borough system might also give scope for Republican ambitions in Queens, on Staten Island, and even in the Bronx, where Republicans hoped to elect officials in years when they failed to elect the mayor. Uncertain about the Bronx, however, party leaders left it a part of New York County, making it the only borough that was not also a county of its own. Recognizing that they might well become the minority party, the Republicans also gave a great deal of attention to schemes designed to provide them with the largest possible delegation on the city council.[158]

Municipal reform proposals that had less direct relevance to the Republican Party received less consideration. In part this was because no single proposal had gathered overwhelming support. Shaw had won strong support for his London County Council plan—a powerful city council elected at large with proportional representation, presiding over tightly centralized municipal departments headed by responsible, highly-qualified commissioners removable by the mayor—but others preferred the strong mayor approach. The modified version of the latter which already characterized the governments of New York and Brooklyn was simply carried over, with none of its muddle clarified, into the greater city. Reform groups also failed to secure the removal of the Bureau of Elections from the Police Department, or the replacement of the highly political Bi-Partisan Police Board by a single professional commissioner.[159] But on the other hand the commission did not consider proposals to abolish such valued reforms as the elected comptroller, the Board of Estimate, and the 1896 centralization of the New York City public school system.[160]

At Seth Low's suggestion, the commission did introduce three provisions designed to give the greater city increased powers over physical improvements. As Low later put it in defending the proposed charter, the commissioners had above all asked themselves: "Have we related the parts to the center, correctly? Have we provided for the proper conduct of public work in all sections; and have we made it possible for the outskirts to secure the development they need, without involving the city in disaster?"[161]

Low believed that the Greater New York Charter would serve these aims in three ways. Most important, it strengthened the city's control over its streets, shifting the right to grant street railway franchises from the state legislature to the City Council and the Board of Estimate, acting jointly, and granting the city the right to own and operate transportation facilities itself.[162] Second, meeting one of Andrew H. Green's great objectives, the new charter "importantly safeguarded . . . the rights of the city as to its harbor," permitting the city to impose conditions on owners of shoreline property.[163]

Finally, at Low's urging and with the advice of several municipal reformers and real estate and banking spokesmen, the new charter set up a Board of Public Improvements with power to order and coordinate public works projects throughout the greater city.[164] Consisting of commissioners from several city departments, this board would have the power to propose plans and policies to the City Council, which could act in such matters only on the board's initiative. At least one contemporary saw in the Board of Public Improvements an agency that might very well promote comprehensive, rational advance planning in the metropolis. Albert Shaw and others, noting that the board was not to have a powerful director, feared that it would encourage logrolling "in a degree never before imagined."[165] Low believed, on the contrary, that the Board of Public Improvements would deny to city councilmen many of their accustomed opportunities for parochialism and corruption. In effect, he expected the new board, whose members would be, he hoped, professional engineers and lawyers removable by a strong mayor, to have an impact on public works planning comparable to that which the Board of Estimate and Appointment, whose members would be elected in the glare of city-wide canvasses, was to have on financial affairs.[166] Together, the two boards would provide the initiative, efficiency, and responsibility to the taxpayers that New York's reformers had sought in vain since the days of the Tilden Commission.

Platt and Morton selected the Charter Commission's members with great care and shrewdness; their proposed charter satisfied the regular Republicans, the Protestants and the promoters of Brooklyn, most other surburban developers, Tammany Hall, and many Manhattan investors, taxpayers, and bondholders. But it imposed higher taxes on Manhattan real estate, offered few new reforms, introduced a large, awkwardly designed City Council, and was thrown together so rapidly, out of so many disparate laws relating to so many distinct jurisdictions, that many of its provisions contradicted one another, or simply made no sense. In addition, Platt (who had secured the election of a new governor, Frank S. Black, without the assistance of Republican Swallowtails like Elihu Root and Joseph Choate) had revived the "adinterim commissioner" idea for use in harassing Mayor Strong. For all these reasons the business and civic groups most closely allied with Strong's administration opposed the charter in the 1897 legislature. Just when the Greater New York it had launched in 1888 was about to pass into law, the Chamber of Commerce of the State of New York urged caution, revision, and delay. Similar counsel came from the Association of the Bar in the City of New York, the City Club, the Reform Club, and the Republican Club.[167]

But Tammany favored consolidation, the Brooklyn opposition had dwindled to a remnant, and Platt was determined to see it through. Joseph B. Bishop, an editor of E. L. Godkin's *Nation* and a close ally of Theodore Roosevelt and other Manhattan independents, asserted that one Republican legislator had said privately "if it were not for the fact that the 'old man' wants it, I doubt if the charter would get a dozen votes in the legislature outside the Brooklyn and Long Island members."[168] That would appear to have been a biased judgment. Only the organized opponents of machine politics on Manhattan spoke out against the measure, and by themselves they could hardly expect to sway the legislature, especially when Seth Low, one of their own leaders, defended the charter as a reform document. As gubernatorial aide Charles Z. Lincoln wrote ex-Governor Morton, "Greater New York had to go through almost as a matter of course."[169]

Conclusion

For all the wealth and diversity of their resources, the closely allied mercantile, banking, real estate, and municipal reform elites that pressed for consolidation between 1887 and 1894 lost control over the plan in 1896 and 1897. Conflicting visions of the metropolis and its purposes, competing political ambitions, and disparate economic interests produced conflicts that dissipated their resources, reducing their ability to determine the greater city's political form. As finally enacted, Greater New York served the immediate personal and political purposes of Republican Party leader Thomas C. Platt. Platt clearly intended to employ his considerable organizing and bargaining talents to secure an acknowledged place among the economic statesmen of the metropolis. Far from standing in opposition to the region's mercantile and corporate elites, he sought their approval. But in order to retain the political position that enabled him to advance his ambition for power and prestige, Platt had to consider other interests .

as well. Above all, these included the interests of Republican Party workers and voters who had helped his party capture the state government. The party needed local patronage in the metropolitan region if it was to secure its new position of dominance in the state. And many of the party's workers also had small investments in local banks, real estate developments, and utilities, or worked closely with those who did. These factors gave party workers a direct interest in the control of local public works projects and little desire for comprehensive planning for the region as a whole. Recent Republican victories had not produced overwhelming margins, especially in the city; so Platt and his associates also had to take account of issues, like taxes and the control of public education in Greater New York, that would sway suburban and upstate Republican voters.

Yet if New York's mercantile elite could not use consolidation to place itself firmly in control of the region's new government or to prevent Platt from using consolidation to threaten Mayor Strong, its leaders secured most of their aims at little cost. Supplemental legislation to create "adinterim commissions" was never placed before the legislature. Greater New York embraced the entire expanse of territory that Andrew H. Green had marked out and that the Chamber of Commerce had sought to include. Further, although the new charter was drawn up hastily and in some confusion, it was an eminently conservative document. It retained the strong mayor, the Board of Estimate, and other features highly valued by taxpayers and bondholders. It preserved the new reforms in the school laws of New York City and provided some protections for the schools of Brooklyn. And it granted the new city some modest but potentially useful new powers over the future development of the Port of New York and the public works of the metropolis.

As enacted in 1896 and 1897, Greater New York represented a compromise among the metropolitan region's mercantile, banking, and real estate elites; the smaller-scale real estate developers in Brooklyn, Queens County, and Staten Island; the leaders of militant Protestantism in Brooklyn; the Manhattan civic reformers; the regular Republicans in Manhattan, Brooklyn, and upstate; and some Tammany Democrats. The poor, even the respectable workingmen and clerks who were to live in the new houses that consolidation was to bring in Brooklyn and Queens, had no direct voice in the matter. The bargain itself was struck in two phases. Andrew H. Green directed the first of these, which spanned the years from 1887 through 1894, in the interest of the mercantile elite. Thomas C. Platt managed the second, from 1895 through 1897, in the interest of the Republican Party. Platt largely worked out the 1897 terms. But once consolidation had taken place, the state legislature could modify its form of government at will. Changes came immediately; as early as 1901 many of the Manhattan independents who had been denied places on the Platt-Morton Charter Commission were appointed to a Charter Revision Commission by Governor Theodore Roosevelt. The balance struck in 1897, as everyone understood at the time, was by no means a stable one.

CHAPTER 8

ECONOMIC POLICY: PLANNING

THE FIRST SUBWAY

PUBLIC MONEY employed by public officials had dredged the Erie Canal, developed New York harbor, and established New York's commercial supremacy early in the nineteenth century. But although New York City retained a strong mayor and a relatively generous set of municipal powers, most of its business leaders had grown deeply suspicious of public officials and had abandoned municipal mercantilism for *laissez-faire* by the 1880s. The rapid transit crisis of the late nineteenth century forced these men to reconsider their outlook. Faced with overcrowded and unhealthy tenement housing, congested streets, and unacceptable commuting times, many business leaders began to ask what initiative the city's government ought to take. Should the city simply encourage private initiative? Or should it move to shape its physical development more directly? These were the issues raised by the most important and controversial issue of economic policy to emerge in Greater New York during the 1880s and 1890s.

New Yorkers had to take a series of intricately related decisions before they could begin to resolve the transit crisis. Which officials, selected in what way and responsible to whom, were to establish the city's policy on rapid transit? Should the city own and operate its rapid transit system, lend its credit to a private entrepreneur, or simply offer a franchise to an entrepreneur who was willing to risk his own money in constructing a system that he would then own and operate for profit? Should the system be located above or below ground; use steam, electricity, or some other motive power; provide a central spine up Broadway or adopt some other route? How soon could the rapid transit system be put into operation? It required a dozen years, endless discussions in the public press, and continuing controversies within New York's leading business and political organizations to make these decisions. In the end, the city tried out a new form of municipal government, put $50 million into a single public improvement, and committed itself to a hybrid policy—of public ownership, private operation, and rather weak public supervision—that lasted another dozen years and was not substantially modified until the 1930s.

These decisions, especially the delay in starting construction, have often been criticized, and responsibility for them has usually been assigned to corrupt or opportunistic politicians, grasping entrepreneurs, and the owners of vested property rights in real estate and local transportation. But in fact both the decisions regarding financing and supervision and the time required to make them must largely be ascribed to stringent technological, legal, financial, and public opinion constraints. When these constraints are taken into consideration, it becomes clear that far from suffering unwarranted delays the subway was planned and built with remarkable speed. That speed was possible because the city's economic elites, guided by the Chamber of Commerce of the State of New York and making good use of professional and technical experts, arrived at a consensus, made the necessary concessions to real estate developers, social reformers, and organized labor, and worked effectively with the state's political leaders.

Early Proposals for Rapid Transit

"Real rapid transit" had been sought in New York since the 1860s. Most cities of the period developed in a roughly circular pattern that made the largest possible area available for residential use. But New York's location on Manhattan Island early forced it into an unusually long, narrow form. This form, together with the concentration of employment around the docks and the central business district, compelled most of the poorer three-quarters of the city's inhabitants to seek homes in the crowded tenement-house districts below Fourteenth Street, where they competed for space with warehouses and office buildings. And it compelled those who sought middle-income neighborhoods of single-family or row houses to accept commuting times of up to an hour or more as they made their way by train, ferry, and railroad to the upper west side, Harlem, Washington Heights, Brooklyn, or several points in New Jersey.[1]

An elevated railroad system, owned by the Manhattan Elevated Railroad

The Bowery, looking north from Grand Street, 1895. Steam-powered elevated railroads, cable car lines, and the last of the horse-car tracks limit the space available for horse-drawn carts and pedestrians. (J. S. Johnston, Courtesy of the Museum of the City of New York)

Company, which was in turn dominated by Jay Gould (and later his son, George Gould), Russell Sage, and J. P. Morgan, had been constructed in the 1870s to meet the needs of commuters within Manhattan. But although this system ran trains up Second and Third avenues into the Bronx on the east side, up Sixth Avenue to 58th Street, and up the continuous line of Ninth, Columbus, and Lenox avenues into Harlem on the west side, it did not provide adequate service. Lacking competitors, the els were heavily used; contemporaries perennially complained that many passengers had to stand. More significantly, the els used heavy (and dirty) steam engines that could not deliver truly rapid transit speeds on the somewhat precarious steel trestles that supported them.[2] The New York Central provided some service from Grand Central Station to remote suburban towns in Westchester County and Connecticut; the Long Island Railroad connected Brooklyn with suburbs to the east. But few people could use these routes.[3] The absence of better transportation facilities hindered the development of residential districts in upper Manhattan and the Bronx, made New York somewhat less attractive than other cities from middle-income people who sought the suburban idyll so well described in Sam Bass Warner, Jr.'s *Streetcar Suburbs*, increased congestion and delays on streets used by the wholesale merchants, and contributed to the heavy crowding of the tenement-house districts.[4]

From the mid 1880s on, a wide variety of economic elites urged that some action be taken to provide faster, safer, and more pleasant transportation between New York City's central business district and its middle-income residential neighborhoods. Real estate and residential groups on the upper west side, in Harlem, and in the Annexed District that later became the southern part of the Bronx made the earliest and most continuous demand. But the most effective demand came from downtown business associations and, above all, from the Chamber of Commerce of the State of New York.

In 1887 the Chamber's *Annual Report* protested that street congestion had become severe enough to delay shipments and increase the cost of doing business.[5] As if in response, Mayor Abram S. Hewitt issued a special *Message on the Harbor, the Docks, the Streets (and street railways), Rapid Transit, the Annexed District, and the Tenement Houses* at the end of January 1888. "Unless additional [rapid transit] facilities are provided," Hewitt argued, "the population which ought to increase at the upper end of the city will be driven to Long Island and New Jersey." This prospect threatened not only the uptown real estate developers, but every property owner in the city, Hewitt insisted. "Our rate of taxation depends upon the growth of the unoccupied portion of the city, particularly north of the Harlem river."[6]

The best solution, in Hewitt's view, would be for the city to arrange for the construction of electrically powered rapid transit subway lines along both the east side and the west side, designed to bring the Annexed District into closer connection with the city center. Hewitt proposed that the city itself borrow the required funds at the prevailing municipal bond rate of 3 percent, then contract for the New York Central Railroad to build the lines, under the supervision of the mayor, the comptroller, and the commissioner of public works. The city would then own the subway. As part of the deal the New York Central would also agree to operate the subway for thirty-five years, supply the needed rolling stock, charge a uniform five-cent fare, and pay 5 percent per year toward the liquidation of the city's investment.[7]

Municipal investment in such a project was both justified and required, Hewitt argued, by the fact that rapid transit was "an essential prerequisite to the development of the Annexed District." But Hewitt did not trust municipal officials to build or operate the subway efficiently, and he recognized that an unrestrained private lessee might inflate his construction costs in order to justify higher dividends. On the other hand a private corporation that had agreed to pay New York 5 percent a year on a construction cost supplied and audited by the city would have adequate incentive to keep that cost down; and the profit motive, together with the 5 percent payment and the five-cent fare, would encourage efficient operation.[8] Like many other Swallowtail Democrats in New York, Hewitt tempered his devotion to the precepts of free trade and a minimal economic role for municipal government by an enthusiasm for government aid to commerce that was worthy of DeWitt Clinton if not of Alexander Hamilton himself.

The Chamber of Commerce, the Cotton and Produce exchanges, and the Board of Trade and Transportation endorsed Hewitt's proposal, as did the *Real Estate Record and Builder's Guide* and the uptown real estate developers whose interests that journal usually supported.[9] Hewitt's message and the views of the Chamber of Commerce persuaded attorney Simon Sterne, a self-professed adherent of "the school of Adam Smith and the Manchester school of political economists" (and a frequent spokesman for the Chamber of Commerce) to "recant some of the doctrines which I have preached for so many years" and to admit "that governmental assistance and management are good things in some cases." But others were not persuaded.[10] Remaining firmly within the limits of Mancunian orthodoxy, E. L. Godkin's *Evening Post* was sure that Hewitt had a bad idea.[11] The *Commercial and Financial Chronicle*, which spoke for investors, agreed.[12] Orlando B. Potter, the Swallowtail Democrat and large owner of downtown real estate who often represented others with similar interests, doubted that Hewitt's proposal was acceptable under an 1884 state constitutional amendment that stated, "No county, city, town, or village shall hereafter . . . be allowed to incur any indebtedness except for county, city, town, or village purposes." Potter added that even if the city could construct a rapid transit system, it ought not to do so, because corrupt politicians would turn it into an invincible patronage machine.[13] Henry R. Beekman, an attorney, real estate heir, and member of the Real Estate Exchange who served as Hewitt's corporation counsel, prepared a brief arguing that Hewitt's plan was constitutional; he denied that it would degenerate into a mere mass of patronage.[14] But the Real Estate Exchange and the New York *Times* found Potter's arguments so persuasive that they backed off from their initial enthusiasm for Hewitt's plan.[15] The New York Central, wary of a new wave of criticism

against it as a monopoly, raised new questions.[16] With many real estate
investors and bankers resisting Hewitt and the commercial groups he
represented, with real estate groups deeply divided, and with Hewitt's
political resources dwindling rapidly, the state legislature refused to provide the necessary legislation.[17] But although Hewitt's plan fell by the
wayside in 1888, it ultimately formed the basis for the arrangement under
which the first subway was built after 1900.

Institutional, Technological, Physical, and Public Opinion Constraints before 1894

Hewitt himself attributed the initial defeat of his rapid transit plan to
"all the bad elements in this city, including the Manhattan Elevated
Railway and all the street railways who have so long abused the patience
of the public."[18] Yet so long as the "bad elements" included both real
estate developers who stood to gain from a rapid transit system and the
bankers who would necessarily provide the funds, Hewitt's plan had little
chance, whether Jay Gould and Russell Sage opposed it or not. Nor were
Hewitt's sometimes abrasive personality and declining stock as a practical
politician crucial to the delay. Institutional arrangements, technology,
topography, and public opinion imposed the real constraints.

Institutional arrangements for the planning, management, construction,
and operation of rapid transit facilities in Greater New York posed a
persistent problem. Hewitt himself recognized the difficulty: He based
his plan on a profound distrust of elected officials and private investors
alike. But if neither set of actors could be trusted, how could the public
need for transit be met?

Throughout the late nineteenth century the development of rapid transit in the cities of New York State was less the concern of the mayors
than of a succession of special-purpose rapid transit commissions. First
authorized in 1875, until 1891 these commissions were temporary bodies
appointed by the mayor at the petition of taxpayers.[19] The commissions
were empowered to define transit routes, secure the consent of abutting
property owners for the construction of the lines, and arrange for the
sale of the appropriate franchises to private corporations that would then
build, operate, and own transit facilities in return for retaining the five-
cent fare and for payments to the city. As historians Augustus Cerillo,
Jr. and Charles R. Cheape have recently observed, the law assigned these
commissions the task of promoting rapid transit, but did not authorize

them to provide transit services themselves, to monitor the performance
of the private operators, or to maintain a permanent professional staff
capable of evaluating existing service and planning for future improvements.[20]

Hewitt might have utilized the temporary commission approach in
1888, but he doubted that any corporation would invest its own funds
in a rapid transit system designed to serve a largely undeveloped area.
He also objected to the established practice of compensating transit corporations for their risk and for their acceptance of the five-cent fare with
the grant of an exclusive 999-year franchise.[21] Thus his plan required
new institutional arrangements; when he failed to secure them he had
to lay it aside.

The Tammany mayors who followed Hewitt, Hugh J. Grant and Thomas
F. Gilroy, could not think of pursuing his initiative. As the first products
of their organization to hold the office since the court house construction
scandals that had led to the ouster of the Tweed Ring, they had to be
very cautious in fiscal matters; they could not start out by proposing to
lead the city into a risky $50 million public works project. Seeking to
demonstrate that his organization now sought to cooperate wholeheartedly
with the city's taxpayers and bondholders, Grant retained Beekman in
the office of corporation counsel long enough to have him draft a new
bill empowering the mayor to appoint a permanent rapid transit commission and giving that commission some much needed new powers to pro-
ceed despite abutting owners' objections to the location of a route.[22] When
the Republicans who controlled the legislature made it party policy to
deny Grant any added powers and to kill his bill in 1889 and again in
1890, he used the old law to appoint a commission that included William
Steinway, the piano manufacturer and independent Democrat, and Samuel
Spencer, an associate of J. P. Morgan and a Republican.[23] Quickly concluding that no rapid transit system could be planned until the provisions
contained in Grant's bill had been passed, this commission issued a tart
report to that effect and disbanded itself in less than the sixty days that
the law allowed it for the selection of a route.[24] In the face of widespread
criticism from the 1890 commission and the business community at large,
the Republicans dropped their resistance. Early in 1891 Grant secured
the permanent commission he sought.[25]

Grant made Steinway the chairman of the new commission and added
Spencer; John Starin, a tug and steamboat millionaire and a Democrat;
Eugene Bushe, a Democratic railroad lawyer; and Frederick Olcott, the
mugwump president of the Central Trust Company, who was soon replaced by John Inman, a millionaire cotton broker, railroad entrepreneur,

and banker.[26] Taking the long-term perspective of a permanently established agency, this body hired two professional engineers, William
Worthen and William Barclay Parsons, and set to work to overcome the
constraints that had delayed action.[27]

Until the middle 1890s, technology placed the most severe limits on
rapid transit planning. Innovations came rapidly after 1888, and one of
the advantages of a permanent, professionally staffed rapid transit commission was its ability to keep up with them. Contemporaries believed that
New York City's long narrow shape forced its transit planners to seek
much faster speeds than seemed necessary in contemporary London, Berlin, Boston, or Chicago. In his 1888 message on the problem, Hewitt
called for "the highest speed yet attained on first-class railways, namely,
forty to fifty miles an hour."[28] The Steinway Commission in 1891 also
called for a speed of at least forty miles an hour, exclusive of stops.[29]
Such speeds were essential if upper Manhattan and the annexed district
were to be made accessible to middle-income commuters, most of whom
were unwilling to spend more than forty-five minutes getting to work.[30]
"Our object," Hewitt had asserted with uncharacteristic hyperbole,
"should be to develop as much of the annexed district as possible, in
order to get the benefit of taxation upon the increased value of property,
which according to the best authority, increases as the square of the
velocity of the travel."[31]

Yet as Hewitt himself understood, in 1888 only steam engines traveling
on solid ground could offer such speeds. The steam-powered elevated
railroads of New York City only made about ten miles an hour, partly
because the elevated structure that carried the rails could not take the
stress of higher speeds.[32] A surface road or an open cut might have provided
a solid foundation for the rails, but both were out of the question in a
narrow city whose surging traffic would brook no interruptions. A masonry
viaduct cutting through the city's long blocks between two avenues, seriously proposed, would have entailed an intolerable expense for the acquisi-
tion of property.[33] Since the City of New York owned most of its streets,
a shallow-cut subway located under the streets offered the cheapest and
most practical alternative. But steam railroads fouled the air in tunnels,
as New Yorkers knew from experience with the New York Central's Park
Avenue tunnel and with London's Metropolitan Line.[34]

If rapid transit technology suitable for New York City was not available
in 1888, Hewitt was correct in his belief that it was coming soon. A
man who always took pride in his knowledge of practical innovations,
Hewitt had followed the growth of electrical technology. He was prepared

for the news, later in 1888, that Frank J. Sprague's electric motors had successfully moved tram cars in Richmond, Virginia. In the next ten years trams would swiftly displace horses on the nation's streetcar lines.[35] But the early motors did not offer great speed. In 1892 the American Street Railway Association proposed that 10 miles per hour be adopted as the standard for streetcar motors. Sprague did not obtain an average speed of fifteen miles an hour until 1898, with a multiple-unit control system for the Chicago elevated line.[36]

Sprague did assert, as early as 1891, that speeds of 120 miles per hour had been achieved in experiments; he offered, in that year, to build a 200-horsepower electric locomotive "which will, under forfeiture, outwork any elevated railroad engine for speed, pulling capacity, steadiness of work, time of operation and continuous mileage."[37] The technological ideas may have been available, but Sprague had not yet demonstrated his ability to deliver the fast motor. When the New York Rapid Transit Commission's William Barclay Parsons studied the problem in 1894, the highest average speed of an electric rapid transit system then in operation was 16 miles per hour on the Liverpool Overhead Railway, a viaduct road.[38]

Even as electric motor technology was becoming available several physical factors—Manhattan's shape, street plan, and patterns of street use, together with long-established legislative and customary limits on the use of certain streets—placed a third set of constraints on rapid transit planners. New York City had only nine major north-south thoroughfares. Three of them—Second, Third, and Ninth (now Columbus) avenues— were already occupied by elevated railroad lines. The New York Central had a shallow-cut tunnel under Park Avenue from 97th to 42nd streets, and held a franchise to go further south (see map 8–1). The Rapid Transit Act of 1879 prohibited the construction of railroads over, under, or at street level along several streets in lower Manhattan, including Broadway below Murray Street, Second Avenue below Twenty-third Street, Park Row, and Nassau, Broad, and Wall streets.[39] Mayor Grant's Act of 1891 permitted an underground road or surface road, though it continued the prohibition against els, on these streets and on Madison Avenue as well, but it forbade the construction of any railroad at all along Fifth Avenue.[40] And it was generally understood that Central Park West, West End Avenue, Riverside Drive, and Lenox Avenue were reserved for luxury or at least upper-middle-income housing and were to be protected from excessive traffic, commercial development, and other intrusive activities. One result was to limit the density of population along these avenues. This,

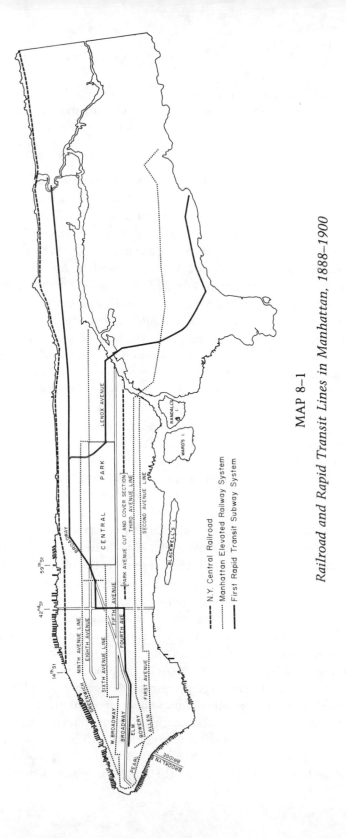

N.Y. Central Railroad

Manhattan Elevated Railway System

First Rapid Transit Subway System

MAP 8–1

Railroad and Rapid Transit Lines in Manhattan, 1888–1900

together with the marginal location of the avenues along Central Park and the rivers, made them poor choices for a rapid transit line, even in the absence of stout resistance from those who wished to reserve them for residential purposes.[41]

In a facetious letter to the *Record and Guide*, "Index" did propose that an el be built up Fifth Avenue, past the mansions of the Astors, Vanderbilts, Huntingtons, Potters, Whitneys, Goulds, Sages, Dillons, and other railway kings: The line would take Harlem and Westchester commuters through "a pleasant and attractive part of the city." But Fifth Avenue was sacred and the other residential streets were in no danger of invasion by rapid transit lines. People wanted to ride in the center of the island; the Manhattan Elevated Railroad Company's statistics showed much heavier traffic on Third and Sixth avenues than on Second and Ninth avenues.[42] Broadway below 59th Street was the great central artery as well as the great shopping and business street; it was the first choice of the Steinway Rapid Transit Commission and its successors.

Yet legal constraints prevented the selection of Broadway for the first subway and ultimately contributed to the oddly off-center, patchwork pattern New York's subway network eventually assumed. These legal constraints were an essential part of the institutional arrangements that dated from the 1870s. The 1891 Rapid Transit Act removed the prohibition against a subway under Broadway.[43] But an 1872 amendment to the New York State Constitution required that a rapid transit commission secure the consent of the owners of at least one-half of the value of all property abutting an urban street railroad before construction could begin. The 1875 Rapid Transit Act and all of its successors through the 1890s retained this requirement, providing that if such consents were not forthcoming, a commission might ask the supreme court to consider whether the road in question was in the general interest, and if the court agreed, to approve the route over the abutters' objections.[44]

Sponsored by Samuel J. Tilden and other Tweed-era Swallowtails, these laws were designed to protect property owners against corrupt officials and self-interested railway promoters. But by the 1890s they almost inevitably produced delay in New York City. On Broadway and some of the other prime streets, a very large portion of the property had fallen into the hands of the executors and guardians of estates, the trustees of charitable institutions, and large corporations, all of whom felt that their fiduciary responsibilities made it impossible to give their consent.[45] And those who owned properties individually often refused to give their consent out of fear that such action might impair their right to claim damages if they suffered injury from construction mishaps or other difficulties.[46] In 1891 and again in 1895, a failure to secure Broadway property owners' consents threw the matter into the courts.

In 1892 the court approved the Steinway Commission's routes: A west side subway up Broadway from the Battery to Fort George, continuing as an el up the Boulevard (Broadway) through the Annexed District, and an east side subway up Fourth and Madison avenues from Fourteenth Street to Ninety-sixth Street, then continuing up Madison and Jerome avenues into the Annexed District.[47] Following the procedures specified in the 1891 Rapid Transit Act, the commission put a 999-year franchise to construct and run a subway along these routes up for auction at the end of the year. But although every major investment bank and railroad syndicate examined the plans, no one was willing to submit a serious bid in 1892.[48]

Disappointed at this result, the *Times* and the *Record and Guide* noted that J. P. Morgan sat on the Manhattan Company's board of directors and that his partner, Samuel Spencer, sat on the Steinway Commission, and asserted that the commission's John H. Inman was a "railroad king" with close connections to the "Gould clique."[49] Perhaps it was true, these journals suggested, that the elevated railroad interests had frightened potential investors off or had made certain that the proffered franchise contained such restrictive terms that no investor would touch it.[50] These charges were probably groundless and may well have been intended more to discourage the commission from dealing with the Manhattan Company than to describe what had occurred.

The subway did threaten to compete with the els, and even to make them obsolete. But in the early nineties the technical and legal risks alone were sufficient to discourage investors. Jacob H. Schiff, one of New York's most respected investment bankers, had concluded that the venture was too risky for private capital in 1891, a year before the Steinway Commission put the franchise up for auction.[51] The *Record and Guide* itself had repeatedly concurred with this judgment.[52] No electric motor had yet demonstrated the necessary speed, power, and durability. No one could be certain that the tunnel could be adequately ventilated. The owners of abutting property had not relinquished their right to claim damages. And the commission's own engineers estimated the necessary initial investment at $55 million.[53]

Apparently persuaded that private capital would not accept the risks involved in its subway plan, the Steinway Commission, acting with what the *Times* and the *Record and Guide* thought was "almost suspicious" speed, turned to a new proposal from the Manhattan Company.[54] Jay Gould had died in early December 1892, and although George Gould had taken his father's position in the company the press now attributed effective leadership to J. P. Morgan. Confident that the subway would not pay and would neither "be sold, nor built," Morgan and his associates proposed that the Steinway Commission permit improvements to the Manhattan Company's existing els and authorize the construction of new els up the east and west sides.[55] Tammany Hall and some annexed district Republicans, as well as several real estate groups and most of the newspapers, urged the acceptance of this proposal as the only way to secure anything approaching rapid transit.[56]

Adopting a different response to the reticence of private capital, a committee of prominent "brokers, auctioneers, owners of real estate, lawyers, and builders" organized under the chairmanship of builder Richard V. Harnett at the Real Estate Exchange to resist the el extension plan and to press for municipal construction of the subway.[57] With the hearty support of Abram S. Hewitt, the *Times,* and the *Record and Guide,* this committee launched a campaign to persuade other economic elites that new els would not provide real rapid transit and that once in place they would "make its construction more than ever difficult."[58]

As this campaign began to make an impact, as more and more real estate owners and merchants concluded that only a subway could meet the need, and as labor organizations began to press for municipal ownership, even Tammany officials urged that the Manhattan Company be required to pay well for the privilege of adding to its lines.[59] At last the Steinway Commission, heavily influenced by its chairman and by John H. Starin, proposed that the Manhattan Company accept a franchise to build new lines on the east and west sides, but not on the avenues most likely to be used for a subway, and that it increase its payments to the city in return.[60] Reluctant to build its lines in advance of demand or to admit any obligation to the city, the company rejected this proposal.[61]

By September it was reported that the mayor and the comptroller had lost patience with the Manhattan Company; in December it was reported that "George Gould refused to contribute to Tammany's 'campaign fund' at the last election, and Tammany ha[d] withdrawn its 'protection'" for his company in the selection of jurors for damage suits as well as in the deliberations of the Steinway Commission.[62] Abandoning the effort to come to terms with the elevated system, the Steinway Commission turned to the William C. Whitney–Thomas Fortune Ryan group behind the Metropolitan Street Railway Company, to the New York Central and the New Haven railroads, and to others for rapid transit facilities in some form. But these interests were also unwilling to act, and then the Panic of 1893, which had begun on May 5, made it impossible to find investors in any quarter.[63]

The Argument for Public Finance

If private funds were not forthcoming, only public money could provide rapid transit. A compelling argument could be made for public investment. Hewitt had forcefully presented the case for his view that rapid transit would bring substantial benefits to the residents and taxpayers of the entire city in 1888, and others had kept it before the public. Public investments would make these benefits available at a lower price. As Jacob H. Schiff observed, if the city financed the subway out of municipal bonds backed by the city's ability to tax, the money could be obtained for 3 percent (or, some suggested, for as little as 2½ percent or even 2 percent). The bonds of a private corporation would have to pay at least 5 percent and for so risky an enterprise might have to pay more. In 1894, during the depths of the depression, the *Real Estate Record and Builder's Guide* suggested that corporate bonds would have to offer 6 percent.[64] Moreover, as Schiff argued, the chief investors in a private transit corporation would expect to issue stock as well as bonds and to receive at least 10 percent on their actual investment.[65] The higher cost of private money would in the end yield less adequate subway facilities, inferior service, and higher fares.

But the New York State constitution, in a clause designed to protect taxpayers from the consequences of corrupt or ill-advised deals between municipal officials and private corporations, forbade the city to loan either funds or credit to a private corporation. Orlando B. Potter had cited this clause in his influential criticism of Hewitt's plan in 1888, and there was little chance that the prohibition would be lifted.[66] Under these circumstances, to propose that the city invest in a subway system was to propose public ownership. Resistance to the notion of public ownership constituted another constraint that both delayed rapid transit planning and helped produce the hybrid policy that was finally adopted.

A wide range of economic and political groups objected to the idea of municipal ownership in 1893. As the *Record and Guide* observed, none of the directors of the Manhattan or Metropolitan companies had ever favored municipal construction or ownership, and it was "a common belief in Albany that the elevated road 'whacked up' most generously last fall in aid of Tammany Hall's campaign fund and as a consequence was promised protection from adverse legislation of any kind. . . ."[67] But narrow self-interest does not account for all opposition to municipal ownership, and even Tammany had more than one reason for its position.

The most principled and unbending opposition came not from Tammany but from Tammany's harshest Democratic critics, the *Evening Post* and the Brooklyn *Eagle*. Neither of these papers had yet followed Simon Sterne in recanting their orthodox adherence to the political economy of the Manchester School, and both denounced the idea of municipal construction as "paternal, communistic, socialistic."[68] Other Democratic voices were also raised in opposition. From 1888 to the end of his life in 1894, Swallowtail Democrat Orlando B. Potter continued to oppose municipal construction on principle, and to assert with Jacksonian enthusiasm that "the people had a right to invest in a new road" themselves.[69] The *Sun*, as cheerfully cynical as the *Post* was earnest, and the *Herald*, edited somewhat erratically from Paris by an aging James Gordon Bennett, also continued to favor the cause of private enterprise and did not hesitate to endorse the schemes emanating from the Manhattan Company.[70]

In view of the widespread Democratic opposition to municipal investment and the odious reputation Tammany had carried since the Tweed Ring, it would have been surprising if Tammany had not taken the position that it did. Tammany and non-Tammany Democratic officials had both made their views perfectly explicit. Following their party's long-standing rhetorical opposition to "monopoly" and its devotion to "free trade" and "home rule," these officials rejected municipal ownership as "undemocratic."[71] Mayor Gilroy's corporation counsel argued before the legislature that the city had no right to go into the transportation business.[72] Gilroy himself worried that a subway investment would bring the city's indebtedness up to its constitutional limit.[73] Comptroller Theodore W. Myers, a widely respected former County Democrat, told the *Record and Guide* that municipal ownership was opposed to the American way of doing things and insisted that the city had no more right to build a rapid transit line than to go into the butcher business.[74] These views suited the Manhattan Company. But they also fit well into a Democratic tradition that held a strong appeal for New York City's many small businessmen, as well as for Catholics and Jews who resisted any action that might strengthen the government and make it possible to impose Protestant values and practices on the city. Some Republicans also opposed municipal construction on *laissez-faire* grounds, and others objected to anything that might give New York's Democratic officials larger responsibilities or more patronage.[75]

But opposition to municipal ownership did not simply pit politicians and railroad interests against the public. After campaigning for two years for municipal construction of the subway and for a more active role for municipal government in general, the *Record and Guide* found that many real estate investors and merchants continued to resist its ideas. In their view, a municipality had fulfilled its responsibilities when it had furnished "sewers, police and fire service, common school education—the crude necessities of civilized life." To do more was to indulge in socialism, to fail to see that all state action constituted an evil interference with individual initiative, and to encourage the plunder of the public purse.[76] Views of this sort continued to be widely shared even after it had become clear that private capital would not invest in the subway. Disagreement between advocates and opponents of an active municipal government split the Board of Trade and Transportation and the Real Estate Exchange in 1893, preventing either organization from throwing its weight behind a new transportation initiative.[77]

The standard histories of economic thought in the United States suggest that advocacy for municipal ownership derived almost entirely from a single source: the Christian socialism of novelist Edward Bellamy and of academic political economists Richard T. Ely and Frank Parsons.[78] But in New York a number of very practical businessmen took up the idea, at least for major public works. Abram S. Hewitt, working out of a tradition that went back to DeWitt Clinton's Erie Canal, started the movement for public investment in the subway; between 1890 and 1894 the *Real Estate Record and Builder's Guide* led the campaign. Although the *Record and Guide* sought an intellectual justification for its challenge to the doctrines of Adam Smith and David Ricardo, it ignored Ely and Parsons and noted the "Bellamyites" only as people who gave municipal ownership a bad name.[79] Instead, the *Record and Guide* cited the views of such leaders of New York's mercantile elite as Hewitt and Simon Sterne, and, as a counterweight to received Manchester liberalism, the contemporary practice of British cities as described in the London *Economist* and in the works of Albert Shaw.[80]

Drawing on the example of London, Glasgow, Birmingham, Berlin, Hamburg, Paris, and other European cities, Shaw met the municipal minimalists on their own grounds of appeal to European experience and theory, and of devotion to property owners' self interest.[81] His works made him an important figure in New York as soon as he arrived in 1892.[82] What Shaw claimed to see in the large European cities was municipal ownership under Chamber of Commerce auspices. In Britain, and even more in Germany, property qualifications severely restricted the number of those eligible to vote in municipal elections, giving propertied persons control over municipal officials. German cities ran their trams, like their slaughter-houses and markets, at a profit, using the proceeds to pay for the general expenses of city government.[83] Picking up this theme, the *Record and Guide* observed that the municipal ownership of gas and light paid profits, and insisted that far from seeking paternalism in New York "we want the City of New York to go into the rapid transit business largely because it is so profitable."[84] But under universal manhood suffrage it was not politic to stress the profits that might be earned from transit fares. Even if it failed to earn a profit, "a good road would pay [the city] immensely were it to earn but bare operating expenses" because it would so greatly increase the value of real property—and hence of tax collections—all along the route.[85] "Indeed, even should dividends be earned, it would be more profitable for the city to spend the excess in betterments and . . . in reduction of the fare than to put it in the Treasury."[86]

These ideas held a strong appeal for uptown real estate developers, especially those whose property would become attractive to an upper-middle-income clientele as soon as the city made substantial investments in streets, parks, transportation, and other facilities. Even before the failure of the subway franchise auction, Frank R. Houghton, a leading developer of upper west side property, observed that the city owned "park systems . . . water supply systems . . . [and] harbor front and dock systems," and dismissed opposition to municipal investment in a subway system as "all this nonsense."[87] The Harnett Committee of leading real estate men, formed just after the unsuccessful Steinway Commission auction of 1892 to push for real rapid transit, asserted that the construction of a rapid transit line belonged with "the building of bridges, viaducts, sewers, aqueducts, or the opening and maintenance of streets, parks, and public places [as] a legitimate function of the municipal government." In the committee's opinion, transportation systems served "as necessary and vital public functions as the street, the sewer, or the water supply systems."[88] Citing the London County Council's takeover of street rail-roads, Harnett waxed enthusiastic. "The tendency of the present age is toward cooperation," he proclaimed, "and cooperation finds one of its expressions in municipal action."[89] The *Record and Guide* would go even further. The municipality had a positive duty to provide such luxuries as speedways and costly municipal buildings, because these contributed to the spiritual well-being of the people. "It is obvious," the journal asserted, "that without an orderly, dignified, and splendid city the highest type of citizen is impossible."[90]

Expressing a wish, or perhaps seeking to change opinion by asserting that opinion had already changed, the *Record and Guide* insisted that it regarded this view "as self-evident," one that had "long ago become commonplace among intelligent citizens, who far from disputing it had as it were incorporated it into the fundamental conception of government."[91] But if this was saying more than the facts justified, it did correctly capture the direction in which opinion was moving. So far as municipal investment in rapid transit was concerned, enthusiasm for increased municipal activity had gained increasing acceptance from the date of Hewitt's first proposal and the first publication of Albert Shaw's observations about European cities. The failure of the subway franchise auction, the refusal of the Manhattan Company, and the discouraging impact of the depression, all gave impetus to the change. By early 1894 most of New York's real estate men and merchants were ready to push for Hewitt's plan.

Labor also produced important support for municipal investment in rapid transit. But labor leaders sought specific benefits for workingmen that the real estate and mercantile elites did not favor, and they found their influence severely circumscribed. In his 1886 campaign Henry George had proposed just the reverse of the *Record and Guide*'s plan: Let the city tax real estate to pay for rapid transit, and let the people ride for free.[92] Real estate interests countered with the argument that "a cheap, well-located system of rapid transit would do much to relieve the congestion in the slums" by permitting the better off of the "poor people to live in a small house rather than in a small part of a big house." This was the pattern in other cities and a good rapid transit system would make it possible in New York. The very poor, of course, could not have their own houses, but even they would benefit from a reduction of density in the most crowded parts of the inner city.[93] Protestant and Jewish philanthropists and charity workers had come to much the same conclusion, and such leaders among them as Hewitt, Seth Low, and Jacob H. Schiff were among the most prominent advocates of municipal investment in rapid transit.[94] But neither the real estate interests nor the philanthropists were willing to propose a municipal subsidy for rapid transit.

A few of the city's more radical social reformers were willing to propose a subsidy, or at least to urge that "a new rapid transit system be built BY THE PEOPLE AND FOR THE PEOPLE," and to work with the labor unions to achieve this goal.[95] The most active of these social reformers was Charles B. Stover, an independently wealthy social worker who was closely connected with the University Settlement.[96] In January 1893 Stover appealed for union support for a plan, very much like that of the Harnett Committee, of opposition to el extensions and support for municipal investment in the subway. But Stover proposed to go farther. He called for municipal investment in, and ownership of, the rolling stock and generating equipment, as well as the hole in the ground and the rails. And once it had been built, Stover proposed that the subway "shall be operated by and at the expense of the city."[97]

In response to Stover's appeal, forty-seven independent, Knights of Labor–affiliated, and American Federation of Labor–affiliated labor organizations endorsed this proposal. Nearly all of these bodies represented the relatively well-paid skilled workers in the building, metal-, and woodworking trades. Several stated in their letters to Stover that their members used the els to get to work, yet at the time the unskilled and most of the semiskilled could not afford either the time or the five-cent fare. Stover had reached out to the aristocracy of labor, whose members might hope for employment in building a new transit system and might even hope to move to a new small house at the end of the line.[98] With this show of labor support, Stover prepared a rapid transit bill calling for a referendum on his proposals and requiring municipal action in the event of a favorable vote. He arranged for it to be introduced in the 1893 legislature. But once the bill had been introduced, it was ignored.[99]

Although Hewitt and the Chamber of Commerce had endorsed municipal investment in rapid transit in 1888, many of the city's merchants and most of its real estate developers and free trade Democrats had opposed the notion. By the end of 1893 the European practices publicized by Albert Shaw, the campaign of the *Real Estate Record and Builders' Guide,* and the failure of a series of efforts to attract private capital had converted many of these opponents, especially among downtown merchants and uptown real estate promoters. Municipal investment had become much more likely. With the appearance of deeply committed social reformers and of increasingly effective labor unions on the scene, a new question had been raised: municipal investment on whose behalf?

The answer was provided in 1894. At the beginning of the year banker and commission merchant R. T. Wilson put together a syndicate that proposed to build the subway if the city would lend it its credit, to the extent of $30 million in 50-year bonds at 3 percent, in return for a first lien on the road. When he appealed to the Chamber of Commerce, the Board of Trade and Transportation, and the Real Estate Exchange to support the constitutional amendment necessary to make this plan permissible, Wilson met a favorable reception from several influential men who, like Simon Sterne, were still wary of municipal ownership.[100] But in all three organizations a majority voted to reject Wilson's scheme in favor of Hewitt's, which the former mayor now revived in substantially the terms he had proposed in 1888.[101]

Wilson had singled out three business organizations in his quest for support. In advocating the Hewitt plan the Chamber of Commerce moved to establish its supremacy. The Chamber's bill established a new permanent Rapid Transit Commission, resembling the Steinway Commission in that it would have a permanent existence, a staff enlarged to include two lawyers as well as a group of engineers, and responsibility for laying out routes, securing abutting owners' consents, and finding entrepreneurs to purchase the franchises it offered. Hewitt's bill modified the existing Rapid Transit Commission in two respects. If it chose, the new commission would have the power to construct a rapid transit line with municipal funds, then lease that line to a private corporation for operation. And the commission's members were no longer to be selected by the mayor. Instead, the bill itself named them: the mayor, the comptroller, the president of the Chamber of Commerce, and five men named in the bill. All five of the latter were to be prominent members of the Chamber of Commerce. The commissioners themselves were empowered to fill vacancies in their ranks.[102]

These two changes were closely connected. If the city was to build the subway, the Chamber of Commerce wanted to retain for itself the power of supervision. In arguing on behalf of his proposal before the state legislature in 1894, Hewitt opposed any plan that would give the city's elected officials the power to build and operate a transit system: "The Chamber of Commerce will wait for rapid transit for a generation before it accepts rapid transit under such conditions," Hewitt declared. "Spare us that horror!"[103] Chamber of Commerce control appealed to the Republicans who controlled the legislature; if rapid transit was to be managed by the Chamber of Commerce, it would not fall into the hands of Democratic officeholders. Further, so long as the commission was constituted in this way, it was safe from the radical low-fare demands of Stover and the labor unions. It was also free from the influence of the Board of Trade and Transportation, which had a well-established interest in the close regulation of railroads and had advanced some very specific ideas about the form of lease the commission was empowered to offer.[104] Hewitt and the Chamber of Commerce rebuffed the Board of Trade and Transportation's proffered assistance in arranging to lobby the legislature in 1894.[105] And in 1896 when Stover sought, with the assistance of James B. Reynolds and other reformers as well as his labor friends, to persuade the commission to select him to fill the vacancy caused by the death of William Steinway, he was rejected in favor of Charles Stewart Smith, the leading Republican and former president of the Chamber of Commerce.[106]

In what was described as a concession to the labor interests, the legislature did include a provision for a referendum on municipal construction, as Stover had requested in 1893. But in the interim at least one Tammany official, Theodore W. Myers, had implied that he did not see how a member of his organization could come out for municipal construction unless the idea was first approved by the voters.[107] Even so, Hewitt and the Chamber of Commerce denounced the idea of a referendum as "anarchical" and briefly threatened to withdraw their support from the bill.[108] But Stover and the AFL had gathered fifty-five thousand signatures in favor of the measure, and the Chamber finally agreed to the referendum in return for legislative acceptance of its proposed commissioners.[109] Upper west side real estate interests also presented fifty thousand petitions. At the active urging of the Chamber of Commerce, the Produce Exchange, the Real Estate Exchange, and the labor group, Governor Flower signed the bill.[110]

That the referendum would receive an overwhelming majority was a foregone conclusion. The Chamber joined the labor and social reform groups, as well as Tammany, the Real Estate Exchange, the State Democracy, and the Committee of Seventy (which in turn had the support of the Republicans and the German American Reform Union) in working for approval, and almost three-quarters of the voters accepted their recommendation.[111] But no one could ever be quite sure what the vote meant. The ballot had contained just six words: For Municipal Construction of Rapid Transit Road. And despite their advocacy of the referendum, neither labor nor Tammany had a single seat on the Chamber of Commerce–dominated commission that was to put Hewitt's plan into effect.

As Charles H. Cheape has observed, the 1891 and 1894 rapid transit acts decisively modified public policy with respect to rapid transit in New York. They established a permanent commission, equipped with a professional staff, to plan, promote, and aggressively push the development of transportation facilities. The 1894 law permitted municipal investment and ownership, though not operation, for the first time.[112] But it should also be noted that the 1894 act made it certain that rapid transit planning would take place under the exclusive direction of the city's mercantile elite, as represented in the Chamber of Commerce. In an important sense the rapid transit commission of 1894 was the product of the sort of thinking that had informed the Tilden Commission in 1876. That commission's proposal for a municipal financial board elected by the taxpayers alone was never taken up. But Simon Sterne, who had served on the Tilden Commission, had later suggested that the same result might be achieved if the leaders of the city's great business and professional organizations were included, simply by virtue of their positions in those private bodies, in the municipal government.[113] The Rapid Transit Act of 1894 carried this idea into effect in the agency that was to handle the city's most important economic activities over the next thirteen years.

Legal and Financial Constraints, 1894–1900

Some of the constraints that had delayed the development of rapid transit in New York had been lifted by 1894, and definitive decisions had been reached regarding the identity of the responsible officials, the form of a possible municipal investment, and the general nature of the road that was to be built. But legal and financial constraints still remained to delay the start of construction and to force the route away from the location that most rapid transit advocates preferred. The contract for construction was not signed until 1900, and traditional accounts have assigned much of the responsibility to Tammany Hall. Tammany did not work to speed construction, but it probably delayed it only slightly—enough, perhaps, to permit a behind-the-scenes agreement that the contract would go to a Tammany contractor.

Other delays intervened before the Rapid Transit Commission could get down to the final selection of a contractor. As soon as the voters had approved the municipal construction referendum, the New York *Sun* brought suit enjoining the commission against the loan of its credit and alleging that construction of a rapid transit railroad was not a legitimate city purpose. The commission successfully defended this suit, using a brief, prepared by its counsel, Edward M. Shepard, that knowledgeable contemporaries called a major document in the history of the movement for municipal ownership. Following the logic suggested earlier by the Harnett Committee, Shepard argued that a railroad rapid transit system was essentially a street, and that it was clearly established that a city had the power to build, maintain, and lease its streets.[114] With the agreement of the courts, municipal ownership had in this case become the established policy of the state.

But the courts were less cooperative in another respect. Like its predecessors, the Rapid Transit Commission sought to design a system based on a trunk road up Broadway from City Hall. The owners of abutting property again refused to give their consents, and, under procedures that had been retained intact from earlier legislation, the commission asked the state supreme court to substitute its consent for that of the owners. But the court now refused. The judges demanded that the Rapid Transit Commission specify exactly what the road would cost. The commission estimated the cost at $50 million but the court accepted a hostile estimate that the actual cost would be twice as great. When the commission would not give ironclad assurances that its figure was correct, the court held that since municipal investment was contemplated, the commission's inability to specify the size of the investment raised a serious doubt as to whether the road could be completed within the city's constitutional debt limit. So long as such a doubt remained, a majority of the court would not substitute its consent for that of the abutting property owners, because the road might be started and then abandoned for lack of funds. Abutters might in that case suffer damages and inconvenience during construction that would never be made up, either in increased value for their property or in improved transit facilities for the public at large.[115] At the same time one judge refused to give consent because the commission's system did not provide what he considered to be adequate facilities to the uptown districts.[116]

The *Street Railway Journal* observed that entrepreneurs took such risks all the time.[117] And in fact municipal construction was contemplated largely because private entrepreneurs would not assume the risk. In ruling that investment in a rapid transit subway was too risky an undertaking for the city, the court in effect now rejected the justification for municipal ownership. The court also refused to accept legislative assignment of authority over the determination of routes and costs to a special commission and sought to reassert the power that judges had exercised in such matters since the early part of the century.

In the face of this ruling, the Rapid Transit Commission could only redraft its proposed transit system so that the projected cost was as small and firmly specified as was consistent with the provision of rapid transit for the entire city. To do this it abandoned the costly Broadway route, dropped a plan (which Hewitt had advocated since 1888) to provide easily accessible water, sewer, and gas utility pipe galleries alongside the subway, reduced the length of the uptown branches, and dropped an upper east side branch entirely. As finally proposed, the first subway line ran from City Hall up the line of Fourth Avenue (Park Avenue South) to Grand Central Station, across Forty-second Street to Broadway, and up into the Annexed District, with a branch from One Hundred and Fourth Street under Central Park and up Lenox Avenue to the Harlem River.[118] The court did approve this plan in December 1897, but it added a proviso that the commission must require any potential contractor to supply a permanent security bond in the amount of $15 million to protect the interests of the abutters and the city.[119] Two months later the commission persuaded the court to reduce the permanent bond to $1 million, but the court continued to insist on a construction bond until 1899.[120]

On the basis of a report on the latest equipment in use in Europe and in other American cities from William Barclay Parsons, who had become its chief engineer, and from a panel of distinguished consulting engineers called together by Abram S. Hewitt, the Rapid Transit Commission had meanwhile decided that the subway should operate on electrical power.[121] Technically it was ready to offer a contract for bids about April 1898. But there was to be one last delay.

The creation of Greater New York on January 1, 1898, had created a monumental set of problems for the city's comptroller. The greater city brought into a single fiscal unit more than forty separate municipalities and local authorities, each of which collected taxes or fees, provided services, and carried a debt. Many of these had kept their books somewhat informally; indeed, one of the arguments in favor of consolidation had been that it would bring all these financial activities into a single office where taxpayers and bondholders might keep them under close scrutiny. In sorting out this mass of detail, the comptroller was required, among other things, to protect the city's interest in the division of debt between the newly divided entities of Nassau and Queens counties and the Town of Hempstead, and in the assignment of burdens to the City of New York and to the four distinct counties that it now contained.[122] Tammany had nominated both the mayor, Robert S. Van Wyck, and the comptroller, Bird S. Coler, who now took on these responsibilities. Although many officials were following Boss Richard Croker in getting what they could out of the city, they wanted to be very careful to avoid the slightest appearance of financial mismanagement. Brooklyn and Kings county were already in debt up to the limit imposed by the value of their property, and with the other debts thrown in it seemed possible that the greater city itself might be barred from the credit markets. By April 1898 Mayor Van Wyck was ordering a halt to many public works that were already underway.[123] The *Record and Guide* suggested that his ulterior motive was to get rid of contractors selected under Mayor Strong, but the real estate journal itself had also suggested, in view of the delays imposed by the debt problem, that private capital carry out such improvements as the construction of municipal buildings, the extension of Riverside Drive, and the addition of new bridges, docks, schools, and transit facilities.[124]

It was also true that under Croker, Tammany was reluctant to cooperate with the Rapid Transit Commission. The commission was, after all, a state agency, dominated by the Chamber of Commerce, and imposed on the City of New York by a Republican legislature concerned to deny patronage to Tammany Hall. Its members were the same sort of Swallowtail Democrats and Republicans who had managed the city through state commissions between 1857 and 1870. And several of the commissioners were actively engaged in politics and would seek to use their service on the commission to build reputations on which they might run for high office, as Seth Low had done. It was not surprising that Croker stated, early in 1898, "As to what the Rapid Transit Board will do, I have but slight notion. I am not in the board's confidence. Moreover, I have but slight respect for it."[125]

State Republican Boss Thomas C. Platt was equally displeased with the men who sat on the Rapid Transit Commission. In the 1898 legislature he cooperated with Croker in pushing a bill to replace it with a new bipartisan commission appointed by the mayor and empowered to sell a franchise for a privately owned and operated subway system.[126] The legislature passed this measure, but in the face of a vigorous protest from all the interests that had favored the 1894 measure, including organized labor, Republican Governor Frank S. Black vetoed it.[127] Whitney's Metropolitan Street Railway Company picked up the idea of a privately owned franchised subway in early 1899, proposing to construct and operate such a line and to pay the city 5 percent of receipts in return for a perpetual franchise and tax relief.[128] But the municipal construction forces again protested. Governor Theodore Roosevelt announced that he would adamantly oppose the granting of any new perpetual franchises, and the Metropolitan withdrew its proposal.[129]

Citing the city's financial difficulties, Comptroller Coler refused to approve the sale of municipal bonds for a subway throughout 1898. But the commissioners felt that he was cooperating with them, and once he had sorted out most of the fiscal problems involved in the creation of the greater city he approved the commission's plan to issue the bonds in lots of $10 million.[130] Corporation Counsel John Whalen added a further delay as he refused until the fall of 1899 to give the necessary approval to the form of the contract that the commission proposed to offer. Contemporary rapid transit advocates impatiently attributed these delays to Tammany.[131] But as late as May 19, 1899, the commission's chairman,

Rapid Transit Commission President A. E. Orr signing Contract #1, March 24, 1900. Seated around the table *clockwise from lower left:* Charles Stewart Smith, Woodbury Langdon, John H. Starin, Orr, August Belmont, Jr., the building contractor John B. McDonald, Mayor Robert A. Van Wyck, Morris K. Jesup, and, with his back to the camera, Comptroller Bird S. Coler. Among the standees are engineer William Barclay Parsons, fourth from the left, and attorney Edward M. Shepard, leaning over to assist Orr. (Courtesy of the Museum of the City of New York)

Swallowtail Democrat Alexander E. Orr, confidentially assured Edward M. Shepard that he did "not believe that at any time since the present administration took office that they have been in a position to act in the line of rapid transit construction. . . . There has not been a day since they took office that they could have authorized the issue of a single bond for rapid transit purposes nor would there have been a single buyer for such a bond had they issued them." Nor did Orr "feel like blaming the Corporation Counsel severely . . . for he knew as well as we did that we could not act [and had in fact been] loyal to his promise."[132]

Once Whalen approved the contract, the commission acted quickly. It offered its contract in the fall of 1899 and in mid-January 1900 accepted the bid of contractor John D. McDonald, a man with good connections to Tammany Hall who had earlier shown an interest in transit.[133] McDonald did not have the necessary funds himself, but as soon as he had been awarded the contract he arranged for the support of August Belmont, the Rothschilds' American representative and a frequent backer of Tammany Hall. Belmont in turn arranged a syndicate that included banker and bonding contractor Andrew Freedman, who had often found it profitable to make Richard Croker a partner in his business.[134] After clearing up a last small delay with a telephone call to William C. Whitney, Belmont committed himself and the subway was on its way to completion.[135] Although no evidence on the point has come to light, it seems likely that the commission had set up some of these arrangements in advance. In any case it had been in close touch with Whitney before he proposed, in 1899, that his company undertake the job.[136]

Conclusion

In the formulation of rapid transit policy, New York's economic elites exerted by far the strongest influence. But those elites were deeply divided. One important line of division was ideological: It separated old-fashioned free-traders who favored a minimal role for municipal government from the increasingly numerous Clintonians who advocated a more active municipal intervention on behalf of commercial prosperity. The ideological division did not entirely follow the cleavages suggested by narrow self-interest, but those who had a special interest in the matter usually followed it. Thus the advocates of municipal construction included the great downtown merchants and the uptown real estate developers who sought the benefits of rapid transit, and their opponents included the various investors who sought profits through the supply of transportation services to the city and the owners of already valuable property along lower Broadway who feared that a subway might somehow damage the value of their real estate. All these groups were very wealthy; it would be difficult to show that one set was wealthier or represented older money than the other.

Most of those who belonged to these wealthy interest groups would greatly have preferred to work out their disagreements among themselves. But they could not do so and were forced to work through public institutions. Some of the wealthy groups did find that these institutions offered them some advantages. Established legal doctrine was hostile to an active economic role for municipal government and effectively protected the rights of property owners. The continuing devotion to an ideology of free trade and municipal minimalism on the part of many of New York's most influential Democrats and publicists also provided a resource to property owners and taxpayers who opposed municipal construction. And so did Tammany Hall's need to live down the appalling reputation for fiscal mismanagement that it had earned in the Tweed era—an era that was fast receding but whose memory was kept alive by hostile journals as well as by the more than occasional misdeeds of contemporary Tammany officials.

Yet the need for legislative action drove all the economic interest groups to seek political support. For several years the opponents of municipal construction looked to Tammany and, occasionally, to the Republican machine as well; advocates of the scheme found similar support among uptown residents and skilled workers. Once public opinion had shifted decisively in favor of the advocates, they were able to use the august forum of the Chamber of Commerce of the State of New York to hammer out a widely acceptable plan. The particular political circumstances of 1894—a year when Thomas C. Platt was seeking to bring New York City's independent and business Republicans into a GOP coalition that might hope to control the state, and when the Democrats were on the defensive—enabled the Chamber to define the problem and arrange for the passage of its solution. But even under these circumstances the Chamber's leaders found it necessary to accept a series of compromises: The Chamber's bill denied the Board of Trade and Transportation and the Real Estate Exchange places on the Rapid Transit Commission, but it included contract restrictions not unlike those that the Board of Trade had sought. The Chamber denied labor a place on the commission and refused to work for a lower fare, but it was forced to accept a referendum and a form of municipal ownership. And the Chamber-dominated Rapid Transit Commission acquiesced when a Tammany contractor, backed by a Tammany-affiliated group of bankers who had not hitherto been able to break into the lucrative traction business, won the subway contract. Nor did all the city's economic elites agree that the Chamber's approach represented their interests. Many conservative taxpayers and bondholders supported the *laissez-faire* position of the New York *Sun,* which argued that the construction of a rapid transit system was not a legitimate city purpose. And many property owners regretted that the policies and procedures favored by the Chamber's Rapid Transit Commission reduced the power of judges to determine the substantive merits of proposed rapid transit schemes.

Moreover, although the leaders of the Chamber of Commerce dominated rapid transit policy in the years between the formation of the Rapid Transit

Commission in 1894 and the creation of the Public Service Commission
in 1907, they were increasingly hard pressed by two quite different elites.
Political party leaders—Republican Thomas Platt no less than Tammany
Democrat Richard Croker—viewed the Rapid Transit Commission skepti-
cally almost from the date of its creation; on more than one occasion
they threatened to abolish it altogether. To defend its very existence as
well as to carry out its engineering and legal responsibilities, the commission relied more and more on professional and technical experts, who
gradually made up a permanent staff. By 1907 the Chamber of Commerce
leaders seemed entirely out of place on a commission intended to serve
all the people. Changing assumptions about government and a heightened
appreciation of the technical requirements for supervising a great rapid
transit system quickly led to the replacement of the Chamber-dominated
Rapid Transit Commission by a Public Service Commission in which experts were accorded a prominence much more in keeping with their real
importance.

CHAPTER 9

CULTURAL POLICY:

CENTRALIZING THE PUBLIC

SCHOOL SYSTEM

IN APRIL 1896 Governor Levi P. Morton signed into law a measure centralizing the New York City public school system. Abrogating arrangements dating to the 1850s, the school centralization law ended all neighborhood participation in school management. Henceforth, a single Board of Education, assisted by a powerful, professionally-trained Board of Superintendents, would take over "the entire administration of public education." In the eyes of contemporaries this was by all odds the most important decision affecting education, and one of the most important affecting cultural policy, taken for the metropolitan region during the 1890s. The New York centralization law had national importance; by making the metropolis one of the first of the large eastern cities to centralize its public schools, it helped establish the pattern that historian David Tyack has called the "one best system" as the standard administrative arrangement for the public schools of all large cities.[1] And locally, the school centralization law set important precedents for the reorganization of all New York City agencies into tightly organized if not always efficiently controlled units in which small numbers of professionally trained directors manage large numbers of civil service employees, most of whom have little chance of advancement.[2]

Organized by Nicholas Murray Butler, who was then an energetic young Columbia University dean, the school centralization movement was in a larger sense a product of the "earnest, public spirited class" that led the professions and managed the charities of Greater New York. Butler provided impetus and direction, but he acted in close conjunction with others, and he carefully shaped the movement to attract the widest possible support from men and women involved in the charity, Protestant outreach, Americanization, and municipal reform movements in Manhattan, and from Republicans across the state. As passed in 1896, the centralization law reflected a compromise among the preferences of these groups.

But the centralization movement also provoked stout resistance. Although it had its origins in the late 1880s, centralization encountered vigorous opposition in 1894 and 1895, and narrowly avoided what might well have been a decisive defeat in 1896. A wide range of groups opposed the move: teachers' and administrators' associations, labor unions, the existing Board of Education and its superintendent, city-wide Catholic and Jewish organizations, neighborhood ethnic and business associations, and the local Tammany and regular Republican organizations. The centralizers carried their point, but since the opponents continued to supply the schools with students, teachers, and administrators even after centralization had taken place, they were to a large extent able to turn the reform to their own purposes. The wide variety of ethnic and religious groups into which late nineteenth-century New Yorkers divided themselves often clashed over the implications of public policy for their basic cultural values. Seeking to establish a vigorous parochial school system, Catholics pressed against increasing Protestant resistance to public aid until a compromise, worked out in the 1894 State Constitutional Convention, produced a flat ban on state aid to religious schools but reaffirmed a long-standing policy of state aid to religious orphanages and other charitable institutions, many of which maintained schools for their wards or inmates.[3] Protestants of New England derivation, in the city as well as upstate, sought to establish the quiet, religious Sunday and to advance the cause of temperance by insisting on a state-wide ban on Sunday sales of alcoholic beverages—and on the futile effort to have city police enforce that ban in Irish and German neighborhoods where a friendly drink at the corner saloon was central to male social life. Sporting men and horse fanciers of British-American, Irish, and German background chafed against the opposition of genteel New Yorkers to the use of Central Park for trotting races and exhibitions.[4] The disagreements were multifarious. But the school centralization controversy stands out for the range of groups it affected, for the articulate arguments it evoked, for its duration, and for the widely accepted belief that schools played an important role in shaping their pupils' values.

The Public School System and Its Critics, 1888–1894

Nicholas Murray Butler and his associates required eight years to bring their movement to fruition. School centralization, like a number of other major reforms, had its origin during the mayoral administration of Abram S. Hewitt, who encouraged the private Public Education Society to look closely into school affairs and suggest improvements.[5] Hewitt failed of re-election and went out of office before the society could report. But early in 1889 it printed a memorial, drafted by Butler and others, urging the Board of Education to prepare an entirely new scheme for the administration of the public schools. The existing system of administration, the P.E.S. complained, was anachronistically decentralized and inefficient. Leaving too much autonomy to school principals, it allowed teachers to work without adequate professional supervision and leadership, deprived pupils of the benefits of up-to-date methods, and allowed the school buildings themselves to fall into neglect. A proper system, by contrast, would lay down strict lines of authority and vest all discretion in a small but powerful central administration.[6] Over the next six years Butler and his associates worked diligently to develop these general suggestions into a firm proposal, and to place that proposal at the top of the public agenda; once they had done so, they needed two more years to get it through the state legislature.

This delay is not surprising: The Public Education Society was calling for a complete transformation of New York City's public school system. Under arrangements that had been modified only in detail over a period of thirty years, New York's schools were managed in a casual, decentralized way that gave a more prominent place to laymen than to professional school administrators. For most children, New York provided just six years of free instruction. There were primary schools for children in grades one, two, and three; grammar schools for grades four, five, and six; night schools that offered grammar and high school instruction to working children and adults; a maritime trade school; a normal school for girls and the famous City College for boys.[7] But only a very small number, selected on the basis of competitive examinations, went beyond grammar school. These public schools served about three quarters of the city's children; Catholic schools enrolled about 13 percent, and about 12 percent attended other nonpublic schools.[8]

In the years since 1871 control over the public schools had been shared by a twenty-one member central Board of Education, aided by a superintendent, and twenty-five boards of ward trustees, each assisted by a clerk who was typically a grammar school principal.[9] Appointed by the mayor, the Board of Education made basic educational policy for the city and provided more general administrative supervision for the system as a whole. The superintendent served as a glorified clerk and general inspector to the board, and prepared a list of teachers eligible for appointment to particular schools.[10] In the 1890s Superintendent John Jasper was famous for his ability to recognize each of the system's 4,000 employees on sight; but he had never made a major policy recommendation.[11] The central board, aided by the superintendent, a few assistant superintendents and inspectors, managed the night and maritime trades schools; the normal school and City College had their own boards.[12]

But most responsibility for the primary and grammar schools that served the overwhelming majority of the children was given over to the ward trustees. Appointed by the Board of Education, the trustees acted under its oversight; but the trustees, who were laymen living in the ward where they held appointments, exercised broad administrative powers under the close but variable supervision of the central board. (See map 9–1, pp. 264–265.) The five trustees for each ward selected sites for new school buildings; let contracts for construction, repairs, and supplies; selected teachers from an eligible list prepared by the central superintendent; controlled teaching assignments and promotions; and advised principals on every aspect of school policy.[13] Their power over construction and repairs gave trustees in the rapidly growing uptown districts the opportunity to aid friendly contractors and real estate developers, but above all they valued their ability to determine who taught in the public schools.

Trustees exercised several controls over school personnel. A young woman who wished to become a teacher (fewer than 8 percent of the city's teachers were men in 1895) had to graduate from the Normal College or ask the chairman of a board of trustees or a school commissioner for a letter attesting to her moral fitness. She could then take an examination, administered by the superintendent of schools, for a probationary license to teach as a substitute. If, after at least sixty days in the classroom, she had won the confidence of the principals, assistant superintendents, and inspectors who had observed her work, she could take a second examination. Success in this test entitled her to a place on the list of persons eligible for appointment to a regular place. Only a principal could select her to fill a vacancy, but each of his selections had to be ratified by his board of trustees.[14] The trustees had an indirect as well as a direct influence over the process, because they had a voice in selecting principals for the schools in their ward and singled out one of those principals to serve as ward clerk, a post that might lead to further promotion to the central administrative post of assistant superintendent.[15]

Butler insisted that these arrangements "divided authority" and created "a system of political catch-basins" that "made the schools a splendid drill-ground for inefficiency, jobbery, and personal pulls." In his view the schools were controlled by an incompetent and corrupt "school ring," "a small clique of individuals who derive either prestige, power, or patronage, from the existing system." The members of the school ring, Butler asserted, should be described "anthropologically, not figuratively," as the "savages and barbarians" of Tammany Hall.[16] *The City Vigilant,* organ of the Reverend Dr. Charles H. Parkhurst, the anti-vice crusader, used similarly inflammatory language that compared a career in New York politics to one in the Catholic Church: The boards of ward trustees were "nurseries where political aspirants serve a novitiate, during which they prove to their superiors whether or not they possess the requisite indifference to public duty, and that subservience of spirit necessary to advancement in the career of machine politics."[17] *The Critic,* an independent Protestant weekly, charged that Tammany agents "hidden from view" among the trustees "can appoint scores of teachers and employ hundreds of workmen each year, exacting political support in return."[18] And Jacob Riis, in the midst of his career as a professional reformer and agent for the Good Government Clubs, added that Tammany Hall relied on the "school vote . . . the men friends and kin of teachers on whom the machine has a grasp, or thinks it has. . . ."[19] For Riis, school reform was part of "the battle against the slum"; another reformer added that "there are regions of the city where the American common school will not thrive if left to local influences."[20] The Reverend William S. Rainsford of St. George's Episcopal Church explained that this was so because the "American" middle class had abandoned the city for the suburbs, leaving immigrant districts in the hands of political hacks.[21]

This rhetoric reflected the professional, religious, and political sources of support for school reform and indicated the breadth of the social gap that lay between the reformers and their opponents. But it did not provide a fair account of the ordinary operations of the school system and it obscured the real issues at stake.

In fact, the ward trustees and their defenders belonged to New York City's increasingly cosmopolitan Irish, German, and old-stock uptown middle class. On the Board of Education, eight of the nine commissioners who supported the decentralized system in 1896 had attended public schools and colleges (making them unusually well educated for their time); seven had migrated from Ireland, Great Britain, Germany, Vermont, Illinois, or Ohio; at least four had amassed considerable wealth (three,

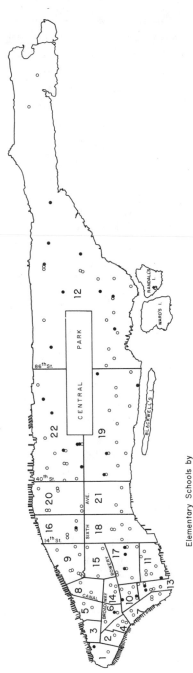

86thSt.

CENTRAL PARK

12

RANDALL'S I.

WARD'S I.

BLACKWELL'S I.

22

19

40thSt.

8 20

21

16

14thSt.

SIXTH AVE.

18

9

15

17

8

CANAL

BROADWAY

5

6 14

10

11

BOWERY

3

2

4

7

13

1

Elementary Schools by
Date of Construction

○ Before 1890

● 1890 – 1895

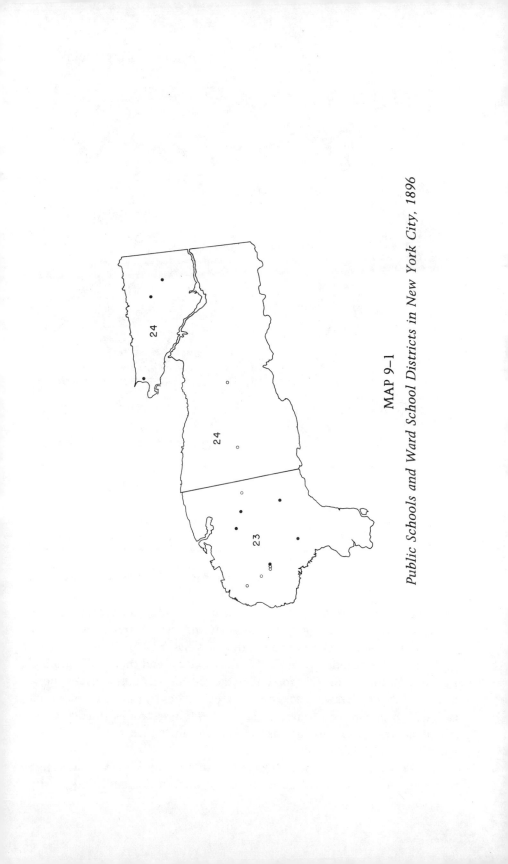

MAP 9–1

Public Schools and Ward School Districts in New York City, 1896

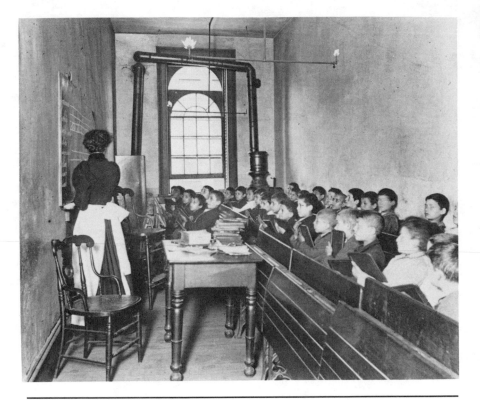

Dark, overcrowded classroom in the temporary Essex Market School, photographed by Jacob A. Riis, 1893. By selecting a room in which it was necessary
to use gaslight at midday, Riis contributed to the campaign to discredit the
decentralized school system. (Jacob A. Riis Collection, Courtesy of the Museum
of the City of New York)

including J. Edward Simmons, the widely respected president of the Fourth
National Bank, were millionaires). Most of these members of the board
lived in the recently built middle- and upper-middle income rowhouse
and apartment districts of upper Manhattan.[22] By contrast all but one
of the board's six advocates of centralization had grown up in New York
or southern New England, four in families able to send them to Columbia,
Harvard, Williams, or Yale for undergraduate or graduate degrees; none
was of Irish or German background; and all held prominent places in
the city's professional or mercantile elites.[23] These groups sought to use
school centralization to increase their own influence over the public
schools.

The ward trustees themselves were less wealthy and less well educated
than their defenders on the Board of Education, but they also were clearly

Children in front of a school on Stanton Street, 1898. Uninvolved in the centralization campaign, Byron recorded a school that was the finest structure on its block. The Riis Collection contains no photograph of a well-kept public school in the 1890s. (Byron Collection, Courtesy of the Museum of the City of New York.)

middle class in background. Angrily refuting charges that the trustees were unworthy of their places, their defenders asserted in 1896 that among the 118 trustees currently in office there were 20 lawyers, 1 judge, and 1 ex-judge; 18 doctors; 6 bank presidents and 2 tellers; 7 retired merchants; and 57 "Merchants, Real estate dealers, Contractors, Clothiers, Grocers, etc. etc., but no manufacturer or dealer in Malt or Spiritous liquors."[24] Others who spoke out in defense of the trustee system had a similar social profile. Of fifty-nine petitioners, meeting organizers, and the like whose occupations can be identified, only eight or nine engaged in more than a local business or profession, but at least twenty-six provided legal, medical, commercial, banking, or real estate services for Harlem and the Bronx. Several of these twenty-six men had achieved local notability; among them were three of the 1895 founders of the North Side Board

of Trade (a chamber of commerce for the Bronx) and the presidents of
the Twelfth Ward Bank in Harlem and the Twenty-third Ward Bank in
the Bronx.[25]

The defenders of the decentralized system were perhaps more distinguished by their cultural and voluntary-association activities than by their
occupations. At least fifteen of the thirty-two for whom more than mere
directory information is available played leading roles in a variety of organizations in Yorkville, Harlem, or the Bronx. Four belonged to German
singing and social clubs such as the Arion, Liederkranz, and Beethoven
societies. Four others were among the leaders of the Harlem Library, the
Harlem Law Library, and the Harlem YMCA. Six had organized and directed such North Side institutions as a Masonic lodge, the Bronx County
Bar Association, and the Bronx Society of Arts, Sciences, and History.[26]
James H. Spellman, the longtime proprietor of a Highbridge (Bronx) liquor
store and a member of the local Knights of Columbus and the Bronx
Sons of Erin, may be typical of the less prominent men who urged the
retention of the trustee system but whose other activities and affiliations
are impossible to trace.[27] Spellman was joined in the anti-centralization
lists by Thomas Rush, who was endorsed for police magistrate in 1895
by the City Vigilance League as an "esteemed . . . school trustee . . .
lawyer of high standing" and one who had been "prominent in the reform
movement."[28]

The trustee system also enjoyed the support of leaders in all the city's
major religious groups. Sponsors of a pro-trustee meeting in Melrose, the
Bronx, claimed that among their vice presidents was "every minister north
of the Harlem River." Eight Bronx ministers did sign a petition circulated
at such a meeting, and they joined with Catholics and Jews to oppose
centralization. Isaac Fromme, a member of the Tammany executive committee and a leader of B'nai B'rith, was supported in his opposition to
centralization by rabbis Dr. De Sola Mendes (vice president of the New
York Board of Rabbis) and Aaron Wise (like Mendes, a member of the
Hebrew Free School Association).[29] Frederick R. Coudert, who delivered
the most impressive single speech on behalf of the trustee system, served
repeatedly throughout the 1890s as the semiofficial spokesman for the
Catholic Archdiocese of New York.[30] The religious diversity of opponents
of reform may be indicated by data on the affiliations of the trustees:
seventy-six were Protestants, thirty-four Catholics, and eight were Jews.[31]

The rapidly growing middle-income communities in the northern sections of New York City afforded opportunities for political as well as
commercial, social, and religious leadership. Ward school boards did play
an important role in local politics, one their defenders did not deny.

But they indignantly did deny that the ward trustees were "ignorant Tammany heelers." Thirty-nine trustees had in fact obtained their positions as Tammany Democrats, but twenty-nine were independent Democrats, thirty-nine were Republicans, one was a Good Government man, and six were "women, whose politics don't count."[32] Bronx and Harlem party leaders, Republican as well as Democratic, joined to oppose centralization because it would prune back the Jacksonian profusion of political offices that provided them with patronage and the opportunity to offer conspicuous service to their communities. Most of these political leaders had first demonstrated their own abilities in minor positions; at least half of the thirty-two leading defenders of the trustee system for whom information is available had held such offices as collector of city taxes, member of the Board of Improvement of Park Avenue above 106th Street, or commissioner of street improvements in the 23rd and 24th wards. John Spellman (brother of James?) had long held the post of watchman at Highbridge.[33]

Tammany had no monopoly on the production of these petty local officials. Among the sponsors of mass meeting protests against centralization were Daniel P. Hays, the president of the independent Harlem Democratic Club; Charles W. Dayton, a founder of that club, Postmaster of New York City under Cleveland between 1893 and 1897, and a supporter of Henry George in the 1897 mayoral election; William H. Ten Eyck, chairman of the executive committee of the North Side Republican Club; James Lee Wells, one of Republican Boss Thomas Platt's closest associates in the Bronx; John Homer Hildreth, a lawyer who belonged simultaneously to both the elite downtown Republican Club and the North Side Board of Trade; and Louis F. Haffen, the successful 1897 Tammany candidate for president of the Borough of the Bronx.[34] Among the Republicans most supporters of the trustee system were Germans or Jews allied with Platt in his battle against the wealthy and increasingly nativist Yankee Republicans of the Union League Club. Edward Lauterbach, a German Jew who was Platt's ally as chairman of the New York County Republican Committee, had his wife join him in speaking out against centralization in Albany as well as in the city.[35] Among the thirteen prominent Democrats who helped organize pro-trustee mass meetings were representatives of every faction in the party, with the exception of the wealthier Cleveland Democrats. All of the pro-trustee politicians had strong ties to their local communities, serving prominently in Catholic, Protestant, or Jewish organizations, and in uptown social clubs as well.[36]

Under the leadership of these men and women from New York City's old-stock, German, and Irish middle classes, the public schools followed clearly discernible patterns of resource allocation and educational policy. Reformers complained that the decentralized system encouraged "incessant wrangling" over money between the central and the local boards and indeed there were continual disputes over the location of new school buildings and the size of the repair budget.[37] But the reformers' chief objection was that the wrong sort of people managed the decentralized schools, and managed them in the wrong sort of way. In the course of defending themselves, the trustees and their allies described their personnel and educational policies in revealing detail.

The central Board of Education controlled financial arrangements within the decentralized system. The board established a single set of salary levels for the entire city and allocated certain operating funds among the wards on the basis of average attendance at a uniform rate—$9.71 per pupil in 1896.[38] These matters were straightforward. But conflict did arise over the allocation of funds for the construction and repair of buildings. School reformers insisted that the decentralized system had failed to provide sufficient classroom space; in 1894 they repeated the estimate of James A. Scrymser, of the Association for Improving the Condition of the Poor, that as many as 163,955 school-age children "could not find seating in our public schools."[39] Scrymser, Riis, and others believed that most of these excluded children lived in the downtown tenement-house districts. The city's rapid growth and the authorities' reluctance to spend money had indeed created a serious problem of overcrowding in the schools, but the reformers exaggerated it. A special school census in 1895 found that only about 50,000 school age children were actually unaccounted for. Over 62,000 attended nonpublic schools, and just under half that number were employed.[40] Not all the 50,000 had been excluded from school. Some may well have completed their six years, and others were probably working, although their parents did not admit the fact to the policemen who took the census. But the president of the Board of Education himself agreed that the schools needed places for at least 20,000 more children.[41]

The Board of Education was already seeking to correct this situation; it repeatedly pressed the municipal authorities who controlled its budget for more construction money. But Tammany mayors in the early nineties felt they had to prove that they could run the city cheaply, and they refused to give the board as much money as it wanted.[42] In allocating the construction funds that it did have, the board favored the uptown wards that lobbied most effectively and produced the strongest support for the decentralized system, but gave more than lip service to its stated policy of erecting "some of the best schoolhouses in the poorest parts of the city."[43] Between 1890 and 1895 the five uptown wards added about 153,000 people; the Board of Education supplied them with nineteen new schools and seven new additions. During these years the lower east side added 58,000 and received seven new school facilities. On a gross per capita basis, uptown districts received one new school for each 5,900 new people; the lower east side, one for each 8,300.[44] The result was apparent in primary school classrooms: On the lower east side twenty of twenty-five primary schools (80 percent) had an average attendance of more than forty-five pupils per class; uptown, thirty-two of fifty-seven (56 percent) were similarly crowded.[45] (See map 9–1.)

In general the children who lived in wealthier neighborhoods had a better chance of attending uncrowded schools, but primary schools had very large classes in all parts of the city. On the lower east side the crowding problem was the result of cultural patterns as well as rapid immigration and poverty. With only 12 percent of its children in Catholic or other nonpublic schools (compared with 18.3 percent uptown and 20 percent or more in half the wards) the lower east side relied more heavily than any other region of the city on the public schools.[46] Children who were neither at work nor in school were distributed more evenly; according to the 1895 school census the proportions ranged from 14 percent to 18 percent in the wards of the lower east side, from 12 percent to 17 percent uptown, and from 8 percent to 18 percent over the entire city.[47]

Reformers also asserted that under the trustees too many schools were dirty and in disrepair. Like the demand for more school buildings, this criticism also reflected a concern of the Board of Education itself. In May 1894 School Commissioner Charles C. Wehrum complained that forty-three schools, located in all parts of the city, needed repairs to correct poor sanitary conditions.[48] The reformers saw in Wehrum's complaint an indictment of the decentralized system, but it also revealed that the system had some built-in checks and balances. The Board of Education asked Dr. Moreau Morris of the Board of Health to examine the schools Wehrum had singled out; he reported in mid-January 1895 that in eighteen cases he could find nothing wrong; that in seventeen cases the necessary repairs had been made; and that fifteen schools still needed repairs. Morris concluded that nine of these last, including four schools in uptown Ward 12, suffered from "dangerously unsanitary conditions" that required immediate attention.[49]

School reformers and their opponents disagreed much less over the allocation of material resources than over the nature of administrative policies and the relationship between the schools and their publics. Although Butler and his associates exaggerated the Tammany influence and perhaps the degree of sheer incompetence in the schools, they did not fundamentally disagree with the defenders of the decentralized system as to the facts of established administrative practices. Butler and others used strong language during the centralization campaign. One member of Mayor Strong's cabinet sententiously declared that "the education of the masses is recognized in all civilized communities as the very foundation of the social structure. . . . Nor is it a good thing in a city like this so largely impregnated with foreign influences, languages, and ideas, that the schools should be controlled locally, for in many localities the influences that would control would be unquestionably un-American."[50]

But once the centralization battle had been won, reformer James B. Reynolds, who as a ward trustee on the lower east side had learned about the system at first hand, defined the issues in more temperate terms. As he put it, "the local boards—in the downtown districts—were composed of local politicians, and their independence and intelligence were not high." And "whenever Tammany is in power teachers find that to secure an appointment or promotion it is well to see certain leading politicians." Yet Reynolds added that while "politics influences school officers in naming teachers . . . , this is probably more personal than general politics. . . . The bad results of political influence . . . are more because of the ignorance of the politicians than because of any intent to degrade the system." In Reynolds's view an equal "evil" in the old school system followed from "the American idea that any man is good for anything if he will only have sufficient enterprise and sufficient confidence." As a result, the decentralized system failed to rely on "first grade experts" or to assign "full authority in their special departments" to such experts as it did have.[51]

Defenders of the trustee system cheerfully conceded many of these points, insisting that what the reformers saw as vices were in fact virtues. The defenders denied that Tammany exerted a pervasive influence over the schools or that the trustees were incompetent. They did not advocate the erection of separate and distinct social systems for the city's several ethnic and religious groups; on the contrary, they insisted that they fully shared the reformers' desire for the creation of an ethnically harmonious, orderly, well-educated citizenry in New York. They did disagree with the reformers about the policy most likely to promote that goal. They argued that they, and not the reformers, should set the terms upon which members of the city's diverse communities would compete for mobility into a single, unified society.

President Robert Maclay of the Board of Education spelled out the key point in an 1896 address:

> New York is a peculiar city. It is a cosmopolitan city. If you do away with the trustee system you do away with the people's schools. The trustees are in touch with the schools and none others are or can be but those who live in the locality of the schools. We have a peculiar population, made up of all nationalities. They are people whose children we want to get in our public schools. There is a fear on the part of these people that we are going to interfere with their religion. If we have ward trustees representing all classes confidence will be maintained.[52]

Henry S. Fuller, editor of *School,* a weekly addressed to the principals and assistant principals at what might be called the middle-management level of the system, went even further. Fuller argued that the trustee system not only served to "maintain the local interest of the people in the schools" but also gave "rise to an active emulation in school districts," and stimulated "a commendable interest in the public schools and a just pride in the public service." These were virtues that "a republic should desire to foster rather than to eradicate."[53] Frederick Coudert added that the trustees, who were "interested in their own neighborhood, knowing the teachers' parents, familiar with the record of the families living about them" found that the decentralized system lifted their sights above the level of petty parochialism. "Animated by a just and natural pride in the success of schools peculiarly their own," he argued, the trustees strove "to excel their rivals in friendly competition because of this very local pride which makes success personal to themselves."[54] Charles Strauss, a school commissioner who was also a member of the Tammany Hall executive committee, put the point in still another way: New York's diverse ethnic and religious groups would inevitably come into conflict over educational policies, he thought; in a decentralized school system that permitted local trustees to interpret system-wide policy, intergroup conflicts could be "harmonized" at the neighborhood level, so that they did not spill across the city as a whole.[55]

In practice, the trustees served these purposes chiefly through their role in the selection of teachers. Reformers charged that the strong role of the trustees made professional schoolmen wholly subservient; as James B. Reynolds put it in 1896, "introduced by a trustee and recommended by a principal, at the request of the trustee [,] a teacher is very sure to pass for the eligible list" from which the trustees could appoint her to a permanent position.[56] Reynolds believed that it was necessary to eliminate the ward trustees in order to make way for the selection of teachers by rigorous examinations administered by trained professionals. Defenders of the trustee system replied that examinations for the eligible list were already managed carefully and honestly, and that the trustees respected the professional judgments of superintendents and principals. More important, in their view, was the fact that examinations could measure only the "scholastic achievements" of prospective teachers. Observing that the "manners, morals and the general personality of the individual" also affected her ability to teach, they maintained that "as to these laymen are not only good but generally the best judges."[57] If laymen might make religion or ethnicity or politics the criterion for judging a candidate's manners and morals, so might a professional superintendent. "On grounds of expediency," defenders of the trustee system preferred to leave such judgments in the hands of numerous boards of local laymen.[58] On the neighborhood level, compromises might be quietly worked out; school commissioner Jacob Mack, who favored the reform, recalled that in one uptown ward the Irish trustees always nominated German teachers and the German trustees returned the favor.[59] These were delicate matters. To concentrate "so much labor, power and responsibility in the hands of the Superintendents" was a dangerous idea in the heterogeneous metropolis.[60]

The evidence suggests that the trustees did in fact play the sort of harmonizing role their defenders attributed to them. At the very least, everyone connected with the schools accepted this theory of the trustee's role. The same arguments were repeated over and over again, with great consistency, not only by the trustees and their neighborhood allies, but also by spokesmen for almost every professional employee of the system. *School*'s Henry Fuller described the trustees as "mediators between parents and teachers, between teachers and principal, in adjusting the innumerable differences and details of a great school system."[61] Leaders of the teachers' and the principals' associations agreed. Jonathan T. Nicholson of the Male Principals' Association stated that when he taught on the lower east side "hardly a day passed . . . when one or another of the trustees was not a visitor to the school, in the interest of the children. . . . All was harmony, the trustees were known to the parents in this community, the children knew them as their friends."[62] Matthew J. Elgas of the New York Teachers' Association, Hester Roberts of the Primary Principals' Association, Mary Tate of the Female Grammar School Principals' Association, Elijah D. Clark of the Male Principals' Association, Mary A. Magovern of the Primary Teachers' Association, and half a dozen others, representing similar organizations, agreed.[63] The leaders of these organizations were all established in their positions; many of them were active in efforts to raise teachers' salaries between 1895 and 1900, and they appeared frequently in the pages of *School*.[64] The teachers seem to have shared their views. Nearly four thousand teachers crowded pro-trustee mass meetings, and the teachers gathered a hundred thousand signatures on anti-centralization petitions.[65]

Butler and his associates asserted that coercion and scare tactics, not sincere conviction, accounted for the teachers' defense of the trustees. But despite several years of effort, Butler was unable to discover any major scandals involving the trustees. No one even suggested that teachers were asked to contribute to political campaigns, a standard practice in Philadelphia.[66] Nor did Butler build a constituency among the teachers. Fear of reprisal might well have prevented teachers from publicly endorsing reform legislation,[67] but the energetic and nearly unanimous opposition to reform described by the press and conceded by the reformers themselves suggests that most teachers preferred the decentralized, trustee-managed system to the proposed alternative. Had the lay officials been entirely arbitrary and incompetent, had teachers stood to lose their jobs every two years on the election of a new mayor, or had their classrooms been universally as foul and overcrowded as the reformers charged, many more teachers would surely have worked covertly with the reformers. At the very least, such conditions would have discouraged the teachers from attending the mass meetings and working so hard on the petition drive. It seems more reasonable to attribute the teachers' defense of the trustees to their understanding of their own occupational and community interests than to unscrupulous Tammany manipulation.

In practice the decentralized administration of the trustees produced mixed results. Joseph M. Rice, a doctor who had studied education in Jena and Leipzig before writing a series of scathing critiques of American school systems for *The Forum* in 1892 and 1893, distinguished between the quality of work in New York City's primary and grammar schools. What he described as the typical primary school drew his most vigorous condemnation: "a hard, unsympathetic, mechanical drudgery school, a school into which the light of science has not yet entered." In the much less crowded grammar schools (grades 4, 5, and 6), by contrast, he found "quite a number of principals . . . who are alive and active, and who exert an excellent influence upon their teachers, and of their own free will have developed very good schools."[68] No one denied that the primary schools stressed order; no one suggested that local officials resisted the use of public schools to train children to become disciplined workers.

The trustees of Ward 17 on the lower east side, where many students had immigrated from Germany, placed a clock on Primary School 26 as "a constant reminder to the pupils to be prompt in their attendance." Throughout the 1880s and 1890s, schools all around the city gave out awards for "Industry, Punctuality, and Good Conduct" or for being "Regular, Punctual and Obedient."[69] According to Henry G. Schneider, who taught in one of the uptown grammar schools, Rice both exaggerated the emphasis on rote drill in New York City classrooms and underestimated the difficulty of maintaining discipline and the need for providing children with simple, carefully ordered lessons.[70]

In an indirect way, *School* explained how tradition and financial constraints, not the trustee system, combined to produce the mechanical classrooms of New York's primary schools. Referring in early 1894 to a recent statement by Harvard President Charles William Eliot, *School* agreed that "a young woman with fifty-six pupils in her class-room has a task before her which no mortal can perform. She may hear the lesson out of one book for all the fifty children during the session of the school; she can keep a certain amount of watching over the children who are not reciting, provided the grading is perfect or nearly so, and she will effect a uniform result with which we must be satisfied." But, *School* went on in further agreement with Eliot, the "new ideas of teaching . . . are entirely different. They are exhaustive. They prove a constant drain on the vitality of the teacher. They require her to be continually on the alert, with constant enthusiasm and sympathy, not only with the subject which she is teaching, but with the pupils themselves." Teaching of this sort was impossible with classes of fifty. President Eliot proposed to meet this difficulty by doubling the number of teachers, setting the standard class size at thirty or even twenty-five. The results, *School* agreed, would be obvious in the children: "their interest would be reached more directly, and their minds more fully, more easily, and more thoroughly developed." But how was the money for all the new teachers to be obtained, when most people did not "fully appreciate the real value, importance, and extent of the teacher's duties?"[71]

The Pro-centralization Coalition

For three years after the 1889 publication of the Public Education Society's memorial on school reform, Butler and his associates made little headway. But it was increasingly clear, even to those who defended the decentralized

system, that reorganization was necessary. The unchanging ward boundaries made less and less sense for school administration: By 1895 Ward
2 had only 112 school-age children, while Ward 22 had 32,741, Ward
19 had 46,797, and Ward 12 had over 70,000.[72] Yet each ward had one
and only one board of five school trustees. The accumulated political
and policy disputes of twenty-odd years had loaded an extraordinary number of checks and balances onto the system, making it difficult to accomplish even the simplest routine tasks. Yet the schools were under strong
and increasing pressure to add a wide variety of new programs: Kindergartens, manual training, high schools, and numerous after-school and summer vacation activities all had vigorous support by the mid-nineties. In
response to these pressures, Mayor Thomas F. Gilroy appointed a special
School Law Revision Commission in the autumn of 1893 and charged
it with the task of devising a new plan of administration for the city's
public schools. This action, followed closely by a substantial increase
in Republican strength in New York State, gave the reformers the opening
they needed.

The Gilroy Commission concluded that school systems in other cities
benefited from "swifter and more efficient exercise of administrative powers than is possible in New York" and proposed a set of remedies quite
similar to those urged by the Public Education Society in 1889. Adopting
the approach recommended by the leading school administrators of the
time, the commission made professional management the key to its
proposal:

> . . . the whole matter of the course of instruction, the management of the
> classes, the examination thereof, the recommendations for appointment, in a
> word, the entire administration of public education itself, should be confined
> to a body of experienced superintendents fully competent to discharge these
> delicate duties and sufficiently numerous to meet the requirements of our
> great city and constantly growing school population.

The commission suggested that twenty superintendents would be "sufficiently numerous" and proposed that Manhattan and the Bronx be divided
into twenty school districts of equal population, and that each new district
be placed under a single district superintendent. Each district superintendent would have full charge of his own area, but would be required to
meet once a week with the other district superintendents and to accept
the ultimate authority of a single top superintendent of schools for the
city as a whole. The commission proposed to reduce the powers of the
Board of Education and the local trustees very sharply, but it did not
suggest that these lay officials be eliminated. Instead, each district was

to have a board of trustees, empowered to meet quarterly to consider the quality and adequacy of school accommodations in its district.[73]

While Mayor Gilroy's school commission deliberated, Joseph M. Rice's muckraking articles on the sorry state of public education in American cities appeared in *The Forum*. The timing won Rice a considerable audience in New York, making his reform program especially significant. Rice defined priorities that Butler and his associates consciously rejected.

Rice agreed with the organized reformers in calling for tighter management, stricter separation of professional administration from lay influence, and stronger leadership from the superintendent. But in contrast to the others he thought that the public schools already suffered from excessive size and overcentralization. Rice believed that the superintendent should be above all an inspiring teacher: "if the superintendent is an educator and spares no pains in endeavoring to improve the minds of his teachers, a few years will suffice to raise the standard of the schools, *provided that the number of teachers in his charge be not too great.*" Teachers were most likely to improve, Rice argued, if they helped to develop the curriculum and pedagogy for their schools, meeting frequently, under a stimulating leader, to exchange ideas and evaluate their work. No superintendent could provide this sort of leadership for more than 400 teachers, he thought, and so he recommended that Manhattan and the Bronx be divided into at least ten largely autonomous school districts, each headed by a district superintendent who should possess "all the powers and responsibilities of a city-superintendent."[74]

In creating districts as in defining the roles of teachers, principals, and superintendents, there was a subtle but fundamental difference between Rice and the other reformers. Rice stressed the need to provide stimulating leadership and to encourage teachers to improve their work; Butler and his associates stressed the need to impose tighter management and control from the top. Rice sought to enhance the professional roles of teachers and principals; the leaders of school reform in New York proposed to turn the schools over to professional administrators and to treat teachers and principals as municipal employees who ought to be made subject to the discipline of a streamlined bureaucracy.

The school reformers stressed administrative centralization, not substantive reform, partly because they had to assemble the largest and most effective possible coalition to support their plan. The members of their coalition disagreed over objectives, so it was safest to avoid matters of substance as far as possible. Instead, the reformers argued that professional administrators working out of a powerful central office would respond more favorably to specific reform proposals than would twenty or twenty-four sets of local officials who were closely tied to their own neighborhoods.

Nicholas Murray Butler played the most important part in the effort to organize the school centralization coalition, but he worked very closely indeed with Wall Street lawyer Stephen H. Olin and a small circle of advisors, just as the manager of one of the city's charities would work with his board of trustees, or as a school superintendent might work with a board of education. As Dean of Columbia University's Faculty of Philosophy and promoter and first president of the new Teachers' College, Butler was the only professional educator among the reform leaders. Although he was only thirty-two in 1894, Butler's reputation was already well established. He had been a member of the Public Education Society in 1889, and in 1893 Abram S. Hewitt singled him out as the one "expert in pedagogy" to whom the Gilroy Commission ought to turn for professional advice.[75]

Acting in effect as the chairman of Butler's circle of advisors, Olin played almost as important a role as Butler himself from 1888 through 1896. Closely associated with the Public Education Society as early as 1888, Olin served on the Gilroy Commission; assigned John C. Clark, one of the young lawyers in his office, to master the intricacies of school administration as it was practiced throughout the United States; and did more than anyone else except Butler to line up support for centralization.[76] Olin and Butler conferred frequently with a very small inner circle: Columbia University President Seth Low, *Evening Post* editor Joseph B. Bishop, ex-mayor Abram S. Hewitt, and Wall Street attorney John B. Pine, who served for many years as a Columbia trustee.[77] Butler was by no means merely the agent of these men; he contributed his own ideas and his formidable energy and talent for organization. But just as the defenders of the decentralized school system had close ties to their own communities, Butler had his own place in a web of educational, social, and economic contacts. Those contacts helped him assemble the procentralization coalition and in general greatly increased his ability to influence events.

In effect the central group of school reformers constituted a subcommittee of New York's organized Protestant charities, and once the Gilroy Commission had issued its report they turned first to organized charity for support. In June 1894 the Association for Improving the Condition of the Poor (AICP), which had asserted that "political influence, indifference or ignorance" had deprived very large numbers of children of seats in the city's schools, announced that it would sponsor summer schools offering the "discipline and personal supervision which the children re-

maining in the city during the summer stand so much in need of." At
the same time, the summer schools would advance the cause of professional teacher training and management, demonstrating the proficiency
of "recent graduates of the Manual Training School, Normal College,
Pratt Institute, and kindergarten training schools," and showing how a
proper school system ought to be managed.[78]

Under such leaders as Wall Street lawyer J. Augustus Johnson and
Century editor Richard Watson Gilder, who was also president of the
Kindergarten Association, Good Government Club E joined the AICP
in sponsoring these summer schools and decided to make school reform
its special concern within the Good Government Club movement. In
the fall of 1894, Club E joined with the Reverend Charles Parkhurst's
City Vigilance League in a vigilante campaign against "the dirty little
candy stores and cigar shops that are found adjoining the girls' and boys'
entrances of the public schools," because with these and the "saloons
on the right of them, saloons on the left of them, and saloons in front
of them, the school children are exposed to many forms of vice."
The fact that the trustees had not enforced an 1893 law prohibiting
saloons from locating within 200 feet of a public school or church
was further evidence, to the Vigilance League and Club E, of the trustees' incompetence or corruption.[79] Pressing the environmental issue
still further, Johnson recommended that poor children be removed as
far as possible from their neighborhoods, to be taught in great block-
square schoolhouses named after the city's most famous conservative
families.[80]

To aid in the school reform campaign Club E organized, in late 1894,
a Women's Committee consisting largely of its members' wives. By mid-
1895 this group had become the independent Public Education Association
(PEA), but its leaders—like the women who were active in the Citizens'
Union after 1897—remained content to follow the lead of the male reformers; during 1895 and 1896 its policies were set by an advisory board,
chaired by Butler.[81] Mariana Griswold Van Rensselaer, the first president
of the PEA, wrote Gilder, who had been abroad, "My! How I have wanted
your advice very often this year. I am a good worker when some man
tells me what to do."[82] The PEA assisted Club E by visiting schools,
especially in immigrant neighborhoods ("special attention turned to the
schools below 14th Street") where its members looked into sanitation
and provisions for kindergartens and manual training.[83] The PEA also
sought the support of women's clubs and alumnae groups, obtained publicity for school reform in newspaper society pages, and lobbied for support
in Albany and New York City.[84] Since women did not have the vote,

the PEA was especially helpful when Butler and Olin wished to insist that their movement was politically nonpartisan.

Leaders of several other charitable or social reform organizations also endorsed centralization. Felix Adler, whose Ethical Culture Society had sponsored a kindergarten as early as 1878, and William S. Rainsford, rector of St. George's, which, as one of the earliest of the Episcopalian "institutional churches," also sponsored kindergartens, manual training classes, and other social and educational services, spoke out in favor of the reform, as did Episcopal Bishop Henry Codman Potter.[85] Head Worker James B. Reynolds of the Columbia University-affiliated University Settlement, served as a pro-reform school trustee in his lower east side ward and played an active part in the battle.[86] Like Butler, each of these men was an independent actor who worked within a web of social and institutional connections. Reynolds had to answer to a board of trustees that was particularly alert to the social and ideological implications of his actions and had already built much of the record that would lead to his appointment as Executive Director of the Citizens' Union.[87] As rector of St. George's, Rainsford had to secure the approval of his chief warden, J. P. Morgan, for each project, but he claimed that he more often followed the advice of Abram S. Hewitt, who was to him "beyond question the first citizen in New York."[88]

A complex set of motives animated these advocates of school reform. None of them considered the implications of the reform plan for the uptown wards that provided the existing system with so many of its leaders and so much of its support. The reformers were deeply influenced by two closely related contemporary notions: the theory that a child's social environment largely determined whether or not it would grow up to pauperism, crime, and depravity; and the liberal Protestant desire to establish the Kingdom of God.[89] Rainsford himself connected the two notions in 1895: "I tell you we are beginning to know today, with a certitude with which our fathers could not know, that the damning influences of the environment have an awful lot to do with the after life of man." Rainsford urged that "the Faith is not in building tabernacles on the mountain but in using the powers of the Christ to transform the places of the world into the similitude of Him who made it and inspires it."[90] Social theory and theology both encouraged these school reformers to focus their attention on the children of the tenements. Oblivious to the cultures and the social patterns of New York's immigrant communities, the members of AICP, the City Vigilance League, Good Government Club E, and the Public Education Association assumed that tenement-house children were growing up in social, moral, and spiritual as well

as physical poverty. Above all, they hoped to use the public school system
to redeem the children of the slums by placing them under wholesome
and uplifting influences.

The reformers certainly sought improved teaching. Butler and Reynolds
joined Rice in criticizing the basic competence of many teachers and
principals, and Hewitt complained to the Gilroy Commission that
"scarcely any graduate" of the public schools "is able to read or write
English correctly." Hewitt went on to urge that the schools help solve
New York's commercial problems by requiring every pupil to learn "ste-
nography, typewriting and telegraphy," and by providing manual training
to replace "the old Apprenticeship system."[91] But the AICP, the City
Vigilance League, Club E, the PEA, and the institutional church leaders
all emphasized the need to get as many children as possible off the streets
and away from temptation, into schools that stressed moral purity, honesty, and thrift, and were under the supervision of men and women of
what Club E called "high character and attainments." Charles Stewart
Smith, former president of the Chamber of Commerce and vice president
of the City Vigilance League, saw no conflict between the commercial
and the religious objectives. Businessmen, he had argued in 1894, "must
look to moral conduct as the principal preservative force [for] the continued commercial supremacy of New York."[92]

German Jews seeking to aid and to Americanize their poor coreligionists
among the eastern European immigrants who were then flooding into
the city shared many of these objectives. Felix Adler expressed their position most directly in an 1894 address to the PEA: "There are only two
things by means of which a people may be unified . . . a national church
and a national school." Since in America "a national church is impossible
. . . the common school and a common language is what we must depend
upon to weld together all the many nationalities in our country."[93] Public
school principal Julia Richman endorsed this view in her 1894 report
to the Hebrew Free School Association. Urging compulsory public attendance for Jewish immigrants, she wrote: "when we force [Jewish boys]
into the old-fashioned 'Cheder,' into influences un-American, unrefined,
uncultured, un-everything but Hebraic, ours is indirectly the responsibility for the evils which are the outgrowth of such surroundings." Jews
should insist, she urged, that no school "in which all instruction is given
in Hebrew or in the jargon [Yiddish]" be accredited as an alternative
to the public schools.[94]

Valuable as it was, the support of the AICP, the City Vigilance League,
Club E, the PEA, and the settlement houses and institutional churches
provided Butler and Olin with too small a base to write their school

centralization plan into law. Accordingly they moved in late 1894 to enlist the support of the successful coalition of business and professional leaders, anti-Tammany Democrats, and Republicans whose Committee of Seventy had just elected reform Mayor William L. Strong.

The Committee of Seventy was willing to help. Some of the anti-Tammany Democrats among its members had seen school reform as an excellent issue as soon as the Gilroy Commission released its report, and the Committee of Seventy itself had used the issue in its campaign.[95] Among the points in the Seventy's "positive program" were demands that

. . . the quality of the public schools be improved, their capacity enlarged and proper playgrounds provided, so that every child within the ages required by law shall have admission to the schools, [that] the health of the children be protected, and that all such modern improvements be introduced as will make our public schools the equal of those in any other city in the world.[96]

Shortly after Strong's November victory, the Committee of Seventy appointed a subcommittee to consider means of implementing school reform. With Olin as its chairman, this group included Butler, John B. Pine, William Ware Locke of Good Government Club E, and Wall Street lawyer Henry Lynde Sprague, a former school commissioner. John C. Clark of Olin's law firm served as secretary to this subcommittee. Stressing the need to establish at the center of the school system "a permanent, dignified, and responsible body of trained experts, to whom is committed the educational administration of the schools," the subcommittee proposed legislation embodying most of the recommendations offered by the Gilroy Commission.[97]

Although it was more critical of the trustees ("a demonstrated interference with progressive and efficient administration . . . relics of a system long since outgrown") than the Gilroy Commission had been, the subcommittee recommended that laymen continue to play a role in the local supervision of the schools. The problem was to make certain that the right sort of laymen replaced the incumbent trustees. The work of Club E and the PEA suggested that "once relieved from the unnecessary and inappropriate duties that now devolve upon them," lay boards "may reasonably be expected to attract to their membership intelligent men and women whose frequent presence in the schools and constant association with the teachers and pupils would be of great public benefit." With such laymen on its local and central boards and with professionally trained superintendents in charge of operations, the subcommittee added, the charity leaders who advocated kindergartens, manual training, after-school playgrounds, vacation schools, improved sanitary conditions, and "increased directness and efficiency of supervision" could all expect a positive response to "prompt and hopeful appeals" for their pet improvements.[98] With the support of the full Committee of Seventy, the subcommittee sent its proposed legislation to Albany, where state Senator Frank D. Pavey, who worked closely with that organization in 1895, introduced the plan as the Committee of Seventy School Bill.[99]

Butler, Olin, Clark, and others worked hard for the measure during the 1895 legislative session, but it quickly became clear that their preparations were still insufficient. None of their pro-centralization arguments met the concerns of uptown residents or of school officials, and the latter rose in vigorous if predictable opposition.[100] The teachers, rejecting the subcommittee's argument that they would "gain in dignity and independence by freedom from the harassing control of local trustees" and foreseeing instead a decline in status if they were placed under the tight control of a small body of professional educators and PEA visitors, joined the protest.[101] Still more important, Butler and Olin had done nothing to secure the support of the German community, whose members, Butler was informed, began to manifest "an ugly spirit . . . with reference to the School Bill."[102] Democrats in the legislature had no reason to aid the Committee of Seventy; many believed that the decentralized system served both their constituents and their organization. United Republican support could have saved the bill, but state Republican boss Thomas C. Platt's patronage war with Mayor Strong and the sharp opposition from New York City administrators, teachers, and Germans persuaded many Republican legislators to withhold their support. The bill died in the assembly in April 1895.[103]

School Centralization as a Republican Measure

Determined to make defeat in 1895 "only the Bull Run that points the way to an Appomattox," the reformers laid more careful plans for 1896.[104] In early January, just before the beginning of the 1896 legislative session, Butler and Olin met once again with their inner circle of advisors. This time the group included Pine, Sprague, and Clark of the Committee of Seventy subcommittee, and added corporation lawyer and legal reformer Henry W. Taft, manufacturer and City Club leader W. Harris Roome, the *Evening Post*'s Joseph B. Bishop, and J. H. Van Amringe, dean of Columbia's School of Arts, vestryman of Trinity Church, and trustee of the Protestant Episcopal Society for the Promotion of Learning in the

State of New York.[105] With the Republicans firmly established in Albany and a critical national election in the offing, Butler, Olin, and their associates changed their strategy. In 1896 they would attempt to make school reform a Republican party measure. To do so they had to place school centralization at the top of the agenda of "reform" and charity measures that the Republicans might choose to support in 1896, distance themselves from the Good Government Club mugwumps who had opposed the Republicans—to Tammany's great advantage—in the 1895 off-year elections, and gain Boss Platt's acquiescence if not his active support.

The first task was to place school reform at the top of the reform agenda. Competing reforms, including proposals for a reorganized police department, for taking the elections bureau out of the police department, for separating the department of charities from the department of correction, and for modifying the city's tenement house, public health, and playground policies all had to be shouldered aside. To demonstrate that school reform stood at the top of the list, Butler and Olin set up a Committee of One Hundred for Public School Reform, and persuaded a cross-section of the city's charity leaders to join it. Butler secured the support of Abram S. Hewitt, patriarch of practical and conservative reform in New York, as chairman of this committee; Olin arranged for the assistance of Elihu Root, the Wall Street lawyer who was president of the elite Republican Club, and of J. Kennedy Tod, a leading investment banker and treasurer of the Committee of Seventy. Hewitt, Root, and Tod joined Butler and Olin in signing invitations to join the Committee of One Hundred; Butler, Taft, Clark, James B. Reynolds, philanthropist William Bayard Cutting, and uptown lawyer W. W. Niles, Jr., formed its executive committee.[106]

The creation of the Committee of One Hundred was a virtuoso exercise in list-making. To indicate that school centralization was indeed at the top of the moral and social reform agenda, Butler and Olin arranged for the committee to include the names of the presidents of the Charity Organization Society, the New York Mission and Tract Society, the Association of the Bar of the City of New York, The National Municipal League, Columbia and New York universities, and many organizations that were only slightly less well known. To indicate that the school centralization met the highest standards of business efficiency, they included eighteen investment and commercial bankers, including leading partners in such firms as J. P. Morgan & Company and Kuhn, Loeb; and forty-nine Wall Street lawyers, of whom at least thirty-one were officers or directors of national corporations, including both the older railroad and coal companies and the newest manufacturers of rubber and electrical products.[107]

Nine members of the committee reputedly possessed at least a million dollars; at least six others had similarly rich relatives; and many more headed or represented banks and corporations capitalized at several million.[108] Fourteen members of the Chamber of Commerce joined the committee, but only four of these were merchants. The committee included representatives of several economic elites, not simply the old-established mercantile elite. '

Including forty-nine lawyers along with nine medical doctors and six university men, the Committee of One Hundred was dominated, however, by professional men. The professionals were as up to date as their colleagues in business. At least forty of the sixty-four had played a leading part in the reorganization of their fields and in the development of the modern university in the decades after the Civil War. Among the forty were founders of the Association of the Bar of the City of New York and the American Bar Association, the dean of the Columbia University School of Law, and founding members of the American Pediatric Society and the American Child Health Association, as well as the presidents and deans of Columbia and New York University. Their presence on the committee provided further assurance that the school reform plan was in line with the best professional practice. The names of such leading municipal reformers as James C. Carter (president of the National Municipal League and reputedly the most influential member of the old Tilden Commission), Horace E. Deming, Frank J. Goodnow, and City Club founder Edmond Kelly, as well as fifty-eight City Club members, demonstrated more specifically that the plan was an integral part of the movement for municipal efficiency and economy.

In selecting men for the committee Butler had hoped, as he told Seth Low, to avoid giving the impression that the reformers were "college men and aristocrats who were endeavoring to get the schools under their control."[109] By comparison with New York's general population the members of the Committee of One Hundred did belong to the city's social as well as its economic elites. No fewer than 92 of the 104 members were listed in the 1896 *Social Register*, and those who were excluded included German Jews Jacob Schiff, Isaac N. Seligman, and Meyer Rothschild, young professional men like John C. Clark who would be listed in later editions, and two young Republican assemblymen. Virtually all of the One Hundred lived in silk stocking neighborhoods: thirty along Fifth Avenue, ten more on Madison, and eleven on the west side. The homes of more than forty were to be found in the older, if outwardly more modest, enclaves of gentility surrounding Washington Square, Irving Place and Gramercy Park, and Madison Square.[110]

Yet Butler and Olin did neglect the city's money- and ancestor-proud social elites, drawing disproportionately on cultivated Protestants (and a few German Jews) of the "earnest, public-spirited" sort. Only 4 of the 104 members of the committee could be described as among Ward McAllister's "400"; only seventeen belonged to either the Union, the Knickerbocker, or the St. Nicholas clubs.[111] But sixty-eight had joined one or both of the two leading clubs that celebrated cultural achievement, the Century and the University.[112] And thirty-six played prominent roles in well-known moral and social reform organizations: eight in the Reverend Charles Parkhurst's militant City Vigilance League, nine in the New York City Mission and Tract Society and other Protestant proselytizing agencies, and twenty-one in the YMCA, the settlement houses, and the institutional churches.[113] Agents for these organizations had urged school reform in 1894 and 1895. In 1896 Butler and Olin used the Committee of One Hundred to bring their boards of directors publicly into the movement.

In many ways the members of the Committee of One Hundred were much more cosmopolitan than the men and women who defended the decentralized system. They were better educated, more widely traveled, held higher and more broadly responsible jobs, and were often at the top of their specialties, in positions that enabled them to respond to and to shape economic and professional developments on an international scale. But in the New York City context the reformers were less cosmopolitan than their opponents in a crucial respect. The militant Protestants among them, caught up in the contemporary enthusiasm for extending religion into everyday life, were intolerant of religious diversity. This was not true of all the centralizers. Although Butler was capable of asserting, without ever adducing the slightest evidence, that "the strongest single influence in the schools at present, except Tammany Hall, is the Roman Catholic Church," he added that "this does not disturb me in the least," and he was eager to bring to New York some school administrators who had been victimized by the anti-Catholic American Protective Association.[114] Yet Butler did play on the issue, and far from discouraging the support of aggressive Americanizers and proselytizers he encouraged them to think that centralization would advance their causes. Defenders of the decentralized system, with their emphasis on harmonizing religious and ethnic conflicts at the neighborhood level, were much more cosmopolitan in this sense.

Once Butler and Olin had assembled the broader range of support indicated by the Committee of One Hundred, they had to make the Republicans in Albany aware of it. In this they were greatly aided by what amounted to an almost complete control of the press. Butler and John C. Clark coordinated the news as well as the editorial policies of the *Evening Post,* the *Times,* the *Tribune,* the *Sun,* the *Mail and Express,* and the *Commercial Advertiser;* with the assistance of Mariana Van Rensselaer they also won the valuable support of Joseph Pulitzer and his *World.*[115] The *Staats Zeitung,* briefly dubious about the reform in 1896, came around as Butler pressed it through Carl Schurz and Frederick W. Holls; the other German-language papers either ignored the school issue or quietly supported it.[116] The genteel literary and religious weeklies— *Harper's Weekly, The Critic,* Lyman Abbott's *The Outlook, The Independent*—also took up the reform, and Butler added his contribution through his own journal, the *Educational Review.* Only two newspapers—the *Herald* and to a lesser degree the *Sun,* both of which seem to have been seeking expanded sales in the middle-income uptown wards—joined *School,* the weekly *Harlem Local Reporter,* and *Dickson's Uptown Weekly* in the Bronx in reporting anti-centralization rallies and arguments at length and without ridicule.[117] Papers directed at an Irish-American audience ignored the issue altogether.[118]

Butler made the fullest possible use of his influence in the press. While school reform proposals lay before the legislature during February and March, he filled the papers with articles designed to discredit the trustees and to show that authorities in finance, law, municipal government, and educational administration all endorsed centralization as sound and efficient. Butler himself contributed anonymous news articles to the *Evening Post* and the *Tribune,* asking one editor to print a piece as an article "because what I want to effect [sic] is public opinion at Albany and letters have no weight with them;" and he helped Mrs. Van Rensselaer draft editorials for the *World.*[119] To reinforce the impact of their press campaign, the reformers took pains to bring selected items to the attention of legislators both directly and through the agency of upstate school administrators whom Butler had met in 1895, while he was president of the National Education Association.[120]

Butler and Olin did not make a secret of their preparations, and by late autumn 1895 the Board of Education and other groups whose bargains had traditionally set school policy realized that they faced a serious challenge. Determined to meet the threat head on, the Board of Education adopted several new ideas, working out its own school reform bill. School Commissioner and Tammany leader Charles Strauss seems to have provided the first draft of the board's bill; in any case Butler succeeded in attaching Strauss's name, with the implication of Tammany dictation, to the measure, although in fact only five of the fifteen commissioners who supported it were Democrats.[121] Nathaniel A. Prentiss and Charles Bulkeley Hubbell, members of the board's reform group of five, sought Butler's support for an effort to modify Strauss's draft. Prentiss proposed to reduce the trustees to a "supervisory and suggestive power;" abolish the inspectors; separate the management of buildings from the management of education *per se*; create eligible lists from which superintendents, not principals or trustees, would select janitors, teachers, and principals; grant long terms and fixed salaries to superintendents to free them from political influence; and establish the policy of rotating assistant superintendents to prevent "the establishment of any purely local influences in school matters."[122] Butler responded to this program with hearty approval, but demanded that reform go still farther, eliminating the trustees, establishing a corps of lay inspectors who would report to the central authorities, and increasing the authority and the salary of the central superintendent. To Hubbell he added that if the trustees had not existed no one would have thought of creating them.[123]

The bill finally advanced by the Board of Education made some concessions to the reformers, but not as many as Hubbell and Prentiss had sought and not nearly enough to satisfy Butler. The board did agree to place control of building construction and maintenance in a separate, central department, to clarify the powers of the superintendent in the licensing of teachers, and to seek authority to establish public high schools. But while the board was willing to deprive the trustees of most of their control over school patronage, it insisted that they continue to perform the function of local lay oversight. Under the board's bill the outmoded ward basis of the trustee system would be replaced by as many as forty-five new districts of equal population. A substantial majority of the twenty-one school commissioners, including several who owed their appointments to Mayor Strong, favored this bill.[124]

When it became clear that the Board of Education would neither abolish the trustee system nor increase the powers of the central administration, Butler and Olin, with the approval of their close advisors, adopted a hard-line strategy. Together with their new press campaign they had state Senator Frank Pavey introduce for bargaining purposes a bill containing a single provision: elimination of the trustees.[125]

Butler sought to have the Pavey and Strauss bills sent to the education committees of the assembly and senate, but he failed in this; they went instead to the committees on cities, where he had fewer friends.[126] Mistrusting Pavey as an ally of Strong's and an enemy of the Thomas Platt's regular Republican organization, and noting that Platt kept his silence while Edward Lauterbach, his closest aide in Manhattan, opposed the measure, a number of upstaters withheld their support.[127] Butler responded by pressing on with his carefully orchestrated press campaign, by keeping up his correspondence with key legislators and upstate school administrators, and by sending a series of impressive delegations to Albany.[128]

In the face of this campaign and of the widespread support Butler and Olin had mobilized, Platt decided not to engage in active opposition to their plan. But he did not favor it, and he warned his associates that they were deluded if they thought that the New York reformers would be satisfied with that measure alone.[129] Platt's decision to stay out of the matter left the reformers free to press for support from those upstate Republicans who were willing to work with the Union League Club and the Committee of Seventy. In mid-February Butler arranged for the ladies of the Public Education Association to testify before the legislators, whom they impressed; then, drawing on their social connections, the ladies paid a call on Governor Morton (who was, after all, a New York banker) and his wife. Assured that "everyone, whose opinion is worth anything" favored centralization, Mrs. Morton joined the movement.[130] Butler and Olin kept in touch with Charles B. Hubbell, leader of the Board of Education's reform faction, and Hubbell met with the governor and the mayor to assure them that he and his associates were working with the reformers.[131] At Butler's request the State Superintendent of Instruction, Danforth E. Ainsworth, assured the Chairman of the Senate Committee on Cities, Nevada N. Stranahan, that in his professional opinion centralization would both improve the quality of instruction and damage the Democratic Party in New York City.[132] And Elihu Root, who had adroitly kept open his lines of communication with both Strong and Platt, added his persuasive powers to the campaign, conferring with the governor and senators Lexow and Brush in Albany, and with Mayor Strong in the city.[133]

Early in March Stranahan and others in the legislature agreed to support school reform, provided, as Butler put it, that they could avoid doing "anything that will rebound to the credit of Mr. Pavey."[134] As "practical men," Butler and his associates made "no objection to this, provided" the legislators came up with a bill that "either wipes out the trustees entirely, or takes away their present powers."[135] Clark was already in Albany, where Butler quickly joined him to work out the final version of the bill with Stranahan and Assembly Speaker Hamilton Fish, and to secure the firm support of Republican senators Lexow and White. The compromise bill that emerged was less a compromise between the Pavey and Strauss bills than a new version of the Committee of Seventy bill offered in 1895. It abolished the trustee system, and in addition provided that district superintendents were not to be assigned to specific districts, but were to work out of a single, central office.[136] In Butler's phrase, the superintendent should be as free as a general to send them where they were needed.[137] With this provision the centralizers completed their break with Joseph M. Rice and his concern that consistent, encouraging leadership be offered to the teachers, within permanent districts of manageable size.

The school bill itself was not a compromise. The real compromise had to do with politics, as reformers dropped their nonpartisan stance and persuaded Republicans that centralization would benefit the party as well as the children. As soon as the new bill had been drafted, Butler wrote one correspondent that it would do more for the Republican organization in New York City than any other measure the legislature could pass, "not . . . because it is framed in the interest of the organization, but simply because it deals a terrific blow at Tammany Hall. Anything that weakens that body strengthens its opponents."[138] But in fact the bill did offer direct advantages to the Republicans. The mayor would now select the only laymen involved in the schools, and Republicans were more likely to elect a mayor than they were to choose a majority on an elective board of education or to dominate neighborhood boards of trustees in most areas of the city.

More immediately and more tangibly, key Republicans received some immediate favors in return for their support. Butler undertook to ask the newspapers to "stop their abuse of Platt . . . in connection with this bill," and "to have the public press confine itself to criticisms of Tammany and of the inefficient system."[139] Hamilton Fish had assured Butler of his support for the measure as early as January 20, but in return he asked for favorable publicity. Butler provided that, as well as a tacit suggestion of support for Fish's contemplated gubernatorial candidacy.[140] When the bill became law in May, Fish asked Butler for praise in the press for senators Stranahan, White, and Ford, and for assemblymen O'Grady, Austin, and Andrews. He noted that much to the disgust of himself and of Governor Morton, Austin had been much maligned in the papers.[141] Butler replied, "I have done everything in my power to see that the gentlemen you name receive their proper public appreciation," and referred Fish to articles in *Harper's Weekly* and the *Illustrated American*, to the report of the Committee of One Hundred, and to his success in suppressing criticism of Austin.[142]

With Republican support assured, the school centralization measure went through the legislature without further change. Seth Low made

NEW YORK HERALD, THURSDAY, APRIL 16, 1896.—TWENTY PAGES.

HEARING BEFORE MAYOR STRONG ON THE "COMPROMISE" SCHOOL BILL.

Opponents (and some advocates) of school centralization at the hearing held by Mayor Strong, April 15, 1896, as pictured by the New York *Herald*. (Courtesy of the New-York Historical Society, New York City)

an eloquent plea for the bill at the last senate hearing, and Senator Pavey, using questions constructed by Butler, disrupted and undermined the testimony of a delegation of teachers who came to Albany to oppose the measure.[143] When the teachers and other opponents of centralization held a rally in New York, Butler assured the legislators that few had attended, and charged that they had been stirred up by Tammany senator John F. Ahearn.[144] Since Ahearn often introduced legislation for the teachers, the influence might well have flowed the other way, but with only the New York *Herald*, the *Sun*, and the uptown and teachers' papers providing coverage of their views, defenders of the decentralized system found it difficult to "effect public opinion at Albany;" as a result many legislators and officials may have underestimated the strength of popular support for the trustees.[145] Tammany leaders certainly believed that centralization was widely opposed: They made their opposition to the measure one of the most prominent issues in their successful 1897 mayoral campaign against Seth Low.[146]

The opposition swelled to a crescendo in April, as the bill passed from the legislature to Mayor Strong for his approval. School commissioners, trustees, inspectors, principals, and teachers, Tammany and anti-Tammany Democrats and uptown Republicans, uptown community leaders, six thousand Bronx businessmen, Protestant ministers, Catholic and Jewish spokesmen, a hundred thousand parents, Joseph M. Rice, and A. F. of L. President Samuel Gompers all urged the mayor to disapprove the bill.[147] But Strong had been nominated by the Committee of Seventy and had been in continual touch with the reformers, and while he listened respectfully to the careful arguments of School Board President Robert Maclay, Teachers' Association President Matthew Elgas, and Catholic spokesman Frederick R. Coudert, and took tea with Mrs. Lauterbach, he could hardly have been impressed by Commissioner Joseph J. Little's jibe that the reformers were "Anglomaniacs!"[148] At the end Butler arranged for Seth Low, the Reverend William S. Rainsford, and Elihu Root to repeat the arguments in favor of the reform, and to remind Strong that opposing it "would involve his running against the Republican Party as well as the Committee of Seventy."[149] On April 23 Strong accepted the bill, and with the governor's signature it became law.[150]

Centralization and School Reform, 1896–1898

The success of the school centralization movement demonstrated that a coalition including the "earnest, public spirited class" of wealthy, generally well-born, well-educated, and able businessmen and professionals that Bryce called the "best men" could indeed exert significant influence over the cultural policy of New York City when they could unite and find leadership as effective as that provided by Nicholas Murray Butler and his associates. But it does not demonstrate that they formed a unified group able to shape cultural policy to its own specifications. Those who joined the school centralization coalition sought disparate and even conflicting objectives, and while they had won a legislative battle they had not displaced the men and women who actually provided public schooling in New York City.

With his usual audacity, Abram S. Hewitt had urged Mayor Gilroy's 1893 School Law Revision Commission to take as a model the antebellum Public School Society, which was, as Hewitt described it, "a close corporation, into which members were admitted by the existing members, and from which the trustees were selected by the Board of Trustees." A system of that sort, he suggested, "would place the control of our schools in the hands of Trustees properly qualified by experience and character to assume the responsibility of their management;" at present, such "men and women do not like to push themselves into prominence and appear as applicants for official favor. They prefer to be sought out."[151] But even if the school reformers had succeeded in placing the city's school system under a "close corporation," they would not have set educational policy on a clear track.

All of the reformers agreed that the schools should speed the assimilation of immigrant children and teach English, arithmetic, and punctuality to new members of the labor force. To these ends they also agreed that the state should rigorously enforce the attendance of more children, for a longer term, in more effectively supervised classrooms.[152] But many of them sought to carry out these objectives through specific programs that others ignored or opposed. One reason for Butler's emphasis on administrative reform was his need to retain the support of groups that would not have been able to agree on a set of priorities for substantive reform. In the course of his campaign he had found it necessary to reassure leaders of movements for kindergartens, manual training, vacation schools, playgrounds, improved sanitary conditions, and tighter supervision of teachers that while centralization would not immediately further their aims, they might expect that under a centralized system school authorities would give their ideas more favorable consideration. All of these programs would cost money to implement, as *School* magazine pointed out.[153] Yet there was no clear consensus among centralizers as to which programs ought to be adopted first.

The reformers were still less able to agree on certain other possible school innovations. Several sought to use the schools to teach thrift; Hubbell enthusiastically promoted anti-cigarette leagues; and still others advocated a classroom campaign against the use of alcoholic beverages.[154] But Butler opposed such schemes in the name of professional control of the curriculum and out of deference to the anti-temperance feeling of German Republicans, whose support had been essential to the centralization movement.[155] He also opposed the use of military drill as a means of instilling patriotism in school children, yet the City Vigilance League and the Union League Club favored this practice.[156] Those who sought to inculcate good citizenship through kindergarten methods were dismissed as utopians by others, like Hewitt, who would have had the children memorize a patriotic "catechism."[157] Felix Adler was almost alone in urging that the objective of school reform ought to be "to provide for each child's mind what will bring out the best in it."[158] Although none of the reformers picked up Harvard President Charles W. Eliot's suggestion that the number of teachers be doubled, their own proposals would increase the cost of schooling. Yet many members of the Committee of One Hundred, including Hewitt himself, wanted to hold down all local government expenditures.[159] Advocates of local economy were even more prominent among the members of the Committee of Seventy, whose support had been critical to the success of the movement.[160] These disagreements over objectives, priorities, and methods among the centralizers remained, of course, once they had secured the compromise school law.

In reaching their objective, the school reformers had fallen far short of establishing a close corporation within which they could restrict debate over school policy to themselves alone. The Board of Education, on which a majority of commissioners had opposed centralization, remained in place, as did all the system's employees, with their established leaders and organizations. School officials and teachers' organizations retained their longstanding connections to the city's political forces and leaders, who in turn remained in their places with all their ties to the city's economic, religious, and ethnic groups. The trustees were gone, Joseph M. Rice's proposal for a ten-district system had been suppressed without a full discussion, and a powerful new bureaucracy was to be established. But it remained to be seen whether the schools would become increasingly responsive to the reformers' goals.

An early test suggested what might happen in the future. In an effort to consolidate the reforms he had secured through the compromise law, Butler persuaded Daniel Coit Gilman, the president of The Johns Hopkins University, to offer himself as a candidate for superintendent of New York's schools in May 1896. A part, if not all, of Butler's purpose in this maneuver was to gain impressive outside endorsement for his approach to school reform and to keep the matter before the public.[161] Gilman explained in an open letter that he was willing to be considered for the job because it was "one of the most important positions, if not the most important, in American education." It was especially important now, when a new law, "secured through the influence of a committee of 100 representative citizens, [permitted] in many respects, the reorganization of [the city's] system of instruction." The unprecedented opportunity thus offered "for the introduction of modern methods [would permit] the permanent separation of the public school system from the influences of parties, sects, and personal preferments. . . ." It would also make it possible to address the problems that chiefly preoccupied the reformers: How "can the old methods of instruction be improved, and the training of the eye and hand be secured without the neglect of the printed page? How may morality and patriotism be promoted in schools that are governed by local self-government and are free from the control of all religious bodies? How may the different requirements of such diverse elements as constitute the population of a cosmopolitan city be wisely and economically supplied? What is the proper training for public school teachers?"[162] Like the reformers, Gilman gave top priority to administrative and pedagogical problems, but did not neglect the moral and social problems that seemed most important to their opponents.

The Gilman candidacy drew substantial support from the Board of Education, but in the face of protests from the Johns Hopkins trustees and faculty Gilman withdrew his name.[163] Butler arranged to substitute the name of Charles B. Gilbert, superintendent of schools in St. Paul, who was, as the reformers on the Board of Education said, "President of the Department of Instruction of the National Education Association" and "a graduate of a New England College."[164] He also had the endorsement of such notables in education as presidents G. Stanley Hall of Clark University, Draper of the University of Illinois, Eliot of Harvard, and Hervey of Teachers College, as well as the liberal Catholic leader, Archbishop John Ireland of St. Paul.[165]

But the reformers had only six votes, and the Board of Education reelected John Jasper for his seventeenth consecutive term as superintendent of New York's schools.[166] Typical of the administrators in the decentralized system, Jasper was himself one of the chief impediments to reform. He had been associated with the city's public school system for every year save one from the day in 1842 when he had entered Public School #9. He had remained in the public schools through the Free Academy, a secondary school, but had no further education, and he had then worked his way up, step by step, through the ranks.[167] Jasper would continue in charge of the system during the first year of centralization, the year when the school system for Greater New York as a whole was to be worked out. To help him, the Board of Education appointed one of the chief defenders of the trustee system in its own ranks, the former teacher, small-time lawyer, and Republican politician John L. N. Hunt, to a six-year term as assistant superintendent of schools and to the key new position of secretary to the new Board of Superintendents.[168] The board also named Teachers' Association President Matthew J. Elgas, who had played a leading part in the teachers' and principals' opposition to centralization, and a Brooklyn principal whom Butler described as "equally bad," to three- and one-year terms on that board.[169]

Yet the reformers did not lose everything. In 1896 they succeeded in electing two of the new assistant superintendents—Teachers College school supervisor Clarence E. Meleney and Holyoke, Massachusetts, Superintendent Albert P. Marble—and blocked the election of Edward H. Boyer, a New York City principal who had helped lead opposition to the reform.[170] They also blocked the selection of former School Commissioner Clara M. Williams, a prominent supporter of the trustee system, as supervisor of kindergartens.[171] Most important of all, Butler successfully urged Elihu Root, Joseph Choate, and others to persuade Governor Morton to "select, as one of his appointees on the Greater New York Commission, some one man sufficiently identified with the school reform movement and well enough informed upon it, to enable us to protect, in the new charter, what we have gained."[172] Morton complied, naming Seth Low to the Greater New York Charter Commission.[173] In drafting the educational portions of the charter, Low conferred and corresponded extensively with Butler, producing an educational chapter that preserved the centralized system for Manhattan and the Bronx, though delaying its application to Brooklyn, Queens, and Staten Island.[174] In 1897 the reformers were satisfied with the selection of William H. Maxwell, Brooklyn's widely respected superintendent, as the Greater City's first superintendent of schools.[175]

Centralization had mixed implications for the teachers as well. Butler, Reynolds, and other reformers had argued that the teachers suffered a good deal of petty tyranny under the trustees. The teachers' spokesmen had responded that they had more to fear from a tyrannical central administration. By concentrating "so much labor, power and responsibility" in the hands of the superintendent, Teachers' Association President Elgas had argued, centralization would create "a kind of educational Pooh-Bah." If the superintendent and his assistants were to have "full charge of all appointments, promotions, and transfers of teachers, to say nothing of payrolls and janitors and other matters," they would need a large staff; soon they would form an expensive, unwieldy bureaucracy, out of touch with the schools, the teachers, and the children.[176] Another memorialist pointed out that anyone "who has any knowledge of the professional fads of different Superintendents will readily comprehend the sacrifice of individuality, the absolute submission, even the servility necessary in a teacher to avoid the possibility of failure, and through that of loss of promotion, and, perhaps, of dismissal."[177] It would take a separate examination to discover how far—and how soon—these fears were realized. But teachers adapted to the new arrangements, and by the end of 1899 their associations found that centralization, together with the creation of Greater New York, enabled them to mount a more successful effort to raise their salaries.[178]

Conclusion

The centralization of the public school system had consequences that were unintended by its advocates and unforeseen by its opponents. It may have had little impact on the actual experience of children in the schools. It did nothing to reduce the size of classes and little to change the sources from which the teachers and their immediate supervisors were recruited. It did not shift control over the schools from one social group to another; certainly it did not simply shift power from the poor— who took no part in the debate—to the rich. Nor did it make inevitable the displacement of local administrators who had worked their way up through the city's educational—and sometimes its political—system by professionals who had made their reputations in the new teachers' colleges and nationally recognized school systems. Indeed the reformers had not really intended to remove politics from administrative appointments; as a practical man Butler understood that his administrative candidates would have the best chance when the Board of Education had been selected by a Republican or an independent Republican mayor with whom Butler was in political alliance.

But if centralization failed to give the reformers a free hand to use the schools for their own educational purposes—whether those purposes had to do with education, moral reform, Americanization, or politics— it did define the terms under which the schools would develop over the next several years. By abolishing the local trustees and establishing a powerful central board of superintendents, the law forced all school employees to pay less attention to neighborhood relationships and more attention to the school bureaucracy. By strengthening the powers and raising the certification standards for officials in that bureaucracy as well as by making an administrative job in New York attractive and sometimes available to superintendents from outside the city, the law served to bring the school system into closer contact with the world of professional school administration as it existed throughout the United States. The most likely result was not the takeover of the city's schools by New England Protestants dedicated to an aggressive program of Americanization, but the gradual creation of a locally recruited corps of school administrators who had deep experience of the city's special social conditions and administrative traditions and who were attuned to the standards and the fashions of the national profession as well. Whatever their ethos, these administrators would attempt to lead the school system through a powerfully centralized apparatus designed to restrict political and neighborhood influence and to ensure professional control over the system.

PART V

*The Distribution of
Power in Greater
New York*

CHAPTER 10

COMPETING ELITES AND THE

DISPERSAL OF POWER

HENRY GEORGE posed the issues addressed in this book as clearly as any of his contemporaries:

> In all the great American cities there is today as clearly defined a ruling class as in the most aristocratic countries of the world. . . . Who are these men? The wise, the good, the learned—men who have earned the confidence of their fellow-citizens by the purity of their lives, the splendor of their talents, their probity in public trusts, their deep study of the problem of government? No; they are gamblers, saloon-keepers, pugilists, or worse, who have made a trade of controlling votes, and of buying and selling offices and official acts. . . . It is through these men that rich corporations and powerful pecuniary interests can pack the Senate and the Bench with their creatures.[1]

In their varying ways E. L. Godkin's lament that the cultivated and well-off had suffered a pervasive Genteel Decline, and Moisei Ostrogorski's theory that an undifferentiated Economic Elite dominated New York and other cities, repeated George's assertions. Many late nineteenth-century New Yorkers shared these perceptions. But larger numbers of the wealthy, the well educated, and the well informed held other views, agreeing with James Bryce that effective power remained in the hands of a Patrician Elite, or with the forgotten but representative Daniel Greenleaf Thompson that the party organizations so scorned by Henry George and so criticized by Ostrogorski were in fact merely syndicates that won the power to govern by offering to perform the most widely desired services at the lowest cost.

Within the limits imposed by their understanding of the city and its social groups, late nineteenth-century New Yorkers asked the questions with admirable clarity. But their answers were heavily influenced by outdated assumptions about the rapidly changing metropolis and by their political and religious beliefs, and they disagreed profoundly among themselves. No retrospective survey of their opinions can possibly determine which view was correct. It is necessary to go beyond inferences derived from the consideration of ideas and attitudes. Defining power as the ability of an individual or a group "to realize their will in a communal action even against the resistance of others," this book has proceeded on the conviction that the best way to uncover the underlying structure of power is through the analysis of events. Accordingly, after establishing the ways in which economic, social, and cultural resources were distributed among the region's people, and the ways in which the people grouped themselves, the preceding chapters have examined in detail the preferences and actions of those who made and were affected by several major decisions made during the 1880s and 1890s.

The evidence indicates that power was concentrated not in one or two but in several distinct economic, social, and political elites. In their efforts to influence decisions these elites engaged in a shifting complex of alliances, bargained with one another, and sometimes made important concessions to secure the support of other elites and of wider publics. The city was neither ruled by a single power elite, nor by a genteel, patrician, or merely rich upper class. Nor was it ruled by an all-powerful political machine. Middle- and lower-income New Yorkers influenced decisions directly, through a variety of increasingly effective organizations, including several political machines and a variety of special-interest groups, and indirectly, through their votes, petitions, demonstrations, strikes, and boycotts.

This distribution of power resembled the pattern found in New York by Wallace S. Sayre and Herbert Kaufman during the 1950s.[2] Nevertheless the distribution of power in Greater New York at the end of the nineteenth century was considerably less dispersed than the political scientists found it to be fifty years later. There were fewer participants, proportionately many more of them were very wealthy or were partners in Wall Street law firms, and fewer of them were university- or union-based experts, government officials, or labor leaders.

The Distribution of Resources

Wealth is not the same as power: The possessors of resources are not always able to turn them to account. There can be no doubt that wealthy men and women exerted more than their share of power over important decisions in late nineteenth-century New York. The region held far more than its share of the nation's millionaires, and through their wealth the very rich controlled other resources, including most of the region's newspapers and access to the services of the largest concentration of lawyers, engineers, bankers, and other professional and business specialists available in any American city. But the very rich did not form a unified and effective power elite.[3] As the national and the metropolitan economies were transformed in these years, Greater New York's wealthy men and women found themselves divided into increasingly diverse and conflicting economic elites. The great import-export merchants who had long dominated the Chamber of Commerce of the State of New York, together with their lawyers and bankers, formed an established mercantile elite. But even before the 1880s this elite was internally divided according to the product lines and markets served by its members, all of whom had also to deal with several competing elites: railroad and shipping moguls, regional wholesalers, complacent real estate owners. By the mid 1890s the mercantile elite was rapidly losing economic primacy to the leaders of the great vertically integrated manufacturing corporations and department stores that were taking over many of the financing, coordinating, and distribution functions that the merchants had traditionally supplied. And throughout these years professionally-trained experts increased rapidly in diversity and developed independent professional interests and outlooks of their own. Individuals and members of the same family sometimes belonged to two or more of these economic elites, yet the elites had distinguishable and often competing economic interests.

Social, cultural, and political cleavages further divided the members of Greater New York's economic elites.[4] Given the well-known religious and ethnic prejudices of the period, it is not surprising that there were distinct Anglo-Protestant, German, German Jewish, and embryonic Catholic social elites. Less well known but equally significant cultural differences further divided the region's wealthy Protestants of British origin into three overlapping but distinct social elites, devoted respectively to the celebration of wealth through expensive sports and display; to ancestor worship; and to cultural achievement. In some contexts the last of these social elites—the "earnest, public-spirited class"—acted as a unit in metropolitan affairs. But this class was divided in turn between evangelicals who sought to convert the heathen and enforce the blue laws and social Christians who sought to establish the Kingdom of God on earth by encouraging tolerance and social reform. Women played important parts in all of these social elites; those who belonged to the "earnest, public-spirited class" and who were active in the churches and charities played the most prominent part in public affairs. Wealthy men who belonged to each of the economic and social elites were active in politics as the financial backers, managers, and leading candidates of the major Democratic, Republican, and Independent factions.

Altogether, Greater New York's economic and social elites were divided so deeply and in so many ways that they could not agree on any single set of economic, cultural, or political initiatives. If they had shared a single set of economic interests, they might have made a unified effort to set the region's political agenda, control its political parties, and shape public opinion in such a way that their own preferences would be accepted as in the interest of all residents of the region. But in fact they could agree on few economic policies apart from the most basic requirements of a market economy—the maintenance of the gold standard because it was the currency of international trade and the continuation of most protections for private property—and these policies were accepted by the great majority of New Yorkers at every income level.

Similarly, if Greater New York's wealthiest men and women had shared a common core of cultural values, they might have been able to unite in a single series of ceremonies, charities, and cultural institutions. Using these to celebrate widely shared values and to provide notable service to the less fortunate and to the region as a whole, they might well have secured the respect and deference of a large proportion of their poorer fellow citizens, adding a formidable cultural resource to their already great economic resources. Instead, they met the increasingly diverse social and cultural universe of the metropolis with half a dozen inconsistent cultural styles. When they sought to exert power, the members of the region's economic and social elites were embarrassed not by their riches but by their numbers and diversity.

When they sought to exert power in these years Greater New York's economic and social elites were also limited by the considerable and increasing resources available to the less affluent. Most major decisions required action by the state or local government and also, therefore, by the political party organizations that supplied government officials. Thus universal manhood suffrage and the contemporary custom of nearly universal voter turnout provided the region's middle- and lower-income citizens with an important resource. As religious enthusiasm reduced the political effectiveness of many Protestants and as ballot and primary reforms produced the largely unintended consequence of strengthening the political party organizations, most party organizations fell into the hands of professional politicians. Generally of middle- or lower-income family background themselves, the successful politicians moved ahead because they were effective organizers. And they retained their leadership by responding effectively to the demands of party workers, civil servants, real estate developers, neighborhood commercial groups, and other middle- and lower- as well as upper-income interest groups. Responding to changing economic conditions as well as to the changing political system, the region's less affluent employers, entrepreneurs, public employees, and skilled workers all organized increasingly effectively to demand that political figures accommodate their interests.

Increasing economic and cultural resources reinforced the increasing political and organizational resources available to the less affluent. So far as we can judge from the available evidence, Greater New York's rapidly expanding population was more and more employed in white-collar, entrepreneurial, and skilled occupations, less and less in unskilled laboring jobs. Although the overall share of the region's wealth and income that was held by the very rich probably did not decline, there is no doubt that the absolute level of wages and salaries received by blue as well as white-collar workers increased. As incomes rose, these workers were able to support their pressure groups more effectively. And as immigrant workers learned to cope with American conditions and to accommodate one another's cultural assumptions and values, they developed strategies and weapons, like "pure and simple" unionism and the boycott, that further strengthened their impact.

The less affluent derived another cultural advantage from the region's ethnic diversity. Whereas the very wealthy were overwhelmingly British or German and Protestant, those who filled the middle-income occupations were increasingly German and Irish Protestants and Catholics and eastern European Jews, and the low-income workers, who more and more were drawn from Italy and eastern Europe as well as from Ireland and Germany, were increasingly Catholic. As a consequence, even a unified upper-income group would have found it difficult to sway the poor through appeals based on shared values and a common sense of cultural identity. It was also true, of course, that the region's increasing ethnic and religious diversity presented a real problem to those who sought to organize low- or middle-income pressure groups. Workers at most levels and in many occupations were themselves divided along ethnic and religious lines. And during the 1890s, just as many Irish and German New Yorkers were developing a cosmopolitan outlook that enabled them to work comfortably together in the craft unions and in the regular Democratic and Republican party organizations, they found themselves confronted by very large numbers of new Italian and eastern European Jewish immigrants whose assumptions and values were very different from their own. Nevertheless, the region's middle-to-lower-income groups enjoyed more resources—higher income and skill levels, more effective organizations, higher rates of literacy, a greater degree of acceptance into the polity, and attitudes and values that permitted them to take effective part in politics—than their counterparts in smaller contemporary cities like Birmingham, Alabama, and Stamford, Connecticut.[5] Altogether, economic, social, and cultural resources were distributed in such complicated and disparate ways that they conferred both advantages and disadvantages on power-seeking New Yorkers of many different backgrounds and many different degrees of wealth.

The Distribution of Power

ECONOMIC AND SOCIAL ELITES

Although some of Greater New York's wealthiest men withdrew into the social life of London, the quiet recesses of the Knickerbocker and Union clubs, or the pursuit of ever larger fortunes, the very rich and their agents supplied a majority of the most active participants in each of the four sets of decisions considered in this study, and collectively they enjoyed power greatly disproportionate to their numbers. Using their money, time, political skill, substantial control of the press, access to (and control over) expertise, and social prestige, they were able to introduce new ideas, deflect some ideas they didn't like, secure new procedures for conducting elections and making appointments to the public service, limit the ability of politicians to loot the public till, establish new standards for police discipline and public health, influence nominations, and win office for themselves. On occasion, several of the economic elites sacrificed some of their preferences regarding local policy in order to advance their preferences for such national economic policies as low tariffs, adherence to the gold standard, federal promotion of commerce, and, as historian Lee Benson has shown, state and then federal regulation of the railroads. Locally they were most successful in developing new economic proposals and in securing a hearing for them.

But the region's extraordinarily large numbers of wealthy men and women divided themselves into an unusually large number of competing economic and social elites, and in their efforts to prevail over one another and to influence regional and national policy they reached for the support of groups that were much less wealthy or prestigious. The political factionalism of the economic elites during the 1880s and 1890s defies brief summary, and that factionalism reflected fundamental disagreements about policy as well as personal ambitions. Apart from tariff reductions and the gold standard, few national economic policies were universally supported. The Chamber of Commerce of the State of New York long sponsored municipal consolidation, yet so influential a member of the Chamber as Abram S. Hewitt never liked the idea; and when the Chamber officially decided to oppose Thomas C. Platt's consolidation plan in 1896, some of the leading bankers in the Chamber applauded Governor Levi P. Morton for accepting it. In the rapid transit decision, most business groups and newspapers ignored Abram S. Hewitt's first proposal, in 1888, that the city finance a rapid transit system, and even when the Chamber of Commerce took up his plan in 1894, wealthy property owners, street and elevated railroad interests, and others who were simply wary of active municipal involvement in the economy continued to resist it. Nicholas Murray Butler's school centralization plan had to overcome equally diverse and conflicting opinions among wealthy people who sought to have the public schools stress economy of operation, moral indoctrination, basic skills, self-realization, or social mobility; and several wealthy men, including the distinguished Catholic attorney Frederic R. Coudert and banker J. Edward Simmons, opposed centralization to the end. Even on the level of basic economic policy, Greater New York's economic elites could not agree on such matters as whether state or local government ought to regulate public service corporations or own and operate gas, electric, and transit utilities; encourage or repress the organization of labor unions; increase or restrict the municipal services offered to the poor.

SPECIALIZATION, THE EXPERT, AND UPPER-INCOME PRESSURE GROUPS

If Greater New York did not possess a single united power elite able to impose its own agenda, to insinuate its own basic objections and assumptions into public policy, and to control the major political parties and fill the city's offices, it did have a large number of economic and social elites that enjoyed considerable success when they sought to devise and introduce specific policy proposals. Their key resource was their access to, and control over, expert knowledge. A single pattern repeated itself in case after case. Experts who enjoyed a good deal of latitude worked out specific policy proposals, but they did so under the close supervision of quasi-expert attorneys or other lay specialists who represented particular economic elites. Once mutual consultation had resulted in a proposal, its expert advocates and representatives of the economic elites that had approved it sought evidence of wider public support and then sought

H

the commitments from the political parties necessary for governmental action. Most successful proposals represented close consultation between experts and representatives of the city's economic elites.

In addition to its millionaires, Greater New York contained dispropor-
tionately large numbers of professional experts, many of whom specialized in developing policy proposals for the city's economic elites. In the Greater New York case Andrew H. Green, aided by Calvert Vaux and Albert E. Henschel, provided the services of a comprehensive regional planner and administrator to large estates and landowners, and to the Swallowtail Democrats who in turn represented the mercantile elite. James C. Carter, John F. Dillon, Dorman B. Eaton, Seth Low, Albert Shaw, and Simon Sterne provided similar expertise on municipal administration. In the rapid transit case, Abram S. Hewitt and Albert Shaw supplied key advice on financing; Henry R. Beekman and Edward M. Shepard provided legal expertise; and William Barclay Parsons and other engineers supplied tech-nical information to a specially constituted board of well-informed but not expert businessmen. On school centralization, Nicholas Murray Butler and Seth Low offered the latest professional advice, while Stephen H. Olin, John C. Clark, and A. Augustus Johnson, as lawyers and concerned laymen, constituted a sort of board of trustees that could both make its own contributions and represent the interests of several economic and social elites. Experts who chiefly advised the economic elite can be found in other controversies as well, particularly those that involved charity. In their different ways the philanthropists Alfred T. White and Jacob Riis, and the experts Lawrence W. Veiller and E. R. L. Gould provided technical advice on tenement house reform. Similarly Richard Watson Gilder, Frederic W. Holls, and R. W. deForest could evaluate its implica-tions for the Charity Organization Society. Eleanora Kinnicutt evaluated the work of George E. Waring and other professional sanitary engineers, and Louisa Lee Schuyler, Josephine Shaw Lowell, and William Rhinelander Stewart evaluated the suggestions of charity professionals like Homer Folks.[6]

The experts' jobs permitted or encouraged most of them to specialize in a single area of public policy. Many were lawyers whose firms had them study nonlegal matters important to clients: Green and Henschel mastered regional development as well as the related law of property transfers and estates; James C. Carter, John F. Dillon, Dorman B. Eaton, Simon Sterne, and many other civil service reformers contributed to the study of public administration; Beekman and Shepard (as well as Whit-ney's attorneys, Elihu Root and Francis Lynde Stetson) specialized in street railway and related matters; Stephen H. Olin, John C. Clark,

J. A. Johnson, and John B. Pine read up on the law governing education; and Frederick W. Holls became an expert on tenement-house reform.[7] Gilder and Shaw found careers in publishing that enabled them to pursue their interests in public affairs. The engineers, including Parsons, Waring, and others involved in such matters as Greater New York and rapid transit, were professional consultants. Several other experts, including E. R. L. Gould, James B. Reynolds, and Lawrence Veiller, held positions in the Protestant charities. Nicholas Murray Butler was one of the few who was then based in a university, but in 1896 he could already call on several other academics for aid in the school centralization affair, and the numbers of university-based experts would increase rapidly after 1900. All these experts had gained their reputations through demonstrated competence and professional recognition. But they retained large professional practices or held their positions at the discretion of wealthy clients or boards of trustees. Greater New York was an international financial center where merchants, bankers, and industrialists could secure the best possible advice on investments. When some of these same wealthy men turned to public policy, they expected and received equally expert advice, tailored to their own preferences.

This is not to say that Greater New York's experts were controlled by a monolithic upper class or that they provided only one line of advice on any given subject. Like those who employed them, they differed widely among themselves. But they owed much of their standing, as experts and even more as advisors on public policy, to their wealthy clients, employers, and sponsors. The progress of an expert was not often so pat as that described by Henry James in the New York scenes of *The Bostonians*, in which "a rich and venerable citizen, conspicuous for his public spirit and his large almsgiving" could, by his "request . . . to be made known to Miss Tarrant . . . mark her for the approval of the respectable. . . ."[8] But it was essential for the experts to retain the confidence of their wealthy sponsors, as Green, acutely aware of the "substantial people" in the mercantile elite, always did. Butler was careful to do the same in the school centralization movement. Joseph M. Rice, by contrast, entered this controversy with less support than Butler and lost his standing altogether when be opposed centralization. Albert Shaw understood the situation clearly when he wrote Richard Ely that he would abandon his strong-city-council plan for fear of being thought eccentric and when he moderated his municipal ownership enthusiasms to suit Chamber of Commerce sentiment. And when Stanton Coit, Headworker of the University Settlement in 1893, tested the limits of his independence by publicly denouncing greedy landlords, he lost his job. He was replaced, as Henry

Holt explained to Francis Lynde Stetson, by "a level-headed Columbia Fellow in Economics, and the managers of the Settlement have learned caution."[9]

Yet while their wealthy clients and employers limited the range of options that the experts were free to propose, those same clients and employers found that reliance on specialized experts limited their own power in turn. Greater New York attracted disproportionately large numbers of experts, and their numbers encouraged them to specialize and to form professional associations. The experts looked for ideas to their professional peers, and to scientific and scholarly sources in Europe and throughout the United States, as well as to their clients and sponsors. Green and Olmsted in regional planning, Low, Shaw, and Goodnow in municipal administration, Butler in education, Hewitt and Parsons in rapid transit engineering, and Hewitt and Shaw in rapid transit financing, all, as experts, learned from these extraneous sources, and recommended ideas not fully acceptable to some of those who first relied on them. As several fields came to constitute specialities in their own right, and as expert advice came less generally from lawyers and more often from specialized professionals and from academics or charity workers holding salaried positions in relatively independent institutions, heterodox ideas were offered with increasing frequency.

The developing specialization and division of labor among experts imposed still another limit on the power of the economic elites: It forced them to set up specialized pressure groups. Few of the individuals involved in school centralization took part in municipal consolidation or rapid transit planning; and there was by no means a complete overlap between those involved in consolidation and transit, despite the close connection between the two decisions. Stephen H. Olin was not a professional expert in education, but he had to specialize in that area if he was to keep up with (and supervise) Butler, and if he was to achieve results. The same was true of George W. Chauncey and other officers of the Brooklyn Consolidation League, or of Eleanora Kinnicutt's work for improved sanitation.

Richard S. Skolnik has argued that the people he describes as New York City's reformers learned by about 1903 that they could exert more influence through single-purpose interest groups than through an independent, progressive political party.[10] A study focused on decisions instead of careers indicates that New York City's wealthy men and women and many of its innovative, if not necessarily progressive, experts had worked this way for many years before 1900. It also suggests that they rarely pursued controversial matters through general-purpose organizations. Even an organization with so broad a purpose as the Union League Club had an explicit policy "to reserve for occasions of special importance the exercise of its political force, and to avoid, save when required by grave reason, such controversies as might disturb the social harmony so happily prevailing among its members."[11] The president of the Produce Exchange used similar language in his 1896 Annual Address: "In the field of legislation it has been the object of the Board of Managers to confine their attention to those measures which particularly affected the branches of trade and commerce represented upon our floor. Aside from the fact that it is no part of the business of an institution of this character to interfere with general legislation, we have felt that our influence would be lessened and the result of our efforts on those matters which directly concerned us made less apparent, if we dissipated our strength on purposes which lay beyond the domain of our chartered purposes."[12]

The few wealthy men who participated in more than one major decision at a time were themselves specialists in general administration. They included elder statesmen like Abram S. Hewitt, Chamber of Commerce leaders like Alexander E. Orr and Charles Stewart Smith, religious leaders like Bishop Henry C. Potter and the Reverend Charles S. Parkhurst, elected executive officers like Governors Morton and Theodore Roosevelt and Mayors Strong and Low, and leaders of political factions like Edward M. Shepard and Elihu Root. A limited number of men had a great deal to say about which issues should be taken up, but no single leader or set of leaders established priorities on all issues for all the economic and social elites, and some of those who established priorities were more clearly members of political than of economic elites.

THE VERY WEALTHY AND PARTY POLITICS

Nor was it possible for all of Greater New York's wealthy men and women to limit participation in major public policy disputes to those within their own ranks. Most major decisions required state legislation and the cooperation of elected city officials. Since elected officials had to consider votes, advocates of change were forced to rally others to their proposals. Thus the early consolidationists brought in Brooklyn political, real estate, and retail interests, and made a general appeal to the public in the 1894 referendum. Butler and Olin felt it necessary to reach beyond the Committee of Seventy and the City Club to the German Jews concerned to Americanize the eastern European immigrants of the lower east side, and to less wealthy groups ranging from the Good Government Clubs, the Public Education Association, the City Vigilance League, and the institutional churches, down to the principals of upstate normal schools. Although the Chamber of Commerce retained extraordinarily close control over rapid transit planning between 1894 and 1907, refusing to work with the Board of Trade and Transportation or the Real Estate Exchange, the Chamber's version of Abram S. Hewitt's plan did have the support of these bodies, and the legislature, at the suggestion of labor organizations, submitted the plan to a referendum in 1894. To impress elected officials and win over possible opponents, innovators often had to appeal to a public almost as large as the one that held the franchise.

A large number of New York's wealthiest men, representing several different economic and social elites, appealed to a broad public not simply to gain support for specific proposals, but to win office and thus to gain the ability to dispose as well as propose. Swallowtail Democrats like Abram S. Hewitt, Edward Cooper, Oswald Ottendorfer, Charles S. Fairchild, William C. Whitney, and William R. Grace in Manhattan, and Edward M. Shepard, George Foster Peabody, and Alexander E. Orr in Brooklyn; Swallowtail Republicans like Joseph H. Choate, Elihu Root, William L. Strong, William C. Brookfield, and their younger associates including Henry L. Stimson; and independents like R. Fulton Cutting, Arthur von Briesen, Edmond Kelly, and Gustav H. Schwab, all used their money, political knowledge and experience, ideas, intelligence, prestige, and social connections to maintain effective and durable political organizations of their own. Others worked through regular political parties that were increasingly managed by self-sufficient professional politicians and that would eventually displace the millionaire-sponsored organizations.

But in the 1890s New York's wealthiest men had by no means been forced out of politics. On the contrary, their high rate of participation further diffused and fragmented their impact on local affairs. As Olmsted observed in the 1870s, it was necessary for wealthy men to form "politico-commercial alliances" if they wished to influence events or advance candidacies in New York. The city's political factions and interest groups formed constantly shifting alliances in their quest for nominations, votes, legislation, and administrative actions. Whatever their personal wealth, leaders of each faction had to play the game like ordinary politicians, or be forced out. "Realizing that the leader of a Machine always becomes a 'boss,' " an unhappy associate once wrote Edward M. Shepard, "I again say I admire your pluck while I deplore your methods."[13] Whatever the truth of this particular charge, the general point was well taken. Through their political factions, the wealthy politicos developed ties to other politicians, responsibilities to assembly district workers, obligations to contractors and suppliers, and sensitivity to the voters. They exerted more influence than they could have done without their political organizations. But they also diminished their ability to act as a unified power elite without consulting others in the city.

One further circumstance, the product of cultural rather than economic and social-organizational forces, further limited the ability of Greater New York's economic elites to gain their own ends through elective politics. Like the experts on whom they relied, those who belonged to the economic elites derived much more frequently than did the rest of their fellow citizens from a British-American Protestant ethnic and religious background. German Protestants and German Jews played as prominent a part in the formulation of public policy as they did in shipping and private banking, and many of the city's wealthiest men adopted a remarkably cosmopolitan social outlook. Many Tammany backers, including August Belmont, Andrew Freedman, and William C. Whitney, mixed easily with their political associates at the race tracks and baseball parks they financed.[14] But a very large portion of the region's wealthiest men adopted increasingly strident anti-Catholic and anti-Semitic social prejudices, and many even of those who supported social reform placed a greater emphasis on an aggressively Protestant cultural and moral reform policy. By emphasizing their cultural distinctiveness, and by seeking to impose their cultural values on others, several economic elites diminished their ability to gain their economic and political ends. In the 1880s their cultural commitments led the Swallowtails to withdraw from the Democratic Party; in the next twenty years cultural issues made it impossible for several groups of wealthy men to put together a stable independent municipal party under their own direction.

Several historians have recently asked whether economic interests or cultural loyalties best account for nineteenth-century voting patterns.[15] In Greater New York, by far the largest proportion of those who were very wealthy belonged to the Anglo-Protestant cultural group, a local minority. When most of the Anglo-Protestant Swallowtail Democrats abandoned their policy of cooperating with the Irish Catholics and failed to reconcile themselves to the increasing cultural heterogeneity of the metropolis, they left the political field free for the emergence of an independent Tammany, and thus permitted Tammany's leaders to combine cultural and class appeals in its propaganda. For the sake of a modest success in their effort to shape the region's cultural policies, a large portion of the mercantile, corporate, and professional elites sacrificed much of their political interests—though they did retain most of their influence over economic policy.

PARTY LEADERS AND MIDDLE-INCOME PRESSURE GROUPS

.   Schemes to restrict the franchise to property owners or at least to those literate in English, and to impose stiff requirements on eligibility for the civil service, were the two political reforms that found most universal support among Greater New York's economic elites. These schemes reflected the general frustration felt by men and women who enjoyed unrivaled facilities for developing proposals, but who could not entirely control the officials who decided whether their proposals became law, or how the laws, once secured, were carried into effect.[16] The regular political organizations of New York City, Brooklyn, and the state as a whole mobilized the greatest concentrations of power over these aspects of decision making, and they grew increasingly independent of the economic elites during the last years of the nineteenth century.

Wealthy political independents made much of Tammany leader Richard Croker's blatant cynicism before the Mazet Committee and his dismissive remarks on such important policy issues as currency ("I'm in favor of all kinds of money—the more the better") and anti-imperialism (he opposed "the fashion of shooting everybody who doesn't speak English"). But the idea that party organizations ignored policy, which Bryce and Ostrogorski picked up from Godkin and other informants, does not hold.[17] Some policies, such as economic and cultural *laissez-faire* for the Democrats, were central to party self-identification; others required careful handling as party leaders sought to arrange coalitions. Nor can we accept the other contemporary charge, that the party organizations had become monoliths dominated by dictatorial bosses. It is true that Republican Thomas C. Platt exerted remarkably complete control over his party's votes in the state legislature between 1893 and 1901 and successfully opposed a fusion between his party and the independent Citizens' Union in support of Seth Low's mayoral candidacy in 1897. It is also true that Tammany leaders (aided by election law reforms intended to reduce their power) imposed increasingly strict discipline on their organization after 1888, and especially after 1903, and that Croker personally directed the nominations of Van Wyck in 1897 and of Shepard in 1901. But even in these cases the bosses were supported by important groups both within their parties and without. As Martin Shefter has observed, although the creation of a highly centralized and disciplined political organization did reduce the patronage opportunities for particular district leaders, in return it gave the organization as a whole both stability and the capacity to charge substantial and predictable fees for the increased services, such as guaranteeing that the legislature would not indulge in unwarranted interference with private business, it could render. Party centralization and discipline thus constituted a "collective benefit" for district leaders.[18] Because these changes rendered an organization independent of direct Swallowtail control, they also enabled political leaders to pay increased attention to the demands of middle-income interest groups.

Increasingly through the nineties, party leaders derived their power from their ability to organize coalitions, mediate and conciliate conflicts among competing factions and interest groups, and win elections. Tammany in particular was able to make itself the champion (in the Greater New York and school centralization controversies as well as in the field of mayoral politics) of the preferences of middle-income, second-generation Irish Catholics, and to a lesser extent of German Catholics and Jews. Tammany leaders also paid close attention to the demands of petty real estate, contracting, and commercial interests in upper Manhattan. And by the mid-nineties Tammany's John Ahearn was paying as much attention to the desires of well-organized civil servants such as the public school teachers as Jacob A. Cantor was paying to those of the Chamber of Commerce. The Republican Party countered by providing similar representation for the preferences of middle-income British-American Protestants and to a lesser extent for Jews and German Lutherans, and for real estate and contracting interests in Brooklyn. Just as the wealthy Swallowtail and independent politicos derived much of their influence from a variety of political, business, professional, charitable, religious, and social organizations, the party bosses could support their pretensions by pointing to the many factions and middle-income interest groups they represented.

Several of the anti-Tammany groups among the economic elites made an earnest effort during the nineties to impose the dry Sunday, to restrict if not eliminate government support for Catholic welfare institutions, to impose stringent "character" tests on Catholic and Jewish applicants for municipal employment and to recruit employees through channels largely supplied by Protestants, and in other ways to impose British-Protestant cultural values and practices on an increasingly Catholic and Jewish population. Together, the Democratic and Republican party organizations resisted these pressures quite successfully. In the sense that most of their leaders were men who had learned to live and work with and to mediate conflicts among people of diverse ethnic and religious backgrounds, they were more cosmopolitan than the members of the wealthiest economic, social, and professional elites; conflicts between the two sets of elites were not necessarily between "locals" and "cosmopolitans."[19]

The cultural give-and-take of middle-income life in New York, the

increasing specialization of economic and professional activities and interests, and the increasingly diverse pressures exerted by middle-income as
well as upper-income interest groups, all made it necessary for successful
party leaders to operate as cosmopolitan brokers responsive to demands
from all ethnic groups and all economic levels. The middle- and lower-
middle-income interest groups, like the party leaders themselves, lacked
the access to specialized expertise enjoyed by the economic and social
elites, and they were not nearly so successful in shaping the views of
experts or in developing policy proposals that reflected their own interests.
But they represented and influenced large numbers of voters, and through
the party organizations and the city government's administrative staff
they exerted significant influence over the final shape of legislation, and
over the administration of such proposals as were adopted. Their influence
was most strongly felt in the making of mayoral nominations, in cultural
policy, and in hiring practices; through the parties, middle-income economic interest groups also gained consideration of their views regarding
Greater New York, rapid transit, and school centralization.

LOWER-INCOME WORKERS AND THEIR UNIONS

Greater New York's workingmen exerted much less influence than
either its wealthiest or its middle-income economic and social elites. Yet
with the Henry George campaign of 1886 the city's increasingly well-
organized craft unions did force their way into the public arena, and
they slowly consolidated their position over the next fifteen years.

After 1886 labor organizations had perhaps their greatest successes in
mayoral politics, preventing the nomination of candidates like Edward
Cooper and George E. Waring who were perceived as anti-labor, and contributing to the decision to nominate Seth Low, who had adopted a generally
pro-labor stance. Through their influence over mayoral nominations labor
leaders secured at least some recognition, in the courts and in police
practices, of their right to conduct orderly strikes, informational boycotts,
and organizing drives. Labor leaders also played an important part in moving the Committee of Seventy and the Citizens' Union platforms slightly
to the left. And as Samuel T. McSeveney has persuasively contended, a
belief on the part of many workingmen that Republican economic policies
would bring an end to the depression of the mid-nineties explains much
of the shift from Democratic to Republican majorities in New York State
after 1892.[20]

On the other hand, labor leaders suffered several clear-cut defeats in
these years. School centralization went through despite Samuel Gompers's

telegram urging Mayor Strong to reject it. Labor leaders provided important support when the Chamber of Commerce sought approval for arrangements under which the city would invest its own funds in the rapid transit subway—a policy that labor had long supported, but the Chamber-dominated Rapid Transit Commission refused to offer one of its seats to a labor representative. The Citizens' Union was controlled by wealthy men who insisted that labor influence be kept to a minimum, lower east side socialists did not persuade the majority of New York's Protestant reformers to value social reform over moral reform, and Seth Low did not become another Hazen S. Pingree.[21]

Largely excluded from the policy-planning groups set up by the region's economic and social elites, labor leaders found it even more difficult than their middle-income counterparts to gain access to expertise or to develop policy proposals tailored to their own preferences. But the skilled workers who accepted Gompers's bread-and-butter approach and the Jewish garment workers developed increasingly effective organizations and demonstrated that they could use their votes with discretion. By the mid-nineties they were able to extract significant concessions from the Tammany Democrats, regular Republicans, and wealthy independents who sought their support at the polls. Gradually and indirectly, the labor organizations and their leaders helped create the conditions that permitted several unions to conduct successful organizing drives after 1896 and that encouraged officials to expand the city's social and educational services, to provide municipal financing for rapid transit, and to create a Greater New York capable of planning public works on a comprehensive scale. Some of these developments benefited semiskilled and unskilled workers outside the garment trades, but they remained poorly organized and without an effective voice in local affairs. They may have been heard as Irishmen or Germans, or as Catholics, but they continued to be ignored as working people.

The Inadequacy of Indirect Evidence

These conclusions differ somewhat from those that would have been suggested by an analysis limited to officeholders or reputations. If we may believe Thomas Mann, when a merchant like Thomas Buddenbrook had established himself as one of the richest and most influential men in late nineteenth-century Lübeck, he could confidently expect to be elected to the town senate—a body whose authority was as unchallenged in its sphere as was that of Parliament in Sir Lewis Namier's eighteenth-century Britain.[22] The relationship between position and power was not nearly so neat in late nineteenth-century New York. New York contained no comparably definitive deliberative institution, and it was not immediately apparent who did participate in decision making.

Studies of the social origins of mayors in a number of American cities suggest that as cities grew larger and economically more complex over the course of the nineteenth century, they became less likely to select their mayors from their economic elites and more likely to select them from the ranks of professional politicians of modest means.[23] In a model study of Ypsilanti, Michigan, Robert O. Schulze suggested that this shift in the social origins of high municipal officeholders reflected a "bifurcation" of the power structure into distinct political and economic elites.[24] The changing social origins of New York's mayors supports this generalization, but the decision-making evidence suggests that its significance was limited. The increasing division of labor affected political roles as it did economic and professional ones, and it did restrict the ability of the wealthy to gain their ends. But their own division into competing economic elites and their reliance on expert specialists also limited their power. The wealthy had developed ways to deal with political organizations before 1886, and they retained much of their ability to shape proposals and influence the local agenda after 1903.

Nor would we learn as much about power in New York from the analysis of the social origins of voluntary association officers as some scholars have believed.[25] The sources that have been preserved give disproportionate attention to the associations of the wealthy, even for so fully documented a society as that of late nineteenth-century New York, and the associations varied widely in their ability to influence decisions. In an effort to increase their organizations' longevity, many association leaders avoided controversy altogether. And simple lists of the members of "committees" of fifty, seventy, or one hundred often reflected little more than a propagandist's notion of the names and affiliations that would impress public officials.

Evidence as to contemporary reputations for power can be derived from lists of this sort, from the press, from formal writings on municipal government, and from private correspondence. But ethnic and class prejudices gave a profound bias to these perceptions. Such keen observers as Bryce, Ostrogorski, and their American informants failed to recognize the development of increasingly potent Irish, German, Catholic, Jewish, civil-servant, middle-level business, and labor organizations in Greater New York, and no doubt in other cities as well, during the last two decades of the nineteenth century.

Peter Bachrach, Morton Baratz, and other scholars have urged that students of power attend to its "other face," to the values, institutions, and behind-the-scenes techniques that can "define the situation" so as to advance proposals favored by the wealthy and established, and to suppress proposals they oppose. The second face of power was much in evidence in late nineteenth-century New York, but in each of its diverse manifestations it constituted only one resource among many. Nor did every effort to rearrange institutions or shape public opinion have its intended consequence. Most of the early advocates of ballot and primary election reform in New York were wealthy men who hoped to reduce the political impact of political machines and illiterate, immigrant voters. But as the reforms assigned more and more of the expenses of primary and general elections to the state, the parties became less and less dependent on their wealthy backers and more responsive to an electorate that did not shrink as registration and voting procedures became more demanding. E. L. Godkin and his contemporaries were able to consign Daniel Greenleaf Thompson's dispassionate analysis of Tammany's effectiveness to oblivion, but in doing so they limited their readers' knowledge even as they encouraged their self-confidence. The Chamber of Commerce and Albert Shaw both served their own purposes when they early promoted the idea of Greater New York. But neither could then effectively oppose the use to which Republican leader Thomas C. Platt put their idea. Nicholas Murray Butler and his associates could bury Joseph M. Rice's argument that an effective school reform plan ought to provide concerned and stimulating leadership for the classroom teachers, but they could not alter the fact that the centralized school system would continue to be staffed by teachers and administrators who retained close ties to the communities they served and who opposed the centralizers' preferred cultural policies.

For New York City at the end of the nineteenth century, at any rate, it is not necessary to rely on indirect evidence about the exercise of power. The great volumes of memoirs, correspondence, memoranda, printed reports, government documents, daily newspapers, and periodicals provide an almost overwhelming body of source material. This material is weighted toward the activities of the wealthy, but for the making of major decisions it also provides a great deal of evidence about the participation—and sometimes the exclusion—of the "other half." To a remarkable degree, the evidence even permits us to observe how some participants sought to mobilize bias and to shape the public agenda.

The Increasing Dispersal of Power in the Cities of the United States during the Twentieth Century

Bryce and Ostrogorski were right to insist that far from falling into precipitous decline, the power exercised by late nineteenth-century New York's richest and best-educated men was stronger and extended over a wider scope of public affairs than that of any other group in the nation's largest city. Like most knowledgeable American observers at the time, the distinguished foreigners did tend to exaggerate the power and the unity of the city's wealthiest men and to ignore the considerable and increasing power exercised by several of the metropolitan region's less wealthy political, economic, and ethnic groups. But although the concentration of power in the hands of the very wealthy was already declining in the 1890s, it remained much more marked than Wallace Sayre and Herbert Kaufman found it to be in their exhaustive study of New York City in the 1950s.[26] How can we account for this long-term dispersion of power away from the very rich?

Several sociologists have concluded that a long-term dispersal of power has taken place and have begun to develop an explanation. David Rogers, Terry N. Clark, Michael Aiken, and others have argued that such factors as increasing size, social heterogeneity, economic diversity, absentee ownership of local economic enterprises, a large number of voluntary associations, and a high level of voting and other forms of citizen involvement in public affairs are all associated with an increasingly broad dispersal of power.[27] In the most carefully considered of these surveys of the social science literature, Michael Aiken concludes that "the older cities, those having had a greater influx of immigrants and other minority groups, and those having non-reformed political structures, are cities that are more likely to have decentralized decision-making arrangements."[28] In a general way, these factors might account for the fact that power was more widely dispersed in late nineteenth-century New York than Estelle Feinstein found it to be in late nineteenth-century Stamford, Connecticut, or than Carl V. Harris found it to be in Birmingham, Alabama, at the same time.[29] And these factors might also account for the increasing dispersal of power in New York City itself over the next fifty years.[30]

Yet all of Aiken's criteria already applied to Greater New York in the

1880s, when power seems to have been even more narrowly concentrated in the hands of an economic elite than it was in 1900. The sociologists' theory, which is based largely on the comparative analysis of data of varying reliability gathered mostly in the 1950s, does not account very well for historical change and fails to specify very clearly how the several factors it singles out might be related to the distribution of power. The New York case suggests that some factors ought to be defined more precisely, and that other factors are also relevant.

In late nineteenth-century New York, economic and cultural conflicts divided the very wealthy into competing elites, providing the opportunity for independent political elites to seize control of the party organizations and leading at least some of the economic elites to reach out to less wealthy groups for support. This would suggest that the relevant question is not "When did city X become industrialized?" or "To what extent do absentees own the productive facilities of city X?", but "To what extent are the wealthiest people in city X divided into competing elites?" And the larger questions—questions that this book has emphasized— ought to be "What conditions tend to divide a city's wealthiest residents into competing elites?" and "Under what circumstances will economic elites bargain for the support of nonelite groups?"

At the end of the nineteenth century, divisions among the very wealthy seem to have multiplied as New York retained its position as the dominant city in the national system of cities during a period in which the economy was undergoing a rapid reorganization. As late as 1880 the richest men in Greater New York were merchants engaged in foreign and domestic wholesale trade, together with the bankers, attorneys, shipowners, and railroad entrepreneurs who served, or sought to exploit, commerce. But the decline of the wholesale merchant and the rise of the vertically integrated manufacturing firm was already under way in 1880, and by 1900 those changes had brought new economic and professional elites, with much more diverse economic perspectives and interests to New York.

Both before and after 1900, New York's economic elites may have been more willing to bargain with their city's less wealthy residents because they employed so few of them in their own firms. Nineteenth-century merchants and bankers employed very few workers of any sort, the national corporations established few plants in the metropolis, and the retired men of wealth who gave New York something of the quality of a *Residenzstadt* by the 1890s supervised no employees except their personal servants. Apart from the sugar and oil refiners and a few others who processed imported goods, manufacturing in Greater New York was confined to the volatile garment, printing, luxury, and related industries in which small firms prevailed. Many of the most active leaders of the Citizens' Union had inherited large fortunes; the other leaders of the organization were merchants, bankers, and lawyers. When they entered into discussions with the leaders of unions in the garment and building trades, they were not talking to their own employees. And when corporate leaders like John D. Rockefeller decided to concern themselves with the moral health of the metropolis, they did not have to consider whether the objects of their concern worked in their own plants.

In these respects, New York was unusual at the time; in other large cities, in Chicago and Philadelphia as well as Pittsburgh and Birmingham, many of the wealthiest men were also very large local employers.[31] The reorganization of American industry probably had a smaller immediate impact on the economic elites of other large cities. As Eric E. Lampard has shown, the division of labor among large cities and their regions was still strongly marked in 1900 and remained so for the next thirty or forty years.[32] With the possible exceptions of Boston and Chicago, New York attracted far more than its share of the owners and managers of the large corporations, and more of the professional and technical experts who advised them, than any other city during these years. It seems likely that New York's wealthiest men and women were unusually likely to divide into competing economic elites.

But Lampard has also shown that the United States system of cities has been radically transformed since the 1930s as the large cities and their regions in all sections of the nation have grown increasingly similar in their economic functions and characteristics.[33] If it follows that each regional metropolis has developed its own diverse sets of economic and professional elites—that the largest cities, at any rate, have become less and less tied to two or three major economic functions—then it should also follow that the New York pattern of division and competition among the very wealthy has come to characterize most of the large cities in the United States.

The New York City case also suggests that the absolute level of a group's living standard and other resources is relevant to its ability to exercise power. If power was more widely dispersed in the metropolis in 1900 than it had been in 1880, the explanation surely lies in the higher absolute, though perhaps not relative, level of the material, cultural, and organizational resources available to the city's less wealthy residents. In 1880 a substantial portion of the population lived very close to the subsistence level, was illiterate and unskilled, had recently suffered through the disorienting experience of immigration, and had not yet overcome the constraints that disparate national backgrounds imposed on the formation of an effective labor movement. Over the next twenty years the absolute level of income and education improved, the death rate, which indicates something about wealth as well as about public health, dropped almost 30 percent, and the Irish and German communities produced large American-born generations more eager to come to terms with life in the United States than to recreate the old country in the new. The established groups were joined by eastern European Jews whose cultural, organizational, and even economic resources already compared favorably to those of the Irish. Drawing on their increased wealth and literacy, and adapting inherited cultural resources like the Irish boycott for use in New York, Irish, German, and eastern European Jewish leaders set up effective religious, ethnic, labor, and political organizations capable of pressing demands on public officials and economic elites. Despite the efforts of the Tilden Commission and those who, like Abram S. Hewitt, would have denied the vote to immigrants, the practice of universal manhood suffrage continued to prevail, so that it was possible to make political use of these resources. Some officials and economic elites had become more willing to listen to the new demands; others found that they had little choice, if they wished to play any part in elective politics.

The significance of the absolute level of economic and cultural resources is also suggested by the Birmingham, Alabama, case. In Birmingham, the level of economic resources and public education available to Birmingham's largely black lower class and its largely foreign-born skilled workers failed to improve between 1871 and 1921. Few of these people had voted in the 1870s, and by 1900 a third to a half of the city's poorest adult males, some whites as well as all blacks, had been permanently disenfranchised. Lacking economic, cultural, and political resources relevant to their situation in Alabama, these groups produced no effective organizations to press their demands.[34] They failed to increase their impact on local decisions, and the explanation would seem to lie as much in their absolute economic, cultural, and organizational poverty as in the relative wealth of Birmingham's often competing manufacturing and commercial elites.

A comparison between late nineteenth-century New York and New York in the 1950s also underlines the significance of the level of economic and cultural resources. Sayre and Kaufman's very thorough study demonstrated that middle-, lower middle-, and even lower-income pressure groups exercised stronger power over a wider scope of affairs in the 1950s than they had done fifty years earlier. By the later period labor leaders in a very wide range of civil service, skilled, semiskilled, and even unskilled occupations, leaders of neighborhood as well as city-wide religious and ethnic organizations, and a greatly expanded array of special-interest groups, were routinely consulted—and heeded—by the professional politicians and career administrators who filled the city's top elective and appointive offices.[35]

The city's economic elites seem to have changed in ways that would account for some of this further dispersal of power. The remnants of the old mercantile elite had long faded from the scene, leaving the economic elite perhaps more fragmented and more concerned with business interests outside New York than before. By the 1950s most members of the economic elites no longer made any active resistance to the political prominence, in New York City, at least, of Germans, Irish Catholics, Jews, or Italians. And labor unions had won an accepted if not always welcome place in the city's life.[36]

But the level of economic, cultural, and organizational resources available to the city's less wealthy whites, though not to its now large and rapidly increasing black and Puerto Rican populations, had risen sharply. Incomes, economic skills, educational achievements, and cultural adaptation to life in New York all improved. Immigration had been largely cut off in the 1920s, so that by the 1950s the proportion of immigrants in the white population had fallen sharply. These increased resources produced effective organizations, which now multiplied their power through their impact on professional and technical experts. In the 1890s experts had found employment largely in Wall Street law firms and in similar firms of engineering and architectural consultants, in the Protestant charities, and in journalism. By the 1950s expertise had become much more widely available as experts found employment in labor unions, Catholic and Jewish as well as Protestant charities, government, universities, and foundations. The cultural resource of expertise had become much more widely diffused, enabling many of the city's less wealthy economic groups to play a much more effective part in the framing of public policy.

These are the broader implications suggested by the study of power distributions in Greater New York. Considerations suggested by the history of regional and metropolitan specialization would lead us to expect that the history of power has been different in most other large cities. But persuasive generalizations about the history of power in urban America, and even confirmation of the explanations offered here for the fragmentation of the economic elites and the increasing effectiveness of less wealthy economic groups in New York, must await comparable studies of other cities.

NOTES

CHAPTER 1

1. Among the most influential contributors to this perspective are Herbert G. Gutman in the essays collected in *Work, Culture, and Society in Industrializing America: Essays in American Working-Class and Social History* (New York: Alfred A. Knopf, 1976); Eugene D. Genovese, *Roll, Jordan, Roll: The World the Slaves Made* (New York: Pantheon Books, 1974); and David Montgomery, "The Shuttle and the Cross: Weavers and Artisans in the Kensington Riots of 1844," *Journal of Social History* 5 (1972):411–46.

2. Steven Lukes, *Power: A Radical View* (London: Macmillan and Co., 1974), p. 26.

3. Estelle F. Feinstein, *Stamford in the Gilded Age: The Political Life of a Connecticut Town, 1868–1893* (Stamford, Conn.: The Stamford Historical Society, Inc., 1973); J. Rogers Hollingsworth and Ellen Jane Hollingsworth, "Expenditures in American Cities," in William O. Adelotte *et al.*, eds., *The Dimensions of Quantitative Research in History* (Princeton: Princeton University Press, 1972), pp. 347–89; Carl V. Harris, *Political Power in Birmingham, 1871–1921* (Knoxville: University of Tennessee Press, 1977); J. Rogers Hollingsworth and Ellen Jane Hollingworth, *Dimensions in Urban History: Historical and Social Science Perspectives on Middle-Size American Cities* (Madison: The University of Wisconsin Press, 1979).

4. Max Weber, "Class, Status, Party," in *From Max Weber: Essays in Sociology,* H. H. Gerth and C. Wright Mills, eds. and trans., (New York: Oxford University Press, 1946), p. 180.

5. For a fuller discussion see David C. Hammack, "Problems in the Historical Study of Power in the Cities and Towns of the United States, 1800–1960," *American Historical Review* 83 (April, 1978): 323–49.

6. On the overrepresentation of the wealthy on New York's City Council and Board of Aldermen between 1838 and 1850, see Edward Pessen, *Riches, Class, and Power Before the Civil War* (Lexington, Mass.: D. C. Heath & Co., 1973), pp. 281–99.

7. George Templeton Strong, *Diary,* Allan Nevins and Milton Halsey Thomas, eds. (New York: Macmillan Co., 1952), vol. 4, p. 236.

8. Ibid., p. 342.

9. Charles Loring Brace, *The Dangerous Classes of New York and Thirty Years Among Them* (New York: Wyncoop and Hallenbeck, 1872), p. 27.

10. Ibid., p. 29. William Osborne Stoddard expressed much the same view in *The Volcano Under the City* (New York: Fords, Howard, & Hulbert, 1887), which he published under the pseudonym A Volunteer Special. Stoddard asserted that "social volcanic forces continuously exist in great cities. Few men have any idea of their extent and power, or of how completely they are prepared for an eruption." These forces were especially dangerous in New York, he insisted: "Somebody has said that a great city is a great sore; but if New York is the sorest city in the country, it is so because it is the largest gathering of elements which are also to be found in all other municipalities. . . . Weakness, timidity, or time-serving compliance with lawlessness in any form provokes attack; sturdy insistence on order, and ready strength, are the only safety" (pp. 316, 317, 333).

11. William C. Redfield, *Taxes and Tenements: A Study of Municipal Conditions* (Brooklyn: League of Loyal Citizens Pamphlet no. 3, Dec. 1894), p. 56.

12. E. L. Godkin, "Problems of Municipal Government," in Godkin, *Problems of Modern Democracy,* Morton Keller, ed. (Cambridge, Mass.: Belknap Press of Harvard University

Press, 1966), p. 2. Godkin originally published this essay in 1894. John Paul Bocock expressed a similar thought in only slightly less violent language in the same year. On the basis of a review of office-holders and press comment, he asserted, "New York has ceased to be an interesting study for municipal experts. It is clean given over to Irish domination." He added that most other large American cities lay under the control of a "Hibernian oligarchy." Bocock, "The Irish Conquest of Our Cities," *The Forum* (1894): 188, 186. In 1887 Frank Goodnow wrote that the displacement of "the middle classes, which had thus far controlled the municipal government, . . . by an ignorant proletariat, mostly of foreign birth, which came under the sway of ambitious political leaders," dated from the rise of the Tweed Ring in the late 1860s; Goodnow, "The Tweed Ring in New York City," in James Bryce, *The American Commonwealth* (London and New York: Macmillan and Co., 1887), vol. 2, p. 335, quoted in Louis Pope Gratacap, *The Political Mission of Tammany Hall* (New York: A. B. King, 1894), p. 22.

13. On this point, see the discussions of the anti-Tammany campaigns of 1890, 1894, and 1901 in chap. 5 of this volume.

14. Quoted in Harold F. Gosnell, *Boss Platt and His New York Machine: A Study of the Political Leadership of Thomas C. Platt, Theodore Roosevelt, and Others* (New York: Russell & Russell 1969 reprint of 1924 first edition), p. 71. In making this assertion Root was conveniently neglecting his own very substantial role in Republican affairs during the 1890s.

15. Ibid., chap. 10.

16. Gosnell's *Boss Platt*, long the best published study of its protagonist, must now be supplemented by Richard L. McCormick, *From Realignment to Reform: Political Change in New York State, 1893–1910* (Ithaca: Cornell University Press, 1981).

17. Simon Sterne, "Administration of American Cities," in John J. Lalor, ed., *Cyclopedia of Political Science, Political Economy, and of the Political History of the United States* (New York: Maynard, Merrill & Co., 1895), vol. 1, p. 464. Richard Hofstadter emphasized Godkin's importance in *The Age of Reform: From Bryan to FDR* (New York: Alfred A. Knopf, 1955), pp. 131–48, as did John G. Sproat in *"The Best Men": Liberal Reformers in the Gilded Age* (New York: Oxford University Press, 1968). Alan Pendleton Grimes, *The Political Liberalism of the New York Nation* (Chapel Hill: The University of North Carolina Press, 1953), is a careful study of Godkin's journal.

18. Hermann Eduard von Holst, *The Constitutional Law of the United States of America*, trans. Alfred Bishop Mason (Chicago: Callaghan & Company, 1887), p. 331. In a remarkable elaboration of his point, von Holst added that "the social, intellectual and moral coherence of the people was becoming less and less, because the rapid growth of the cities under the influence of modern means of intercourse and production. The destruction of the vitalizing communal spirit, as it had existed in the conservative times of the early republic, a nation of small tradesmen and farmers, was greatly promoted by the immense influx of Europeans of different nations. Power was delivered up to the mass, and the mass was a fluctuating chaos. . . ." (p. 333). In writing of municipal government, von Holst took all of his examples from the history of New York City and relied heavily on the views of Dorman B. Eaton, another reform-minded lawyer.

19. Sterne, "Administration of American Cities," p. 464.

20. On court-imposed limitations on municipal activities, see Clyde E. Jacobs, *Law Writers and the Courts: The Influence of Thomas M. Cooley, Christopher G. Tiedeman, and John F. Dillon Upon American Constitutional Law* (New York: Da Capo Press 1973 reprint of Berkeley and Los Angeles: University of California Press edition of 1954), chaps. 4 and 5.

21. Henry George, "Open Letter to the Hon. Abram S. Hewitt, October 20, 1886," reprinted in Louis F. Post and Fred C. Leubuscher, *Henry George's 1886 Campaign: An Account of the George–Hewitt Campaign in the New York Municipal Election of 1886* (Westport, Conn.: Hyperion Press, Inc., 1976 reprint of 1887 first edition), p. 57.

22. Carl's testimony is reprinted in Sigmund Diamond, ed., *The Nation Transformed: The Creation of an Industrial Society* (New York: George Braziller, 1963), pp. 176–77.

23. The New York *World* published a large number of interviews with George supporters, Oct. 1, 1886.

24. Henry George, *Progress and Poverty* (San Francisco: W. M. Hinton & Co., 1879),

pp. 270, 305, quoted in Eric Foner, "Class, Ethnicity, and Radicalism in the Gilded Age: The Land League and Irish-America," *Marxist Perspectives* 1 (Summer 1978): 34.

25. Samuel Gompers, *Seventy Years of Life and Labor: An Autobiography* (New York: E. P. Dutton & Co., 1925), pp. 210, 311–20. As he recalled in his autobiography, Gompers wound up his campaign for George by appealing to established republican virtues: "Do not attempt to spread the schism [between capital and labor] wider, Mr. Hewitt . . . for fear lest instead of using this constitutional and legal method men may turn to less constitutional" (p. 319).

26. William H. Form and Joan Rytina, "Ideological Beliefs on the Distribution of Power in the United States," *American Sociological Review* 83 (Feb. 1969): 19–30.

27. Letter, Theodore Roosevelt to Henry Cabot Lodge, Mar. 25, 1889, reprinted in Elting E. Morison et al., eds., *The Letters of Theodore Roosevelt* (Cambridge, Mass.: Harvard University Press, 1951), vol. 1, p. 154.

28. On the anti-party ideology, see Richard Hofstadter, *The Idea of a Party System: The Rise of Legitimate Opposition in the United States, 1780–1840* (Berkeley: The University of California Press, 1970). On its persistence through the nineteenth century, see David J. Rothman, *Politics and Power: The United States Senate 1869–1901* (Cambridge, Mass.: Harvard University Press, 1966), chap. 8.

29. For evidence that a Patrician Elitist outlook was more widely held than any other among New York's men of property and education at the end of the nineteenth century, see Hammack, "Elite Perceptions of Power in the Cities of the United States, 1880–1900: The Evidence of James Bryce, Moisei Ostrogorski, and Their American Informants," *Journal of Urban History* 4 (1978): 363–96.

30. James Bryce, *The American Commonwealth*, vol. 2, p. 26.

31. For the development of these points, see Hammack, "Elite Perceptions of Power," pp. 372–78. Stated this way, Bryce's interpretation of power in American cities contrasts clearly with the "stratificationist" interpretation developed by Floyd Hunter and other sociologists and political scientists in the 1950s. As stated by Nelson Polsby (one of its most severe critics), the stratificationist interpretation of power holds: "1. There is an upper class power elite which rules in local community life. 2. Political and civic leaders are subordinate to this elite. 3. There is only one elite in each community, possessing a common will, and exerting its dominance on all non-trivial community issues. 4. The elite rules in its own interests exclusively, and largely to the detriment of the lower classes. 5. As a consequence, social conflict takes place between the elite and the non-elite" (Polsby, *Community Power and Political Theory* [New Haven: Yale University Press, 1963], pp. 129–32). Floyd Hunter presented his version of this interpretation in *Community Power Structure: A Study of Decision Makers* (Chapel Hill: University of North Carolina Press, 1953).

32. Godkin's belief in the possibility of success for the best men spurred him to the production of quantities of anti-Tammany propaganda in the 1880s and 1890s; among his most notable works in this genre were his *Tammany Biographies* (New York: The Evening Post, 1890, 1894), and *The Triumph of Reform* (New York: The Evening Post, 1895). Indeed, in the mid-eighties he defended the contribution of the Irish to American life as in many ways comparable to that of "the far richer and more cultivated Germans" (New York *Tribune*, May 31, 1884). After reading the proofs of some *American Commonwealth* chapters in 1887, Godkin wrote Bryce, "I know of nothing about the United States nearly as acute and accurate and as lucid as your talk in these chapters." He made no objection to Bryce's interpretation of power, though he did hope that Bryce understood that the bar had "much degenerated since Tocqueville's day." In 1889 he objected that Bryce had been "unnecessarily cautious" in his criticism of the United States. By the time of Seth Low's defeat in 1897, Godkin had grown "very much disappointed" with elective politics and was persuaded that Greater New York's "poor ignorant Tammany population" did not want what Bryce meant by "good government." Letters, Godkin to Bryce, Nov. 26, 1887, Mar. 24, 1889, and Nov. 19, 1897, Bryce Papers, Bodleian Library, Oxford. In late 1897 Godkin wrote to another friend, "I am tired of having to be continually hopeful; what I long for now is a little private gloom in despair." Quoted by Morton Keller in his introduction to Godkin, *Problems of Modern Democracy*, p. xxxvii; letters, Brace to Bryce, Mar. 12, 1884; Feb. 12, 1886; and Jan. 1, 1889, Bryce Papers.

33.   On Curtis and Gilder, see John Tomsich, *A Genteel Endeavor: American Culture and Politics in the Gilded Age* (Stanford: Stanford University Press, 1971), pp. 75–83, 103–7, 171–88. Gilder was more confident about the possibility of Americanizing the immigrants than Bryce himself. Compare Gilder's presidential address to the New York Kindergarten Association, reprinted in the association's 1894 *Annual Report*, with Bryce's letter to Gilder, Feb. 22, 1895, Gilder Papers, New York Public Library.

34.   Letter, Roosevelt to Bryce, Jan. 6 and Feb. 5, 1888, Bryce Papers.

35.   Letter, Goodnow to Bryce, Nov. 10, 1893, Bryce Papers. Goodnow had commended Bryce's treatment of American municipal institutions when he read the relevant chapters in proof. Goodnow to Bryce, Nov. 10, 1893, Bryce Papers.

36.   Letter, Albert Shaw to William Howe Tolman, Mar. 12, 1897, Shaw Papers, New York Public Library. This letter endorsed Tolman's proposals for the Citizens' Union mayoral campaign of 1897, and it is quite possible that Shaw's statement was a calculated flattery of the CU's financial backers. But it is consistent with other statements by Shaw, including a letter, Shaw to Bryce, Jan. 5, 1894, Shaw Papers.

37.   Letter, Clark to Bryce, Nov. 6, 1896, Bryce Papers.

38.   Letter, Bryce to Low, Jan. 9, 1892; and Low to Bryce, Nov. 2, 1897, Bryce Papers.

39.   Moisei Ostrogorski, *Democracy and the Organization of Political Parties*, vol. 2: *The United States* (London and New York: Macmillan and Co., 1902), p. 105; Rodney Barker and Xenia Howard-Johnston, "The Politics and Political Ideas of Moisei Ostrogorski," *Political Studies* 22 (1975): 415–29. For a discussion of his research on the United States, see Hammack, "Elite Perceptions of Power," pp. 395–96, n. 107.

40.   Ostrogorski, *Democracy*, pp. 94, 162–63, 166, 187–91, 204–5, 223, 248–49, 285–86, 314–17.

41.   Ibid., p. 248.

42.   For further discussion of these points, see Hammack, "Elite Perceptions of Power," pp. 382–86. The similarity between this view of power and that of the stratificationists is obvious.

43.   *The Nation* 76 (Apr. 30, 1903): 356–58.

44.   Notable among these were several of the younger anti-machine political organizers in New York, including journalist and civil service reformer George McAneny, attorney Edward M. Shepard, an independent Democrat, and social worker James B. Reynolds, the Citizens' Union's organizer on the lower east side and an ally of Theodore Roosevelt. Letters, Ostrogorski to McAneny, June 18, 1896, June 19, 1898, Mar. 4, 1900, and May 30, 1900; McAneny Papers, Princeton University; Shepard to Ostrogorski, Oct. 16, 1896, Letterpress copybook no. 7, Shepard Papers, Special Collections, Columbia University; and James B. Reynolds to Police Commissioner Bernard York requesting information for "a Russian economist who is studying constitutional government in Paris," July 31, 1899, University Settlement Society of New York Papers, State Historical Society of Wisconsin.

45.   Daniel Greenleaf Thompson, *Politics in a Democracy* (New York: Longmans, Green, and Co., 1894), pp. 44–45, 51.

46.   Ibid., p. 51.

47.   Although two leading literary periodicals, *The Critic* 23 (Dec. 1893): 389–90 and *The Dial* 16 (Apr. 1894): 214–15 reviewed *Politics in a Democracy*, most other journals ignored it. In response to a query from James Bryce, Wendell Phillips Garrison of *The Nation* "inquired about D. G. Thompson & . . . glanced at his book. He is little known in this office," Garrison wrote, "and very lightly esteemed, & you are safe in treating him as a negligible quantity." Letter, Garrison to Bryce, Dec. 20, 1893, Bryce Papers.

48.   A memorial volume, *Daniel Greenleaf Thompson, Feb. 9, 1850, July 10, 1897,* (New York, 1898), contains accounts of Thompson's life, as do obituaries in the New York *Times* and New York *World*. A member of the Century Association, the Authors and Lawyers Clubs, and the Association of the Bar of the City of New York, Thompson was also for many years the president of the Nineteenth Century Club.

49.   Cited in Richard Skolnik, "The Crystallization of Reform in New York City, 1890–1917" (Ph.D. diss., Yale University, 1971) p. 109.

50.   *The Banker's Magazine* 52 (1896): 714.

51.   Thompson, *Politics in a Democracy*, p. 44.

52.   *The Banker's Magazine* 53 (1896): 272–76.

53.   A number of Richard Croker's most direct statements on self-interest in politics

are pulled together in New York State (Legislature), Assembly, Special Committee to Investigate the Public Offices and Department of the City of New York (the Mazet Committee), *Report of Counsel,* Dec. 22, 1899, p. 44. Plunkitt's statements are contained in William L. Riordan, *Plunkitt of Tammany Hall* (New York: E. P. Dutton & Co., 1963), pp. 6, 25. An acute observer on the reform side similarly observed in 1897, "New Yorkers are suspicious or nothing; especially the lower classes," and were inclined to believe that the city had been "administered for fifty years on the theory of every party's getting all they could out of it." Letter, Franklin Pierce to James B. Reynolds, June 30, 1897, University Settlement Society Papers.

54. Paul Leicester Ford, *The Honorable Peter Stirling and What People Thought of Him* (New York: Henry Holt and Company, 1894), p. 242.

55. Arthur Bartlett Maurice, *The New York of the Novelists* (New York: Doubleday, Page, & Co., 1901), p. 53.

56. Henry Jones Ford, *The Rise and Growth of American Politics: A Sketch of Constitutional Government* (New York: Macmillan Co., 1898), pp. 296–97. Edward Lauterbach, an attorney and chairman of the New York County Republican Committee, offered much the same argument in his defense of Republican partisanship in a speech to the Nineteenth Century Club in New York, Dec. 11, 1895, reprinted in the club's pamphlet, *How Far Can Municipal Government be Divorced from National Party Lines* (New York, 1896).

57. J. Bleeker Miller, *Trade, Professional, and Property-Owners' Organizations in Public Affairs* (New York, 1884), p. 29; Simon Sterne, "Some Reflections on Recent Changes and Proposed Reform in the City of New York," 1885 ms. in the Simon Sterne Papers, New York Public Library.

58. Miller, *Trade, Professional, and Property-Owners' Organizations,* p. 31.

59. Sterne, "Some Reflections."

60. Notable critiques of the use of attitudes as indices of the distribution of power include Robert A. Dahl, "A Critique of the Ruling Elite Model," *American Political Science Review* 52 (1958): 463–69; and Raymond E. Wolfinger, "Reputation and Reality in the Study of Community Power," *American Sociological Review* 25 (1960): 636–44. The most persuasive defense is William A. Gamson, "Reputation and Resources in Community Politics," *American Journal of Sociology* 72 (1966): 121–31.

61. Form and Rytina, in "Ideological Beliefs on the Distribution of Power in the United States," similarly found their wealthier respondents inclined to say that power is widely dispersed among competing elites, including union leaders, and their poorer respondents inclined to say that the rich dominate. But they interpret this evidence somewhat differently, suggesting that the poor base their opinions on experience, while the rich base theirs on fashionable works of David Riesman and Robert A. Dahl, frequently read in college. Yet it appears that well-educated professional men in late nineteenth-century New York not only agreed with Bryce's Patrician Elitist theory but also helped him formulate it. There seems to be no reason to believe that the rich rely on experience any less—or any more—than the poor.

62. On court-imposed restrictions on municipal expenditures, see Jacobs, *Law Writers and the Courts.* We still lack a good study of the development of legislative and state constitutional limits on municipalities, though such devices as the debt limit and the board of estimate are well known. For a study of the powers of American municipalities before 1825 see Jon C. Teaford, *The Municipal Revolution in America* (Chicago: University of Chicago Press, 1975).

63. Cf. Gamson, "Reputation and Resources in Community Politics;" and Peter Bachrach and Morton S. Baratz, *Power and Poverty: Theory and Practice* (New York: Oxford University Press, 1970).

64. Arthur M. Schlesinger, *The Rise of the City, 1878–1898* (New York: Macmillan Co., 1933); Allan Nevins, *Abram S. Hewitt: With Some Account of Peter Cooper* (New York: Harper & Brothers, 1935). For a fuller discussion of the historiography of power in American cities, see Hammack, "Problems in the Historical Study of Power." For fuller documentation, see Hammack, "Participation in Major Decisions in New York City, 1890–1900: The Creation of Greater New York and the Centralization of the Public School System," (Ph.D. diss., Columbia University, 1973), chap. 4.

65. Richard Hofstadter, *The Age of Reform;* Frederick C. Jaher, "The Boston Brahmins in the Age of Industrial Capitalism," in Jaher, ed., *The Age of Industrialism in America:*

Essays in Social Structure and Cultural Values (New York: The Free Press, 1968); Jaher, "Nineteenth-Century Elites in Boston and New York," *Journal of Social History* 6 (1972): 32–77; Jaher, "Style and Status: High Society in Late Nineteenth-Century New York," in Jaher, ed., *The Rich, the Well Born, and the Powerful: Elites and Upper Classes in History* (Urbana: University of Illinois Press, 1973), pp. 258–84; Stow Persons, *The Decline of American Gentility* (New York: Columbia University Press, 1973).

66. Gabriel A. Almond, "Power and Plutocracy in New York City" (Ph.D. diss., University of Chicago, 1939); Gabriel Kolko, "Brahmins and Business, 1870–1914: A Hypothesis on the Social Basis of Success in American History," in Kurt H. Wolff and Barrington Moore, Jr., eds., *The Critical Spirit: Essays in Honor of Herbert Marcuse* (Boston: Beacon Press, 1967), pp. 343–63; James Weinstein, *The Corporate Ideal in the Liberal State, 1900–1918* (Boston: Beacon Press, 1968), chap. 4.

67. Robert K. Lamb, "The Entrepreneur and the Community," in William Miller, ed., *Men in Business: Essays in the History of Entrepreneurship* (Cambridge, Mass.: Harvard University Press, 1952), pp. 91–119; Charles N. Glaab, *Kansas City and the Railroads: Community Policy in the Growth of a Railroad Metropolis* (Madison: State Historical Society of Wisconsin, 1962); Julius Rubin, *Canal or Railroad? Imitation and Innovation in the Response to the Erie Canal in Philadelphia, Baltimore, and Boston,* in *Transactions of the American Philosophical Society,* n.s., vol. 51, pt. 7, Philadelphia, 1961.

68. Oscar Handlin, *Boston's Immigrants* (Cambridge, Mass.: Harvard University Press, 1941); Herbert G. Gutman, "The Worker's Search for Power: Labor in the Gilded Age," in H. Wayne Morgan, ed., *The Gilded Age: A Reappraisal* (Syracuse: Syracuse University Press, 1963), pp. 38–68; Gutman, *Work, Culture, and Society,* pts. 3 and 4.

69. Robert K. Merton, *Social Theory and Social Structure* (rev. ed., New York: The Free Press, 1957), chap. 1; Richard C. Wade, "The City in History: Some American Perspectives," in Werner Z. Hirsch, ed., *Urban Life and Form* (New York: Holt, Rinehart & Winston, 1963), pp. 71–75; and Wade, "An Agenda for Urban History," in Herbert J. Bass, ed., *The State of American History* (Chicago: University of Chicago Press, 1970), pp. 50–58.

70. For a review and critique of this work see Richard L. McCormick, "Ethno-Cultural Interpretations of Nineteenth-Century American Voting Behavior," *Political Science Quarterly* 89 (1974): 351–77.

71. Samuel P. Hays, "The Politics of Reform in Municipal Government in the Progressive Era," *Political Science Quarterly* 55 (1965): 157–69; and "The Changing Political Structure of the City in Industrial America," *Journal of Urban History* 1 (1974): 6–38.

72. Hays, "The Changing Political Structure of the City," p. 38.

73. Arthur S. Link, *American Epoch* (New York: Alfred A. Knopf, 1955), pp. 84–86 and passim; George E. Mowry, *The Era of Theodore Roosevelt and the Birth of Modern America, 1900–1912* (New York: Harper & Bros., 1958), pp. 66–67 and passim.

74. Wallace S. Sayre and Nelson Polsby, "American Political Science and the Study of Urbanization," in Philip Hauser and Leo Schnore, eds., *The Study of Urbanization* (New York: Wiley, 1965), p. 132.

75. Terry N. Clark, "Power and Community Structure: Who Governs, Where, and When?" in Charles Bonjean et al., eds., *Community Politics: A Behavioral Approach* (New York: The Free Press, 1971), pp. 174–87; John Walton, "The Vertical Axis of Community Organization and the Structure of Power," in Bonjean, et al., *Community Politics,* pp. 188–97; Walton, "A Systematic Survey of Community Power Research," in Michael Aiken and Paul E. Mott, eds., *The Structure of Community Power* (New York: Random House, 1970), pp. 443–64; and Michael Aiken, "The Distribution of Community Power: Structural Bases and Social Consequences," in Aiken and Mott, *The Structure of Community Power,* pp. 487–525.

76. Dahl, "A Critique of the Ruling Elite Model," pp. 463–69.

77. Robert A. Dahl, "The Concept of Power," *Behavioral Science* 2 (1957): 201–15.

78. For attempts to examine all decisions taken in particular communities over long periods see Wallace Sayre and Herbert K. Kaufman, *Governing New York City: Politics in the Metropolis* (New York: The Russell Sage Foundation, 1960); and Harris, *Political Power in Birmingham.*

79. On the criteria appropriate for selecting decisions see Robert A. Dahl, *Who Governs? Democracy and Power in an American City* (New Haven: Yale University Press, 1961),

pp. 124–25, 148–49; Nelson E. Polsby, *Community Power and Political Theory*, pp. 96, 128; Linton C. Freeman et al., "Locating Leaders in Local Communities," *American Sociological Review* 28 (1963): 791–98.

80.   Cf. Linton C. Freeman, et al., "Locating Leaders in Local Communities." In fact, local communities in the United States have been directly subordinate to state governments since the revolution, and during the nineteenth century came increasingly under state control. See Jon C. Teaford, "City vs. State: The Struggle for Legal Ascendancy," *American Journal of Legal History* 17 (1973): 51–65.

81.   Peter Bachrach and Morton S. Baratz, "Decisions and Nondecisions: An Analytical Framework," *American Political Science Review* 57 (1963): 632–42. For a detailed discussion of these issues, see Hammack, "Problems in the Historical Study of Power," pp. 341–48.

82.   Bachrach and Baratz, *Power and Poverty*; Matthew Crenson, *The Un-Politics of Air Pollution* (Baltimore: The Johns Hopkins University Press, 1971); Lukes, *Power: A Radical View*.

83.   Bachrach and Baratz, "The Two Faces of Power," *American Political Science Review* 56 (1962): pp. 947–52, quoting E. E. Schattschneider's *The Semisovereign People*; Norton E. Long, "Political Science and the City," in Leo Schnore, ed., *Social Science and the City: A Survey of Urban Research* (New York: Wiley, 1968), p. 250.

84.   Carl V. Harris, "The Underdeveloped Historical Dimension of the Study of Community Power Structure," *Historical Methods Newsletter* 9 (1976): 195–201.

85.   Carl J. Friedrich, *Man and His Government* (New York: McGraw-Hill, 1963), pp. 199–215.

86.   Hollingsworth and Hollingsworth, "Expenditures in American Cities," pp. 347–89.

87.   For a review of this work, see Hammack, "Problems in the Historical Study of Power," pp. 342–44; for a recent assertion of the significance of elites, see Harold Perkin, "The Recruitment of Elites in British Society Since 1800," *Journal of Social History* (1978): 222–24.

88.   All of these phrases were employed in late nineteenth-century New York. Theodore Roosevelt is famous for the phrase "bully pulpit;" William C. Whitney was widely described as the Warwick or kingmaker of the Democratic party; and the term *locum tenens* came naturally to Edward M. Shepard when he sought to persuade a leading banker to join "directly or indirectly" the Gold Democrats' campaign committee in 1896. Shepard to James Loeb, Aug. 14, 1896, Shepard Papers.

89.   For this distinction, see John Day's forward to Emmanuel LeRoy Ladurie, *The Peasants of Languedoc*, trans. John Day (Urbana, Illinois: University of Illinois Press, 1974), p. ix.

90.   Among the model works of this school are Ladurie's *The Peasants of Languedoc*; Marc Bloch's *Feudal Society*, trans. by L. A. Manyon (Chicago: University of Chicago Press, 1963); and Fernand Braudel's *The Mediterranean and the Mediterranean World in the Age of Philip II*, trans. by Sian Reynolds (New York: Harper & Row, 1972–73).

CHAPTER 2

1.   Moses King, *Handbook of New York City* (Boston: Moses King, 1893), especially pp. 69–76.

2.   Bayrd Still, *Mirror For Gotham* (New York: New York University Press, 1956) pp. 257–59. Compare Henry James, *The American Scene* (Bloomington: University of Indiana Press, 1968), pp. 72–79, and *Harper's Weekly* 38 (1894): 756–57.

3.   The population of the New York State portion of the metropolitan region for these dates is given in Walter Laidlaw, *Population of the City of New York, 1890–1930* (New York: Cities Census Committee, 1932), p. 25. The urban population of the United States as a whole is given in U.S. Bureau of the Census, *Historical Statistics of the United States: Colonial Times to 1957* (Washington, D.C.: U.S. Government Printing Office, 1960).

4. Allan R. Pred, *Urban Growth and the Circulation of Information: The United States System of Cities, 1790–1840* (Cambridge, Mass.: Harvard University Press, 1973), pp. 28–42.

5. Robert G. Albion, *The Rise of New York Port, 1815–1860* (New York: Charles Scribner's Sons, 1939), chap. 5; David T. Gilchrist, ed., *The Growth of the Seaport Cities, 1790–1825* (Charlottesville: University of Virginia Press for the Eleutherian Mills–Hagley Foundation, 1967), pp. 32–37.

6. Benjamin Chinitz, *Freight and the Metropolis: The Impact of America's Transport Revolutions on the New York Region* (Cambridge: Harvard University Press, 1960), pp. 9, 19–31.

7. Lee Benson, *Merchants, Farmers, and Railroads: Railroad Regulation and New York Politics, 1850–1887* (Cambridge: Harvard University Press, 1955), chap. 3.

8. Glenn Porter and Harold C. Livesay, *Merchants and Manufacturers: Studies in the Changing Structure of Nineteenth-Century Marketing* (Baltimore: The Johns Hopkins University Press, 1971).

9. *Appleton's Dictionary of New York And Its Vicinity* (New York: D. Appleton and Company, 1898), p. 320.

10. Robert M. Lichtenberg, *One-Tenth of a Nation: National Forces in the Economic Growth of the New York Region* (Cambridge: Harvard University Press, 1960), p. 13.

11. Edward Ewing Pratt, *Industrial Causes of Congestion of Population in New York City* (New York: Columbia University Studies in History, Economics, and Public Law, no. 109, 1911), chap. 3; *Real Estate Record and Builder's Guide*, Apr. 26, 1890. Moses King's *Handbook of New York City* contains descriptions and photographs of many of these plants.

12. Alfred D. Chandler, Jr., *The Visible Hand: The Managerial Revolution in American Business* (Cambridge: Harvard University Press, 1977), part III.

13. Pratt, *Industrial Causes of Congestion*, p. 94.

14. Pratt, in *Industrial Causes of Congestion*, reviews the reasons for the expansion of these industries in chaps. 3 and 4.

15. For New York City, see table 2–3. Only 4 percent of all manufacturing employees in New York City worked in an industry of which 45 percent or more of the firms in New York State employed 250 or more employees; comparable figures for Chicago and Philadelphia are 37.6 percent and 21.4 percent.

16. Sidney M. Robbins and Nestor E. Terleckyj, *Money Metropolis: A Locational Study of Financial Activities in the New York Region* (Cambridge: Harvard University Press, 1960), chap. 1.

17. Michael P. Conzen, "The Maturing Urban System in the United States, 1840–1910," *Annals of the American Association of Geographers* 67 (1977): 92.

18. Alfred D. Chandler, Jr., "Patterns of Railroad Finance, 1830–1850," *Business History Review* 28 (1954): 248–63.

19. Vincent P. Carosso, *Investment Banking in America: A History* (Cambridge: Harvard University Press, 1970) p. 15; Thomas R. Navin and Marian V. Sears, "The Rise of a Market for Industrial Securities, 1887–1902," *Business History Review* 29 (1955): 105–38.

20. Navin and Sears, "The Rise of a Market for Industrial Securities."

21. Useful discussions of investment banking in New York include Fritz Redlich, *The Molding of American Banking: Men and Ideas* (New York: Johnson Reprint Corporation, 1968), chap. 21; Carosso, *Investment Banking in America*, chaps. 1 and 2; and Barry E. Supple, "A Business Elite: German-Jewish Financiers in Nineteenth-Century New York," *Business History Review* 31 (1957): 143–51.

22. Carosso, *Investment Banking in America*, pp. 16, 30.

23. Ibid., chap. 2.

24. Conzen, "The Maturing Urban System in the United States," pp. 92–99.

25. E. M. Patterson, "Certain Changes in New York's Position as a Financial Center," *Journal of Political Economy* 21 (1913): 539.

26. See table 2–18.

27. James Willard Hurst, *The Growth of American Law: The Law Makers* (Boston: Little, Brown, and Company, 1950), pp. 295–313; Erwin O. Smigel, *The Wall Street Lawyer: Professional or Organization Man?* (New York: The Free Press of Glencoe, 1964); Jerold

S. Auerbach, *Unequal Justice: Lawyers and Social Change in Modern America* (New York: Oxford University Press, 1976), chaps. 1 and 2.

28. These figures are derived from an inspection of R. G. Dun & Company, *Reference Book (And Key) Containing Ratings of Merchants, Manufacturers, and Traders Generally, throughout the United States & Canada* (New York: 1880, 1895, 1910).

29. Joseph Frazier Wall, *Andrew Carnegie* (New York: Oxford University Press, 1970), p. 483.

30. Allan Nevins, *John D. Rockefeller: The Heroic Age of American Enterprise* (New York: Charles Scribner's Sons, 1940), p. 158. Beginning in 1880 Rockefeller and his family had spent the winter in New York, staying, like Carnegie, at the Windsor Hotel.

31. *The Tribune Monthly*, vol. 4 (1892), reprinted in Sidney Ratner, ed., *New Light on the History of Great American Fortunes* (New York: Augustus M. Kelley, Inc., 1953). The 30 percent figure includes reputed millionaires in New York City, Brooklyn, and the adjacent communities that were consolidated into Greater New York in 1898. Based on reports from newspapermen and Republican party officials throughout the United States, the *Tribune* survey was designed as a contribution to the 1892 Republican presidential campaign. Antitariff Democrats were certain to examine it with a critical eye, so it had to be as accurate as possible.

32. Of the £1,000,000 estates inherited in Britain between 1880 and 1899, 38 percent had been earned in the London region; the proportion rose to 57 percent in the 1900–1914 period. W. D. Rubinstein, "Wealth, Elites and the Class Structure of Modern Britain," *Past and Present* no. 76 (1977): 105.

33. Compare the similar table presented by Carl V. Harris in *Political Power in Birmingham* (Knoxville: The University of Tennessee Press, 1977), p. 48.

34. These offices still concentrated on financial matters. American railroads never did develop full-scale central managements. Alfred D. Chandler, Jr., *The Visible Hand*, pp. 183–87.

35. Capitalization figures taken from *The Manual of Statistics* (New York, 1883, 1910).

36. Daniel Bell, *The End of Ideology*, rev. ed. (New York: The Free Press, 1962), pp. 42–43, quoted in Carosso, *Investment Banking in America*, p. 50.

37. William Miller, "American Historians and the Business Elite," *Journal of Economic History* 9 (1949): 184–208; Miller, "The Recruitment of the American Business Elite," *Quarterly Journal of Economics* 64 (1950): 242–53; Miller, "The Business Elite in Business Bureaucracies," in Miller, ed., *Men in Business* (Cambridge: Harvard University Press, 1952), pp. 286–305; Frances W. Gregory and Irene D. Neu, "The American Industrial Elite in the 1870's," in Miller, ed., *Men in Business*, pp. 193–211; Mabel Newcomer, *The Big Business Executive: The Factors that Made Him* (New York: Columbia University Press, 1975), pp. 53–54. The argument presented here for the relations among economic elites in New York is consistent with the data presented in Jocelyn Maynard Ghent and Frederic Cople Jaher, "The Chicago Business Elite: 1830–1930. A Collective Biography," *Business History Review* 50(1976): 288–328.

38. Carosso, *Investment Banking in America*, chaps. 1 and 2.

39. Chandler, *The Visible Hand*, pt. 4; Carosso, *Investment Banking in America*, p. 50.

40. Harold C. Passer, *The Electrical Manufacturers, 1865–1900: A Study in Competition, Entrepreneurship, Technical Change and Economic Growth* (Cambridge, Mass.: Harvard University Press, 1953).

41. *The New York Sun, The Sun's Guide to New York* (New York, 1892), p. 200.

42. The best source of information on the Chamber of Commerce of the State of New York remains the Chamber's *Annual Reports*. Joseph B. Bishop's *A Chronicle of One Hundred & Fifty Years: the Chamber of Commerce of the State of New York, 1768–1918* (New York: Charles Scribner's Sons, 1918), reviews some of the ceremonial highpoints. Eight of the fourteen mayoral elections held between 1872 and 1901 were won by members of the Chamber; and William L. Wickham, who was elected mayor in 1874, was elected to the Chamber in 1883.

43. Benson, *Merchants, Farmers, and Railroads*, passim. Benson points out that "the very size of the city (Brooklyn included), its dispersed locational patterns, the large number of individual firms and companies, and the variety of business and property interests in-

volved" make it very difficult to generalize about "the heterogeneous mass comprising the New York merchants" (p. 55).

44. *The Sun's Guide to New York*, p. 199; *Appleton's Dictionary of New York*, pp. 231–32.

45. *Harper's Weekly*, Nov. 1, 1890, pp. 857–60; ibid., June 13, 1891; King's *Handbook of New York City*, pp. 794–804; Lee Benson, *Merchants, Farmers, and Railroads*, pp. 56–57.

46. The best source on the Reform Club remains the Club's *Annual Reports*, together with the papers of its members, including Henry DeForest Baldwin (at Yale University), Charles S. Fairchild (at the New-York Historical Society), and Edward M. Shepard (at Columbia University). On the Merchants' Association, see Arnold J. Bornfriend, "The Business Group in Metropolis: The Commerce and Industry Association of New York" (Ph.D. diss., Columbia University, 1967).

47. King's *Handbook of New York City* and *Appleton's Dictionary of New York* describe these organizations.

48. King's *Handbook of New York*, p. 805; *Real Estate Record and Builder's Guide*, Jan. 13, 1894.

49. See Benson, *Merchants, Farmers, and Railroads*, chap. 7.

50. The charter and by-laws of the Chamber were reprinted in each of its *Annual Reports*.

51. The predominance of legal writers on public questions is suggested by the large proportion of legal works consulted by James Bryce when he was preparing *The American Commonwealth* and by Woodrow Wilson when he was preparing lectures on American cities and other contemporary public issues in the 1880s and 1890s. See Hammack, "Elite Perceptions," p. 389, n. 15; and Arthur S. Link, ed., *The Papers of Woodrow Wilson* (Princeton: Princeton University Press, 1970), vol. 8, pp. 81–116.

52. King's *Handbook of New York City*, p. 557.

53. George Martin, *Causes and Conflicts: The Centennial History of the Association of the Bar of the City of New York, 1870–1970* (Boston: Houghton, Mifflin Company, 1970), p. 48 and passim; the bar association's *Annual Reports* provide the fullest record of its work. On the organization of the New York County Lawyers' Association, see the New York *Times*, May 22, 1908.

54. For one example of this phenomenon, see chap. 7 in this volume.

55. Daniel H. Calhoun, *The American Civil Engineer* (Cambridge, Mass.: MIT Press, 1960), pp. 1–90; Monte A. Calvert, *The Professional Engineer in America, 1830–1910* (Baltimore: The Johns Hopkins University Press, 1967), pp. 220–21; Raymond H. Merritt, *Engineering in American Society, 1850–1875* (Lexington: The University Press of Kentucky, 1969); Deborah S. Gardner, "The Professionalization of American Architects, 1857–1875," unpublished Davis Center Seminar Paper, May 2, 1980.

56. Graduate study in such fields formed a key part of the background of several men active in policy formation in New York City during the 1890s, including Albert Shaw, editor of the American *Review of Reviews;* James B. Reynolds, Headworker of the University Settlement; E. R. L. Gould of the City and Suburban Homes Company; and Nicholas Murray Butler, Dean of the Faculty at Columbia and the leading advocate of reform for New York City's public schools.

57. Frank B. Houghton, quoted in the *Real Estate Record and Builder's Guide*, Nov. 3, 1894. This theme was repeatedly sounded by advocates of Greater New York between 1888 and 1896.

58. The history of *Municipal Affairs*, which published a remarkable series of articles during the six years of its existence and then abruptly ceased publication, remains unexplored.

59. For one study of this process see Gerald D. Kurland, *Seth Low: The Reformer in an Urban and Industrial Age* (New York: Twayne Publishers, Inc., 1971).

60. The best of the generally disappointing studies of the Astors is Harvey O'Connor, *The Astors* (New York: Alfred A. Knopf, 1941); on this point see chap. 3.

61. These attitudes were most strongly expressed during the debates over the financing of the rapid transit system.

62. *The Sun's Guide to New York*, p. 2.

63. Richard Hofstadter, *The Age of Reform: From Bryan to FDR* (New York: Alfred A. Knopf, 1956), p. 75.

CHAPTER 3

1. James D. McCabe, Jr., *Lights and Shadows of New York Life* (New York: Farrar, Straus and Giroux 1970 reprint of the Philadelphia: National Publishing Company edition of 1872), p. 57.

2. Karl Baedeker, ed., *The United States: With an Excursion Into Mexico* (New York: Da Capo Press 1971 reprint of the 1893 edition), pp. 22–23.

3. Theodore Dreiser, *The Color of a Great City* (New York: Boni & Liveright, 1923), pp. 1–2.

4. King's *Handbook of New York City* (Boston: Moses King, 1893), p. 545, 148–53; *Appleton's Dictionary of New York And Its Vicinity* (New York: D. Appleton and Company, 1898), pp. 101–2.

5. Wayne Andrews, *Architecture, Ambition and Americans: A Social History of American Architecture* (London: Collier-Macmillan, Ltd.–The Free Press of Glencoe, 1947), chap. 5; Grace M. Mayer, *Once Upon a City: New York from 1890 to 1910 as Photographed by Byron* (New York: The Macmillan Company, 1958).

6. "Fifth Avenue and its Characteristics," the *Times* (London), Sept. 5, 1887, reprinted in Bayrd Still, *Mirror for Gotham: New York As Seen by Contemporaries from Dutch Days to the Present* (New York: New York University Press, 1956), pp. 241–42.

7. Jacob A. Riis, *How the Other Half Lives* (New York: Dover Publications, Inc., 1971), p. 17. To be more precise, Riis might have said that the tenements were filling up east Harlem and the south Bronx; in the 1890s these areas were inhabited largely by Irish, German, and Italian immigrants, not by blacks.

8. William Dean Howells, *A Hazard of New Fortunes* (New York: Harper & Brothers, 1890), vol. 1, p. 195.

9. W. D. Rubinstein, "Wealth, Elites and the Class Structure of Modern Britain," *Past and Present* no. 76 (1977): 108–12.

10. Henry James, *The American Scene* (Bloomington and London: Indiana University Press, 1968 reprint of 1904 first edition), p. 178.

11. *The Sun's Guide to New York* (New York, 1892), pp. 1–2.

12. Riis's reforming intentions are stressed throughout *How the Other Half Lives* and are described in detail in *The Battle with the Slum* (New York, 1902).

13. Tenement House Department of the City of New York, *First Report*, 1902–1903, vol. 1, pp. 62–65. This report does not make it clear whether Manhattan had 6,763 buildings served by school sinks, or 6,763 school sinks serving perhaps only 1,000 buildings.

14. Tenement House Department of the City of New York, *First Report*, 1902–1903, vol. 2, pp. 12–15.

15. Tenement House Department of the City of New York, *First Report* 1902–1903, vol. 1, pp. 143–45.

16. James, *The American Scene*, p. 135.

17. Thomas Kessner, *The Golden Door: Italian and Jewish Immigrant Mobility in New York City, 1880–1915* (New York: Oxford University Press, 1977), p. 165.

18. Dreiser, *The Color of a Great City*, p. 99.

19. Richard Harding Davis, *The Exiles*, quoted in Arthur Bartlett Maurice, *New York in Fiction* (New York: Dodd, Mead and Company, 1900), pp. 121–22.

20. Dreiser, *The Color of a Great City*, pp. 120–24.

21. Barry E. Supple, "A Business Elite: German-Jewish Financiers in Nineteenth-Century New York," *Business History Review* 31 (1957): 143–78.

22. King's *Handbook of New York City*, p. 319; Regular Meeting Minutes, Apr. 13, 1893, Union League Club (manuscript in the possession of the club); Samuel T. McSeveney, *The Politics of Depression: Political Behavior in the Northeast, 1893–1896* (New York: Oxford University Press, 1972), p. 104.

23. The *Social Register* and the *Society-List and Club Register* listed New York's gentile clubs alone, as did Francis Gerry Fairfield, *The Clubs of New York* (New York: Henry L. Hinton, 1873; Arno Press reprint, 1975). King's *Handbook of New York City* and the *Sun's Guide to New York* provide brief descriptions of the Jewish clubs, but while *Appleton's Dictionary of New York* lists these clubs it describes them as "German." King omits the Jewish clubs from his list of "leading" clubs, p. 68, as does Henry L. Nelson in

his account of "Some New York Clubs," *Harper's Weekly*, Mar. 15, 1890, pp. 193–96, 211.

24. New York *Times*, Oct. 29, 1878; Oct. 23, 1892, reporting that Einstein gave his first mayoral campaign speech at the Hebrew Institute on the lower east side.

25. Based on an analysis of the 1896 *Social Register*; King's *Handbook of New York City*, pp. 319, 551; *The Sun's Guide to New York*, pp. 88–91.

26. *The Sun's Guide to New York*, pp. 88–89.

27. *The Sun's Guide to New York*, p. 89; King's *Handbook of New York City*, pp. 333, 557, 559; *Appleton's Dictionary of New York*, p. 111.

28. The phrase is from May King Van Rensselaer and Frederic Van de Water, *The Social Ladder* (New York: Henry Holt and Company, 1924). Frederic Cople Jaher lists the other studies of New York society in this period in "Style and Status: High Society in Late Nineteenth-Century New York," in Jaher, ed., *The Rich, the Well Born, and the Powerful: Elites and Upper Classes in History* (Urbana: University of Illinois Press, 1973), pp. 258–59, n.2.

29. Edith Wharton, *The Age of Innocence* (New York: D. Appleton and Company, 1920; Charles Scribner's Sons reprint, 1968), pp. 33–34.

30. Ibid., pp. 102–3.

31. Junius Henry Browne, *The Great Metropolis: A Mirror of New York* (New York, 1869; Arno Press reprint edition, 1975), p. 32.

32. Ibid.; Browne did not, however, make it explicit that he was considering only Protestant New York.

33. Frederic Cople Jaher, "Nineteenth-Century Social Elites in Boston and New York," *Journal of Social History* 6 (1972): 54.

34. Ibid., p. 54.

35. Ibid., p. 61.

36. Ibid.

37. Ibid., p. 55.

38. Willard Glazier, *Peculiarities of American Cities* (Philadelphia: Hubbard Brothers, 1884), p. 397. E. Digby Baltzell quotes a similar observation, from Robert Douglas Bowden, *Boies Penrose* (New York: Greenberg, 1937), pp.7–8, in *Philadelphia Gentlemen: The Making of a National Upper Class* (Glencoe, Illinois: The Free Press, 1958), p. 31.

39. Martha J. Lamb and Mrs. Burton Harrison, *History of the City of New York: Its Origin, Rise, & Progress* (New York: The A. S. Barnes Company, 1896), p. 790.

40. James, *The American Scene*, p. 165.

41. Harvey O'Connor, *The Astors* (New York: Alfred A. Knopf, 1941), p. 197.

42. Frederic Cople Jaher places McAllister's activities in their social context in his "Style and Status: High Society in Late Nineteenth-Century New York," pp. 263–73.

43. Gabriel A. Almond, "Plutocracy and Politics in New York City" (Ph.D. diss., University of Chicago, 1938), pp. 152–60.

44. *The Nation* 54 (Feb. 1892): 127. Edgar Fawcett made the same points in "Plutocracy and Snobbery in New York," *The Arena* 4 (1891): 142–51.

45. Baltzell, *Philadelphia Gentlemen*, pp. 336, 349–54.

46. Fairfield, *The Clubs of New York*, p. 15.

47. Henry L. Nelson, "Some New York Clubs," *Harper's Weekly*, Mar. 15, 1890, p. 195.

48. *The Sun's Guide to New York*, p. 92.

49. The sources for these observations are indicated in note 23, above. For another analysis of the varied purposes of the elite social clubs of a major American city, focusing on the years around 1940, see Baltzell, *Philadelphia Gentlemen*, pp. 337–54. Baltzell places Philadelphia's clubs on a single hierarchy of social prestige, although he does recognize the existence of roughly parallel Catholic and Jewish prestige hierarchies; for the latter, see pp. 274–91, 307, 343.

50. The *Social Register* listed first the club at which a man received mail.

51. *National Cyclopedia of American Biography* (New York: James T. White and Company, 1898), vol. 26, p. 85; for the argument that a shared culture unified the upper class of another city, see Baltzell, *Philadelphia Gentlemen*, pp. 345–52.

52. Charles Philips Trevelyan to Sir George Otto Trevelyan, Apr. 1, 1898, in Charles

Philips Trevelyan, *The Great New People: Letters from North America and the Pacific,*
ed. G. L. Trevelyan (New York: Doubleday & Company, Inc., 1971), p. 12.

53. Everett P. Wheeler, "The Unofficial Government of Cities," *Atlantic Monthly*
86 (1900): 375.

54. Josephine Shaw Lowell to Mrs. Robert Gould Shaw, May 23, 1882, printed in
William Rhinelander Stewart, *The Philanthropic Work of Josephine Shaw Lowell* (New
York: The Macmillan Company, 1911), pp. 129, 124–25.

55. Stewart, *The Philanthropic Work of Josephine Shaw Lowell,* pp. 175–89; Gregory
H. Singleton, "Protestant Voluntary Organizations and the Shaping of Victorian America,"
American Quarterly 27 (1975): 557–58.

56. *The Sun's Guide to New York,* p. 245; *King's Handbook of New York City,*
p. 419.

57. The *Charities Directory* (New York: The Charity Organization Society, 1890–
1900), an annual description of charitable organizations in New York, describes Catholic
and Jewish charities to the extent that they cooperated with the C.O.S. George Paul Jacoby,
Catholic Child Care in Nineteenth Century New York (Washington, D.C.: The Catholic
University of America Press, 1941; New York: Arno Press reprint edition, 1974), describes
several of the Catholic charities. For Catholic scepticism of the Protestant parish plan, see
The Catholic World 67 (Sept. 1897): 846–49. Moses Rischin describes the pattern of charita-
ble activities among Jews in *The Promised City: New York's Jews, 1870–1914* (Cambridge:
Harvard University Press, 1962; New York: Corinth Books reprint, 1964), pp. 98–111; his
analysis is confirmed by Arthur A. Goren, *New York Jews and the Quest for Community*
(New York: Columbia University Press, 1970), pp. 12–17.

58. There is no adequate study of the organization of the German community in
New York. King's *Handbook of New York City* describes several German charities; Jerold
S. Auerbach's *Unequal Justice: Lawyers and Social Change in Modern America* (New
York: Oxford University Press, 1976), offers the most recent (and the most critical) account
of the origins of the Legal Aid Society.

59. Accounts of the 1894 state constitutional convention include John Webb Pratt,
Religion, Politics and Diversity: The Church-State Theme in New York History (Ithaca:
Cornell University Press, 1967), chap. 9; McSeveney, *The Politics of Depression,* chap.
3; and Richard L. McCormick, "Shaping Republican Strategy: Political Change in New York
State, 1893–1910" (Ph.D. diss., Yale University, 1976), chap. 2.

60. Wheeler, "The Unofficial Government of Cities," provides the most succinct account of these arrangements. Although the New York Public Library, the Metropolitan
Museum of Art, and the American Museum of Natural History have all been the subjects
of histories, an incisive account of the origins of the New York City pattern of public
support for private cultural institutions remains to be written. For a study of the cultural
institutions of another major city, see Helen Lefkowitz Horowitz, *Culture and the City:
Cultural Philanthropy in Chicago from the 1880s to 1917* (Lexington: University Press
of Kentucky, 1976). Horowitz's article, "Animal and Man in the New York Zoological
Park," *New York History* 56(1975): 426–55, is suggestive.

61. There is no good secondary study of these conflicts, most of which were well
reported in the New York *Times,* the New York *Evening Post,* and the religious weeklies.

62. These conflicts also await a thorough historical examination. But Samuel McSeveney's *The Politics of Depression,* pp. 69–79, is very good on the school issue, and Moses
Rischin describes the variety of Jewish educational initiatives in *The Promised City,*
pp. 98–103.

63. The U.S. Census recorded information on wealth holding in 1850, 1860, and
1870, but not in later years. One of the best studies of this data is Lee Soltow, *Men and
Wealth in the United States, 1850–1870* (New Haven: Yale University Press, 1975). Robert
E. Gallman's "Trends in the Size Distribution of Wealth in the Nineteenth Century: Some
Speculations," in Soltow, ed., *Six Papers on the Size Distribution of Wealth and Income*
(New York: Columbia University Press for the National Bureau of Economic Research,
1969), pp. 1–30, employs this data together with several late nineteenth-century lists of
top wealth holders to argue that rich people were increasingly inclined to live in large
cities by 1900. James L. Sturm, in *Investing in the United States, 1798–1893: Upper Wealth
Holders in a Market Economy* (New York: Arno Press, 1977), pp. 14, 20, used probate

records to identify patterns of investment and consumption behavior among the wealthy but notes that these records ignore the majority who die with little property and are, in any case, not available for research in New York City. Edward Pessen used New York City's tax assessment books for his study of the wealthiest New Yorkers in the antebellum period; but this source largely ignores personal wealth, including the stocks and bonds that had become so important by the 1890s; Pessen, *Riches, Class, and Power Before the Civil War* (Lexington, Mass.: D.C. Heath and Company, 1973), chap. 2. Nor do assessment data tell us anything about the poorer half or two-thirds of the population.

64.   That is to say, 13% of all men who told the census taker that they had an occupation in 1900 were the children of mothers born in Russia, Poland, Austria, or Hungary. Men from these backgrounds were significantly underrepresented in unskilled, semiskilled, and skilled occupations. They constituted altogether 66% of all garment workers; and they claimed a surprisingly high 6.3%, 10.2%, 5.5%, and 20.8% of the high white-collar, semiprofessional, clerical, and entrepreneurial jobs, respectively. See table 3–7.

65.   Thomas Kessner, *The Golden Door: Italian and Jewish Immigrant Mobility in New York City, 1880–1915* (New York: Oxford University Press, 1977), p. 169 and passim.

66.   An 0.8 percent sample of the firms rated by R. G. Dun & Company turned up 14 tailors and dressmakers, of whom 10 had German or Irish names, in 1880; but only 4 German or Irish tailors and dressmakers in 1910. The best account of the history of garment making is still Jesse E. Pope, *The Clothing Industry in New York* (Columbia: University of Missouri Studies in History, 1905).

67.   Altogether, Dun rated only about 40,000 New York City, Brooklyn, and Long Island City firms in 1895. Many of the retail dealers and manufacturers reported by the census must have been employees rather than proprietors; but many persons included in other occupations were also independent proprietors.

68.   The Brooklyn *Daily Eagle Almanac* for 1899 gives what appears to be a remarkably complete list of the Greater City's "Business and Commercial Societies and Associations," pp. 240–43.

69.   Apart from the jewelry industry, these fields were still unrepresented in the list of "business and commercial societies and associations" provided by the Brooklyn *Daily Eagle Almanac* in 1904, pp. 294–95. Melvyn Dubofsky describes the activities of employers' organizations in the garment trades after 1909 in *When Workers Organize: New York City in the Progressive Era* (Amherst: The University of Massachusetts Press, 1968), chap. 3.

70.   Moses Rischin, *The Promised City*, p. 64–65, describes the organization of the garment manufacturing business.

71.   Abraham Cahan, *The Rise of David Levinsky* (New York: Harper and Brothers, 1917; Harper Torchbook edition, 1960).

72.   Taking the figures for the number of employees and the number of firms supplied by the United States Census of Manufactures for 1880, 1900, and 1910, it appears that the average firm in the ladies' garment industry declined from 51 employees to 32 in 1900 and in 1910; that the average men's garment or shirt firm declined from 46 employees to 18 in 1900, then rose to 28 in 1910; and that the average firm in the millinery industry declined from 36 employees to 34 and then to 25.

73.   Cahan, *The Rise of David Levinsky*, p. 209. Dubofsky, in *When Workers Organize*, chaps. 3–5, emphasizes the roles of German Jewish and Protestant philanthropists in settling strikes and securing recognition for unions in the garment trades. The organization of the industry at the end of the nineteenth century is described in some detail in Pope, *The Clothing Industry in New York*, chap. 2.

74.   *Eagle Almanac*, 1899, p. 242.

75.   Petitions and correspondence from these local commercial organizations appear with some frequency among the Mayors' Papers. One of the moving spirits in the North Side Board of Trade was James Lee Wells, a Republican who was considered for the post of public works commissioner under Mayor Strong and who later served as secretary of state for the State of New York.

76.   *Eagle Almanac*, 1899, pp. 282–93.

77.   *School* magazine reported on the activities of these associations in detail. For further discussion, see chap. 7 of this volume.

78.   Neither contemporaries nor historians have paid much attention to the German

community in late nineteenth-century New York. Suggestive contemporary references include Henry L. Nelson, "Some New York Clubs," *Harper's Weekly*, Mar. 15, 1890, p. 211, and George J. Manson, "The 'Foreign Element' in New York City: 1. The Germans," *Harper's Weekly*, August 4, 1888, pp. 581–84. One listing of German societies and organizations is provided in the *Eagle Almanac*, 1904, pp. 233–43. Much of *The Promised City* focuses on the organizations created by eastern European Jews; see especially chaps. 6 and 10.

79. The standard studies of this problem are Fergus MacDonald, *The Catholic Church and The Secret Societies in the United States* (New York: The United States Catholic Historical Society, 1946), and Henry J. Browne, *The Catholic Church and The Knights of Labor* (Washington, D.C.: The Catholic University of America Press, 1949).

80. In addition to the discussion of the school centralization controversy presented in chap. 7 of this volume, see the studies of the 1894 state constitutional convention cited in note 59, above.

81. Goren, *New York Jews and the Quest for Community; Eagle Almanac*, 1899, pp. 178–207, provides some membership information for Greater New York. Charles W. Ferguson, *Fifty Million Brothers: A Panorama of American Lodges and Clubs* (New York: Farrar & Rinehart, Inc., 1937), characterizes most of the secret societies active during the 1890s. The largest societies in Greater New York were the Masons, the Royal Arcanum, and the Odd Fellows. Several identifiable ethnic or sectarian societies also had considerable memberships: the Catholic Benevolent Legion (16,205), the (Jewish) Independent Order of B'rith Abraham (14,018), the (nativist Protestant) Junior Order of American Mechanics (3,710), and the Deutcher Order der Harugari (2,800): Brooklyn *Daily Eagle* Almanac (1901), pp. 209–42.

82. Department of the Interior, U.S. Census Office, *Vital Statistics of New York City and Brooklyn*, compiled by John S. Billings (Washington, D.C.: Government Printing Office, 1894), provides data regarding both the residential patterns of New York's ethnic groups (pp. 234–37) and the death rates of the city's various neighborhoods (pp. 250–51). Death rates can be used as a crude index of the prosperity of the residents of a neighborhood. On the balanced ticket, see chap. 4 of this volume.

83. "Harmonize" was the phrase of Tammany Law Committee and New York City Board of Education member Charles S. Strauss, quoted in the New York *Herald*, Mar. 27, 1896.

84. For a detailed study, see chap. 7 of this volume.

85. The *Annual Reports* of the New York State Bureau of Labor Statistics provide extensive information on wage rates and days worked per year. See the *Eighteenth Annual Report*, 1900, p. 459.

86. Ibid., pp. 12–18, 135. *The Real Estate Record and Builder's Guide*, the authoritative trade paper, reported on Jan. 6, 1894, that the threat of strikes had prevented wage reductions in the building trades during the depression.

87. Ibid., p. 459.

88. Louise Bolard More's *Wage-Earners' Budgets: A Study of Standards and Cost of Living in New York City* (New York: Henry Holt and Company, 1907), p. 269, advanced the "conservative conclusion" that "a 'fair living wage' for a workingman's family of average size in New York City should be at *least* $728 a year, or a steady income of $14 a week." Reporting a study undertaken by the New York State Conference of Charities and Correction and supported by The Russell Sage Foundation, Robert Coit Chapin maintained in 1909 that "an income under $800 is not enough to permit the maintenance of a normal standard" with regard to housing, food, fuel, clothing, medical care, insurance, and support of labor unions, churches, and other voluntary associations; Chapin, *The Standard of Living Among Workingmen's Families in New York City* (New York: Charities Publication Committee, 1909), p. 245. These are the earliest systematic studies of living standards in New York City; they reflect prices that had risen somewhat from the levels of the nineties.

89. Edward Ewing Pratt, *Industrial Causes of Congestion of Population in New York City* (New York: Columbia University Studies in History, Economics, and Public Law, vol. 43, 1911), p. 129.

90. Tenement House Department of the City of New York, *First Report*, 1902–1903, vol. 1, map p. 144–45, locates each "New Law" tenement built during the first eighteen months after the law went into effect on Jan. 1, 1902, and indicates which sections of

the city were attracting new, high-quality tenements. Of the New Law tenements constructed during this period, 45 percent were located in the more prosperous parts of the lower east side.

91. New York State Bureau of Labor Statistics, *Eighteenth Annual Report*, 1900, p. 459; Selig Perlman and Philip Taft, *History of Labor in the United States, 1896–1932* (New York: Macmillan, 1935), p. 289, quoted in Dubofsky, *When Workers Organize*, p. 97.

92. Pratt, *Industrial Causes of Congestion*, pp. 144–46, 185–88.

93. Tenement House Committee of 1894, *Report* (Albany, 1895), p. 207.

94. Robert Graham, *Social Statistics of a City Parish* (New York: Church Temperance Society, 1894), pp. 40–41.

95. Tenement House Committee of 1894, *Report*, p. 161. A similar account of cigar makers appears in the New York State Bureau of Labor Statistics, *Fourteenth Annual Report*, 1896, pp. 917–18.

96. Dubovsky, *When Workers Organize*, chaps. 6 and 7.

97. Michael Gordon, "Irish Immigrant Culture and the Labor Boycott in New York City, 1880–1886," in Richard L. Ehrlich, *Immigrants in Industrial America, 1850–1920* (Charlottesville: University of Virginia Press for the Eleutherian Mills–Hagley Foundation and the Balch Institute, 1977), pp. 111–22.

98. Rischin, *The Promised City*, p. 180.

99. Pratt, *Industrial Causes of Congestion*, p. 100.

100. Rischin, *The Promised City*, p. 172.

101. See chap. 6 of this volume. In *Labor and the Left: A Study of Socialist and Radical Influences in the American Labor Movement, 1881–1924* (New York: Basic Books, Inc., 1970), John H. M. Laslett argues that previous historians credited union leaders with more influence over the fate of socialism than they did in fact exert. According to Laslett, "the intense strains created by the process of rapid industrial change, which in Europe served to accentuate profound divisions which already existed in pre-industrial society, in America found no such permanent roots in which to grow. In the end, high wage levels, political pluralism, and the lack of a strong sense of class consciousness were strong enough to prevail" (p. 304). The New York City case suggests that the diversity of workers' national and ideological backgrounds also constituted an important barrier to the adoption of a political program by the labor unions.

102. Rischin, *The Promised City*, p. 184. There are several histories of labor organizations in New York City; Rischin provides the best synthesis of the basic facts, so far as those have been ascertained. Rischin's own emphasis is of course on the Jewish unions.

103. Rischin, *The Promised City*, pp. 184–86.

104. An excellent recent review of the evidence on these points is found in Susan Previant Lee and Peter Passell, *A New Economic View of American History* (New York: W. W. Norton & Company, 1979), pp. 341–46.

105. New York City voting data taken from the *City Record* and the *Tribune Almanac*; southern and nonsouthern turnout estimates from J. Morgan Kousser, *The Shaping of Southern Politics* (New Haven: Yale University Press, 1974), p. 12. On ballot reform, see Herbert J. Bass, *"I Am a Democrat:" The Political Career of David Bennett Hill* (Syracuse: Syracuse University Press, 1961), pp. 147–54, and Peter H. Argersinger," "A Place on the Ballot: Fusion Politics and Antifusion Laws," *American Historical Review* 85 (1980): 287–306.

106. Department of the Interior, Census Office, *Report on Population of the United States at the Eleventh Census, 1890* (Washington, D.C.: Government Printing Office, 1897), pp. 126, lxvii.

107. Department of the Interior, Census Office, *Twelfth Census of the United States . . . 1900: Population*, pt. 2 (Washington, D.C.; 1902), table 25, p. 173.

108. See chap. 4, in this volume.

109. On London politics in this period, see Paul Thompson, *Socialists, Liberals and Labour: The Struggle for London, 1885–1914* (London: Routledge & Kegan Paul, 1967), pp. 71, 72–76, 85–89; on class relations, see Gareth Stedman Jones, *Outcast London: A Study in the Relationship Between Classes in Victorian Society* (Oxford: The Clarendon Press, 1971). A telling anecdote on the importance of sport in English politics appears in Simon Knott, *The Electoral Crucible: The Politics of London, 1900–1914*, (London: Greene & Co., n.d., after 1974), pp. 12, 26, 28: "When the future King [Edward VI] visited East

London he was greeted with a banner—'The East End welcomes the noble owner of Persimmon' [a famous thoroughbred]." The sporting activities of the leading Tammany–and of several Republican—millionaires have yet to receive careful study. Whitney, Ryan, and Belmont were all famous for their involvement in thoroughbred racing as well as for their association with Tammany Hall; Andrew Freedman, a financier who worked closely with Tammany Boss Richard Croker, was president of the New York Baseball Club; Herman Oelrichs, one of the city's most prominent German-American Democrats and for a time a member of the Democratic National Committee, sat on the board of Madison Square Garden, Inc. In 1890 Republicans Cornelius Van Cott and Edwin A. McAlpin had served as president and director of the New York Baseball Club.

110.   On the race track incident see Robert Muccigrosso, "The City Reform Club: A Study in Late Nineteenth-Century Reform," *New-York Historical Society Quarterly* (1968), pp. 250–51, and the contemporary pamphlet, "The Central Park Race Track Law Was Repealed by Public Sentiment." (New York, 1892). Jesup's remarks appear in the Chamber of Commerce of the State of New York, *Annual Report* (1895), part 1, p. 95.

111.   New York State Bureau of Labor Statistics, *Eighteenth Annual Report, 1900,* p. 372. This was the statement of the settlement house associated with Grace Episcopal Church.

112.   William R. Hutchison's *The Modernist Impulse in American Protestantism* (Cambridge: Harvard University Press, 1976) provides the best survey of the theology of this religious persuasion, but although he explores its implications for American imperialism, Hutchison has surprisingly little to say about the impact of liberal Protestantism on municipal policy.

113.   The increasing employment of women in office jobs was evident in the occupational data for New York City published in the 1890, 1900, and 1910 censuses. For observations on the national scope of this phenomenon, see W. Elliot Brownlee, *Dynamics of Ascent: A History of the American Economy* (New York: Alfred A. Knopf, 1974), p. 218.

CHAPTER 4

1.   Wallace S. Sayre and Herbert Kaufman, *Governing New York City: Politics in the Metropolis* (New York: Russell Sage Foundation, 1960), p. 44.

2.   For a discussion of the city charter that defined the rules for New York City between 1873 and 1898, see Seymour J. Mandelbaum, *Boss Tweed's New York* (New York: John Wiley & Sons, Inc., 1965), chap. 10.

3.   Theodore Roosevelt, *Autobiography* (New York: 1913), pp. 62–63.

4.   William L. Riordan, *Plunkitt of Tammany Hall* (New York: E. P. Dutton & Co., 1963), pp. 17, 19.

5.   Letter, Roosevelt to Lodge, March 25, 1889, in Elting E. Morison, *The Letters of Theodore Roosevelt* (Cambridge: Harvard University Press, 1951) vol. 1, p. 154.

6.   Peter Alexander Speek, *The Singletax and the Labor Movement* (Madison, Wisconsin: Bulletin of the University of Wisconsin, Economic and Political Science Series, 1917) vol. 8, no. 3, pp. 32–33, 58–64; Louis F. Post and Fred C. Leubuscher, *Henry George's 1886 Campaign: An Account of the George-Hewitt Campaign in the New York Municipal Election of 1886* (Westport, Connecticut: Hyperion Press, Inc., 1976 reprint of the New York: J. W. Lovell Co., 1887 1st ed.), pp. 6–7, 15, 46.

7.   Post and Leubuscher, *George's Campaign,* pp. 152–53.

8.   New York *World,* Oct. 31, 1886.

9.   Ibid., Oct. 27, 1886.

10.   The New York *World,* Oct. 27, 1886, printed a version of Hewitt's speech that differs somewhat from that given in Post and Leubuscher, *George's Campaign,* pp. 91–96.

11.   New York *World,* Oct. 27, 1886.

12.   Ibid., Oct. 7, 1897.

13.   Ibid., Oct. 14 and 15, 1897.

14.   The New York State laws governing primary elections were pulled together in *Throop's Revised Statutes of the State of New York* (Albany: Banks and Bros., 1886), and in Clarence F. Birdseye, *Revised Statutes, Codes and General Laws of the State of*

New York (New York: Baker, Voorhis and Co., 1896 and 1901). An excellent contemporary account of the effects of these laws in practice is A. C. Bernheim, "Party Organizations and Their Nominations to Public Office in New York City," *Political Science Quarterly* 3(1888): 99–122.

15. In other states, political interest groups manipulated the rules of the game to limit popular participation in elections during these years. J. Morgan Kousser has shown that southern Democrats used new ballot and especially registration laws to prevent blacks and poor whites who favored the Republican and Populist parties from voting in *The Shaping of Southern Politics: Suffrage Restriction and the Establishment of the One-Party South, 1880–1910* (New Haven: Yale University Press, 1974); Peter H. Argersinger has shown that Republicans used the publicly printed blanket ballot to limit the effectiveness of Democratic–Populist fusion campaigns in the Midwest and Far West in " 'A Place on the Ballot': Fusion Politics and Antifusion Laws," *American Historical Review* 85 (April 1980): 287–306.

16. The New York State laws governing ballots and other election matters are provided by *Throop's Revised Statutes* and Birdseye's *Revised Statutes*. William C. Ivins, *Machine Politics and Money in Elections in New York City* (New York: Arno Press 1970 reprint of Harper and Bros., 1887), provides a valuable commentary by a pragmatic insider; Joseph B. Bishop, "The Secret Ballot in Thirty-three States," *The Forum* (Jan. 1892), p. 595, offers a critique by an editor of Godkin's *Nation.* Herbert J. Bass, "The Politics of Ballot Reform in New York State, 1888–1890," *New York History* (July 1961): 253–72, describes voting practices and their first modern revision; Richard L. McCormick, *From Realignment to Reform: Political Change in New York State, 1893–1910* (Ithaca: Cornell University Press, 1981), discusses later changes. Additional detail on the 1890 ballot reform can be found in the letters of Wendell Philips Garrison and Joseph B. Bishop to James Bryce, especially in Bishop to Bryce, Jan. 26, 1892, Bryce Papers, Bodleian Library, Oxford University; and in J. H. Work to Charles S. Fairchild, Dec. 29, 1889, Fairchild Papers, New-York Historical Society. Information on later ballot reform campaigns in New York include a People's Municipal League circular dated Feb. 19, 1892, signed by Gustav H. Schwab, in the Fairchild Papers, and a circular addressed "To the Allied Political Clubs of New York City," dated Feb. 14, 1897, in the James B. Reynolds Papers of the University Settlement Society of New York Papers, State Historical Society of Wisconsin.

CHAPTER 5

1. For a review of studies of office-holding in American cities, see David C. Hammack, "Problems in the Historical Study of Power in the Cities and Towns of the United States, 1800–1960," *American Historical Review* 83 (Apr. 1978): 342–43; on Wood, see Samuel A. Pleasants, *Fernando Wood* (New York: Columbia University Press, 1948).

2. On state control of New York City affairs between 1857 and 1870 see pp. 188–190 of this volume. On Hall, see Croswell Bowen, *The Elegant Oakey* (New York: Oxford University Press, 1956). The best study of the Tweed scandals is Alexander B. Callow, Jr., *The Tweed Ring* (New York: Oxford University Press, 1966).

3. Samuel T. McSeveny, *The Politics of Depression: Political Behavior in the Northeast, 1893–96* (New York: Oxford University Press, 1972), pp. 3–7. Allan Nevins describes many of the objectives of the mercantile elite in *Abram S. Hewitt: With Some Account of Peter Cooper* (New York: Harper & Brothers, 1935), chap. 21. Also helpful for understanding the politics of this group is Robert Kelley, *The Transatlantic Persuasion: The Liberal-Democratic Mind in the Age of Gladstone* (New York: Alfred A. Knopf, 1969). For the term Swallowtails, see Martin Shefter, "The Emergence of the Political Machine: an Alternative View," in Willis D. Hawley and Michael Lipsky, et al., eds., *Theoretical Perspectives on Urban Politics* (Englewood Cliffs, New Jersey: Prentice-Hall, Inc., 1976), p. 27.

4. Open letter, Roosevelt to Elihu Root and William H. Bellamy, Oct. 16, 1886, in Elting E. Morison, ed., *The Letters of Theodore Roosevelt* (Cambridge, Mass.: Harvard University Press, 1951), volume 1, pp. 110–11.

5. Shefter, "Emergence of the Political Machine," p. 27; Mark D. Hirsch, *William C. Whitney, Modern Warwick* (New York: Dodd, Mead & Company, 1948), pp. 53–71;

Howard B. Furer, *William Frederick Havemeyer: A Political Biography* (New York: The American Press, 1965), pp. 144–54; Gustavus Myers, *The History of Tammany Hall* (New York: Boni & Liveright, Inc., 1917), pp. 252–54. Myers's useful compendium of facts about the history of New York City politics must be used carefully. In the preface to the first edition of 1901 Myers asserts that no established publisher would accept his manuscript, out of fear of provoking Tammany officials. But although Myers denies that the wealthy men who underwrote the private printing and distribution of the work did not insist "upon a censorship of the manuscript or its alteration in any way for political purposes," he did in fact submit the work for approval to James B. Reynolds, James W. Pryor, and Milo Roy Maltbie, representatives respectively of the Citizens' Union, the City Club, and the Reform Club's Committee on Municipal Reform; and he did accept some of their suggestions, including apparently a proposal that he entirely recast his account of mayoral politics between 1874 and 1897. See Myers, *Tammany*, pp. x–xi, 258; letters, James B. Reynolds to L. J. Callanan, Oct. 29, 1899(?), to Mortimer L. Schiff, Nov. 22, 1900(?), and to Milo R. Maltbie, Dec. 19, 1900(?), Reynolds Papers, University Settlement Society of New York Papers, State Historical Society of Wisconsin.

6. Hirsch, *Whitney*, pp. 214, 239, 407; Nevins, *Hewitt*, p. 524; Louis F. Post and Fred C. Leubuscher, *Henry George's 1886 Campaign* (Westport, Conn.: Hyperion Press, Inc., 1976 reprint of 1887 1st ed.), pp. 62–63; William Mills Ivins, *Machine Politics and Money in Elections in New York City* (New York: Arno Press 1970 reprint of Harper and Bros., 1887 1st ed.), p. 56; Seymour J. Mandelbaum, *Boss Tweed's New York* (New York: John Wiley & Sons, Inc., 1965), chap. 9. Henry George insisted that mayoral candidates usually contributed as much as $75,000 in support of their campaigns: Post and Leubuscher, *George's Campaign*, p. 24. "Contributions to the Campaign of the Democratic National Committee," dated "February 5, 1885," Cleveland Papers, Library of Congress, indicates that the New York City Swallowtails provided a very large share of Cleveland's campaign funds. (I am indebted to Perry Blatz for a copy of this document.)

7. Hirsch, *Whitney*, pp. 71, 130; Myers, *Tammany*, pp. 255–57, 259; New York *Times*, Oct. 5, 17, 18, & 31, 1874, Oct. 20 and Nov. 2, 6, & 8, 1876. Letter, Hewitt to Dr. Thomas Cottman, Oct. 9, 1874, quoted in Hirsch, *Whitney*, pp. 80–81.

8. Hirsch, *Whitney*, p. 176.

9. Matthew P. Breen, *Thirty Years of New York Politics, Up-to-Date* (New York: the author, 1899), p. 633. Hirsch, *Whitney*, pp. 105, 131–32; Myers, *Tammany*, pp. 259–60. New York *Times*, Oct. 20 & 22, 1878.

10. Nevins, *Hewitt*, pp. 432–35.

11. Breen, *Thirty Years*, pp. 632–46; Hirsch, *Whitney*, p. 159; Myers, *Tammany*, p. 260; Nevins, *Hewitt*, p. 435; New York *Times*, Oct. 23 and Nov. 22, 1880.

12. Breen, *Thirty Years*, pp. 665–88; Hirsch, *Whitney*, pp. 161–67, 170–81; Nevins, *Hewitt*, pp. 437–38.

13. Hirsch, *Whitney*, p. 172.

14. Ibid., pp. 181–87.

15. Breen, *Thirty Years*, pp. 687–88; Hirsch, *Whitney*, pp. 188–91; Myers, *Tammany*, pp. 261–62; New York *Times*, Oct. 23 & 24, 1882.

16. Breen, *Thirty Years*, pp. 701–6; Hirsch, *Whitney*, p. 240; Myers, *Tammany*, p. 262, New York *Times*, Oct. 1–12, 1884.

17. Hirsch, *Whitney*, pp. 248–59, 269, 350–54.

18. Breen, *Thirty Years*, pp. 704–7; Hirsch, *Whitney*, pp. 352–53.

19. Breen, *Thirty Years*, pp. 763–66; Hirsch, *Whitney*, p. 357.

20. Henry George, Jr., *The Life of Henry George* (Garden City, New York: Doubleday, Page & Company, 1911), vol. 2, p. 463; New York *Times*, Sept. 20 and Oct. 10, 1886; Breen, *Thirty Years*, pp. 687–88; Hirsch, *Whitney*, pp. 131–34; New York *World*, Oct. 3, 1886.

21. New York *World*, Oct. 1, 1886.

22. Ibid., Oct. 3, 6, & 9, 1886.

23. New York *Times*, Sept. 26 and Oct. 6 & 12, 1886. More than any other Swallowtail, Hewitt had repeatedly sought to promote cooperation with Tammany. New York *World*, Oct. 5, 7, 8, 9, 12, & 15, 1886.

24. Nevins, *Hewitt*, p. 462.

25. Harold F. Gosnell, *Boss Platt and His New York Machine* (New York: Russell

& Russell, 1969 reprint of Chicago, 1924, 1st ed.), p. 33; Morison, *Letters of Theodore Roosevelt*, vol. 1, pp. 68 n.2, 110–13; Howard L. Hurwitz, *Theodore Roosevelt and Labor in New York State, 1880–1900* (New York: Columbia University Press, 1943), pp. 119–21; letters, Roosevelt to Henry Cabot Lodge, Oct. 17 & 20, 1886; Roosevelt to Elihu Root and William H. Bellamy, Oct. 16, 1886, in Morison, *Letters of Theodore Roosevelt*, vol. 1, pp. 110–13.

26. Nevins, *Hewitt*, pp. 264–66, 409–19, 426–31; Post and Leubuscher, *George's Campaign*, pp. 34–35, 39–40.

27. Nevins, *Hewitt*, p. 418.

28. Post and Leubuscher, *George's Campaign*, pp. 52, 95.

29. Martin Shefter's "The Electoral Foundations of the Political Machine: New York City, 1884–1897," in Joel Silbey et al., eds., *American Electoral History: Quantitative Studies in Popular Voting Behavior* (Princeton: Princeton University Press, 1978), is a valuable statistical study of voting patterns in this and succeeding elections (see especially pp. 282 and 288); New York *City Record*, Dec. 6, 1886, p. 15. The social composition and the political histories of many assembly districts are described in the *Evening Post*, Apr. 3, 1890, and in that paper's *Tammany Biographies* (Oct. 1890 and 1894); in articles in the New York *Times*, Dec. 7, 1888; May 5 and July 20, 1892; July 7, 10, 18, 20, 21, 24, & 31; and Aug. 7, 14, 21, 28, & 31, and Sept. 4, 11, 18, & 25 and Oct. 2, 1893; and in Daniel Greenleaf Thompson, *Politics in a Democracy* (New York: Longmans, Green, and Co., 1893), chap. 10.

30. New York *City Record*, Dec. 6, 1886, p. 15.

31. Myers, *Tammany Hall*, pp. 275–76; M. R. Werner, *Tammany Hall* (Garden City, New York: Doubleday, Doran & Co., Inc., 1928), pp. 305, 436, 438.

32. Post and Leubuscher, *George's Campaign*, p. 133.

33. Letter, Hewitt to Frederick R. Coudert, Mar. 24, 1887, Hewitt Mayoral Letterpress Copybook, New-York Historical Society; Nevins, *Hewitt*, pp. 489–90; New York *City Record*, Jan. 18 and Feb. 1, 1888.

34. Nevins, *Hewitt*, pp. 402, 460; letter, Hewitt to Orlando B. Potter, June 23, 1885, quoted in Hirsch, *Whitney*, p. 181.

35. New York *Times*, May 10 and Oct. 28, 1887 and Jan. 2 and 26, 1888; Nevins, *Hewitt*, pp. 472–87; New York *World*, Oct. 18, 1888.

36. The New York *World* reviewed Hewitt's nativist outbursts in a comprehensive article, Oct. 18, 1888.

37. Breen, *Thirty Years*, pp. 766–76.

38. Nevins, *Hewitt*, pp. 512–513.

39. Ibid., p. 511; New York *World*, Oct. 18, 1888.

40. New York *City Record*, Dec. 14, 1888, p. 57; Shefter, "Electoral Foundations," pp. 273, 280, 282, 288.

41. Nevins, *Hewitt*, p. 266.

42. That Choate had been Roosevelt's early sponsor is made clear in the letters and notes contained in Morison, *Letters of Theodore Roosevelt*, vol. 1, pp. 34, 55, 58, 136; and vol. 2, p. 882. Harold F. Gosnell notes the solidarity and significance of this group in *Boss Platt*, p. 128.

43. Gosnell's *Boss Platt* remains the best account of the workings of the state's Republican party in the 1890s.

44. Robert Muccigrosso, "The City Reform Club: A Study in Late Nineteenth-Century Reform," *New-York Historical Society Quarterly* 52 (July 1968); Richard Skolnik, "Civic Group Progressivism in New York City," *New York History* 51 (1970): 411–39. City Reform Club, *Record of Assemblymen and Senators from the City of New York in the Legislature of 1884* (New York, 1886), and similar titles for the years through 1894; City Club of New York, *Annual Reports* for 1895–1900.

45. New York *Times*, Aug. 15, 1894.

46. Letter, Bryce to Gilder, Feb. 22, 1895, Bryce Papers.

47. William R. Hutchison, *The Modernist Impulse in American Protestantism* (Cambridge: Harvard University Press, 1976).

48. Moses Rischin, *The Promised City: New York's Jews, 1870–1914* (Cambridge: Harvard University Press, 1962), p. 179.

49. Ibid., p. 204; Clyde Griffen, "Rich Laymen and Early Social Christianity," *Church*

History 36 (March 1967): 3–23, and "Christian Socialism Instructed by Gompers," *Labor History* 12 (Spring 1971):195–214.

50. The Frederick W. Holls Papers at Columbia University contain extensive discussion of tenement house reform proposals. Writing as chairman of the Charity Organization Society's Tenement Reform Committee on Mar. 1, 1899, Holls had assured State Republican Chairman Benjamin B. Odell, Jr., that tenement reform was "a very important subject and one upon which the people of the East Side feel very strongly. The Republican Party," he added, "can do nothing more calculated to gain support further than to champion the cause of healthy and attractive homes for the poor against the greed of builders and tenement house owners."

51. Rischin, *The Promised City*, pp. 178, 204.

52. Letter, Theodore Roosevelt to Henry Cabot Lodge, Oct. 16, 1897, in Morison, *Letters of Theodore Roosevelt*, vol. 1, pp. 697–98.

53. The Citizens' Union made extensive, though carefully controlled, use of women from its inception. Franklin Pierce urged that the CU enlist women in a letter to James B. Reynolds, Feb. 4, 1897; Nicholas Murray Butler wrote to Reynolds defining the CU's policy, Apr. 12, 1897. Women could, Butler wrote, "advertise the movement by exploiting it and keeping it before the attention of large numbers of people," and they could "assist materially by making an active canvass for members as soon as the enrollment blanks are ready." But, he added, care must be taken to avoid "the criticism perhaps of being a women's movement;" the women should not be seen to act "until our own Executive Committee gets under a full head of steam." Both letters in the Reynolds Papers. The Reynolds Papers contain no letters from Mrs. Lowell, but Seth Low wrote Reynolds, Dec. 18, 1897, to ask why she had requested $5,000 to cover election expenses in a single assembly district; Low Papers, Columbia University; and Roosevelt decried her campaign deeds in a letter, Oct. 25, 1897, to Jacob A. Riis in Morison, *Letters of Theodore Roosevelt*, vol. 1, pp. 698–99. Mrs. Eleanora Kinnicutt, the leader of the Women's Health Protective Association, was also among those who early urged Low to accept the CU mayoral nomination; letter, Mar. 23, 1897, Low Papers, cited by Gerald Kurland in *Seth Low: The Reformer in an Urban and Industrial Age* (New York: Twayne Publishers, Inc., 1971), p. 365, n.12.

54. Melvin G. Holli, *Reform in Detroit: Hazen S. Pingree and Urban Politics* (New York: Oxford University Press, 1969), pp. 161–69.

55. Ibid., pp. 169–72. The PML platform is in the New York *Times*, Sept. 6, 1890.

56. James B. Reynolds, University Settlement Headworker's Report, March 1897, quoted in the A. J. Kennedy Notes in the Reynolds Papers.

57. Quoted in Werner, *Tammany Hall*, p. 348.

58. Letter, Holls to the Rev. W. A. Passanant, Jr., Apr. 6, 1896, Holls Papers.

59. New York *Times*, Sept. 18, 19, 21, 23, & 24, 1888; New York *Herald*, Sept. 24, 1888; letter, Hewitt to William Hogg, Sept. 24, 1888, Hewitt Mayoral Letterpress Copybooks; New York *Times*, Oct. 24, 1888; New York *Herald*, Oct. 2, 1888.

60. New York *World*, Oct. 5, 6, 12, & 16, 1888; New York *Times*, Sept. 15 and Oct. 12, 17 & 21, 1888; Breen, *Thirty Years*, pp. 820–30.

61. The New York *Times* covered the organization of the People's Municipal League in minute detail; the only published account appears in Muccigrosso, "The City Reform Club." Richard Skolnik provides much useful information in "The Crystallization of Reform in New York City, 1890–1917," (Ph.D. diss., Yale University, 1964).

62. New York *Times*, Aug. 27, 1890.

63. New York *Herald*, Oct. 10, 1890.

64. New York *Times*, Sept. 27, 1890; New York *Herald*, Oct. 2, 1890; letters, Charles S. Fairchild to Gustav Schwab, n. d., Fairchild Papers, New-York Historical Society; New York *Times*, *World*, and *Herald*, Oct. 9 & 10, 1890. The *Herald* provided the fullest detail on these negotiations.

65. New York *Herald*, Oct. 1 & 10, 1890.

66. Skolnik, "The Crystallization of Reform," p. 138; New York *Herald*, Oct. 1 & 13, 1890; letter, Charles S. Fairchild to *The Evening Post*, Oct. 27, 1891, Fairchild Papers.

67. New York *City Record*, Dec. 8, 1890, p. 17; Thompson, *Politics in a Democracy*, provides what amounts to a sophisticated, if verbal and not statistical, multivariate analysis of the Tammany vote. Using assembly district and even election district percentages, Thompson shows that Tammany drew votes from all sectors of the city, especially from the middle-

and lower-middle income residents of Irish and German extraction. Shefter, "Electoral Foundations," does not deal with the 1890 election.

68. New York *Herald*, Sept. 17, 1891; Memorandum, Committee of Democrats Opposed to the February Convention, Feb. 5, 1892, Fairchild Papers; Herbert J. Bass, *"I Am A Democrat:"* The Political Career of David Bennett Hill (Syracuse: Syracuse University Press, 1961), chap. 8; and Hirsch, *Whitney*, chap. 13. New York *Times*, Sept. 23 & 29, and Oct. 5, 1892; *Herald*, Oct. 1, 1892. Hirsch, *Whitney*, pp. 405–6. Letters, William R. Grace to "My Dear Secretary," Feb. 27, 1892 (with accompanying plans for organizing the anti-Hill movement), Fairchild Papers; E. L. Godkin to Henry Villard, June 7, 1893, reprinted in William M. Armstrong, *The Gilded Age Letters of E. L. Godkin* (Albany: State University of New York Press, 1974), pp. 446–48; New York *Times*, Sept. 23 and Oct. 8, 1892.

69. New York *Times* and New York *Tribune*, Oct. 15, 16, 17, & 18, 1892. Among the candidates most seriously considered, according to these reports, were GAR favorites Horace Porter, E. A. McAlpin, and William L. Strong, and the Jewish bankers and philanthropists Jesse Seligman and Jacob H. Schiff. New York *Times*, Oct. 19, 1892.

70. Muccigrosso, "The City Reform Club," p. 246; Werner, *Tammany Hall*, pp. 349–56. Letter, Charles R. Flint to Edward M. Shepard, Dec. 19, 1893, Shepard Papers, Columbia University, on the New York *Times'* policy of stressing the police corruption issue.

71. Werner, *Tammany Hall*, p. 356; archives of the Chamber of Commerce of the State of New York.

72. Werner, *Tammany Hall*, pp. 356–94; New York *Evening Post, Tammany Biographies*, pp. 9, 12–14. The New York *Herald*, Oct. 20, 1891, identified one district leader, George R. Roesch, as a member of the often independent Stecklerite faction on the lower east side, not, *contra* Werner, a Tammany regular.

73. The organization of the Committee of Seventy was described in detail in the New York *Times*, Sept. 7, 16, & 20, 1894; Elsie R. Koetl, "New York in 1894: Case Study of a Reform Movement," (Master's Essay, Columbia University, 1967), provides a careful analysis of the social origins of the committee's members.

74. New York *Times*, Sept. 9 and Oct. 2, 3, 4, 11, 14, & 31, 1894; Jan. 20 & 21, 1893; New York *Herald*, Oct. 20, 1891.

75. New York *Times*, Sept. 16 and Oct. 4 & 5, 1894; Kurland, *Low*, pp. 74–76; letters, Theodore Roosevelt to Anna Roosevelt, Aug. 12, 1894; Roosevelt to Henry Cabot Lodge, Sept. 30, Oct. 8 & 22, 1894, all reprinted in Morison, *The Letters of Theodore Roosevelt*, vol. 1, pp. 393, 399, 400, 407.

76. New York *Times*, Sept. 16 and Oct. 5 & 6, 1894.

77. New York *Times* and New York *World*, Oct. 5, 9, 10, & 11, 1894; letters, Theodore Roosevelt to Henry Cabot Lodge, Sept. 30 and Oct. 8, 1894, in Morison, *The Letters of Theodore Roosevelt*, vol. 1, pp. 399, 400.

78. New York *Times*, Oct. 5, 9, 10, & 11, 1894.

79. Ibid., Oct. 4, 6, 9, 10, & 12, 1894 and Jan. 20, 1893.

80. Ibid., Oct. 9, 1894; letter, E. L. Godkin to Edward M. Shepard, Dec. 27, 1897, asserting that Strong had stated, following his election, that he had promised a police commissionership to O'Brien in return for his support; Shepard Papers.

81. New York *Times*, Oct. 11 & 17, 1894; letter, Theodore Sutro to Charles S. Fairchild, Nov. 11, 1894, Fairchild Papers.

82. New York *Times*, Oct. 11, 1894; Thomas Collier Platt, *The Autobiography of Thomas Collier Platt*, ed. Louis J. Lang (New York: B. W. Dodge & Co., 1910), pp. 268–93, provides Platt's version of his bargain with Strong.

83. New York *Times*, Oct. 10, 16, & 17, 1894.

84. Ibid., Oct. 16, 1894.

85. Ibid., Oct. 20, 1894.

86. Ibid., Oct. 5, 1894.

87. New York *City Record*, Dec. 15, 1894, p. 15.

88. For the sources on the ethnicity and wealth of New York's assembly districts, see note 29, above. For a statistical analysis, see Shefter, "The Electoral Foundations of the Political Machine," pp. 273, 280.

89. On Josiah Quincy's Boston, see Geoffrey Blodgett, *The Gentle Reformers: Massa-*

chusetts Democrats in the Cleveland Era (Cambridge: Harvard University Press, 1966); on Pingree's Detroit, see Holli, *Reform in Detroit;* on the contradictions in Mayor Strong's administration see Hurwitz, *Theodore Roosevelt and Labor in New York State,* pp. 150–75; letters, Theodore Roosevelt to Carl Schurz, July 13 & 17 and Aug. 6, 1895, in Morison, *Letters of Theodore Roosevelt,* vol. 1, pp. 465–66, 468, 472–74; the Citizens' Union, *The City for the People! Campaign Book of the Citizens' Union* (New York, 1897), pp. 50–51, 59–70; Frank D. Pavey, "Mayor Strong's Experiment in New York City," *The Forum* 23 (1897): 539–53. The leading municipal officers under Strong are listed in the *Tribune Almanac,* 1897, pp. 271–72. Letters describing their factional loyalties include Seth Low to Theodore Roosevelt, Oct. 12, 1895, Low Papers, Columbia University; and Theodore Roosevelt to Henry Cabot Lodge, Dec. 20, 1895, in Morison, *Letters of Theodore Roosevelt,* vol. 1, pp. 500–501. Frederick W. Holls wrote Joseph Choate, May 18, 1895, Holls Papers, to urge the appointment of Herman C. Kudlich as police magistrate and to insist that Germans would not accept the appointment of German Jews as recognition for their group. Richard Skolnik reviews the career of Strong's street cleaning commissioner in "George E. Waring, Jr., A Model for Reformers," *New-York Historical Society Quarterly* 52 (1968): 354–78. George F. Knerr, "The Mayoral Administration of William L. Strong" (Ph.D. diss., New York University, 1957) provides a general review.

    90. No historian has undertaken a full-scale prosopographic analysis of the Citizens' Union, and none will be provided here. This characterization is based on a thorough reading of the Seth Low, Nicholas Murray Butler, and especially the James B. Reynolds papers, and a careful study of CU activities as reported in the New York *Times* and other papers, 1897–1903.

    91. Letters, Franklin Pierce to James B. Reynolds, Feb. 4, 1897, and Everett P. Wheeler to Reynolds, June 16, 1897, Gustav Schwab to Reynolds, Feb. 15, 1897, and John B. Pine to Reynolds, Mar. 25 and Apr. 14, 1897, Reynolds Papers.

    92. James B. Reynolds, University Settlement Headworker's Report, March 1897, quoted in the A. J. Kennedy Notes in the Reynolds Papers. Gerald Kurland, "The Amateur in Politics: The Citizens' Union and the Greater New York Campaign of 1897," *New-York Historical Society Quarterly* 53 (1969): 354–55.

    93. Kurland, *Low,* p. 111.

    94. Letter, R. Heber Newton to Reynolds, May 5, 1897, Reynolds Papers.

    95. Letters, Charles Stewart Smith to John B. Pine, Apr. 28 and May 1, 1897; Charles H. Parkhurst to Charles Stewart Smith, Apr. 30, 1897; John Frankenheimer to James B. Reynolds, May 1, 1897, Reynolds Papers.

    96. "You could do nothing," Schiff wrote, "more certain to destroy the influence of the University Settlement both among the people whom the influence of the settlement is intended to benefit and among a considerable part of the friends who are willing and desirous to support the work of the settlement." Letter, Schiff to Reynolds, May 6, 1896, Reynolds Papers.

    97. Letter, Henry White to Reynolds, Mar. 4, 1897, Reynolds Papers; New York *Times,* June 6, 1897; Rischin, *The Promised City,* pp. 177–78.

    98. Letter, Daniel Harris to Reynolds, Mar. 27, 1897.

    99. The best account of Low's life is Kurland, *Seth Low;* Charles Stewart Smith reviewed some of Low's qualifications in a letter to James B. Reynolds, July 16, 1897, Reynolds Papers.

    100. Letters, Charles J. Edwards to Edward M. Shepard, Aug. 25, 1897, Shepard Papers; Frederick W. Holls to Seth Low, July 26, 1897, Holls Papers; Edward D. Page to James B. Reynolds, Sept. 11, 1897; Franklin Pierce to Reynolds, July 7 & 13, 1897; James Loeb to James B. Reynolds, July 25, 1897; Charles Stewart Smith to Reynolds, Aug. 19, 20, & 29, 1897; Bolton Hall to Reynolds, Sept. 1, 1897; all in Reynolds Papers.

    101. Gosnell, *Boss Platt,* chap. 14, provides an excellent discussion of Platt's character and purposes; Platt, *Autobiography,* pp. 358–61; Kurland, *Low,* p. 93; letters, Theodore Roosevelt to Seth Low, June 23 & 29 and Sept. 4, 1897, in Morison, *The Letters of Theodore Roosevelt,* vol. 1, pp. 631–32, 633–34, 666–67; Nicholas Murray Butler to James B. Reynolds, Aug. 23 & 28, 1897; Lemuel E. Quigg to Reynolds, Aug. 28, 1897; F. B. Thurber to Reynolds, June 18, 1897, Reynolds Papers.

    102. New York *Times,* Sept. 24 & 25 and Oct. 8, 1897; Kurland, *Low,* p. 99.

103. Letter, Charles J. Edwards to Edward M. Shepard, Sept. 14, 1897, Shepard Papers; New York *Times*, Sept. 24, 28, & 30, and Oct. 2, 12, 13, 14, 15, & 16, 1897.
104. Letters, Charles J. Edwards to Edward M. Shepard, Aug. 25 and Sept. 3, 14, & 24, 1897; George Foster Peabody to Shepard, Sept. 14, 1897; Shepard Papers.
105. Election totals are given in the New York *City Record,* Dec. 30, 1897, p. 79. These comparisons are based as closely as possible on the returns for assembly districts in the same areas in 1894 and 1897; actual district boundaries had been changed in the interim. Sources of information on the social and ethnic characteristics of the various districts are identified in note 29 to this chapter. Frederick W. Holls suggested that even if the Citizens' Union/Republican split had "not taken place, there would have been sufficient diminution of Low's vote to elect Van Wyck after all." Letter to Andrew Dickson White, Nov. 27, 1897.
106. Shefter, "Electoral Foundations of the Political Machine," pp. 273, 280.
107. New York (State) Assembly, Special Committee to Investigate the Public Offices and Departments of the City of New York (the Mazet Committee), *Report of Counsel,* Dec. 22, 1899, provides a convenient synopsis.
108. Quoted in Kurland, *Low,* p. 117.
109. Jeremy P. Felt, "Vice Reform as a Political Technique: The Committee of Fifteen in New York, 1900–1901," *New York History* 54 (1973):26–33.
110. Kurland has traced these negotiations in detail in his *Seth Low,* pp. 123–29.
111. Kurland, *Seth Low,* pp. 129–30.
112. Ibid., pp. 128–35.
113. Ibid., pp. 132–36; manuscript Minutes, Board of Managers of the New York Produce Exchange, May 31, 1888, New-York Historical Society.
114. New York *Times,* Oct. 4, 1901. Jack Gabel, "Edward M. Shepard: Militant Reformer" (Ph.D. diss., New York University, 1967), provides the only comprehensive review of his life. Shepard's papers, now at Columbia University, are extraordinarily full.
115. John DeWitt Warner, "Municipal Betterment in the New York City Elections," *Municipal Affairs* 5 (1901): 625–27.
116. Quoted in Kurland, *Low,* p. 126.
117. Warner, "Municipal Betterment," pp. 630–38; New York *Times,* Oct. 1901, passim.
118. See note 50 in this chapter.
119. Kurland, *Low,* p. 126.
120. Warner, "Municipal Betterment," p. 632–35.
121. The *City Vigilant,* Sept. and Oct. 1901, passim; Alfred Hodder, *A Fight for the City* (New York: The Macmillan Company, 1903), pp. 138–39, 159–97; Felt, "Vice Reform," p. 108. Jerome so far discounted the Irish vote as to use anti-Irish jokes in his campaign: Hodder, *Fight,* p. 149.
122. For the official canvass of the vote in 1901, see the New York *City Record,* Jan. 4, 1902.
123. Citizens' Union, *The City for the People! The Best Administration New York Ever Had: Campaign Book of the Citizens' Union, 1903* (New York, 1903).
124. Low's first appointments are listed in the *Tribune Almanac,* 1902, p. 397. Kurland, *Low,* pp. 145–47, and Theodore Lowi, *At The Pleasure of the Mayor* (New Haven: Yale University Press, 1964), pp. 134–39, evaluate his choices. Other evaluations of Low's mayoralty include Kurland, *Low,* pp. 159–90, and Steven C. Swett, "The Test of a Reformer: A Study of Seth Low, New York City Mayor, 1902–1903," *New-York Historical Society Quarterly* 44 (1960): 20–22, 30–31.
125. Kurland, *Low,* chap. 8.
126. Ibid., p. 186; George B. McClellan, Jr., *The Gentleman and the Tiger: The Autobiography of George B. McClellan, Jr.* (Philadelphia and New York: J. B. Lippincott Company, 1956), pp. 169–71; Marvin G. Weinbaum, "New York County Republican Politics, 1897–1922: The Quarter Century After Municipal Consolidation," *New-York Historical Society Quarterly* 50 (1966): 70–74; Gosnell, *Boss Platt,* chap. 11.
127. Skolnik, "Civic Group Progressivism in New York City;" Augustus Cerillo, Jr., in "The Reform of Municipal Government in New York City, From Seth Low to John Purroy Mitchell," *New-York Historical Society Quarterly* 57 (1973): 51–71, describes the activities of upper-income pressure groups in New York City after 1906, but underestimates their significance in the 1890s.

CHAPTER 6

1. Martin Shefter, "The Emergence of the Political Machine: An Alternative View," in Willis D. Hawley et al., eds., *Theoretical Perspectives on Urban Politics* (Englewood Cliffs, New Jersey: Prentice-Hall, Inc., 1976), pp. 35–36; A. C. Bernheim, "Party Organizations and Their Nominations to Public Office in New York City," *Political Science Quarterly* 3 (1888): 107–8. Shefter's essay is the most valuable account of Tammany Hall's history in this period, but the following pages dispute several of its conclusions. Underestimating the resources employed by the Swallowtail Democrats, Shefter fails to appreciate that Hewitt's nativist outbursts and the Swallowtail decision to join the independent movements of the 1890s were at least as responsible as Tammany leader Richard Croker's leadership techniques for his organization's success in 1890, 1892, 1894, and 1897. Unaware of the role of the Hugh Grant–Thomas F. Gilroy uptown crowd in the late eighties through the nineties, Shefter overestimates Croker's importance and exaggerates the continuity of his regime. As a result he dates Tammany's hegemony over mayoral nominations from 1890 rather than from Charles F. Murphy's ascension to the leadership in 1903, and, more significantly, obscures the diversity of New York City politics between 1886 and 1903.

2. Quoted in M. R. Werner, *Tammany Hall* (Garden City, New York: Doubleday, Doran, & Co., Inc., 1928) p. 276.

3. Mark D. Hirsch, *William C. Whitney, Modern Warwick* (New York: Dodd, Mead, & Co., 1948), pp. 154–55, 160–62.

4. Ibid., pp. 53–71.

5. Every successful mayoral candidate between 1872 and 1884 could be described as a Swallowtail Democrat, as could eleven of the seventeen mayoral nominees (counting each man once for each year in which he was nominated). Of the other six nominees, Bank of North America President William Dowd, running as the Republican candidate in 1880, secured the largest share of the vote. Only two Democrats and three Republicans who had worked their way up through the ranks secured mayoral nominations in these years. See table 4–1, in this volume.

6. William Mills Ivins, *Machine Politics and Money in Elections in New York City* (New York: Arno Press 1970 reprint of Harper & Bros. 1887 1st edition), p. 9.

7. Matthew P. Breen, *Thirty Years of New York Politics, Up-to-Date* (New York: the author, 1899), pp. 685–86, 703–6; Hirsch, *Whitney,* pp. 160, 179, 202–3.

8. The evidence on these points is widely scattered; for accounts of the careers of several County Democracy men who later became Tammany district leaders, see the New York *Evening Post,* Apr. 3, 1890.

9. At various times Murphy, Sullivan, Campbell, White, and Purroy supported County Democracy or other anti-Tammany candidates; Steckler, Reilly, Plunkitt and Murray often resisted the leadership of Richard Croker. Steckler's organization sometimes opposed Tammany, and in 1894 it actually supported Committee of Seventy mayoral candidate William L. Strong, a Republican.

10. Martin Shefter, "The Electoral Foundations of the Political Machine: New York City, 1884–1897," in Joel Silbey, et al., eds., *American Electoral History: Quantitative Studies in Popular Voting Behavior* (Princeton: Princeton University Press, 1978), pp. 282, 287.

11. New York *Evening Post,* Apr. 3, 1890; *Harper's Weekly,* July 13, 1890.

12. Ibid.

13. See my biographical sketches of Grant and Gilroy in Melvin Holli and Peter d'A. Jones, *Biographical Directory of American Mayors,* (Westport, Conn.: Greenwood Press, 1981).

14. New York *Times,* Oct. 6 & 14, 1888; New York *Herald,* Sept. 20 and Oct. 11, 1890.

15. Tammany's mayoral nominations and platforms can best be followed through the daily newspapers, especially the *Times,* the *Herald,* and the *World.*

16. Werner, *Tammany Hall,* pp. 314–18.

17. These appointments are described in the New York *Evening Post,* Apr. 3, 1890.

18. Ibid.

19. The Tammany clubs are described in ibid. and in a series of New York *Times* articles on the Tammany organizations in a number of assembly districts, May 5 and July

20, 1892; and on July 7, 10, 18, 20, 21, 24, & 31; Aug. 7, 14, 21, & 28; and Sept. 4, 11, 18, & 25 and Oct. 2, 1893. County Democrats had made the Amsterdam Club their headquarters in the mid-eighties, but with the exception of the Narragansett Club, founded as early as 1879 in Hugh Grant's uptown 19th A.D., the Onawanda and perhaps the Home clubs in the heavily Tammany 12th and 16th "gashouse" districts, and Henry Purroy's Annexed District Club, most Tammany clubs were established in the late eighties or early nineties, after Grant's 1888 victory.

20.   Martin Shefter's account of the "Emergence of the Political Machine" emphasizes the increasing discipline that Tammany leaders exerted over their district leader followers but fails to note the significance of the decay of competing Democratic factions when the Swallowtails pulled out of them—and lost their ability to win votes—after 1886.

21.   Werner, *Tammany Hall*, pp. 320–21; New York *Herald*, Sept. 28 and Oct. 11, 1890; and New York *City Record*, Dec. 8, 1890, p. 17.

22.   New York *World*, Jan. 17, 1892, p. 13; *Evening Post*, *Tammany Biographies* (New York: 1890 and 1894) pp. 9, 10, 16, 17.

23.   On the public reputations of the Big Four, see *Harper's Weekly*, July 13, 1889; on Parkhurst's attack and the Lexow investigation see Werner, *Tammany Hall*, pp. 349, 394; on Tammany's election campaign, see the New York *Times*, Oct. 1894.

24.   Evidence of Whitney's increasingly close relations with Croker appears in letters of Daniel S. Lamont to Governor David B. Hill, May 17, 1889, Hill Papers, and in several undated letters from Whitney to William F. Sheehan, Sheehan Papers, all in the Syracuse University Library. In 1892, Whitney made certain of Croker's support for Cleveland by making it possible for him to "win" $100,000 through a wager that Cleveland would defeat Harrison, Hirsch, *Whitney*, pp. 406, 407; De Alva Stanwood Alexander, *Four Famous New Yorkers: The Political Careers of Cleveland, Platt, Hill, and Roosevelt* (New York: Henry Holt & Company, 1923), p. 191. Among Croker's closest associates in 1897, according to Werner (*Tammany Hall*, pp. 455–56), were Daniel McMahon, Charles F. Murphy, George Washington Plunkitt, John C. Sheehan, and Thomas J. Dunn—all contractors of one sort or another—and Patrick Divver, Bernard Martin, Edward J. Fitzpatrick, and other notorious downtown saloonkeepers. Uptown leaders Jacob Seabold, John B. Sexton, and William E. Stillings, who had been closely associated with Grant and Gilroy, had moved into the background.

25.   New York *Times*, Oct. 27 and Nov. 1, 1897; letter, Charles J. Edwards to Edward M. Shepard, Sept. 24, 1897, Shepard Papers, Columbia University.

26.   Letter, Charles J. Edwards to Edward M. Shepard, Sept. 28, 1897.

27.   New York *Times*, Oct. 1, 1897.

28.   New York *Times*, Oct. 1, 20, 21, & 27, 1897. Godkin found Gardner's remark especially offensive: letter, E. L. Godkin to James Bryce, Oct. 22, 1897, in William M. Armstrong, ed., *The Gilded Age Letters of E. L. Godkin* (Albany: State University of New York Press, 1974), pp. 497–98.

29.   The New York *World* published Tammany's full platform and several speeches, Oct. 1, 1897; also relevant is Thomas C. O'Sullivan, chairman of the Committee on Resolutions, "Address at Tammany Hall," Jan. 26, 1897, in Tammany Minutes, vol. 2 of Kilroe Additions from the New York County Democratic Committee, Kilroe Collection of Tammaniana, Columbia University Library.

30.   Steven Kelman's paper is quoted in Shefter, "The Emergence of the Political Machine," p. 35.

31.   These observations are based on an examination of changes in the percentage of the vote going to the Tammany, Republican, and Citizens' Union mayoral candidates in 1897 compared with the percentage going to the Tammany and the Republican or Fusion candidates in 1890, 1892, and 1894, by assembly district. Since assembly district boundaries were changed between 1894 and 1897, comparisons can only be approximate.

32.   Shefter, "Electoral Foundations of the Political Machine," pp. 273, 280.

33.   New York (State) Assembly, Special Committee to Investigate the Public Offices and Departments of the City of New York (Mazet Committee), *Report of Counsel*, Dec. 22, 1899, p. 51 and passim.

34.   Mazet Committee, *Report of Counsel*; New York *Times*, Oct. 4, 1901.

35.   See chaps. 5 and 6 in this volume.

36.   New York *Times*, Oct. 4, 1901.

37. Jack Gabel, "Edward M. Shepard: Militant Reformer" (Ph. D. diss., New York University, 1967). Shepard's papers provide important additional detail.

38. For the official canvass of the vote in 1901, see the New York *City Record*, Jan. 4, 1902. The analysis offered here is again based on a study of the assembly district vote.

39. The best account of Murphy is Nancy Joan Weiss, *Charles Francis Murphy, 1858–1924: Respectability and Responsibility in Tammany Politics* (Northampton, Mass.: Smith College, 1968).

40. George B. McClellan, Jr.'s autobiography, *The Gentleman and the Tiger*, ed. Harold C. Syrett (Philadelphia: J. B. Lippincott Co., 1956), provides the best account of McClellan's career and of his relations with Croker and Murphy.

41. New York *City Record*, Dec. 31, 1903.

42. McClellan, *The Gentleman and the Tiger*, chap. 13.

43. Wallace S. Sayre and Herbert Kaufman, *Governing New York City: Politics in the Metropolis* (New York: Russell Sage Foundation, 1960), pp. 688–89.

44. Peter Alexander Speek, *The Singletax and the Labor Movement* (Madison, Wisconsin: Bulletin of the University of Wisconsin, Economic and Political Science Series, 1917) vol. 8, no. 3, pp. 25–27.

45. Ibid., p. 41.

46. Ibid.

47. Michael Gordon, "Irish Immigrant Culture and the Labor Boycott in New York City, 1880–1886," in Richard L. Ehrlich, ed., *Immigrants in Industrial America, 1850–1920* (Charlottesville: University of Virginia Press for the Eleutherian Mills–Hagley Foundation and the Balch Institute, 1977), pp. 111–22.

48. Samuel Gompers, *Seventy Years of Life and Labor: An Autobiography* (New York: E. P. Dutton & Company, 1925), p. 311.

49. Speek, *The Singletax*, pp. 58–60. Barrett had presided at the trial at which Tammany boss Richard Croker was tried and acquitted of murder in connection with an affray during the 1874 election (Croker was working for Abram S. Hewitt at the time); in 1885 and 1899 Barrett was renominated, over a labor protest, with Croker's support. Breen, *Thirty Years*, pp. 791–95; letter, James B. Reynolds to J. Noble Hays, Nov. 9, 1899, attributing the poor showing of the Citizens' Union to the "effect of placing Barrett at the head of our ticket," Reynolds Papers, University Settlement Society of New York Papers, State Historical Society of Wisconsin.

50. Speek, *The Singletax*, p. 63.

51. Ibid., pp. 32–33, 62–64; Gompers, *Seventy Years*, pp. 311–13.

52. Gompers, *Seventy Years*, p. 313; Louis F. Post and Fred C. Leubuscher, *Henry George's 1886 Campaign*, (Westport, Conn.: Hyperion Press, Inc., 1976 reprint of New York, 1887, 1st ed.) pp. 6–7, 15; Speek, *Singletax*, pp. 62–66.

53. Post and Leubuscher, *George's Campaign*, pp. 6–7, 15.

54. Gompers, *Thirty Years*, p. 316; Post and Leubuscher, *George's Campaign*, p. 12, chaps. 5, 7, 9, and 10; Speek, *Singletax*, chap. 6.

55. Post and Leubuscher, *George's Campaign*, pp. 26–28.

56. George's most important speeches are reproduced in Post and Leubuscher, *George's Campaign*, chaps. 2, 5, and 7.

57. Post and Leubuscher, *George's Campaign*, p. 22.

58. Ibid., p. 23.

59. Ibid.

60. Allan Nevins, *Abram S. Hewitt: With Some Account of Peter Cooper* (New York: Harper & Bros., 1935), p. 468; Breen, *Thirty Years*, pp. 687–88; Hirsch, *Whitney*, pp. 188–91; Gustavus Myers, *The History of Tammany Hall* (New York: Boni & Liveright, Inc., 1917) pp. 261–62; New York *City Record*, Dec. 6, 1886.

61. Shefter, "Electoral Foundations of the Machine," pp. 282, 288.

62. New York *City Record*, Dec. 6, 1886, p. 15; accounts of the political history and social composition of assembly districts are identified in note 29 to chapter 5 in this volume.

63. Henry George, Jr., *The Life of Henry George* (Garden City, New York: Doubleday, Page & Co., 1911), vol. 2, p. 462.

64. Post and Leubuscher, *George's Campaign*, pp. 132–34, reprints an Oct. 25, 1886 letter of the Right Reverend Monsignor Thomas S. Preston, Vicar-General of the Archdiocese of New York, to Joseph J. O'Donohue, Chairman of the Tammany Committee on Resolutions,

assuring O'Donohue that "the great majority of the Catholic clergy of this city are opposed to the candidacy of Mr. George." According to Post and Leubuscher, this letter was widely distributed in front of Catholic churches on the Sunday before the election.

65. Howard L. Hurwitz, *Theodore Roosevelt and Labor in New York State, 1880–1900* (New York: Columbia University Press, 1943), p. 143.

66. Ibid., p. 141.

67. Ibid., p. 138.

68. Speek, *Singletax*, p. 133.

69. Ibid., pp. 138–40.

70. Ibid., pp. 130, 139, 144–45; George, Jr., *George*, pp. 494–95.

71. Speek, *Singletax*, pp. 144–48.

72. George, Jr., *George*, pp. 511–12.

73. Speek, *Singletax*, pp. 127, 150; New York *World*, Oct. 11, 1888.

74. Speek, *Singletax*, p. 135.

75. Gompers, *Seventy Years*, p. 321.

76. Speek, *Singletax*, pp. 116–17.

77. Gompers describes the struggle for control of the cigarmakers' organizations in *Seventy Years*, chap. 12.

78. New York *Times, World, Herald*, Oct. 9 & 10, 1890.

79. New York *Herald*, Oct. 1 & 10, 1890.

80. The PML platform is in the New York *Times*, Sept. 6, 1890. Frank Scott repeated the points of this platform in accepting the PML mayoral nomination; *Times*, Oct. 14, 1890.

81. New York *Times*, Sept. 7 & 16 and Oct. 4 & 6, 1894.

82. The James B. Reynolds Papers contain several letters that discuss the disaffection of labor, including George McAneny to Reynolds, Jan. 26, 1897; John B. Pine to Reynolds, April 14, 1897; Henry White to Reynolds, May 11, 1897; Thomas Clegg to Reynolds, May 28, 1897; and Arthur H. Ely to Reynolds, n.d. [1897].

83. Hurwitz, *Theodore Roosevelt and Labor*, pp. 153–54, 163–75.

84. Gerald Kurland, *Seth Low, The Reformer in an Urban and Industrial Age* (New York: Twayne Publishers, Inc., 1971), p. 102; New York *Times*, Oct. 11, 1987.

85. Letter, Charles J. Edwards to Edward M. Shepard, Sept. 14, 1897, Shepard Papers; New York *Times*, Oct. 12, 13, 14, 15, & 16, 1897.

86. New York *World*, Oct. 30, 1897.

87. Ibid., Oct. 15, 1897.

88. For Tammany platforms, see the New York *Times* and the New York *World*, Oct. 11, 1894; Oct. 15, 1897; Oct. 4, 1901; and Oct. 3, 1903. For an extended statement of the position taken by the uptown group that dominated Tammany between 1886 and 1896 see Thomas F. Gilroy, "The Wealth of New York," *North American Review* 157 (1893): 307–14, 403–4, 541–49. For other sources see notes 29 and 30 to this chapter.

89. These included the demands for recognition of the right to organize, for the eight-hour day for employees of the city and its contractors, and for city ownership and control of a new rapid transit system.

90. Moses Rischin, *The Promised City: New York's Jews, 1879–1914* (Cambridge, Mass.: Harvard University Press, 1962), pp. 224–35, describes the evolution of the city's socialist politics during this period.

91. Harold U. Faulkner, *The Decline of Laissez-Faire, 1897–1917* (New York: Holt, Rinehart and Winston, 1951), pp. 280–87, provides an excellent survey of the development of the political policy of the American Federation of Labor.

CHAPTER 7

1. The *Evening Post* manuscript index is now at the New-York Historical Society.

2. Telephone conversation with Professor Pomerantz, Nov. 1970; E. Hagaman Hall, *The Second City of the World* (New York: The Republic Press, 1898), p. 7. An excellent analysis of the stages of decision making is provided in Robert E. Aggar et al., *The Rulers and the Ruled* (New York: John Wiley & Sons, 1964), p. 40.

3. George Mazaraki, "Andrew H. Green" (Ph.D. diss., New York University, 1966), pp. 316–24; Hall, *The Second City*, pp. 47–49; Harold C. Syrett, *The City of Brooklyn, 1865–1890* (New York: Columbia University Press, 1948), p. 247.

4. Samuel A. Pleasants, *Fernando Wood* (New York: Columbia University Press, 1948), pp. 77–83; Syrett, *Brooklyn*, pp. 41–43.

5. John Foord, *The Life and Public Services of Andrew H. Green* (New York: Doubleday, Page & Company, 1913), p. 176; Pleasants, *Fernando Wood*, pp. 73–76.

6. Gerald W. McFarland, "Partisan of Nonpartisanship: Dorman B. Eaton and the Genteel Reform Tradition," *Journal of American History* 54 (1968): 808–9; James C. Mohr, *The Radical Republicans in New York During Reconstruction* (Ithaca: Cornell University Press, 1973), chaps. 2–4.

7. Andrew H. Green, *Communication . . . Relative to . . . the Sixth and Seventh Avenues . . . to the Board of Commissioners of the Central Park* (New York: William Cullen Bryant & Co., 1866).

8. James B. Hodgskin, "A Brief Sketch of the General Plan and Principles of the Proposed New Charter for the City of New York and Brooklyn, Submitted for Fellowmembers of the Committee of Seventy of New York, and of the Citizens Reform Committee of Brooklyn" (New York: privately printed, Dec. 1, 1871); The Brooklyn *Eagle, Consolidation Number*, Jan. 2, 1898, p. 50; Hall, *The Second City*, p. 47; Mazaraki, "Andrew H. Green," pp. 320–21; Foord, *Andrew H. Green*, pp. 176–77.

9. Foord, *Andrew H. Green*, pp. 3–11, 28–32; Alexander C. Flick, *Samuel Jones Tilden: A Study in Political Sagacity* (New York: Dodd, Mead and Company, Inc., 1939), pp. 70–77, 87–90, 115–17, 125, 161–62, 418, 478, 487. Tilden's railroad investments became so lucrative, and so well known, that his opponents in the 1876 presidential election campaign derisively dubbed him "Old Usufruct." ibid., p. 287. It was through his work in Tilden's firm that Green became executor of the estate of William B. Ogden, the first mayor and a leading real estate and railroad promoter of Chicago; this connection may also have helped Green's brother become one of Ogden's business associates in Chicago. Flick, *Tilden*, p. 115; Foord, *Andrew H. Green*, p. 216; Mazaraki, "Andrew H. Green," p. 290.

10. Foord, *Andrew H. Green*, pp. 32–40.

11. *Address of A. H. Green on his re-election as President of the Board of Education* (New York: William Cullen Bryant & Co., 1857), pp. 11, 35; Foord, *Andrew H. Green*, pp. 36–39.

12. Foord, *Andrew H. Green*, pp. 51–53.

13. Olmsted also objected to what he called Green's "constitutional reluctance to pay" even the most patently legitimate bills. Letter, Frederick Law Olmsted to John Bigelow, reprinted without date in Bigelow, *Retrospections of an Active Life* (New York: The Baker and Taylor Co., 1909), p. 342. Several years later, Olmsted spoke critically of Green's "politico-commercial alliances;" letter, Olmsted to H. R. Towne, Oct. 2, 1889, Olmsted Papers, Library of Congress.

14. Frederick Law Olmsted, "Public Parks and the Enlargement of Towns" (1870), reprinted in S. B. Sutton, ed., *Civilizing America's Cities: A Selection of Frederick Law Olmsted's Writings on City Landscapes* (Cambridge: The MIT Press, 1971), p. 98.

15. Alexander Callow, Jr., *The Tweed Ring* (New York: Oxford University Press, 1966), pp. 271–72; Foord, *Andrew H. Green*, pp. 98–165; Seymour J. Mandelbaum, *Boss Tweed's New York*, (New York: John Wiley & Sons, Inc., 1965), pp. 80–84. Green was himself a member of the anti-Tweed Committee of Seventy.

16. Foord, *Andrew H. Green*, p. 159; Mandelbaum, *Boss Tweed's New York*, pp. 90–91, 100, 108–9, 118, 133–34.

17. John Bigelow described Green as a sour, difficult, irascible man in journal entries during the 1890s; the unpublished (and unedited) typescript of Bigelow's Journal, vol. 9, pt. 30, Mar. 14, 1893, p. 9; Mar. 31, 1893; Apr. 14, 1893, p. 21; vol. 9, pt. 31, Jan. 21, 1894, pp. 36–37; Bigelow Papers, New York Public Library. On the 1870s, see Mandelbaum, *Boss Tweed's New York*, pp. 133–34; Foord, *Andrew H. Green*, pp. 158–60, 208–12; and Oswald Ottendorfer, circular advocating the nomination of Andrew H. Green for mayor of the City of New York in 1876, in the Andrew H. Green Papers, New-York Historical Society. These papers contain several items of interest, but the great bulk of Green's papers have been lost.

18. Foord, *Andrew H. Green*, pp. 203–5; Hall, *The Second City*, pp. 22, 27; William R. Hutton, *The Washington Bridge: A Description of its Construction* (New York: Leo Von Rosenberg, 1889?), pp. 9–10. I am indebted to Professor David P. Billington for this reference.

19. The Brooklyn *Eagle*, Nov. 15, 1894; Syrett, *Brooklyn*, pp. 246–47.

20. Green, *Communication . . . to the Board of Commissioners of the Central Park*, 1866, pp. 47–49 and passim.

21. Andrew H. Green, *Communication to the Board of Commissioners of the Central Park* (New York: privately printed, 1868), pp. 17–18 and passim.

22. Andrew H. Green, *Public Improvements in the City of New York* (New York: privately printed, 1874), pp. 5–7, 11, 16–27. Neither the New York *Times Index* nor Green's various memorialists and biographers indicate that he said anything at all on the subject of consolidation between 1874 and 1889.

23. The standard history of its subject is Edward Dana Durand, *The Finances of New York City* (New York: The Macmillan Company, 1898).

24. On his retirement as comptroller of the City of New York in 1876, Green became trustee of the estate of William B. Ogden, who owned a good deal of Manhattan real estate; later he helped Tilden draw up his will, and served as executor and trustee of Tilden's estate. John Bigelow, another of the Tilden trustees, referred to the size of the estate's holdings in his Journal, vol. 9, pt. 32, July 28, 1894, pp. 17–18, New York Public Library. Further discussion and documentation of Green's planning activities during the 1870s and 1880s is provided in David C. Hammack, "Participation in Major Decisions in New York City, 1890–1900: The Creation of Greater New York and the Centralization of the Public School System," (Ph. D. diss., Columbia University, 1973) pp. 136–40.

25. Chamber of Commerce of the State of New York, *Annual Report*, 1887–1888, pp. 22–23, 63–64, 98–99, 104–6, 109–10. Letter, Abram S. Hewitt to George Wilson, secretary of the Chamber of Commerce, Nov. 4, 1887, Archives of the Chamber of Commerce of the State of New York.

26. City of New York, *City Record*, Feb. 1, 1888; see also the *City Record*, Jan. 18, 1888.

27. Chamber of Commerce of the State of New York, *Annual Report*, 1887–1888, pp. xliv–xlvii. According to its published records the Chamber had not formally discussed or acted upon the notion of municipal union. Hence this proposal was probably advanced by Chamber Secretary George Wilson, who wrote the *Annual Report*, and had presumably been approved by the Chamber's officers. Wilson was credited with authorship of the *Annual Report* by the New York *Times*, May 1, 1888. His career is described in Chamber of Commerce of the State of New York, *Tribute to the Memory of Mr. George Wilson, Secretary, 1868–1908* (New York: Oct. 12, 1908).

28. *Real Estate Record and Builder's Guide*, May 5, 1888. On June 16, this periodical added that Baltimore had just annexed areas containing nearly 41,000 people and that Chicago, Philadelphia, and Boston were also adding to their populations through annexation. The *Record and Guide* urged that a permanent commission be established to achieve the same results for New York.

29. New York *Times*, May 1, 1888. On May 3 the *Tribune* rejected the idea of consolidation as premature.

30. New York *Times*, Mar. 13 & 17, 1889; *Record and Guide*, Jan. 5 & 19 and Mar. 9, 1889.

31. New York *Times*, Mar. 17, 1889.

32. New York *Times*, Mar. 13 & 17, 1889; Foord, *Andrew H. Green*, p. 182; Mazaraki, "Andrew H. Green," p. 326.

33. Chamber of Commerce of the State of New York, *Annual Report*, 1888–1889, p. xxix. The Chamber once again argued that the shift of funds from U.S. bonds to real estate mortgages and municipal bonds made consolidation desirable. Andrew H. Green, *Communication on the Subject of a Consolidation of Areas About the City of New York Under One Government* (Albany: New York State Assembly Document no. 71, Mar. 31, 1890), p. 7. A copy of this document, now in Columbia University's Butler Library, is inscribed to Seth Low from O[rlando] B. Potter with the comment, "A very able paper will repay perusal."

34. Green, *Communication on the Subject of a Consolidation*, pp. 7–13. Lee Benson

has shown that the Chamber of Commerce and Green's anti-Tweed associate, Simon Sterne, employed similar anti-monopoly rhetoric against the railroads in their effort to secure government regulation of railroad practices and rates: *Merchants, Farmers, and Railroads* (Cambridge: Harvard University Press, 1955), pp. 68–79, 119–20, 144–47. In 1887 Green had hoped for appointment to a major railroad commission: letter, Green to Thomas B. Carroll, Apr. 1, 1887, Green Papers, New-York Historical Society. There can be no doubt that Green was working closely with the Chamber of Commerce as well as with the city's major landowners in these years.

35.   New York State Assembly *Journal*, 1890, pp. 615, 1140–41, 1790, 1867–68; New York State Senate *Journal*, 1890, pp. 788, 974, 1115, 1297. Albert E. Henschel, Green's lobbyist, wrote an account of these events in *Municipal Consolidation: A Historical Sketch of the Greater New York* (New York: 1895), pp. 5–6; Hall, *The Second City*, p. 69; New York *World*, May 5, 1890; New York *Tribune*, Dec. 14, 1889; New York *Times*, May 3, 1889; New York *Sun*, May 4, 1889; *Record and Guide*, May 10, 1889. The Assembly vote was an overwhelming seventy-nine to six; twenty-four of the thirty-two state senators voted for the bill in its final form. Hill himself had insisted on the right to name the commissioners. Green's bill had named Green himself; James S. T. Stranahan, his counterpart as a public works coordinator in Brooklyn; Calvert Vaux, Green's old subordinate from the Central Park Commission who was still landscape architect for the New York City Parks Department; Frederick DeVoe, a paint manufacturer and merchant and sometime County Democrat who had served as Brooklyn Bridge trustee and Board of Education commissioner; John L. Hamilton, a builder and prominent leader of builders' organizations; and John Foord, the journalist and later biographer of Green. Governor Hill appointed all of these men, with the exception of Foord, for whom he substituted Union League Republican George Rhett Cathcart, a businessman who had once worked for the *Times*. Stranahan and DeVoe belonged to the Chamber of Commerce. Neither Hill's biography—Herbert J. Bass, *"I Am a Democrat:" The Political Career of David Bennett Hill* (Syracuse: Syracuse University Press, 1961)—nor Hill's papers, at the New York State Library, Albany, throw any light on his actions in this instance.

36.   Foord, *Andrew H. Green*, pp. 186–87; Hall, *The Second City*, pp. 54–70. Mayor Hugh J. Grant of New York City, a Tammany Democrat, asked F. W. DeVoe, who had already accepted appointment to the commission from Governor Hill, to represent his city's interests. Mayor Alfred C. Chapin of Brooklyn named Republican real estate developer Edward F. Linton. Charles P. McClelland, the Dobbs Ferry Democratic politician chosen by the Westchester County supervisors, did not participate in the commission's meetings and opposed consolidation in the state legislature. The Queens County supervisors selected Democrat John H. Brinckerhoff, another local politician. The Kings County supervisors chose William D. Veeder, one of their county's leading Democrats. The Richmond County supervisors first asked the distinguished civil service reformer and mugwump, George William Curtis, who declined to serve and who probably opposed consolidation, then turned to George J. Greenfield, a Democrat and a lawyer who was closely associated with the local Chamber of Commerce and with taxpayer groups. Hall, *The Second City*, pp. 59–61, 67, and various biographical sources; letter, Frederick W. DeVoe to Mayor Grant, June 5, 1890, Mayors' Papers, New York City Municipal Archives and Records Center; New York *Times*, Apr. 30, 1891, May 27, 1893; New York *Tribune*, Apr. 30, 1891; Mazaraki, "Andrew H. Green."

37.   Green, *Communication on the Subject of a Consolidation*, passim.

38.   New York *Evening Post*, Apr. 2, 1891; New York *Tribune*, Mar. 28 and Apr. 3, 7, & 14, 1891; New York *Times*, Mar. 28 and Apr. 3, 7 & 14, 1891. I have been unable to locate a copy of the commission's minutes. The newspapers covered its deliberations selectively: the *Times* and the *World*, which supported consolidation, ignored the disagreements within the commission; the *Tribune* and the *Evening Post*, which opposed the movement, stressed the commission's internal difficulties in an effort to discredit its objectives.

39.   After extensive discussions, the commission agreed to submit to the legislature the bill that Green favored, calling for immediate consolidation and assigning to the commission the task of devising a charter for the Greater City. But with Brooklyn representative Edward F. Linton and King's County representative William D. Veeder opposed, the commission did not present a united front to the legislature. Green had also refused to endorse the renomination of Tammany Mayor Hugh J. Grant in New York, and, as the Democratic

Swallowtails declined in importance, he found his political base eroding. Grant and his closest Tammany associates were identified with the real estate development of upper Manhattan and the Bronx; the *Tribune* reported, Dec. 21, 1892, that Grant favored a northward expansion of the city, but opposed the annexation of Brooklyn. Grant had neither stressed this position during his two terms in office, nor had he supported Green's initiatives. In 1891 Green's bill, opposed by upstate and Brooklyn representatives and without strong backing in the legislature, died in the assembly. New York State Assembly, *Journal,* 1891, p. 1968; New York *Times, Tribune,* and *World,* Apr. 30, 1891.

40.   New York *Tribune,* Apr. 3, 1891. Graves's address was published as a pamphlet, under the title given here, in New York City on June 1, 1892.

41.   Graves, "How Taxes Can Be Reduced," New York *Times,* Jan. 19 & 23, 1892.

42.   Hall, *The Second City,* pp. 76–79; *Eagle Consolidation Number,* p. 38; New York *Times,* Dec. 16 & 18, 1892; for a detailed analysis of the Consolidation League activists, see Hammack, "Participation in Major Decisions," pp. 176–82.

43.   In the absence of a good study of Brooklyn politics, the best source is the extraordinarily full collection of Edward M. Shepard Papers at Columbia University. On Gaynor, see Louis Heaton Pink, *Gaynor: The Tammany Mayor Who Swallowed the Tiger: Lawyer, Judge, Philosopher* (New York: The International Press, 1931); and Mortimer Smith, *William Jay Gaynor: Mayor of New York* (Chicago: Henry Regnery & Co., 1951). Discussions of Gaynor's relations to Brooklyn reform Democrats appear in Syrett, *Brooklyn,* and in David C. Hammack, "Edward M. Shepard and the Gravesend Affair," *Columbia Library Columns* 23 (May 1974): 3–10. For a critical discussion of the various sources, see Hammack, "Participation in Major Decisions," pp. 180–85.

44.   Hall, *The Second City,* p. 99. Cleveland carried Brooklyn by 30,000 votes in 1892. On the Sunday following the election his elated followers in that city restated their plan, first discussed by Gaynor the previous July, to run a candidate for mayor on a pro-consolidation, economy-and-efficiency-in-local-government platform. New York *Times,* July 17 and Nov. 13, 1892.

45.   Hall, *The Second City,* p. 99; statement of Sanders Shanks, secretary of the Brooklyn Consolidation League, on the fly-leaf of Edward Graves's second pamphlet, *Greater New York: The Reasons Why* (New York: The Brooklyn Consolidation League, 1894). The league also printed and distributed large numbers of Edward A. Bradford's contribution, *Great New York* (Brooklyn, 1894). The *Evening Post,* the *Tribune,* and the Brooklyn *Eagle* all covered the Consolidation League's activities as fully as the pro-consolidation *Times.* In earlier years the *Eagle* had largely ignored consolidation, but the *Eagle Annual Index* reveals a dramatic upsurge of interest in the matter with the formation of the Consolidation League in late 1892. The *Evening Post* manuscript index reveals a similar, though less marked, shift of attention.

46.   On the capacity of the Brooklyn Bridge, see the proposal of August Belmont, James Jourdan, Frederick Uhlmann, and George W. Wingate to run a privately owned streetcar line across the bridge, discussed in New-York Board of Trade and Transportation, "Continuous Transit Between New York and Brooklyn" (New York: printed for the private use of the Board of Trade and Transportation, Apr. 8, 1896), New-York Board of Trade and Transportation Papers, New-York Historical Society. Albert Shaw discussed the question before the New York State Assembly Special Committee to Investigate the Desirability of Municipal Ownership of the Street and Elevated Railroads of the Various Cities of the State, as reported in the committee's *Report and Testimony* (Albany: Wynkoop Hallenbeck Crawford Co., State Printers, Feb. 11, 1896), p. 1083. Several of the consolidationists called for specific public works in their testimony before the New York State Legislature, Joint Committee on the Affairs of the City of New York, reported in the committee's *In The Matter of . . . Greater New York* (Albany: 1896 New York State Senate Document no. 44, 1897), pp. 63–65, 69, 96, 98, 152–54, 156–57, 166–67, 217, 223–26, 229–31, 275–79, 280–84, 291, 293, 508. Letter, Leonard Moody to Seth Low, June 9, 1896, Low Papers, Columbia University Library.

47.   Syrett, *Brooklyn,* chap. 12 and p. 216.

48.   Ibid. St. Clair McKelway, speeches of Feb. 2 and Mar. 11, 1893, McKelway Papers, New York Public Library. In the second of these speeches McKelway, whose eloquence and position as editor of the *Eagle* made him one of Brooklyn's most prominent Cleveland Democrats, declared "I am in favor of the annexation of the county towns to Brooklyn

because, if it made the aldermen more, it would make the [county] supervisors less; indeed, it would abolish them altogether."

49.   In May 1892, the East River Savings Institution refused to complete the purchase of $90,000 in Kings County bonds, on the ground that the county had exceeded its debt limit; New York *Times*, July 17, 1892. Brooklyn's financial difficulties after absorbing the county towns are discussed in detail in a series of letters from Fred W. Hinrichs to Edward M. Shepard, Feb. 24 and Mar. 1 & 5, 1894, from Alfred Treadway White to Shepard, Apr. 30 and May 6 & 8, 1894; and from Shepard to White, May 3, 1894, all in Shepard Papers. "The absorbtion of the county towns, which are largely rural," Hinrichs argued on Feb. 24, "would mean, I fear, practical bankruptcy of the present city." Syrett touches on these problems in *Brooklyn*, pp. 190–93.

50.   Letter, George W. Chauncey to Seth Low, June 8, 1896, Low Papers.

51.   Statement of Abraham Abraham, recorded in New York State Legislature, Joint Committee on the Affairs of the City of New York, *In the Matter of Greater New York*, p. 64 (similar statements appear at, e.g., pp. 159 and 173. *Record and Guide*, Dec. 10, 1892.

52.   Syrett, *Brooklyn*, p. 253; New York *Tribune*, Dec. 21, 1892 (Mayor Grant's views); letter, G. Carson Brevoort to Mayor Thomas F. Gilroy, Feb. 10, 1893, Mayors' Papers; *Record and Guide*, Mar. 11 and July 22, 1893.

53.   For Shaw's career, see Lloyd J. Graybar, *Albert Shaw of the Review of Reviews, An Intellectual Biography* (Lexington: University Press of Kentucky, 1974).

54.   Albert Shaw, *Municipal Government in Great Britain* (New York: The Century Company, 1895), pp. 246–47.

55.   Ibid.

56.   Ibid., p. 63.

57.   Albert Shaw, "The Municipal Problem and Greater New York," *Atlantic Monthly* 79 (June, 1897): 739–40.

58.   Ibid., pp. 738–39; Albert Shaw, memorandum for Horace E. Deming on the purposes of municipal government, June 3, 1897, Albert Shaw Papers, New York Public Library.

59.   Shaw, "The Municipal Problem and Greater New York," pp. 735–6, 739–40.

60.   Ibid., p. 740. In addition to his implicit advocacy of this idea in his two books, *Municipal Government in Great Britain* and *Municipal Government in Continental Europe* (New York: The Century Company, 1895), Shaw's correspondence reveals that he pressed it on such leading figures in New York City as Horace E. Deming, Dorman B. Eaton, Abram S. Hewitt, and Frederick W. Holls, arranged for others to advocate it in the pages of his *Review of Reviews*, and may well have written a series of articles on "Self-Government of Cities" which the New York *Times* published on the occasion of the 1894 New York State Constitutional Convention. For detailed discussion of these points, see Hammack, "Participation in Major Decisions," pp. 198–210.

61.   Commission to Devise a Plan for the Government of Cities in the State of New York, *Report*, submitted to the Senate and Assembly of the State of New York, Feb. 24, 1877. Reprinted in *Municipal Affairs* 3 (Sept. 1899): 426.

62.   Manuscript of an address by Simon Sterne, "Some Reflections on Recent Changes and Proposed Reforms in Legislation Affecting the City of New York," delivered before the Constitution Club, Jan. 21, 1885, Sterne Papers, New York Public Library.

63.   Eaton discussed the charter for the Greater City in a lengthy correspondence with Seth Low: letters, Eaton to Low, Aug. 1 & 17 and Sept. 9, 1896, Low Papers. In *The Government of Municipalities* (New York: The Macmillan Company for Columbia University Press, 1899), the large book that capped his career of forty years as a municipal reformer in New York, Eaton generously acknowledged Shaw's contributions (p. vii).

64.   Andrew H. Green, "Greater New York: History of the Consolidation Movement— Its Advantages," *The Independent* 48 (1896): 509–10.

65.   Letter, Albert Shaw to Richard T. Ely, Nov. 30, 1896, Shaw Papers. Shaw's proposal that Greater New York be governed by a city council similar to the London County Council did win significant support. In addition to Eaton, Frederick W. Holls, sanitary reformer Eleanora Kinnikutt, and Columbia University trustee John B. Pine, among others, urged the proposal on Seth Low while he served on the Greater New York Charter Commission in 1896 and 1897; City Club President John E. Parsons made the commission's failure to adopt the plan one of the reasons for his objection to the charter as a whole in 1897.

Letters, Mrs. Kinnikutt to Low, Jan. 7, 1897; Pine to Low, Sept. 21, 1896; Parsons to Low, Jan. 16, 1897, Low Papers. Similar arguments were made by Sidney V. Lowell in his leaflet "Consolidation from European Experience" (1896), Low Papers; and by George Gunton in *Gunton's Magazine* 10 (Mar. 1896): 167–72, and ibid. (May 1896): 341–47. But most active political figures continued to agree with Abram S. Hewitt, who insisted in 1901 that "the real remedy for our troubles in New York is an honest and able mayor, with plenty of power, and his continuance in office until he ceases to be a useful servant." Letter, Hewitt to David A. Munro, Jan. 4, 1901, Cooper-Hewitt Papers, New-York Historical Society. Edward M. Shepard, too, was "a strong believer in the consolidation of power in the hands of the Mayor"; letter, Shepard to J. Warren Greene, July 6, 1899; similar sentiments appear in Shepard to Frank L. Babbott, Mar. 12, 1896, Shepard Papers. The Greater New York Charter Commission on which Low served in 1896–1897 proposed a strong-mayor charter; Low's papers indicate that he favored that plan.

66. Edward A. Bradford, *Great New York.*
67. Edward C. Graves, *Greater New York: The Reasons Why.*
68. *Record and Guide,* Sept. 29, 1894.
69. Ibid., July 30, 1892.
70. Ibid., Sept. 29, 1894.
71. Ibid.
72. Henschel, *Municipal Consolidation,* pp. 31–33, 37, 54–57, 60–64. Erastus Wiman, a Staten Island developer, stressed the argument that consolidation would speed the introduction of rapid transit facilities between Manhattan and Brooklyn, Queens, and Staten Island, in "Manhattan, City of the Future—New York—Brooklyn—Staten Island," speech delivered before the Brooklyn Real Estate Exchange, May 3, 1892 (New York: n.d.). Seth Low made similar arguments in his pro-consolidation letter to the New York *Times,* Nov. 2, 1894, Low Papers.
73. New York *Times,* Mar. 30 and Apr. 5, 6, & 12, 1893; New York *Tribune,* Apr. 6, 7, & 16, 1893; New York *Evening Post,* Mar. 29 and Apr. 5, 1893; Brooklyn *Eagle,* Apr. 4, 5, & 6, 1893.
74. New York *Times,* Jan. 30, 1893; Brooklyn *Eagle,* Feb. 7, 1893; New York *Tribune,* Apr. 7, 1893.
75. Brooklyn *Eagle,* Apr. 11, 12, 29, & 31, May 3 & 7, and Oct. 21, 1893; New York *Evening Post,* Oct. 25, 1893; New York *Times,* Oct. 25, 26, & 30 and Nov. 10, 1893; New York *Tribune,* Oct. 26 and Nov. 20, 1893; *Record and Guide,* Dec. 16, 1893 and Feb. 10, 1894. For a modern interpretation of these election results, see Samuel T. McSeveney, *The Politics of Depression: Political Behavior in the Northeast, 1893–1896* (New York: Oxford University Press, 1972), p. 53.
76. In January, Tammany Mayor Thomas Gilroy had declared consolidation to be "the manifest destiny of the vast population and immense business interests of which our port is the center" and had endorsed Green's call for a referendum: Board of Aldermen of the City of New York, *Proceedings* 213 (1894): 16–29. With Tammany, the Republican leadership, and most Brooklyn legislators in favor of the referendum, the vocal opposition of the two assemblymen from New York City's uptown Annexed District (the Bronx) failed to attract support. New York *Times,* Feb. 9, 1894; *Record and Guide,* Jan. 27 and Feb. 3 & 10, 1894; *Eagle Consolidation Number,* p. 38.
77. *Record and Guide,* Jan. 27, Feb. 3, 10, & 17, and Mar. 3, 1894; New York *Tribune,* Feb. 9, 1894; Brooklyn *Eagle,* Feb. 14, 20, 21, 23, 24, 26, & 27 and Mar. 1, 1894; New York *Times,* Feb. 22, 23, 27, & 28 and Mar. 1, 1894. Syrett, *Brooklyn,* pp. 250–51. Brooklyn Republican Senator William H. Reynolds pressed the equal-assessment–equal-taxation demand, which was quickly taken up by the Consolidation League's Edward M. Grout and by the anti-consolidation *Eagle.* The *Times* successfully insisted that Green resist this demand; by Mar. 3, 1894, the *Record and Guide* was quoting Democratic state senator Jacob A. Cantor, who represented Green in the legislature, as agreeing with the *Times* that no equal-taxation clause should be included in the referendum. On the eve of the referendum Frank R. Houghton, a promoter of real estate on Manhattan's upper west side, stated that Green had assured him that the various parts of Greater New York would retain their varying tax rates: *Record and Guide,* Nov. 3, 1894.
78. Brooklyn *Eagle,* Dec. 12 & 23, 1893; New York *Times,* Dec. 13 & 24, 1893; Jan. 3, 18, 26, & 31, 1894; Syrett, *Brooklyn,* p. 257.

79. Hall, *The Second City*, pp. 99–100; Henschel, *Municipal Consolidation*, pp. 17–18, 35, 51, 67–69.

80. Henschel, *Municipal Consolidation*, pp. 17–18.

81. Hall, *The Second City*, p. 99.

82. Henschel, *Municipal Consolidation*, pp. 17–18, 54–67; New York *Times*, Oct. 27, 1894; New York *World*, Oct. 1894, passim; New York *Tribune*, Feb. 6, 1895. Henschel himself takes credit for coordinating this campaign; but he was working as Green's aide and had passed his entire career as an assistant to Tilden, Green, and Henry R. Beekman, all of whom were leading Swallowtail Democrats: Hall, *The Second City*, pp. 67–69.

83. Brooklyn *Eagle*, Oct. 1894, passim. The Brooklyn *Union* said nothing on the issue until the day before the election, when it came out in opposition to consolidation; the Brooklyn *Citizen* ignored the question entirely. Syrett, *Brooklyn*, p. 256.

84. *The Irish-American*, Mar. 5, 1894.

85. Ibid., Oct. 29, 1894.

86. The *Record and Guide* printed statements that both advocated and opposed consolidation: Dec. 16, 1893; Jan. 27, Feb. 3 & 10, Mar. 10, Oct. 27, and Nov. 3, 1894. On the one hand, the *Record and Guide* suggested that consolidation would raise Manhattan taxes, retard the development of the Annexed District, and produce political confusion. Yet it stated, "New York would undoubtedly lose a great deal in prestige the world over—and in actual dollars and cents, too—should Chicago or any other city on the continent count a larger population." Also, consolidation would hasten the development of areas suited for the provision of inexpensive homes for working men. Like the leaders of Tammany, and the leaders of municipal reform, New York's real estate developers were unable to take a clear position on consolidation.

87. See note 83, in this chapter.

88. Foord, *Andrew H. Green*, p. 191. The town of Mount Vernon also voted on consolidation in 1894, and it voted negatively; but it was included in the referendum at the request of some of its residents, and had never constituted part of Green's plan. Henschel, *Municipal Consolidation*, pp. 15–16.

89. [Brooklyn] League of Loyal Citizens, circular (no place, date, or title), in the Papers of Mayor William L. Strong, Mayors' Papers. The validity of the returns is further cast in doubt by contemporary rumors that McLaughlin's Democratic organization had instructed Brooklyn policemen to count the proposal out, and by the Consolidation League's attempt to offset this instruction by reminding Brooklyn policemen that their New York counterparts enjoyed higher salaries. Syrett, *Brooklyn*, p. 254; New York *Times*, Oct. 18 and Nov. 2, 1894.

90. Data from the official election returns, reported in the *City Record* 22 (Dec. 15, 1894): 21, 62, 63; and from the various sources on the geographical location of New York City's and Brooklyn's ethnic and income groups indicated in chap. 5, note 29, in this volume. Map 7–1 indicates the geographical distribution of the proconsolidation vote.

91. Note the vote in New York A.D.'s 29 and 30 (map 7–1), and in Brooklyn wards 17, 23, 24, 25, 26, 28, 29, 30, and 31 (map 7–2).

92. These are Pearsonian product-moment correlations between the percentage of all voters in each district who favored consolidation and the percentage who voted for the other candidate or proposition indicated. In Brooklyn the correlation between the consolidation vote and the basic revision of the state constitution was 0.676.

93. *Record and Guide*, Dec. 16, 1893.

94. Brooklyn League of Loyal Citizens, Pamphlets nos. 1–7; New York State Legislature, Joint Committee on the Affairs of the City of New York, *In the Matter of Greater New York*, Brooklyn anticonsolidation testimony, passim. The Brooklyn Public Library has apparently lost its file of the League's periodical, *Greater Brooklyn*, and I have not been able to find this source.

95. Data on the Loyal League leaders from the various biographical sources for the period.

96. William C. Redfield, *Taxes and Tenements: A Study of Municipal Conditions* (Brooklyn: League of Loyal Citizens Pamphlet no. 3, Dec. 1894).

97. Ibid., pp. 34–56. Robert D. Benedict echoed the point in his "Objections to Consolidation," *The Independent* 48 (1896): 510. He opened his argument with the assertion "the great cities are the danger points of the nation."

98. The Reverend R. S. Storrs, "Remarks at an anti-consolidation mass meeting, January 13, 1896," in League of Loyal Citizens Pamphlet no. 6, p. 10. Similar statements recur frequently in the Loyal League's publications and testimony.
99. Letter, Wurster to Morton, Jan. 10, 1896, Levi P. Morton Papers, New York Public Library.
100. Storrs, "Remarks," p. 12.
101. St. Clair McKelway, printer's proof of speech to the Montauk Club, Mar. 11, 1893, McKelway Papers.
102. St. Clair McKelway, printer's proof of speech to the New York Real Estate Exchange, Feb. 2, 1893, McKelway Papers.
103. Speeches and other records of these occasions are in the McKelway Papers.
104. League of Loyal Citizens, *Hearing Before the Senate Committee on Cities, February 12, 1895: Arguments in Opposition to the Lexow and Reynolds Bills* (Brooklyn: 1895), p. 5; Brooklyn *Eagle*, Jan. 18 & 19 and Mar. 7, 1895; New York *Tribune*, Apr. 26, 1895.
105. New York *Tribune*, Apr. 26, 1895.
106. New York *Tribune* and *Times*, and Brooklyn *Eagle*, February, March, April, and May 1895, passim.
107. The demand for resubmission, and the failure of the legislature to act in 1895, were extensively reported in the contemporary press. For a detailed discussion, see Hammack, "Participation in Major Decisions," pp. 248–57.
108. Harold F. Gosnell, *Boss Platt and His New York Machine* (New York: Russell & Russell 1969 reprint of 1924 1st edition) provides an excellent study of its subject. In 1882 Platt followed the lead of New York Republican Senator Roscoe Conkling and resigned from the U.S. Senate in a patronage dispute with President Chester A. Arthur. The New York State legislature then shocked Conkling and Platt by refusing to return them to the Senate with a vote of confidence—and Platt was further embarrassed by a charge that he had entertained a prostitute in his Albany hotel room.
109. Ibid., pp. 23, 24, 37–38, 66–67, 274–90; Louis J. Lang, ed., *The Autibiography of Thomas Collier Platt* (New York: B. W. Dodge & Co., 1910), p. 303.
110. McSeveney, *The Politics of Depression*, pp. 20–25.
111. The phrase is from Lang, *Autobiography of Thomas Collier Platt*, p. 303.
112. Ibid.
113. *Record and Guide*, Mar. 9 & 16, 1895.
114. New York *Tribune*, Mar. 16 and Apr. 17 & 19, 1895.
115. New York *Tribune* and *Times*, Apr. 19, 1895.
116. Lang, *The Autobiography of Thomas Collier Platt*, pp. 301–02 (statement contributed to the *Autobiography* by Clarence Lexow).
117. New York *Tribune*, May 9 & 10, 1895; *Record and Guide*, May 11 & 18, 1895.
118. Letters, Platt to Morton, Dec. 17, 1895; Morton to Benjamin F. Tracy, Dec. 31, 1895; Morton Papers. Letter, Platt to Morton, Jan. 3, 1896, printed in Lang, *The Autobiography of Thomas Collier Platt*, p. 307; letter, Platt to Morton, quoted in Robert McElroy, *Levi Parsons Morton, Banker, Diplomat, and Statesman* (New York: G. P. Putnam's Sons, 1930), p. 259. McElroy places this letter in 1895, but its reference to the Raines liquor control law indicates that it was written in early 1896.
119. Letter, Morton to Tracy, Dec. 31, 1895, Morton Papers.
120. *Record and Guide*, Dec. 21, 1895, Jan. 4, 1896; New York *Times*, Dec. 30, 1895. By mid-December Police Commissioner Theodore Roosevelt had already concluded that Morton could be "relied upon to support some of the bills aimed at the Police Department and especially at me," and that "there will evidently be a resolute effort to legislate me out of office, in some manner this year." Letter, Roosevelt to Henry Cabot Lodge, Dec. 13, 1895, printed in Elting E. Morison, ed., *The Letters of Theodore Roosevelt* (Cambridge: Harvard University Press, 1951), vol. 1, p. 499. Roosevelt made the point still more explicitly in a letter to Lodge on Dec. 23; Ibid., p. 502.
121. Letter, Morton to Tracy, Dec. 31, 1895, Morton Papers.
122. Letter, Platt to Morton, Jan. 3, 1896, Morton Papers.
123. Ibid.
124. Letter, Morton to Platt, Jan. 4, 1896, Morton Papers.
125. Brooklyn *Eagle*, Feb. 4, 1896, quoting the New York *Sun* of the same date. The

Eagle discussed the same scheme on Feb. 19 and Mar. 5; the *Times*, which dubbed it "Platt's scheme," described it on Jan. 25 & 29, Feb. 5, 13, & 22, Mar. 1, 4, & 15; and Apr. 22, 23, & 29, 1896. The *Tribune* and the *Evening Post* also reported on the special commission plan throughout the legislative session.

126. Letter, Morton to Lauterbach, Mar. 14, 1896, Morton Papers.

127. Letter, Lauterbach to Morton, Mar. 16, 1896, Morton Papers.

128. *Dickson's Uptown Weekly*, Jan. 25, 1896. Opposition to consolidation was also voiced by the *Harlem Local Reporter*, Apr. 1, 1896; and by representatives of the Taxpayers' Anti-Equalization League (most of whose spokesmen doubled as leaders of the West End Association on Manhattan's upper west side); Legislature of the State of New York, Joint Committee on the Affairs of New York City, *In the Matter of . . . Greater New York*, pp. 420–32. Similar opposition was reported in the *Record and Guide*, Jan. 25 and Feb. 1 & 29, 1896, and in the New York *Sun*, Apr. 3 & 7, 1896.

129. *Record and Guide*, Jan. 25, 1896.

130. New York *Times*, Oct. 12 & 31 and Nov. 19, 1895; *Record and Guide*, Nov. 2, 1895; New York State Legislature, Joint Committee on the City of New York, *In the Matter of . . . Greater New York*, pp. 194, 151–56; letter, Edward M. Shepard to William C. Redfield, Oct. 21, 1895, Shepard Papers; letter, Frederick W. Wurster to Levi P. Morton, Feb. 7, 1896, Morton Papers.

131. Union League Club meeting minutes, Feb. 13, May 14, and June 11, 1896; Union League Club circular, Feb. 25, 1896; Union League Club Archives. Further details on opposition to consolidation in 1896 are provided in Hammack, "Participation in Major Decisions," pp. 264–73.

132. New York State Legislature, Joint Committee on the City of New York, *In the Matter of . . . Greater New York*.

133. Ibid., pp. 487–521, 620; New York *Times*, Jan. 7 and Apr. 24, 1896; New York *Sun*, Apr. 5, 9, 10, & 23, 1896; New York *World*, Apr. 3, 4, 5, 21, 22, & 23, 1896. In addition, the generally pro-Platt *Press* and *Herald* also supported consolidation during the spring of 1896.

134. *Record and Guide*, Apr. 11 & 18, 1896; New York *World*, Apr. 3, 1896. Roswell P. Flower, a Democrat who had served as governor in 1893 and 1894, who had remained on good terms with Tammany although close to Tilden, and who owned a great deal of Manhattan real estate, now came out strongly for consolidation for the first time: New York State Legislature, Joint Committee on the Affairs of the City of New York, *In the Matter of . . . Greater New York*, pp. 493–95.

135. New York *Times*, Jan. 7, 1896.

136. New York *Times*, Feb. 26, 1896; *Record and Guide*, Feb. 29, 1896.

137. *Record and Guide*, Mar. 7, 1896; New York *World*, Apr. 11, 1896.

138. New York *Times*, Apr. 3, 4, 7, & 8, 1896; New York *World*, Apr. 2, 3, 4, & 5, 1896.

139. Memorandum, Mayor Frederick W. Wurster to "The Honorable The Legislature of the State of New York," Apr. 9, 1896, Morton Papers; Memorandum, Mayor William L. Strong to the State of New York, Apr. 9, 1896, Strong Papers, Mayors' Papers.

140. New York *World*, Apr. 23, 1896; New York *Sun*, Apr. 22, 23, & 27, 1896.

141. Two Henry F. Purroy Democrats voted for consolidation on this occasion. Green had taken care to endorse Purroy in the 1895 elections; New York *Sun*, Apr. 23, 1896; New York *Times*, Nov. 3, 1896. Platt secured the support of assembly leader Hamilton Fish, State Republican Committee Chairman Benjamin B. Odell, and State Senator Timothy E. Ellsworth, all of whom had earlier been described as opposed to consolidation. Lieutenant Governor Charles T. Saxton and ex-Senator Warner Miller remained opposed, but three of "Miller's" assemblymen voted with Platt; New York *World*, Apr. 9, 11, 15, 16, 17, 18, 19, 22, & 23, 1896; New York *Sun*, Apr. 15, 20, & 23, 1896; letter, Ellsworth to Morton, May 5, 1896, Morton Papers. Lexow's account of the Greater New York legislation, written at Platt's request some years later, appears in Lang, *The Autobiography of Thomas Collier Platt*, pp. 299–306.

142. New York *Times*, Apr. 23, 25, 26, & 29 and May 2 & 7, 1896; New York *World*, Apr. 23, 24, 26, & 29, 1896; Union League Club, "Meeting Minutes," May 14, 1896, Union League Club Archives; letters, St. Clair McKelway to Morton, Apr. 28, 1896; Francis

M. Scott to Morton, May 4, 1896; Joseph Larocque, R. W. G. Welling, J. H. Van Amringe to Morton, all on May 8, 1896; William E. Rogers to Morton, May 20, 1896. Morton Papers.

143. Letter, Platt to Morton, Apr. 23, 1896, Morton Papers.

144. Letter, Platt to Morton, Apr. 28, 1896, Morton Papers.

145. Letter, Morton to Platt, May 1, 1896, Morton Papers.

146. Letter, Morton to Tracy, May 7, 1896, Morton Papers.

147. New York *Times*, May 12, 1896.

148. Letters, Platt to Morton, Apr. 28, 1896; Morton to Platt, May 1, 5, 11, & 28, 1896, Morton Papers.

149. Letters, Morton to Tracy, May 29, 1896; Morton to Low, May 29, 1896; Low to Morton, May 25, 1896; McKelway to Morton, Apr. 28, 1896, Morton Papers.

150. For a full discussion, see Hammack, "Participation in Major Decisions," pp. 282–89.

151. New York *Times*, June 10, 1896; New York *Sun*, June 9 & 10, 1896; Syrett, *Brooklyn*, p. 57; Lang, *The Autobiography of Thomas Collier Platt*, pp. 244, 357, 511; Gosnell, *Boss Platt*, pp. 66–67, 246, 254. Dutcher campaigned for Tracy in the 1897 mayoral election; see his speech, dated Oct. 18, 1897, in the Silas B. Dutcher Papers, Long Island Historical Society. Letter, Benjamin B. Odell to Morton, Aug. 7, 1896, recommending Garretson for appointment to the State Supreme Court, Morton Papers.

152. Letter, St. Clair McKelway to Morton, Apr. 28, 1896, Morton Papers; Charles J. Edwards to Edward M. Shepard, Sept. 14, 1897 (on Gleason), Shepard Papers; New York *World*, Apr. 26 & 29, 1896. On the Platt-Tammany alliance, see Gosnell, *Boss Platt*, pp. 231–34.

153. Dillon's career and his standing as a defender of the rights of property are described in Clyde E. Jacobs, *Law Writers and the Courts* (Berkeley: University of California Press, 1954).

154. New York *World*, Apr. 24, 1896; New York *Times* and *Sun*, June 10, 1896; *Record and Guide*, June 13, 1896. Low's appointment won praise from Brooklyn reform Democrat Alexander E. Orr, Lieutenant Governor Charles T. Saxton, and veteran civil service reformer Dorman B. Eaton: letters, Orr to Low, June 9, 1896, Low Papers; Saxton to Morton, June 11, 1896; Eaton, *The Government of Municipalities*, p. 472. Franklin Pierce expressed a widely shared view when he wrote to Low, "I find there are a multitude of good citizens in this community who are looking both to you and to the Hon. John F. Dillon for such action as will defeat what are believed to be many bad features of this proposed charter": letter, Pierce to Low, Jan. 11, 1897, Low Papers.

155. The major collections of papers left by leading reform Democrats—Henry deForest Baldwin, Charles S. Fairchild, Abram S. Hewitt, and Edward M. Shepard—contain almost no correspondence with Green at all in the 1890s.

156. *Record and Guide*, June 27, 1896. The Low Papers contain many documents referring to the Charter Commission, but I have been unable to locate a set of minutes or other direct record of the commission's deliberations.

157. Syrett, *Brooklyn*, p. 271; memorandum "To the Greater New York Commission" from the Committee on Draft, n.d., Low Papers; William C. DeWitt, "Molding the New Metropolis," *Munsey's Magazine* 17 (Sept. 1897): 924–25; New York *World*, Apr. 26, 1896; letters, Franklin W. Hooper to Seth Low, Oct. 19, Nov. 20, and Dec. 7, 1896; the Brooklyn Board of Education to Low, n.d.; George W. Chauncey to Low, Jan. 5, 1897, Low Papers; and Frank L. Babbott to Edward M. Shepard, Jan. 8 & 13, 1897, Shepard Papers; Shepard to William C. Redfield, Oct. 18, 1895, Albert Shaw Papers.

158. Committee on Draft, memorandum "To the Greater New York Commission"; letters, Low to Tracy, Jan. 12, 1897; Low to Dillon, Dec. 22, 1896; Low to Dorman B. Eaton, Aug. 5 & 24 and Oct. 19, 1896; Low to Alfred T. White, Jan. 8, 1897, Low Papers.

159. New York *World*, Apr. 26, 1896; letters, Seth Low to Tracy, Jan. 30, 1897, Low Papers; Henry deForest Baldwin to George M. Pinney, expressing Reform Club views, Jan. 4, 1897, Henry deForest Baldwin Papers, Yale University; Republican Club of New York, printed *Report* of the Committee on the New York Charter, and City Club of New York, memorandum of Objections to the Greater New York Charter, both in Low Papers.

160. Letters, Low to Mrs. Francis P. Kinnicutt, Mar. 23, 1897; Low to Governor Frank S. Black, Apr. 17, 1897, Low Papers.

161. Letter, Low to Mrs. Francis P. Kinnicutt, Mar. 23, 1897, Low Papers.
162. Letters, Low to Governor Black, Apr. 17, 1896; Low to Charles Stewart Smith, Apr. 8, 1897; Low to Mrs. Kinnicutt, Mar. 23, 1897, Low Papers.
163. Letters, Low to Black, Smith, and Kinnicutt, cited in note 162; William C. Dewitt, "Molding the New Metropolis," p. 929.
164. Seth Low, "memorandum . . . proposing a Board of Local Improvements," Nov. 2, 1896; letter, James R. Sheffield to Low, Jan. 21, 1897, Low Papers; James R. Sheffield, "Memorandum for the Greater New York Commission," Sheffield Papers, Yale University; letters, Henry deForest Baldwin to Charles D. Olendorf, Oct. 17, 1896, and Baldwin to George M. Pinney, Dec. 22, 1896 and Jan. 23, 1897; Henry deForest Baldwin, manuscript diary, entries for Jan. 5–23, 1897, Baldwin Papers; letter, Frank Harvey Field to Edward M. Shepard, Jan. 15, 1897, Shepard Papers.
165. Julius F. Harder, "The City's Plan," *Municipal Affairs* 2 (1898): 45; *Commercial and Financial Chronicle* 64 (Jan. 23, 1897); letter, Albert Shaw to N. F. Hawley, Mar. 1, 1897, Shaw Papers. Shaw criticized the charter as "the most cumbrously complicated . . . ever constructed" in that letter; more circumspectly, he suggested in his article, "The Municipal Problem and Greater New York," pp. 741–44, that the Board of Local Improvements might not work as intended.
166. Letter, Low to Charles Stewart Smith, Apr. 8, 1897, Low Papers.
167. The public manifestations of protest against the charter are described in Syrett, *Brooklyn*, p. 271. The Morton and Low papers contain statements of opposition from these and other sources.
168. Quoted in Gosnell, *Boss Platt*, p. 165, citing E. L. Godkin, *Unforeseen Tendencies of Democracy* (Boston: Houghton Mifflin & Company, 1898), p. 167. The clearest contemporary statement of the decline of anti-consolidation sentiment in Brooklyn is provided in a series of letters from Alfred T. White to Edward M. Shepard. Of nine prominent men who had opposed consolidation in 1896 and who met with White to consider a renewal of their protest in 1897, only one, Robert L. Benedict, was willing to continue. The others were all "tired of the subject." Letters, White to Shepard, Mar. 27 & 30 and Apr. 8, 1897, Shepard Papers.
169. Letter, Charles Z. Lincoln to Morton, June 5, 1897, Morton Papers.

CHAPTER 8

1. The *Real Estate Record and Builder's Guide* often commented on the unusually long commuting times of New York City's middle-income residents; on Dec. 24, 1892, it stated that New Yorkers would accept train rides of up to forty-five minutes, with additional time needed to get to and from train terminals. The New York *Times*, July 22, 1888, described the precarious facilities then available for travel to the district above the Harlem River.
2. *Record and Guide*, Jan. 29, 1898. James Blaine Walker, *Fifty Years of Rapid Transit, 1865 to 1917* (New York: the author, 1918) describes the elevated system. Under Gould management, the els were run in such a way as to maximize profits; the ability of the system to provide "real rapid transit" was never seriously tested.
3. *Record and Guide*, July 2, 1892, describes the growth of population in uptown areas served by the elevated railroads. Frank J. Sprague persuasively argued that the technical characteristics of steam railways (shallow grades, long headways, etc.) made them unsuitable for heavily-traveled commuter lines; "The Future of the Electric Railway," *Forum* 12 (1891): 120–30.
4. Sam Bass Warner, Jr., *Streetcar Suburbs: The Process of Growth in Boston, 1870–1900* (Cambridge: Harvard University Press, 1962).
5. Chamber of Commerce of the State of New York, *Annual Report* 1887–1888, pp. 22–23, 63–64, 98–99, 104–6, 109–10; letter, Abram S. Hewitt to George Wilson, secretary of the Chamber of Commerce, Nov. 4, 1887.
6. New York *City Record*, Feb. 1, 1888.
7. Ibid.

8. Ibid.; letter, Abram S. Hewitt to George Foster Peabody, Feb. 16, 1894, Cooper-Hewitt Letterpress Copybooks, New-York Historical Society.

9. Letters, Hewitt to Alexander E. Orr, president of the New York Produce Exchange, Feb. 7, 1888, Hewitt Mayoral Letterpress Copybooks, New-York Historical Society; Hewitt to Morris K. Jesup, president of the Chamber of Commerce of the State of New York, Apr. 13, 1888, Chamber of Commerce archives; *Record and Guide*, Feb. 4 & 11, 1888; New-York Board of Trade and Transportation Meeting Minutes, Apr. 10, 1888, New-York Historical Society; New York *Times*, Feb. 8, 11, & 19, 1888.

10. New York *Times*, Feb. 28, 1888.

11. *Record and Guide*, Feb. 11, 1888.

12. Ibid.

13. New York *Times*, Feb. 28 and Apr. 12, 1888.

14. Henry R. Beekman, counsel to the Corporation of the City of New York, memorandum to Mayor Abram S. Hewitt, Feb. 23, 1888, autograph copy in the Abram S. Hewitt Papers, Cooper Union.

15. *Record and Guide*, Feb. 18, Apr. 28, and May 5, 1888; New York *Times*, Feb. 4 & 5 and Apr. 12, 1888.

16. New York *Times*, Feb. 2, 1888.

17. Allan Nevins, *Abram S. Hewitt: With Some Account of Peter Cooper* (New York: Harper & Brothers, 1935), pp. 503–4.

18. Hewitt to Parke Godwin, Nov. 15, 1888, Hewitt Mayoral Letterpress Copybooks.

19. The relevant laws are chap. 606 of the New York Laws of 1875, chap. 529 of the Laws of 1879, chap. 4 of the Laws of 1891, and chap. 752 of the Laws of 1894.

20. Augustus Cerillo, Jr. "Reform in New York City: A Study of Urban Progressivism" (Ph.D. diss. Northwestern University, 1969)," p. 83.

21. Hewitt, statement in the New York *City Record*, Feb. 1, 1888.

22. *Record and Guide*, Mar. 16, 1889; New York *Times*, Mar. 15, 1889.

23. New York *Times*, Apr. 10 & 23 and May 29, 1890; *Record and Guide*, Apr. 12 and June 28, 1890.

24. New York *Times*, June 22, 1890.

25. Ibid., Jan. 6, 1891.

26. Ibid., Dec. 15, 1890 and Jan. 6, 1891; biographical data from the various sources used for this book.

27. Rapid Transit Commission, *Report . . . to the Common Council of the City of New York, October, 1891; Record and Guide*, July 3, 18 & 25, Sept. 19 & 26, and Oct. 24, 1891. Over the summer the Rapid Transit Commission also engaged four independent engineers (the distinguished Octave Chanute, Theodore Cooper, Joseph Wilson, and the politically well-connected John Bogart) to prepare separate reports on the advantages and disadvantages of alternative rapid transit schemes; *Record and Guide*, Sept. 19, 1891.

28. New York *City Record*, Feb. 1, 1888.

29. *Street Railway Journal* 8 (Dec. 1892), p. 770.

30. *Record and Guide*, Dec. 24, 1892.

31. New York *City Record*, Feb. 1, 1888.

32. Ibid.

33. Such a project was endorsed both by the New York *Times*, Dec. 21, 1888, and by the *Record and Guide*, May 12 and June 2, 1888; Oct. 24, 1891. Viaduct railways had become common in the large cities of Great Britain during the 1860s, but they had also acquired a reputation for destroying the value of the property they touched; John R. Kellett, *The Impact of Railways on Victorian Cities* (London: Routledge & Kegan Paul, 1969), pp. 16–17.

34. *Record and Guide*, Dec. 19, 1891.

35. New York *City Record*, Feb. 1, 1888; Harold C. Passer, *The Electrical Manufacturers, 1865–1900* (Cambridge: Harvard University Press, 1953), pp. 248–50.

36. American Street Railway Association, *Report of the Tenth Annual Meeting*, Oct. 21–22, 1891, p. 163; Idem., *Report of the Eleventh Annual Meeting*, Oct. 19–20, 1892, p. 190; Passer, *The Electrical Manufacturers*, p. 273.

37. Frank J. Sprague, "Ideal Rapid Transit," *Street Railway Journal* 7 (March 1891), Supplement on Rapid Transit, pp. 1–6 (reprinting, with Sprague's corrections, an interview with Sprague first published in the New York *Commercial Advertiser*, Sprague), "Consider-

ations Which Should Govern the Selection of a Rapid Transit System," *Street Railway Journal* 7 (June 1891): 319–22.

38. William Barclay Parsons, *Report to the Board of Rapid Transit Railroad Commissioners in and for the City of New York on Rapid Transit in Foreign Cities* (New York, 1894), pp. 36–39. The Liverpool Overhead Railway was, however, capable of reaching speeds of 28 mph between its stops.

39. Chapter 529 of the New York Laws of 1879.

40. Chapter 4 of the New York Laws of 1891, section 4.

41. New York *Times*, May 24, 1890; *Record and Guide*, Dec. 19, 1891.

42. *Record and Guide*, Feb. 4, 1893; Nov. 24, 1888; Nov. 19, 1892.

43. Chapter 4 of the New York Laws of 1891.

44. Walker, *Fifty Years of Rapid Transit*, p. 128.

45. *Record and Guide*, Dec. 12, 1891. The fact that rapid transit would require, as the experts increasingly agreed, four parallel tracks on one level, further constrained planners to select routes up the city's widest streets; *Record and Guide*, Sept. 19, 1891.

46. *Record and Guide*, Dec. 5, 1891.

47. Rapid Transit Commission, *Report*, Oct. 1891.

48. *Record and Guide*, Nov. 19 and Dec. 24, 1892; New York *Times*, Dec. 15, 29, & 30, 1892.

49. *Record and Guide*, Dec. 24 & 31, 1892.

50. New York *Times*, Dec. 31, 1892.

51. *Record and Guide*, Sept. 26, 1891.

52. Ibid., Sept. 26, Oct. 24, Nov. 5, and Dec. 31, 1891; Nov. 19, 1892. Andrew Carnegie had also been overheard to doubt whether the subway could attract the necessary capital; Ibid., Dec. 19, 1891.

53. Ibid., Oct. 24, 1891; Nov. 19 and Dec. 3, 1892.

54. Ibid., Dec. 31, 1892.

55. New York *Times*, Jan. 21, 1893; *Record and Guide*, Dec. 10, 24, & 31, 1892; Jan. 7 and Apr. 15, 1893.

56. *Record and Guide*, Jan. 7 & 14, 1893.

57. Ibid.; New York *Times*, Dec. 31, 1892 and Jan. 1 & 5, 1893.

58. Ibid.; New York *Times*, Jan. 5, 1893. Hewitt opposed any extension of the elevated railroad system, but he did favor a proposal to add a third track to the existing els, in order to permit them to offer express service.

59. Ibid., Mar. 18, 1893. This journal covered the issue in detail through the 1890s. New York *Times*, Jan. 5 & 17, 1893.

60. New York *Times*, Apr. 2, 1893; *Record and Guide*, Apr. 15, 1893.

61. *Record and Guide*, May 15 & 22, 1893.

62. Ibid., Sept. 9 and Dec. 16, 1893.

63. Ibid., May 13 & 27, 1893.

64. Ibid., Sept. 26, 1891; Nov. 19, 1892; and Nov. 3, 1894.

65. Letter, Jacob H. Schiff to Mayor Hugh J. Grant, Mar. 16, 1891, Mayors' Papers, New York City Municipal Archives and Records Center, cited in Charles W. Cheape, III, "The Evolution of Urban Public Transit, 1880–1912: A Study of Three Cities" (Ph.D. diss., Brandeis University, 1976) pp. 128–29.

66. New York *Times*, Feb. 28, 1888.

67. *Record and Guide*, Dec. 24, 1892; Mar. 25, 1893.

68. Ibid., Dec. 31, 1892; Jan. 14, 1893.

69. Ibid., Jan. 7 & 14, 1893. Franklin Edson, a Swallowtail ex-mayor, also opposed municipal ownership in 1893: Ibid., Jan. 7.

70. Ibid., Jan. 14, 1893; Nov. 3, 1894.

71. Ibid., Aug. 20, 1892.

72. Ibid., Mar. 25, 1893.

73. Ibid., Sept. 30, 1893.

74. Ibid., Nov. 19, 1892; June 10, 1893.

75. Ibid., Nov. 19, 1892; Jan. 7, 1893.

76. Ibid., Mar. 18, 1893.

77. New-York Board of Trade and Transportation, Minutes, Feb. 8 and Mar. 8 & 22, 1893; *Record and Guide*, June 14, 1893.

78. Joseph Dorfman, *The Economic Mind in American Civilization* (New York: Viking Press, 1949), vol. 3; Harold U. Faulkner, *The Decline of Laissez-Faire* (New York: Holt, Rinehart and Winston, 1951); Sidney Fine, *Laissez-Faire and the General Welfare State* (Ann Arbor: The University of Michigan Press, 1956).

79. *Record and Guide*, Aug. 20, 1892.

80. Ibid., Nov. 5, 1892.

81. Albert Shaw, *Municipal Government in Great Britain* (New York: The Century Company, 1895), and *Municipal Government in Continental Europe* (New York: The Century Company, 1896).

82. The *Record and Guide* began to reprint Shaw's articles on municipal ownership in 1889: see its issues of Jan. 26 and Feb. 2, as well as July 11, 1891; Aug. 20, 1892; Dec. 28, 1895.

83. *Record and Guide*, Mar. 18, 1893.

84. Ibid., Jan. 14, 1893. New York City already derived a significant—and celebrated—income from the East River ferry and other franchises that it let to the highest bidder; Frank R. Houghton, a west side real estate developer, quoted in the *Record and Guide*, Dec. 10, 1893. Although the size of this income was sometimes exaggerated, it constituted about one-quarter of the city's total expenditures in the 1890s, as Edward Dana Durand demonstrated in *The Finances of New York City* (New York: The Macmillan Company, 1898), p. 221.

85. *Record and Guide*, June 3, 1893.

86. Ibid.

87. Ibid., Dec. 10, 1892.

88. Ibid., Jan. 7, 1893. The New York *Times* reported that Henry R. Beekman made an identical argument at a large meeting of real estate men, Jan. 5, 1893.

89. *Record and Guide*, Mar. 18, 1893. Comparable pressures had led the chairman of the Manchester Chamber of Commerce to state, in the early 1850s, "I am strongly of the opinion there ought to be a controlling power" capable of regulating the activities of railway companies within British cities; Kellett, *The Impact of Railways on Victorian Cities*, pp. 18–19.

90. *Record and Guide*, Mar. 18, 1893.

91. Ibid.

92. Louis F. Post and Fred C. Leubuscher, *Henry George's 1886 Campaign: An Account of the George-Hewitt Campaign in the New York Municipal Election of 1886* (Westport, Connecticut: Hyperion Press, Inc., 1976 reprint of New York: John W. Lovell Company, 1887 1st ed.), p. 28.

93. *Record and Guide*, July 30, 1892.

94. The support of Hewitt and Schiff has already been noted: Low stated his support in a letter to Hewitt (Feb. 1, 1888, Low Papers, Columbia University), and acted with a Chamber of Commerce that supported Hewitt's plan before the city council (New York *Times*, Feb. 11, 1888). Thomas Ash has shown that nearly all social work leaders in New York saw electrified rapid transit as the key to reducing overcrowding in the city's slums between 1890 and 1900: Ash, "The Reformers' Illusion: Mass Transit and the Urban Poor, 1870–1910" (unpublished Princeton University seminar paper, June 13, 1977).

95. Charles B. Stover, "To the Wage-Earners of New York" (New York, Jan. 6, 1893), pamphlet in the Charles B. Stover Papers, contained in the University Settlement Society of New York Papers, Wisconsin State Historical Society, p. 1.

96. A sketch of Stover's life is included in the "A. J. Kennedy Notes" filed with the Stover Papers.

97. Stover, "To the Wage-Earners of New York."

98. Ibid. The exceptions were two unions of clothing cutters, one of upholsterers, and two of cigar makers. For the living standard of workers in these trades, see chap. 3, in this volume; for union members' use of the elevated roads, see Stover, "To the Wage-Earners of New York," pp. 15–16.

99. New York *Times*, Jan. 17 and Mar. 24, 1893; *Record and Guide*, Feb. 18 & 25, Mar. 18 and Apr. 1, 1893. Stover's Chadwick Civic Club joined with the Central Labor Union to sponsor a mass meeting in January, at which Father Edward McGlynn, Samuel Gompers, James P. Archibald, and Henry George—the four men who had played the most

prominent roles in George's 1886 mayoral campaign—all endorsed municipal ownership and operation of the rapid transit system.

100. New York *Times*, Jan. 24 & 25 and Mar. 8 & 16, 1894; *Record and Guide*, Jan. 27 and Mar. 13 & 17, 1894; New-York Board of Trade and Transportation, Meeting Minutes for Feb. 14 and March 7, 1894; letters, F. B. Thurber to Frank S. Gardner, Feb. 8, 1894, and R. T. Wilson & Co. to Frank S. Gardner, Feb. 9, 1894; memorandum to the New-York Board of Trade and Transportation from Simon Sterne and James T. Young, Mar. 6, 1894, Board of Trade and Transportation Papers.

101. Chamber of Commerce of the State of New York, *Annual Report 1893–1894*, 84–105, 112–125; New-York Board of Trade and Transportation, Meeting Minutes, Mar. 7, 1894; *Record and Guide*, Mar. 3 & 17, 1894.

102. New York *Times*, Mar. 16, 1894. The men named in the bill were Samuel D. Babcock, John Claflin, Seth Low, and Alexander E. Orr.

103. *Record and Guide*, Apr. 7, 1894. Speaking in favor of a proposal to improve the els in 1893, Hewitt had taken a similar line: Tammany-nominated and appointed officials were not to be trusted, so New York's citizens must turn to private corporations for any immediate relief from congestion; New York *Times*, Jan. 5, 1893.

104. Memorandum, L. J. Callanan, James Talcott, and George F. Morgan to the New-York Board of Trade and Transportation, Mar. 7, 1894; New-York Board of Trade and Transportation, Meeting Minutes, Mar. 7, 1894.

105. Memorandum, George F. Morgan to the Board of Trade and Transportation, filed with notes to the Board's meeting of May 9, 1894.

106. Letter, J. Kennedy Tod to James B. Reynolds, Dec. 8, 1896, Reynolds Papers in the University Settlement Society of New York Papers; New York *Tribune*, Dec. 14, 1896.

107. *Record and Guide*, Sept. 30, 1893.

108. New York *Times*, Apr. 6, 1894.

109. *Record and Guide*, Apr. 7, 1894; New York *Times*, Apr. 17, 1894.

110. Cheape, "The Evolution of Urban Public Transit," p. 131.

111. *Record and Guide*, Oct. 13, 20, & 27 and Nov. 3, 1894.

112. Cheape, "The Evolution of Urban Public Transit," p. 136.

113. Simon Sterne, manuscript of an address entitled "Some Reflections on Recent Changes and Proposed Reforms in Legislation Affecting the City of New York," Sterne Papers, New York Public Library.

114. Sun Publishing Assn. v. The Mayor, 152 *New York Reports*, 257–75 (March 1897). Shepard's brief, printed separately, was hailed at the time as "a municipal ownership document" by such advocates of that policy as Edward M. Grout (letter to Shepard, Feb. 1, 1897) and John DeWitt Warner (letter to Shepard, Aug. 20, 1897), Edward M. Shepard Papers, Columbia University; *Record and Guide*, Apr. 3, 1897; New York *Times*, Mar. 24, 1897.

115. *Record and Guide*, Jan. 15 and May 30, 1896; *Matter of Rapid Transit Comm.*, 5 N.Y. App. Div. 290 (1896).

116. Letter, Shepard to Richard Rogers Bowker, May 23, 1896, Shepard Papers.

117. *Street Railway Journal* 12 (June 1896): 366.

118. *Record and Guide*, Aug. 8 and Nov. 7, 1896; New York City Board of Rapid Transit Railroad Commissioners, *Proceedings*, Jan. 14, 1897.

119. *Matter of Rapid Transit Comm.*, 23 N.Y. App. Div. 472 (1897).

120. Cheape, "The Evolution of Urban Public Transit," p. 144; *Matter of Rapid Transit Comm.*, 26 N.Y. App. Div. 608 (1899).

121. Rapid Transit Railroad Commissioners, *Proceedings*, Oct. 2, 1894; Jan. 29, 1895.

122. *Record and Guide*, Jan. 8, 1898. New York County included the Bronx.

123. Ibid., Mar. 26 and Apr. 16, 1898.

124. Ibid., May 14, 1898.

125. Interview with Croker quoted from the New York *Journal* in the New York *Times*, Feb. 3, 1898.

126. *Record and Guide*, Mar. 19, 1898.

127. Ibid., Mar. 26 and Apr. 2, 1898; letters, Seth Low to Arthur von Briesen, Mar. 30, 1898, and Low to Governor Black, Apr. 11, 1898, Low Papers, Columbia University; Arthur von Briesen, Chairman, Central City Committee of the Citizens' Union, to Everett

P. Wheeler, Mar. 19, 1898, asking Wheeler to lobby against this bill and enclosing lists of the members of a Committee of Fifty appointed by the Citizens' Union on Rapid Transit, Everett P. Wheeler Papers, New York State Library, Albany. With Hewitt as chairman, this committee included Stover and labor leader George Tombleson as well as representatives of the Chamber of Commerce, the Board of Trade and Transportation, the Citizens' Union, the Gold Democrats, the Civil Service Reform Association, the German American Reform Union, and the Charity Organization Society.

128. *Record and Guide*, Apr. 1, 1899.

129. State Republican boss Thomas C. Platt had favored legislation to allow the Metropolitan to receive the terms it sought. Roosevelt refused to go along. Letters, Platt to Roosevelt, Mar. 21, 1899, Platt Papers, Yale University; Roosevelt to Platt, Mar. 15 & 17 and Apr. 4, 1899, in Elting E. Morison, ed. *The Papers of Theodore Roosevelt* (Cambridge: Harvard University Press, 1951), vol. 2, pp. 964, 966, 978–79; Roosevelt to E. R. A. Seligman, Apr. 17, 1899, ibid., p. 989; Seth Low to Roosevelt, Mar. 21 and Apr. 18, 1899; and Low to Charles Sprague Smith, Apr. 7, 1899, Low Papers; Roosevelt to Platt, Apr. 14, 1899, Platt Papers; New York *Times*, Apr. 18, 1899.

130. Letter, Edward M. Shepard to William Barclay Parsons, Jan. 21, 1899, Shepard Papers; Rapid Transit Railroad Commissioners, *Proceedings*, Feb. 2, 1899.

131. Letters, Henry Demarest Lloyd to Seth Low, Jan. 8, 1898, Low Papers in the Columbia University Files; letter, Alexander E. Orr to Edward M. Shepard, May 19, 1899, Shepard Papers.

132. Letter, Orr to Shepard, May 19, 1890. Five days later A. Augustus Healy wrote Shepard that Whalen had similarly refused to approve the issuance of bonds for the construction of an addition to the Brooklyn Museum. Both letters in Shepard Papers. As Comptroller Bird S. Coler insisted, it was politically impossible for the city authorities to approve a major bond issue for Manhattan, so long as the city's total indebtedness appeared to be so great that it could not undertake comparable projects in the other boroughs; New York *Times*, Dec. 17, 1898.

133. Rapid Transit Railroad Commissioners, *Proceedings*, Sept. 21, 1899, Jan. 16, 1900. McDonald had indicated an interest in building the subway as early as February, 1895: *Proceedings*, Feb. 5 & 12, 1895. New York *Times*, Jan. 16, 1900.

134. Cheape, "The Evolution of Urban Public Transit," p. 155.

135. Continental Securities Company v. Belmont, 83 N.Y. Misc. 340, at 344, cited by Walker, *Fifty Years of Rapid Transit*, p. 171. Anthony N. Brady later testified that in 1898 Whitney had "thought" that Brady, who had considerable investments in Brooklyn transit facilities, "ought not to be interested on this [Manhattan] side of the river, as it might create some friction and interfere with the friendly relations that existed between Mr. Whitney and his associates and myself," State of New York, Public Service Commission, First District, *Investigation of Interborough Metropolitan Company and Brooklyn Rapid Transit Company* (New York: 1907), vol. 4, p. 1613.

136. Whitney had closely monitored all rapid transit legislation for New York City; letters, Francis Lynde Stetson to Whitney, Apr. 12, 1894; New York State Democratic Chairman James W. Hinckley to Whitney, Nov. 1, 1894; Henry A. Robinson to Whitney, Apr. 8, 1897; all in Whitney Papers, Library of Congress; Edward M. Shepard to William Barclay Parsons, Jan. 21, 1899, Shepard Papers.

CHAPTER 9

1. David B. Tyack, *The One Best System: A History of American Urban Education* (Cambridge: Harvard University Press, 1974), provides by far the best comprehensive study of this movement. In dealing with the centralization of schools in New York City, Tyack demonstrates that New York set a pattern followed during the next twenty years by most other large cities. Several of the smaller midwestern and far western cities had anticipated elements of the New York pattern in the 1870s and 1880s.

2. On the twentieth-century structure of New York City's municipal agencies, see Wallace S. Sayre and Herbert Kaufman, *Governing New York City: Politics in the Metropolis* (New York: The Russell Sage Foundation, 1960), chap. 8.

3. On cultural issues in the 1894 New York State Constitutional Convention, see John Webb Pratt, *Religion, Politics, and Diversity: The Church-State Theme in New York History* (Ithaca: Cornell University Press, 1967), and Samuel T. McSeveney, *The Politics of Depression: Political Behavior in the Northeast, 1893–1896* (New York: Oxford University Press, 1972). Peter Romanofsky, "Saving the Lives of the City's Foundlings: The Joint Committee and New York Child Care Methods, 1860–1907," *New-York Historical Society Quarterly* 61 (1977): 49–68, describes one conflict over orphans.

4. On the prohibition issue, see Harold F. Gosnell, *Boss Platt and His New York Machine* (New York: Russell and Russell 1969 reprint of Chicago, 1924, 1st ed.), pp. 162–5; on trotting in Central Park, see the pamphlet, *The Central Park Race Track Law Was Repealed by Public Sentiment*, no author (New York: n.p., 1892).

5. Letters, Abram S. Hewitt to William E. Dodge, May 24, 1887; Hewitt to Mrs. J. M. Thurber, June 13, 1888; and Hewitt to Stephen H. Olin, Nov. 23, 1888, all in Hewitt Mayoral Letterpress Copybooks, New-York Historical Society.

6. Public Education Society, "Memorial to the Board of Education," Feb. 6, 1889. The committee that submitted this memorial included Butler and Columbia University trustee John B. Pine; among the society's officers were Abraham Jacobi, M.D., D. B. St. John Roosa, M.D., and Mrs. Joseph H. Choate, all of whom played important parts in the school centralization movement through its successful conclusion in 1896. The later Public Education Association grew out of this movement, but was not a direct descendent of the Public Education Society; see Sol Cohen, *Progressives and Urban School Reform* (New York: Teachers' College Press, 1964), pp. 26–28.

7. The annual *Directory* and *Journal* of the Board of Education of the City of New York describe the city's school system in detail. For a contemporary account, see A. Emerson Palmer, *The New York Public School* (New York: The Macmillan Company, 1905).

8. Good Government Club E, *Publication* No. 9, "Progress in School Reform" (New York: 1895), printed the results of an 1895 school census; for enrollment in the city's Catholic parochial schools, see the *Irish World and American Industrial Liberator*, May 4, 1895, reporting a Catholic school attendance in New York City of 33,301. New York *Times*, Feb. 21, 1896.

9. For a general account, see Palmer, *The New York Public School*. The position of clerk to a board of trustees is noted in Board of Education of the City of New York, *Handbook* (New York, 1896), pp. 1–18.

10. Commission to Revise the Laws Affecting the Common Schools and Public Education in the City of New York, *Report* (New York: Mar. 10, 1894).

11. According to James B. Reynolds, one school commissioner had argued that Jasper's great qualification was that he "remembered each school in the city by its number," letter, Reynolds to Butler, Apr. 3, 1899, Reynolds Papers, in the University Settlement Society of New York Papers, State Historical Society of Wisconsin.

12. Board of Education of the City of New York, *Handbook*, 1896.

13. Commission to Revise the Laws Affecting the Common Schools, *Report*; Stephen H. Olin, "Public School Reform in New York," *Educational Review* 8 (June 1894):1–6.

14. Among the clearest accounts of the appointment process are Stephen H. Olin, "Public School Reform in New York;" Olin, "The New York Common Schools," *Harper's New Monthly Magazine* 90 (Mar. 1895): 584–89; an account of a disputed appointment appears in *School*, Oct. 5, 1893, p. 37.

15. Additional accounts of the appointment process appear in statements by defenders of the decentralized system including Henry S. Fuller, editor of *School*, in a letter to the New York *Sun*, Apr. 16, 1896, and School Commissioner Robert Maclay, in an "Argument" presented to Mayor Strong on Mar. 31, 1896, Mayors' Papers, New York City Municipal Archives and Records Center.

16. Butler, editorials in the *Educational Review*, 15 (Jan. 1898): 95 and (Mar. 1898): 300; letter, Butler to Assemblyman, George C. Austin, Mar. 6, 1896, Butler Papers, Columbia University. Butler elaborated upon and repeated these views in letters to other legislators and in editorials in *Educational Review* through 1895 and 1896.

17. Committee on Education of the City Vigilance League, "Report," in *The City Vigilant* 1 (Oct. 1894): 261.

18. *The Critic*, Feb. 1, 1896, p. 71.

19. Jacob A. Riis, *The Making of an American* (New York: The Macmillan Company, 1904), p. 354.

20. Olin, "The New York Common Schools," p. 588.

21. William S. Rainsford, "The Church's Opportunity in the City Today," address reprinted in *Publications* of the Church Social Union (Boston: The Diocesan House, 1895).

22. Biographical information derived from widely scattered sources, including those consulted in studying the city's economic elites and more specialized sources such as Sidney Marsden Fuerst, *New York Teachers' Annual* (New York, 1896); David McAdam et al., ed., *History of the Bench and Bar of New York* (New York: New York History Company, 1897); Otto Spengler, *Das Deutsche Element der Stadt New York* (New York: the author, 1913); and James Lee Wells et al., *The Bronx and Its People: A History, 1609–1927* (New York: Lewis Publishing Company, 1927). The nine commissioners who certainly opposed school centralization in 1896 included Richard H. Adams, Dr. Walter Edson Andrews, Charles L. Holt, William H. Hurlbut, John L. N. Hunt, Alexander P. Ketchum, Robert Maclay, Charles Strauss, and Charles C. Wehrum. Joseph E. Simmons had been president of the board, 1886–1891. Commissioners Emile Benneville, Hugh Kelly, Joseph J. Little, and William J. Van Arsdale also opposed centralization, but they did not take such prominent positions. Adams, Maclay, and Simmons were millionaires, according to the list in the *Tribune Monthly*, vol. 4 (1892), reprinted in Sidney Ratner, ed., *New Light on the History of Great American Fortunes* (New York: Augustus M. Kelley, Inc., 1953).

23. The advocates of centralization in 1896 included Charles B. Hubbell, Jacob A. Mack, Philip Meirowitz, M.D., Auguste Phillipe Montant, Edward H. Peaslee, M.D., and Nathaniel Appleton Prentiss. Of the opponents, only Hurlbut (Yale 1860, trustee of the Bowery Savings Bank, member of the Union League Club Executive Committee), had a similar profile.

24. "Petition Against the Compromise Bill," signed by Dr. Abbie Hamlin McIvor and the school inspectors, in Mayors' Papers, box 6063, item 81, no. 6.

25. The names of these defenders of the decentralized system were derived from petitions and other documents in the Mayors' Papers, box 6063, and from the *Harlem Local Reporter*, Mar. 11, 1896; *Dickson's Uptown Weekly*, Jan. 4, 1896; the New York *Commercial Advertiser*, Mar. 27, 1896; the New York *Herald*, Mar. 27 and Apr. 2, 5, & 15, 1896; and the New York *Sun*, Apr. 16, 17, & 19, 1896. Altogether directors or officers of five of the six commercial or savings banks in Harlem and the Bronx opposed centralization, as did a purported 6,000 uptown shopkeepers, who signed an anti-centralization petition noted in the New York *Tribune*, Apr. 16, 1896.

26. These data, like those discussed above, are derived from scattered bits of biographical information, not from a systematic check of the membership records of the relevant organizations. Such records are unavailable. Hence the numbers of memberships and leadership positions given are minima, and the actual numbers were probably much larger. Since membership records are available for many of the elite social and economic organizations to which the advocates of centralization belonged, the latter appear to have held a larger number of memberships; but this in part reflects gaps in our data. More detail as to the names and activities of opponents of centralization is provided in David C. Hammack, "Participation in Major Decisions in New York City, 1890–1900: The Creation of Greater New York and the Centralization of the Public School System" (Ph.D. diss., Columbia University, 1973), pp. 374–87.

27. Wells, *The Bronx and its People*; vol. 3, p. 199.

28. *The City Vigilant*, vol. 1, p. 275; vol. 2, p. 96.

29. New York *Herald*, Apr. 3, 1896; "Petition of Citizens and Taxpayers of the Twenty-third and Twenty-fourth Wards," n.d., Mayors' Papers, box 6063, item 49; New York *Herald* and *Commercial Advertiser*, Mar. 27, 1896. Other Jews who opposed centralization included New York Republican County Committee Chairman Edward Lauterbach, who had earlier played a part in German Jewish charitable activities; Mrs. Lauterbach; school trustees Samuel Samuels and Samuel D. Levy; and Joseph M. Rice, whose articles in *The Forum* had criticized the quality of public education in New York and other cities and who had been recommended for appointment to Mayor Gilroy's School Law Revision Commission by Nathan Bijur, Registrar Ferdinand Levy, and DeWitt J. Seligman. Letters, Bijur, Levy, and Seligman to Mayor Gilroy, May 4 & 5, 1893, Mayors' Papers, box 6143. Trustee Samuel D. Levy spoke

against centralization at a meeting of the Federation of East Side Workers, according to an article in the New York *Herald,* Mar. 27, 1896.

30.   John Webb Pratt, *Religion, Politics, and Diversity: The Church-State Theme in New York History* (Ithaca: Cornell University Press, 1967), pp. 247–48, describes Coudert's role as a spokesman for the Church. Coudert's defence of the decentralized system is preserved in the Mayors' Papers, box 6063, item 47.

31.   "Petition Against the Compromise Bill," Mayors' Papers.

32.   Ibid.

33.   Among the uptown Republicans who opposed centralization were James Lee Wells, Platt's candidate for New York City public works commissioner in 1895 and later president of the Borough of the Bronx, and Assemblyman Alonzo Bell. Uptown Tammany leaders who opposed centralization included Louis F. Haffen, later commissioner of public works and also president of the Borough of the Bronx, and Isaac Fromme. Other data derived from the sources indicated in notes 20 and 23, in this chapter. For John Spellman, see Wells, *The Bronx and Its People,* vol. 3, p. 119.

34.   New York *Herald,* Mar. 27 and Apr. 2, 1896.

35.   Mayor Strong appointed at least two "representative Germans" to the Board of Education; both of these men opposed centralization. Letter, Nicholas Murray Butler to Carl Schurz, May 21, 1895, Butler Papers.

36.   Although opposition to centralization was concentrated in the uptown portion of the city, evidence of opposition from other locations can also be found. The following table indicates the residential locations of school officials, school commissioners, and of persons who corresponded with the mayor in opposition to centralization:

	Officials	*Commissioners*	*Correspondents*
Uptown (Wards 12, 23, 24)	12	7	5
East Side, West Side,			
40th–86th Streets (Wards 19, 22)	4	4	5
14th–40th Streets			
(Wards 9, 16, 18, 20, 21)	1	2	10
Below Fourteenth Street			
(Wards 1–8, 10, 11, 13–15, 17)	6	1	12

37.   These disputes were covered in *School;* for example, see *School* 5 (Jan. 25, 1894):170, for a conflict between Commissioner Charles C. Wehrum and Mayor Gilroy over the allocation of construction funds.

38.   Board of Education of the City of New York, *Annual Report,* 1896, pp. 96–97. The figure of $9.71 is produced by dividing the average attendance given for each ward into the amount of funds allocated to that ward by the central Board of Education. In five lower east side wards the amount per pupil ranged from $9.70 to $9.73; in five uptown wards, from $9.69 to $9.73.

39.   Good Government Club E, *Publication No. 1.* For Scrymser's estimate, see The New York Association for Improving the Condition of the Poor, *Annual Report,* 1893–94, pp. 204–5.

40.   Good Government Club E, *Publication No. 9,* "Progress in School Reform," table 1, pp. 55ff.

41.   New York *Sun,* Apr. 16, 1896. Accurate figures are apparently not available. For Superintendent Jasper's charge that the school census of Dec. 1895 contained serious errors, see the New York *Times,* Feb. 21, 1896, p. 7. That census reported 983 certified truants, together with 2,211 at work who by law ought to have been at school, and 39,778 between the ages five and eight and 6,949 between the ages of eight and sixteen who were not at school, for a total of 49,861 children between the ages of five and sixteen not accommodated. A census conducted by the Health Department in Apr. 1895 found 50,069 school-age children who were not attending classes. According to the *Times,* it was generally conceded that the schools needed space for 35,000 or 40,000 more children. New York *Times,* Feb.

21, 1895; Oct. 9 & 14, Nov. 20, and Dec. 15 & 31, 1895; and Feb. 6, 1895. Neither census inquired as to the number of years a child had spent in school.

42. In the early stages of the centralization movement, advocates of school reform recognized that the school commissioners understood the need for additional accommodations and that they "would, if they could, remedy the evils," but that funds were "deliberately withheld by the Board of Apportionment," dominated by the mayor and the comptroller. Good Government Club E, *Publication No. 1,* describing a meeting on behalf of school reform held June 6, 1894.

43. *The Tribune Monthly, Public Schools of New York,* Mar. 1896 (New York: The Tribune Association), pp. 70, 88–89. Edgar S. Maclay, the author of this collection of sketches of most of New York's grammar and primary schools, asserted that "under Tammany domination in school matters, the rights of the Hebrews have been almost entirely ignored and their schools have been allowed to remain overcrowded and badly ventilated," as in the case of Primary School 31 in Ward 11. But he praised two grammar schools in the same ward, noting that the trustees had secured a playground and improved light and air for GS 71, and cited GS 88, which opened in 1889 under Hugh J. Grant's mayoral administration and received an addition in 1895 as a result of action under Mayor Gilroy, as an example of the policy of erecting "some of the best schoolhouses in the poorest parts of the city." Following a *Tribune* tendency, Maclay mixed anti-Tammany rhetoric with straight reporting. In opposing centralization, the North Side Board of Trade argued that the change would be "especially threatening" to the "progress and growth of the North Side, because people will not purchase or rent property where there are no good school accommodations." Petition of the North Side Board of Trade, Mar. 9, 1896, Mayors' Papers; *Harlem Local Reporter,* Mar. 11, 1896.

44. Population changes calculated from Department of the Interior, Census Office, *Eleventh Census, 1890. Population of the United States by Minor Civil Divisions: Census Bulletin on New York State,* Robert P. Porter, Superintendent of the Census (Washington, D.C.: 1891), p. 10; Health Census of the City of New York, Apr. 1895; school construction dates from Board of Education of the City of New York, *Annual Report,* 1896.

45. Attendance data from Board of Education of the City of New York, *Annual Report,* 1896.

46. The 1895 School Census printed in Good Government Club E, *Publication No. 9,* "Progress in School Reform," p. 55ff, provides data on attendance at nonpublic as well as public schools.

47. Good Government Club E, *Publication No. 9,* p. 55ff.

48. Good Government Club E, *Publication No. 7,* "Public School Buildings in New York City. Their Condition as Shown in Official Reports" (New York: 1895), items 3–5.

49. Ibid., p. 11.

50. Letter, M. Phinby to Mayor William L. Strong, Apr. 17, 1896. Mayors' Papers, box 74. *Harper's Weekly* similarly disliked the sort of trustee usually appointed, it believed, in the "regions of the city which most need good schools;" editorial, Mar. 23, 1895. Still more explicitly, an unsigned letter from several correspondents to Mayor Strong, dated Nov. 16, 1895, asserted that under Tweed, "the Board of Education was run in the interests of the Catholic Church & the bad element in the dominant political party." Mayor Havemeyer then appointed a new board, containing "but one pronounced Roman Catholic, Mr. Eugene Kelly, and one Hebrew, Mr. Joseph Seligman, both men of high standing and broad views." Succeeding mayors followed this pattern, the letter continued, until Mayor William R. Grace "came out quite boldly and introduced both politics and religion, by making several appointments with these as the prime qualifications." Mayors Grant and Gilroy had gone still further, until under the latter "the mask was thrown entirely to one side and the Board of Education put entirely into the hands of Tammany Hall and the Roman Catholic Church. Not only was the Board of Education thus prostituted, but Boards of Inspectors were in like manner made up, as in our own District, of two Roman Catholics and one Protestant. Boards of Trustees were already changed. . . . Investigation would show how far this went in the appointments of Assistant Superintendents, Teachers, Janitors, Clerks, and other employees." Sentiments of this sort certainly lay behind many critiques of the trustee system, but it would not be accurate to say that they dominated. While Butler did not repudiate them, he did not stress them himself. His only reference to Protestant

opinion in his correspondence asserts that "Principal Boyer, who is insane on the subject of the Pope, thinks that the whole machinery of the Roman Catholic Church will move Rome to New York if this bill passes." Butler added, "You will understand that the question of sectarianism in the schools is an awkward one to raise and to talk about; but the fact of the matter is that the strongest single influence in the schools at present, except Tammany Hall, is that of the Roman Catholic Church." He concluded, "This is not a matter that disturbs me in the least, but I simply wanted to point out to you that any evil results that come from the presence of Roman Catholics in the schools are there already and do not wait on the passage of our school bill." Letter, Butler to Seth Low, Mar. 19, 1896, Butler Papers. While he held these views, Butler also opposed the bigotry of the American Protective Association and sought to bring to New York City a school administrator who had been the victim of the APA in Denver; letter, Butler to Norman Hapgood, June 4, 1896, Butler Papers.

51.   Letter, James B. Reynolds to Jane W. Bartlett, Feb. 17, 1899, Reynolds Papers. In 1896, Reynolds had charged that he knew at least ten incompetent teachers who had gained their places through pull; but when a committee of the Board of Education challenged him to name them in executive session, he refused, on the ground that he did not wish to hound individual teachers, but to bring about a reform in the system as a whole; New York *Tribune*, Apr. 16, 1896, and letters, Reynolds to the New York State Senate Committee on Cities, n.d., Butler Papers; and Nevada N. Stranahan to Reynolds, Feb. 29, 1896, Reynolds Papers. Similarly, the Rev. R. S. MacArthur charged in 1895 that "teachers in the public schools are obliged to pay tribute to political leaders" but refused (or was unable) to support his charge with specific evidence; Board of Education of the City of New York, *Journal*, Feb. 6, 1895; New York *Times*, Feb. 21 & 22, 1895. The charges that could be proved involved favoritism of the sort Reynolds described to Miss Bartlett: New York *Evening Post*, Feb. 13, 1896 (editorial); Elijah D. Clark, clerk of the trustees in Ward 24 and an opponent of centralization, testimony in Wells, *The Bronx and Its People*, vol. 2, p. 541; Thomas Hunter (president of the New York Normal, later Hunter, College), *Autobiography of Thomas Hunter* (New York: the Knickerbocker Press, 1936), pp. 320–21. It was also true that William E. Stillings was both a school trustee in the 12th Ward and an important Tammany district leader, that three of the other trustees in that ward were also members of the Tammany general committee, and that the ward's 56,000 pupils numbered more than those of Albany, Troy, Rochester, and Syracuse combined; Olin, "The New York Common Schools." Yet the press never launched an attack on Stillings' school work, and at least one schoolman under his charge defended him as "faithful, honest, efficient—is for everything that goes for the good of the children—nor threat, nor cajolery can win him from meritorious appointments in the schools, nor compel him to unworthy appointments. With him, politics, religion, race do not influence him in his school work." Letter, Joseph J. Casey to Ashley W. Cole, Oct. 22, 1895, Levi P. Morton Papers, New York Public Library.

52.   *School*, Mar. 5, 1896, p. 212.

53.   New York *Sun*, Apr. 16, 1896.

54.   Frederick R. Coudert, Statement, Mayors' Papers, box 6063, item 47.

55.   New York *Herald*, Mar. 29, 1896.

56.   Letter, Reynolds to the New York State Senate Committee on Cities, n.d., Butler Papers.

57.   "Memoranda of Points in Favor of the Board of Education Bill," Mayors' Papers, box 6063, item 81, p. 5.

58.   Matthew J. Elgas, "Argument against 'The Compromise School Bill,' " Apr. 18, 1896, Mayors' Papers, box 6063. Elgas was president of the New York City Teachers' Association.

59.   New York *Herald*, Mar. 27, 1896.

60.   Elgas, "Argument against 'The Compromise School Bill.' "

61.   Fuller, letter to the editor of the New York *Sun*, Apr. 16, 1896.

62.   Jonathan T. Nicholson, GS 10, 117th Street and Amsterdam Avenue, "School Trustees and the Children," Mayors' Papers, box 6063.

63.   These statements, all of which were delivered at Mayor Strong's hearing on the school bill, Apr. 18, 1896, are in the Mayors' Papers.

64. *School* was not alone in covering the activities of these teachers; the New York *Teachers' Magazine* reported Jonathan T. Nicholson's election as president of the New York State Teachers' Association in its issue for Sept. 1899, p. 229.

65. New York *Herald*, Mar. 27, 1896; New York *Sun*, Apr. 19, 1896.

66. Adele Marie Shaw, "The Public Schools of a Boss-Ridden City," *World's Work* 7 (Feb. 1904):4462; Clinton R. Woodruff, "A Corrupt School System," *Educational Review* 26 (Dec. 1903):433–36. I am indebted to Elaine Soffer for these references.

67. A few individuals mentioned such threats, including Arthur H. Lee in a letter to Butler, n.d., Butler Papers, and Joseph Francis Darling in a letter to Mayor Strong, Apr. 15, 1896, Mayors' Papers. Darling asserted that he had been removed from his teaching post in 1895 because he had opposed the trustee system. An anonymous "school official" complained of such pressure in a letter printed in the *Evening Post*, Apr. 16, 1896.

68. Joseph M. Rice, "The Public Schools of New York City," *The Forum* 14 (Jan. 1893):616–30.

69. *The Tribune Monthly, Public Schools of New York*, account of P.S. 26; "awards of merit" of the New York City Public Schools at the Museum of the City of New York.

70. *Education* 16 (Nov. 1895):182–85.

71. *School* 5 (Feb. 15, 1894):192.

72. Good Government Club E, *Publication No. 9*, pp. 55ff.

73. Commission to Revise the Laws Affecting the Common Schools, *Report*, pp. 4, 6, 21.

74. Rice, "The Public School System of New York City," p. 628.

75. Letter, Hewitt to E. Ellery Anderson, Oct. 24, 1893 (copy), Hewitt Papers, Cooper Union Library. There is as yet no good published account of Butler's life; but Richard F. W. Whittemore's "Nicholas Murray Butler and Public Education, 1862–1917" (doctoral diss., Teachers' College, 1962) is very useful. Hewitt had been ready to support Butler for commissioner of education in 1889; letter, Hewitt to Charles H. Ham, Jan. 26, 1889 (copy), Hewitt Papers, Cooper Union.

76. Butler's voluminous correspondence on the school centralization movement, largely contained in a single letter file, filed under the name "New York Schools" in the Butler Papers, Special Collections, Columbia University, documents these relationships. According to Sol Cohen, Butler himself gave this letter file the title, "The School War"; Cohen, *Progressives and Urban School Reform*, p. 43n.

77. Evidence as to meetings and the flow of ideas among these men is contained in the Butler Papers and is supplemented by the Low and Hewitt papers at Columbia University, the New-York Historical Society, and the Library of Congress.

78. Good Government Club E, "Report of the Committee on Schools," William Ware Locke, chairman, Nov. 26, 1894; the AICP *Annual Report*, 1893–94, pp. 200–222, contains additional material on that organization's school reform efforts.

79. Good Government Club E's *Publications* list its organizers and leaders; a complete series is available at the New-York Historical Society and the New York Public Library. On the anti-candy store campaign, see Good Government Club E, *Publication No. 8*, "Circular Letter to the Delegates to a Conference on the Public Schools of New York, April 12, 1895," pp. 3–4 and passim.

80. Good Government Club E, "Public School Buildings in New York City," sec. 6.

81. Sol Cohen describes the early history of the PEA in *Progressives and Urban School Reform*, pp. 1–3, 26–28, 45. Susan Abbot Mead of the PEA executive committee underlined Butler's controlling influence when she sent him the PEA's endorsement of his reform bill with a note, "You see what entire confidence we have in our Advisory Board"; letter, Mead to Butler, Feb. 1896, Butler Papers. Butler received similar acknowledgments of his influence from Mrs. Schuyler Griswold Van Rensselaer; letter, Mrs. Van Rensselaer to Butler, Dec. 4, 1895, Butler Papers.

82. Letter, Mrs. Van Rensselaer to Richard Watson Gilder, Apr. 1, 1896, Gilder Papers, New York Public Library. Mrs. Van Rensselaer's self-subordinating remarks to Butler and Gilder were not simply conventional or ironic; to judge from her extensive correspondence with Butler and from press reports, she accepted his direction in all phases of the school centralization movement.

83. Public Education Association, *Annual Report*, 1895, pp. 4–8; PEA *Annual Report*, 1896, pp. 6–10.

84. Public Education Association, *Annual Report*, 1896, p. 10; letters, E. Alma Rainsford, Martha L. Draper, and Cornelia E. Marshall to Mrs. Levi P. Morton, Feb. 22, 1896, Levi P. Morton Papers; Mrs. Van Rensselaer to Gilder, Apr. 1, 1896, Gilder Papers.

85. Letters, William S. Rainsford to Mrs. Levi P. Morton, Feb. 22, 1896, and (Episcopal Bishop) Henry Codman Potter to Governor Levi P. Morton, Mar. 28, 1896, Morton Papers; Rainsford to Butler, Apr. 7, 1896, Butler Papers. New York *Herald*, Jan. 14, 1895 and Mar. 28, 1896.

86. Letters, James B. Reynolds to New York State Senate Committee on Cities, n.d., Butler Papers; Butler to Reynolds, Mar. 21, 1896, and Nevada N. Stranahan to Reynolds, Feb. 29, 1896, Reynolds Papers.

87. Letter, Henry Holt to Francis Lynde Stetson, June 1, 1894, Stetson Papers, Williams College; see discussion of this letter in chap. 10, n.9.

88. William S. Rainsford, *The Story of a Varied Life: An Autobiography* (Garden City, New York: Doubleday, Page, & Co., 1922), pp. 342–43. Of Hewitt, Rainsford wrote that "I went and sat at his feet, and learned more from him about New York, its needs and its dangers, and what might and might not be possible to do for it, than any other man in its two and a half millions could have taught me."

89. William R. Hutchison, *The Modernist Impulse in American Protestantism* (Cambridge: Harvard University Press, 1976), p. 2.

90. William S. Rainsford, "The Church's Opportunity in the City Today," *Publications* of the Church Social Union (Boston: The Diocesan House, Nov. 1, 1895), pp. 6, 9. Altogether, at least twenty-one of the members of the Committee of One Hundred for School Reform that Butler and his associates put together in 1896 were members of the boards of trustees of the Educational Alliance, the University Settlement, the Young Men's Christian Association, St. George's Church, the Kindergarten Association, and similar enterprises dedicated to moral uplift and the practical application of religious sentiment. For a full-scale analysis, see Hammack, "The Centralization of New York City's Public School System" (Master's Essay, Columbia University, 1969), chap. 2.

91. Letter, Abram S. Hewitt to E. Ellery Anderson, Oct. 24, 1893 (copy), Hewitt Papers, Cooper Union.

92. Good Government Club E, *Publication no. 8*, "Circular Letter to the Delegates to a Convention on the Public Schools of New York, April 12, 1895," p. 5.

93. Adler's address was quoted in the New York *Herald*, Mar. 28, 1896.

94. Hebrew Free School Association of the City of New York, *Annual Report*, 1895, pp. 19–20.

95. Letter, Henry deForest Baldwin to Walter Hines Page, Mar. 5, 1894, urging Page to publish a magazine article exposing "the manner in which Tammany has interfered with the public schools in this city, with the idea that it can be made a powerful issue in our next municipal campaign." Baldwin Papers, Yale University Library. Baldwin provided no detail on Tammany interference, and the article was not published, in Page's *Forum* or elsewhere. Baldwin was closely associated with William R. Grace's organization. John D. Townsend, another Democrat who remained independent from Tammany Hall during the 1890s, sought to make Tammany cronyism in the selection of school trustees an issue in the 1894 mayoral election; Townsend, *New York in Bondage* (New York: 1901), pp. 247–48. Committee of Seventy, No. 2, "Report of Sub Committee on Public School Reform," New York, 1894.

96. Committee of Seventy, No. 2, "Report of Sub Committee on Public School Reform."

97. Ibid.

98. Ibid.

99. An unpaginated volume of clippings, papers, and letters apparently kept by Butler and titled "Citizens Committee of One Hundred: Public School Reform," kept in the rare book section, Teachers College Library, hereafter referred to as Scrapbook, gives 1895 details.

100. New York *Times*, Mar. 12, 1895; letter to the editor from "School Reform," New York *Evening Post*, Mar. 12, 1895.

101. New York *Times*, Apr. 18 & 22, 1895; New York *Sun*, Apr. 18, 21, 22, & 24, 1895; New York *Tribune*, Apr. 23, 1895. Both the *Sun* and the *Tribune* reported that over 4,000 teachers had gathered to hear New York City Teachers' Association President Matthew J. Elgas and others denounce the bill.

102. Letters, Frederick W. Holls to Butler, Feb. 13 & 14, 1895, Holls Papers, Columbia University; in response, Butler hastened to write Carl Schurz for support in *Harper's Weekly;* letter, Feb. 15, 1895, Butler Papers.

103. Butler had secured the support of the influential Hamilton Fish, but despite assiduous effort had failed to gain the support or assure the neutrality of state Republican leader Thomas C. Platt; letter, Frederick W. Holls to Butler, Nov. 10, 1894, Holls Papers; New York *Sun,* Apr. 18 & 26, 1895. Butler attributed his defeat in 1895 to "followers of Platt . . . in open alliance with Tammany," and to "the mercenary and destructive elements in the school system;" editorial, *Educational Review* 10 (June 1895):99–101.

104. *Educational Review* 10 (June 1895):102.

105. Letters, Butler to Olin, Pine, Sprague, Clark, Taft, Roome, Bishop, Van Amringe, and John E. Eustice, Jan. 20, 1896, Butler Papers.

106. Letter, Butler to Joseph B. Bishop, Jan. 29, 1896, Butler Papers. A copy of the invitation to join this committee and a copy of its "Platform" which lists its offices and members, are included in Butler's Scrapbook.

107. These data are compiled from Milo T. Bogard, *The Redemption of New York* (New York, 1906); *Dictionary of American Biography* (New York: Charles Scribner's Sons, 1943); Moses King, *King's Notable New Yorkers of 1896–99* (New York: Moses King, 1899); McAdam et al., *History of the Bench and Bar of New York; National Cyclopedia of American Biography* (New York: James T. White and Company, 1898ff); Spengler, *Das Deutsche Element der Stadt New York; Trow's New York City Directory 1895/1896* (New York: Trow Publishing Company, 1895); Daniel Van Pelt, *Leslie's History of the Greater New York* (New York: Arkell Publishing Co., 1898); *Who's Who in New York* (New York: L. R. Hammersly, 1904).

108. Data on millionaires taken from the New York *Tribune* list of 1892; data on the capital of business firms from R. G. Dun & Company *Reference Book* (New York, 1895).

109. Letter, Butler to Low, Feb. 7, 1896, Butler Papers.

110. The *Social Register* and *Trow's New York City Directory* provide addresses.

111. Club memberships from the *Social Register;* "400" memberships from the patriarchs and matrons of the Assembly Balls listed in the *Social Register* and from the lists in the New York *Times,* Feb. 2 & 16, 1892.

112. One member of the Committee of One Hundred was president of the ancestor-worshiping St. Nicholas Club in 1896, and thirty of its bankers and lawyers did belong to the Metropolitan, the more open of the clubs that celebrated wealth. But the conclusion that the Committee of One Hundred was disproportionately drawn from the social elite that celebrated cultural achievement is supported by the fact that of the thirty-two committee members who belonged to the Union or the Metropolitan clubs, twenty-seven also belonged to either the Century or the University. Compare the analysis of club memberships among selected economic and social elites presented above, pp. 65–79.

113. Religious and moral reform membership data from the sources cited in note 107, above, the organizations' annual reports, and the *Charities Directory*.

114. Letters, Butler to Seth Low, Mar. 19, 1896; Butler to Norman Hapgood, June 4, 1896, Butler Papers.

115. Butler dealt with the *Tribune,* the *Times,* and the *Evening Post;* Clark attended to the *Sun,* the *Mail and Express,* and the *Commercial Advertiser.* Mrs. Van Rensselaer, under Butler's direction, went directly to Pulitzer and secured his permission "to let me run the editorial page on that subject and write all the editorials I wished in the *World.*" Documentation of these points is contained in Butler's 1896 correspondence with John E. Milholland, F. L. Murlin, and A. E. Palmer of the *Tribune;* with Joseph B. Bishop of the *Evening Post;* with John C. Clark regarding their difficulties in securing the complete cooperation of the *Sun* and the *Herald,* which persisted in printing news stories favorable to the teachers and community groups opposed to centralization despite their editorial support of the reform; and with Mrs. Van Rensselaer concerning editorials for the *World.* Also relevant is Mrs. Van Rensselaer to Richard Watson Gilder, Apr. 1, 1896, Gilder Papers. Bishop of the *Evening Post,* Francis P. Church of the *Sun,* and Charles R. Miller, chief editor of the *Times,* all joined the Committee of One Hundred, as did Joseph P. Gilder, editor of *The Critic;* Robert U. Johnson, editor of *Century* magazine; Edmund Clarence

Stedman, a frequent contributor to *Harper's, Atlantic, Scribner's,* and *Century* magazines and a *Century* editor; and the publisher Henry Holt. Butler also corresponded frequently with Lillian Betts of the editorial staff of Lyman Abbot's *Outlook* magazine.

116. Letters, Butler to Schurz, Feb. 15, 1895 and Apr. 2, 1896, Butler Papers; Holls to Butler, Feb. 14 & 15, 1895, Holls Papers; *Staats-Zeitung,* Feb. 13 and April 18, 24, 25, 26, & 27, 1895; Apr. 25, 1896. The *New Yorker Zeitung,* a sentimental and sensational sheet, noted the issue only on Apr. 25, 1896, when it praised Mayor Strong for signing the reform bill. The *New Yorker Herald* entirely ignored the matter. The *New Yorker Review* reported only that teachers appeared against the bill at a mayor's hearing, Apr. 19, 1896. All three of these papers were published at 7 Frankfort Street and may have shared the same management. The socialist *New Yorker Volkszeitung* had no time for the matter at all.

117. Clippings in Butler's Scrapbook document these points.

118. Neither the often pro-Tammany *Irish-American,* Patrick Ford's *Irish World and American Industrial Liberator,* nor the clerically edited *New-York Freeman's Journal & Catholic Register* paid any attention at all to the school centralization issue.

119. Letters, Butler to John E. Milholland, Jan. 13 & 30 and Feb. 4 & 5, 1896; Butler to Joseph B. Bishop, Dec. 20, 1895, and Jan. 29, 1896; Butler to John C. Clark, Feb. 5, 1896; Mrs. Van Rensselaer to Butler, Dec. 4, 1895; Butler to Mrs. Van Rensselaer, Jan. 25 and Feb. 3 & 5, 1896, Butler Papers. Mrs. Van Rensselaer wrote Gilder that her editorials in the *World* "have made more visible effect than any other papers and been quoted on the floor of the Senate—think of that!" Apr. 1, 1896, Gilder Papers.

120. James B. Reynolds and Mrs. Van Rensselaer independently testified to Butler's success in making school centralization the great reform measure of 1896. On Mar. 27, 1896, Reynolds wrote to R. W. Gilder, who was traveling in Europe for several months, that "most of the reform strength has been spent for the last two months on the school bill." On April 1 Mrs. Van Rensselaer added that "tenements have seemed a back number this year—schools seem to have taken their place in the public mind." Both letters in the Gilder Papers. Butler brought his press campaign home to the Republican legislators in Albany through letters, clippings, leaflets full of favorable editorials, and commentaries on news articles. Carbons of his letters to Assembly Speaker Hamilton Fish, Assembly Committee on Cities Chairman George C. Austin, Senate Committee on Cities Chairman Nevada N. Stranahan, and State Senators Frank Pavey and Horace White, among others, are in the Butler Papers; leaflets are in the Butler Scrapbook.

121. The *Tribune,* the *World,* the *Times,* the *Journal,* the *Mail and Express,* the *Commercial Advertiser,* and the *Evening Post* helped denounce the Strauss Bill, as did *Harper's Weekly* and *The Critic;* Butler then used statements from all these publications in leaflets printed by the Committee of One Hundred for its lobbying campaign. Butler's letters to key Republican legislators emphasized Strauss's responsibility for the Board of Education bill and insisted on his Tammany connections.

122. Letter, Prentiss to Butler, Dec. 17, 1895, Butler Papers. The last of these proposals would have consolidated authority in the central administration and discouraged the development of viable local districts within the city.

123. Letters, Butler to Prentiss, Dec. 18, 1895; Butler to Hubbell, Dec. 16, 1895. When he learned that Butler would support no plan that preserved the trustees, Hubbell, who believed that insistence on that point would destroy the chance for reform, turned to the *Evening Post* but found that Butler set that paper's editorial position on the matter. Letter, Joseph B. Bishop to Butler, Dec. 20, 1895, Butler Papers.

124. Board of Education of the City of New York, *Journal,* Jan. 16, 1896, pp. 123–27.

125. For Butler's attacks on the trustees as agents of Tammany and therefore corrupt, inefficient, and lacking in devotion to "American" ideals, see his editorials in the *Educational Review* 9 (Jan. 1895):102; 10 (June 1895):99–101; 11 (Mar. 1896):301, 305; (Apr. 1896): 412–13; (May 1896): 512–13. Butler employed similar language in his correspondence with Republican legislators.

126. Letters, Butler to A. A. Wray, Chairman of the Senate Committee on Education, Feb. 6, 1896; Wray to Butler, Feb. 12, 1896; Nevada N. Stranahan to Butler, Feb. 7, 1896; Butler to Stranahan, Feb. 12, 1896, Butler Papers.

127. Letter, Butler to Elihu Root, Mar. 2, 1896, Butler Papers.

128. In addition to Root, Butler sent Frank Goodnow, the expert on municipal administration, and a delegation of women from the PEA to Albany. Details of his campaign are provided in Hammack, "Participation in Major Decisions," pp. 349–64.

129. Letters, Mrs. Van Rensselaer to Richard Watson Gilder, Apr. 1, 1896, Gilder Papers; Thomas C. Platt to Hamilton Fish, Feb. 19, 1896, Fish Papers in private hands. I am indebted to Prof. Richard L. McCormick for this reference.

130. Letters, Caroline S. Spencer to Mrs. Levi P. Morton, Feb. 12, 1896; E. Alma Rainsford, Martha Lincoln Draper, and Cornelia E. Marshall to Mrs. Morton, Feb. 22, 1896; and Stephen H. Olin to Mrs. Morton, Feb. 20, 1896; Morton Papers.

131. Letter, Hubbell to Butler, Feb. 27, 1896, Butler Papers.

132. Letters, Butler to Ainsworth, Feb. 24 and Mar. 5, 1896; Ainsworth to Butler, Mar. 4, 1896, Butler Papers.

133. Letter, Root to Butler, Feb. 29, 1896, Butler Papers. Root's intervention was critical to the effort to secure the support of senators Lexow and Brush, who were skeptical of mugwumps and independent Republicans of the *Evening Post* and New York *Times* varieties.

134. Letter, Butler to Root, Mar. 2, 1896, Butler Papers.

135. Ibid.

136. Letters, Butler to Stranahan, Mar. 2 & 4, 1896; Butler to Hubbell, Mar. 4, 1896; Butler to Joseph B. Bishop, Mar. 4, 1896; Butler to Hamilton Fish, Mar. 4, 1896; Butler to George C. Austin, Mar. 4, 1896; Butler Papers. *Educational Review* 11 (Apr. 1896): 411–13; Mrs. Van Rensselaer told Richard Watson Gilder (letter, Apr. 1, 1896, Gilder Papers) that "the whole success at Albany . . . has been due to Senator Stranahan. . . . He . . . fought for us in more ways than could be discreetly told in print."

137. Butler reviewed the essential provisions of the bill in the *Educational Review* 11 (Apr. 1896):412–13.

138. Letter, Butler to James A. Milne, Mar. 9, 1896, Butler Papers.

139. Letters, Butler to W. H. Merrill of the *World*, Mar. 4, 1896, Butler to Joseph B. Bishop, Mar. 4, 1896, Butler Papers. Attacks on Platt, Butler wrote to Bishop, "embarrass some of the Senators who are supporting our bill vigorously. . . . Inasmuch as they are in a pretty delicate position I am not disposed to regard this suggestion of theirs as wholly unreasonable." Frederick W. Holls also suggested that the school centralization bill would offset the "iniquity" of the Raines liquor control law passed by the Republican legislature in 1896 over the objections of temperance advocates, charity reformers, and Germans; letter, Holls to William Cary Sanger, Mar. 11 & 18, 1896, Holls Papers.

140. Letters, Fish to Butler, Jan. 20, 1896; Butler to Fish, May 9, 1896, Butler Papers.

141. Letter, Fish to Butler, May 8, 1896, Butler Papers.

142. Letters, Butler to Fish, May 9, 1896; Mrs. Van Rensselaer to Butler, Mar. 23, 1896.

143. Letters, Butler to John C. Clark, Mar. 14, 1896; Butler to Low, Mar. 19, 1896; Butler to Pavey, Mar. 17, 1896, Butler Papers. Editorial, *Educational Review* 11 (Apr. 1896): 413.

144. Letters, Butler to George C. Austin, Mar. 6, 1896; Butler to George C. Horton, Mar. 6, 1896; Butler to Nevada N. Stranahan, Mar. 6, 12, & 27, 1896; Butler to Horace White, Mar. 12 & 18, 1896, Butler Papers.

145. Ahearn entered the state senate as a candidate of Abram S. Hewitt's County Democracy in 1888, defeated a Tammany candidate in 1889, and joined Tammany in 1891 only after the rival organization had disintegrated. In 1894 he introduced a pension bill for New York City's teachers, as well as measures for the benefit of the city's policemen and firemen. The New York *Teachers' Magazine* followed the ultimately successful progress of the "Ahearn Bill," designed to raise teachers' salaries according to qualifications, length of service, and duties, through the spring of 1899.

146. In an address at Tammany Hall, Jan. 26, 1897, Thomas C. O'Sullivan (chairman of the Tammany Committee on Resolutions) gave more attention to school centralization than to any other action of the Strong administration except its decision to raise taxes. "The reorganization of the Board of Education," O'Sullivan asserted, "followed by the introduction of new methods, suggested by reformers who know nothing about the practical operation of our public schools, has been a source of embarrassment and dismay to every principal and teacher in the system and materially interferes with the education of the children, who have but a few years to devote to study." In addition, school reorganization

had "encouraged factional strife, fostered bigotry and intolerance and by its appointments packed the Board of Education with a view to race, sectarian and geographical discriminations." Tammany Minutes, 1891–1915, vol. 2 of Kilroe Additions from the New York County Democratic Committee, Kilroe Collection of Tammaniana, Columbia University Library. An anticentralization edition of *Tammany Times* is retained among the Mayors' Papers.

147. Evidence for most of these points has been presented in this chapter, pp. 263–275; Samuel Gompers's telegram to Mayor William L. Strong, Apr. 15, 1896, is in the Mayors' Papers; Rice's opposition is noted in the New York *Sun*, Apr. 19, 1896.

148. Statements from Maclay, Elgas, Coudert, and others are in the Mayors' Papers; Little's remark was reported in the *Commercial Advertiser*, Apr. 16, 1896. A postcard distributed by the opponents to encourage large numbers to attend anti-centralization meetings read "Aristocracy Against the People. Danger to the Public Schools," Mayors' Papers, box 72.

149. Letters, Butler to Rainsford, Apr. 8, 1896; Butler to Root, Apr. 2, 1896; John C. Clark to Butler, Apr. 18, 1896. To make certain that Strong would find no last-minute reason to oppose the measure, Butler arranged for Olin and Hubbell to meet with him to define the financial powers of the Board of Education in such a way as not to encroach upon those of the mayor and the comptroller; letters, Olin to Butler, Mar. 13, 1896; Butler to Olin, Mar. 14, 1896; Butler to Hubbell, and Hubbell to Butler, both Mar. 14, 1896, Butler Papers.

150. New York *Sun*, Apr. 24, 1896; *Educational Review* 11 (May 1896): 512–14.

151. Letter, Hewitt to E. Ellery Anderson, Oct. 24, 1893 (copy), Hewitt Papers, Cooper Union.

152. Detailed discussion of these points appears in Hammack, "Participation in Major Decisions," pp. 368–69.

153. *School* 5 (Feb. 15, 1894):192.

154. Letter, Hewitt to Otto T. Bannard, Sept. 16, 1895 (copy), Hewitt Papers, Cooper Union. Bannard, "The Penny Provident Fund," in William Howe Tolman and William I. Hull, eds., *Handbook of Sociological Information with Especial Reference to New York City*, prepared for the City Vigilance League (New York: The Knickerbocker Press of G. P. Putnam's Sons, 1895), pp. 119–20. Charles Bulkeley Hubbell, *Recollections of an Inconsequential Man* (Brookside Farm, Williamstown, Mass., 1928), p. 36, describes the anti-cigarette campaign of the leading advocate of centralization on the Board of Education. On the anti-alcohol campaign, see letters, Frederick W. Holls to Charles R. Skinner, June 17, 1895; Skinner to Holls, June 22, 1895, Holls Papers; Skinner to Butler, Feb. 5, 1896, Butler Papers.

155. Butler expressed his opposition to state laws mandating the teaching of specific anti-alcohol doctrines in several *Educational Review* editorials in 1894 and 1895.

156. Merle Curti, *The Social Ideas of American Educators*, 2nd ed. (Paterson, N.J.: Littlefield, Adams and Co., 1963), p. 225; *The City Vigilant*, vol. 2 (Apr. 1895), pp. 57–58; Union League Club, Minutes of General Meetings, May 8 and June 12, 1895, Union League Club Archives.

157. Letters, Hewitt to Robert U. Johnson, Aug. 23, 1895; Hewitt to the Rev. T. J. Morgan, Aug. 23, 1895; Hewitt to the Rev. John Lewis Clark, Aug. 20, 1896; and Hewitt to Wilson T. Gill, Oct. 22, 1897; Hewitt Papers, New-York Historical Society.

158. Adler's remark, in a speech to the PEA, was reported in the New York *Herald*, Mar. 28, 1896.

159. Letter, Hewitt to E. Ellery Anderson, Oct. 24, 1893 (copy), Hewitt Papers, Cooper Union.

160. The Committee of Seventy Platform is reprinted in William Howe Tolman, ed., *Municipal Reform Movements in the United States: The Textbook of the New Reformation* (New York: Fleming H. Revell Co., 1895), pp. 86–88.

161. Letters, Butler to Frederick W. Holls, May 22, 1896; Butler to Daniel Coit Gilman, May 1896, Butler Papers.

162. New York *Times*, May 29, 1896.

163. Ibid.

164. Ibid.; letters, Butler to E. H. Peaslee, May 29, 1896, and Butler to N. A. Prentiss, May 9, 1896.

165. New York *Times*, May 29, 1896.
166. Ibid.
167. Ibid.
168. Ibid., July 9, 1896.
169. Ibid., June 25, 1896; letter, Butler to James B. Reynolds, June 19, 1896, Reynolds Papers.
170. New York *Times*, June 25, 1896; letters, Butler to Reynolds, June 19, 1896, Reynolds Papers; Butler to Meleney, June 18, 1896; Butler to N. A. Prentiss, June 12, 1896; Butler to J. B. Bishop, June 19, 1896; Butler Papers, protesting the newspapers' unwillingness to "open up" on Boyer.
171. New York *Times*, June 25, July 9, and Sept. 17, 1896; letter, Butler to Reynolds, June 19, 1896, Reynolds Papers.
172. Letters, Butler to Root, Mar. 6 and May 4, 1896; Butler to Choate, Mar. 6, 1896; Butler to Hamilton Fish, Mar. 6 & 14, 1896; Butler to Holls, Mar. 6, 1896, Butler Papers; Nevada N. Stranahan to Governor Levi P. Morton, May 4, 1896, Morton Papers; Butler to Root, Feb. 29 and May 4, 1896, Root Papers, Library of Congress.
173. Letter, Low to Butler, Sept. 2, 1896, Butler Papers.
174. Letters, Butler to Low, Oct. 19, Nov. 5, and Dec. 2, 1896; Jan. 9 & 13, 1897; Low to Butler, Feb. 6, 1897, Butler Papers. Butler conferred with Olin and with Brooklyn Superintendent of Schools William H. Maxwell before submitting his final set of suggestions to Low, Jan. 13, 1897. Most of the 1896 reforms were preserved in the new charter, but until 1902 each borough retained its own school district. A 1901 charter revision commission appointed by Governor Theodore Roosevelt extended the tightly centralized system to the entire greater city. Cohen, *Progressives and Urban School Reform*, p. 44.
175. *Educational Review*, 15 (Apr. 1898): 414–15.
176. Matthew J. Elgas, "Argument against 'The Compromise School Bill,'" Mayors' Papers.
177. "Protest Against the Compromise Bill," no author or date, but probably by Commissioner Maclay, Mayors' Papers, box 6063, item 46.
178. New York *Teachers' Magazine* (Dec. 1899): 520–23.

CHAPTER 10

1. Louis F. Post and Fred C. Leubuscher, *Henry George's 1886 Campaign: An Account of The George-Hewitt Campaign in the Municipal Election of 1886* (Westport, Conn.: Hyperion Press, Inc., 1976 reprint of 1887 1st ed.), p. 57.
2. Wallace S. Sayre and Herbert Kaufman, *Governing New York City: Politics in the Metropolis* (New York: Russell Sage Foundation, 1960), Robert A. Dahl, *Who Governs? Democracy and Power in an American City* (New Haven: Yale University Press, 1961), and Wallace S. Sayre and Nelson W. Polsby, "American Political Science and the Study of Urbanization," in Philip M. Hauser and Leo F. Schnore, eds., *The Study of Urbanization* (New York: John Wiley & Sons, Inc., 1965), pp. 115–56, report similar power distributions for New Haven and for a wide range of other cities in the 1950s.
3. The most influential application of the power elite thesis to a city is still that of Floyd Hunter, *Community Power Structure: A Study of Decision Makers* (Chapel Hill: The University of North Carolina Press, 1953); sophisticated restatements of the thesis are provided in Peter Bachrach and Morton Baratz, *Power and Poverty: Theory and Practice* (New York: Oxford University Press, 1970), and Matthew Crenson, *The Un-Politics of Air Pollution* (Baltimore: The Johns Hopkins University Press, 1971). One of the best of the several attempts to catalogue the continuously proliferating literature on community power is provided by Willis D. Hawley and James H. Svara, in *The Study of Community Power: A Bibliographic Review* (Santa Barbara, Calif.: ABC–CLIO, Inc., 1972).
4. The existence of a single social hierarchy is asserted or implied in E. Digby Baltzell, *Philadelphia Gentlemen: The Making of a National Upper Class* (Glencoe, Illinois: The Free Press, 1958); Frederic C. Jaher, "Nineteenth Century Elites in Boston and New York," *Journal of Social History* 6 (1972): 32–77; and John N. Ingham, "Rags to Riches Revisited:

The Effect of City Size and Related Factors on the Recruitment of Business Leaders," *The Journal of American History* 63 (1976): 624–27 (on Pittsburgh).

5. Carl V. Harris, *Political Power in Birmingham, 1871–1921* (Knoxville: University of Tennessee Press, 1977); Estelle F. Feinstein, *Stamford in the Gilded Age: The Political Life of a Connecticut Town, 1868–1893* (Stamford: Stamford Historical Society, Inc., 1973).

6. Roy Lubove stressed the contribution of Lawrence Veiller to tenement house reform in *The Progressives and the Slums* (Pittsburgh: University of Pittsburgh Press, 1962), but, as Anthony Jackson makes clear in *A Place Called Home: A History of Low-Cost Housing in Manhattan* (Cambridge: The MIT Press, 1976), other experts also played important roles. For the roles of Gilder, Holls, and deForest as evaluators of tenement reform proposals, see the files on this subject in the papers of Richard Watson Gilder at the New York Public Library, and the following letters in the Frederick W. Holls Papers at Columbia University: to Holls from Gilder, Oct. 15, 1895; from Edward T. Devine, Dec. 15, 1898; from R. W. deForest, Feb. 26, 1899, and Mar. 23 and Apr. 21, 1903; and a long series from Veiller, dated between Dec. 28, 1898 and Oct. 10, 1901; and Holls to Theodore Roosevelt, Jan. 5, 9, & 31, Mar. 9, and Apr. 13, 1901. Mrs. Kinnicutt's work for sanitary reform has been neglected by historians; her contemporary standing is indicated in a letter from Carl Schurz to Richard Watson Gilder, Sept. 25, 1894, Gilder Papers; on the management of the charities, see David M. Schneider and Albert Deutsch, *The History of Public Welfare in New York State, 1867–1940* (Chicago: The University of Chicago Press, 1941), pp. 96–97 and 142–43, and Walter I. Trattner, *Homer Folks: Pioneer in Social Welfare* (New York: Columbia University Press, 1968), pp. 31–55.

7. Evidence on these points has been presented in chaps. 5, 6, and 7 of this volume.

8. Henry James, *The Bostonians* (New York: Random House–Modern Library edition, 1956), p. 279. James is here describing New York City during the late 1870s or early 1880s.

9. Letter, Henry Holt to Francis Lynde Stetson, June 1, 1894, Stetson Papers, Williams College Library. Holt was seeking a contribution from J. P. Morgan's attorney. According to the *Real Estate Record and Builder's Guide* of Dec. 23, 1893, Coit had charged that "the greed of the landlords" contributed to the suffering of those who were thrown out of work by the depression that had begun in 1893. The New York *Times* reported only that Coit had made a Christmastime "remember the poor" speech; but three months later it noted that he had left for a European tour a few days after the settlement society's annual benefit at the Metropolitan Opera. In 1895 a *Times* profile of Coit failed to note his earlier connection with the University Settlement. New York *Times*, Dec. 22, 1893; Mar. 29, 1894; Mar. 24, 1895. The Papers of the University Settlement Society of New York, now at the Wisconsin State Historical Society, contain the society's official minutes for this period, but fail to throw any light on this incident. James B. Reynolds, who would later work so closely with Seth Low in the Citizens' Union and with Nicholas Murray Butler in the school centralization campaign, replaced Coit as Head Worker of the University Settlement in 1894.

10. Richard S. Skolnik, "Civic Group Progressivism in New York City," *New York History* 51 (1970): 354–78.

11. Report of the Union League Club Committee on Political Reform, Jan. 13, 1887. On Jan. 12, 1888, the same committee, then chaired by New York *Tribune* publisher Whitelaw Reid, added that "it was not desirable to diminish the influence of this Club by embracing too many opportunities for urging its opinions upon the community on topics not of the first importance or not carefully considered (with a considerable degree of unanimity) by the Club itself." Both statements are recorded in the manuscript book "Minutes, 1884–1894" still retained in the library of the Union League Club.

12. New York Produce Exchange, "Minutes," New-York Historical Society. Making a related point, Edward M. Shepard quoted with approval the statement "that those who are likely to participate as advisers in the formation of policy, will weaken their influence if they commit [? illegible] themselves to hard and fast lines." Letter, Shepard to Horace E. Scudder, Nov. 23, 1892, Shepard Papers, Columbia University.

13. Letter, C. Augustus Haviland to Edward M. Shepard, Oct. 16. 1894, Shepard Papers. The papers of Shepard, Abram S. Hewitt, Henry deForest Baldwin (William R. Grace's aide), and Republicans James Rockwell Sheffield and Henry L. Stimson contain many references to routine patronage matters through the 1890s. Hewitt intervened on behalf of

former supporters in letters to New York Postmaster Charles W. Dayton, Mar. 7, 1894, and to Deputy Commissioner of Street Cleaning Charles K. Moore, Feb. 2, 1895. Cooper-Hewitt Letterbooks, New-York Historical Society.

14.   See the relevant sketches in *Who's Who in New York City and State* (New York: L. R. Hamersly Company, 1904), and subsequent editions.

15.   The best exploration of these themes for New York is in Samuel T. McSeveney, *The Politics of Depression: Political Behavior in the Northeast, 1893–1896* (New York: Oxford University Press, 1972). Richard L. McCormick, "The Party Period and Public Policy: An Exploratory Hypothesis," *Journal of American History* 66 (1979): 279–98, places the voting studies in perspective.

16.   The best review of northern and western efforts to restrict the franchise by manipulating the ballot at the end of the nineteenth century is Peter H. Argersinger, " 'A Place on the Ballot': Fusion Politics and Antifusion Laws" *American Historical Review* 85 (1980): 287–306. On the use of civil service reform to increase "middle-class" influence over the implementation of municipal policy, see Martin J. Schiesl, *The Politics of Efficiency: Municipal Administration and Reform in America, 1800–1920* (Berkeley: University of California Press, 1977), chap. 1 and 2. Argersinger does not discuss the New York case because it is so much more complex than that of any other state; Schiesl draws heavily on New York for his evidence. For a discussion of the New York evidence in terms of the social distinctions employed here, see chap. 1, in the present volume.

17.   David C. Hammack, "Elite Perceptions of Power in the Cities of the United States, 1880–1900: The Evidence of James Bryce, Moisei Ostrogorski, and their American Informants," *Journal of Urban History* 4 (1978): 372, 373–74, 379, 384. Croker's statements are reported in William L. Riordan, *Plunkitt of Tammany Hall* (New York: E. P. Dutton, 1963), p. 88, and in M. R. Werner, *Tammany Hall* (Garden City, New York: Doubleday, Doran & Co., Inc., 1928), p. 441.

18.   Martin Shefter, "The Emergence of the Political Machine: An Alternative View," in Willis D. Hawley et al., *Theoretical Perspectives on Urban Politics* (Englewood Cliffs, N.J.: Prentice-Hall, Inc., 1976), p. 28.

19.   Robert K. Merton proposed the distinction between "cosmopolitans" and "locals" in his influential essay, "Patterns of Influence: Local and Cosmopolitan Influentials," in Merton, *Social Theory and Social Structure*, rev. ed. (New York: The Free Press, 1957). Samuel P. Hays has sought to apply this distinction to the study of American politics during the Progressive Era in "Political Parties and the Community–Society Continuum," in *The American Party Systems: Stages of Political Development*, William Nisbet Chambers and Walter Dean Burnham, eds. (New York: Oxford University Press, 1967). In New York City, lines of division followed economic interest, ethnic identity, and religious persuasion; if men with more education and greater experience of foreign travel were often grouped against those who lacked such advantages, they were never unified in their position on an issue: and they were often less tolerant of cultural diversity–and in that sense less cosmopolitan–than the city's "local" politicians. New York's status as a major port, its very large foreign-born and second-generation population, and its unusually marked degree of ethnic diversity may well have set it apart from other cities in the years of the present study. Carl V. Harris found that a somewhat similar conflict between a "Liberal Element" and a "Moral Element" characterized the politics of Birmingham, Alabama, in the 1890s; Harris, *Political Power in Birmingham*, pp. 70–79.

20.   On the politics of mayoral nominations, see chap. 4, in this volume. McSeveney, *The Politics of Depression*, pp. 224–25.

21.   On Pingree, see Melvin G. Holli, *Reform in Detroit* (New York: Oxford University Press, 1969).

22.   Thomas Mann, *Buddenbrooks* (New York: Alfred A. Knopf, 1924), pt. 7, chaps. 3 and 4; Lewis Namier, *The Structure of Politics at the Accession of George III* (London: Macmillan and Company, 1929).

23.   For a detailed discussion of these studies, see Hammack, "Problems in the Historical Study of Power," pp. 342–44.

24.   Robert O. Schulze, "The Bifurcation of Power in a Satellite City," in Morris Janowitz, ed., *Community Power Systems* (Glencoe, Ill.: The Free Press, 1961), pp. 19–80.

25.   Walter S. Glazer, "Participation and Power: Voluntary Associations and the Functional Organization of Cincinnati in 1840," *Historical Methods Newsletter* 5 (1972): 151–

68; Edward Pessen, "The Role of the Rich and Elite in Local Voluntary Associations," in Pessen, *Riches, Class, and Power Before the Civil War* (Lexington, Mass.: D. C. Heath and Company, 1973), pp. 251–80.

26. Wallace S. Sayre and Herbert Kaufman, *Governing New York City*, passim.

27. David Rogers, "Community Political Systems: A Framework and Hypothesis for Comparative Studies," in Bert E. Swanson, ed., *Current Trends in Comparative Community Studies* (Kansas City, Mo.: Community Studies, Inc., 1962); Terry N. Clark, "Power and Community Structure: Who Governs, Where, and When?" in Charles Bonjean, Terry Clark, and Robert Lineberry, eds., *Community Politics: A Behavioral Approach* (New York: The Free Press, 1971), pp. 174–87; Michael Aiken, "The Distribution of Community Power: Structural Bases and Social Consequences," in Aiken and Paul E. Mott, eds., *The Structure of Community Power* (New York: Random House, 1970), pp. 487–525; John Walton, "The Vertical Axis of Community Organization and the Structure of Power," in Bonjean et al., *Community Politics*, pp. 188–97; Claire W. Gilbert, "Some Trends in Community Politics: A Secondary Analysis of Power Structure Data from 166 Communities," in Bonjean et al., *Community Politics*, pp. 210–15.

28. Aiken, "The Distribution of Community Power," p. 506.

29. Feinstein, *Stamford in the Gilded Age;* Harris, *Political Power in Birmingham.*

30. The conclusion that power became more widely dispersed in New York City is based largely on a comparison of my findings for the 1890s with those reported in Sayre and Kaufman, *Governing New York City*, which rests heavily (although not explicitly) on the 1950s. Sayre and Kaufman summarize their results in chap. 19. The studies collected in Jewell Bellush and Stephen M. David, eds., *Race and Politics in New York City* (New York: Praeger Publishers, 1971), raise questions about the adequacy of Sayre and Kaufman's analysis for an understanding of the relation between New York City's black population and local decision making. But they describe a series of decisions in which participation was much more widely dispersed than it had been in comparable decisions during the 1890s.

31. See pp. 39–42.

32. Eric E. Lampard, "The Evolving System of Cities in the United States: Urbanization and Economic Development," in Harvey S. Perloff and Lowdon Wingo, Jr., *Issues in Urban Economics* (Baltimore: The Johns Hopkins Press, 1968), pp. 81–139.

33. Ibid., pp. 130–34.

34. Harris, *Political Power in Birmingham*, chap. 12.

35. Sayre and Kaufman, *Governing New York City*, chap. 3.

36. Ibid., pp. 508–10. To move to still later events, the ability of the public employee unions to use their pension funds to save New York City from bankruptcy during the fiscal crisis of the late 1970s reflects the growth of power and wealth in their hands that would have been inconceivable at the end of the nineteenth century.

BIBLIOGRAPHIC ESSAY

The footnotes in this book identify the primary and secondary sources on which it is based, but the literature on the New York metropolitan region is so widely dispersed, and so frequently partial, narrowly purposeful, or contentious, as to call for an extended comment.

DESCRIPTIONS AND GUIDES

As a "great place to visit," New York City has had more than its share of guidebooks since the middle of the nineteenth century. By far the best comprehensive description of the metropolitan region in the nineties is Moses King's extraordinary *Handbook of New York City* (Boston: Moses King, 1893), an illustrated guide to an unusually wide range of social and economic activity. King's portfolio of photographic *Views of New York* (Boston: Benjamin Bloom, Inc., 1896), is similarly comprehensive. Arthur Fremont Rider, *Rider's New York City* (New York: Henry Holt & Co., 1916), provides a marvelously detailed description of the notable buildings on nearly every street in Manhattan. *Appleton's Dictionary of New York And Its Vicinity* (New York: D. Appleton & Co., 1898), and the slightly more democratic competitor issued by a leading newspaper, *The Sun's Guide to New York* (New York: The New York Sun, 1893), provide concise accounts of a wide variety of places and institutions. Karl Baedeker's *United States: With an Excursion Into Mexico* (New York: Da Capo Press, 1971 reprint of 1893 ed.), opens with an extensive discussion of the metropolis.

Arthur Bartlett Maurice's *New York in Fiction* (New York: Dodd, Mead, and Company, 1901, 1917), written for the traveler, evokes the New York City described in the best-selling novels of its time. Theodore Dreiser's *The Color of a Great City* (New York: Boni and Liveright, 1923), is the classic of its genre; a large share of William Dean Howells's *A Hazard of New Fortunes* consists of wryly informed comments on the city's residential neighborhoods and people; Henry James's *The American Scene* (New York: Harper & Bros., 1907), while not always up to the standard of his best fiction, offers striking observations on a remarkably wide range of New York City places—as does his 1886 novel, *The Bostonians*; and Edith Wharton's *Age of Innocence* (New York: Modern Library, 1920), provides a wider but no less schematic view of the city than her other New York novels and stories. Bayrd Still's *Mirror for Gotham: New York as Seen by Contemporaries from Dutch Days to the Present* (New York: New York University Press, 1956) is an indispensable compendium of impressions.

Two classic works are essential to anyone who seeks to visualize New York City in earlier eras: Isaac Newton Phelps Stokes, *The Iconography of Manhattan Island, 1498–1909* (New York: R. H. Dodd, 1915–1928), and John A. Kouwenhoven, *The Columbia Historical Portrait of New York* (Garden City: Doubleday, 1953). Grace M. Mayer's *Once Upon a City: New York From 1890 to 1910 as Photographed by Byron* (New York: Macmillan, 1958) contains the definitive image of Fifth Avenue during the period. *Harper's Weekly* consistently published the best illustrated descriptions of the city and its institutions. James D. McCabe, Jr., *Lights and Shadows of New York Life* (New York: Farrar, Straus & Giroux, 1970 reprint of 1872 edition) and Junius Henry Browne, *The Great Metropolis: A Mirror of New York* (New York: Arno Press, 1975 reprint of 1869 edition), are notable examples of a comprehensive type that had gone out of fashion by the 1890s; Helen Campbell, Thomas W. Knox, and Thomas Byrnes, *Darkness and Daylight; Or, Lights and Shadows of New York Life. A Pictorial Record* (Hartford, Conn.: A. D. Worthington & Co., 1897) confined its attention to those who were the objects of missionary, charitable, or police attention.

New York City's unrivaled business and social services produced equally valuable guidebooks and manuals designed more for residents than for tourists. Among the business guides, the annual *Manual of Statistics*, the *Annual Report* of the Chamber of Commerce of the State of New York, and R. G. Dun and Company, *Reference Book (And Key) Containing Ratings of Merchants, Manufacturers, and Traders Generally, Throughout the United States and Canada* proved most useful. The weekly *Real Estate Record and Builder's Guide* is an invaluable repository of information and incisive editorial commentary on its field. The Charity Organization Society's annual *Charities Directory* provided an increasingly comprehensive and systematic listing of Protestant, and of many Catholic and Jewish, charities; the United Hebrew Charities reported extensively on the latter; William Howe Tolman and William I. Hull, eds., *Handbook of Sociological Information with Especial Reference to New York City* (New York, 1894), and Frank Moss, *The American Metropolis* (three volumes, New York: P. F. Collier, 1897), provide helpful descriptions of many charities and social and religious reform movements. Among the newspaper almanacs, those of the New York *World* and the Brooklyn *Eagle* provided unusually full lists of business, social, fraternal, and religious organizations. The official New York *City Record* annually listed all tax-exempt religious and charitable properties in the city; in December 1902, *Federation* provided a classified analysis of the properties listed in the *City Record* on June 29, 1902.

LIVING CONDITIONS

Two influential and complementary movements of the era, the Protestant campaign to create a closer facsimile of God's kingdom on earth and the increasingly scientific public health and charities efforts, both encouraged the production of systematic social surveys—as well as the compilation of complete lists of charitable and religious agencies and organizations. The most famous of the surveys was certainly Jacob A. Riis's classic, *How The Other Half Lives* (New York, 1890; the 1971 Dover Publications, Inc., reprint contains an excellent selection of Riis's remarkable photographs). But with its impressionistic, sensational, judgmental style *How The Other Half Lives* belonged as much to an older tradition as to the systematic approach of the next twenty years. One of the first of the newer works was *Vital Statistics of New York City and Brooklyn* (Washington, D.C.: U.S. Department of the Interior, Census Office, 1894), an extraordinary volume compiled by public health pioneer John S. Billings, M.D. In this study Billings introduced the "health district," a direct antecedent of the census tract, and made a systematic effort to relate national origin and neighborhood environment data to death rates from a wide variety of diseases for the years between 1885 and 1890.

Housing surveys became reasonably comprehensive and precise somewhat less rapidly than studies of public health problems. Two official publications, the inadequately financed report of the United States Bureau of Labor, *The Slums of Baltimore, Chicago, New York, and Philadelphia* (Washington, D.C., 1894), and the *Report* of the 1894 New York State Tenement House Commitee (Albany, 1894), remained impressionistic (and vivid). Former Charity Organization Society President Robert W. deForest and COS housing specialist Lawrence Veiller brought out the earliest publications that presented housing data with something like the systematic thoroughness employed by Billings in his study of public health: the *First Report of the Tenement House Department of the City of New York, 1902–1903* (two volumes, New York, 1903), and *The Tenement House Problem* (two volumes, New York: Macmillan, 1903). But the first of these was still devoted more to dramatizing problems, advancing its authors' preferred solutions, and promoting the reelection of Mayor Seth Low than to a dispassionate test of hypotheses, and the second, which was also intended to support specific policy proposals, provided extensive data on population density but little on the quality or number of rooms per person.

Employing Presbyterian minister Walter Laidlaw (who had studied at the universities of Toronto and Berlin before receiving an NYU Ph.D. in religion in 1897) as "supervisor and tabulator," the Federation of Churches and Christian Workers in New York City produced a fascinating series of surveys of housing and social conditions, and of religious affiliation and observance, in several areas of Manhattan in the mid- and late nineties. The Federation published the first three of these, beginning with the *First Sociological Canvass: The Fifteenth Assembly District* (New York, 1896), on the middle west side, in pamphlet form, then issued others in the pages of its new quarterly *Federation*, established in 1901. Like Robert Graham's remarkably careful and analytic *Social Statistics of a City Parish* (New York: Church Temperance Society, 1894), these canvasses were intended to support a proposal that the leading denominations put aside their sectarian disputes and act as a single church, dividing the city into geographically discrete "parishes" and maintaining in each at least one Protestant church, as the basis for a systematic effort to meet the city's social and religious needs. The religious and public health reform impulses came together in the Cities Census Committee, whose interim reports were eventually incorporated in Laidlaw's monumental *Population of the City of New York, 1890–1930* (New York: Cities Census Committee, 1932), a work that is richer in detail and more useful for this period than Ira Rosenwaike's more recent *Population History of New York City* (Syracuse: Syracuse University Press, 1972).

The earliest careful studies of the cost of living in New York City are Louise Bolard More, *Wage Earner's Budgets: A Study of Standards and Cost of Living in New York City* (New York: Henry Holt and Company, 1907), and Robert Coit Chapin, *The Standard of Living Among Workingmen's Families in New York City* (New York: Russell Sage Foundation, 1909). Otho G. Cartwright, *The Middle West Side* (New York: Russell Sage Foundation, 1914) and Katherine Anthony, *Mothers Who Must Earn* (New York: Russell Sage Foundation, 1914), two volumes in the West Side Studies series, describe housing and living standards in a section of the city that historians have largely neglected. The *Annual Reports* of the New York State Bureau of Labor Statistics provide a great deal of information on such matters as wage rates, days worked per year, working conditions, and union membership in many skilled and semiskilled crafts, as well as on such related matters as settlement house activity. The United States census published increasingly complete data on the occupations of New Yorkers between 1880 and 1910; the census of occupations for 1910 was particularly detailed. Edward Ewing Pratt's *Industrial Causes of Congestion of Population in New York City* (New York: Columbia University Studies in History, Economics and Public Law, 1911) is a minor classic of systematic social investigation; Thomas Jesse Jones, *The Sociology of a New York City Block* (New York: Columbia University Press, 1904), a curious study of culture and psychology, contains an unusually full report of neighborhood social information.

IMMIGRANT COMMUNITIES

Neither the Protestant commitment to the City of God nor the scientific attack on poverty and disease led early social investigators to pay much attention to immigrant culture or community life. The public health and the religious investigators, and the U.S. Census, did gather a good deal of information on the national origins of the region's residents; Kate Holladay Claghorn made excellent use of this information in her study, "The Foreign Immigrant in New York City," in U.S. Industrial Commission, *Reports*, volume 15 (Washington, D.C., 1901), pp. 449–92. Several of the works issued by the U.S. Immigration Commission, including volume 26, *Immigrants in Cities* (Washington, D.C., 1910), and volume 32, *Immigrants in Schools* (Washington, D.C.), also contain lengthy reports on New York City that are useful despite the anti-new immigrant bias of the commission's work as a whole.

Journalists like Riis and Hutchings Hapgood (*The Spirit of the Ghetto* [New York: Funk & Wagnalls Company, 1902]), convey the flavor of contemporary impressions of immigrant neighborhoods; novelist Abraham Cahan's *The Rise of David Levinsky* (New York, 1971) provides an invaluable inside view. But Moses Rischin's richly detailed *The Promised City: New York's Jews, 1870–1914* (Cambridge, Mass.: Harvard University Press, 1962), supplied the first and on the whole still the most satisfactory account of a New

York City immigrant community as a whole. Three later works, Ronald Sander's *The Downtown Jews: Portraits of an Immigrant Generation* (New York: Harper & Row, 1966), Arthur A. Goren's sophisticated study of the politics of communal organization, *New York Jews and the Quest for Community* (New York: Columbia University Press, 1970), and Irving Howe's literary *The World of Our Fathers* (New York: Harcourt, Brace, Jovanovich, 1976), are all excellent. Arthur M. Silver's 1964 Yeshiva University Ph. D. dissertation, "Jews in the Political History of New York City, 1865–1897," describes its subject with an extraordinary wealth of detail. Barry E. Supple's article, "A Business Elite: German-Jewish Financiers in Nineteenth Century New York," *Business History Review* 31 (1957): 143–178, remains the most valuable publication on the city's German Jews.

Apart from two comparative works, other immigrant groups have received much less attention than the Jews. Nathan Glazer and Daniel Patrick Moynihan's brilliant and influential *Beyond The Melting Pot: The Negroes, Puerto Ricans, Jews, Italians, and Irish of New York City* (Cambridge: The MIT Press, 1963), reaches back to the nineteenth century for material but ignores the Germans, who constituted the largest single immigrant group in the 1880s and 1890s. In *The Golden Door: Italian and Jewish Mobility in New York City, 1880–1915* (New York: Oxford University Press, 1976), Thomas Kessner confronts almost intractable statistical problems with considerable success in providing the only notable "new" social history of occupational mobility in New York City. Two historians have recently opened up intriguing approaches to the Irish: Eric Foner, "Class, Ethnicity, and Radicalism in the Gilded Age: The Land League and Irish-America," *Marxist Perspectives* I (1978):6–55; and Michael Gordon, "Irish Immigrant Culture and the Labor Boycott in New York City, 1880–1920," in Richard Ehrlich, ed., *Immigrants in Industrial America, 1850–1920* (Charlottesville, Virginia: University of Virginia Press, 1977):111–122. James S. Lapham, "The German-Americans of New York City, 1860–1890," St. John's University Ph.D. dissertation, became available only after work on this book was completed. Ferdinand C. Valentine's *Gotham and the Gothamites* (London: Field & Tuer, 1887), published under the pseudonym Heinrich Oscar von Karlstein, persuasively purports to offer the impressions of a sophisticated German visitor to the city. Neither the Federation of Churches nor the authors of the West Side Studies sought to identify viable immigrant communities, but so far as their information may be believed, the mixed Irish and German areas on the west side were too heterogeneous to support a highly developed community life. There is no equivalent, for the late nineteenth century, of Robert Ernst's pioneering *Immigrant Life in New York City, 1825–1863* (New York: Columbia University Press, 1949), of Jay Dolan's *The Immigrant Church: New York's Irish and German Catholics, 1815–1865* (Baltimore: The Johns Hopkins University Press, 1975), or of Ronald H. Bayor's *Neighbors in Conflict: The Irish, Germans, Jews and Italians of New York City* (Baltimore: The Johns Hopkins University Press, 1978). But all three of these excellent books throw some light on the cultural history of the city in the intervening years.

SOCIAL ELITES

Contemporary writings about the social life of the well-to-do largely ignored the German gentiles, the German Jews, and the Catholics, and in focusing on the Anglo-Protestant social elites emphasized moral disapproval of snobbery, ridicule of the nouveau riche, techniques for the social climber, or the social pretensions of the writer's own group. Each of these emphases encouraged contemporary writers—and later historians—to believe that the city sustained a single social hierarchy. Although his own work is not entirely free of this assumption, Frederick C. Jaher provides the best introduction to these writings in his two articles, "Nineteenth-Century Elites in Boston and New York," *Journal of Social History*, 6 (1972): 32–77, and "Style and Status: High Society in Late Nineteenth-Century New York," in Jaher, ed., *The Rich, The Well Born, and the Powerful: Elites and Upper Classes in History* (Urbana: University of Illinois Press, 1973). Two books with a non-New York focus, E. Digby Baltzell, *Philadelphia Gentlemen: The Making of a National Upper Class* (Glencoe, Illinois: The Free Press, 1959), and Stow Persons, *The Decline of Gentility* (New York: Columbia University Press, 1973), provide stimulating perspectives. Stephen Birmingham's superficial *"Our Crowd": The Great Jewish Families of New York* (New York: Harper & Row, 1967), offers the best available introduction to the social world of the German-Jewish economic elite.

The most important studies of the attitudes of urban social and economic elites at the end of the nineteenth and the beginning of the twentieth centuries frequently refer to New York City: Alan Pendleton Grimes's careful account of *The Political Liberalism of the New York Nation* (Chapel Hill: The University of North Carolina Press, 1953); Richard Hofstadter's brilliant and influential *The Age of Reform: From Bryan to FDR* (New York: Alfred A. Knopf, 1955); John G. Sproat, *"The Best Men": Liberal Reformers in the Gilded Age* (New York: Oxford University Press, 1968); Robert Kelley, *The Transatlantic Persuasion: The Liberal-Democratic Mind in the Age of Gladstone* (New York: Alfred A. Knopf, 1969); John Tomsich, *A Genteel Endeavor: American Culture and Politics in the Gilded Age* (Stanford: Stanford University Press, 1971); and Geoffrey Blodgett's thoughtful essays, "Reform Thought and the Genteel Tradition," in H. Wayne Morgan, ed., *The Gilded Age: A Reappraisal* (Syracuse: Syracuse University Press, revised and enlarged edition, 1970), and "A New Look at the Gilded Age: Politics in a Cultural Context," in Daniel W. Howe, ed., *Victorian America* (Philadelphia: University of Pennsylvania Press, 1976). Edmond S. Ions, *James Bryce and American Democracy* (London: Macmillan, 1968), provides a very useful narrative of Bryce's travels in the United States. The best account of Ostrogorski's life and work is Rodney Barker and Xenia Howard-Johnson, "The Politics and Political Ideas of Moisei Ostrogorski," *Political Studies* 22 (1975):415–29. For my own discussion of these writers and of elite opinion in several cities in addition to New York, see David C. Hammack, "Elite Perceptions of Power in the Cities and Towns of the United States, 1889–1900: The Evidence of James Bryce, Moisei Ostrogorski, and Their American Informants," *Journal of Urban History* 4 (1978): 363–96.

None of these studies of elite attitudes takes full account of religious influences during the period. The best account of the theology that encouraged Protestants to seek to create the City of God on earth is William R. Hutchison, *The Modernist Impulse in American Protestantism* (Cambridge, Mass.: Harvard University Press, 1976), but this book stresses the impact of the modernist impulse on foreign policy, not on urban affairs. The standard surveys of the social gospel, Charles H. Hopkins, *The Rise of the Social Gospel in American Protestantism* (New Haven: Yale University Press, 1940), and Henry F. May, *Protestant Churches and Industrial America* (New York: Harper, 1949), emphasize the role of the clergy. Two valuable articles by Clyde Griffen, "Rich Laymen and Early Social Christianity," *Church History* 36 (1967): 3–23, and "Christian Socialism Instructed by Gompers," *Labor History* 12 (1971):195–213, explore the effects of the modernist impulse on the urban policies favored by New York Episcopalians and other Protestants. Gregory H. Singleton's essay, "Protestant Voluntary Organizations and the Shaping of Victorian America," *American Quarterly* 28 (1975): 549–60, raises some intriguing questions about social patterns. John Webb Pratt's excellent *Religion, Politics, and Diversity: The Church-State Theme in New York History* (Ithaca: Cornell University Press, 1967), describes the religious controversies of the 1890s. Paul S. Boyer, *Urban Masses and Moral Order in America, 1820–1920* (Cambridge, Mass.: Harvard University Press, 1978), emphasizes social rather than religious concerns.

Among the most useful contemporary sources are William S. Rainsford's *The Story of a Varied Life* (Garden City, New York: Doubleday, Page & Co., 1922), by the wonderfully outspoken rector of St. George's Episcopal Church, and the religious weeklies, including the Episcopalian *Churchman*, the Baptist *Examiner*, and the Congregationalist *Independent*. Allen F. Davis, *Spearheads for Reform: The Social Settlements and the Progressive Movement, 1890–1914* (New York: Oxford University Press, 1967), reflects the views of settlement house workers but not their trustees. In the absence of a good history of the religious and other charitable activities of late nineteenth-century New York, the best introduction to the subject is provided by Walter I. Trattner, *Homer Folks: Pioneer in Social Welfare* (New York: Columbia University Press, 1968); David M. Schneider and Albert Deutsch, *The History of Public Welfare in New York State, 1867–1940* (Chicago: The University of Chicago Press, 1941); William Rhinelander Stewart, *The Philanthropic Work of Josephine Shaw Lowell* (New York, 1905); and the contemporary periodical, *Charities*. There is no equivalent, for New York, of Nathan I. Huggins, *Protestants Against Poverty: Boston's Charities, 1870–1900* (Westport, Conn.: Greenwood Press, 1971). Everett P. Wheeler provides an incisive analysis of the significance of charitable activities in "The Unofficial Government of Cities," *Atlantic Monthly* 86 (1900):375.

THE ECONOMY AND THE ECONOMIC ELITES

New York City's economy has often attracted scholarly scrutiny, especially during periods when it appeared to be ailing. Robert G. Albion's *The Rise of New York Port, 1815–1860* (New York: Charles Scribner's Sons, 1939) was the first noteworthy historical approach to its subject; its conclusions are largely supported by the essays in David T. Gilchrist, ed., *The Growth of the Seaport Cities, 1790–1825* (Charlottesville, Virginia: University of Virginia Press, 1967). Benjamin H. Bechhart, ed., *The New York Money Market* (four volumes, New York: Columbia University Press, 1932–34), describes the financial institutions of the metropolis; Fritz Redlich's engaging study, *The Molding of American Banking: Men and Ideas* (New York: Johnson Reprint Corporation, 1968), and Vincent P. Carosso's more recent *Investment Banking in America: A History* (Cambridge, Mass.: Harvard University Press, 1970), place the New York institutions in their national context. Alfred D. Chandler, Jr., "Patterns of Railroad Finance, 1830–1850," *Business History Review* 28 (September, 1954): 248–263, describes New York's triumph over Boston and Philadelphia in the competition to become the national financial center; Thomas R. Navin and Marion V. Sears, "The Rise of a Market for Industrial Securities, 1887–1902," *Business History Review* XXIX (1955): 105–38, pursue later developments in that story. Glenn Porter and Harold C. Livesay's *Merchants and Manufacturers: Studies in the Changing Structure of Nineteenth Century Marketing* (Baltimore: The Johns Hopkins University Press, 1971), and Alfred D. Chandler, Jr.'s magisterial *The Visible Hand: The Managerial Revolution in American Business* (Cambridge, Mass.: Harvard University Press, 1977), provide the essential background for an understanding of New York's place in the evolving business system. Allan Nevins's *John D. Rockefeller: The Heroic Age of American Enterprise* (New York: Charles Scribner's Sons, 1940), Alfred D. Chandler, Jr.'s *Henry Varnum Poor, Business Editor, Analyst, and Reformer* (Cambridge, Mass.: Harvard University Press, 1956), and Joseph Frazier Wall's *Andrew Carnegie* (New York: Oxford University Press, 1970), are, in their very different ways, the best of the biographies of the city's leading businessmen. Ralph M. Hower's *History of Macy's of New York, 1858–1919* (Cambridge: Harvard University Press, 1943) is far broader than most works on a single firm. Jesse E. Pope, *The Clothing Industry in New York* (Columbia, Missouri: University of Missouri Studies in History, 1905), remains the best introduction to its subject.

Richard P. Morgan, *The Decline of Commerce of the New York Port* (Urbana, Illinois: University of Illinois Press, 1901), and E. M. Patterson, "Certain Changes in New York's Position as a Financial Center," *Journal of Political Economy* 21 (1913), reflected a widespread interest in the city's economic problems at the time they were written. Several of the volumes commissioned by the Regional Plan Association of New York in 1960 looked back over the city's economic history from a period of renewed concern: Benjamin Chinitz, *Freight and the Metropolis: The Impact of America's Transport Revolutions on the New York Region*, Robert M. Lichtenberg, *One-Tenth of a Nation: National Forces in the Economic Growth of the New York Region*, Sidney M. Robbins and Nestor E. Terleckyj, *Money Metropolis: A Locational Study of Financial Activities in the New York Region* (all published in Cambridge by Harvard University Press, 1960). Three studies of surpassing value for an understanding of the changing relationship between the New York metropolitan region and the other regions of the United States are Eric E. Lampard, "The Evolving System of Cities in the United States: Urbanization and Economic Development," in Harvey S. Perloff and Lowdon Wingo, Jr., eds., *Issues in Urban Economics* (Baltimore: The Johns Hopkins University Press, 1968): 81–139; Allan R. Pred, *Urban Growth and the Circulation of Information: The United States System of Cities, 1790–1840* (Cambridge, Mass.: Harvard University Press, 1973); and Michael P. Conzen, "The Maturing Urban System of the United States, 1840–1910," *Annals of the American Association of Geographers* 67 (1977): 88–108.

Historians have neglected the history of New York's business organizations. The best study of their activities in the late nineteenth century is Lee Benson, *Merchants, Farmers, and Railroads: Railroad Regulation and New York Politics, 1850–1887* (Cambridge: Harvard University Press, 1955), which emphasizes the role of the New-York Board of Transportation. Arnold J. Bornfriend, "The Business Group in Metropolis: The Commerce and Industry Association of New York," (Ph.D. diss., Columbia University, 1967), describes the early history of the Merchants' Association. Joseph B. Bishop's sponsored, commemorative *Chronicle of One Hundred and Fifty Years: The Chamber of Commerce of the State of New York* (New York: Charles Scribner's Sons, 1918), remains the only introduction to the most important such organization in the 1880s and 1890s; the Chamber's *Annual Reports* are far more informative.

New York City's professions have received much less historical attention than its economic activities. James Willard Hurst's pathbreaking work, *The Growth of American Law: The Law Makers* (Boston: Little, Brown, & Co., 1950), suggests numerous lines of analysis that still await pursuit. R. T. Swaine, *The Cravath Firm* (New York, 1946), an insider's view, remains the best account of the evolution of the Wall Street law firm; George Martin, *Causes and Conflicts: The Centennial History of the Association of the Bar of the City of New York, 1870–1970* (Boston: Houghton, Mifflin Co., 1970), is an unusually useful commemorative volume. Erwin O. Smigel, *The Wall Street Lawyer: Professional or Organization Man?* (New York: The Free Press of Glencoe, 1964) and Jerome Carlin, *Lawyers' Ethics: A Survey of the New York City Bar* (New York: Russell Sage Foundation, 1966) are sophisticated studies of the more recent period that throw some light on earlier decades; Jerold S. Auerbach's deeply engaged *Unequal Justice: Lawyers and Social Change in Modern America* (New York: Oxford University Press, 1976), reviews tendencies since the turn of the century.

Although the history of labor in New York is more intricate and of greater political significance than that of the professions, it has suffered a similar neglect. Three major works do provide a good introduction to the Jewish unions: Rischin's *The Promised City*, Melvyn Dubofsky's incisive *When Workers Organize: New York City in the Progressive Era* (Amherst: The University of Massachusetts Press, 1968), and John H. M. Laslett's *Labor and the Left: A Study of Socialist and Radical Influences in the American Labor Movement, 1881–1924* (New York: Basic Books, 1970), chapter 4. Samuel Gompers's classic statement, *Seventy Years of Life and Labor: An Autobiography* (New York: E. P. Dutton & Co., 1925) provides much detail on the New York labor scene in the 1870s and 1880s; John R. Commons et al., *History of Labor in the United States* (four volumes, New York: Macmillan, 1918–1935), frequently refers to developments in the metropolis. Also useful are Joel Seidman, *The Needle Trades* (New York: Farrar & Rinehart, 1942); Benjamin Stolberg, *Tailor's Progress: The Story of a Famous Union and the Men Who Made It* (New York: Doubleday, 1944); and Melech Epstein's readable though far from definitive *Jewish Labor in U.S.A.* (two volumes, New York: Trades Union Sponsoring Committee, 1950–53). Eric Foner and Michael Gordon have written important articles, noted above, on Irish workers in New York; Fergus MacDonald, *The Catholic Church and the Secret Societies in the United States* (New York: The United States Catholic Historical Society, 1946), and Henry J. Browne, *The Catholic Church and the Knights of Labor* (Washington, D.C.: The Catholic University of America Press, 1949), throw some light on New York events. The literature contains no references to historical studies of the city's German, Bohemian, Scandinavian, or British workers or their unions, despite their considerable numbers and political importance.

POLITICS: THE TRADITIONAL REFORM PERSPECTIVE

The perspective of self-proclaimed late nineteenth-century political reformers—a perspective compounded of devotion to a Kingdom of God Protestantism (and a concomitant scepticism if not hostility toward Catholicism), dedication to the rights of property, loyalty to the all-but-outmoded antiparty sentiments of eighteenth-century Anglo-America, and a self-confident Patrician Elitist belief in the legitimacy of rule by a cultivated moral, social, and economic elite—has cast a long shadow over the voluminous literature on New York

City's politics. The late nineteenth-century reform perspective shaped nearly all of the works on the city's politics that were published at the time. Among the most important of these are Samuel J. Tilden, *The New York City Ring, Its Origin, Maturity, and Fall* (New York: T. Polhemus, 1873); the City Reform Club's annual *Record of Assemblymen and Senators from the City of New York in the Legislature of 1886* (New York, continued through the volume for 1894); William Mills Ivins, "Municipal Government," *Political Science Quarterly* 2 (1887): 291–312, and his intriguingly detailed *Machine Politics and Money in Elections in New York City* (New York, 1887; Arno Press reprint, 1970)—a close political associate of independent Democratic mayor William R. Grace in the mid- and late 1880s, Ivins ran for mayor himself on the Republican ticket in 1905; A.C. Bernheim, "Party Organizations and Their Nominations to Public Office in New York City," *Political Science Quarterly* 3 (1888):99–122, a valuable description and analysis of the actual working of party primaries; the New York *Evening Post's Tammany Biographies* (1890; second edition 1894)—hostile portraits of Tammany's less reputable leaders, published in support of anti-Tammany candidates for mayor; John Paul Bocock, "The Irish Conquest of Our Cities," *The Forum* (1894):180–190; E. L. Godkin's essays, notably "Problems of Municipal Government," collected in Godkin's *Problems of Modern Democracy*, edited with a valuable introduction by Morton Keller (Cambridge, Mass.: Harvard University Press, 1966); the great journalist's letters, industriously gathered from widely scattered locations but unevenly edited by William M. Armstrong, *The Gilded Age Letters of E. L. Godkin* (Albany, New York: State University of New York, 1974); Albert Shaw, "The Municipal Problem and Greater New York," *The Atlantic Monthly* 79 (1897): 733–48; Simon Sterne's *laissez-faire* critique of the Strong administration, "The Reconquest of New York by Tammany," *The Forum* (1898):553–67; John DeWitt Warner's shrewd but not entirely reliable critique of *laissez-faire* influence in the 1897 campaign, "Municipal Betterment in New York City Elections," *Municipal Affairs* 5 (1901):625–40; the remarkably clear-eyed report of P. Tecumseh Sherman, *Inside the Machine: Two Years in the Board of Aldermen, 1898–1899* (New York, 1901); and Lincoln Steffens, *The Shame of the Cities* (New York: McClure, Phillips, 1904), a book whose readability and intelligence compensate for its doubtful reliability as regards statements of fact.

Several programmatic and celebratory statements define the acknowledged objectives and campaign themes of successive New York City reform movements—and through their titles reflect their Protestant religious basis: The Committee of One Hundred, *Plan for the Organization of the Democratic Party of the City and County of New York* (New York, 1881); The Reverend Leighton Williams, et al., *Municipal Program Leaflets* (New York, 1894); E. L. Godkin, *The Triumph of Reform: November 6, 1894* (New York: Souvenir Publishing Company, 1895); William Howe Tolman, ed., *Municipal Reform Movements in the United States: The Textbook of the New Reformation* (New York: Fleming H. Revell Co., 1895); Citizens' Union of New York, *The City for the People! Campaign Book of the Citizens' Union* (New York, 1897, 1901), and *The City for the People! The Best Administration New York Ever Had: Campaign Book of the Citizens' Union* (New York: 1903); Milo T. Bogard, ed., *The Redemption of New York* (New York: R. F. McBreen & Sons, 1902), on Seth Low's 1901 mayoral victory; Alfred Hodder, *A Fight for the City* (New York: Macmillan, 1903) on the 1901 William Travers Jerome campaign for district attorney; and a special number of *Federation,* entitled *The Redemption of our City,* January 1902, containing the numerous papers presented at a conference on "the religious condition of our city at the beginning of the Twentieth Century and in particular to record the progress of religious forces" since 1888. The periodical and occasional publications of several organizations also reflect the range of reform perspectives: the *Monthly Bulletin,* 1895ff, of the City Club of New York, as well as the publications of the Confederation of Good Government Clubs and of the individual clubs, issued mostly in 1895 and 1896; the City Vigilance League's *City Vigilant,* 1894ff; *Federation,* 1901–1905; the *Annual Report* of the Reform Club, and the excellent quarterly sponsored by that organization's Committee on Municipal Reform, *Municipal Affairs,* 1896–1901. John D. Townsend's *New York in Bondage* (New York, 1901) is an anti-Tammany tract that was written in the reform mode but was designed to serve an immediate tactical partisan purpose. Matthew P. Breen, *Thirty Years of New York Politics Up-to-Date* (New York, 1899), similarly employed the reform mode to rebuke officials and organizations that had failed to speed the development of the author's home area, the Annexed District (later the south Bronx).

Relying heavily on the reformers' observations and campaign literature, and identifying themselves with the cause, the authors of the era's most influential treatises on municipal government generally offered fuller, more systematic statements of the reform perspective. See in particular Worthington C. Ford, *The American Citizens' Manual* (New York, 1882); Hermann Eduard von Holst, *The Constitutional Law of the United States* (Chicago: A. B. Mason, 1887), section 102; James Bryce, *The American Commonwealth* (London and New York: Macmillan, 1887); Woodrow Wilson, *The State* (Boston: D. C. Heath & Co., 1889), sections 1029–1040; Simon Sterne, "The Administration of American Cities," in John J. Lalor, ed., *Cyclopedia of Political Science, Political Economy, and of the Political History of the United States* (New York: Maynard, Merrill & Co., 1895), vol. 1, pp. 460–68; and Dorman B. Eaton, *The Government of Municipalities* (New York: Macmillan, 1899). Albert Shaw's two substantial studies, *Municipal Government in Continental Europe* and *Municipal Government in Great Britain* (both New York: The Century Co., 1895), contain a good deal of incidental comment on New York as well as other American cities.

The reform perspective further dominated a succession of interpretations of late nineteenth-century New York politics, written after the event. The first of these, memorials and biographies by and about participants, must be read in every sense as primary sources: Edward Cary, *George William Curtis* (Boston: Houghton Mifflin, 1895); John Foord, *The Life and Public Services of Simon Sterne* (New York: Macmillan, 1903); Foord, *The Life and Public Services of Andrew H. Green* (New York: Doubleday, Page & Co., 1913); Jacob A. Riis, *The Making of an American* (New York: Macmillan, 1904); John Bigelow, ed., *Letters and Literary Memorials of Samuel Jones Tilden* (New York: Harper & Brothers, 1908); Bigelow, *Retrospections of an Active Life* (New York: The Baker & Taylor Co., 1909); William Adams Brown, *Morris Ketchum Jesup: A Character Sketch* (New York: Charles Scribner & Sons, 1910); Theodore Roosevelt, *An Autobiography* (New York: Macmillan, 1913); Jeremiah Augustus Johnson, *The Life of a Citizen: At Home and in Foreign Service* (New York: The Vail Ballou Press, 1915); De Alva Stanwood Alexander, *Four Famous New Yorkers: The Political Careers of Cleveland, Platt, Hill, and Roosevelt* (New York: Henry Holt & Co., 1923); Benjamin R. C. Low, *Seth Low* (New York: G. P. Putnam's Sons, 1925); Charles Bulkeley Hubbell, *Recollections of an Inconsequential Life* (New York: Charles Scribner's Sons, 1939); Nicholas Murray Butler, *Across the Busy Years: Recollections and Reflections* (New York: Charles Scribner's Sons, 1939); Richard W. G. Welling, *As the Twig is Bent* (New York: G. P. Putnam's Sons, 1942). Lincoln Steffens's *Autobiography* (New York: Harcourt Brace, 1931) is in a class by itself.

These works were immediately succeeded by a series of books that utilized the reform view to shape highly selective histories of New York politics designed for contemporary anti-Tammany or local color purposes: Gustavus Myers, *The History of Tammany Hall* (New York: Boni & Liveright, 1901), a work that fails to note the significance of the County Democracy or to acknowledge reformers' editing of its text; Denis Tilden Lynch, *Boss Tweed: The Story of a Grim Generation* (New York, Alfred A. Knopf, 1927); Herbert Asbury, *The Gangs of New York* (New York: Alfred A. Knopf, 1927); W. R. Werner, *Tammany Hall* (New York: Doubleday, 1928); and Roy V. Peel, *The Political Clubs of New York* (New York: G. P. Putnam's Sons, 1935). A related genre consists of books that defend major political leaders from reform critiques: Alfred Henry Lewis's idealized *Richard Croker* (New York: Life Publishing Company, 1901); Thomas C. Platt's revealing *Autobiography*, compiled and edited by Louis J. Lang (New York: B. W. Dodge & Co., 1910); Robert McElroy's authorized *Levi Parsons Morton: Banker, Diplomat, and Statesman* (New York: G. P. Putnam's Sons, 1930); Theodore Lothrop Stoddard's *Master of Manhattan: The Life of Richard Croker* (New York: Longman's, 1931); Louis Heaton Pink's *Gaynor: The Tammany Mayor Who Swallowed the Tiger* (New York: The International Press, 1931); and James McGurrin's *Bourke Cochran: A Free Lance in Politics* (New York: Charles Scribner's Sons, 1958).

Relying on these sources and sharing their assumptions, the first generation of urban historians enthusiastically embraced the reform perspective. Albert Bushnell Hart set an early example in "The Rise of American Cities," in *The Quarterly Journal of Economics* (January 1890): 129–57. The most influential of his successors were Arthur M. Schlesinger, *The Rise of the City* (New York: Macmillan, 1933), and, especially for New York, Allan Nevins, through his many biographies of the city's institutions and leaders: *The Evening Post: A Century of Journalism* (New York: Boni and Liveright, 1922), on the paper that had employed Godkin and Steffens as well as himself; *Grover Cleveland: A Study in Courage* (New York: Dodd, Mead and Company, 1932); *Abram S. Hewitt, With Some Account of Peter Cooper* (New York: Harper & Brothers, 1935); *John D. Rockefeller* (1940); and with John A. Kraut, *The Greater City: New York, 1898–1948* (New York: Columbia University Press, 1948). Nevins's version of the reform perspective in turn exerted a heavy influence on a number of Columbia University Ph.D. dissertations published in the 1930s and 1940s: Alexander C. Flick, *Samuel Jones Tilden: A Study in Political Sagacity* (New York: Dodd, Mead, and Company, 1939); Harold C. Syrett, *The City of Brooklyn, 1865–1898* (New York: Columbia University Press, 1948); Samuel A. Pleasants, *Fernando Wood of New York* (New York: Columbia University Press, 1948) on a politician who did not clearly follow either a "reform" or a "Tammany" pattern; Mark D. Hirsch, *William C. Whitney, Modern Warwick* (New York: Dodd, Mead, and Company, 1948)—a richly detailed study of a very complex man that comes closer than most comparable books to an independent view; E. McClung Fleming, *R. R. Bowker, Militant Liberal* (Norman: University of Oklahoma Press, 1952); and Frederick Shaw, *History of the New York City Legislature* (New York: Columbia University Press, 1954). Several unpublished studies, cast in the same mold, review some of the notable careers or events of the period: Jack Gabel, "Edward M. Shepard, Militant Reformer" (New York University Ph.D. dissertation, 1967); George F. Knerr, "The Mayoral Administration of William L. Strong" (New York University Ph.D. dissertation, 1957); Robert H. Mucigrosso, "Richard W. G. Welling: A Reformer's Life" (Columbia University Ph.D. dissertation, 1966); and Lurton W. Blassingame, "Frank J. Goodnow and the American City" (New York University Ph.D. dissertation, 1968). Limited though they are by their point of view, these works do devote a good deal of attention to New York City affairs during the 1880s and 1890s; the biographies and memoirs of such notable New York political figures as Joseph H. Choate, Elihu Root, Henry L. Stimson, Oscar S. Straus, Bourke Cochran, and even Theodore Roosevelt treat the city briefly as a backdrop to careers of national significance.

POLITICS: THE HOFSTADTER ERA

Richard Hofstadter sought more to explain than to reexamine the accepted distinctions between reformers and practical politicians in *The Age of Reform*; a number of later works, several of which employ a sophistication and irony comparable to Hofstadter's, retain the reformer/politician framework while enriching our understanding of the period. The most useful of these works are Albert Fein, "New York City Politics from 1897–1903: A Study in Political Party Leadership" (Columbia University Master's Essay, 1954); David M. Ellis, James A. Frost, Harold C. Syrett, and Harry J. Carman, *A Short History of New York State* (Ithaca: Cornell University Press, 1957); Steven C. Swett, "The Test of a Reformer: A Study of Seth Low, New York City Mayor, 1902–1903," *New-York Historical Society Quarterly* 44 (1960):5–41; Ari Hoogenboom, *Outlawing the Spoils: A History of the Civil Service Reform Movement, 1865–1883* (Urbana: University of Illinois Press, 1961); J. Joseph Huthmacher, "Charles Evans Hughes and Charles Francis Murphy: The Metamorphosis of Progressivism," *New York History* 44 (1965):28–34; Marvin G. Weinbaum, "New York County Republican Politics, 1897–1922: The Quarter Century After Municipal Consolidation," *New-York Historical Society Quarterly* 50 (1966):62–94; Alfred Connable and Edward Silberfarb's journalistic but comprehensive *Tigers of Tammany: Nine Men Who Ran New York* (New York: Holt, Rinehart and Winston, 1967); Robert F. Wesser, *Charles Evans Hughes: Politics and Reform in New York, 1905–1910* (Ithaca: Cornell University Press, 1967); Elsie R. Koetl's collective biography of the Committee of Seventy, "New York in 1894: Case Study of a Reform Movement" (Columbia University Master's Essay, 1967); Gerald W. McFarland, "Partisan of Non-Partisanship: Dorman B. Eaton and the Genteel Reform Tradition," *Journal of American History* 54 (1968):3–22; Robert Mucigrosso, "The City Reform Club: A Study in Late Nineteenth Century Reform," *New-York Historical Society Quarterly* 52 (1968):235–54; Matthew T. Downey, "Grover Cleveland and Abram S. Hewitt: The Limits of Factional Consensus," *New-York Historical Society Quarterly* 54 (1970):223–40; Gerald Kurland, *Seth Low: The Reformer in an Urban and Industrial Age* (New York: Twayne Publishers, 1971); Jeremy P. Felt, "Vice Reform as a Political

Technique: The Committee of Fifteen in New York, 1900–1901," *New York History* 54 (1973): 24–51; and Lloyd J. Graybar, *Albert Shaw of the Review of Reviews: An Intellectual Biography* (Lexington: University of Kentucky Press, 1974). The two most concise and influential restatements of the reform perspective are Elting E. Morison's Appendix III to his model edition of the invaluable *Letters of Theodore Roosevelt* (Cambridge, Mass.: Harvard University Press, 1951), vol. 2, pp. 1478–83; and Arthur Mann's Introduction to his edition of William L. Riordan, *Plunkitt of Tammany Hall* (New York: E. P. Dutton, 1963), pp. vii–xxii.

The late nineteenth-century reform view stressed the battle between good reformers and bad politicos, denying that interest-group conflict—especially labor, Catholic, or political faction interest-group conflict—over municipal policy could be legitimate, or ought to be the object of serious inquiry. The brevity of the list of useful books on the impact of labor in New York City politics testifies to the reform view's pervasive and durable impact: Louis F. Post and Fred C. Leubuscher, *Henry George's 1886 Campaign: An Account of the George-Hewitt Campaign in the New York Municipal Election of 1886* (New York, 1886; Westport, Conn.: Hyperion Press reprint ed., 1976), containing speeches of George and Hewitt together with narratives by George's press aides; Henry George, Jr., *The Life of Henry George* (New York: Doubleday, McClure & Co., 1900); Peter Alexander Speek's wonderfully detailed account of George's 1886 campaign and its immediate aftermath, *The Singletax and the Labor Movement* (Madison, Wisconsin: The University of Wisconsin Press, 1917); Howard L. Hurwitz's carefully argued *Theodore Roosevelt and Labor in New York State, 1880–1900* (New York: Columbia University Press, 1943); Irwin Yellowitz's equally careful *Labor and the Progressive Movement in New York State, 1897–1916* (Ithaca, New York: Cornell University Press, 1965); Jeremy P. Felt, *Hostages of Fortune: Child Labor Reform in New York State* (Ithaca: Cornell University Press, 1965).

POLITICS: THE REALISTIC PERSPECTIVE

Michael Wallace has argued, in "Changing Conceptions of Party in the United States, 1814–1828," *American Historical Review* 74 (1968):453–91, that New York political leaders had broken with the antiparty assumptions of the Founding Fathers and developed a rationale for the activities of permanent political parties and pressure groups as early as the Jacksonian period. Political leaders certainly acted on this new rationale at the end of the century, but the few writers who attempted to apply it to municipal politics, to the activities of the affluent no less than to those of labor, continued to encounter resistance and hostility until well into the twentieth century. J. Bleeker Miller's argument for the legitimacy of *Trade, Professional, and Property-Owners' Organizations in Public Affairs* (New York, 1884) was ignored by contemporary writers. Daniel Greenleaf Thompson's extraordinary *Politics in a Democracy* (New York: Longmans, Green, and Co., 1893) argued at length for a dispassionate recognition of the interest-group basis of the city's politics, but was resolutely ignored on publication and was quickly forgotten by political scientists who have more recently emulated its theoretical and empirical approaches. Louis Pope Gratacap's pamphlet, *The Political Mission of Tammany Hall* (New York: A. B. King, 1894), repeated several of Thompson's arguments to no effect.

Yet these early works did inaugurate a vigorous tradition of realistic, straightforward writing on New York City politics. Several products of this tradition are especially useful to any attempt to understand the 1890s: a series of sketches of Tammany assembly district organizations and their leaders that appeared weekly in the New York *Times* between July and October, 1893; Riordan's *Plunkitt of Tammany Hall;* Louis Eisenstein and Elliot Rosenberg's memoir of machine politics on the lower east side at the beginning of the twentieth century, *A Stripe of Tammany's Tiger* (New York: R. Speller, 1966), and George B. McClellan, Jr., *The Gentleman and the Tiger: The Autobiography of George B. McClellan, Jr.,* ed. by Harold C. Syrett (Philadelphia: J. B. Lippincott, 1956). This tradition also produced such classics as James A. Farley's *Behind the Ballots* (New York: Viking, 1938), and Edward J. Flynn's *You're The Boss* (New York: Harcourt, Brace and Co., 1947), and influenced several historians, most notably Herbert J. Bass, *"I Am A Democrat": The Political Career of David Bennett Hill* (Syracuse: Syracuse University Press, 1961); John Webb Pratt, "Boss

Tweed's Public Welfare Program," *New-York Historical Society Quarterly* 45 (1961):396–411; Alexander B. Callow, Jr., *The Tweed Ring* (New York: Oxford University Press, 1965); Nancy J. Weiss, *Charles Francis Murphy, 1858–1924: Respectability and Responsibility in Tammany Politics* (Northampton, Mass.: Smith College, 1968); and Leo Hershkowitz, whose *Tweed's New York: Another Look* (Garden City, New York: Doubleday/Anchor, 1977) offers a vigorous critique of Tweed's prosecutors. Neither participants in nor historians of the 1880s and 1890s have applied the realistic approach to that period; Thomas J. Condon noted the absence of an objective history of the County Democracy or of Tammany for that period in his "Politics, Reform and the New York City Election of 1886," *New-York Historical Society Quarterly* 44 (1960): 363–93, and that gap remains. There is no equivalent, for the late nineteenth century or the early twentieth century, of Jerome Mushkat's carefully researched *Tammany: The Evolution of a Political Machine, 1789–1865* (Syracuse: Syracuse University Press, 1971).

POLITICS: PARTIES AND INTEREST GROUPS

Several political and historical studies transcend the traditional approaches to New York City affairs. The first two of these were the products of Charles E. Merriam's seminar on politics at the University of Chicago: Harold F. Gosnell's *Boss Platt and His New York Machine* (New York: Russell & Russell, 1969 reprint of 1924 first edition), a work that builds a realistic approach into a classic analysis of interest groups and party politics; and Gabriel A. Almond's unpublished "Power and Plutocracy in New York City," a 1938 University of Chicago Ph.D. dissertation that sought systematically to explore the political activities of the very wealthy. Three others are also by political scientists. Wallace Sayre and Herbert Kaufman's *Governing New York City: Politics in the Metropolis* (New York: Russell Sage Foundation, 1960), focuses on the 1950s but suggests how a clearsighted political analysis might reinterpret the past. Theodore Lowi's *At the Pleasure of the Mayor: Patronage and Power in New York City, 1898–1958* (New York: The Free Press, 1964), applies such an analysis on a limited scale, with notable results. Martin Shefter's over-reliance on biased primary and secondary sources makes "The Emergence of the Political Machine: An Alternative View," in Willis D. Hawley et al., *Theoretical Perspectives on Urban Politics* (Englewood Cliffs, New Jersey: Prentice-Hall, Inc., 1976), more valuable for its intriguing review of recent political science literature than for its history; his "The Electoral Foundations of the Political Machine: New York City, 1884–1897," in Joel Silbey, et al., eds., *American Electoral History: Quantitative Studies in Popular Voting Behavior* (Princeton: Princeton University Press, 1978) offers an original and persuasive quantitative analysis of voting patterns.

Every historian of late nineteenth-century New York owes a considerable debt to a group of historians whose work has moved beyond the traditional preoccupation with bosses and reformers. Neither of Lee Benson's two books on New York State, *Merchants, Farmers, and Railroads* and *The Concept of Jacksonian Democracy: New York as a Test Case* (Princeton: Princeton University Press, 1961), deals directly with the city at the end of the nineteenth century, but both offer interpretations and raise questions that are now basic to our understanding of it. Seymour J. Mandelbaum's *Boss Tweed's New York* (New York: John Wiley & Sons, Inc., 1965), offers an intriguing application of communication theory to the city's politics during the 1860s. Clifton K. Yearly's *The Money Machines: The Breakdown and Reform of Governmental and Party Finance in the North, 1860–1920* (Albany: State University of New York Press, 1970), is unusually suggestive. Samuel T. McSeveney's *The Politics of Depression: Political Behavior in the Northeast, 1893–1896* (New York: Oxford University Press, 1972) provides a careful statistical and historical test of the hypothesis that cultural and not economic factors shaped voting behavior in New York, New Jersey, and Connecticut during that era. James C. Mohr's *The Radical Republicans in New York During Reconstruction* (Ithaca: Cornell University Press, 1973) offers an important reinterpretation of the policies of the state's Republicans during the late 1860s; Richard L. McCormick, "Prelude to Progressivism: The Transformation of New York State Politics, 1890–1910," *New York History* 59 (1978):252–76, performs a comparable task for the later period (McCormick's *From Realignment to Reform: Political Change in New*

York, 1893–1910 [Ithaca: Cornell University Press, 1981], not yet available as this book was being completed, presents his argument in detail). Two earlier articles, Richard Skolnik, "Civic Group Progressivism in New York City," *New York History* 51 (1970): 411–39, and Augustus Cerillo, Jr., "The Reform of Municipal Government in New York City, From Seth Low to John Purroy Mitchell," *New-York Historical Society Quarterly* 57 (1973):51–71, open new perspectives on the purposes and strategies of the city's reformers.

Whatever perspective the historian adopts, he or she finds that the data of New York City politics is as voluminous as the subject is complex. The annual New York *Tribune Almanac* is especially valuable for its summaries of party platforms, election results, and frequent lists of party and municipal officials. The official New York City *City Record* published more information than any historian has yet been able to use, including not just the annual speeches of the mayor, official decisions and transactions, and voting results by election district (precinct), but also the names, addresses, and party affiliations of election officials down to the precinct level. E. Dana Durand, *The Finances of New York City* (New York: Macmillan, 1898), is an intelligent and objective guide to the tangled history of the city's financial affairs in the nineteenth century.

Three usefully annotated compilations make the historical writings on the politics of New York and other cities readily available: Bruce M. Stave, ed., *Urban Bosses, Machines, and Progressive Reformers* (Lexington, Mass.: D.C. Heath, 1972); Blaine A. Brownell and Warren E. Stickle, *Bosses and Reformers: Urban Politics in America, 1880–1920* (Boston: Houghton Mifflin, 1973); and Alexander B. Callow, Jr., *The City Boss in America: An Interpretive Reader* (New York: Oxford University Press, 1976). Among the studies of other cities, I have found most stimulating Samuel P. Hays, "The Politics of Reform in Municipal Government in the Progressive Era," *Pacific Northwest Quarterly* 55 (1964):157–69; Geoffrey Blodgett, *The Gentle Reformers: Massachusetts Democrats in the Cleveland Era* (Cambridge, Mass.: Harvard University Press, 1966); Robert R. Dykstra, *The Cattle Towns* (New York: Alfred A. Knopf, 1968); Sam Bass Warner, Jr., "If All The World Were Philadelphia: A Scaffolding for Urban History," *American Historical Review* 74 (1968):26–43; Melvin Holli, *Reform in Detroit: Hazen S. Pingree and Urban Politics* (New York: Oxford University Press, 1969); Estelle F. Feinstein, *Stamford in the Gilded Age: The Political Life of a Connecticut Town* (Stamford: Stamford Historical Society, 1973); and Carl V. Harris, *Political Power in Birmingham, 1871–1921* (Knoxville: University of Tennessee Press, 1977).

PUBLIC POLICY

Until very recently scholars paid much less attention to the history of public policy than to the history of politics in New York City. Contemporary memorials and memoirs long constituted the only literature on the creation of Greater New York. Of these, the most important are the proconsolidation arguments published by Andrew H. Green, his assistant, Albert E. Henschel, the Brooklyn Consolidation League, and the Brooklyn League of Loyal Citizens. The fullest contemporary chronicle is E. Hagaman Hall, *The Second City of the World* (New York: The Republic Press, 1898), designed for sale to those who participated in the decision to create the greater city. Also useful are Gustav Herzfeld, *Gross New York: Eine Studie zur Einverleibunsfrage* (Berlin: Dietrich Reimer, 1898), and John Foord's intelligent but selective biography of Green. Mandelbaum offers an interesting perspective on Green in *Boss Tweed's New York;* Syrett reflects the Brooklyn *Eagle's* opposition to consolidation in *The City of Brooklyn.*

Three dissertations discuss Green and Greater New York in detail: George Mazaraki's chronicle, "Andrew H. Green" (New York University, 1966); my own "Participation in Major Decisions in New York City, 1890–1900: The Creation of Greater New York and the Centralization of the Public School System" (Columbia University, 1973); and Barry J. Kaplan's "A Study in the Politics of Metropolitanization: The Greater New York City Charter of 1897" (State University of New York at Buffalo, 1975), a work that emphasizes the relationship between consolidation and some ideas about regional government. Kaplan generally supports my own interpretation of Green's role in "Andrew H. Green and the Creation of a Planning Rationale: The Formation of Greater New York City, 1865–1890,"

Urbanism Past and Present 8(1979):32–41. Jon Alvah Peterson, "The Origins of the Comprehensive City Plan Ideal in the United States, 1840–1911" (Harvard University Ph.D. dissertation, 1967), provides an invaluable account of the public policy context in which Greater New York took shape.

The history of rapid transit was also neglected until very recently. James Blaine Walker's *Fifty Years of Rapid Transit, 1864–1917* (New York: Arno Press 1970 reprint of 1918 1st edition) provides an informed chronicle, although it entirely accepts the contemporary inclination to attribute undesirable results to evil intent. The Public Service Commission of the State of New York, First District, *Report for the Six Months Ending December 31, 1907* (Albany: New York State Senate Document no. 20, January 20, 1908), supplies a clear account of official efforts to provide rapid transit from 1865 on, pp. 454–65. Augustus Cerillo, Jr., "Reform in New York City: A Study of Urban Progressivism," (Northwestern University Ph.D. dissertation, 1969), devotes a chapter to the rapid transit planning of the period 1890–1907, noting the role of the Chamber of Commerce but underestimating the constraints on New York's transit planners. Cynthia M. Latta kindly permitted me to examine the careful narrative of official events she prepared for her 1975 Columbia University Ph.D. dissertation, "The Return on the Investment in the Interborough Rapid Transit Company." The germ of my own interpretation first appeared in my dissertation. Charles W. Cheape III's 1976 Brandeis University Ph.D. dissertation, "The Evolution of Urban Public Transit, 1880–1921: A Study of Three Cities," emphasizes management policy and places that aspect of the story in its national context; his book, *Moving the Masses: Urban Public Transit in New York, Boston, and Philadelphia, 1880–1912* (Cambridge, Mass.: Harvard University Press, 1981), appeared after this book was completed.

The history of public education in New York City has received somewhat more attention. A. Emerson Palmer, *The New York Public School* (New York: Macmillan, 1905), is a valuable contemporary account; *The Tribune Monthly, Public Schools of New York* (New York: The Tribune Association, March, 1896) provides detailed sketches of many schools by reporter Edgar S. Maclay. The New York City Board of Education's *Annual Report* and *Directory*, and the independent magazine, *School*, provide great detail on school affairs. Sol Cohen, *Progressives and Urban School Reform: The Public Education Association of New York City, 1895–1954* (New York: Teachers' College Press, 1964), describes the school centralization movement from the point of view of the Public Education Association. The first version of my own interpretation appears in my unpublished 1969 Columbia University Master's Essay, "The Centralization of New York City's Public School System, 1896: A Social Analysis of a Decision." By far the best comprehensive survey of the centralization movement in the United States is David B. Tyack, *The One Best System: A History of American Urban Education* (Cambridge, Mass.: Harvard University Press, 1974). Diane Ravitch uncritically adopts the biased evaluation of New York City's public schools put forward by Nicholas Murray Butler and Jacob Riis and underestimates the significance of cultural and economic conflict in her discussion of centralization in *The Great School Wars: New York City, 1805–1973* (New York: Basic Books, 1974). Wayne Urban, "Organized Teachers and Educational Reform in the Progressive Era, 1890–1920," *History of Education Quarterly* 16 (1976), offers an alternative to my interpretation of the teachers' motives. Richard F. W. Whittemore, "Nicholas Murray Butler and Public Education, 1862–1911" (Columbia University Ph. D. dissertation, 1962), is a helpful introduction; Charles M. Spatz, "New York City Public Schools and the Emergence of Bureaucracy, 1868–1917" (University of Chicago Ph. D. dissertation, 1975), became available too late for use.

There are notable studies on three other areas of municipal policy in late nineteenth-century New York. James F. Richardson's *The New York Police* (New York: Oxford University Press, 1970) emphasizes the late nineteenth century and avoids most of the pitfalls left by the political battles of the era. John Duffy, *A History of Public Health in New York City, 1866–1966* (New York: Russell Sage Foundation, 1974), provides a good comprehensive introduction to its subject. And several works examine the history of housing reform in the city: James Ford, *Slums and Housing With Special Reference to New York City: History, Conditions, Policy* (Cambridge, Mass.: Harvard University Press, 1936), a judicious summary from the Charity Organization Society point of view; Roy Lubove, *The Progressives and the Slums* (Pittsburgh: University of Pittsburgh Press, 1962), an independent critique of that viewpoint; and Anthony Jackson, *A Place Called Home: A History of Low-Cost Housing in Manhattan* (Cambridge, Mass.: The MIT Press, 1976), which stops far short of a full-scale economic analysis but makes good use of the published sources. David C. Hammack, "Small Business and Urban Power: Some Notes on the History of Economic Policy in Nineteenth-Century American Cities," in Stuart Bruchey, ed., *Small Business in American Life* (New York: Columbia University Press, 1980), reviews our knowledge of the history of economic policy in New York and other cities.

PRIMARY SOURCES

New Yorkers congratulate themselves on their ability to forget their past, and they view that characteristic as an aspect of their city's openness to newcomers. But they have also created several extraordinary collections of historical documents and have made these collections especially rich in materials from the late nineteenth century. Indeed both the technology and the social customs of that period (typewriters used with letterpress copybooks instead of carbon paper, literate and carefully filed correspondence, written appointments for telephone conversations) produced some almost unmanageably large sets of records.

The detailed reconstructions of the decision-making process reported in chaps. seven, eight, and nine of this book are very largely based on such records, produced by individuals and organizations and held above all in three collections. At the New York Public Library, the papers of Richard Watson Gilder, Albert Shaw, and Levi P. Morton are especially extensive and rewarding; those of Timothy Shaler Williams, R. W. G. Welling, and John Bigelow (including the latter's remarkable typescript journal) are full and useful for a narrower range of topics; those of Andrew Haswell Green, George E. Jones, Henry M. Leipziger, St. Clair McKelway, Lemuel E. Quigg, Simon Sterne, and Calvert Vaux are fragmentary but contain some gems; and the voluminous papers of Frank J. Sprague and William Rhinelander Stewart had not, when I examined them, been put into usable order. At the New-York Historical Society, the [Edward] Cooper–[Abram S.] Hewitt letterpress copybooks are so voluminous that they belong in a class of their own; Hewitt's Mayoral letterpress copybooks, the papers of the New-York Board of Trade and Transportation, and the papers of Charles S. Fairchild are also extensive and valuable; the much less complete papers of Bourke Cochran, Lewis L. Delafield, Andrew Haswell Green, Charles H. Marshall, and Lemuel E. Quigg contain many useful pieces of information. Four very large collections at Columbia University are unusually revealing: those of Nicholas Murray Butler (not entirely open at the time I used it), Frederick W. Holls, Seth Low, and Edward M. Shepard; the much smaller collection of the William Barclay Parsons papers contains several useful items; but the Edwin R. Kilroe collection of Tammaniana is disappointingly thin for this period. The William R. Grace papers and the papers of the Community Service Society of New York (successor to the Charity Organization Society) were given to Columbia after I had completed archival research.

Several other New York institutions also hold useful materials. The Municipal Archives and Records Center of the City of New York holds a large collection of the papers of the city's mayors and departments, and is especially rich in letters and petitions to the mayor; during the fiscal crisis of the 1970s these papers were not always accessible, but they are now receiving appropriate care. The Long Island Historical Society in Brooklyn holds a number of valuable small collections, including papers of the Brooklyn Elevated Railroad, the Civitas Club, and of Silas B. Dutcher. The Cooper Union for the Advancement of Science and Art has a helpful collection of transcripts from the papers of Abram S. Hewitt, organized by topic.

Outside of New York City, the most valuable collections of papers are at Yale University, the Library of Congress, and the State Historical Society of Wisconsin. At Yale the Henry deForest Baldwin, Thomas C. Platt, and James Rockwell Sheffield papers are all limited in extent but full of useful items; although the more extensive Henry L. Stimson papers are relatively thin for the 1890s, they do reveal the extent of his involvement in the Republican politics of the silk stocking district. The papers of several New Yorkers who held federal office have found their way to the Library of Congress, but in most cases these collections include few items relevant to city affairs. The Cooper-Hewitt letterpress copybooks, here as at the New-York Historical Society, do contain political letters among the business correspondence; Frederick Law Olmsted's papers contain several intriguing references to the city;

Whitelaw Reid's papers contain a few references to news items that posed policy questions for his *Tribune;* Elihu Root's papers throw some light on the 1894 state constitutional convention; and William C. Whitney's papers contain several useful items on New York City transit and Democratic political matters. The papers of Joseph H. Choate, William C. Redfield, Oscar S. Straus, and Benjamin F. Tracy include almost nothing of interest on the city where these men spent most of their careers. The State Historical Society of Wisconsin has made a specialty of papers on progressive politics; its materials on left-wing politics in New York City had few items on the 1880s or 1890s when I examined it, but its microfilmed collection of the papers of the University Settlement Society of New York is invaluable on the reform politics of the 1890s as well as on the activities of the settlement. Within the State of New York, the David B. Hill and Everett P. Wheeler papers at the New York State Library in Albany, the S. Fred Nixon papers on microfilm at Cornell University, and the Henry E. Huntington papers, and the miscellaneous collection of autographed letters by New York State leaders at Syracuse University all contain useful material.

SOCIAL SCIENCE AND THE HISTORICAL STUDY OF POWER

The social science literature on community power is as complex and contentious as the literature on New York City, but since I review it in chapter 1 of this book and elsewhere I will not discuss it in detail here. Several excellent collections make the leading articles on community power easily available to those who wish to explore the field: Willis D. Hawley and Frederick M. Wirt, eds., *The Search for Community Power* (Englewood Cliffs, New Jersey: Prentice-Hall, Inc., 1968); Roderick Bell, David V. Edwards, and R. Harrison Wagner, eds., *Political Power: A Reader in Theory and Research* (New York: The Free Press, 1969); Michael Aiken and Paul E. Mott, eds., *The Structure of Community Power* (New York: Random House, 1970); Charles Bonjean, et al., eds., *Community Politics: A Behavioral Approach* (New York: The Free Press, 1971); and Daniel N. Gordon, ed., *Social Change and Urban Politics: Readings* (Englewood Cliffs: Prentice-Hall, Inc., 1973). Willis D. Hawley and James H. Svara, *The Study of Community Power: A Bibliographic Review* (Santa Barbara, California: ABC-CLIO Press, 1972), provides a useful annotated list of the articles and books in the field to its date. Geraint Parry, *Political Elites* (New York: Praeger, 1969), provides an excellent introduction to the theoretical issues.

Among the historians who have discussed the implications of this literature for history see especially Dykstra, *The Cattle Towns,* Appendix B, and "Stratification and Community Political Systems: Historians' Models," in Allan G. Bogue, ed., *Emerging Theoretical Models in Social and Political History* (Beverly Hills, California: Sage Publications, 1973); Lee Benson, "Political Power and Political Elites," in Benson, et al., *American Political Behavior: Historical Essays and Readings* (New York: Harper & Row, 1974), pp. 281–310; and Carl V. Harris, "The Underdeveloped Historical Dimension of the Study of Community Power Structure," *Historical Methods Newsletter* 9 (1976):195–201. My own views appear in two articles, "Problems in the Historical Study of Power in the Cities and Towns of the United States, 1800–1960," *American Historical Review* 83 (1978): 323–49, and "Economic Interest Groups and Path Analysis: Two Approaches to the History of Power," in *The Journal of Interdisciplinary History* 12 (1981):695–704. Many historical works are concerned with the distribution of power, but few have employed an approach comparable to the one used in this work. Among those that have, see Dykstra, *The Cattle Towns;* Feinstein, *Stamford in the Gilded Age;* Harris, *Political Power in Birmingham;* and J. Rogers Hollingsworth and Ellen Jane Hollingsworth, *Dimensions in Urban History: Historical and Social Science Perspectives on Middle-Size American Cities* (Madison: University of Wisconsin Press, 1979).

INDEX